FOR STUDENTS

Over the past four years we have spent time in classrooms across Canada, speaking to students just like you.

We've asked what you want to see in a textbook, how you learn, how many hours a week you spend online, and what you find most valuable when preparing for a test. Based on your feedback, we've developed a new hybrid learning solution—**CRIM**. Your textbook, the Chapter Review cards, and the online resources found at **www.icancrim2.com** present a new, exciting, and fresh approach to learning. Check out the website for great tools like

- Interactive quizzing
- Interactive ebook
- Flashcards
- Games
- Test Yourself
- Videos
- **And more!**

Purestock/Getty Images

NELSON EDUCATION

CRIM, Second Canadian Edition
by Larry J. Siegel, Gregory P. Brown, and Ron Hoffman

Vice President, Editorial Higher Education:
Anne Williams

Executive Editor:
Lenore Taylor-Atkins

Marketing Manager:
Terry Fedorkiw

Developmental Editor:
Liisa Kelly

Photo Researcher:
Indu Arora

Permissions Coordinator:
Indu Arora

Content Production Manager:
Jennifer Hare

Copy Editor:
Karen Rolfe

Proofreaders:
Erin Moore and Kelli Howey

Indexer:
Belle Wong

Manufacturing Coordinator:
Joanne McNeil

Design Director:
Ken Phipps

Managing Designer:
Franca Amore

Interior Design Revisions:
Jennifer Stimson

Cover Design:
Peter Papayanakis

Cover Image:
Simone van den Berg/Shutterstock

Compositor:
Kyle Gell Design

Printer:
RR Donnelley

Printed and bound in the United States
1 2 3 4 15 14 13 12

For more information contact Nelson Education Ltd., 1120 Birchmount Road, Toronto, Ontario, M1K 5G4. Or you can visit our Internet site at http://www.nelson.com

Library and Archives Canada Cataloguing in Publication Data

Siegel, Larry J.
Crim / Larry J. Siegel, Gregory P. Brown, Ron Hoffman.—2nd Canadian ed.

Previous ed. has title: Criminology, the core.
Includes bibliographical references and index.
ISBN 978-0-17-650444-1

1. Criminology—Textbooks. 2. Crime—Canada. I. Brown, Gregory Paul II. Hoffman, Ron, 1952- III. Title.

HV6025.S55 2012 364
C2012-900826-5

ISBN-13: 978-0-17-650444-1
ISBN-10: 0-17-650444-3

CRIM Brief Contents

CRIM Contents

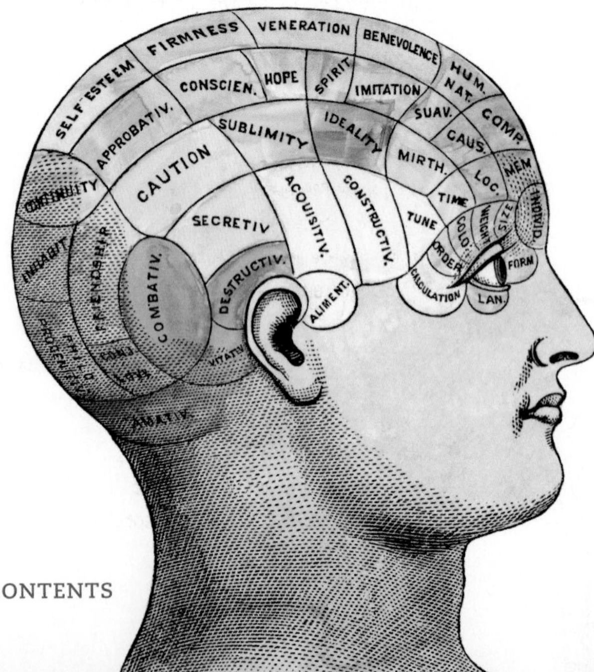

© North Wind Picture Archives/Alamy

THE CANADIAN PRESS/Ryan Remiorz

Scott Rothstein/Shutterstock.com

© ACE STOCK LIMITED/Alamy

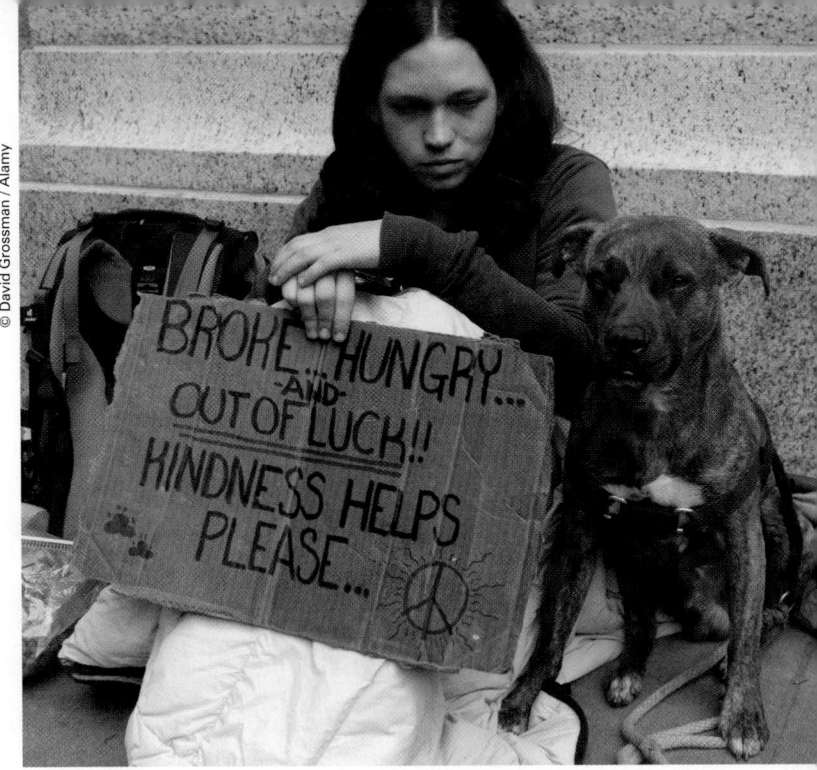

© David Grossman / Alamy

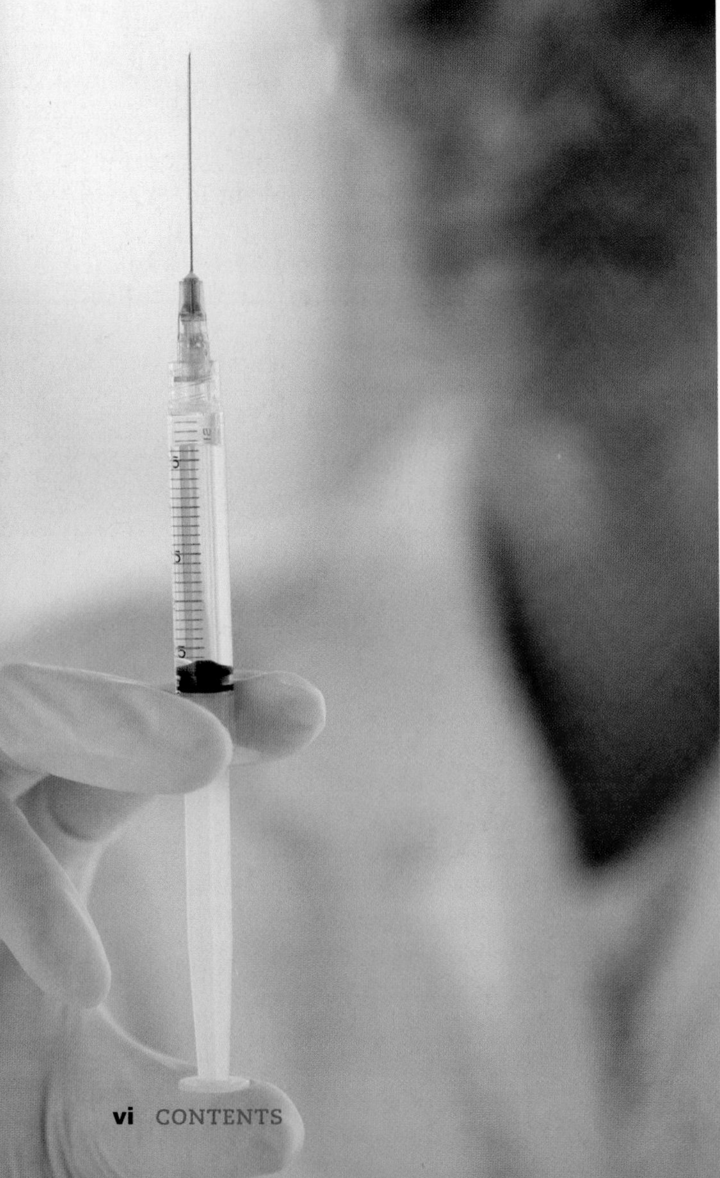
© Royalty-Free/Masterfile

AP Photo/John Miller

© Steve Debenport/iStockPhoto

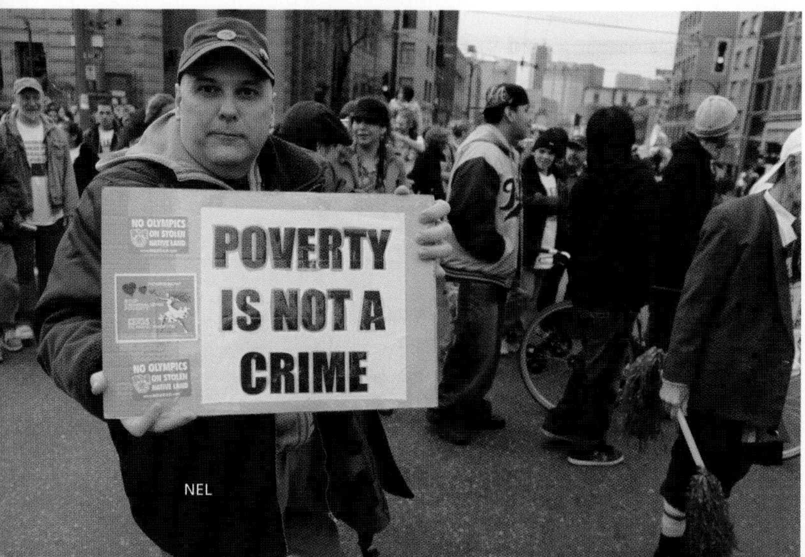

© ryan koopmans/Alamy

© Oleksiy Maksymenko/Alamy

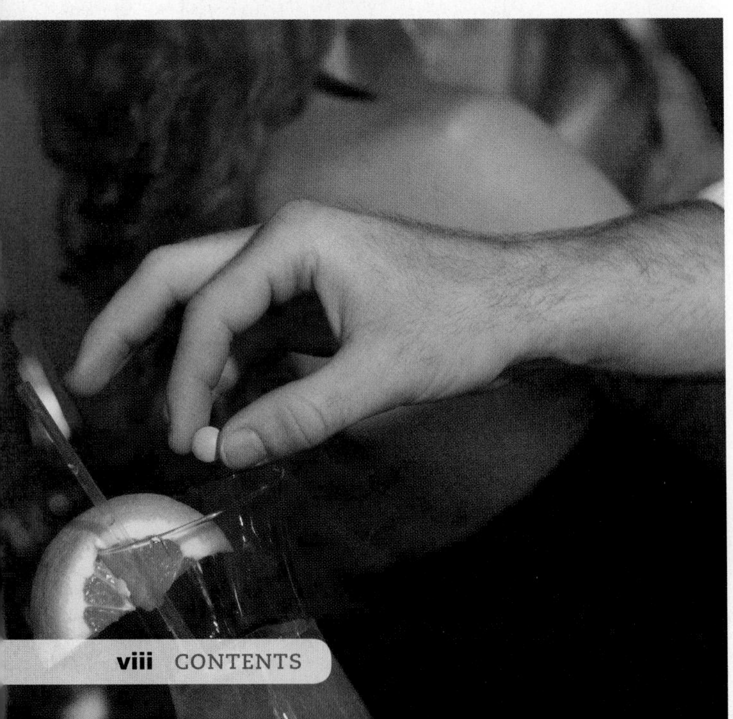
Monkey Business Images/Shutterstock.com

© Alex Slobodkin/iStockPhoto

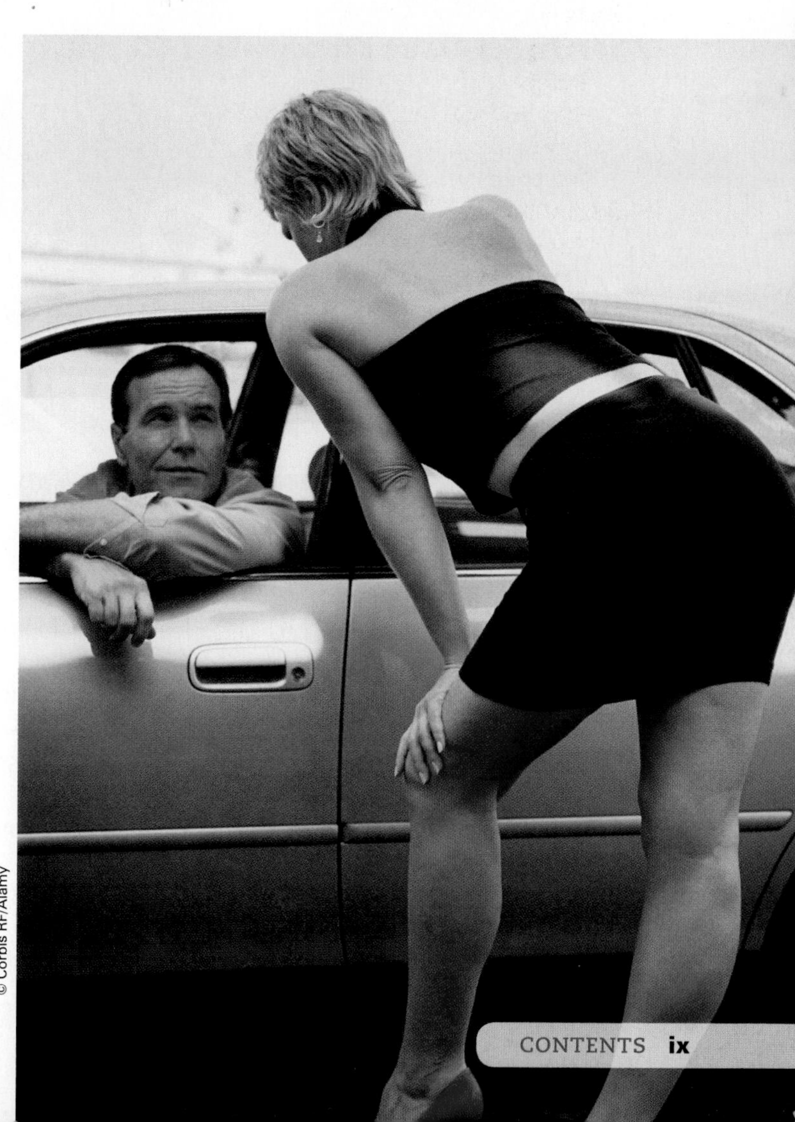
© Corbis RF/Alamy

CHAPTER 1

Crime *and* Criminology

Learning Outcomes

LO1 Define criminology.

LO2 Describe the development of the discipline of criminology.

LO3 Identify the subareas that constitute the discipline of criminology.

LO4 Identify the major perspectives of criminology and the focus of each.

LO5 Define common law and its relationship to the Criminal Code of Canada.

LO6 Explain the purpose of criminal law.

LO7 Define the elements of a crime.

LO1 Introduction

Between 1980 and 2002 more than 60 women, many of Aboriginal descent, were reported missing from Vancouver's downtown Eastside, an area known for its prevalence of sex trade workers.[1] In February 2002, after growing pressure from families of some of the missing women, a joint task force of Vancouver police and the RCMP descended with a search warrant on a Coquitlam-area pig farm owned by Robert "Willie" Pickton, 54, and his younger brother David, 53. So began the largest and most expensive homicide investigation in Canadian history, estimated to have cost taxpayers nearly $130 million.[2] Dozens of police, forensic specialists, anthropologists, and others were called in to search the property, sifting through mountains of soil to find DNA evidence to identify victims. Within two weeks, Robert Pickton was charged with the first-degree murders of two of the missing women, and as the excavations continued to unearth evidence of additional victims, the number of charges increased to 27. The trial commenced on January 30, 2006, and one of the first witnesses to take the stand was an undercover police officer who posed as Pickton's cellmate. The officer asserted that Pickton confessed to a total of 49 murders and that he wanted to kill another woman to make it an even 50 but was caught because he was "sloppy." On December 9, 2007, the jury returned a verdict that Pickton was guilty on six counts of second-degree murder and was eventually sentenced to life imprisonment with no possibility of parole for 25 years.[3]

DID YOU KNOW?

- The Canadian legal system is a direct descendant of the British common law.
- The criminal law has a number of different goals, including social control, punishment, retribution, deterrence, and the representation of morality.
- Each crime has both a physical and a mental element.
- Persons accused of crimes can defend themselves either by denying the criminal act or by presenting an excuse or justification for their actions.
- The criminal law is constantly changing in an effort to reflect social values and contemporary issues and problems.

The Robert Pickton case is an extreme example, but it is representative of the complex problems and issues that face criminologists and shape their field of study. How common is serial murder? Why are some groups (e.g., Aboriginal women) more likely to be victimized by a serial killer? Are serial killers more common now than in the past? What should be done with a serial killer such as Pickton? Offer him rehabilitative treatment, or lock him up for the rest of his life? Should we bring back the death penalty for individuals convicted of serial killings? How can criminologists use their knowledge to help law-enforcement agencies prevent these crimes from happening?

© Andy Clark/Reuters/Corbis (inset); RCMP/Reuters/Landov

Robert William Pickton, 54, is accused of brutalizing and killing 27 women. What is a "serial killer"? What could cause someone to prey on and kill other people? Is it the environment that person grew up in? Is it some kind of physical or mental illness? How can we prevent such crimes in the future?

Such questions about crime and its control have spurred the development of criminology, an academic discipline that makes use of scientific methods to study the nature, extent, cause, and control of criminal behaviour. Unlike political figures and media commentators, whose opinions about crime may be coloured by personal experiences, biases, and election concerns, criminologists must remain objective as they study crime and its consequences. For example, some politicians have sought to capitalize on public fear by advocating restrictive immigration laws. However, criminologists John Hagan and Alberto Palloni have conducted objective, scientific research that shows that immigrants are actually less involved in crime than citizens and by many measures of personal well-being do better than citizens.[4]

criminology
The scientific study of the nature, extent, cause, and control of criminal behaviour.

interdisciplinary
Involving two or more academic fields.

REUTERS

Convicted murderer, rapist, and former colonel in the Canadian Air Force, Russell Williams had a strange habit of taking self-photos at crime scenes as pictured here.

Criminology is an **interdisciplinary** science. Criminologists hold degrees in a variety of diverse fields, most commonly sociology, but also criminal justice, political science, psychology, anthropology, economics, and the natural sciences. For most of the 20th century, criminology's primary orientation was sociological, but today it can be viewed as an integrated approach to the study of criminal behaviour.

A Brief History of Criminology

The scientific study of crime and criminality is a relatively recent development.

During the Middle Ages (1200–1600), people who violated social norms or religious practices were believed to be witches or possessed by demons.[5] It was common practice to use torture to extract confessions. Those convicted of violent or theft crimes suffered extremely harsh penalties, including whipping, branding, maiming, and execution. For example, between 1575 and 1590, Nicholas Remy, head of the Inquisition in the French province of Lorraine, ordered 900 sorcerers and witches burned to death. According to Anne Llewellyn Barstow in her book *Witchcraze: A New History of the European Witch Hunts*, estimates of the number of individuals tortured or burned to death during the European Inquisition period (the

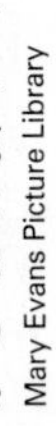

Mary Evans Picture Library

Witchcraft in early modern Europe

15th, 16th, and 17th centuries) range from 100 000 to possibly several millions.[6]

Classical Criminology

By the mid-18th century, social philosophers began to argue for a more rational approach to punishment. They sought to eliminate cruel public executions, which were designed to frighten people into obedience. Reformers stressed that the relationship between crime and punishment should be balanced and fair. This more moderate view of criminal sanctions can be traced to the writings of an Italian scholar, Cesare Beccaria (1738–1794), who was one of the first scholars to develop a systematic understanding of why people committed crime.

Archive Photos/Getty Images

Cesare Beccaria (1738–1794) argued that the effectiveness of criminal justice depended on the certainty of punishment rather than on its severity.

Beccaria believed in the concept of **utilitarianism**: In their behaviour choices, people want to achieve pleasure and avoid pain. Crimes occur when the potential pleasure and reward from illegal acts outweigh the likely pains of punishment. To deter crime, punishment must be swift, certain to occur if the law is broken, and severe enough to deter any future law-breaking behaviour. Beccaria also believed that the law should set out what the punishments for different crimes are, that punishments should fit the severity of the crime, and that they should be public, to deter (warn) citizens about what would happen to law breakers.[7]

utilitarianism
The view that people's behaviour is motivated by the pursuit of pleasure and the avoidance of pain.

classical criminology
The theoretical perspective suggesting that (1) people have free will to choose criminal or conventional behaviours; (2) people choose to commit crime for reasons of greed or personal need; and (3) crime can be controlled only by the fear of criminal sanctions.

The writings of Beccaria and his followers form the core of what today is referred to as classical criminology. As originally conceived in the 18th century, **classical criminology** theory had several basic elements:

1. In every society, people have free will to choose criminal or lawful solutions to meet their needs or settle their problems.
2. Criminal solutions may be more attractive than lawful ones because they usually require less work for a greater payoff.
3. A person's choice of criminal solutions may be controlled by his or her fear of punishment.
4. The more certain, swift, and severe the punishment, the better able it is to control criminal behaviour.

The classical perspective influenced judicial philosophy, and sentences were geared to be proportionate to the seriousness of the crime. Executions were still widely used but gradually came to be employed for only the most serious crimes. The catch phrase was "let the punishment fit the crime."

© James W. Porter/CORBIS

Auguste Comte attempted to discover the successive stages through which the human race evolved. He believed that in the beginning man was not much superior to the great apes, but evolved to the state at which he found the civilized society of Europe of his time.

Positivist Criminology

During the 19th century, a new vision of the world challenged the validity of classical theory and presented an innovative way of looking at the causes of crime. The scientific method was beginning to take hold in Europe and North America. Scientists were using careful observation and analysis of natural phenomena to explain how the world worked. New discoveries were being made in biology, astronomy, and chemistry. If the scientific method could be applied to the study of nature, then why not use it to study human behaviour?

positivism
The branch of social science that uses the scientific method of the natural sciences and suggests that human behaviour is a product of social, biological, psychological, or economic forces.

Auguste Comte (1798–1857), considered the founder of sociology, argued that societies pass through stages that can be grouped on the basis of how people try to understand the world in which they live. People in primitive societies believe that inanimate objects have life (e.g., the sun is a god); in later social stages, people embrace a rational, scientific view of the world. Comte called this the positive stage, and those who followed his writings became known as positivists.

© Mary Evans Picture Library/Alamy

Auguste Comte (1798–1857) was a French philosopher, known as the founder of the discipline of sociology and the doctrine of positivism.

Positivism has two main elements:

1. Positivists see human behaviour as a function of external forces that are often beyond individual control. Some are social, such as wealth and class; others are political and historical, such as war and famine. Personal factors, such as an individual's brain structure and biological makeup or mental ability, also influence human behaviour.
2. Positivists rely on the scientific method. They would agree that an abstract concept such as "intelligence" exists because it can be measured by an IQ test. They would challenge a concept such as the "soul" because it cannot be verified by the scientific method.

Early Positivism

The earliest "scientific" studies examining human behaviour now seem quaint and primitive. Physiognomists, such as J.K. Lavater (1741–1801), studied the facial features of criminals and found that the shape of ears, nose, and eyes and the distances between them were associated with antisocial behaviour. Phrenologists, such as Franz Joseph Gall (1758–1828) and Johann K. Spurzheim (1776–1832), studied the shape of the skull and bumps on the head and concluded that these physical attributes were linked to criminal behaviour.

By the early 19th century, abnormality in the human mind was being linked to criminal behaviour patterns. Philippe Pinel, one of the founders of French psychiatry, coined the phrase *manie sans delire* to denote what eventually was referred to as a psychopathic personality. In 1812, an American, Benjamin Rush, described patients with an "innate preternatural moral depravity."[8] English physician Henry Maudsley (1835–1918) believed that insanity

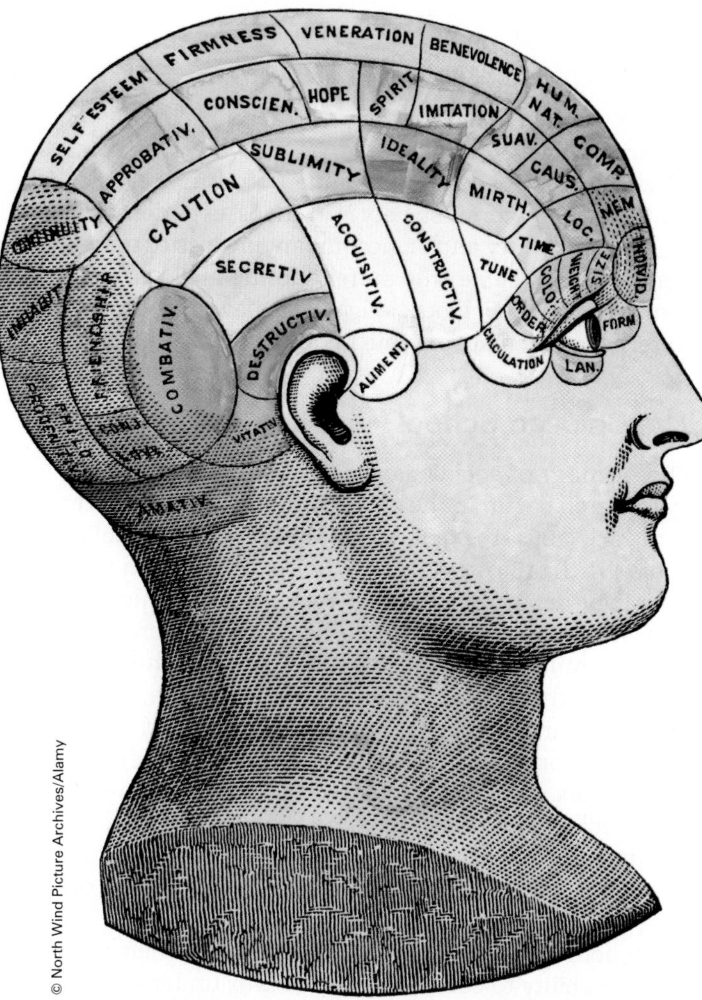

Viennese physician Franz-Joseph Gall (1758–1828) believed that a person's character and mental capacity could be determined by studying the skull. Different areas of the skull corresponded to various aspects of a person's personality as shown in the image above.

and criminal behaviour were strongly linked.[9] These early research efforts shifted attention to brain functioning and personality as the key to criminal behaviour.

Biological Determinism

In Italy Cesare Lombroso (1835–1909), known as the "father of criminology," began to study the cadavers of executed criminals in an effort to determine scientifically how criminals differed from noncriminals. His research soon convinced Lombroso that serious and violent offenders had inherited criminal traits. These "born criminals" suffered from "atavistic anomalies"; physically, they were throwbacks to more primitive times when people were savages and were believed to have the enormous jaws and strong canine teeth common to carnivores and savages who devour raw flesh. Lombroso's version of criminal anthropology was brought to North America via articles and textbooks that adopted his ideas.[10]

Although Lombroso's version of strict biological determinism is no longer taken seriously, some criminologists have recently linked crime and biological traits. Because they believe that social and environmental conditions also influence human behaviour, the term **biosocial theory** has been coined to reflect the assumed link between physical and social traits and their influence on behaviour.

biosocial theory Approach to criminology that focuses on the interaction between biological and social factors as they relate to crime.

sociological criminology Approach to criminology, based on the work of Quetelet and Durkheim, that focuses on the relationship between social factors and crime.

Sociological Criminology

At the same time that biological views were dominating criminology, another group of positivists was developing the field of sociology to study scientifically the major social changes that were taking place in 19th-century society. The foundations of **sociological criminology** can be traced to the work of pioneering

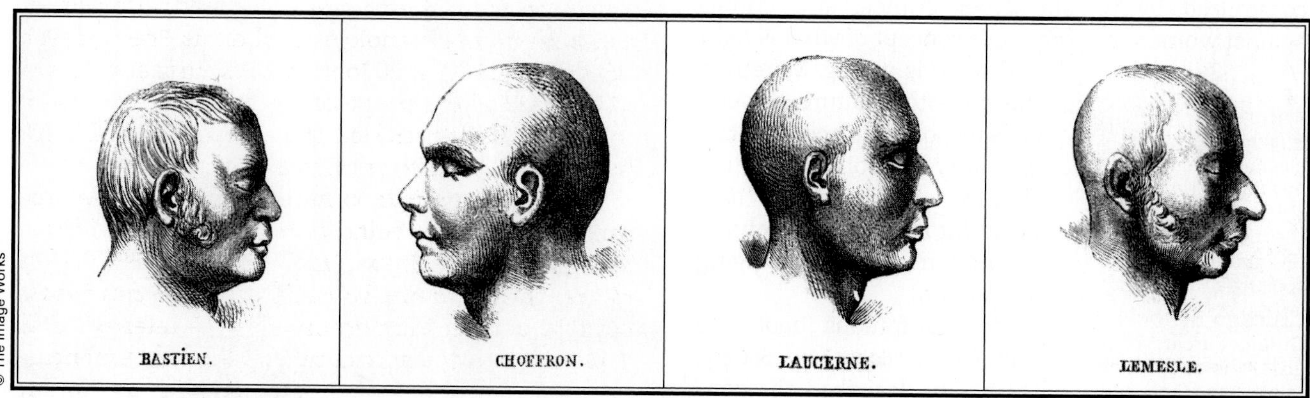

Early positivists believed that the shape of the skull was a key determinant of behaviour. These drawings from the 19th century illustrated "typical" criminally shaped heads.

© The Art Gallery Collection / Alamy

Emile Durkheim (1858–1917)

sociologists L.A.J. (Adolphe) Quetelet (1796–1874) and (David) Emile Durkheim (1858–1917).[11]

Quetelet was a Belgian mathematician who (along with a Frenchman, Andre-Michel Guerry) used social statistics that were just being developed in Europe to investigate the influence of social factors on the propensity to commit crime. In addition to finding a strong influence of age and sex on crime, Quetelet uncovered evidence that season, climate, population composition, and poverty were also related to criminality.[12] He was one of the first criminologists to link crime rates to alcohol consumption.[13]

According to Emile Durkheim, criminality was the result of cultural or societal forces as opposed to being rooted in the individual. He viewed crime as inevitable and even necessary because it is functionally useful in maintaining a healthy society. In part it does this by reaffirming boundaries between what is considered "good" and "bad" behaviour in society.[14] For example, society's response to crimes such as sexual offences committed by priests, cyber crimes, and crimes against women reinforces our concept of what is right and what is wrong. Moreover, the collective nature of society's response promotes social solidarity and cohesion. Crime is also a way to inject new ideas into society, preventing stagnation and encouraging adaptation.

anomie
A lack of norms or clear social standards. Because of rapidly shifting moral values, the individual has few guides to what is socially acceptable.

Chicago School
Group of urban sociologists who studied the relationship between environmental conditions and crime.

In his famous book *The Division of Labor in Society*, Durkheim described the consequences of the shift from a small, rural society, which he labelled "mechanical," to the more modern "organic" society with a large urban population, division of labour, and personal isolation.[15] From the resulting structural changes flowed anomie, or norm and role confusion. An anomic society is in chaos, experiencing moral uncertainty and an accompanying loss of traditional values. People who suffer anomie may become confused and rebellious. Might the dawning of the "Internet age" create **anomie** in our own culture?

The Chicago School

The primacy of sociological positivism was secured by research begun in the early 20th century by Robert Ezra Park (1864–1944), Ernest W. Burgess (1886–1966), Louis Wirth (1897–1952), and their colleagues in the sociology department at the University of Chicago. The scholars who taught at this program created what is still referred to as the **Chicago School** in honour of their unique style of doing research.

These urban sociologists examined how neighbourhood conditions, such as poverty levels, influenced crime rates. They found that social forces operating in urban areas created a crime-promoting environment; some neighbourhoods were "natural areas" for crime.[16] In urban neighbourhoods with high levels of poverty, the fabric of critical social institutions, such as the school and the family, became undone. Their traditional ability to control behaviour was undermined, and the outcome was a high crime rate.

Chicago School sociologists argued that crime was not a function of personal traits or characteristics, but rather a reaction to an environment that was inadequate for proper human relations and development. Thus, they challenged the widely held belief that criminals were biologically or psychologically impaired or morally inferior. Instead, crime was a social phenomenon and could be eradicated by improving social and economic conditions.

© Janusz Wrobel/Alamy

High poverty levels in a neighbourhood can influence crime rates.

© Josh Rinehults/iStockPhoto

Fighting in front of children can lead to children who are less able to trust and feel secure in the idea that their world and the authority figures in it will be stable and long lasting.

Socialization Views

During the 1930s and 1940s, another group of sociologists began conducting research that linked criminal behaviour to the quality of an individual's relationship to important social processes, such as education, family life, and peer relations. They found that children who grew up in homes wracked by conflict, attended inadequate schools, or associated with deviant peers became exposed to pro-crime forces. One position, championed by the criminologist Edwin Sutherland, was that people learn criminal attitudes from older, more experienced law violators. Another view, developed by Chicago School sociologist Walter Reckless, was that crime occurs when children develop an inadequate self-image, which renders them incapable of controlling their own misbehaviour. Both of these views linked criminality to the failure of **socialization**—the interactions people have with the various individuals, organizations, institutions, and processes of society that help them mature and develop.

Conflict Criminology

In his *Communist Manifesto* and other writings, Karl Marx (1818–1883) had sown the seeds for a new approach in criminology.[17] Documenting the oppressive labour conditions prevalent during the rise of industrial capitalism, he was convinced that the character of every civilization is determined by its mode of production—the way its people develop and produce material goods. The most important relationship in industrial culture is between the owners of the means of production, the capitalist bourgeoisie, and the people who do the actual labour, the proletariat. The economic system controls all facets of human life; consequently, people's lives revolve around the means of production. The exploitation of the working class, he believed, would eventually lead to class conflict and the end of the capitalist system.

Although these writings laid the foundation for a Marxist criminology, it was not until the social and political upheaval of the 1960s, fuelled by the war in Vietnam, the civil rights movement, and the anti-establishment "hippie" counterculture, that **conflict theory** took hold. Young sociologists, interested in applying Marxist principles to the study of crime, began to analyze the social conditions that promoted class conflict and crime. What emerged from this intellectual ferment was a Marxist-based radical criminology that indicted the economic system which produced the conditions that support a high crime rate. The Marxist tradition has played a significant role in criminology ever since.

socialization
Process of human development and enculturation. Socialization is influenced by key social processes and institutions.

conflict theory
The view that human behaviour is shaped by interpersonal conflict and that those who maintain social power will use it to further their own ends.

© Lebrecht Music and Arts Photo Library/Alamy

Karl Marx (1818–1883)

LO2 Contemporary Criminology

These various schools of criminology, developed over 200 years, have been constantly evolving. Classical theory has evolved into modern **rational choice theory**, which argues that criminals are rational decision makers. They use available information to choose criminal or conventional behaviours, and their choice is structured by the fear of punishment. Lombrosian theory has evolved into contemporary biosocial and psychological views. Criminologists no longer believe that a single trait or inherited characteristic can explain crime, but some are convinced that biological and psychological traits interact with environmental factors to influence all human behaviour, including criminality. Biological and psychological theorists study the association between criminal behaviour and factors such as diet, hormonal makeup, personality, and intelligence. (See Figure 1.1.)

rational choice theory
The view that crime is a function of a decision-making process in which the potential offender weighs the potential costs and benefits of an illegal act.

social structure theory
The view that disadvantaged economic class position is a primary cause of crime.

The original Chicago School vision has been updated in **social structure theory**, which maintains that the social environment directly controls criminal behaviour. According to this view, people at the bottom of the social structure, who cannot achieve success through conventional means, experience anomie, strain, failure, and frustration; they are the most likely to turn to criminal solutions to their problems. The social process view is also still prominent. Some theorists believe that children learn to commit crime by interacting with and modelling their behaviour after others they admire; others find that criminal offenders are people whose life

CONNECTIONS

Criminologists have sought to reconcile the differences among these visions of crime by combining or integrating them into unified but complex theories of criminality. At their core, these integrated theories suggest that as people develop over the life course, a variety of factors—some social, others personal—shape their behaviour patterns. What these factors are and the influence they have on human behaviour will be discussed in Chapter 9.

CLASSICAL/ CHOICE PERSPECTIVE	**Situational forces** Crime is a function of free will and personal choice. Punishment is a deterrent to crime.
BIOLOGICAL/ PSYCHOLOGICAL PERSPECTIVE	**Internal forces** Crime is a function of chemical, neurological, genetic, personality, intelligence, or mental traits.
STRUCTURAL PERSPECTIVE	**Ecological forces** Crime rates are a function of neighbourhood conditions, cultural forces, and norm conflict.
PROCESS PERSPECTIVE	**Socialization forces** Crime is a function of upbringing, learning, and control. Peers, parents, and teachers influence behaviour.
CONFLICT PERSPECTIVE	**Economic and political forces** Crime is a function of competition for limited resources and power. Class conflict produces crime.
INTEGRATED PERSPECTIVE	**Multiple forces** Biological, social-psychological, economic, and political forces may combine to produce crime.

FIGURE 1.1

Criminology Perspectives

The major perspectives of criminology focus on *individual* (biological, psychological, and choice theories), *social* (structural and process theories), *political and economic* (conflict), and *multiple* (integrated) factors.

experiences have shattered their social bonds to society.

The writings of Marx and his followers continue to be influential. Many criminologists still view social and political conflict as the root cause of crime. The inherently unfair economic structure of advanced capitalist countries, such as Canada and the United States, is the engine that drives the crime rate. Some contemporary criminologists are now combining elements from each of these views into complex integrated theories of criminal career development.

Each of the major perspectives is summarized in Figure 1.1.

LO3 What Criminologists Do: The Criminological Enterprise

Regardless of their background or training, criminologists are primarily interested in studying crime and criminal behaviour. Their professional training, occupational role, and income are derived from a scientific approach to the study and analysis of crime and criminal behaviour.[18]

Several subareas exist within the broader arena of criminology. Taken together, they make up the criminological enterprise. Criminologists may specialize in a subarea in the same way that psychologists might specialize in a subfield of psychology, such as child development, perception, personality, psychopathology, or sexuality. Some of the more important criminological specialties are described in the following sections and summarized in Figure 1.2.

valid
Actually measuring what one intends to measure; relevant.

reliable
Producing consistent results from one measurement to another.

Criminal Statistics

The subarea of criminal statistics involves measuring the amount and trends of criminal activity. How much crime occurs annually? Who commits it? When and where does it occur? Which crimes are the most serious?

Criminologists interested in criminal statistics try to create **valid** and **reliable** measurements of criminal behaviour. For example, they create techniques to analyze the records of police and court agencies. They develop methods such as questionnaires to measure the percentage of people who actually commit crimes but escape detection by the justice system. They also develop techniques to identify the victims of crime: how many people are victims of crime and what percentage report crime to the police. The study of criminal statistics is one of the most crucial aspects of the criminological enterprise because without valid and reliable data sources, efforts to conduct research on crime and create criminological theories would be futile.

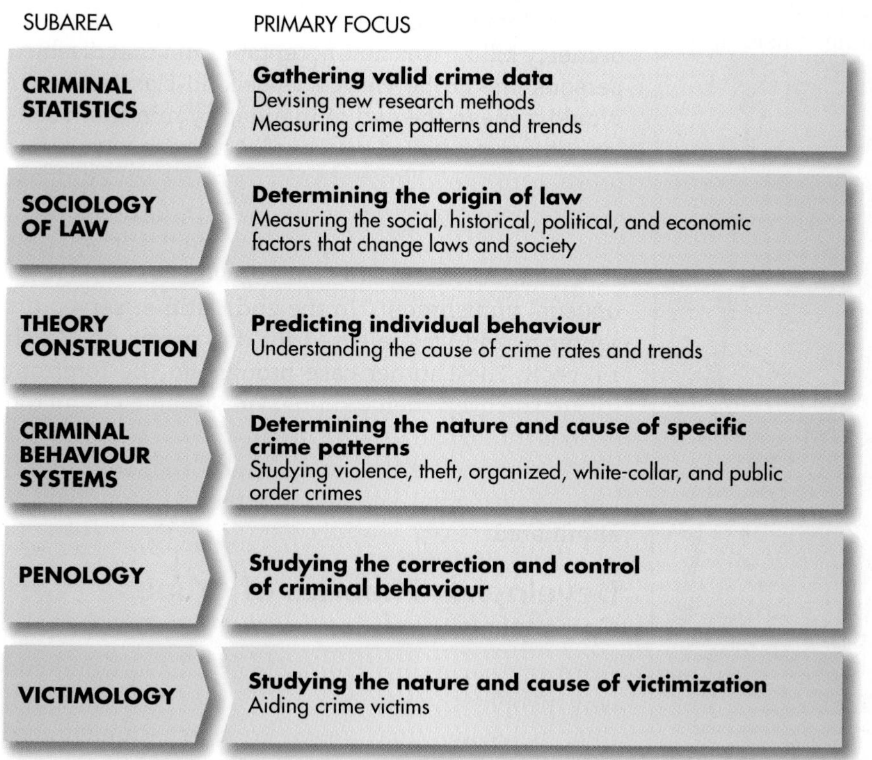

SUBAREA
PRIMARY FOCUS
CRIMINAL STATISTICS
Gathering valid crime data
Devising new research methods
Measuring crime patterns and trends
SOCIOLOGY OF LAW
Determining the origin of law
Measuring the social, historical, political, and economic factors that change laws and society
THEORY CONSTRUCTION
Predicting individual behaviour
Understanding the cause of crime rates and trends
CRIMINAL BEHAVIOUR SYSTEMS
Determining the nature and cause of specific crime patterns
Studying violence, theft, organized, white-collar, and public order crimes
PENOLOGY
Studying the correction and control of criminal behaviour
VICTIMOLOGY
Studying the nature and cause of victimization
Aiding crime victims

FIGURE 1.2

The Criminological Enterprise

These subareas constitute the field discipline of criminology.

The Sociology of Law

The sociology of law is a subarea of criminology concerned with the role social forces play in shaping criminal law and the role of criminal law in shaping society. Criminologists study the history of legal thought in an effort to understand how criminal acts, such as theft, sexual assault, and murder, evolved into their present form.

Often criminologists are asked to join the debate when a new law is proposed to outlaw or control a particular behaviour. For example, in Canada debate continues to rage over Bill C-68 (1995), the Firearms Act, which requires Canadians to register their firearms. In November 2011, the newly elected Harper majority government followed through on a campaign promise by introducing Bill-C19, "An Act to amend the Criminal Code and the Firearms Act," which would eliminate the contested long-gun registry. Criminologists are being drawn into the debate to help answer important questions: Did mandatory registration make it more difficult for criminals to obtain firearms? Will there be fewer murders and other kinds of violent crimes because of mandatory registration? Will eliminating the long-gun registry make it more dangerous for police officers attending a call? The answers to these questions will help shape any future changes in Canadian laws regarding firearms and their use.[19]

AP PHOTO/HO Maclean's

Robert Latimer with his 12-year-old daughter Tracy.

Criminologists also participate actively in updating the content of criminal law, helping lawmakers respond to changing times and conditions. For instance, computer fraud, hijacking, theft from automated teller machines, Internet scams, identity theft, copyright issues related to downloading music and videos from the Internet, and distribution of child pornography over the Internet are behaviours that did not exist when criminal law was originally conceived. The law must be constantly revised to reflect cultural, societal, and technological adaptations of common acts.

For example, in 2001 Saskatchewan farmer Robert Latimer went to jail to begin serving a minimum ten-year sentence for the second-degree murder of his 12-year-old daughter Tracy, in spite of calls from the trial jury itself and the public for mercy and a much lighter sentence. In 1993 Mr. Latimer confessed to killing his severely disabled daughter with carbon monoxide gas, but claimed he acted out of compassion to end the constant pain his daughter suffered. The Latimer case raised several major legal and social issues. For example, should courts abide by the letter or the spirit of the law? If the courts were lenient to Latimer, would this send a message that euthanasia or mercy killing was now acceptable and that disabled persons should be viewed as second-class citizens? Would it mean the end of mandatory minimum sentences for convicted persons? Although one judge referred to the killing of Tracy Latimer as "compassionate homicide," the Supreme Court of Canada did not accept this as a legal defence nor did it accept that the mandatory ten-year sentence would be "cruel and unusual punishment." In the end, Latimer served his sentence and was released for day parole on March 13, 2008. The Latimer case brought to the forefront the debate over "mercy killing," or euthanasia, and the serious moral and legal issues involved.[20]

Criminologists can help make the determination when a law should be changed, updated, or eliminated.

Developing Theories of Crime Causation

From the beginning, criminologists have wondered why people engage in criminal acts even though their behaviour may result in harsh punishment

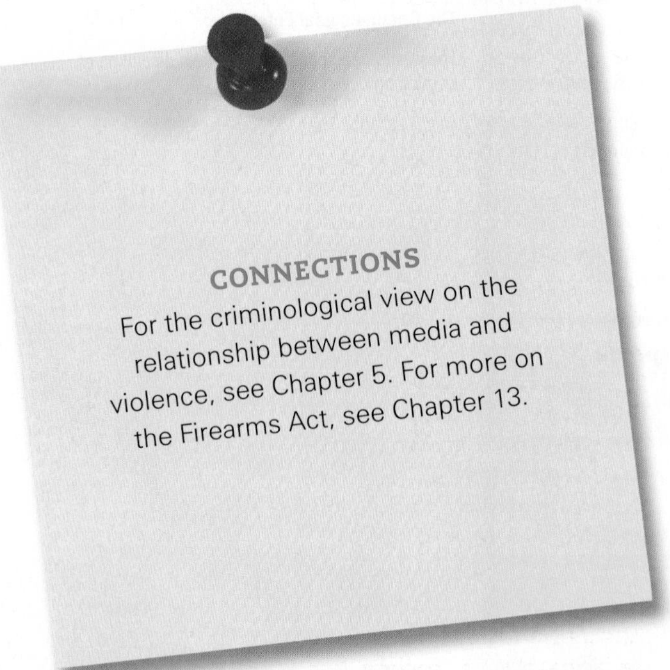
CONNECTIONS
For the criminological view on the relationship between media and violence, see Chapter 5. For more on the Firearms Act, see Chapter 13.

and social disapproval. Some criminologists with a psychological orientation view crime as a function of personality, development, social learning, or cognition. Others investigate the biological correlates of antisocial behaviour and study the biochemical, genetic, and neurological linkages to crime. Sociologists look at the social forces producing criminal behaviour, including neighbourhood conditions, poverty, socialization, and group interaction.

Understanding the true cause of crime remains a difficult problem. Criminologists are still unsure why, given similar conditions, some people choose criminal solutions to their problems while others conform to accepted social rules of behaviour.

Understanding and Describing Criminal Behaviour

Another subarea of criminology involves research on specific criminal types and patterns: violent crime, theft crime, public order crime, organized crime, cyber crime, and so on. Numerous attempts have been made to describe and understand particular crime types. Marvin Wolfgang's famous 1958 study, *Patterns in Criminal Homicide*, is considered a landmark analysis of the nature of homicide and the relationship between victim and offender.[21] Edwin Sutherland's analysis of business-related offences helped coin a new phrase, **white-collar crime**, to describe economic crime activities of the affluent.

Penology

The study of **penology** involves the correction and control of known criminal offenders. Some criminologists are advocates of **rehabilitation**; they direct their efforts at identifying effective treatment strategies for individuals convicted of law violations. Others argue that crime can be prevented only through a strict policy of social control; they advocate measures such as **capital punishment** and **mandatory sentences**. Criminologists also help evaluate correctional initiatives to determine if they are effective and how they impact people's lives.

Victimology

Criminologists recognize the critical role of the victim in the criminal process and that the victim's behaviour is often a key determinant of crime.[22] **Victimology** includes the following areas of interest:

- Using victim surveys to measure the nature and extent of criminal behaviour and calculate the actual costs of crime to victims
- Calculating probabilities of victimization risk
- Studying victim culpability in the precipitation of crime
- Designing services for crime victims, such as counselling and compensation programs

Victimology has taken on greater importance as more criminologists focus attention on the victim's role in the criminal event.

LO4 Deviant or Criminal—How Criminologists Define Crime

Criminologists devote themselves to measuring, understanding, and controlling crime and deviance. How are these behaviours defined, and how do we distinguish between them?

Criminologists view deviant behaviour as any action that departs from the social norms of society.[23] **Deviance** thus includes a broad spectrum of behaviours, ranging from the most socially harmful, such as rape and murder, to the relatively inoffensive, such as joining a religious cult or cross-dressing. A deviant act becomes a **crime** when it is deemed socially harmful or dangerous; it then will be specifically defined, prohibited, and punished under the criminal law.

Criminologist John Hagan developed a useful breakdown for understanding the relationship between deviance and crime (see Table 1.1 on the next page).[24] Some kinds of behaviours or practices, such as body tattooing and piercing, may be unusual, but are viewed by most of us as relatively harmless; this is an example of what Hagan calls a "social diversion." Other kinds of deviant behaviour, such as mental illness, may be seen as potentially more threatening or dangerous to the public, and so bring forth a stronger societal response such as commitment to a hospital, or community supervision; Hagan terms this type of deviance "social deviation." "Conflict crimes" are kinds of deviance that a society has

white-collar crime
Illegal acts that capitalize on a person's status in the marketplace. White-collar crimes may include theft, embezzlement, fraud, market manipulation, price fixing, and false advertising.

penology
Subarea of criminology that focuses on the correction and control of criminal offenders.

rehabilitation
Treatment of criminal offenders aimed at preventing future criminal behaviour.

capital punishment
The execution of criminal offenders; the death penalty.

mandatory sentences
A statutory requirement that a certain penalty shall be carried out in all cases of conviction for a specified offence.

victimology
The study of the victim's role in criminal events.

deviance
Behaviour that departs from the social norm but is not necessarily criminal.

crime
An act, deemed socially harmful or dangerous, that is specifically defined, prohibited, and punished under the criminal law.

TABLE 1.1

John Hagan's Breakdown of Deviance and Crime

Kind of Deviance	Severity of Social Response	Perceived Harmfulness	Degree of Agreement	Examples
Consensus crimes	Severe	Extremely harmful	Consensus	Homicide; incest
Conflict crimes	Punitive	Somewhat harmful	Conflict	Drugs; prostitution; gambling
Social deviations	Indeterminate	Potentially harmful	Uncertainty	Mental illness; delinquency
Social diversions	Mild	Relatively harmless	Apathy	Fads and fashions

Source: From HAGEDOR. *Sociology 4/E*. © 1990 Nelson Education Ltd. Reproduced by permission. www.cengage.com/permissions

consensus view
The belief that the majority of citizens in a society share common values and agree on what behaviours should be defined as criminal.

defined in law as criminal, but there is still not a lot of agreement about whether these acts are really criminal; marijuana use is a good example. Finally, some kinds of deviance virtually everyone agrees are wrong, cause severe harm, and are criminal; Hagen calls these acts, such as child abuse or murder, "consensus crimes."

Hagan points out that what is considered deviant or criminal can change over time and can be culturally specific; for example, running lottery games (like the Irish Sweepstakes) used to be illegal in Canada (a conflict crime), but such a practice is now considered, at worst, a social diversion, and homosexual relationships are still considered illegal in some countries while in Canada they are not.

Criminologists are often concerned with the concept of deviance and its relationship to criminality. The shifting definition of deviant behaviour is closely associated with our concepts of crime: Where should society draw the line between behaviour that is merely considered deviant and unusual, and behaviour that is considered dangerous and criminal? For example, when does sexually oriented material stop being merely erotic and suggestive (deviant) and become obscene and pornographic (criminal)? Can a clear line be drawn separating sexually oriented materials into two groups, one that is legally acceptable and a second that is considered depraved or obscene? And if such a line can be drawn, who gets to draw it?

Though crimes may be defined as acts that are socially harmful or dangerous, criminologists still differ over what acts are truly "harmful" and who decides that they are "dangerous." As you may recall, professional criminologists usually align themselves with one of several schools of thought or perspectives. Each of these perspectives maintains its own view of what constitutes criminal behaviour and what causes people to engage in criminality. A criminologist's choice of orientation or perspective thus depends, in part, on his or her definition of crime. The three most common concepts of crime used by criminologists are the consensus view, the conflict view, and the interactionist view.

Mondelo/EPA/Landov

Is smoking marijuana deviant? A majority of Canadians support the decriminalization of marijuana, which would make possession a minor offence, punishable by only a small fine. Is marijuana possession deviant? Should it be decriminalized?

The Consensus View of Crime

According to the **consensus view**, crimes are behaviours that all elements of society consider to be repugnant. The rich and powerful as well as the poor and indigent are believed to agree on which behaviours are so repugnant that they should be outlawed and criminalized. Therefore, the criminal law—the written code that defines crimes and their punishments—reflects the values, beliefs, and opinions of society's majority. The term *consensus* implies general agreement among a majority of citizens on what behaviours should be prohibited by **criminal law** and hence be viewed as crimes.[25]

This approach to crime implies that it is a function of the beliefs, morality, and rules that are inherent in Western civilization. Ideally, the laws apply equally to all members of society and their effects are not restricted to any single element of society. Whereas laws banning break and enter and robbery are directed at controlling the neediest members of society, laws banning insider trading, embezzlement, and corporate price-fixing are aimed at controlling the wealthiest.

The Conflict View of Crime

Although most practising criminologists accept the consensus model of crime, others take a more political orientation toward its content. The **conflict view** depicts society as a collection of diverse groups—such as owners, workers, professionals, and students—who are in constant and continuing conflict. Groups able to assert their political power use the law and the criminal justice system to advance their economic and social position. Criminal laws, therefore, are viewed as acts created to protect the haves from the have-nots. Conflict criminologists often contrast the harsh penalties exacted on the poor for their "street crimes" (break and enter, robbery, and theft) with the minor penalties the wealthy receive for their white-collar crimes (securities violations and other illegal business practices). Whereas the poor go to prison for minor law violations, the wealthy are given lenient sentences for even the most serious breaches of law.

According to the conflict view, the definition of crime is controlled by wealth, power, and position and not by moral consensus or the fear of social disruption.[26] Crime, according to this definition, is a political concept designed to protect the power and position of the upper classes at the expense of the poor. Even laws prohibiting violent acts, such as robbery, sexual assault, and murder, may have political undertones. Banning violent acts ensures domestic tranquility and guarantees that the anger of the poor and disenfranchised classes will not be directed at their wealthy capitalist exploiters. Spousal assault may be inspired by the capitalist system's devaluation of women, which may increase their vulnerability to this act. The conflict view of crime, then, includes the following in a comprehensive list of "real" crimes[27]:

- Violations of human rights due to racism, sexism, and imperialism
- Unsafe working conditions
- Inadequate child care
- Inadequate opportunities for employment and education and substandard housing and medical care
- Crimes of economic and political domination
- Pollution of the environment
- Price-fixing
- Police brutality
- Assassinations and war making
- Violations of human dignity
- Denial of physical needs and necessities, and impediments to self-determination
- Deprivation of adequate food and blocked opportunities to participate in political decision making*

criminal law
The written code that defines crimes and their punishments.

conflict view
The belief that criminal behaviour is defined by those in a position of power to protect and advance their own self-interest.

interactionist view
The belief that those with social power are able to impose their values on society as a whole, and these values then define criminal behaviour.

The Interactionist View of Crime

According to the **interactionist view**, the definition of crime reflects the preferences and opinions of people who hold social power in a particular legal jurisdiction. These people use their influence to impose their definition of right and wrong on the rest of the population. Criminals are individuals that society labels as outcasts or deviants because they have violated social rules. In a classic statement, sociologist Howard Becker argued, "The deviant is one to whom that label has successfully been applied; deviant behavior is behavior people so label."[28] Crimes are outlawed behaviours because society defines them that way, not because they are inherently evil or immoral acts.

The interactionist view of crime is similar to the conflict perspective in that behaviour is outlawed when it offends those with sufficient social, economic, and political power to make the law conform to their interests or needs. However, unlike the conflict view, the interactionist perspective does not attribute capitalist economic and political motives to the process of defining crime. Instead, interactionists see criminal law as conforming to the beliefs of "moral crusaders" or moral entrepreneurs, who use their influence to shape the legal process as they see fit.[29] Laws against pornography, prostitution, and drugs are believed to be motivated more by moral crusades than by capitalist sensibilities. Consequently, interactionists are concerned with shifting moral and legal standards.

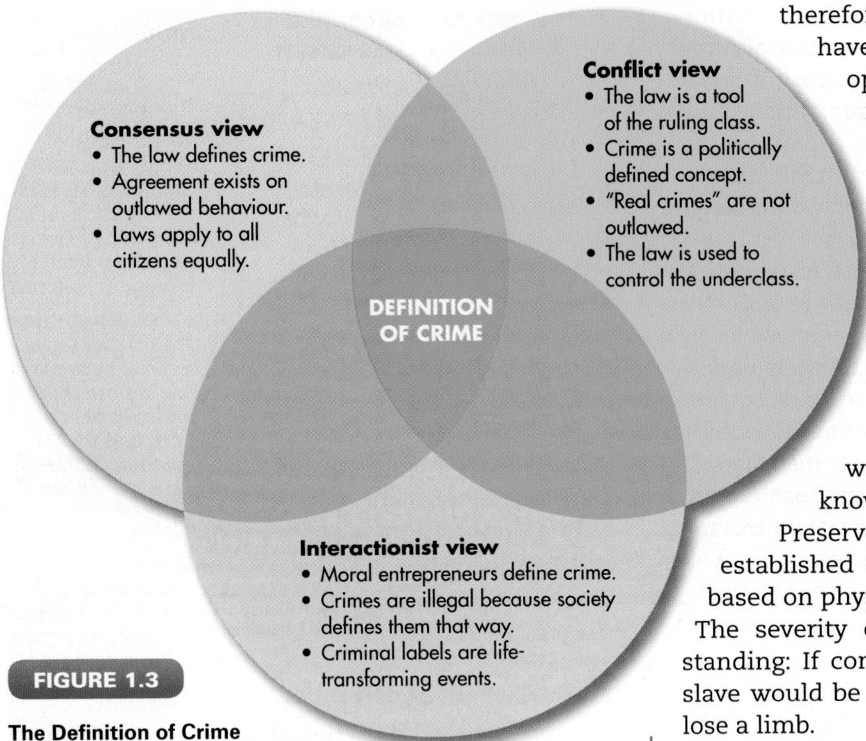

Consensus view
- The law defines crime.
- Agreement exists on outlawed behaviour.
- Laws apply to all citizens equally.

Conflict view
- The law is a tool of the ruling class.
- Crime is a politically defined concept.
- "Real crimes" are not outlawed.
- The law is used to control the underclass.

DEFINITION OF CRIME

Interactionist view
- Moral entrepreneurs define crime.
- Crimes are illegal because society defines them that way.
- Criminal labels are life-transforming events.

FIGURE 1.3

The Definition of Crime

A Definition of Crime

Because of their diverse perspectives, criminologists have taken a variety of approaches in explaining crime's causes and suggesting methods for its control (see Figure 1.3). Considering these differences, we can take elements from each school of thought to formulate an integrated definition of crime such as the following:

> Crime is a violation of societal rules of behaviour as interpreted and expressed by the criminal law, which reflects public opinion, traditional values, and the viewpoint of people currently holding social and political power. Individuals who violate these rules are subject to sanctions by state authority, social stigma, and loss of status.

The definition of crime affects how criminologists view the cause and control of illegal behaviour and shapes their research orientation.

This definition combines the consensus view that the criminal law defines crimes, the conflict perspective's emphasis on political power and control, and the interactionist concept of stigma. Thus, crime as defined here is a political, social, and economic function of modern life.

Code of Hammurabi
The first written criminal code, developed in Babylonia about 1780 B.C.

Mosaic Code
The laws of the ancient Israelites, found in the Old Testament of the Judeo-Christian Bible.

No matter which definition of crime we embrace, criminal behaviour is tied to the criminal law. It is therefore important for all criminologists to have some understanding of the development of criminal law, its objectives, its elements, and how it evolves.

Crime and the Criminal Law

The concept of criminal law has been recognized for more than 3000 years. Hammurabi (1792–1750 B.C.), the sixth king of Babylon, created the most famous set of written laws of the ancient world, known today as the **Code of Hammurabi**. Preserved on basalt rock columns, the code established a system of crime and punishment based on physical retaliation ("an eye for an eye"). The severity of punishment depended on class standing: If convicted of an unprovoked assault, a slave would be killed, whereas a free person might lose a limb.

More familiar is the **Mosaic Code** of the Israelites (1200 B.C.). According to tradition, God entered into a covenant or contract with the tribes of Israel in which they agreed to obey his law (the 613 laws of the Old Testament, including the Ten Commandments), as presented to them by Moses, in return for God's special care and protection. The Mosaic Code is not only the foundation of Judeo-Christian moral teachings but also a basis for the Canadian legal system. Prohibitions against murder, theft, and perjury preceded, by several thousand years, the same laws found in Canada today.

Though ancient formal legal codes were lost during the Dark Ages, early German and Anglo-Saxon societies developed legal systems featuring monetary compensation for criminal violations. Guilt was determined by two methods. One was compurgation, in which the accused person swore an oath of innocence with the backing of 12 to 25 oath helpers, who would attest to his or her character and claims of innocence. The second was trial by ordeal, which was based on the principle that divine forces would not allow an innocent person to be harmed. It involved measures such as having the accused place his or her hand in boiling water or hold a hot iron. If the wound healed, the person was found innocent; if the wound did not heal, the accused was deemed guilty. Another version, trial by combat, allowed the accused to challenge the accuser to a duel, with the outcome determining the legitimacy of the accusation. Punishments included public flogging, branding, beheading, and burning.

LO5 Common Law

After the Norman conquest of England in 1066, royal judges began to travel throughout the land, holding court in each county several times a year. When court was in session, the royal administrator, or judge, would summon a number of citizens who would, on their oath, tell of the crimes and serious breaches of the peace that had occurred since the judge's last visit. The royal judge would then decide what to do in each case, using local custom and rules of conduct as his guide. Courts were bound to follow the law established in previous cases unless a higher authority, such as the king or the pope, overruled the law.

The present English system of law came into existence during the reign of Henry II (1154–1189), when royal judges began to publish their decisions in local cases. Judges began to use these written decisions as a basis for their decision making, and eventually a fixed body of legal rules and principles was established. If a new rule was successfully applied in a number of different cases, it would become a **precedent**. These precedents would then be commonly applied in all similar cases—hence the term **common law**. Crimes such as murder, break and enter, arson, and sexual assault are common-law crimes whose elements were initially defined by judges. They are referred to as *mala in se*, or inherently evil and depraved. When the situation required, the English Parliament enacted legislation to supplement the judge-made common law. Crimes defined by Parliament, which reflected existing social conditions, were referred to as *mala prohibitum*, or **statutory crimes**.

Canada inherited English common law and standardized crimes such as murder, break and enter, arson, and sexual assault by putting them in statutory form in criminal code. As in England, whenever common law proved inadequate to deal with changing social and moral issues, the Canadian Parliament supplemented it with legislative statutes, creating new sections of the Criminal Code. Table 1.2 lists a number of crimes that were first defined in common law.

LO6 Contemporary Criminal Law

Canadian laws are divided into indictable and summary conviction offences. The distinction is based on seriousness: An **indictable offence** is a serious offence; a **summary conviction offence** is a less serious offence. Crimes such as murder, aggravated sexual assault, and robbery are indictable offences; they are punished with long prison sentences. Crimes such as personating a police officer, causing a disturbance of the peace, trespassing at night, or soliciting for the purposes of prostitution are summary conviction offences.

Regardless of their classification, acts prohibited by the criminal law constitute behaviours considered unacceptable and impermissible by those in power. People who engage in these acts are eligible for severe sanctions. By outlawing these behaviours, the government expects to achieve a number of social goals:

- *Enforcing social control.* Those who hold political power rely on criminal law to formally prohibit behaviours believed to threaten societal well-being or to challenge their authority. For example, Canadian law incorporates centuries-old prohibitions against the following behaviours harmful to others: taking another person's possessions, physically harming another person, damaging another person's property, and cheating another person out of his or her possessions. Similarly, the law prevents actions that challenge the legitimacy of the government, such as planning its overthrow, collaborating with its enemies, and so on.
- *Discouraging revenge.* By punishing people who infringe on the rights, property, and freedom of others, the law shifts the burden of revenge from the individual to the state. The famous American jurist Oliver Wendell Holmes stated that this prevents "the greater evil of private retribution."[30] Although state retaliation may offend the sensibilities of many citizens, it is greatly preferable to a system in which people would have to seek justice for themselves.
- *Expressing public opinion and morality.* Criminal law reflects constantly changing public opinions and moral values. *Mala in se*, or inherently evil and depraved crimes such as murder and sexual assault, are almost universally prohibited; however, the prohibition of legislatively created *mala prohibitum*, or statutory crimes such as traffic offences and gambling violations, changes according to social conditions and attitudes. Criminal law is used to codify these changes.
- *Deterring criminal behaviour.* Criminal law has a social control function. It can control, restrain, and direct human behaviour through its sanctioning power. The threat of punishment associated with violating the law is designed to prevent crimes before they occur. During the Middle Ages, public executions drove this point home. Today criminal law's impact is felt through news accounts of long prison sentences.
- *Punishing wrongdoing.* The deterrent power of criminal law is tied to the authority it gives the state to sanction or punish

precedent
A rule derived from previous judicial decisions and applied to future cases; the basis of common law.

common law
Early English law, developed by judges, that became the standardized law of the land in England and eventually formed the basis of the criminal law in Canada.

statutory crimes
Crimes defined by legislative bodies in response to changing social conditions, public opinion, and custom.

indictable offence
A serious offence where an "indictment" is issued requiring the accused to stand trial before a judge alone, or a judge and jury; the Canadian equivalent to the American "felony."

summary conviction offence
A minor offence punishable by a fine of up to $2000, six months in jail, or both; the Canadian equivalent to the American "misdemeanour."

TABLE 1.2

Common-Law Crimes

Crimes	Examples
Crimes Against the Person	
First-degree murder. Unlawful killing of another human being that is planned and deliberate.	A woman buys some poison and pours it into a cup of coffee her husband is drinking, intending to kill him. The motive—to get the insurance benefits of the victim.
Manslaughter. Unlawful killing of another human being committed in the heat of passion caused by sudden provocation.	A man, taunted in front of his co-workers by the man who is having an affair with his wife, grabs an iron bar and uses it to beat and kill his wife's lover.
Infanticide. Unlawful killing of her newly born child by a female person who, at the time, is not fully recovered from the effects of giving birth or the effect of lactation, and whose mind is thereby disturbed.	A new mother, suffering from a severe postpartum depression and fearful she may physically hurt her three-week-old baby, drowns the infant in the bathtub, in the belief that the baby will return to God and be safe from any harm the mother might do.
Assault. Threat of or actual use of force against another without his or her consent.	Leaving a bar at closing time after a night of drinking, a university student accuses his girlfriend of flirting with other men, and slaps her in the face.
Sexual assault. An assault of a sexual nature against another without his or her consent.	After a party a man offers to drive a young female acquaintance home. He takes her to a wooded area and, despite her protests, forces her to perform oral sex on him.
Robbery. Use of violence or the threat of violence to steal from a person or property.	A man armed with a hunting knife enters a gas bar and demands that the attendant hand over all the cash in the till.
Inchoate (Incomplete) Offences	
Attempt. An intentional act or omission for the purpose of committing a crime that is more than mere preparation or planning of the crime. The crime is not completed, however.	A person intending to kill another person places a bomb in the intended victim's car so that it will detonate when the ignition key is turned. The bomb is discovered before the car is started. Attempted murder has been committed.
Conspiracy. Voluntary agreement between two or more persons to undertake to commit an indictable offence.	Two men meet and, on paper, draw out a plan and a list of materials necessary to kidnap an elderly woman. The two are guilty of conspiracy.
Crimes Against Property	
Break and enter. To break in and enter a place with the intent to commit an indictable offence.	Intending to steal a DVD player and any other easy-to-carry electronic equipment, a young man breaks a window and enters another's house.
Arson. Intentional or reckless damage by fire or explosion of another's property.	A man, upset that his boss did not give him a raise, goes to his boss's house and sets fire to it.
Theft. Without permission or right, to take or convert to one's own use property that belongs to another person.	While in the music store, a young woman spots a newly released CD by her favourite singer, but she doesn't have enough money to purchase it, so she slips it into her purse and walks out of the store.

offenders. Those who violate criminal law are subject to physical coercion and punishment.

- *Maintaining social order.* All legal systems are designed to support and maintain the boundaries of the social system they serve. In medieval England, the law protected the feudal system by defining an orderly system of property transfer and ownership. Laws in some socialist nations protect the primacy of the state by strictly curtailing profiteering and individual enterprise. Our own capitalist system is also supported and sustained by criminal law. In a sense, the content of criminal law is more a reflection of the needs of those who control the existing economic and political system than a representation of some idealized moral code.

actus reus
An illegal or "guilty" act. It may be an affirmative act, such as killing, or a failure to act when legally required to do so.

mens rea
A "guilty mind"; the intent to commit a criminal act.

LO7 The Elements of a Crime

In order for a crime to occur, the state must show that the accused committed the guilty act, or ***actus reus***, and had the ***mens rea***, or criminal intent, to commit the act. The *actus reus* may be an aggressive act, such as taking someone's money, burning a building, or shooting someone; or it may be a failure to act when there is a legal duty to do so, such as a parent's neglecting to seek medical attention for a sick child. The *mens rea* (guilty mind) refers to an individual's state of mind at the time of the act or, more specifically, the person's intent to commit the crime.

For most crimes, both the *actus reus* and the *mens rea* must be present for the act to be considered a crime. For example, if George decides to kill Bob and then takes a gun and shoots Bob, George can be convicted of the crime of murder, because both elements are present. George's shooting of Bob is the *actus reus*; his decision to kill Bob is the *mens rea*. However, if George only thinks about shooting Bob but does nothing about it, the element of *actus reus* is absent, and no crime has been committed. Thoughts of committing an act do not, in themselves, constitute a crime. Let us now look more closely at these issues.

Actus Reus

To satisfy the requirements of *actus reus*, guilty actions must be voluntary. Even though an act may cause harm or damage, it is not considered a crime if it was done by accident or was an involuntary act. For example, it would not be a crime if a motorist obeying all the traffic laws hit a child who had run into the street. If the same motorist were drinking or speeding, then this action would be considered a crime because it was a product of negligence. Similarly, it would not be considered a crime if a babysitter accidentally dropped a child and the child died. However, it would be considered manslaughter if the sitter threw the child down in anger or frustration and the blow caused the child's death. In some circumstances of *actus reus*, the use of words is considered criminal. For example, according to the Canadian Criminal Code (R.S. 1985), if a person makes a speech or distributes literature that incites hatred against an "identifiable" group distinguished by colour, race, religion, or ethnic origin, that person is guilty of an illegal act, punishable by up to two years in prison.[31]

Typically, the law does not require people to aid people in distress, such as entering a burning building to rescue people trapped by a fire. However, failure to act is considered a crime in certain instances:

1. *Relationship of the parties based on status.* Some people are bound by relationship to give aid. These relationships include parent–child and husband–wife. If a husband finds his wife unconscious because she took an overdose of sleeping pills, he is obligated to try to save her life by seeking medical aid. If he fails to do so and she dies, he can be held responsible for her death.
2. *Imposition by statute.* Some laws require that any adult must provide assistance by reporting suspected physical, sexual, or emotional abuse of a child.
3. *Contractual relationships.* These relationships include lifeguard and swimmer, doctor and patient, and babysitter and child. Because lifeguards have been hired to ensure the safety of swimmers, they have a legal duty to come to the aid of drowning persons. If a lifeguard knows a swimmer is in danger and does nothing about it and the swimmer drowns, the lifeguard is legally responsible for the swimmer's death.

Mens Rea

In most situations, for an act to constitute a crime, it must be done with criminal intent, or *mens rea*. Intent, in the legal sense, can mean carrying out an act intentionally, knowingly, and willingly. However, the definition also encompasses situations in which

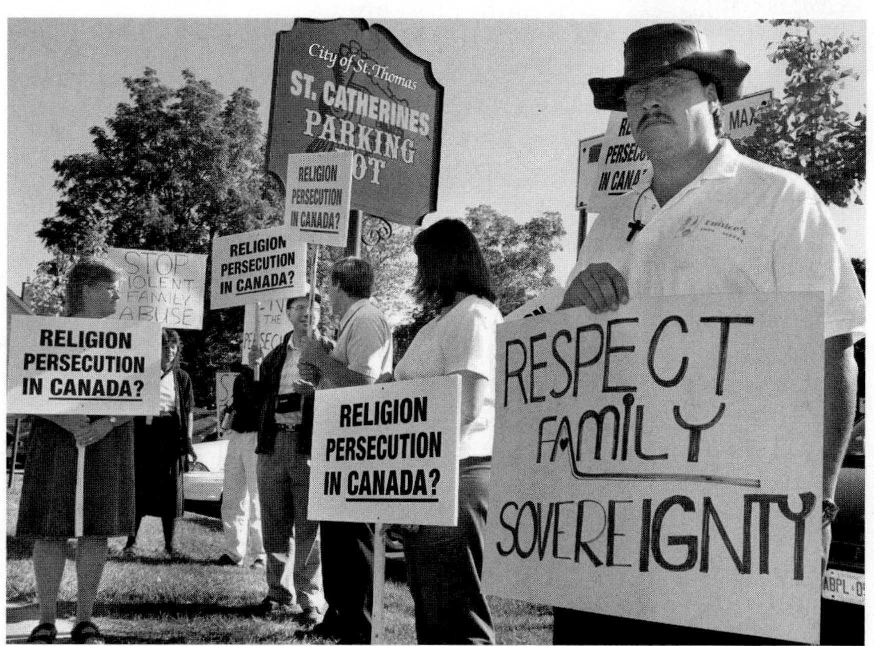

London Free Press/Ken Wightman

In 2002, a St. Thomas, Ontario, court heard evidence during the so-called "Aylmer spanking case" that a mother and father used belts, sticks, electrical cords, a clothes hanger, and a broken metal fly swatter to discipline their seven children. Section 43 of the Criminal Code has allowed spanking by parents and school teachers since 1892, but only for the purpose of "correction," and only if "reasonable." On January 30, 2004, in response to a legal challenge to Section 43 launched by the Canadian Foundation for Children, Youth and the Law that argued Section 43 was discriminatory, infringed the right of children to security of the person, and opened the door to cruel and unusual punishment, the Supreme Court upheld Section 43 and the right of parents and teachers to use "reasonable" force "by way of correction." However, the Court went further to identify that parents cannot use corporal punishment with children under the age of two or with teenagers, cannot use objects while disciplining, must use an open hand, and cannot administer blows or slaps to the head.[32]

absolute liability crimes
Illegal acts in which guilt does not depend on intent, or *mens rea*. They are usually acts that endanger the public welfare, such as violations of health and safety regulations.

excuse defence
Criminal defence based on a lack of criminal intent (*mens rea*). Excuse defences include mental disorder, automatism, intoxication, and ignorance.

justification defence
Criminal defence that claims an illegal action was justified by circumstances and therefore not criminal. Justification defences include necessity, duress, self-defence, and entrapment.

recklessness or negligence establishes the required criminal intent.

Criminal intent also exists if the results of an action, although originally unintended, are certain to occur. For example, when Timothy McVeigh planted a bomb in front of the Murrah Federal Building in Oklahoma City, he did not intend to kill any particular person in the building. Yet the law would hold that McVeigh or any other person would be substantially certain that people in the building would be killed in the blast, and McVeigh therefore had the criminal intent to commit murder.

Absolute Liability

Though common-law crimes require that both the *actus reus* and the *mens rea* must be present before a person can be convicted of a crime, several crimes defined by statute do not require *mens rea*. In these cases, the person accused is guilty simply by doing what the statute prohibits; intent does not enter the picture. These **absolute liability crimes**, or public welfare offences, include violations of health and safety regulations, traffic laws, and hunting or fishing out of season. For example, a person stopped for speeding is guilty of breaking the traffic laws regardless of whether he or she intended to go over the speed limit or did it by accident. The underlying purpose of these laws is to protect the public; therefore, intent is not required.[33]

Criminal Defences

When people defend themselves against criminal charges, they must refute one or more of the elements of the crime of which they have been accused. A number of different approaches can be taken to create this defence.

First, defendants may deny the *actus reus* by arguing that they were falsely accused and that the real culprit has yet to be identified. Second, defendants may claim that although they engaged in the criminal act of which they are accused, they lacked the *mens rea* (intent) needed to be found guilty of the crime.

If a person whose mental state is impaired commits a criminal act, it is possible for the person to excuse his or her criminal actions by claiming that he or she lacked the capacity to form sufficient intent to be held criminally responsible. Mental disorder, automatism, intoxication, and ignorance are types of **excuse defences**. For example, the defence of automatism was successfully used in the *Parks* (1992) case. Parks claimed to be sleepwalking when he drove 23 kilometres through Toronto to the home of his parents-in-law whom he then murdered. The Supreme Court of Canada accepted the argument by Parks's lawyers that he was not criminally responsible for the murders.[34]

Another type of defence is justification. Here the individual usually admits committing the criminal act but maintains that he or she should not be held criminally liable because the act was justified. Among the **justification defences** are necessity, duress, self-defence, and entrapment. For example, in *R. v. Ruzic* (1998),[35] the accused (Ruzic) used the defence of duress, claiming she smuggled two kilograms of heroin into Canada because she had been told by a man that if she didn't do it her elderly mother living in Belgrade would be beaten up or even killed.

Persons standing trial for criminal offences may thus defend themselves by claiming that they did not commit the act in question, that their actions were justified under the circumstances, or that their behaviour can be excused by their lack of *mens rea*. If either the physical or mental elements of a crime cannot be proven, then the defendant cannot be convicted.

In recent years, Canadian defence lawyers have tried to convince the courts that some women accused of the murder of their male partners may actually have been acting out of self-defence after having suffered years of emotional or physical abuse. The accompanying Policy and Practice in Criminology feature discusses the "battered woman" defence in detail.

The Evolution of Criminal Law

Criminal law is constantly evolving in an effort to reflect changing circumstances in society. For example, in response to the September 11, 2001, terrorist attacks in the United States, the Canadian government introduced the Anti-Terrorism Act (Bill C-41) to amend the Criminal Code so that terrorist groups could be more easily identified and investigated, through the use of electronic surveillance, detention of suspected terrorists and their associates for up to 72 hours without charge, and requiring individuals who have knowledge about the activities of a terrorist group to report that knowledge to authorities.[36] Similarly, after public calls for more accountability for young people who commit serious offences, the Youth Criminal Justice Act was introduced in 2001.

POLICY AND PRACTICE IN CRIMINOLOGY

A LANDMARK CASE: THE "BATTERED WOMAN" DEFENCE

In September 1986, Angelique Lyn Lavallee, a 22-year-old Manitoba woman, was charged with the second-degree murder of her common-law spouse, Kevin Rust. Lavallee admitted to shooting Rust in the back of the head in the midst of a "boisterous party" being held at their home. According to Lavallee, Rust confronted her in an upstairs bedroom and pushed and slapped her. Rust then handed her a .303 rifle kept in the home and a shot was fired through the screen in the bedroom window. Rust chambered a second shell and handed it to Lavallee, with the threat "Wait till everybody leaves, you'll get it then." Meaning to scare Rust off, Lavallee fired the rifle, hitting Rust in the back of the head as he left the bedroom, killing him.

At her trial, Lavallee's lawyer argued that her action was a case of "self-defence" as defined in Section 34(2) of the Criminal Code, which states:

(2) Every one who is unlawfully assaulted and who causes death or grievous bodily harm in repelling the assault is justified if
- (a) he causes it under reasonable apprehension of death or grievous bodily harm from the violence with which the assault was originally made or with which the assailant pursues his purposes, and
- (b) he believes on reasonable and probable grounds, that he cannot otherwise preserve himself from death or grievous bodily harm.

The introduction of this defence was surprising; in the past, the courts had required that (1) the perceived harm be "imminent" (about to occur or actually underway) and that (2) there be no means to escape or avoid the harm. Indeed, Lavallee's actions did not appear to meet either test; Rust was leaving the room to go back to the party when he was killed, removing the imminent threat of harm, and providing Lavallee the opportunity to leave the bedroom and the house to seek help.

Lavallee's lawyer introduced evidence at trial that from the very beginning of their relationship, Lavallee was frequently physically abused by Rust, and made several trips to the hospital as a result. Friends of the couple testified to their "stormy" relationship and to the recurring physical abuse of Lavallee.

Lavallee's lawyer capped the defence argument with expert testimony from psychiatrist Dr. Fred Shane, who testified that Lavallee demonstrated the symptoms of "battered woman syndrome." Dr. Shane explained that, like other women characterized by this syndrome, Lavallee had "been terrorized by Rust to the point of feeling trapped, vulnerable, worthless and unable to escape the relationship despite the violence." Based on their past experiences, battered women know that their abusers will make good on their threats, but they feel helpless to escape the inevitable physical assault. For battered women, then, attacks are always "imminent" and, at some point, will probably be fatal.

The Manitoba jury acquitted Lavallee, in large part based on Dr. Shane's testimony that battered woman syndrome characterized the actions of the accused in the case. However, the acquittal was overturned by the Manitoba Court of Appeal, on the ground that Dr. Shane's testimony was "unnecessary and superfluous," as the facts of the case spoke for themselves; and his comment that he found the accused "credible" was improper, given that Lavallee did not testify, and so her credibility could not be tested in cross-examination. The Court of Appeal recommended the Crown proceed with a lesser charge of manslaughter.

On May 3, 1990, the Supreme Court of Canada restored Lavallee's acquittal on the basis that Dr. Shane's testimony was relevant to the issue of self-defence—and the "battered woman syndrome" was therefore accepted as a legitimate defence to homicide and other forms of bodily harm committed in self-defence.

CRITICAL THINKING

1. What standard should the courts use to determine whether the defence of battered woman syndrome is valid? Will the Supreme Court's acceptance of the battered woman's defence mean a significant increase in cases where women claim this type of self-defence? Should the syndrome of "battering" be restricted to women?
2. Is it fair to punish someone suffering from severe emotional trauma who committed a murder in the same manner as someone who killed for money? Why or why not? Should motive influence punishment?

© Judith Collins / Alamy

Sometimes legal changes are prompted by highly publicized cases that generate fear and concern. For example, a number of highly publicized cases of criminal harassment or "stalking" (including the murder of Arlene May in Toronto in 1996) prompted the Canadian government to amend the Criminal Code in 1997 and again in 2002 to implement penalties of up to ten years in prison for engaging in stalking behaviour.[37] Similarly, the 1988 murder of 11-year-old Christopher Stephenson by a convicted pedophile who had recently been released from a nearby federal prison led the Ontario government to enact "Christopher's Law" (Sex Offender Registry 2000), which requires convicted sex offenders living in Ontario to report to their local police service on an annual basis, and to notify the police within 15 days of any change in address.[38]

The future direction of Canadian criminal law remains unclear. Certain actions, such as crimes by corporations and political corruption, will be labelled as criminal and given more attention. Other offences, such as recreational drug use, may be reduced in importance or removed entirely from the criminal law system. In addition, changing technology and its ever-increasing global and local roles in our lives will require modifications in criminal law. For example, technologies such as automated teller machines, cellular phones, and the Internet have already spawned a new generation of criminal acts such as theft of access numbers, software piracy, identity theft, and distribution of child pornography. As the information highway sprawls toward new expanses, computer networks advance, and biotechnology produces new substances, criminal law will be forced to address threats to the public safety that today are unknown.

Ethical Issues in Criminology

A critical issue facing criminology students involves recognizing the field's political and social consequences. All too often criminologists forget the social responsibility they bear as experts in the area of crime and justice. When government agencies request their views of issues, their pronouncements and opinions may become the basis for sweeping social policy.

The lives of millions of people can be influenced by criminological research data. Debates over firearms control, decriminalization of marijuana possession, and mandatory sentences are ongoing and contentious. Some criminologists have argued successfully for social service, treatment, and rehabilitation programs to reduce the crime rate; others consider these a waste of time, suggesting instead that building more prisons, coupled with tough criminal sentences, can bring the crime rate down. By accepting their roles as experts on law-violating behaviour, criminologists place themselves in a position of power. The potential consequences of their actions are enormous. Therefore, they must be both aware of the ethics of their profession and prepared to defend their work in the light of public scrutiny. Major ethical issues include what to study, whom to study, and how to conduct those studies:

- *What to study.* Criminologists must be concerned about the topics they study. It is important that their research not be directed by the sources of funding on which research projects rely. The objectivity of research may be questioned if studies are funded by organizations that have a vested interest in the outcome of the research. For example, a study on the effectiveness of home alarm systems to stop break and enters may be tainted if the funding for the project comes from a security company or alarm manufacturer whose sales may be affected by the research findings.
- *Whom to study.* Another ethical issue in criminology concerns selection of research subjects. Too often criminologists focus their attention on the poor and minorities while ignoring middle-class white-collar crime, organized crime, and government crime. For example, a few social scientists have suggested that criminals have lower intelligence quotients than the average citizen and that because the average IQ score is lower among some minority groups, their crime rates are high.[39] This was the conclusion reached in *The Bell Curve*, a popular but highly controversial book written by Richard Herrnstein and Charles Murray.[40] In Canada, the availability of funding has led to a flood of research studies about crime in Aboriginal communities, unfairly depicting these communities as crime "hot spots," while ignoring other issues and the many positive aspects of life in Aboriginal communities.[41] Although such research is often methodologically unsound, it brings to light the tendency of criminologists to focus on one element of the community while ignoring others.
- *How to study.* A third area of concern involves the methods used in conducting research. One issue is whether subjects are fully informed about the purpose of research. For example, when European-Canadian and visible-minority youngsters are asked to participate in a survey of their behaviour, are they told in advance that the data they provide may later be used to demonstrate racial differences in their self-reported crime rates? Criminologists must also be careful to keep records and information confidential in order to maintain the privacy of research participants. In studies that involve experimentation and treatment, care must be taken to protect those subjects who have been chosen for experimental and control groups. For example, is it ethical to provide a special program for one group while depriving others of the same opportunity just so they can later be compared? Conversely, criminologists must be careful to protect subjects from experiments that may actually cause harm. An examination of the highly publicized "Scared Straight" program, which brings youngsters into contact with hard-core felons in a prison setting, found that participants may have been harmed by their experience. Rather than being frightened into conformity, subjects actually increased their criminal behaviour.[42] Finally, criminologists must take extreme care to ensure that research subjects are selected in a random and unbiased manner.[43]

CHAPTER 2

The Nature *and* Extent *of* Crime

Learning Outcomes

LO1 Name three primary sources of crime statistics used in Canada.

LO2 Explain the benefits of the Crime Severity Index.

LO3 Identify the strengths and weaknesses of crime statistics.

LO4 Identify the important trends over time in the Canadian crime rate.

LO5 Identify major factors that influence the crime rate.

LO6 Define aging out or desistance.

LO7 Define racial profiling.

Introduction

Saturday, July 21, and Sunday, July 22, 2007, marked another deadly weekend in greater Toronto, the urban ring where nearly one-fifth of Canadians live. Early Saturday morning, Kimel Foster, 21, was shot to death, and another man wounded by multiple gunshots fired outside the Town Talk Bar, in downtown Toronto. More than 50 bar patrons witnessed the shooting. At about 1 A.M. on the Sunday morning, a young child, Ephraim Brown, aged 11, was fatally shot when caught in the shooting crossfire between two rival gangs in the neighbourhood. At 2 A.M. Toronto police responded to another homicide of a young male gunned down outside his apartment building in a hail of bullets fired from a passing cab. Later on Sunday morning another young male, Amin Aafi, 24, was shot and killed, and another man wounded outside a dance club in Toronto's Entertainment District.[1]

DID YOU KNOW?

- The Uniform Crime Report (UCR), first introduced in 1961, is an annual tally of crime reported to local police departments. The UCR2 was implemented in the mid-1980s and contains more detailed information about the circumstances of each criminal incident. The UCR2 was revised and updated in 1998 and again in 2004.
- The Personal Risk and Victimization Survey (PRVS) was conducted in 1988, 1993, 1999, 2004, and 2009 with a sample of about 20 000 people. The PRVS provides an estimate of the total number of criminal incidents, including those not reported to police.
- Self-report surveys ask respondents about their own criminal activity. They are useful in measuring crimes rarely reported to police, such as drug usage.
- Crime rates peaked in the early 1990s and have been in decline ever since.
- A number of factors influence crime rate trends, including the economy, drug use, firearms availability, and crime control policies.
- It is difficult to gauge future trends. However, some experts forecast a decrease in crime rates through the year 2041 as the Canadian population continues to age, and as young people make up a smaller proportion of the population.

Stories like these help convince most Canadians that we live in a violent society. Are Canadians justified in their fear of violent crime? Should they, in fact, barricade themselves in their homes? Are crime rates actually rising or falling? Where do most crimes occur? To answer these and similar questions, criminologists have devised elaborate methods of crime data collection and analysis. Without accurate data on the nature and extent of crime, it would not be possible to formulate theories that explain the onset of crime or to devise social policies that facilitate its control or elimination.

In this chapter, we review how data are collected on criminal offenders and offences and what this information tells us about crime patterns and trends. We also examine the concept of criminal careers and discover what available crime data can tell us about the onset, continuation, and termination of criminality. We begin with a discussion of the most important sources of crime data.

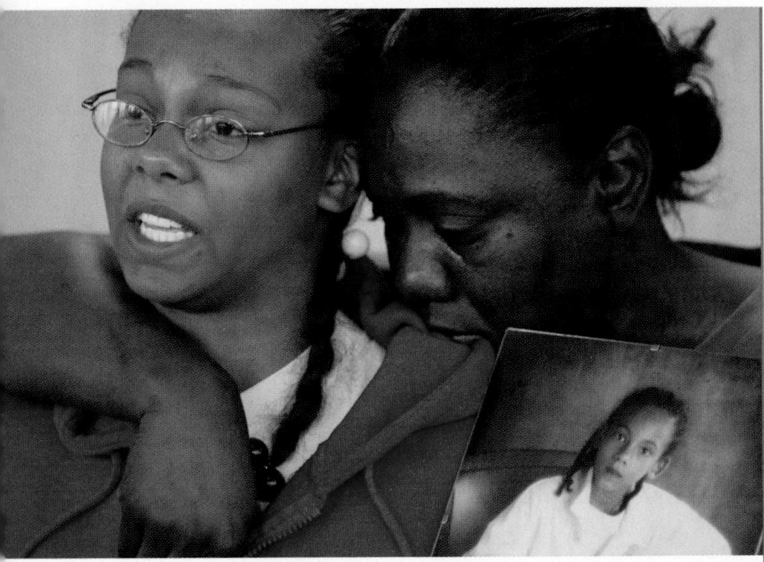

Toronto Star/GetStock.com

Distraught family members mourn the tragic death of 11-year-old Ephraim Brown, another innocent victim of gang violence in Toronto.

LO1 Sources of Crime Statistics

The Uniform Crime Report

First introduced in 1961, the **Uniform Crime Report (UCR)** is a listing of the number of criminal offences that occurred in each police agency's jurisdiction, the clearance status of each reported offence, and the number of persons charged (see Figure 2.1). Every police agency in Canada is required each month to complete the survey.[2] Completed UCR surveys are forwarded to the Canadian Centre for Justice Statistics, where the information is grouped together or "aggregated" to get a total of the number of crimes reported across Canada, in each of the provinces, and for the larger cities. In the mid-1980s, a second "revised Uniform Crime Report" survey, or **UCR2**, was introduced to capture more detailed information about each criminal incident, including the characteristics of victims and accused; the location, date, and time of day of the incident; use and type of weapons; type of property stolen; and so forth. Most of the larger police agencies, accounting for about 60 percent of crime, now also report information using the UCR2, which was revised and updated in 1998 and 2004 in order to reflect new changes in the law and types of offences.[3] The UCR surveys are the most widely cited sources of Canadian criminal statistics.

Uniform Crime Report (UCR)
A yearly crime report used by all police agencies in Canada.

UCR2
Revised crime-reporting system introduced in the mid-1980s. It collects detailed information about accused persons, victims, location, and weapons involved in each criminal incident. Most of the larger police agencies use the UCR and the UCR2.

Every year, the Canadian Centre for Justice Statistics publishes *Canadian Crime Reports*, a summary of the data collected from the UCR surveys.[4] The crime data are reported in large tables, using three different methods. First, the number of crimes reported to the police and arrests made are expressed as raw figures (e.g., 554 murders occurred in 2010). Second, crime rates per 100 000 people are computed. That is, when it is reported that the homicide rate was 2.0 in 2010, this means that 2 people in every 100 000 were murdered between January 1 and December 31, 2010. This is the equation used:

$$\frac{\text{Number of reported crimes}}{\text{Total Canadian population}} \times 100{,}000 = \text{Rate per } 100{,}000$$

Third, the Canadian Centre for Justice Statistics computes changes in the number and rate of crime over time. For example, the number of homicides in Canada increased by about 1.4 percent between 2000 and 2010, from 546 to 554.

The accuracy of the data reported on the UCR surveys is, however, suspect. Research indicates that fewer than half of all crime victims report incidents to police. Nonreporters may believe that the victimization was "a private matter," that "nothing could be done," or that the victimization was "not important enough."[5]

There is also evidence that local police agencies make errors in their reporting practices. Some agencies may define crimes loosely—for example, reporting an aggravated assault on a woman as an attempted murder—whereas others pay strict attention to the UCR reporting guidelines.[6] Some local police departments make unintentional but systematic errors in UCR reporting, and others may deliberately alter reported crimes to improve their department's public image. Police administrators interested in lowering the crime rate may falsify crime reports by, for example, classifying a break and enter as a trespass.[7] Ironically, what appears to be a rising crime rate may be simply an artifact of improved police record-keeping ability.[8]

Methodological issues also contribute to questions regarding the validity of UCR data. The complex scoring procedure used on the UCR surveys means that many serious crimes are not counted. For example, during a robbery of a gas bar, the offender strikes the clerk with an iron pipe. The robber runs out the door and steals an automobile parked at the gas pump. Although the offender has technically committed robbery, aggravated assault, and motor vehicle theft, because robbery is the most serious offence, it

FIGURE 2.1

Uniform Crime Report, Crime Statistics

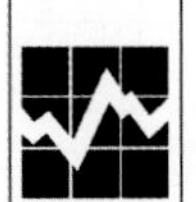

Canadian Centre for Justice Statistics

Form "C" – Crime Statistics

Month of

Confidential when completed

Complete and **return this copy to Statistics Canada** in the enclosed envelope on or before the 15th of the month

Si vous préférez ce questionnaire en français, veuillez cocher ☐

Date submitted		
Day	Month	Year
Signature of head of department		

INFORMATION FOR RESPONDENTS

Authority:
Statistics Act, Revised Statutes of Canada, 1985, Chapter S19

Objective:
This survey was designed to produce an indicator on the incidence of crime in Canadian society. The information is used by federal and provincial policy makers as well as public and private researchers. The data are also widely disseminated by the media for purposes of general public information.

Confidentiality:
Statistics Canada is prohibited by law from publishing any statistics which would divulge information obtained from this survey that relates to any identifiable respondent/individual without the previous written consent of that respondent/individual. The information reported on this questionnaire will be treated in confidence, used for statistical purposes and published in aggregate form only. The confidentiality provisions of the Statistics Act are not affected by either the Access to Information Act or any other legislation.

Correspondence:
If you require assistance in the completion of this questionnaire or any questions regarding the survey, please contact the;

Policing Services Program,
Canadian Centre for Justice Statistics,
Statistics Canada
Ottawa, Ontario
K1A 0T6,
Telephone: 1-800-387-2231

OFFENCES	Reported or known to police	Un-founded	Actual Number	OFFENCES CLEARED		PERSONS DATA				
				By charge	Otherwise	Adults		Young offenders		
						Charged		Charged		Not Charged
						Male	Female	Male	Female	
1	2	3	4	5	6	7	8	9	10	11
HOMICIDE * TOTAL 001										
Murder, First degree 002										
Murder, Second degree 003										
Manslaughter 004										
Infanticide 005										
ATTEMPTED MURDER – TOTAL 006										
ROBBERY TOTAL 018										
Firearms 019										
Other offensive weapons 020										
Other Robbery 021										

8-1000-92.1: 1998-09-09 STC/CCJ-140-60100

* **(See Supplementary Homicide instructions on page four)**

Statistics Canada Statistique Canada

Canadä

FIGURE 2.1 *(continued)*

- 2 -

OFFENCES	Reported or known to police	Un-founded	Actual Number	OFFENCES CLEARED		PERSONS DATA				
				By charge	Otherwise	Adults		Young offenders		
						Charged		Charged		Not Charged
						Male	Female	Male	Female	
1	2	3	4	5	6	7	8	9	10	11
BREAKING AND ENTERING TOTAL 022										
Business premises 023										
Residence 024										
Other Break and Enter 025										
THEFT – MOTOR VEHICLE TOTAL 026										
Automobiles 027										
Trucks 028										
Motorcycles 029										
Other Motor Vehicles 030										
THEFT OVER $5,000 TOTAL 031										
Bicycles 032										
From motor vehicles 033										
Shoplifting 034										
Other thefts over $5,000 035										
THEFT $5,000 AND UNDER TOTAL 036										
Bicycles 037										
From motor vehicles 038										
Shoplifting 039										
Other thefts $5,000 and under . 040										
HAVE STOLEN GOODS 041										
FRAUDS TOTAL 042										
Cheques 043										
Credit Cards 044										
Other frauds 045										
PROSTITUTION TOTAL 046										
Bawdy house 047										
Procuring 048										
Other prostitution 049										

8-1000-92.1: 1998-09-09

FIGURE 2.1 *(continued)*

- 3 -

OFFENCES	Reported or known to police	Un-founded	Actual Number	OFFENCES CLEARED		PERSONS DATA				
				By charge	Otherwise	Adults		Young offenders		
						Charged		Charged		Not Charged
						Male	Female	Male	Female	
1	2	3	4	5	6	7	8	9	10	11
GAMING AND BETTING TOTAL 050										
Betting house 051										
Gaming house 052										
Other gaming and betting offences 053										
OFFENSIVE WEAPONS TOTAL 054										
Firearms usage 055										
Weapons possession 056										
Trafficking import/export 057										
Other weapon offences 058										
OTHER CRIMINAL CODE (EX. TRAFFIC) – TOTAL 059										
Arson 060										
Bail Violations 061										
Counterfeiting currency 062										
Disturb the peace 063										
Escape custody 064										
Indecent Acts 065										
Kidnapping 066										
Public Morals 067										
Obstruct public peace officer . . 068										
Prisoner unlawfully at large . . . 069										
Trespass at night 070										
Mischief (property damage) over $5,000 071										
Mischief (property damage) $5,000 and under 072										
Other Criminal Code Offences 073										
HEROIN TOTAL 074										
Possession 075										
Trafficking 076										
Importation/Production 077										
COCAINE TOTAL 078										
Possession 079										
Trafficking 080										
Importation/Production 081										
OTHER DRUGS TOTAL 082										
Possession 083										
Trafficking 084										
Importation/Production 085										

8-1000-92.1: 1998-09-09

FIGURE 2.1 *(continued)*

- 4 -

OFFENCES	Reported or known to police	Un-founded	Actual Number	OFFENCES CLEARED		PERSONS DATA				
				By charge	Otherwise	Adults		Young offenders		
						Charged		Charged		Not Charged
						Male	Female	Male	Female	
1	2	3	4	5	6	7	8	9	10	11
CANNABIS TOTAL 086										
Possession 087										
Trafficking 088										
Importation 089										
Production 090										
OTHER FEDERAL STATUTES TOTAL (EX.TRAFFIC) 095										
Bankruptcy Act 096										
Canada Shipping Act 097										
Customs Act 098										
Excise Act 099										
Immigration Act 100										
Firearms Act 101										
Other Federal Statute Offences 102										
PROVINCIAL STATUTES (EX. TRAFFIC) TOTAL 103										
Liquor Acts 104										
Securities Act 105										
Other Provincial Statutes 106										
MUNICIPAL BY-LAWS (EX. TRAFFIC) 107										
SPECIAL *										
991										
992										
993										
994										
995										

SUPPLEMENTARY HOMICIDE RETURN

In view of the importance of homicide statistics, it is requested that the following supplementary information be supplied for all homicides occurring in your jurisdiction. Statistics Canada will send the investigating police force a Homicide Return for completion and return to Statistics Canada.
The names of victim(s) and person(s) charged must equal the actual number of offences and persons charged as reported for Items 002 to 005 – Form "C".

Offence	Date of offence	Location of offence	Victim(s)	Person(s) charged

8-1000-92.1: 1998-09-09 ***TO BE UTILIZED FOR SPECIAL SURVEYS OR NON-APPLICABLE OFFENCES**

Source: Adapted from Statistics Canada website, Definition, Data Sources and Methods Module, SDDS 3302, Uniform Crime Reporting Survey, Uniform Crime Reporting, Version 1.0, Reporting Manual (http://www.statcan.gc.ca/imdb-bmdi/document/3302_D7_T1_V1-eng.pdf).

would be the only one recorded in the UCR.[9] The most common issues affecting the validity of the UCR are summarized in the box below:

Factors Affecting the Validity of the Uniform Crime Reports

1. Many criminal incidents are never reported to the police. This is especially true of more minor crimes, but even a large percentage of sexual assaults and assaults are not reported. Victims may believe that there is nothing the police can do, or the crime was not important enough to go to the bother of reporting it. In other cases, the crime may have gone undetected. Sometimes victims are afraid to report a crime for fear of further reprisals from their victimizer. In rare cases, the victim may have died or disappeared.
2. Reports can vary in accuracy and completeness.
3. Sometimes, police agencies don't make a report, and the Canadian Centre for Justice Statistics has to "estimate" the amount of crime that would have occurred in that agency's jurisdiction.
4. Not all Canadian police agencies use the UCR2 form, although completion rates have improved greatly over time. In 2010, 152 police agencies across the 10 provinces and 3 territories reported complete data, covering approximately 99 percent of the Canadian population. Most agencies that do complete the UCR2 are urban, and so the data may not be representative regionally or nationally.
5. If an accused commits multiple crimes during one incident, only the most serious offence is recorded. For example, if a man sexually assaults, robs, and murders a victim, only the murder is recorded. Consequently, many lesser crimes go unreported.
6. All criminal incidents are not counted the same way. For example, one incident is counted for each separate occurrence of a property crime, such as theft, no matter how many victims are involved. But in the case of violent crime, one incident is counted for each victim involved in the occurrence.

Sources: Shannon Brennan and Mia Dauvergne, "Police-reported Crime Statistics in Canada, 2010" *Juristat*, July 2011, Statistics Canada Cat. no. 85-002-X, 21; Robert A. Silverman, James J. Teevan, and Vincent F. Sacco, *Crime in Canadian Society* (Toronto: Harcourt Brace Canada, 2000).

Every month, Statistics Canada and the Canadian Centre for Justice Statistics publish the *Juristat* report, which contains articles, special studies, and statistics about crime in Canada. *Juristat* can be found in most college libraries, and some of the articles are available free online at http://www.statcan.ca.

LO2 Crime Severity Index

Recognizing the limitations of UCR surveys and in an attempt to enhance the quality of the data collected on crime in Canada, a third instrument, the Crime Severity Index, was introduced in 2009. (See Table 2.1.) The Crime Severity Index was the first major change in the method of reporting of police-reported crime statistics since the collection of these data began in 1961. In the past, the crime rate was heavily influenced by less serious offences, which research has shown often went unreported. Additionally, these less serious crimes were assigned exactly the same weight as more serious crimes. What was needed was a

TABLE 2.1

Defining Criminal Victimization in Canada

Type of Victimization	Description
Violent victimization	
Sexual assault	Forced sexual activity, an attempt at forced sexual activity, or unwanted sexual touching, grabbing, kissing, or fondling.
Robbery	Theft or attempted theft in which the perpetrator had a weapon or there was violence or the threat of violence against the victim.
Physical assault	An attack (victim hit, slapped, grabbed, knocked down, or beaten), a face-to-face threat of physical harm, or an incident with a weapon present.
Non-violent victimization Household victimization	
Break and enter	Illegal entry or attempted entry into a residence or other building on the victim's property.
Motor vehicle/parts theft	Theft or attempted theft of a car, truck, van, motorcycle, moped, or other vehicle or part of a motor vehicle.
Theft of household property	Theft or attempted theft of household property such as liquor, bicycles, electronic equipment, tools, or appliances.
Vandalism	Wilful damage of personal or household property.
Theft of personal property	Theft or attempted theft of personal property such as money, credit cards, clothing, jewellery, a purse or a wallet (unlike robbery, the perpetrator does not confront the victim).

method to capture the overall picture of trends in crime severity. The **Crime Severity Index** helps to determine the severity of police-reported crime in relation to the past and to Canada overall. The mechanics involve assigning a "seriousness" weight to each type of offence that is derived from actual sentences handed down by courts in all provinces and territories, with more serious crimes being assigned higher weight than less serious ones. It should be noted that the new Index does not replace, but rather complements, existing measures of crime.[10]

Crime Severity Index
A yearly crime report used by all police agencies in Canada that measures both volume and severity of crime across the country.

Victim Surveys

The second source of crime data is surveys that ask crime victims about their encounters with criminals.

Personal Risk and Victimization Survey (PRVS) National study carried out in 1988, 1993, 1999, 2004, and 2009 by Statistics Canada that surveys approximately 20 000 Canadians about their personal experiences of criminal victimization.

self-report surveys A research approach that requires subjects to reveal their own participation in delinquent or criminal acts.

Because many victims do not report their experiences to the police, victim surveys are considered a method of getting at the unknown figures of crime.

General Social Survey

Every year since 1985, Statistics Canada has conducted a General Social Survey (GSS) of the Canadian population. The primary objective of the GSS is to gather data on current and emerging social trends to monitor changes in living conditions and quality of life. About 20 000 people are asked to complete a 30-minute interview over the telephone. Some of the issues dealt with are so important that they are repeated at regular intervals. For example, questions pertaining to victimization were included in the following years: 1988, 1993, 1999, 2004, and 2009. According to the latest 2009 survey, victimization rates have remained stable since 2004 with the majority of criminal incidents reported being nonviolent. More specifically, theft of personal property (34 percent), theft of household property (13 percent), vandalism (11 percent), break-ins (7 percent), and theft of motor vehicles/parts (5 percent) accounted for 70 percent of incidents recorded by the GSS. Violent incidents, namely physical assault (19 percent), sexual assault (8 percent), and robbery (4 percent) accounted for the remaining self-reported incidents. The rates of violent and household victimization were also similar to those reported in 2004. However, the rate of theft of personal property increased 16 percent, up from 93 incidents per 1000 people in 2004 to 108 incidents in 2009.[11]

Personal Risk and Victimization Survey

The data collected by the national **Personal Risk and Victimization Survey (PRVS)** is the most comprehensive source of information about victimization in Canada. Because of the care with which the samples are drawn and the high completion rate, the PRVS data are considered a relatively unbiased, valid estimate of all victimizations for the target crimes included in the survey.

Findings and Validity of the GSS

Results from the 2009 General Social Survey on victimization revealed that 27 percent of Canadians said that they had been a victim of a crime in the previous 12 months. Interestingly, only about one-third of these incidents were actually reported to police.[12] The reason for such discrepancies is that fewer than half of violent crimes, and only about one-third of personal theft crimes (e.g., theft of money from a purse) and household thefts (e.g., lawn ornaments) are reported to police. Victims seem to report to the police only crimes that involve considerable loss or injury. If we are to believe GSS findings, the official UCR statistics do not provide an accurate picture of the crime problem because many crimes go unreported to the police.

Validity of the PRVS

Like the UCR and GSS, the PRVS may also suffer from some methodological problems. As a result, its findings must be interpreted with caution. Among the potential problems are the following:

- Overreporting due to victims' misinterpretation of events. For example, a lost wallet may be reported as stolen, or an open door may be viewed as a break and enter attempt.
- Underreporting due to the embarrassment of reporting crime to interviewers, fear of getting in trouble, or simply forgetting an incident.
- Inability to record the personal criminal activity of those interviewed, such as drug use or child abuse; murder is also not included, for obvious reasons.
- The PRVS does not record crimes committed in the workplace, forms of organized crime, and corporate crimes.
- Sampling errors, which produce a group of respondents who do not represent the nation as a whole.[13]

CONNECTIONS

Victim surveys provide information not only about criminal incidents that have occurred, but also about the individuals who are most at risk of falling victim to crime, and where and when they are most likely to become victimized. Data from the PRVS surveys will be used in Chapter 3 to draw a portrait of the nature and extent of victimization in Canada.

Self-Report Surveys

Self-report surveys ask people to reveal information about their own law violations. Most often,

FIGURE 2.2

Self-Report Survey Questions

During the past 12 months, did you:

	Never did act	One time	2–5 times	6–9 times	10+ times
take some school property worth $5.00 or more?					
sell any kind of drugs?					
skip school without a legitimate excuse?					
have a fistfight with another person?					
purposely damage or destroy public or private property that did not belong to you?					
take something from a store without paying?					

Source: M. Leblanc and M. Fréchette (1989), *Male Criminal Activity from Childhood through Youth: Multilevel and Developmental Perspectives*, pp. 195-196. With kind permission of Springer Science and Business Media.

self-report surveys are administered to groups of subjects through a mass distribution of questionnaires. The basic assumption of self-report studies is that the assurance of anonymity and confidentiality will encourage people to describe their illegal activities accurately. Self-reports are viewed as a mechanism to get at the "dark figures of crime," the figures missed by official statistics. Figure 2.2 above illustrates some typical self-report items.

Most self-report studies have focused on juvenile delinquency and youth crime, for three reasons.[14] First, the school setting makes it convenient to test thousands of subjects simultaneously because they all have the means to respond to a research questionnaire (pens, desks, and time). Second, because school attendance is universal, a school-based self-report survey represents a cross-section of the community. Finally, juveniles have the highest reported crime rates; measuring delinquent behaviour, therefore, is a key to understanding the nature and extent of crime.

Self-reports are not restricted to youth crime, however. They are also used to examine the offence histories of prison inmates, drug users, and other segments of the population, including American college students.[15] Also, because most self-report instruments contain items measuring subjects' attitudes, values, personal characteristics, and behaviours, the data obtained from them can be used for various purposes, including testing theories, measuring attitudes toward crime, and computing the association between crime and important social variables, such as family relations, educational attainment, and income.[16]

Self-Report Findings

In general, self-reports, like victimization surveys, indicate that the number of people who break the law is far greater than the number projected by official statistics. Almost everyone questioned is found to have violated some law at some time.[17] Furthermore, self-reports dispute the notion that criminals and delinquents specialize in one type of crime or another; offenders seem to engage in a "mixed bag" of crime and deviance.[18]

Self-report studies typically indicate that the most common offences are truancy, alcohol abuse, trespassing, shoplifting, or theft under $50, fighting, marijuana use, and damage to the property of others. What is surprising is the consistency of these findings in samples taken around the United States and in Canada. Table 2.2 contains data from a self-report study included in the National Longitudinal Survey of Children and Youth started in 1994–95. This long-term national survey includes about 1800 children 12 to 13 years of age, and shows that, consistent with other studies, females are less likely than males to engage in delinquent acts against property or to engage in aggressive behaviours such as fighting, sexual assault, or arson.[19]

As Table 2.2 shows, 56 percent of males and 30 percent of females 12 to 13 years of age report "some" or a "high" level of involvement in delinquent acts against property. The fact that 56 percent of the males and 30 percent of the females report that they have committed aggressive acts of a criminal nature against others suggests that violence and property

TABLE 2.2

Gender Differences in Self-Report Delinquency at Age 12–13, 1996–97

Type of Delinquent Behaviour	Gender	Level of Delinquency			
		None	*Some*	*High*	*Total*
Delinquent acts involving property	Females	70%	23%	7%	100% (967)
	Males	60%	27%	13%	100% (964)
Aggressive behaviour	Females	71%	22%	7%	100% (981)
	Males	44%	40%	16%	100% (974)

Source: Adapted from Statistics Canada publication JURISTAT, Catalogue 85-002, Vol. 21, No. 4 page 3 (http://www.statcan.gc.ca/bsolc/olc-cel/olc-cel?catno=85-002-x&lang=eng).

crime may be widespread and not restricted to a few "bad apples."

Accuracy of Self-Reports

Although self-report data have profoundly affected criminological inquiry, some important methodological issues have been raised about their accuracy. Critics of self-report studies frequently suggest that it is unreasonable to expect people to candidly admit illegal acts. This is especially true of those with official records, who may be engaging in the most criminality. At the same time, some people may exaggerate their criminal acts, forget some of them, or be confused about what is being asked. Some surveys contain an overabundance of trivial offences, such as shoplifting small items or using false identification, often lumped together with serious crimes to form a total crime index. Consequently, comparisons between groups can be highly misleading.

The "missing cases" phenomenon is also a concern. Even if 90 percent of a school population voluntarily participate in a self-report study, researchers can never be sure whether the few who refuse to participate or are absent that day comprise a significant portion of the school's population of persistent high-rate offenders. Research indicates that offenders with the most extensive prior criminality are also the most likely to "be poor historians of their own crime commission rates."[20] It is also unlikely that the most serious chronic offenders in the youth population are the most willing to cooperate with university-based criminologists administering self-report tests.[21] Institutionalized youths, who are not generally represented in the self-report surveys, are not only more delinquent than the general youth population, but also are considerably more misbehaving than the most delinquent youths identified in the typical self-report survey.[22] Consequently, self-reports may measure only nonserious, occasional delinquents while ignoring hard-core chronic offenders who may be institutionalized and unavailable for self-reports.

LO3 Evaluating Crime Data

Each source of crime data has strengths and weaknesses. The UCR surveys and the Crime Severity Index are carefully tallied by the Canadian Centre for Justice Statistics and contain data on the number of murders and people arrested, information that the other data sources lack. However, the UCR omits the many crimes victims choose not to report to police, and it is subject to the reporting caprices of individual police departments.

The PRVS includes unreported crime and important information on the personal characteristics of victims. However, the data consist of estimates made from relatively limited samples of the total Canadian population, so that even narrow fluctuations in the rates of some crimes can have a major impact on findings. It also relies on personal recollections that may be inaccurate. The PRVS does not include data on important crime patterns, including murder and drug abuse.

Self-report surveys can provide information on the personal characteristics of offenders, such as their attitudes, values, beliefs, and psychological profiles, that is unavailable from any other source. Yet, at their core, self-reports rely on the honesty of criminal offenders and drug abusers, a population not generally known for accuracy and integrity.

Although their tallies of crimes are certainly not in synch, the crime patterns and trends these sources record are often quite similar.[23] For example, all three sources generally agree about the personal characteristics of serious criminals (such as age and gender) and where and when crime occurs (such as urban areas, nighttime, and summer months). In addition, the problems inherent in each source are consistent over time. Therefore, even if the data sources are incapable of providing a precise and valid count of crime at any given time, they are reliable indicators of changes and fluctuations in yearly crime rates.

What do these data sources tell us about crime trends and patterns?

LO4 Crime Trends

Crime is not new to this century. Historical data from Statistics Canada show that the crime rate in Canada grew steadily from 1886 through to the beginning of World War I in 1914. During World War I the crime rate declined, but immediately after the war the increase resumed, reaching a peak in 1939, just prior to the beginning of World War II.[24] During World War II and into the 1950s, the crime rate remained below prewar levels. However, in the late 1950s and early 1960s the Canadian crime rate began a steady increase that continued until the 1990s, as is clearly shown in Table 2.3.

Both the number and rate of crime have been steadily declining since the early 1990s. Between 1991 and 1998, the crime rate declined by 22 percent and, according to the Canadian Centre for Justice Statistics, both the overall Crime Severity Index and the traditional police-recorded overall crime rate declined again in 2010, matching similar declines in the previous five years[25] (see Table 2.3). Even youth

TABLE 2.3

Overall Crime Severity Index and Traditional Police Reported Crime Rate Canada; 2000 to 2010

Year	Total Crime Severity Index		Police Reported Total Crime Rate Per 100 000 Population	
	Index Number	*Percentage Change from Previous Year*	*Total Rate*	*Percentage Change from Previous Year*
2000	106.7	–4	7607	–1
2001	105.3	–1	7587	0
2002	104.1	–1	7512	–1
2003	106.8	3	7770	3
2004	104.1	–3	7600	–2
2005	101.3	–3	7325	–4
2006	100.0	–1	7244	–1
2007	95.2	–5	6898	–5
2008	90.4	–5	6617	–4
2009	87.6	–3	6444	–3
2010	82.7	–6	6145	–5

Source: Adapted from Shannon Brennan and Mia Dauvergne, "Police-reported Crime Statistics in Canada", 2010, *Juristat*, July 2011 Statistics Canada Cat. No. 85-002-X, Tables 1A and 1B, pp. 24, 25.

crime, a continuing source of public concern, has been declining since 2001, including a 7 percent decrease in 2010.[26]

Trends in Violent Crime

The violent crimes reported in the UCR survey include homicide, attempted murder, sexual assault, assault, robbery, and abduction. In 2010, about 437 000 violent crimes were reported to police, a rate of around 1282 per 100 000 Canadians. According to the Canadian Centre for Justice Statistics, the Violent Crime Severity Index decreased by 6 percent in 2010, and the traditional police-reported violent crime rate decreased by 3 percent, following decreases in each of the previous three years (see Table 2.4).[27]

Common assaults account for nearly two-thirds of violent crime. Sexual assaults are the next most frequently occurring form of violent crime, accounting for 8 percent of the total. After peaking in the mid-1970s, the national homicide rate generally declined until 1999 and has been relatively stable ever since.[28] The number of homicides committed with a firearm has been declining since the 1970s (see Figure 2.3).

TABLE 2.4

Violent Crime Severity Index and Traditional Police-Reported Violent Crime Rate Per 100 000 Population; Canada, 2000 to 2010

Year	Violent Crime Severity Index		Police Reported Violent Crime Rate Per 100 000 Population	
	Index Number	*Percentage Change from Previous Year*	*Total Rate*	*Percentage Change from Previous Year*
2000	97.8	–2	458 559	4
2001	97.2	–1	457 043	–1
2002	96.2	–1	451 733	–2
2003	97.6	1	453 963	0
2004	96.0	–2	448 514	–2
2005	98.5	3	447 857	–1
2006	100.0	2	451 652	0
2007	97.7	–2	445 252	–2
2008	94.9	–3	443 608	–2
2009	94.1	–1	444 533	–1
2010	88.9	–6	437 316	–3

Source: Adapted from Shannon Brennan and Mia Dauvergne, "Police-reported Crime Statistics in Canada", 2010, *Juristat*, July 2011 Statistics Canada Cat. No. 85-002-X, Tables 1A and 1B, pp. 24, 25.

The use of handguns surpassed rifles or shotguns for the first time in 1991 and by 2006, three times as

FIGURE 2.3

Homicide in Canada: Homicide Rates Peaked in the 1970s

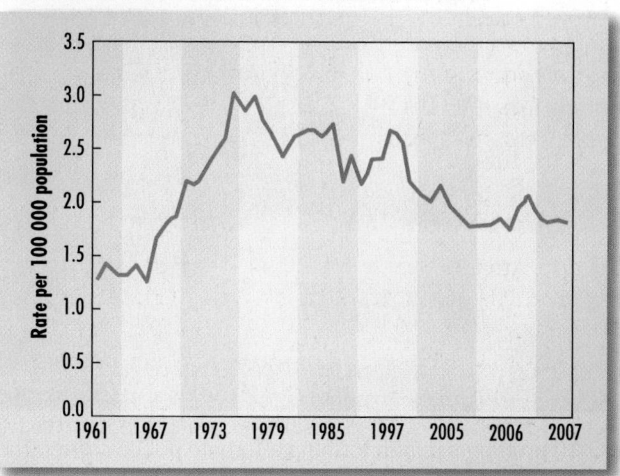

Source: Adapted from Statistics Canada website (http://www.statcan.gc.ca/daily-quotidien/101026/dq101026a-eng.htm).

many victims were killed with a handgun than with a rifle or shotgun.[29]

Even though the official crime data tell us that the violent crime rate has been declining for the last decade, highly publicized cases such as the fatal shooting of teenager Jane Creba, 15, on Boxing Day, 2005, in Toronto help convince the general public that Canadian society is growing more violent and crime ridden. Politicians sometimes seize on these tragedies to advocate a quick fix for what is seen to be a growth in violence—ban violent videogames, give police more powers, prohibit rap and heavy metal music with violent lyrics. Can such measures possibly deter violence such as occurred in the Jane Creba case?

Trends in Property Crime

The property crimes reported in the UCR include theft, break and enter, fraud, motor vehicle theft, and possession of stolen goods. Thefts under $5000 are the most common type of property crime committed in Canada and in 2010 they accounted for 41 percent of all property crimes. Interestingly, although they are still prevalent, the rate has dropped 27 percent since 2000.[30]

Trends in Victimization

The rate of victimization in Canada has remained relatively unchanged over the past decade with just over one-quarter of the population aged 15 years and older reporting being a victim of a crime. The majority of crimes reported in 2009 were nonviolent including theft of personal property (34 percent), theft of household property (13 percent), vandalism (11 percent), break-ins (7 percent), and theft of motor vehicles/parts (5 percent); these accounted for 70 percent of incidents recorded by the GSS. Violent incidents, namely physical assault (19 percent), sexual assault (8 percent), and robbery (4 percent), have been stable but highest among youth. Single people are more likely to be victims as opposed to those who are married, and sexual assault rates are higher among females than males. Not surprisingly, physical assault has been highly associated with alcohol and drug use.[31]

© WARREN TODA/epa/Corbis

THE CANADIAN PRESS/Ryan Remiorz

G-20 protesters join in trashing a Toronto police cruiser. Those who participated and were later apprehended by police were likely charged with the property crime of mischief—wilful damage to the property of another.

What the Future Holds

It is always risky to speculate about the future of crime trends because current conditions can change rapidly. But contemporary criminologists such as Marc Ouimet may have provided some important clues. Ouimet explains that Canadian property crime rates began to level off in the 1980s, as the youth population aged 15 to 24 began to decline in numbers.[32] Ten years later, this same large group or "cohort" of youth, now 25 to 34, moved out of the prime risk years for committing violence, coinciding with the decline in violent crime that began in 1991.

Peter Carrington's research shows that as the Canadian population continues to age, crime rates will continue to decrease right through the year 2041, when decreases will begin to slow down. Until another large youth cohort comes along, like the baby boom, it is likely that Canada will continue to have relatively low crime rates.[33]

While overall in Canada crime rates may continue to decrease, the aging of the baby boomers is having other impacts on the crime rate, in particular in changing the nature of the kinds of crimes that police must respond to. The oldest of the Canadian baby boomers are now in their 60s, and the youngest are in their late 40s. Most of the members of this age group are now well established, have good incomes, own their own homes, have numerous credit cards, and are looking for good investments to assure their retirement income. Law-enforcement experts point to increases in the number of complaints about telemarketing scams, Internet fraud, and identity theft, along with mounting concerns about elder abuse, as early indications of what could be serious problems as the baby boomers mature into old age.[34]

Although Carrington's predictions that crime rates will continue to decline is reassuring, there is no way of telling what unanticipated future changes may influence crime rates. The overall recorded crime rate is forecast to fall to 85 percent of its 1999 level by 2026 and to 81 percent by 2041 (see Figure 2.4). Technological developments such as the rapid expansion of e-commerce have created new classes of crime. Concern about the environment in rural areas may produce a rapid upswing in environmental crimes ranging from vandalism to violence.[35] Terrorism, both at home and abroad, will put new demands on law enforcement.

FIGURE 2.4

Actual and Forecast Recorded Rates of Three Categories of Crime, Canada, 1999–2041

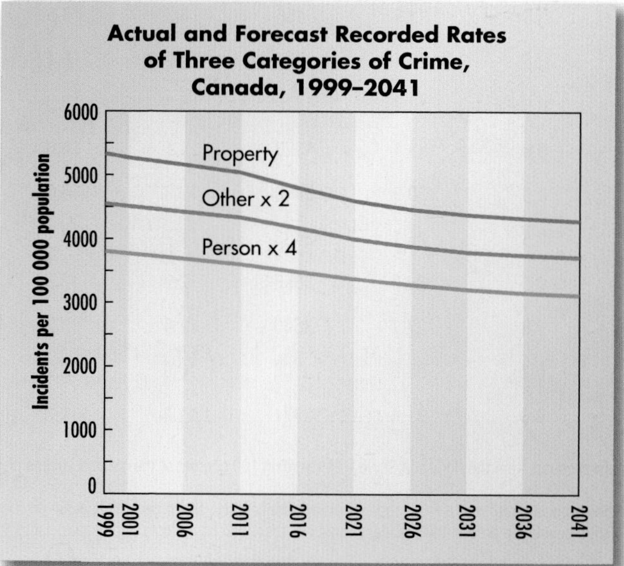

Source: Carrington (2001), "Population Aging and Crime in Canada, 2000-2041," *Canadian Journal of Criminology*, 43(3), 331-56. Reprinted with permission from University of Toronto Press Incorporated (www.utpjournals.com).

LO5 Crime Patterns

To gain insight into the nature of crime, criminologists look for stable crime rate patterns. If crime rates are consistently higher at certain times, in certain areas, and among certain groups, this knowledge might help explain the onset or cause of crime. For example, if criminal statistics show that crime rates are consistently higher in poor neighbourhoods in large urban areas, then crime may be a function of poverty and neighbourhood decline. If, in contrast, crime rates were spread evenly across the social structure, this would provide little evidence that crime has an economic basis; instead, crime might be linked to socialization, personality, intelligence, or some other trait unrelated to class position or income. In this section we examine traits and patterns that may influence the crime rate.

The Ecology of Crime

Most reported crimes occur during the warm summer months of July and August. During the summer, teenagers and young adults, who usually have the highest crime levels, are out of school and have greater opportunity to commit crime. People also spend more time outdoors, making them easier targets. Two exceptions to this trend are murders and robberies, which occur frequently in December and January (although rates are also high during the summer). Robbery rates increase in the winter partly because the Christmas shopping season means more money in the cash registers of potential targets.[36] Repeat burglary attempts tend to occur at the same time of day as the previously successful burglary.[37]

Crime rates also may be higher on particular days of the month than at any other time. Government welfare and social assistance cheques typically arrive at the end of the month, and with them come increases in activities such as breaking into mailboxes and accosting recipients on the streets. Also, people may have more disposable income at this time, and the availability of extra money may relate to behaviours associated with crime, such as drinking and gambling.[38]

Weather effects, such as temperature swings, may also affect violent crime rates. Crime rates increase with rising temperatures up to a point (about 30°C), but then begin to decline, perhaps because it becomes too hot for physical exertion.[39] However, the rates of some crimes, such as domestic assault, continue to increase as temperatures rise.[40]

Use of Firearms

According to international criminologists Franklin Zimring and Gordon Hawkins, the proliferation of

street crimes
Crimes such as robbery, assault, sexual assault, theft, and murder that often occur in public places, and are easy to detect.

handguns and the high rate of lethal violence they cause is the single most significant factor separating the crime problem in the United States from the rest of the developed world.[41]

In contrast, Canada has a long history of firearms control legislation dating back to 1892. With the passage of the Firearms Act in 1998, Canada put in place some of the toughest firearms control legislation in the world, including mandatory registration of all firearms.[42] The rate of firearm-related robberies has been relatively stable since 2001 following sharp declines throughout the 1990s. The current rates of firearm-related robbery reported by police are at the lowest levels since the late 1970s. See Table 2.5.[43]

Social Class and Crime

Criminologists can't agree on whether there is a direct link between social class and crime. Crime statistics show that the poor, those with little education, and those with menial jobs are more likely to be arrested, convicted, and incarcerated, especially for "**street crimes**" such as assaults, prostitution, and theft. After all, common sense tells us that people at the lowest rungs of the social structure have the greatest incentive to commit crimes. Those unable to obtain desired goods and services through conventional means may decide to resort to so-called instrumental crimes such as theft and other illegal activities—for example, selling narcotics—to obtain them, or perhaps they may take out their rage, frustration, and anger against society by committing "expressive" violent crimes such as sexual assault or murder.[44]

Official statistics confirm that victimization rates for both males and females in inner-city, high-poverty areas are generally higher than those in suburban or wealthier areas.[45] Studies using aggregate police statistics (arrest records) have consistently shown that crime rates in lower-class areas exceed

TABLE 2.5

Firearm-Related Homicides and Robbery, Canada, 1977–2006

Year	Firearm-related homicide[1]			Firearm-related robbery[2]		
	Number	*Rate[3]*	*% of all homicides*	*Number*	*Rate[3]*	*% of all robberies*
1977	260	1.1	36.6	7507	31.6	38.5
1978	250	1.0	37.8	7203	30.1	36.6
1979	207	0.9	32.8	7439	30.7	35.6
1980	195	0.8	32.9	8594	35.1	35.0
1981	199	0.8	30.7	9040	36.4	34.4
1982	248	1.0	37.2	8954	35.6	32.9
1983	224	0.9	32.8	7505	29.6	30.9
1984	228	0.9	34.2	6886	26.9	29.5
1985	222	0.9	31.5	6789	26.3	29.8
1986	175	0.7	30.8	6710	25.7	28.8
1987	202	0.8	31.4	5960	22.5	26.5
1988	169	0.6	29.3	6072	22.7	25.1
1989	218	0.8	33.2	6439	23.6	25.0
1990	196	0.7	29.7	7426	26.8	26.4
1991	271	1.0	35.9	9006	32.1	27.1
1992	247	0.9	33.7	8736	30.8	26.3
1993	195	0.7	31.1	8038	28.0	26.8
1994	196	0.7	32.9	7361	25.4	25.4
1995	176	0.6	29.9	6692	22.8	22.1
1996	212	0.7	33.4	6737	22.8	21.2
1997	193	0.6	32.9	5486	18.3	18.5
1998	151	0.5	27.1	5324	17.7	18.4
1999	165	0.5	30.7	5122	16.8	17.8
2000	184	0.6	33.7	4323	14.1	16.0
2001	171	0.6	30.9	3818	12.3	14.0
2002	152	0.5	26.1	3483	11.1	13.1
2003	161	0.5	29.3	3856	12.2	13.6
2004	173	0.5	27.7	3645	11.4	13.3
2005	223	0.7	33.6	3508	10.9	12.2
2006	190	0.6	31.4	3671	11.3	12.0

1. Homicide data reflect victim counts from the Homicide Survey representing 100 percent of the national volume of homicides.
2. Robbery data reflect incident counts from the UCR Aggregate Survey representing 100 percent of the national volume of robberies. ... Victim counts are greater than incident counts as there can be multiple victims associated with the same incident.
3. Rates are calculated per 100 000 population.

Source: Adapted from Statistics Canada publication, *Juristat*, Catalogue 85-002-XWE2008002, vol. 28, no. 2 (http://www.statcan.gc.ca/pub/85-002-x/2008002/article/tbl/tbl02-eng.htm).

Ho New/REUTERS

Bank heist rate plunges: Vancouver is no longer the bank robbery capital of Canada, according to the latest statistics released by the Vancouver Police Department in 2009.

those in wealthier neighbourhoods. Another "official" indicator of a class–crime relationship comes from surveys of prison inmates, which consistently show that prisoners were members of the lower class and unemployed or underemployed in the years before their incarceration.

But do those in the lowest social class positions really commit more crimes? Or, because they are poor, uneducated, and powerless, are they just more likely to get caught, convicted, and sent to jail? Some criminologists suggest that the relationship between official crime and social class is a function of law-enforcement practices, not actual criminal behaviour patterns. Police may devote more resources to poor areas, and consequently apprehension rates may be higher there. Others observe that middle- and upper-class Canadians probably commit just as many crimes as those in the lower classes, but these **suite crimes**, such as fraud, embezzlement, stock market manipulation, and price fixing, are much harder to detect.[46]

Class and Self-Reports

Self-report data have been used extensively to test the class–crime relationship. If people in all social classes self-report similar crime patterns, but only those in the lower class are formally arrested, that would explain higher crime rates in lower-class neighbourhoods. However, if lower-class people report greater criminal activity than their middle- and upper-class peers, it would indicate that official statistics accurately represent the crime problem.

Surprisingly, self-report studies generally do not find a direct relationship between social class and youth crime.[47] Socioeconomic class is related to official processing by police, courts, and correctional agencies, but not to the actual commission of crimes. While lower- and middle-class youths self-report equal amounts of crime, lower-class youths have a greater chance of getting arrested, convicted, and incarcerated and becoming official delinquents.[48] More than 25 years ago, Charles Tittle, Wayne Villemez, and Douglas Smith concluded that little if any support exists for the contention that crime is primarily a lower-class phenomenon. They argued that official statistics probably reflect class bias in processing lower-class offenders.[49]

suite crimes
Crimes such as price-fixing, insider trading, embezzlement, and improper disposal of toxic waste that often occur behind closed doors in corporate boardrooms and offices, and are hard to detect.

Weighing the Evidence for a Class–Crime Relationship

Tittle's research has sparked significant debate. Many self-report instruments include trivial offences such as using false identification or drinking alcohol. Their inclusion may obscure the true class–crime relationship because affluent youths frequently engage in trivial offences such as petty theft, using drugs, and simple assault. Those who support a class–crime relationship suggest that if only serious indictable offences are considered, a significant association can be observed.[50] Studies showing middle- and lower-class youths to be equally delinquent rely on measures weighted toward minor crimes (e.g., using false identification or skipping school); when serious crimes, such as break and enter and assault,

CONNECTIONS

If class and crime are unrelated, then the causes of crime must be found in factors experienced by members of all social classes—psychological impairment, family conflict, peer pressure, school failure, and so on. Theories that view crime as a function of problems experienced by members of all social classes are reviewed in Chapter 7.

are compared, lower-class youths are significantly more delinquent.[51] There is also debate over the most appropriate measure of class. Should it be parents' income? Occupation? Educational attainment? Findings may be skewed if the measurement of class used is inappropriate or invalid.

Like so many other criminological controversies, the debate over the true relationship between class and crime will most likely persist. The weight of recent evidence seems to suggest that serious, official crime is more prevalent among the lower classes, whereas less serious, self-reported crime is spread more evenly throughout the social structure.[52] Income inequality, poverty, and resource deprivation are all associated with the most serious violent crimes, including homicide and assault.[53] Communities that lack economic and social opportunities also produce high levels of frustration; their residents believe that they are relatively more deprived than residents of more affluent areas and may turn to criminal behaviour to relieve their frustration.[54] In these communities, family life is disrupted, and law-violating youth gangs thrive in a climate that undermines adult supervision.[55] Conversely, when the poor are provided with economic opportunities via welfare and social assistance, crime rates drop.[56]

Nonetheless, although crime rates may be higher in lower-class areas, poverty alone cannot explain why a particular individual becomes a chronic violent criminal; if it did, the crime problem would be much worse than it is now.[57]

LO6 Age and Crime

There is general agreement that age is inversely related to criminality—the older you are, the less likely you are to engage in criminal activity.[58] Regardless of economic status, marital status, race, sex, or other factors, younger people commit crime more often than their older counterparts. Research indicates this relationship has been stable across time periods ranging from the early 1900s to the present era.[59] Figure 2.5 shows the relationship between age and crime.

Official statistics tell us that young people are arrested at a disproportionate rate to their numbers in the population; victim surveys generate similar findings for crimes in which assailant age can be determined. Whereas people aged 12 to 17 collectively make up about 8 percent of the total Canadian population, they account for about 20 percent of all criminal charges. The rate at which youth are charged for crimes of violence is double the adult rate; and the charge rate for youth accused of property crimes is more than triple the adult rate. In the case of motor vehicle theft, youth aged 15–18 years account for 30 percent of those accused of motor vehicle theft, and three-quarters of those charged are under the age of 25.[60]

FIGURE 2.5

Visual Depiction of Crime Data by Age

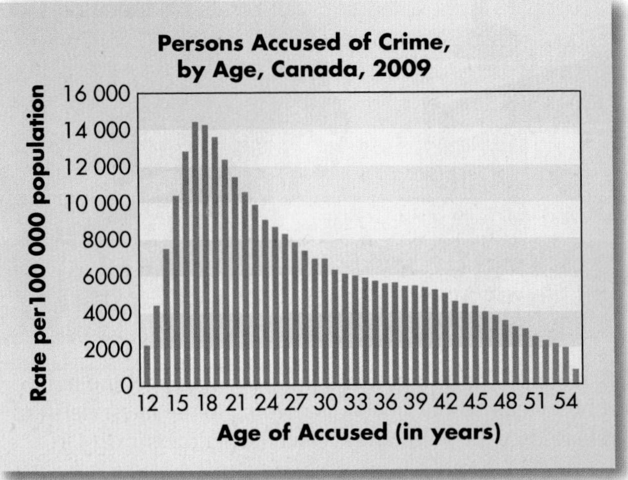

Source: Adapted from Statistics Canada publication, *Juristat,* Catalogue 85-002-XWE2010002 (http://www.statcan.gc.ca/pub/85-002-x/2010002/article/11292-eng.htm#a15).

As a general rule, property crime is a young person's activity, peaking at around age 16, and dropping off significantly after age 20. Violent crime peaks at about age 18, but persists much longer, dropping off in frequency only after about age 35.[61]

Older Canadians, those over the age of 55, are particularly resistant to the temptations of crime; they make up about 22 percent of the population but account for only 4 percent of those charged with a criminal offence. Males aged 55 and over are most frequently arrested for impaired driving, theft, and common assault; and females over 55 are most

AP Photo/FBI, File

The "Geezer Bandit," believed to be somewhere between 60 and 70 years of age, is suspected by the FBI of robbing as many as 16 banks in Southern California.

frequently arrested for theft, fraud, and impaired driving.[62] Even those convicted and put in prison experience the effects of age, as research shows that offenders over the age of 40 who have been released from prison are less likely to commit additional crimes, compared to younger offenders.[63] There has been little change in the crime rate for older Canadians for the past 20 years. The fact that people commit less crime as they mature is referred to as **aging out** or **desistance**.

Why does aging out occur? One view is that there is a direct relationship between aging and crime. Psychologists note that young people, especially the indigent and antisocial, tend to discount the future.[64] They are impatient, and, because their future is uncertain, they are unwilling or unable to delay gratification. As they mature, troubled youths are able to develop a long-term life view and resist the need for immediate gratification.[65] Kids may view crime as fun, a risky but exciting social activity. As they grow older, life patterns such as job and marriage become inconsistent with criminality; people literally grow out of crime.[66]

James Q. Wilson and Richard Herrnstein argue that aging out is a function of the natural history of the human life cycle.[67] Deviance in adolescence is fuelled by the need for conventionally unobtainable money and sex and reinforced by close relationships with peers who defy conventional morality. At the same time, teenagers are becoming independent from parents and other adults who enforce conventional standards. They have a new sense of energy and strength and are involved with peers who are similarly vigorous and frustrated. Adults, on the other hand, develop the ability to delay gratification and forgo the immediate gains that law violations bring. They also start wanting to take responsibility for their behaviour and to adhere to conventional mores, such as establishing long-term relationships and starting a family.[68] Research shows that young people may turn to crime as a way to solve the problems of adolescence, including loneliness, frustration, and fear of peer rejection. As they mature, conventional means of problem solving become available and their life experience helps them seek out nondestructive solutions to their personal travails.[69]

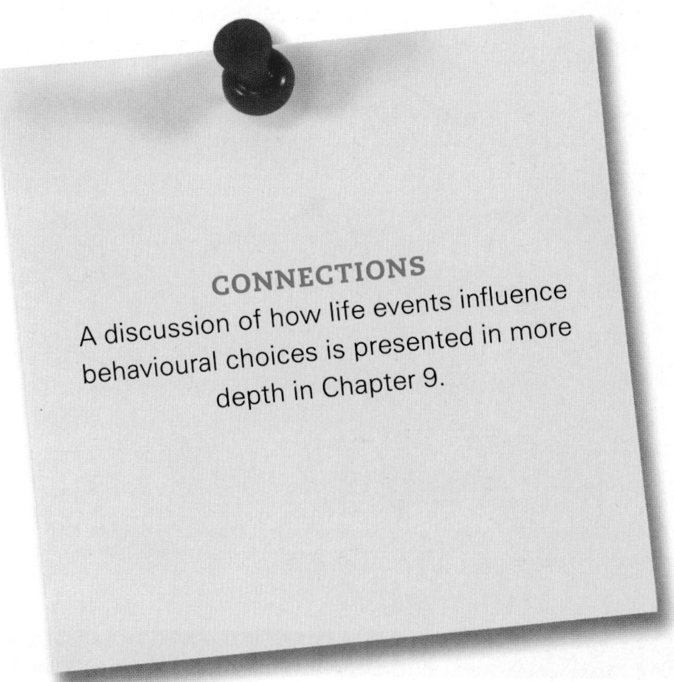
CONNECTIONS
A discussion of how life events influence behavioural choices is presented in more depth in Chapter 9.

aging out (desistance)
The fact that people commit less crime as they mature.

masculinity hypothesis
The view that women who commit crimes have biological and psychological traits similar to those of men.

Although most people age out of crime, some do pursue a criminal career. Yet even career criminals eventually slow down as they age. Crime is too dangerous, physically taxing, and unrewarding (and punishments too harsh and long lasting) to become a long-term way of life for most people.[70] By middle age, many of even the most chronic offenders terminate their criminal behaviour.

Gender and Crime

Crime is for the most part a male activity. In 2008/2009 of all adult criminal court cases, 77 percent involved a male accused, while 17 percent involved a female accused. Offences for which males had the highest involvement included sexual assault (98 percent), other sexual offences (97 percent), being unlawfully at large (91 percent), weapons offences (91 percent), and break and enter (90 percent). On the other hand, females were most highly represented in cases of prostitution (31 percent), fraud (31 percent), and theft (30 percent).[71] Significantly, the pattern of sex differences in criminal activity is consistent across different societies, and over time.

Why are there gender differences in the crime rate? Early criminologists pointed to emotional, physical, and psychological differences between males and females to explain the differences in crime rates. They maintained that because females were weaker and more passive, they were less likely to commit crimes. Cesare Lombroso argued that a small group of female criminals lacked "typical" female traits of "piety, maternity, undeveloped intelligence, and weakness."[72] Lombroso's theory became known as the **masculinity hypothesis**; in essence, a few "masculine" females were responsible for the handful of crimes that women commit.[73]

According to Canadian sociologists Elizabeth Comack and Selena Brickey (2007), women who

POLICY AND PRACTICE IN CRIMINOLOGY

THE CANADIAN RESPONSE TO YOUTH CRIME

Despite the overall decline in the youth crime rate, there are still calls by the public and media to "get tough" on youth crime. The summer of 2010 saw the first release of the Youth Crime Severity Index (Table 1) and the Youth Violent Crime Severity Index (Table 2). Based on the same concept as the general Crime Severity Index (CSI) offences received a weight based on their seriousness.[74]

As can be seen in Table 1, overall both the number and seriousness of crimes committed by youth has been declining since 2001.

In addition, despite media calls for action on youth crime to the contrary, the rate of violent crime committed by youth declined by more than 5 percent between 2000 and 2010, as shown in Table 2.[75]

Historically, the public response to youth crime in Canada is one of controversy and contradiction. The first federal act designed to specifically address youth crime was the Juvenile Delinquents Act (JDA), passed in 1908. Under the JDA, youth were not charged with crimes. Instead, young people who came into conflict with the law were brought before the court to plead "true" or "not true" to the charge of being a "delinquent"

© Ocean/Corbis

TABLE 1

Youth Crime Severity Index and Rate of Youth Accused of Police Reported Crime Canada, 2000 to 2010

Year	Youth Crime Severity Index		Police Reported Youth Crime Rate Per 100 000 Population	
	Index Number	*Percentage Change from Previous Year*	*Total Rate*	*Percentage Change from Previous Year*
2000	103.5	4	6914	7
2001	106.0	2	7159	4
2002	101.1	–5	6945	–3
2003	106.0	5	7280	5
2004	100.8	–5	6959	–4
2005	97.3	–4	6596	–5
2006	100.0	3	6812	3
2007	101.6	2	6782	0
2008	96.2	–5	6577	–3
2009	96.6	0	6593	0
2010	90.5	–6	6147	–7

Source: Adapted from Statistics Canada publication, *Juristat*, Catalogue 85-002-XWE 2011 001, pp. 35-36 (http://www.statcan.gc.ca/bsolc/olc-cel/olc-cel?catno=85-002-X&chropg=1&lang=eng).

TABLE 2

Youth Violent Crime Severity Index and Rate of Youth Accused of Police Reported Violent Crime; Canada, 2000 to 2010

Year	Youth Violent Crime Severity Index		Police Reported Youth Violent Crime Rate Per 100 000 Population	
	Index Number	*Percentage Change from Previous Year*	*Total Rate*	*Percentage Change from Previous Year*
2000	89.3	7	1944	13
2001	91.4	2	1984	2
2002	87.3	–5	1898	–4
2003	92.6	6	1961	3
2004	87.8	–5	1925	–2
2005	94.1	7	1895	–2
2006	100.0	6	1960	3
2007	102.2	2	1955	0
2008	96.3	–6	1903	–3
2009	97.8	2	1895	0
2010	93.7	–4	1838	–3

Source: Adapted from Statistics Canada publication, *Juristat*, Catalogue 85-002-XWE 2011 001, pp. 35-36 (http://www.statcan.gc.ca/bsolc/olc-cel/olc-cel?catno=85-002-X&chropg=1&lang=eng).

in need of treatment and supervision. Even youth accused of minor transgressions such as truancy, running away from home, underage drinking, or just being incorrigible could be declared delinquent and institutionalized or put on probation. Unfortunately, the *parens patriae* basis of the JDA, where the state takes on the role of parent for children in need of guidance and treatment, meant that youth had very few legal rights and no way to challenge the decisions of the courts.

By the late 1960s it was clear that the JDA needed to be replaced by legislation that could better address the growth in youth crime taking place at the time, a consequence of the baby-boom children now maturing into teenagers. After years of debate and many versions of the statute, the Young Offenders Act (YOA) was proclaimed law in April 1984. The new act did away with the status of "juvenile delinquent" so that young people could now be held accountable for the specific criminal offences they had committed. At the same time, the YOA introduced legal rights similar to those held by adults. Still, under the YOA children and young persons were to receive special consideration, in the form of guidance and treatment and lighter sentences for their crimes. Unfortunately, in attempting to make youth accountable for their crimes, while at the same time providing for shorter sentences to encourage rehabilitation, the YOA failed to satisfy both the "get tough" and the "child saver" camps. Research showed that too many youth convicted of minor offences were placed in custody.[76] The media consistently point to high-profile cases of violent crime as evidence that we needed to get tough on youth crime.

THE CANADIAN PRESS/Nathan Denette

Police officers stand by as a lockdown was ordered at Central Technical School in Toronto after at least one shot was reportedly fired shortly after 1 P.M. in a stairwell of the school on the afternoon of September 30, 2010. Do we need tougher laws to deal with youth violent crime?

On April 1, 2003, the **Youth Criminal Justice Act (YCJA)** became law, introducing the "justice model" to deal with crimes committed by young people. According to this model and to the "Declaration of Principle" that guides the YCJA, crime prevention through rehabilitation, in combination with the application of meaningful consequences, should be the goal of the youth justice system. To achieve this goal, alternative measures to avoid criminal charges and sentences of custody for minor offences are emphasized, while at the same time "fair and proportionate accountability" will ensure that serious crimes committed by youth are punished with stiffer sentences. In addition, youth will be afforded enhanced protections to ensure that their legal rights are protected.

Youth Criminal Justice Act (YCJA) Law that provides for a range of alternate measures to divert minor cases out of the courts and out of custody sentences, but will mean stiffer sentences for serious crimes.

Will the YCJA end the controversy about how to deal with youth who commit crimes? Not likely. Critics argue that the YCJA does not go far enough and is "too soft" on serious offenders. Sociologist Bernard Schissel argues that young people have become a sort of scapegoat for a growing fear of crime in society, an easy target to blame for a host of society's ills and fears. Others observe that youth crime is only a symptom—of social inequality and poverty, lack of educational resources, lack of perceived opportunity, and inadequate parenting.

CRITICAL THINKING

1. Do you think there is a youth crime problem in Canada? Why or why not?
2. What do you think is the most effective way to deal with youth crime? Should we treat youth exactly the same as adults? Why or why not?

Sources: Bernard Schissel, *Social Dimensions of Canadian Youth Justice* (Toronto: Oxford University Press, 1993); Bernard Schissel, *Blaming Children: Youth Crime, Moral Panics and the Politics of Hate* (Halifax, Fernwood Publishing, 1997); W. Gordon West, "Reconstructing Canadian Moral Panic: Youth and School Violence," in Thomas O'Reilly-Fleming (ed.), *Post Critical Criminology* (Scarborough, Ontario: Prentice-Hall, 1996); Thomas Gabor, "Methodological Orthodoxy or Eclecticism? The Case of Youth Violence," *Canadian Journal of Criminology 42* (2000): 77–83; Jim Hackler and Wasanti Paranjape, "Juvenile Justice Statistics: Mythmaking or Measure of System Response," *Canadian Journal of Criminology, 25* (1983): 209–26; Peter Carrington, "Factors Affecting Police Diversion of Young Offenders: A Statistical Analysis," Report to the Solicitor General Canada, 1998; Robert Hoge, D.A. Andrews, and Alan Leschied, "Tests of Three Hypotheses Regarding the Predictors of Delinquency," *Journal of Abnormal Child Psychology 22* (1994): 547–59.

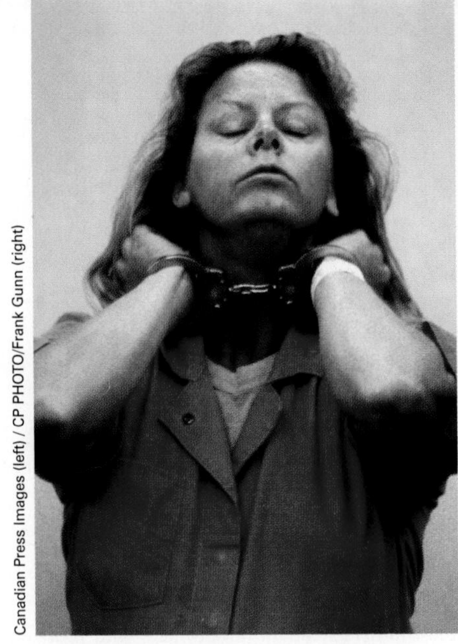

Aileen Wuornos. Her life and crimes, including the murders of seven men, were depicted in the 2003 movie *Monster*.

Karla Homolka. Convicted of manslaughter in the murders of Lesley Mahaffy and Kristen French, she claimed she was a victim and unwilling accomplice of the real killer, Paul Bernardo.

Canadian Press Images (left) / CP PHOTO/Frank Gunn (right)

commit crimes continue to be characterized as somehow more morally reprehensible than men because they violate strict moral beliefs about how we expect women to behave—while at the same time we tolerate much greater latitude in the behaviour of men. In the case of women who commit violent offences, the media even go so far as to characterize them as "monsters." In fact, despite the many assumptions writers have made about female criminality, we still know little about how and why females commit the crimes they do.[77]

Some criminologists still consider trait differences a key determinant of crime rate differences. For example, some criminologists link antisocial behaviour to hormonal influences by arguing that male sex hormones (androgens) account for more aggressive male behaviour; thus, gender-related hormonal differences can explain the gender gap in the crime rate.[78]

By the mid-20th century, criminologists commonly portrayed gender differences in the crime rate as a function of socialization. Female criminals were described as troubled individuals, alienated at home, who pursued crime as a means of compensating for their disrupted personal lives.[79] The streets became a "second home" to girls whose physical and emotional adjustment was hampered by a strained home life marked by conditions such as absent fathers or overly competitive mothers. The relatively few females who commit violent crimes report having home and family relationships that are more troubled than those experienced by males.[80]

In the 1970s, liberal feminists focused their attention on the social and economic role of women in society and its relationship to female crime rates.[81] They suggested that the traditionally lower crime rate for women could be explained by their "second-class" economic and social position. They predicted that as women's social roles changed and their lifestyles became more like those of men, their crime rates would converge.[82] Though much progress has been made in addressing the economic and social inequality of women in Canadian society, working women still make only three-quarters the money men make, often for doing the same work; continue to shoulder the burden for most childrearing and housework; and are much more likely than males to live in poverty.[83]

Crime rates are still considerably higher for males than for females. However, criminologists have pointed to rapid increases in the female violence rate as evidence of a troubling trend. Between 1994

CONNECTIONS

Gender differences in the crime rate may be a function of androgen levels; these hormones cause areas of the brain to become less sensitive to environmental stimuli, making males more likely to seek high levels of stimulation and to tolerate more pain in the process. Chapter 5 discusses the biosocial causes of crime and reviews this issue in greater detail.

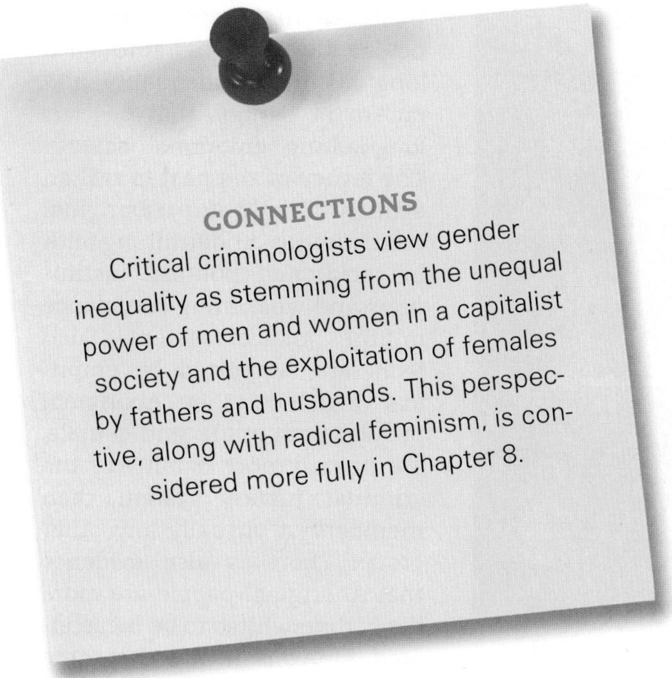

CONNECTIONS

Critical criminologists view gender inequality as stemming from the unequal power of men and women in a capitalist society and the exploitation of females by fathers and husbands. This perspective, along with radical feminism, is considered more fully in Chapter 8.

and 2009, the number of adult females appearing in court accused of serious violent crimes including homicides, attempted murder, sexual assaults, major assaults, and robbery grew by 124 percent (from 2058 to 4621). In comparison, the male rate grew by only 35 percent. More disturbing, other research on youth crime shows that rates of overall crime and especially violent crime may be increasing much more rapidly for girls than boys, as much as two or three times faster.[84]

Betsie Van der Meet/Stone/Getty Images

Rates of female violence are rising faster than rates for males. One reason may be the breakdown of the old stereotype that girls don't display aggression.

LO7 Race and Crime

There is not a lot of Canadian research about the link between race and crime. In fact, due to the sensitivity of the issue, most Canadian police and correctional agencies do not collect or publish data that link racial characteristics with crimes. Criminologist Scot Wortley reports that government statistics show that blacks and especially Aboriginal people are overrepresented in the criminal justice system.[85] However, it is difficult to carry out research into the reasons that these racial groups are overrepresented: Do they commit more crimes, or are these groups just more likely to be targeted for arrest, conviction, and incarceration?

In 2007/2008, Aboriginal adults accounted for 22 percent of admissions to sentenced custody, while representing 3 percent of the Canadian population.[86] Rates of violent crime are especially high on First Nations reserves.

Causes of Racial Disparity

Racial differences in the crime rate remain an extremely sensitive issue. Research shows that suspects who are poor, minority, and male are more likely to be formally arrested than suspects who are white, affluent, and female.[87] Some critics charge that police officers may use "racial profiling" to target certain visible minority groups for arrest.[88] For example, a 2005 study conducted by Scot Wortley in Kingston, Ontario, found that a young black male was 3.7 times more likely to be stopped and questioned by police than a Caucasian and an Aboriginal person was 1.4 times more likely to be stopped than a Caucasian.[89]

While UCR data may reflect discriminatory police practices, Aboriginal people are arrested for a disproportionate amount of violent crime, such as assaults and murder, and it is improbable that police discretion alone could account for these proportions. It is doubtful that police routinely ignore white killers and robbers, while arresting violent Aboriginal offenders. Many criminologists today concede that recorded racial differences in violent crime arrest rates cannot be explained away solely by racism or differential treatment within the criminal justice system.[90] To do so would be

The standoff at Caledonia. Members of the Six Nations of the Grand River laid claim to a tract of land that a developer planned to turn into a residential subdivision. Protests, violence, and claims of racism characterized the five-year dispute.

Colin Mcconnell/GetStock.com

to ignore the social problems that may explain why crime is more frequent in some racial groups.

Racism and Crime

How, then, can racial patterns be explained? Most explanations focus on the impact of economic deprivation, social disorganization, subcultural adaptations, and the legacy of racism and discrimination on personality and behaviour.[91]

CONNECTIONS

According to some criminologists, racism has created isolated subcultures that espouse violence as a way of coping with conflict situations. Exasperation and frustration among minority group members who feel powerless to fit within middle-class society are manifested in aggression. This view is discussed further in Chapter 10's review of the subculture of violence theory.

Aboriginal people in particular have suffered through a long history of inequality and racism in Canada that has left long-lasting emotional scars.[92] The legacy of the past is still an element of daily life in Aboriginal communities, undermining faith in social and political institutions and weakening confidence in the justice system. Such fears are supported by empirical evidence that Aboriginal people, both male and female, are treated more harshly by the criminal justice system than members of virtually any other group. There is also evidence that Aboriginal people are more likely than whites to be incarcerated for committing the same crimes, and are much less likely to be granted parole. It is possible that some judges view many Aboriginal offenders as "poor risks," considering them more likely to reoffend than white offenders.[93] Yet, Aboriginal victims of crime receive less public concern and media attention than white victims.[94]

Is Convergence Possible?

Considering these overwhelming social problems, is it possible that racial crime rates will soon converge? One argument is that if economic conditions improve in minority communities, then differences in crime rates will eventually disappear.[95] A trend toward Aboriginal self-government, underway since the late 1980s, may help to reduce race-based crime rate differentials.[96]

DID YOU KNOW?

- There are stable and enduring patterns in the crime rate.
- Crime is more common during the summer and in urban areas.
- While the true association between class and crime is still unknown, the official data tell us that crime rates are highest in areas with high rates of poverty.
- Young people have the highest crime rates. People commit less crime as they mature.
- Males have a higher crime rate than females. However, the female crime rate appears to be rising.
- Some criminologists suggest that institutional racism, such as police profiling, accounts for the racial differences in the crime rate. Others believe that high Aboriginal crime rates are a function of living in poverty.

The Chronic Offender

Crime data show that most offenders commit a single criminal act and, upon arrest, discontinue their antisocial activity. Others commit a few less serious crimes. Finally, a small group of persistent offenders accounts for a majority of all criminal offences. These persistent offenders are referred to as career criminals or **chronic offenders**.

The concept of the chronic or career offender is most closely associated with the research efforts of Marvin Wolfgang, Robert Figlio, and Thorsten Sellin.[97] In their landmark 1972 study, *Delinquency in a Birth Cohort*, they used official records to follow the criminal careers of a cohort of 9945 boys born in Philadelphia in 1945, from the time of their birth until they reached 18 years of age in 1963. Official police records were used to identify delinquents. About one-third of the boys (3475) had some police contact. The remaining two-thirds (6470) had none. The best-known discovery of Wolfgang and his associates was the phenomenon of the chronic offender. They identified a group of 627 boys who had been arrested five times or more. This group was responsible for a total of 5305 offences, or 51.9 percent of all the offences committed by the cohort. Even more striking was their involvement in serious criminal acts. Though comprising only about 6 percent of the entire sample, they committed 71 percent of the homicides, 73 percent of the rapes, 82 percent of the robberies, and 69 percent of the aggravated assaults.

Wolfgang and his associates found that arrests and court experience did little to deter the chronic offender. In fact, punishment was inversely related to chronic offending: The more stringent the sanction chronic offenders received, the more likely they were to engage in repeated criminal behaviour.

chronic offenders
A small group of persistent offenders who account for a majority of all criminal offences.

Wolfgang's pioneering effort to identify the chronic career offender has since been replicated by a number of other researchers in a variety of locations in the United States, Canada, and abroad.[98]

The findings of the cohort studies and the discovery of the chronic offender have revitalized criminological theory. If relatively few offenders become chronic, persistent criminals, then perhaps they possess some individual trait that is responsible for their behaviour. Most people exposed to troublesome social conditions, such as poverty, do not become chronic offenders, so it is unlikely that social conditions alone can cause chronic offending.

Traditional theories of criminal behaviour failed to distinguish between chronic and occasional offenders. They concentrated more on explaining why people begin to commit crime and paid scant attention to why people stop offending. The discovery of the chronic offender 25 years ago forced criminologists to consider issues such as persistence and desistance in their explanations of crime; more recent theories account for not only the onset of criminality but also its termination.

CHAPTER 3

Victims and Victimization

Learning Outcomes

LO1 Define victimology.

LO2 Identify major problems faced by victims of crime.

LO3 Identify major risk factors for being victimized.

LO4 Explain the victim precipitation theory, lifestyle theories, and routine activities theory.

LO5 List organizations created to assist victims of violence in Canada.

LO6 Identify victims' services programs.

LO7 Identify major legislation pertaining to victims' rights.

LO8 Describe major programs designed to prevent crime.

© Alistair Heap/Alamy

LO1 Introduction

Eight-year-old Victoria Stafford went missing on the afternoon of April 8, 2009, while walking home from Oliver Stephens Public School in Woodstock, Ontario. Surveillance camera footage from a nearby high school showed Victoria walking away from the school engaged in conversation with an unidentified woman. Terri-Lynne McClintic, 18, the woman in the surveillance video, and boyfriend Michael Rafferty, 28, were arrested by Ontario Provincial Police on May 20, 2009, and charged with first-degree murder and abduction. McClintic explained that she had approached Victoria on the street and engaged the little girl in a conversation about her dog, a shih tzu named Precious. She asked Victoria if she would like to see the dog. The little girl readily agreed, and the two headed off to a waiting car. Later that day, McClintic and Rafferty drove to a rural area near Guelph, Ontario, where they murdered Victoria and concealed the body in a field under a pile of rocks. At her trial on April 30, 2010, McClintic pleaded guilty to first-degree murder in connection with Victoria's death, explaining that she had never intended to steal a child that afternoon, and that she had been under the influence of drugs. "Every day I think that maybe if I hadn't walked down the street that day, that precious little angel would still be here. Every day I ask myself why. Why did I tell myself that everything would be OK?"[1] Michael Rafferty, her accomplice in the murder, is scheduled to be tried in 2012.

DID YOU KNOW?

- Victimology is the branch of criminology that examines the nature and extent of crime victimization.
- The total economic loss from crime victimization amounts to billions of dollars annually.
- Victims may suffer long-term trauma, including posttraumatic stress disorder.
- Many victims become fearful and go through a fundamental life change.
- People who are victims may be more likely to engage in antisocial acts themselves.

The horrific acts of a seemingly cold-blooded child killer such as Terri-Lynne McClintic illustrate the terrible impact crime can have on victims, their families, and society in general. Why do people become targets of predatory criminals? Is victimization a matter of chance, or are there ways victims can somehow deflect or avoid criminal behaviour? What can be done to protect victims, and, failing that, what can be done to help them in the aftermath of crime?

For many years, crime victims were not considered an important topic for criminological study. Victims were viewed as the passive recipients of a criminal's anger, greed,

THE CANADIAN PRESS/Dave Chidley

On July 19, 2009, police found "suspicious remains" in a secluded country field near Mount Forest, Ontario, which were later identified as those of Victoria Stafford, a grade 3 student who was abducted and murdered. Is it possible to protect children from such irrational acts, or is victimization a random event that can happen to anyone at any time?

victimology
The study of the victim's role in criminal events.

victimologists
Criminologists who focus on the victims of crime.

or frustration; like 8-year-old Victoria Stafford, they were considered to be people "in the wrong place at the wrong time." In the late 1960s, a number of pioneering studies found that, contrary to popular belief, the victim's own behaviour is important in the crime process. Victims were found to influence criminal behaviour by playing an active role in a criminal incident, as when an assault victim initially provokes an eventual attacker. Victims can also play an indirect role in a criminal incident, as when a woman adopts a lifestyle that continually brings her into high-crime areas.

CP PHOTO/Toronto Star-Bernard Weil

Evidence of children who are victims of abuse or neglect such as Jeffrey Baldwin (pictured on t-shirt) stirs deep emotions in all of us.

The discovery that victims play an important role in the crime process has prompted the scientific study of victims, or **victimology**. Criminologists who focus their attention on crime victims refer to themselves as **victimologists**.

In this chapter, we examine victims and their relationship to the criminal process. First, using available victim data, we analyze the nature and extent of victimization. We then discuss the relationship between victims and criminal offenders. In this context, we look at various theories of victimization that attempt to explain the victim's role in the crime problem. Finally, we examine how society has responded to the needs of victims and consider the special problems they still face.

LO2 Problems of Crime Victims

The most comprehensive source of information about victimization in Canada is the Personal Risk and Victimization Survey (PRVS). Every five years, a sample of about 20 000 Canadians are asked about their experiences of personal injuries and accidents, and of being a victim of a crime. In 2004 and 2009, the PRVS crime questions concentrated on eight types of criminal victimization: assault, sexual assault, robbery, theft of personal property, break and enter, theft of household property, motor vehicle/parts theft, and vandalism.

© David R. Frazier Photolibrary, Inc./Alamy

Home break-ins can have severe psychological effects, particularly in children, including feeling unsafe and fear and distrust of others.

The results from the 2009 PRVS revealed that about 25 percent of Canadians aged 15 and over were the victim of a crime in 2009 (7.4 million), about the same percentage as in 2004.[2] Being the target or victim of a sexual assault, a break and enter, or an assault is a terrible burden that can have considerable long-term consequences. In this section we explore some of the effects of these incidents.

Economic Loss

Given that only about one-third of all crimes are reported to police, it is difficult to arrive at a figure representing the real costs of crime in Canada in any given year. Based on PRVS data, the Department of Justice estimates that crime cost Canadians $70 billion in 2003, or $2200 for every man, woman, and child in Canada every year.[3] As can be seen in Figure 3-1, more than two-thirds of the costs of crime are borne directly by victims, estimated at $47 billion annually, including the value of property stolen or damaged, pain and suffering, lost time from work, and health-care costs.[4]

Police, court, and correctional services costs for dealing with crime are estimated at $13 billion each year, with the remainder of the costs of crime, $10 billion, spread out over various crime prevention measures including alarm systems and security services. Add it all up, and the total costs of crime ($70 billion) are more than every level of government in Canada spends each year on education.[5]

In terms of the costs of various types of crime, as can also be seen in Figure 3.1, property crime, including victim costs, criminal justice system costs, and prevention, is the most expensive type of crime, estimated to cost Canadians $40 billion in 2003. Violent crime is next, costing Canadians an estimated $18 billion that year, followed by "Other" types of crime (including drug and traffic offences) at $12 billion.[6]

In addition to the annual costs, victims may suffer long-term losses in earnings and occupational attainment. Research by Ross Macmillan shows that Americans who suffer a violent victimization during adolescence earn about US$82 000 less than nonvictims; Canadian victims earn $237 000 less. Macmillan reasons that victims bear psychological and physical ills that inhibit first their academic achievement and later their economic and professional success.[7]

Costs of Crime in Canada—An Update

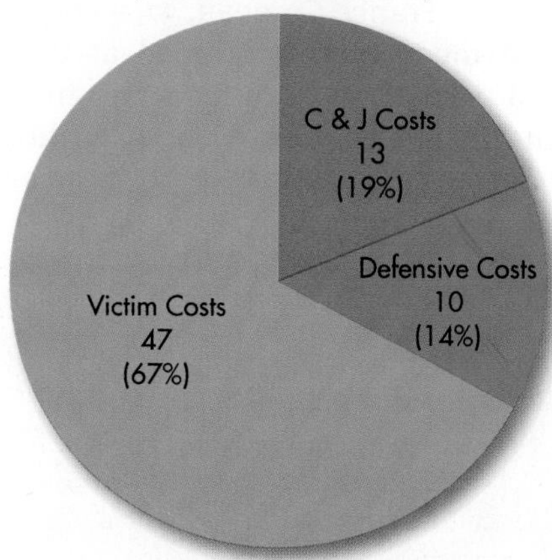

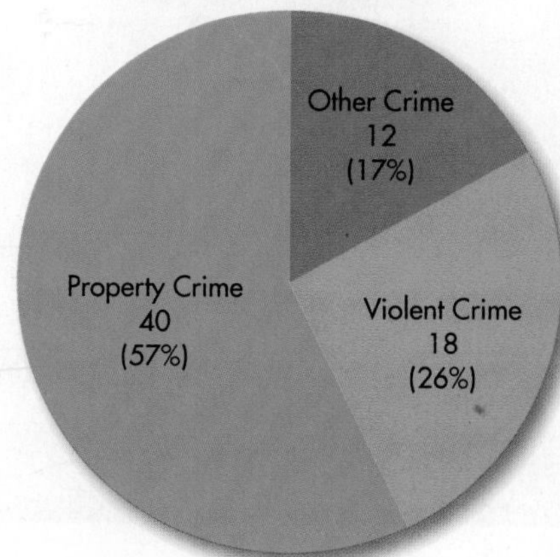

Source: JustResearch, 2005, Issue No. 12, Figures: Costs of Crime in Canada an Update, page 58, http://www.justice.gc.ca/eng/pi/rs/rep-rap/jr/jr12/jr12.pdf, Department of Justice Canada, 2005. Reproduced with the permission of the Minister of Public Works and Government Services Canada, 2011.

System Abuse

The suffering endured by crime victims does not end when their attacker leaves the scene of the crime. They may suffer more victimization by the justice system.

While the crime is still fresh in their minds, victims may find that the police interview following the crime is handled callously, with innuendos or

DID YOU KNOW?

- Males and females are equally likely to be the victim of a crime. Women are much more likely to be the victim of a sexual assault or personal theft, while males are more likely to be the victim of a physical assault or robbery.
- The poor are much more likely than the affluent to be the victims of violent crime; the wealthy are more likely to be the targets of personal theft.
- Younger, single people are more often targets than older, married people.
- Some people and places are targets of repeat victimization.

posttraumatic stress disorder
Psychological reaction to a highly stressful event; symptoms may include depression, anxiety, flashbacks, and recurring nightmares.

insinuations that they were somehow at fault. They have difficulty learning what is going on in the case; property is often kept for a long time as evidence and may never be returned. Some sexual assault victims report that the treatment they receive from legal, medical, and mental health services is so destructive that they can't help feeling revictimized.[8] Victims may also suffer economic hardship because of wages lost while they testify in court and find that authorities are indifferent to their fear of retaliation if they cooperate in the offenders' prosecution.[9]

Long-Term Stress

Victims may suffer stress and anxiety long after the incident is over and the justice process has been forgotten. For example, girls who were psychologically, sexually, or physically abused as children are more likely to have lower self-esteem and be more suicidal as adults than those who were not abused.[10] Children who are victimized in the home are more likely to run away to escape their environment, which puts them at risk for juvenile arrest and involvement with the justice system.[11]

Stress does not end in childhood. Spousal abuse victims suffer an extremely high prevalence of depression, **posttraumatic stress disorder** (an emotional disturbance following exposure to stresses outside the range of normal human experience), anxiety disorder, and obsessive-compulsive disorder (an extreme preoccupation with certain thoughts and compulsive performance of certain behaviours).[12] One reason may be that abusive spouses are as likely to abuse their victims psychologically with threats and intimidation as they are to use physical force; psychological abuse can lead to depression and other long-term disabilities.[13]

Some victims are physically disabled as a result of serious wounds sustained during episodes of random violence, including a growing number that suffer paralyzing spinal cord injuries and while the health-care system may cover the costs of any required medical procedures, many victims must live with severe long-term emotional and physical consequences.[14]

Fear

People who have suffered crime victimization remain fearful long after their wounds have healed. Even if they have escaped attack themselves, hearing about another's victimization may make people timid and cautious. For example, women who are being abused by their partner may be fearful of reporting the abuse to authorities, especially when they read media reports about women who have been stalked and murdered by their partners following disclosure of the abuse to police.[15]

Victims of violent crime are the most deeply affected, fearing a repeat of their attack. There may be a spillover effect in which victims become fearful of other forms of crime they have not yet experienced; people who have been assaulted develop fears that their house will be burglarized.[16] Many go through a fundamental life change, viewing the world more suspiciously and less as a safe, controllable, and meaningful place. These people are more likely to suffer psychological stress for extended periods of time.[17]

Communities may live in fear when news of a violent incident grips the neighbourhood. Sometimes local incidents become national news. Beginning in September 2009, Ontario Provincial Police began the search for a male suspect who had tied up and sexually assaulted two women after breaking into their homes in the tiny community of Tweed, Ontario. Then, in November 2009, in a seemingly unrelated incident, Marie-France Comeau, 37, a corporal in the Canadian Armed Forces stationed at CFB Trenton, was found sexually assaulted and murdered in her Brighton, Ontario, home, about an hour's drive west of Tweed. On January 28, 2010, Jessica Elizabeth

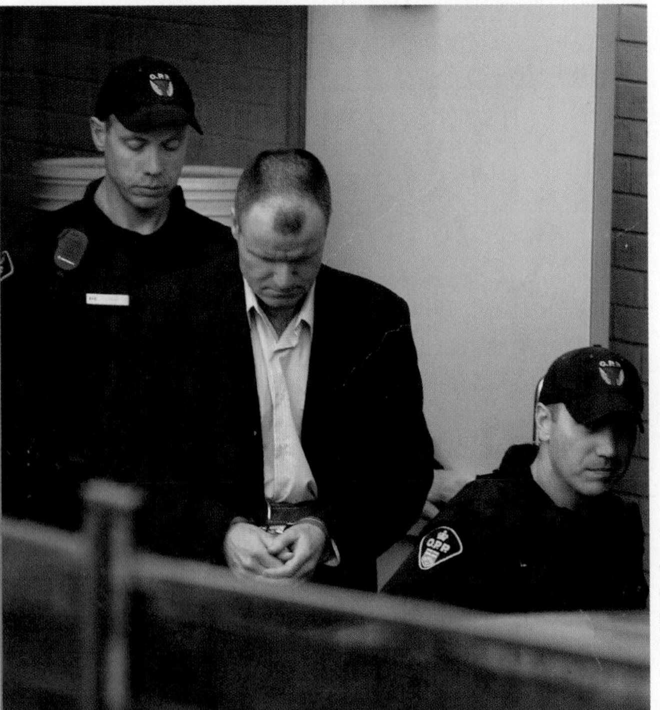
Steve Russell/GetStock.com

Escorted by police, Russell Williams leaves Tweed-area courthouse after pleading guilty to the murders of Marie-France Comeau and Jessica Elizabeth Lloyd.

Lloyd, 27, who worked for the local school bus company as a schedule coordinator, was found sexually assaulted and murdered in her home on Highway 37, about 25 kilometres south of Tweed. On October 2010, Colonel Russell Williams, base commander at CFB Trenton and a decorated air-force officer, pled guilty in the first-degree murders of Marie-France Comeau and Jessica Elizabeth Lloyd, in two separate counts of sexual assault and forcible confinement, and in more than 80 break and enters and attempted break and enters in Tweed and the surrounding area in which women's underwear and other clothing was stolen.[18]

Antisocial Behaviour

There is growing evidence that crime victims are more likely to commit crime themselves. Being abused or neglected as a child increases the odds of being arrested, both as a juvenile and as an adult.[19] Young people, especially those who were physically or sexually abused, are much more likely to smoke, drink, take drugs, and become involved in criminal activities than are nonabused youth (see Figure 3.2). Incarcerated offenders report significant amounts of posttraumatic stress disorder as a result of prior victimization, which may in part explain their violent and criminal behaviours.[20]

The abuse–crime phenomenon is referred to as the **cycle of violence**.[21] Research shows that both boys and girls are more likely to engage in violent behaviour if they were (a) the target of physical abuse and (b) exposed to violent behaviour among adults they know or live with, or exposed to weapons.[22]

cycle of violence
Victims of crime, especially childhood abuse, are more likely to commit crime themselves.

The Nature of Victimization

How many crime victims are there in Canada, and what are the trends and patterns in victimization? According to the 2009 GSS, about 7.4 million Canadians, or just over one-quarter of the population, reported being a victim of a criminal incident in the preceding 12 months. This proportion was essentially unchanged from that reported in 2004.

Patterns in the victimization survey findings are stable and repetitive, suggesting that victimization is not random but a function of personal and ecological factors. The stability of these patterns allows judgments to be made about the nature of victimization; policies can then be created in an effort to reduce the victimization rate. Who are victims? Where does victimization take place? What is the relationship between victims and criminals? The following sections discuss some of the most important victimization patterns and trends.

LO3 The Social Ecology of Victimization

According to a 2009 Statistics Canada report on victimization,[23] the risk of being a victim of a violent crime increases for those who are often engaged in evening activities outside the home, such as working nights, visiting friends, or going out to bars. Men and women are equally likely to be victims, though of different types of crime: women are more likely to be victims of sexual assault; males are more likely to be victims of assault or robbery. Marital status is another factor impacting on victimization. Single people, either never-married or those who are separated or divorced, are at the

FIGURE 3.2

Percentage of U.S. Male High School Students (Grades 9–12) Reporting Smoking, Drinking, or Using Drugs, by Physical/Sexual Abuse Status

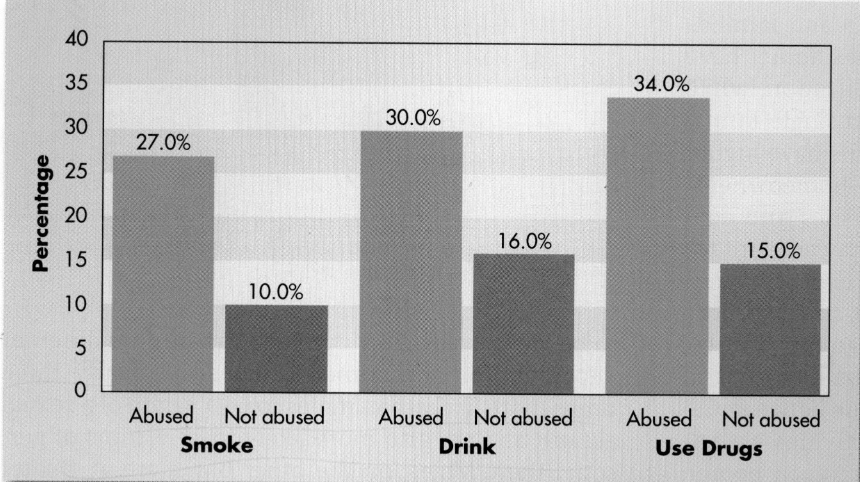

Notes: Smoke: smoked at least several cigarettes in the past week; Drink: drank at least once a month; Use drugs: used illegal drugs at least once in the past month. The survey was an in-class questionnaire completed by 3162 boys in grades 5–12 at a nationally representative sample of 265 public, private, and parochial schools from December 1996 to June 1997. The survey included roughly equal samples of adolescent boys in grades 5–8 and 9–12. All responses were weighted to reflect grade, region, race and ethnicity, and gender.

Source: Cathy Schoen et al., *The Health of Adolescent Boys: Commonwealth Fund Survey Findings* (New York: Commonwealth Fund, 1998). Figure prepared by the Center for Substance Abuse Research, University of Maryland, College Park.

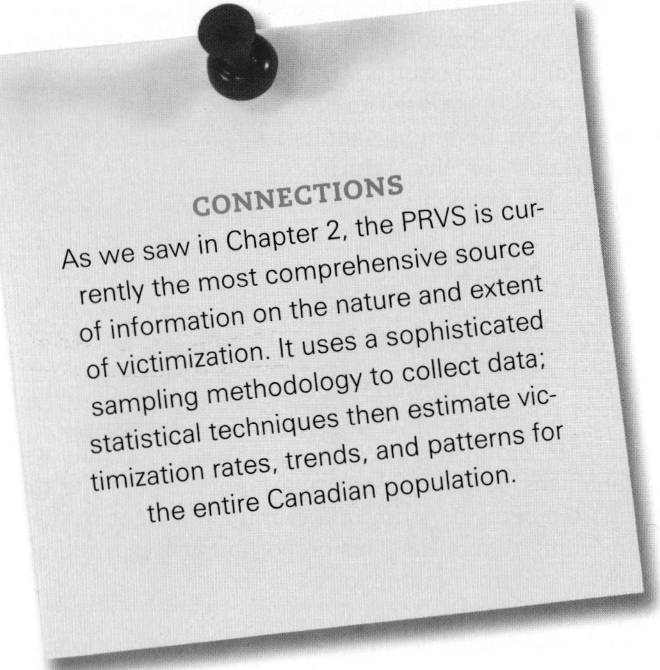

highest risk of victimization. Neighbourhood characteristics also affect the chances of victimization. Those living in cities, especially in Western Canada, have higher rates of both personal and household victimization.

The Victim's Household

The PRVS tells us that in Canada, low-income households are at a higher risk for violent victimization. On the other hand, households that reported an annual income of $60 000 or more have a greater risk of personal property theft. Individuals and families living in semi-detached, row, and duplex homes have the highest risk for household victimization, while apartment dwellers and those living in single-family dwellings have the lowest rates. Tenants have higher rates of household victimization than homeowners.

Changes in population characteristics and economic changes in Canadian society may account for the victimization patterns. As individuals' incomes and buying power continue to grow, and as more and more Canadians reside in large urban centres, personal and household theft may be expected to increase. At the same time, as the divide between the poor and the rich grows, criminal activities associated with violence will remain common in poorer, low-income neighbourhoods.

Victim Characteristics

Social and demographic characteristics also distinguish victims and nonvictims. The most important of these factors are gender, age, social status, marital status, and race.

Gender

As Figures 3.3 and 3.4 show, gender affects victimization risk: While males and females are equally likely to be victimized, the victimization rates are different depending on the crime. Females are nearly three times more likely than males to be a victim of a sexual assault and are also more likely to be victims of personal theft. Males, on the other hand, are at greater risk of being a victim of a robbery or a physical assault.

FIGURE 3.3

Self-Reported Violent Victimization and Theft of Personal Property by Gender, 2009—Rate per 1000 population age 15 years and older

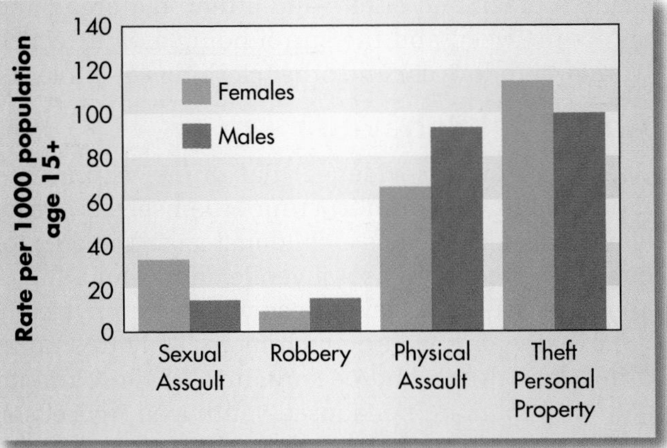

Source: Adapted from Statistics Canada publication JURISTAT - Criminal Victimization in Canada, 2009, Summer 2010, Vol. 30, No. 2, page 22 (http://www.statcan.gc.ca/pub/85-002-x/2010002/article/11340/tbl/tbl4-eng.htm).

FIGURE 3.4

Victimization by Violent Crime, by Gender

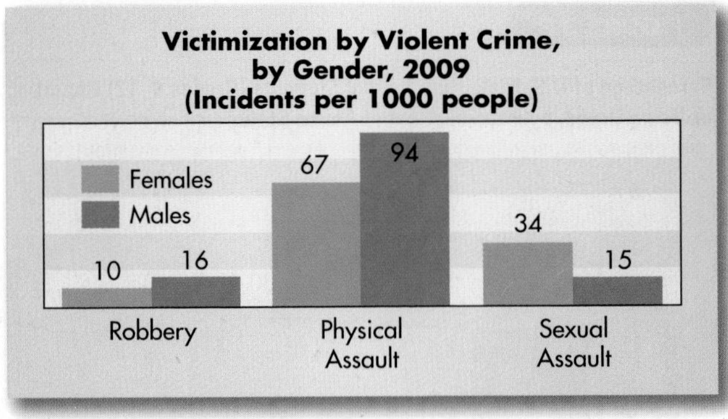

Source: Adapted from Statistics Canada publication JURISTAT, vol. 30, no. 2, 2010 (http://www4.hrsdc.gc.ca/.3ndic.1t.4r@-eng.jsp?iid=61).

Age

Victim data reveal that young people face a much greater victimization risk than do older persons. As Figure 3.5 shows, victim risk diminishes rapidly after age 25. The elderly, who are thought of as the helpless

FIGURE 3.5

Criminal Victimization and Age

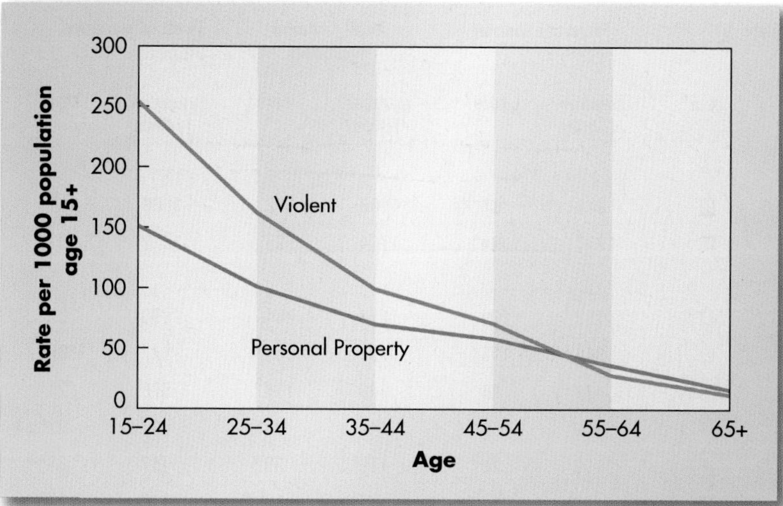

Source: Adapted from Statistics Canada publications JURISTAT, vol. 25, no. 7, and Vol. 30, No 2, 2009, retrieved on HRDSC Website (http://www4.hrsdc.gc.ca/.3ndic.1t.4r@-eng.jsp?iid=61).

targets of predatory criminals, are actually much safer than their grandchildren. People over 65, who make up about 13 percent of the population, account for only 2 percent of violent victimizations; young people ages 15 to 24, who also make up about 13 percent of the population, typically account for more than 30 percent of victimizations. For example, the 15-to-24 age group is about four times more likely to be sexually assaulted than people ages 45 to 54 (see Figure 3.6).[24]

Social Status

The poorest Canadians, those with the lowest level of reported household income, are also the most likely victims of sexual assault and physical assaults (see Figure 3.7). Although the poor are more likely to suffer violent crimes, the wealthy are more likely targets of personal theft crimes such as muggings and theft of belongings. Perhaps the affluent, who sport more expensive attire and frequent trendy restaurants and theatres, attract the attention of thieves (See Table 3.1.).

FIGURE 3.6

Self-Reported Violent Victimization and Theft of Personal Property by Age, 2009—Rate per 1000 population age 15 years and older

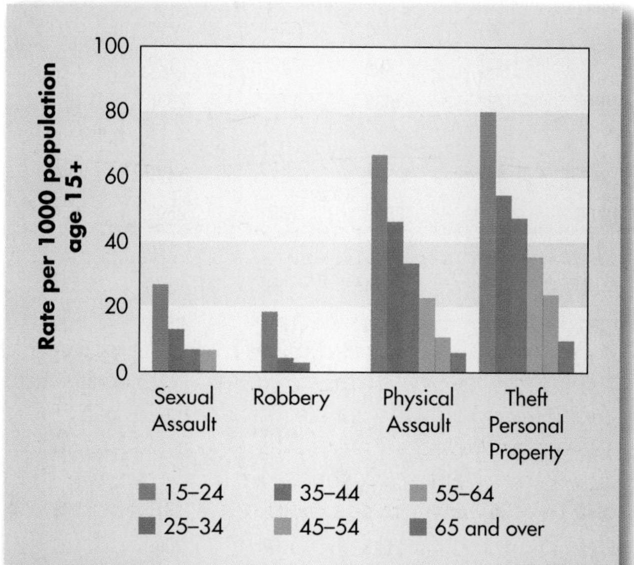

Note: Due to small numbers, it is not possible to calculate some rates for older age groups.

Source: Adapted from Statistics Canada publications JURISTAT, vol. 25, no. 7, and Vol. 30, No 2, 2009, retrieved on HRDSC Website (http://www4.hrsdc.gc.ca/.3ndic.1t.4r@-eng.jsp?iid=61).

FIGURE 3.7

Criminal Victimization and Social Status

Criminal Victimization Rates by Household Income Group, Canada, 2004—household income in dollars

	0–14,999	15,000–29,999	30,000–39,999	40,000–59,999	60,000 and over
	rate per 1000 population[1]				
Total violent victimization	**156**	**104**	**105**	**94**	**106**
Physical assault[2]	102	68	77	66	80
Sexual assault[3]	38[E]	24[E]	19[E]	21	16
Robbery	17[E]	12[E]	F	7[E]	9[E]
Personal property theft	71	76	92	81	116
	rate per 1000 households				
Total household victimization	**160**	**223**	**257**	**267**	**300**
Break and enter	41	36	50	41	42
Motor vehicle theft	21[E]	42	39	49	56
Theft of household property	59	84	93	93	104
Vandalism	39	60	74	84	98

[E] use with caution, coefficient of variation is high (16.6% to 33.3%)
F too unreliable to be published
1. Rates calculated per 1000 population aged 15 and over.
2. Includes incidents of spousal physical assault.
3. Includes spousal sexual assault.

Note: Figures may not add to total due to rounding.

Source: Adapted from Statistics Canada publication Household Income and Victimization in Canada, 2004, Catalogue 85F0033MWE, no. 20 (http://www.statcan.gc.ca/pub/85f0033m/85f0033m2009020-eng.pdf).

TABLE 3.1

Self-Reported Violent Victimization and Theft of Personal Property by Selected Demographic Characteristics, 2009

Characteristics	Sexual assault		Robbery		Physical assault		Total—violent incidents		Theft of personal property	
	number (1000s)	*rate[1]*	*number (1000s)*	*rate[1]*	*number (1000s)*	*rate[1]*	*number (1000s)*	*rate[1]*	*number (1000s)*	*rate[1]*
Sex										
Female†	472	34	146	10	945	67	1563	112	1609	115
Male	204[E]	15[E]*	222	16	1277	94*	1704	125	1372	101
Age										
15 to 24†	307	69	209[E]	47[E]	757	169	1273	284	898	200
25 to 34	161[E]	35[E]*	56[E]	12[E]*	545	118*	761	165*	642	139*
35 to 44	92[E]	19[E]*	43[E]	9[E]*	413	86*	548	114*	578	121*
45 to 54	96[E]	18[E]*	F	F	316	59*	444	84*	487	92*
55 to 64	F	F	F	F	118	29*	156	39*	257	63*
65 and over	F	F	F	F	73[E]	17[E]*	84[E]	19[E]*	118	27*
Marital status										
Married†	131[E]	9[E]	66[E]	5[E]	677	48	874	62	1112	79
Common-law	82[E]	26[E]*	F	F	335	105*	440	137*	442	138*
Single	385	54*	237	34*	1011	143*	1633	231*	1207	171*
Widowed	F	F	F	F	F	F	F	F	26[E]	19[E]*
Separated/divorced	74[E]	40[E]*	36[E]	19[E]*	184[E]	99[E]*	293	158*	192	103*
Household income										
Less than $20 000†	41	29[E]	F	F	148	103	212	147	112	78
$20 000 to $39 999	85[E]	26[E]	F	F	246	75	364	112	302	93
$40 000 to $59 999	83[E]	22[E]	F	F	294	76	406	105	343	89
$60 000 to $99 999	138[E]	22[E]	72[E]	12[E]	536	86	746	120	633	102
$100 000 or more	220[E]	31[E]	113[E]	16[E]	598	83	932	129	1037	143*
Aboriginal identity										
Aboriginal people†	63[E]	71[E]	F	F	123	141[E]	204	232	127	145
Non-Aboriginal people	612	23*	347	13	2081	78*	3039	114*	2838	107
Immigrant status										
Immigrant†	F	F	F	F	244	43	355	62	477	84
Non-immigrant	598	27	334	15	1977	90*	2909	133*	2502	114*
Visible minority										
Visible minority†	F	F	F	F	189[E]	51[E]	279[E]	76[E]	376	102
Non-visible minority	604	25	332	14	2009	85*	2945	124*	2578	109
Sexual orientation[2]										
Heterosexual†	509	20	262	10	1779	71	2550	102	2483	99
Homosexual	F	F	F	F	F	F	108[E]	405[E]*	F	F
Activity limitations										
Limited in activities†	229	27	173[E]	20[E]	832	96	1234	143	916	106
No limitation	445	24	194	10*	1384	73*	2023	107*	2060	109

† reference category
* significantly different from reference category ($p < 0.05$)
1. Rates are calculated per 1000 population age 15 years and older.
2. Data for those who self-identified as bisexual have been suppressed due to the unreliability of the estimates.

Note: Excludes responses of "Don't know and Not stated." Excludes data from the Northwest Territories, Yukon, and Nunavut, which will be published at a later date.
Source: Adapted from Statistics Canada publication JURISTAT - Criminal Victimization in Canada, 2009, Summer 2010, Vol. 30, No. 2, page 22 (http://www.statcan.gc.ca/pub/85-002-x/2010002/article/11340/tbl/tbl4-eng.htm).

Marital Status

Marital status also influences victimization risk. Never-married and separated/divorced males and females are victimized more often than married people. Widows and widowers have the lowest victimization risk. This association between marital status and victimization is probably influenced by age, gender, and lifestyle:

1. Many young people, who have the highest victim risk, are actually too young to have been married.
2. Young single people also go out in public more often and sometimes interact with high-risk peers, increasing their exposure to victimization.
3. Widows and widowers suffer much lower victimization rates because they are older, interact with older people, and are more likely to stay home at night and to avoid public places.

Race and Ethnicity

Compared to European Canadians, visible minorities and recent immigrant groups are more likely to experience hate crimes.[25] Also, as can be seen in Figure 3.8, Jews and Muslims reported considerably higher rates of hate crimes than Catholics and other religions.

Morton Beiser reports that while Southeast Asian refugees to Canada were more likely to experience more subtle forms of racism (e.g., rudeness or insulting remarks), 11 percent reported acts of vandalism directed against their ethnic community as a whole, and 5 percent of the study group had been physically threatened/manhandled or had personal property defaced with racial graffiti.[26]

Why do these discrepancies exist? Because of income inequality, racial and ethnic minority group members are often forced to live in deteriorated urban areas beset by alcohol and drug abuse, poverty, racial discrimination, and violence. Consequently, their lifestyle places them in the most "at risk" population group.

© Kuttig - People - 2 / Alamy

FIGURE 3.8

Police-Reported Hate Crime by Type of Religion, Canada, 2006

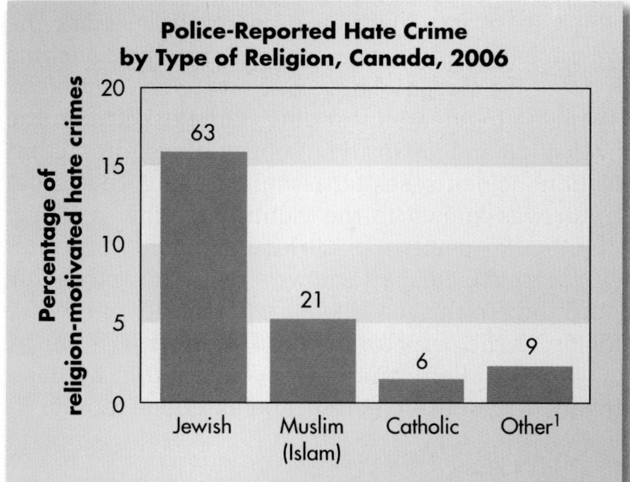

[1] Includes all other hate crimes where the type of religion is not otherwise stated (e.g., Protestant, Buddhist, Hindu, and Sikh).

Source: Adapted from Statistics Canada publication Hate Crime in Canada, Catalogue 85F0033MWE2008017, vol. 29, no. 3 (http://www.statcan.gc.ca/pub/85f0033m/2008017/c-g/5200138-eng.htm).

CONNECTIONS

The association between age and victimization is undoubtedly tied to lifestyle: Young people often stay out late at night, go to public places, and hang out with other young people who have a high risk of criminal involvement. Teens also face a high victimization risk because they spend a great deal of time in the most dangerous building in the community: the local school!

Repeat Victimization

Does prior victimization enhance or reduce the chances of future victimization? Individuals who have been crime victims have a significantly higher chance of future victimization than people who have remained nonvictims.[27] Households that have experienced victimization in the past are the ones most likely to experience it again in the future.[28]

What factors predict chronic victimization? Most repeat victimizations occur soon after a previous crime has occurred, suggesting that repeat victims share some personal characteristic that makes them a magnet for predators.[29] For example, children who are shy, physically weak, or socially isolated may be prone to being bullied in the schoolyard.[30] David Finkelhor and Nancy Asigian have found that three specific types of characteristics increase the potential for victimization:[31]

1. *Target vulnerability.* The victims' physical weakness or psychological distress renders them incapable of resisting or deterring crime and makes them easy targets.
2. *Target gratifiability.* Some victims have some quality, possession, skill, or attribute that an offender wants to obtain, use, have access to, or manipulate. Having attractive possessions such as a leather coat may make one vulnerable to predatory crime.
3. *Target antagonism.* Some characteristics increase risk because they arouse anger, jealousy, or destructive impulses in potential offenders. Being gay or effeminate, for example, may bring on undeserved attacks in the street; being argumentative and alcoholic may provoke barroom assault.*

*Source: VIOLENCE AND VICTIMS by UNIVERSITY OF NEW HAMPSHIRE. Copyright 1996 Reproduced with permission of SPRINGER PUBLISHING COMPANY, INC. in the format Textbook and Other Book via Copyright Clearance Center.

© ACE STOCK LIMITED/Alamy

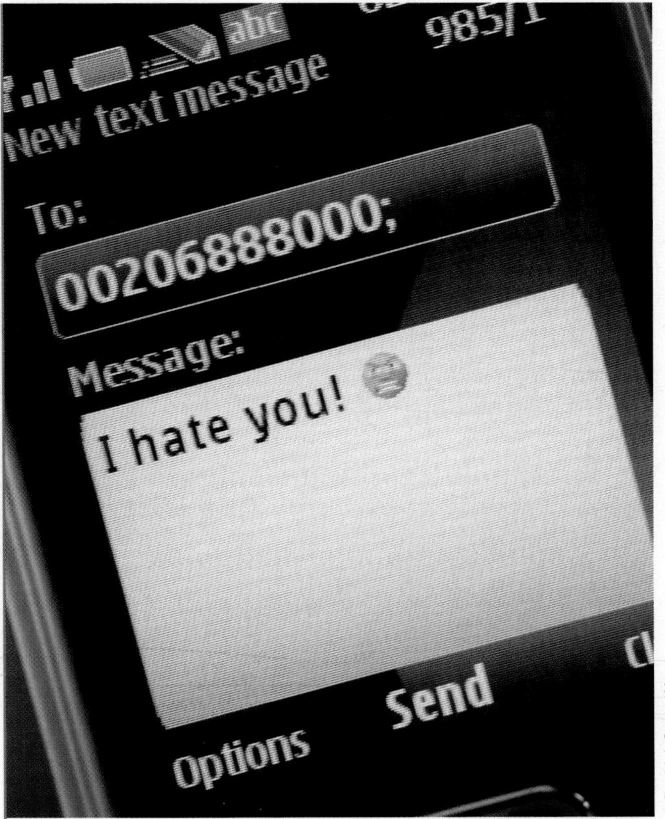

© David J. Green/Alamy

Repeat victimization may occur when the victim does not take defensive action. For example, if an abusive husband finds out that his battered wife will not call the police, he repeatedly victimizes her; or if a hate crime is committed and the police do not respond to reported offences, the perpetrators learn they have little to fear from the law.[32]

The Victims and Their Criminals

The victim data also tell us something about the relationship between victims and criminals. Victims report that most violent crimes were committed by a single offender, almost always male, between the ages of 18 and 34. In the majority of violent victimization incidents (sexual assault, assault), the perpetrator was known to the victim, as either a family member (37 percent) or a friend/acquaintance/other (36 percent). Robbery, however, is the exception. According to the 2009 PRVS, in a majority of robbery incidents the perpetrator was a stranger.[33]

Victimization commonly occurs within families, involving parents, children, and extended family.

Theories of Victimization

For many years, criminological theory focused on the actions of the criminal offender; the role of the victim was virtually ignored. However, more than

50 years ago, scholars began to realize that the victim was not simply a passive target in crime, but someone whose behaviour can influence his or her own fate, who "shapes and molds the criminal."[34] These early works helped focus attention on the role of the victim in the crime problem and led to further research efforts that have sharpened the image of the crime victim. Today a number of different theories attempt to explain the causes of victimization.

U.S. Representative Gabrielle Giffords was shot in the head in Tucson, Arizona at a Safeway store.

AP Photo/Susan Walsh

DID YOU KNOW?

- Victim precipitation theory suggests crime victims may trigger attacks by acting provocatively.
- Some experts link victimization to high-risk lifestyles.
- Some people live in places that are magnets for criminals.
- The routine activities approach suggests that the risk of victimization may be an interaction among suitable targets, ineffective guardians, and motivated criminals. Victims present attractive targets with insufficient protection to motivated criminals.

LO4 Victim Precipitation Theory

According to **victim precipitation theory**, some people may actually initiate the confrontation that eventually leads to their injury or death. Victim precipitation can be either active or passive.

Active precipitation occurs when victims act provocatively, use threats or fighting words, or even attack first.[35] In 1971, Menachem Amir suggested that female sexual assault victims often contribute to their attacks by dressing provocatively or pursuing a relationship with the perpetrator.[36] Amir's findings are controversial, and Canadian courts have taken a strong stand in finding that "implied consent" is not a defence in the case of sexual assault, regardless of the actions or attire of the victim.[37]

In contrast, **passive precipitation** occurs when the victim exhibits some personal characteristic that unknowingly either threatens or encourages the attacker. The crime can occur because of personal conflict—such as when two people compete over a job, promotion, love interest, or some other scarce and coveted commodity. For example, a woman may become the target of intimate violence when she improves her job status and her success results in a backlash from a jealous spouse or partner.[38] In other situations, although the victim may never have met the attacker or even known of his or her existence, the attacker feels menaced and acts accordingly.[39]

Passive precipitation may also occur when the victim belongs to a group whose mere presence threatens the attacker's reputation, status, or economic well-being. For example, hate crime violence may be precipitated by immigrant group members' arriving in the community to compete for jobs and housing. Research indicates that passive precipitation is related to power: If members of the target group can establish themselves economically or gain political power in the community, their vulnerability will diminish. They are still a potential threat, but they become too formidable a target to attack; they are no longer passive precipitators.[40] By implication, economic power reduces victimization risk.

victim precipitation theory
The view that victims may initiate, either actively or passively, the confrontation that leads to their victimization.

active precipitation
Aggressive or provocative behaviour of victims that results in their victimization.

passive precipitation
Personal or social characteristics of victims that make them "attractive" targets for criminals; such victims may unknowingly either threaten or encourage their attackers.

Lifestyle Theories

Some criminologists believe that people may become crime victims because their lifestyles increase their exposure to criminal offenders. Victimization risk is increased by behaviours such as associating with young men, going out in public places late at night, and living in an urban area. Conversely, one's

lifestyle theories
The view that people become crime victims because of lifestyles that increase their exposure to criminal offenders.

chances of victimization can be reduced by staying home at night, moving to a rural area, staying out of public places, earning more money, and getting married. The basis of such **lifestyle theories** is that crime is not a random occurrence, but rather a function of the victim's lifestyle.

DID YOU KNOW?

Statistics Canada suggests that to NOT become a victim, people do the following:

- Get married
- Stay home at night
- Don't drink alcohol
- Get older
- Retire

Source: http://dsp-psd.pwgsc.gc.ca/collection_2010/statcan/85F0033M/85f0033m2010022-eng.pdf.

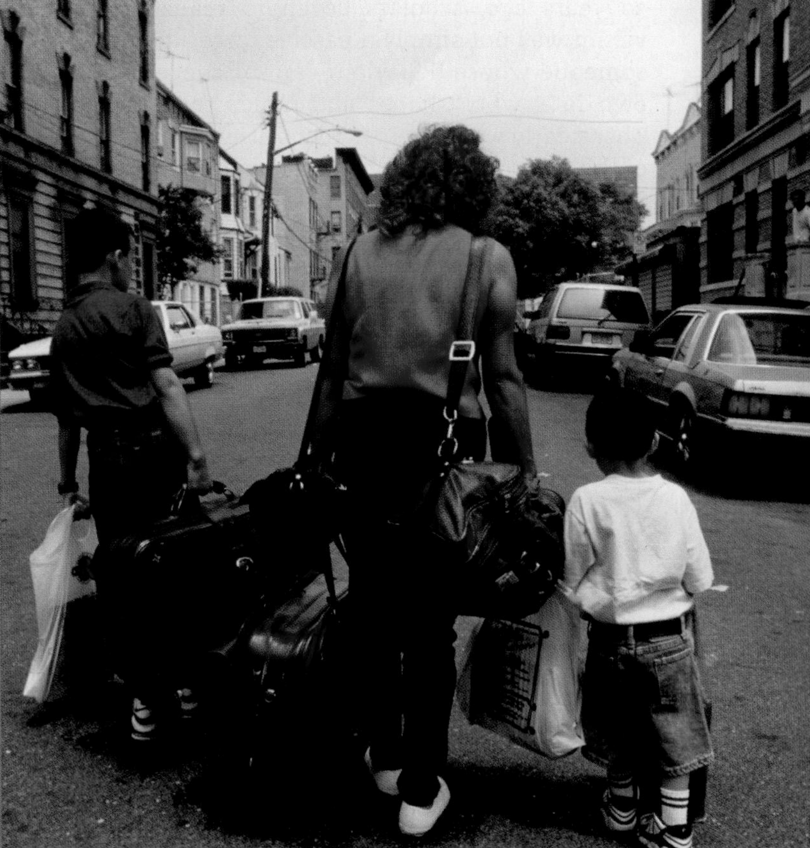

© Viviane Moos/CORBIS

High-Risk Lifestyles

People who have high-risk lifestyles have a much greater chance of victimization. For example, young runaways are at high risk for victimization; the more time they are exposed to street life, the greater their risk of becoming crime victims.[41]

Teenage males have an extremely high victimization risk because their lifestyle places them at risk both at school and once they leave the school grounds.[42] They spend a great deal of time hanging out with their friends and pursuing recreational fun.[43] Their friends may give them a false identification so they can go drinking in the neighbourhood bar. They may hang out in taverns at night, which places them at risk because many fights and assaults occur in places that serve liquor. Those who have a history of engaging in serious delinquency, getting involved in gangs, carrying weapons, and selling drugs have an increased chance of themselves being a target of serious violence.[44]

AP Photo/Pier Paolo Cito

Lifestyle risks continue into young adulthood. College and university students who spend several nights each week partying and who take recreational drugs are much more likely to be victims of violent crime than those who avoid such risky academic lifestyles.[45]

Because almost every Canadian will one day become a crime victim, victim/witness assistance programs (VWAP) have been developed across Canada to help victims deal with the stress they may endure when they or their family members become crime victims. Available to both children and adults, the programs provide emotional support and referrals to community agencies, case information and court preparation, needs assessment, and intervention.

© Rich Legg/iStockPhoto

Deviant Place Theory

According to **deviant place theory**, victims do not encourage crime, but are victim prone because they reside in socially disorganized high-crime areas where they have the greatest risk of coming into contact with criminal offenders, irrespective of their own behaviour or lifestyle.[46] Consequently, there may be little reason for residents in lower-class areas to alter their lifestyle or take safety precautions because personal behaviour choices do not influence the likelihood of victimization.[47] Neighbourhood crime levels may be more important for determining the chances of victimization than individual characteristics.

Deviant places are poor, densely populated, highly transient neighbourhoods in which commercial and residential properties exist side by side.[48] The commercial establishments provide criminals with easy targets for theft crimes, such as shoplifting. Successful people stay out of these stigmatized areas. They are home to "demoralized kinds of people" who are easy targets for crime: the homeless, the addicted, the mentally ill, and the elderly poor.[49]

People who live in more affluent areas and take safety precautions significantly lower their chances of becoming crime victims; the effect of safety precautions is less pronounced in poor areas. Residents of poor areas have a much greater risk of becoming victims because they live in areas with many motivated offenders; to protect themselves, they have to try harder to be safe than do the more affluent.[50]

Routine Activities Theory

Routine activities theory was first articulated in a series of papers by Lawrence Cohen and Marcus Felson.[51]

Cohen and Felson assume that both the motivation to commit crime and the supply of offenders are constant.[52] Every society will always have some people who are willing to break the law for revenge, greed, or some other motive. The volume and distribution of predatory crime (violent crimes against a person and crimes in which an offender attempts to steal an object directly) are closely related to the interaction of three variables that reflect the routine activities of the typical North American lifestyle:

1. The availability of **suitable targets**, such as homes containing easily saleable goods
2. The absence of **capable guardians**, such as police, homeowners, neighbours, friends, and relatives
3. The presence of **motivated offenders**, such as a large number of unemployed teenagers†

deviant place theory
The view that victimization is primarily a function of where people live.

routine activities theory
The view that victimization results from the interaction of three everyday factors: the availability of suitable targets, the absence of capable guardians, and the presence of motivated offenders.

suitable targets
Objects of crime (persons or property) that are attractive and readily available.

capable guardians
Effective deterrents to crime, such as police or watchful neighbours.

motivated offenders
People willing and able to commit crimes.

†Source: Crime and everyday life by FELSON, MARCUS Copyright 1998 Reproduced with permission of SAGE PUBLICATIONS INC BOOKS in the format Textbook and Other Book via Copyright Clearance Center.

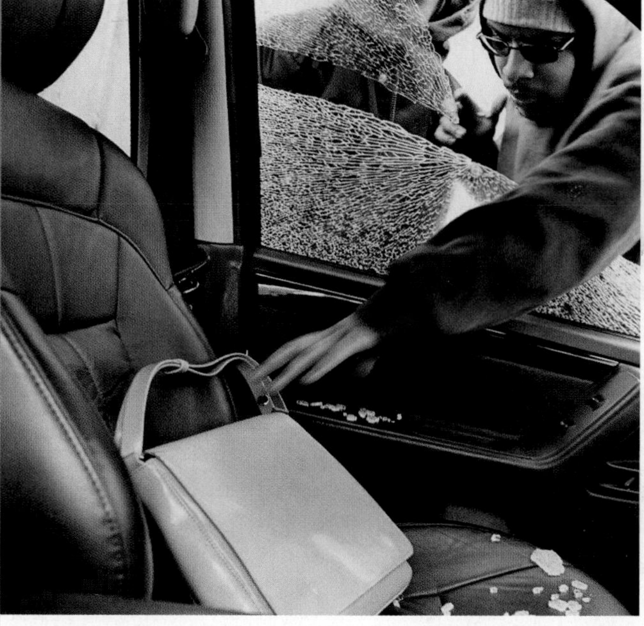
© Ocean/Corbis

Leaving valuables in open view is an invitation to potential criminals.

The presence of these components increases the likelihood that a predatory crime will take place. Targets are more likely to be victimized if they are poorly guarded and exposed to a large group of motivated offenders such as teenage boys.[53] The interacting components of routine activities theory are illustrated in Figure 3.9.

Cohen and Felson argue that crime rates in the United States increased between 1960 and 1980 because the number of adult caretakers at home during the day (guardians) decreased as a result of increased female participation in the workforce. While mothers are at work and children in daycare, homes are left unguarded. Similarly, with the growth of suburbia and the decline of the traditional neighbourhood, the number of such familiar guardians as family, neighbours, and friends diminished. At the same time, the volume of easily transportable wealth increased, creating a greater number of available targets.[54] Skyrocketing drug use in the 1980s created an excess of motivated offenders, and the rates of some crimes, such as robbery, increased dramatically. Falling crime rates in the 1990s would be explained by a robust economy, which decreases the pool of motivated offenders, and the growing number of police officers, which increases guardianship. The Canadian experience has been much the same.

Routine Activities and Lifestyle

Routine activities theory and the lifestyle approach have a number of similarities. They both assume that a person's living arrangements can affect victim risk and that people who live in unguarded areas are at the mercy of motivated offenders. These two theories both rely on four basic concepts: (1) proximity to criminals, (2) time of exposure to criminals, (3) target attractiveness, and (4) guardianship.[55]

Based on the same basic concepts, these theories share the following predictions: People increase their victimization risk if they (1) live in high-crime areas, (2) go out late at night, (3) carry valuables such as an expensive watch, (4) engage in risky behaviour such as drinking alcohol, and (5) are without friends or family to watch or help them.[56] For example, young women who drink to excess in bars and fraternity houses may elevate their risk of date rape because (1) they are easy targets and (2) their attackers can rationalize sexually assaulting them because they are intoxicated ("she's loose and immoral so I didn't think she'd care"). Intoxication is sometimes used to try to make it seem as though the victim is responsible for the crime.[57] Conversely, people can reduce their chances of repeat victimization if they change their lifestyle and adopt crime-suppressing routines such as getting married, having children, or moving to a small town.[58]

FIGURE 3.9

Routine Activities Theory

Crime and victimization involve the interaction of three factors.

LO5 Caring for the Victim

Victim surveys tell us that almost every Canadian over the age of 15 will one day become the victim of a crime, such as theft or break and enter, and in the aftermath may suffer financially and experience mental stress or even physical hardship.[59] Surveys show that upward of 75 percent of the general public have been victimized by crime at least once in their lives. As many as 25 percent of the victims develop posttraumatic stress syndrome, with symptoms that last for more than a decade after the crime occurred.[60]

Helping the victim to cope is the responsibility of all of society. Law enforcement agencies, courts, and correctional and human service systems have come to realize that due process and human rights exist not only for the criminal defendant but also for the victim of criminal behaviour.

In Canada, recognition of the rights of victims in the criminal justice process dates from the 1970s,

CP Photo/Hamilton Spectator-Ron Pozzer

Priscilla de Villiers, whose daughter Nina was murdered in 1991, founded and was president of CAVEAT (Canadians Against Violence Everywhere Advocating Its Termination), a victims' rights organization that played a major role throughout the 1990s in lobbying all levels of government to implement legislative and policy changes that recognize the role of victims in the Canadian criminal justice system. CAVEAT closed its doors in May 2001.

when criminal injuries compensation programs were first introduced to provide limited compensation to victims of violent crime.[61] Victim–offender reconciliation programs (VORPs) began to be implemented in the mid-1970s. However, it was not until the 1980s and 1990s, under pressure from women's advocacy groups and victims' rights organizations (e.g., CAVEAT), that the rights of victims were explicitly expressed in criminal justice legislation, policies, and practice.

In 1983 Bill C-127 introduced the new offence of sexual assault, which included significant provisions for more equitable and humane treatment of victims, including recognition that sexual assault happens to both women and men; removal of spousal immunity; disqualification of evidence from the victim's background unless it is proven to be directly relevant; and introduction of new rules of evidence regarding consent, corroboration, and recency of complaint.[62] In 1988, the Criminal Code was amended to permit the introduction of a victim impact statement at the sentencing stage, and included an explicit definition of "victim" for this purpose, as follows:

> Criminal Code S. 722(4)
>
> Definition of "victim"—For the purposes of this section, "victim," in relation to an offence
>
> (a) means the person to whom harm was done or who suffered physical or emotional loss as a result of the commission of the offence; and
>
> (b) where the person described in paragraph (a) is dead, ill or otherwise incapable of making a statement referred to in subsection (1), includes the spouse or any relative of that person, anyone who is in law or fact the custody of that person or is responsible for the care or support of that person or any dependant of that person.

In 1995, further revisions to the Criminal Code were introduced that now require courts to consider victim impact statements at the time of sentencing. In 1999, Bill C-79 introduced a broader definition of "victim" as "the victim of an alleged offence." Bill C-79 included additional amendments that require officials in the criminal justice system to ensure "the safety and security of any victim of or to the offence," including considerations in relation to granting bail and imposing special conditions on a bail release.[63]

Other recent changes to the Criminal Code that involve victim rights include the use of publication bans to protect the identity of sexual assault victims and children, the use of videotaped testimony

THE CANADIAN PRESS/Sean Kilpatrick

Sue O'Sullivan, Federal Ombudsman for Victims of Crime. The Office of the Federal Ombudsman for Victims of Crime was created in 2007 as an independent resource for victims in Canada. The mandate of the office is to ensure the federal government meets its commitments to victims by addressing their needs, promoting their interests, and making recommendations to the federal government on issues that negatively impact victims. "The Government of Canada has made victims of crime a priority, and we will continue to contribute to that important work by helping victims directly and by actively promoting positive, system-wide change."

MADD

Mothers Against Drunk Driving

Les mères contre l'alcool au volant

CP PHOTO/Nathan Denette

MADD Canada's aim is to offer support services to victims, heighten awareness about the dangers of impaired driving by alcohol and/or drugs, and save lives and prevent injuries on our roads.

compensation Financial aid awarded to crime victims to repay them for their loss and injuries; may cover medical bills, loss of wages, loss of future earnings, and/or counselling.

for children who are victims or witnesses, the imposition of victim surcharges as an additional component of sentencing in order to fund victim assistance programs, the ordering of restitution for victims, and victim notification of "faint hope clause" hearings for offenders serving a life sentence.[64] The Corrections and Conditional Release Act, which governs the operations of the Correctional Service of Canada, now contains provisions for the release of information to victims regarding the institution in which the offender is located and any releases from custody and their location. In addition, victims are notified of parole board hearings and are allowed to attend and introduce a victim impact statement for consideration in parole decision making.[65] Numerous acts, regulations, and policies in each of the provinces and territories contain additional provisions for the support and protection of victims and victims' rights.

DID YOU KNOW?

MADD Canada provides the following services for victims:

- Court accompaniment
- Helping victims know their rights under the law
- Referrals
- Emotional support
- Annual Candlelight Vigil of Hope and Remembrance and Victims' Weekend
- Memorial Wall
- On-line Tribute to Victims
- Advocating for victim rights in law

Source: Victim Services, MADD Canada. Reprinted with permission by MADD Canada.

Since 1999 the federal government has operated the Policy Centre for Victim Issues with the goal of promoting research on, new initiatives for, and awareness of victims and victims' rights.

LO6 Victim Service Programs

A wide variety of victim service programs have been developed throughout Canada. These programs are organized on a variety of government levels and serve a variety of clients. We will look briefly at some prominent forms of victim assistance operating in Canada.[66]

Victim Compensation

One of the goals of victim advocates has been to lobby for legislation creating crime victim **compensation** programs.[67] As a result of such legislation, victims may apply to provincial agencies to receive financial compensation for expenses incurred as a consequence of injuries or death resulting from a criminal offence. Compensation may be provided for medical bills, loss of wages, loss of future earnings, and counselling. In the case of death, the victim's survivors may receive burial expenses and aid for loss of support.[68] Personal and household property losses are not normally compensated.

Court Services

Among the victim services now provided through the court system, victim witness assistance programs (VWAP) play a key role in providing information, assistance, and support to victims and witnesses of crime. VWAP programs provide a range of services, including crisis intervention/counselling, referrals to community agencies, emotional support, information about the progress of the case, hearing dates, bail conditions, and court preparation and support.

IT SHOULDN'T HURT TO BE A CHILD
CANADIAN CENTRE FOR MISSING CHILDREN

Canadian Centre for Missing Children

The Canadian Centre for Missing Children has a number of services available to victims of crime and families of missing children.

Some provinces have also implemented domestic violence court (DVC) programs that bring together police, Crown attorneys, VWAP staff, probation staff, and others to ensure coordination in prosecution efforts, to ensure the safety and needs of domestic assault victims and their children, and to monitor court outcomes.[69]

Public Education

More than half of all victim programs include public education programs that help familiarize the general public with their services and with other agencies that help crime victims. In some instances, these are primary prevention programs, which teach methods of dealing with conflict without resorting to violence. For example, school-based programs present information on spousal and dating abuse, followed by discussions of how to reduce violent incidents.[70]

Crisis Intervention

Most victim programs refer victims to specific services to help them recover from their ordeal. Clients are commonly referred to the local network of public and private social service agencies that can provide emergency and long-term assistance with transportation, medical care, shelter, food, and clothing. In addition, more than half of all victim programs provide **crisis intervention** for victims who feel isolated, vulnerable, and in need of immediate services. Some programs counsel at their offices, while others visit victims in their homes, at the crime scene, or in the hospital.

Victim–Offender Reconciliation Program (VORP)

Victim–offender reconciliation programs use mediators to facilitate face-to-face encounters between victims and offenders. The first VORP in North America was established in Kitchener, Ontario, in 1974. The aim is to engage in direct negotiations that lead to restitution agreements and, possibly, reconciliation between the two parties involved.[71] With the support of the Crown attorney and the court, professionally trained staff are used to facilitate mediation for a wide range of property crimes and simple assaults.[72]

LO7 Victims' Rights

Victim advocates argue that crime victims have legal rights that should assure them basic services from the government.[73] Just as the defendant has the right to counsel and a fair trial, society is also obliged to ensure basic rights for law-abiding citizens. These rights range from adequate protection from violent crimes to victim compensation and assistance from the criminal justice system. In 1988, and again in 2003, the federal, provincial, and territorial justice ministers recognized these rights in a "Canadian Statement of Basic Principles of Justice for Victims of Crime," which states that[74]

CONNECTIONS

Reconciliation programs are based on the concept of restorative justice, which rejects punitive correctional measures and instead suggests that crimes of violence and theft should be viewed as interpersonal conflicts that need to be settled in the community through non-coercive means. See Chapter 8 for more on this approach.

crisis intervention Emergency counselling for crime victims.

victim–offender reconciliation programs Mediated face-to-face encounters between victims and their attackers, designed to produce restitution agreements and, if possible, reconciliation.

1. Victims of crime should be treated with courtesy, compassion, and respect.
2. The privacy of victims should be considered and respected to the greatest extent possible.
3. All reasonable measures should be taken to minimize inconvenience to victims.
4. The safety and security of victims should be considered at all stages of the criminal justice process and appropriate measures should be taken when necessary to protect victims from intimidation and retaliation.
5. Information should be provided to victims about the criminal justice system and the victim's role and opportunities to participate in criminal justice processes.
6. Victims should be given information, in accordance with prevailing law, policies, and procedures, about the status of the investigation; the scheduling, progress, and final outcome of the proceedings; and the status of the offender in the correctional system.
7. Information should be provided to victims about available victim assistance services, other programs and assistance available to them, and means of obtaining financial reparation.

8. The views, concerns, and representations of victims are an important consideration in criminal justice processes and should be considered in accordance with prevailing law, policies, and procedures.

9. The needs, concerns, and diversity of victims should be considered in the development and delivery of programs and services, and in related education and training.

10. Information should be provided to victims about available options to raise their concerns when they believe that these principles have not been followed.†

Assuring victims' rights involves an eclectic mix of advocacy groups—some independent, others government-sponsored, and some self-help. Advocates can be especially helpful when victims need to interact with the agencies of justice. For example, advocates can lobby police departments to keep investigations open as well as request the return of recovered stolen property. They can demand that prosecutors and judges provide protection from harassment and reprisals by, for example, making "no contact" a condition of bail. They can help victims make statements during sentencing hearings as well as probation and parole revocation procedures. Victim advocates can also interact with news media, making sure that reporting is accurate and that victim privacy is not violated.

LO8 Self-Protection

Although the general public mostly approves of the police, fear of crime and concern about community safety have prompted many people to become their own "police force," taking an active role in community protection and citizen crime-control groups.[75] The more crime in an area, the greater the amount of fear, and the more likely residents will be to engage in self-protective measures.[76] Research indicates that a significant number of crimes may not be reported to police simply because victims prefer to take matters into their own hands.[77]

One manifestation of this trend is the concept of **target hardening**, or making one's home and business crime-proof through the use of locks, bars, alarms, and other devices.[78] Commonly used crime-prevention techniques include a fence or barricade at the entrance; a doorkeeper, guard, or receptionist in an apartment building; an intercom or phone to gain access to the building; surveillance cameras; window bars; warning signs; and dogs chosen for their ability to guard property. The use of these measures is inversely proportional to perception of neighbourhood safety: People who fear crime are more likely to use crime-prevention techniques.

target hardening
Making one's home or business crime-proof through the use of locks, bars, alarms, and other devices.

†Source: *Canadian Statement of Basic Principles of Justice for Victims of Crime, 2003* (http://www.justice.gc.ca/eng/pi/pcvi-cpcv/pub/03/princ.html). Department of Justice Canada, 2003. Reproduced with the permission of the Minister of Public Works and Government Services Canada, 2011.

Campaigns such as "lock it or lose it" are meant to combat high rates of automobile thefts.

OPP Lock It or Lose It logo. Reprinted by permission of the OPP.

Although the true relationship is still unclear, there is mounting evidence that people who protect their homes are less likely to be victimized by property crimes.[79] One study conducted in the United States found that people who install burglar alarms are less likely to suffer burglary than those who forgo similar preventive measures.[80]

Community Organization

Some communities have organized on the neighbourhood level against crime. Citizens have been working independently and in cooperation with local police agencies in neighbourhood patrol and block-watch programs. These programs organize local citizens in urban areas to patrol neighbourhoods, watch for suspicious people, help secure the neighbourhood, lobby for improvements (such as increased lighting), report crime to police, put out community newsletters, conduct home-security surveys, and serve as a source for crime information or tips.[81]

Although such programs are welcome additions to police services, there is little evidence that they appreciably affect the crime rate. There is also concern that their effectiveness is spottier in low-income, high-crime areas, which need the most crime-prevention assistance.[82] Block watches and neighbourhood patrols seem more successful when they are part of general-purpose or multi-issue community groups, rather than when they focus directly on crime problems.[83]

With **CRIM** you have a multitude of study aids at your fingertips. After reading the chapters, check out these ideas for further help:

Chapter Review cards include learning outcomes, definitions, and visual summaries for each chapter.

Printable flashcards give you three additional ways to check your comprehension of key **criminology** concepts.

Other great ways to help you study include **interactive games, videos, quizzes, and flashcards**.

"I like the flashcards, the videos, and the quizzes. Great format! I love the cards in the back of the book!"

—Asha Thtodort, Algonquin College

Visit **www.icancrim2.com** to find the resources you need today!

CHAPTER

4

Choice Theory: Because They Want To

Learning Outcomes

LO1 State the major premises underlying choice theory.

LO2 Explain the concept of situational crime prevention.

LO3 Explain general deterrence.

LO4 Explain specific deterrence.

LO5 Explain the logic of incapacitation as a means of crime reduction.

LO6 Outline the policy implications of choice theory.

LO1 Introduction

As the price of precious metals such as copper, bronze, platinum, and rhodium continues to increase, police services across the country are dealing with a rash of thefts of precious metals from hydroelectric companies, construction sites, businesses, auto dealerships, and even cemeteries, where York Region police officers arrested two men in September 2009 after they were spotted by cemetery workers attempting to pry bronze nameplates from grave headstones.[1] In November 2010, thieves pulled $10 000 worth of copper wiring out of hydroelectric generators in Calgary,[2] and in April 2010 Vancouver police arrested seven men after thieves in search of copper wire sawed through an underwater hydroelectric cable, causing an estimated $2.8 million in damage.[3] But such daring thefts of metals are not without risks. In June 2008 a Calgary man was found face-down inside a manhole after having been electrocuted trying to remove copper from underground electric cables.[4] In Canada, the United States, the United Kingdom, and other countries around the world, theft of precious metals is now a major crime problem, with serious economic consequences for public utilities, business owners, and taxpayers.[5]

DID YOU KNOW?

- Choice theory can be traced to Beccaria's view that crime is rational and can be prevented by punishment that is swift, severe, and certain.
- Crime is said to be offence-specific because criminals evaluate the characteristics of targets to determine their suitability.
- Crime is offender-specific because criminals evaluate their skills, motivations, and needs before committing a specific crime.
- Criminal choice involves actions such as choosing the place of crime, selecting targets, and learning criminal techniques.

rational choice
The view that crime is a function of a decision-making process in which the potential offender weighs the potential costs and benefits of an illegal act.

choice theory
The school of thought holding that people choose to engage in delinquent and criminal behaviour after weighing the consequences and benefits of their actions.

The planning and actions of thieves devoted to finding and stealing precious metals suggests that the decision to commit crime can involve rational and detailed planning and decision making, designed to maximize personal gain and avoid capture and punishment. Some criminologists go as far as suggesting that any criminal violation—committing a theft or a robbery, selling drugs, attacking a rival, or filing a false tax return—is based on rational decision making. Such a decision may be motivated by a variety of personal reasons, including greed, revenge, need, anger, lust, jealousy, thrill seeking, or vanity. But if it is made after weighing the potential benefits and consequences, then the illegal act is a **rational choice**. This view of crime is referred to here as **choice theory**.

Reuters/Landov

The theft of precious metals, now a major crime problem, requires rational and detailed planning on the part of thieves. Here, building materials at a construction site appear vulnerable to robbery.

In this chapter, we review the philosophical underpinnings of choice theory—the view that criminals rationally choose crime. We then turn to theories of crime prevention and control that flow from the concept of choice: situational crime control, general deterrence theory, specific deterrence theory, and incapacitation. Finally, we take a brief look at how choice theory has influenced criminal justice policy.

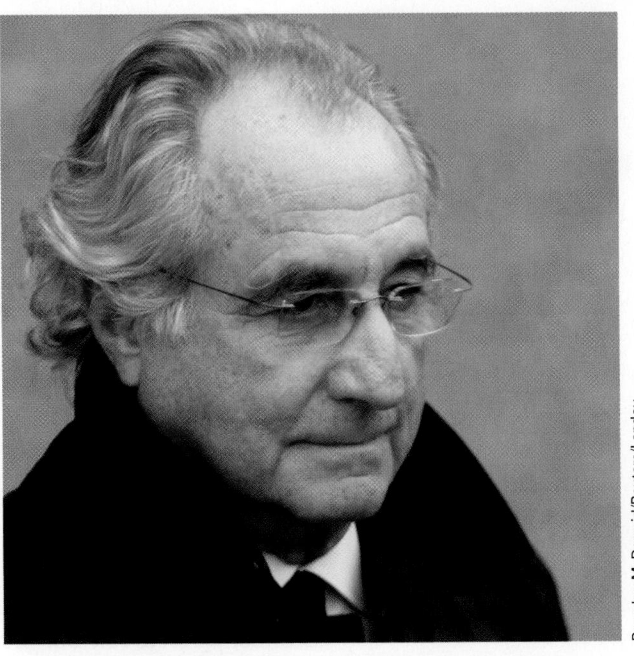
Brendan McDermid/Reuters/Landov

People choose to commit crime for reasons of greed or personal need. The former was the case with Bernie Madoff, who took billions of dollars in one of the largest Ponzi schemes in U.S. history. He is now serving a 150-year prison sentence.

The Development of Rational Theory

Rational choice theory has its roots in the classical school of criminology developed by Italian social thinker Cesare Beccaria, whose utilitarian approach powerfully influenced the criminal justice system and was widely accepted throughout Europe and North America.[6] It seemed more rational to let the "punishment fit the crime" than to punish criminals in a cruel and capricious manner. Beccaria's vision was influential in the move away from torture and physical punishment in the 19th century toward prison sentences geared to fit the severity of crime. These practices were the cornerstone of what is today known as **classical criminology**, a view that remained popular for a century.

classical criminology
The theoretical perspective suggesting that (1) people have free will to choose criminal or conventional behaviours; (2) people choose to commit crime for reasons of greed or personal need; and (3) crime can be controlled only by the fear of criminal sanctions.

By the end of the 19th century, the popularity of the classical approach began to decline, and, by the middle of the 20th century, the perspective was neglected by mainstream criminologists. During this period, positivist criminologists focused on internal and external factors—poverty, IQ, education—rather than personal choice and decision making.

Beginning in the late 1970s, a number of criminologists began to revisit classical ideas, producing books and monographs expounding the theme that criminals are rational actors who plan their crimes, could

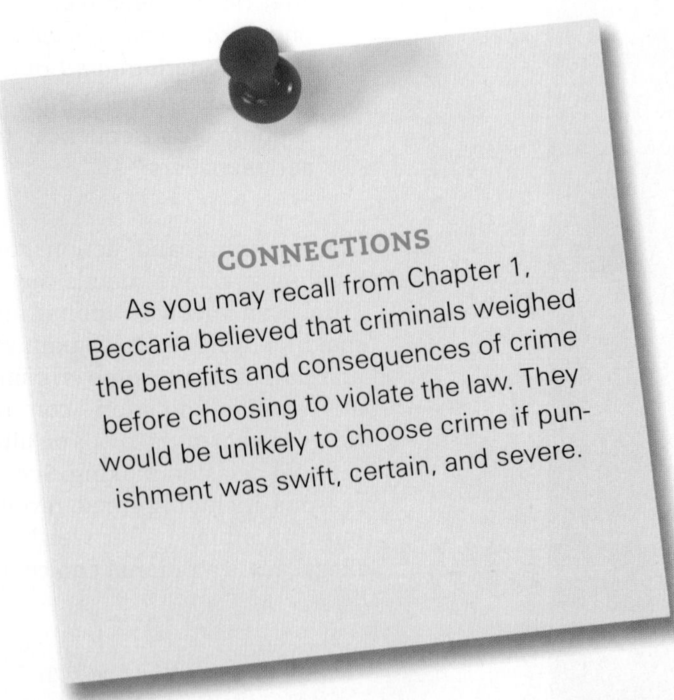
CONNECTIONS

As you may recall from Chapter 1, Beccaria believed that criminals weighed the benefits and consequences of crime before choosing to violate the law. They would be unlikely to choose crime if punishment was swift, certain, and severe.

be controlled by the fear of punishment, and deserve to be penalized for their misdeeds. In *Thinking About Crime*, political scientist James Q. Wilson observed that people who are likely to commit crime are unafraid of breaking the law because they value the excitement and thrills of crime, have a low stake in conformity, and are willing to take greater chances than the average person. If they could be convinced that their actions would bring severe punishment, only the totally irrational would be willing to engage in crime.[7]

From these roots has evolved a more contemporary version of classical theory, based on intelligent thought processes and criminal decision making; today this is referred to as the rational choice approach to crime causation.[8]

The Concept of Rational Choice

According to the rational choice approach, law-violating behaviour or "criminality" is the product of careful thought and planning. Offenders choose to engage in criminal behaviour after considering both personal needs—money, revenge, thrills, entertainment—and situational factors, such as how well a target is protected and the efficiency of the local police force. The reasoning criminal evaluates the risk of apprehension, the seriousness of expected punishment, the potential value of the criminal enterprise, and his or her immediate need for criminal gain.

© MBI/Alamy

Conversely, the decision to forgo committing a crime may be based on the criminal's perception that the potential rewards of the criminal act are not worth the risk of apprehension. For example, burglars may choose not to commit a crime if they believe that a neighbourhood is well patrolled by police.[9] In fact, when police concentrate patrols in a particular area of the city, crime rates tend to increase in adjacent areas because calculating criminals view them as being safer.[10]

structuring crime According to the rational choice approach, the decision to commit crime, regardless of its substance, is structured by (1) where it occurs, (2) the characteristics of the target, and (3) available means.

Structuring Criminality

A number of personal factors condition people to choose criminality. Offenders are likely to desist from crime if they believe (1) that their future criminal earnings will be relatively low and (2) that attractive and legal opportunities to generate income are available.[11] In contrast, criminals may be motivated when they know people who have made "big scores" and are quite successful at crime. Though the prevailing wisdom is that "crime does not pay," a small but significant subset of criminals enjoy earnings of $50 000 or more per year from crime, and their success may help motivate other would-be offenders.[12] In this sense, rational choice is a function of a person's perception of conventional alternatives and opportunities.

Learning and experience may be important elements in **structuring crime**.[13] Career criminals may learn the limitations of their powers; they know when to take a chance and when to be cautious. Experienced criminals may turn from a life of crime when they develop a belief that the risk of crime is greater than its potential profit.[14]

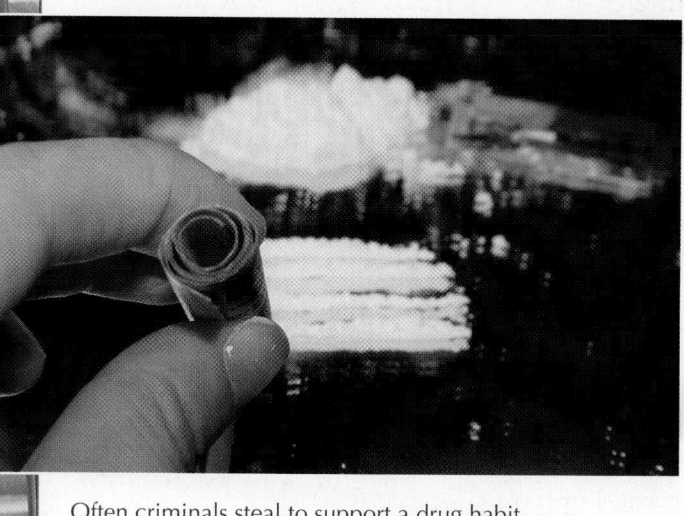

© sx70/iStockPhoto

Often criminals steal to support a drug habit.

Personality and lifestyle also affect criminal choices. Criminals appear to be more impulsive and have less self-control than other people; they seem unaffected by fear of criminal punishment.[15] They are typically under stress or facing some serious personal problem or condition that forces them to choose risky behaviour.[16] (See Table 4.1.)

Choosing the Place

Criminals carefully choose where they will commit their crime. Criminologist Bruce Jacobs's interviews with 40 active crack cocaine street dealers in a Midwestern U.S. city showed that dealers carefully evaluate the desirability of their sales area before setting up shop.[17] Dealers consider the middle of a long block the best choice because they can see everything in both directions; police raids can be spotted before they occur.[18] Another tactic is to entice new buyers into spaces between apartment buildings (see photo at left). Although the dealers may lose the tactical edge of being on a public street, they gain a measure of protection because their colleagues can watch over the operation and come to the rescue if the buyer tries to "pull something."[19]

Dennis MacDonald/World of Stock

CONNECTIONS

Rational choice theory dovetails with routine activities theory, which you learned about in Chapter 3. Although not identical, these approaches both claim that crime rates are a product of criminal opportunity. They suggest guardians, decreasing the suitability of targets, or reducing the offender population should lower crime rates. Conversely, increased opportunity and reduced guardianship will increase crime rates.

Choosing Targets

Evidence of rational choice may also be found in the way criminals locate their targets. Victimization data indicate that while the affluent are rarely the victims of violent crimes, high-income households are the most likely targets of break and enter.[20] Interviews with burglars find that they check to make sure that no one is home before they enter a residence. Some call ahead, whereas others ring the doorbell, preparing to claim they had the wrong address if someone answers. Some find out which families have star high school athletes because those that do are sure to be at the weekend football game, leaving their houses unguarded.[21] Others seek unlocked doors and avoid the ones with deadbolts; houses with dogs are usually considered off-limits.[22]

CP PICTURE ARCHIVE/Ottawa Citizen

Patrick (Paddy) Mitchell of Ottawa (right), leader of the notorious Stopwatch Gang of bank robbers, died in 2007 while serving a 65-year sentence in a U.S. prison hospital for stealing an estimated $15 million. "This brings the end to North America's most famous, most successful and, especially, most likeable bank robber of our time," one observer noted.

TABLE 4.1

Robbing Banks for a Living

The Motivation to Rob Banks
According to Canadian criminologist Fred Desroches, "Bank robbers need money for the same reasons we all do"—to pay debts, buy a car, take a vacation, pay day-to-day expenses. In addition, about 15 percent of robbers need the money to support an alcohol, gambling, or drug habit, and a majority report that the initial motivation to get into the bank robbery business was to support their "partying lifestyle"—drinking, drugs, hitting the bars with friends, and living for the moment. Sometimes the motivation to rob a bank is simply for the thrill of it.
Planning the Bank Robbery
Surprisingly, little planning goes in to most bank robberies—in some cases, as little as five minutes. According to Desroches, "minimization of risk" is the primary factor in selecting a target and constructing a plan. Usually, robbers will pick times when there are likely to be only a few "civilians" present who could disrupt the robbery; choose locations based on access to a means of "getaway" (either automobile or public transit); and prefer large cities over small towns because getaway will be easier. In many cases, individuals will rob banks within or close to the neighbourhood they live, as they are most familiar with these locations and can quickly and easily construct a robbery plan.
Learning from Experience
Desroches found that a majority of bank robbers report using information gleaned from the local media about robberies, their own and those committed by others, to revise plans and techniques or determine the need to escape the community based on what the police are reported to know about them. In addition, bank robbers may search for information about the wording of notes handed to tellers, successful getaway strategies, bank policies and practices in the event of a robbery, the need to use a weapon to overcome resistance, the nature of the police response to bank robberies, and the amount of cash taken (as an indicator of potentially good targets).
A Winning Formula
Desroches reports that most bank robbers do not vary their modus operandi very much—which can greatly assist the police in their capture. Why don't they change their M.O.? Simple. If they haven't been caught yet, why tamper with a winning formula they don't believe can be improved on anyway?

Sources: Frederick J. Desroches, *Force and Fear: Robbery in Canada* (Toronto: Nelson Canada, 1995); Frederick J. Desroches, *Behind the Bars: Experiences in Crime* (Toronto: Canadian Scholars Press, 1996).

Burglars also report being sensitive to the activities of their victims. They note that homemakers often develop predictable behaviour patterns, which helps burglars plan their crimes.[23]

Burglars seem to prefer "working" between 9 A.M. and 11 A.M. and in midafternoon, when parents are either working or dropping off or picking up children at school. Burglars appear to monitor car and pedestrian traffic and avoid selecting targets on heavily travelled streets.[24] It does not seem surprising that well-organized communities that restrict traffic and limit neighbourhood entrance and exit routes have experienced significant declines in property crime.[25]

DID YOU KNOW?

- Theft crimes appear rational because thieves and burglars typically choose targets that present little risk and they plan their attacks carefully.
- Robbers report that they select vulnerable targets who are unlikely to fight back. They avoid armed victims.
- Drug users and dealers use elaborate ploys to avoid detection. They employ businesslike practices in their commercial enterprises.

In sum, rational choice involves both shaping criminality and structuring crime. Personality, age, status, risk, and opportunity seem to influence the decision to become a criminal; place, target, and techniques help to structure crime.[26]

Is Crime Rational?

It is relatively easy to show that some crimes are the product of rational, objective thought, especially when they involve an ongoing criminal conspiracy centred on economic gain. For example, when American stockbroker Bernard Madoff was convicted in June 2009 for criminal fraud after operating a "Ponzi" scheme that bilked thousands of clients out of billions of dollars,[27] his elaborate financial scheme not only showed signs of rationality but exhibited brilliant, though flawed, financial expertise. Similarly, the drug dealings of organized crime bosses demonstrate a reasoned analysis of market conditions, interests, and risks. But what about crimes that are immediate rather than ongoing? Do they show signs of rationality?

Are Street Crimes Rational?

There is evidence that even seemingly "unplanned" street crimes may also be the product of careful risk assessment, including environmental, social, and structural factors. Target selection seems highly rational. Ronald Clarke and Patricia Harris found that auto thieves are very selective in their choice of targets. Vehicle selection seems to be based on attractiveness and suitability for a particular purpose; for example, German cars are selected for stripping because they usually have high-quality audio equipment that has good value on the second-hand market.[28]

There are also signs of rationality in the choices made by armed robbers. They generally choose targets close to their homes or in areas that they routinely travel. Familiarity with the area gives them ready knowledge of escape routes; this is referred to as their "awareness space."[29] Robbers may be wary of

Bank robbers are known to use police scanners to track the movement of police in the area surrounding their target.

© Piotr Marcinski/Alamy

people who are watching the community for signs of trouble: research by Paul Bellair shows that robbery levels are relatively low in neighbourhoods where residents keep a watchful eye on their neighbours' property.[30] Many robbers avoid freestanding buildings because they can more easily be surrounded by police; others select targets that are known to do a primarily cash business, such as bars, supermarkets, and restaurants.[31]

Frederick Desroches found that bank robbers use specific techniques to avoid being apprehended by police. Some go as far as using police scanners to monitor police activity in the area of the bank they plan to rob.[32] One bank robber told Desroches

> I can recall listening to the police scanner after the alarm went off. I could hear the dispatcher, "We have an alarm . . ." as they were coming out the door . . . Meanwhile my cohorts are getting into the car and one partner says, "Now it's your job." I got out onto the expressway and I could see the lights of a police cruiser coming down the road and turning into the parking lot. They were there fast! We were in the bank three minutes. [Over the scanner] I hear the police say, "The suspects left in a Chevy Nova." I can't believe my luck because this car is not even similar looking.[33]

Is Drug Use Rational?

Did actor Charlie Sheen make an objective, rational choice to abuse drugs and potentially sabotage his career? Did the "King of Pop," entertainer Michael Jackson, make a rational choice when he abused prescription drugs to the point that it killed him?[34]

Is it possible that drug users and dealers, a group not usually associated with clear thinking, make rational choices? Research does in fact show that at its onset, drug use is controlled by rational decision making. Users report that they begin taking drugs when they believe that the benefits of substance abuse outweigh its costs: They believe that drugs will provide a fun, exciting, thrilling experience. They choose what they consider safe sites to buy and sell drugs.[35] Their entry into substance abuse is facilitated by their perception that valued friends and family members endorse and encourage drug use and abuse substances themselves.[36]

Drug dealers approach their profession in a businesslike fashion. According to criminologist George Rengert's study of drug markets, drug dealers face many of the same problems as legitimate retailers. If they are too successful in one location, rivals will be attracted to the area, and stiff competition may drive down prices and cut profits. The dealer can fight back by discounting the cost of drugs or increasing quality, as long as it doesn't reduce profit margins.[37]

© Allstar Picture Library/Alamy

Is drug use rational? If so, how can persistent abuse by such well-known celebrities as Charlie Sheen be explained? After all, they have everything to lose and nothing to gain from their behaviour.

Even in what appear to be senseless killings among strangers,[38] it can be argued that the underlying motives are rational—the desire of murderers to avoid retaliation from the victims they assaulted or to avoid future prosecution.[39]

Why Do People Commit Crimes?

Assuming that crime is rational, why—knowing its often-unpleasant consequences—do people choose to commit crime? Rational choice theorists believe the answer is both simple and obvious. For many people, crime is a more attractive alternative than law-abiding behaviour. It brings rewards, excitement, prestige, or other desirable outcomes without lengthy work or effort. Whether it is violent or profit oriented, crime has an allure that some people cannot resist. Crime may produce a natural "high" and other positive sensations that are instrumental in maintaining and reinforcing criminal behaviour.[40] Some law violators describe the "adrenaline rush" that comes from successfully executing illegal activities in dangerous situations. This has been termed **edgework**: the "exhilarating, momentary integration of danger, risk, and skill" that motivates people to try a variety of dangerous criminal and noncriminal behaviour.[41]

Ronen Boidek/Shutterstock.com

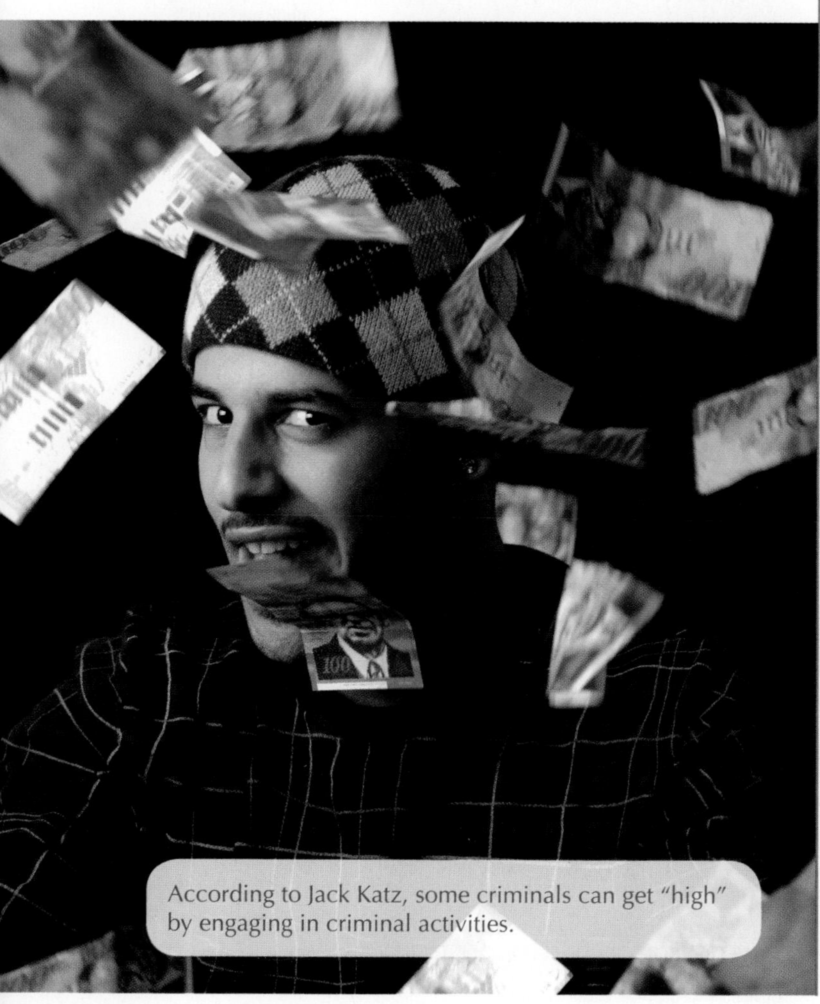

According to Jack Katz, some criminals can get "high" by engaging in criminal activities.

edgework
The excitement or exhilaration of successfully executing illegal activities in dangerous situations.

seductions of crime
The situational inducements or immediate benefits that draw offenders into law violations.

offender-specific crime
Theories of criminality that look at why people commit crime and the factors that explain criminality.

Sociologist Jack Katz argues that there are, in fact, immediate benefits to criminality. These situational inducements, which he labels the **seductions of crime**,[42] directly precede the commission of crime and draw offenders into law violations. For example, someone challenges their authority or moral position, and they vanquish their opponent with a beating; or they want to do something exciting, so they break into and vandalize a school building.

According to Katz, choosing crime can help satisfy personal needs. For some people, shoplifting and vandalism are attractive because getting away with crime is a thrilling demonstration of personal competence (Katz calls this "sneaky thrills"). Even murder can have an emotional payoff: Killers behave like the avenging gods of mythology, choosing to have life-or-death control over their victims.[43]

If committing crime is a rational choice, it follows that crime can be controlled or eradicated by convincing potential offenders that crime is a poor choice—that it will bring them not rewards, but pain, hardship, and deprivation. Evidence shows that jurisdictions with relatively low incarceration rates also experience the highest crime rates.[44] As we have seen, according to rational choice theory, street-smart offenders know which areas offer the least threat and plan their crimes accordingly. A number of potential strategies flow from this premise. The following sections discuss each of these crime reduction or control strategies based on the rationality of criminal behaviour.

LO2 Situational Crime Prevention

Rational choice theory suggests that because criminal activity is **offender-specific**, crime prevention, or at least crime reduction, can be achieved through policies that convince potential criminals to desist from criminal activities, delay their

situational crime prevention A method of crime prevention that seeks to eliminate or reduce particular crimes in narrow settings.

defensible space The principle that crime can be prevented or displaced by modifying the physical environment to reduce the opportunity individuals have to commit crime.

actions, or avoid a particular target. Criminal acts will be avoided if (1) potential targets are carefully guarded, (2) the means to commit crime are controlled, and (3) potential offenders are carefully monitored. Desperate people may contemplate crime, but only the truly irrational will attack a well-defended, inaccessible target and risk strict punishment.

One way of preventing crime, then, is to reduce the opportunities people have to commit particular crimes. This approach is known as **situational crime prevention**. It was first popularized in the early 1970s by Oscar Newman, who coined the term **defensible space**. The idea is that crime can be prevented or displaced through the use of residential designs that reduce criminal opportunity, such as well-lit housing projects that maximize surveillance.[45] (See Table 4.2.)

Crime Prevention Strategies

Situational crime prevention involves developing tactics to reduce or eliminate a specific crime problem (such as shoplifting in an urban mall or street-level drug dealing). According to criminologists Ronald Clarke and Ross Homel, crime prevention tactics used today generally fall into one of four categories:

TABLE 4.2

Sixteen Techniques of Situational Prevention

Increasing Perceived Effort	Increasing Perceived Risks	Reducing Anticipated Rewards	Inducing Guilt or Shame
Target hardening	Entry/exit screening	Target removal	Rule setting
Slug rejector devices	Automatic ticket gates	Removable car radio	Harassment codes
Steering locks	Baggage screening	Women's shelters	Customs declaration
Bandit screens	Merchandise tags	Phone card	Hotel registrations
Access control	Formal surveillance	Identifying property	Strengthening moral condemnation
Parking lot barriers	Burglar alarms	Property marking	"Shoplifting is stealing"
Fenced yards	Speed cameras	Vehicle licensing	Roadside speedometers
Entry phones	Security guards	Cattle branding	"Bloody idiots drink and drive"
Deflecting offenders	Surveillance by employees	Reducing temptation	Controlling disinhibitors
Bus stop placement	Pay phone location	Gender-neutral phone lists	Drinking-age laws
Tavern location	Park attendants	Off-street parking	Ignition interlock
Street closures	Closed-circuit TV systems	Denying benefits	Server intervention
Controlling facilitators	Natural surveillance	Ink merchandise tags	Facilitating compliance
Credit card photo	Defensible space	PIN for car radios	Improved library checkout
Caller ID	Street lighting	Graffiti cleaning	Public lavatories
Gun controls	Cab driver ID		Trash bins

Source: CRIME PREVENTION AT THE CROSSROADS by STEVEN LAB. Copyright 1997 Reproduced with permission of ANDERSON PUBLISHING COMPANY, INC. in the format Textbook and Other Book via Copyright Clearance Center.

- Increase the effort needed to commit crime.
- Increase the risks of committing crime.
- Reduce the rewards for committing crime.
- Induce guilt or shame for committing crime.*

Hisham Ibrahim/Photographer's Choice/Getty Images

Cameras have been installed in many intersections, such as this one in Vancouver, to prevent crime.

*CRIME PREVENTION AT THE CROSSROADS by STEVEN LAB. Copyright 1997 Reproduced with permission of ANDERSON PUBLISHING COMPANY, INC. in the format Textbook and Other Book via Copyright Clearance Center.

These basic techniques and some specific methods that can be used to achieve them are summarized in Table 4.2.

Some of the tactics to increase effort include target-hardening techniques such as putting unbreakable glass on storefronts, locking gates, and fencing yards. Even simple prevention measures can work. Removing signs from store windows, installing brighter lights, and instituting a pay-first policy have helped reduce thefts from gas stations and convenience stores. Many police services now offer Crime Prevention Through Environmental Design (CPTED) audits to assist individuals and businesses to identify and implement environmental changes to reduce the risk of being victimized.[46]

Technological advances can also make it more difficult for would-be offenders to commit crimes; for example, having an owner's photo on credit cards should reduce the use of stolen cards. New security products such as steering locks on cars have reduced the incidence of theft.[47] Similarly, installing a locking device on cars that prevents drunk drivers from starting the vehicle significantly reduces drunk-driving rates.[48]

Target reduction strategies are designed to reduce the value of crime to the potential criminal. These include making car stereos removable so they can be kept at home at night, marking property so that it is more difficult to sell when stolen, and having gender-neutral phone listings to discourage obscene phone calls. Tracking systems can help police locate and return stolen vehicles.

Inducing guilt or shame might include such techniques as setting strict rules to embarrass offenders. For example, publishing "John lists" in the newspaper punishes those arrested for soliciting prostitutes. Facilitating compliance by providing trash bins might shame chronic litterers into using them. Widespread use of caller ID–equipped telephones has resulted in significant reductions in the number of obscene and prank phone calls, presumably because of the shame presented by the threat of exposure.[49]

© digitallife/Alamy (t); © mambo/Alamy (b)

As the popularity of Facebook, Twitter, and other forms of social media increase, there are applications to, for example, Neighbourhood Watch where homeowners could receive instantaneous messages from others in the community with warnings about suspicious persons nearby.

displacement
An effect of crime prevention efforts in which efforts to control crime in one area shift illegal activities to another.

extinction
The phenomenon in which a crime prevention effort has an immediate impact that then dissipates as criminals adjust to new conditions.

Displacement, Extinction, Discouragement, and Diffusion

Situational crime prevention efforts, however, may produce unforeseen and unwanted consequences. Preventing crime in one location does not address or deter criminal motivation. People who desire the benefits of crime may choose alternative targets, so that crime is not prevented but deflected or displaced.[50] For example, beefed-up police patrols in one area may shift crimes to a more vulnerable neighbourhood.[51] Although crime **displacement** certainly does not solve the general problem of crime, it has been shown to reduce the frequency of crime or produce less serious offence patterns.[52]

Scott Rothstein/Shutterstock.com

There is also the problem of **extinction**: Crime reduction programs may produce a short-term positive effect, but benefits dissipate as criminals adjust to new conditions. They learn to dismantle alarms or avoid patrols. They may also try new offences they had previously avoided. For example, if every residence in a neighbourhood has a foolproof burglar

Warren Toda/EPA /Landov

Big Brother is watching you. Toronto police have installed closed-circuit television cameras throughout downtown Toronto; the one pictured is in the shadow of the CN Tower.

diffusion of benefits An effect that occurs when efforts to prevent one crime unintentionally prevent another, or when crime-control efforts in one locale reduce crime in other nontarget areas.

discouragement An effect that occurs when limiting access to one target reduces other types of crime as well.

general deterrence A crime control policy that depends on the fear of criminal penalties, convincing the potential law violator that the pains associated with crime outweigh its benefits.

alarm system, motivated offenders may turn to armed robbery, a riskier and more violent crime.

Although displacement and extinction may create problems, there may also be advantages.[53] **Diffusion of benefits** occurs (1) when efforts to prevent one crime unintentionally prevent another and/or (2) when crime-control efforts in one locale reduce crime in other nontarget areas. What causes diffusion? First, crime prevention efforts may produce a generalized fear of apprehension. For example, video cameras set up in a mall to reduce shoplifting can also reduce property damage because would-be vandals fear they will be caught on camera. Or intensive police patrol efforts targeting neighbourhood drug dealers may convince prostitutes that it is too dangerous to ply their trade in that area.[54]

Situational crime prevention efforts may also produce **discouragement**: Limiting access to one target convinces would-be lawbreakers that crime no longer pays in general. For example, evaluations of auto protection systems that use hidden radio transmitters to track stolen cars have found that these devices help lower car theft rates. The auto protection systems not only deter auto thieves, but also seem to disrupt the operation of "chop shops," where stolen vehicles are taken apart for the resale of parts. Stolen car buyers cannot be sure if a stolen vehicle they purchase contains an auto protection system, which the police can trace to their base of operations.[55] Thus, a device designed to protect cars from theft also has the benefit of disrupting the sale of stolen car parts.

Shevelev Vladimir/Shutterstock.com

As electronic security measures have made car stereos increasingly difficult to steal, criminals are turning to stealing airbags, xenon headlights, and GPS and DVD systems.

DID YOU KNOW?

- Situational crime prevention efforts are designed to reduce or redirect crime by making it more difficult to profit from illegal acts.
- General deterrence models are based on the fear of punishment that is severe, swift, and certain.
- Specific deterrence aims at reducing crime through the application of severe punishments. Once offenders experience these punishments, they will be unwilling to repeat their criminal activities.
- Incapacitation strategies are designed to reduce crime by taking known criminals out of circulation, preventing them from having the opportunity to commit further offences.

LO3 General Deterrence

According to the rational choice view, motivated people will violate the law if left free and unrestricted. The concept of **general deterrence** is that, conversely, the decision to commit crime can be controlled by the threat of criminal punishment. If people fear being apprehended and punished, they will not risk breaking the law. An inverse relationship should exist between crime rates and the severity, certainty, and speed of legal sanctions. If, for example, the punishment for a crime is increased and the effectiveness and efficiency of the criminal justice system are improved, then the number of people engaging in that crime should decline.

The factors of severity, certainty, and speed of punishment may also be interactive. For example, if a crime—say, robbery—is punished severely, but few robbers are ever caught or punished, the severity of punishment for robbery will probably not deter people from robbing. On the other hand, if the certainty of apprehension and conviction is increased by modern technology, more efficient police work, or some other factor, then even minor punishment might deter the potential robber.

Do these factors actually affect the decision to commit crime and, consequently, general crime rates?

Certainty of Punishment

According to deterrence theory, if the certainty of arrest, conviction, and sanctioning increases, crime rates should decline. Rational offenders will soon realize that the increased likelihood of punishment outweighs any benefit they perceive from committing crimes. According to this view, crime persists because most criminals believe (1) that there is only a small chance they will get arrested for committing a particular crime, (2) that police officers are sometimes reluctant to make arrests even if they are aware of crime, and (3) that even if apprehended there is a good chance of receiving a lenient punishment.[56]

Although this view seems logical enough, the relationship between certainty of punishment and crime rates is far from settled. While a few research efforts do show a direct relationship between crime rates and the certainty of punishment,[57] a great deal of contradictory evidence indicates that the likelihood of being arrested or imprisoned has little effect on crime.[58]

One reason for this ambivalent finding is that the association between certainty of punishment and crime may be time-, crime-, and group-specific. For example, research shows that when the number of arrests increases, the number of serious crimes reported to police declines the next day.[59] It is possible that news of increased and aggressive police activity is rapidly diffused through the population and has an immediate impact, but that the effect erodes over time.

Research carried out in the United States also finds that the certainty of punishment may be race-specific. Arrests of blacks may influence only black offence rates, whereas arrests of whites probably affect only white offending patterns. In large cities, the threat of arrest may be communicated within neighbourhoods, some of which may be racially segregated. This threat affects residents of each racial grouping independently.[60]

Some research efforts have found a crime-specific deterrent effect. For example, using national data sets measuring crime and arrest rates in the United States, criminologist Edwin Zedlewski found that an increased probability of arrest may help lower the burglary rate, whereas theft rates remain unaffected by law enforcement efforts.[61]

crackdown
The concentration of police resources on a particular problem area to eradicate or displace criminal activity.

Level of Police Activity

If certainty of apprehension and punishment deters criminal behaviour, then increasing the number of police officers on the street should cut the crime rate. Moreover, if these police officers are active, aggressive crime fighters, would-be criminals should be convinced that the risk of apprehension outweighs the benefits they can gain from crime. However, the evidence that adding police leads to reduced crime rates is spotty.[62] Numerous studies have failed to show that increasing the number of police officers in a community can, by itself, lower crime rates.[63]

It is possible that while adding police may not work, adding more effective police could reduce crime. Research indicates that if police could make an arrest in at least 30 percent of all reported crimes, the crime rate would decline significantly.[64] But how can that figure be achieved, considering that arrest rates today hover at 20 percent?

To lower crime rates, some police services have instituted **crackdowns**—sudden changes in police activity designed to increase the communicated threat or actual certainty of punishment.

© C. Anthony Redpath/CORBIS

A prison term has historically been the deterrent of choice.

brutalization effect
The belief that capital punishment creates an atmosphere of brutality that enhances rather than deters the level of violence in society.

For example, a police task force might target street-level narcotics dealers by using undercover agents and surveillance cameras in known drug-dealing locales. However, these efforts have not proven to be successful mechanisms for lowering crime rates.[65] An analysis of 18 police crackdowns by Lawrence Sherman found that while they initially deterred crime, crime rates resumed earlier levels once the crackdown ended.[66] Although these results contradict the deterrence concept, research shows that more focused efforts may reduce crime levels. Crime rates are reduced when police officers use aggressive problem-solving and community improvement techniques, such as increasing lighting and cleaning vacant lots, to fight particular crimes in selected places.[67] A good example of the effectiveness of the crackdown strategy is the success of Ontario's RIDE (Reduce Impaired Driving Everywhere) program, which has had a significant impact in reducing impaired-driving-related accidents and fatalities on Ontario highways.[68]

Why do we kill people who kill people to show killing people is wrong?

Severity of Punishment

The introduction or threat of severe punishment should also bring the crime rate down. Although some studies have found that increasing sanction levels can control common criminal behaviours, there is little consensus that strict punishments alone can reduce criminal activities.[69] Because the likelihood of getting caught for some crimes is relatively low, the impact of deterrent measures is negligible over the long term.[70] For example, laws that provide expanded or mandatory sentences for crimes committed with guns have received mixed reviews. While some experts believe that these laws can lower crime rates, others question their deterrent effect. In sum, there is little empirical evidence that they have worked as planned.[71]

Capital Punishment

In May 2004, Cobourg Police Chief Garry Clement called for the reinstatement of the death penalty for those who kill officers of the law. Clement was reacting to the death of one of his officers, Constable Chris Garrett, slain by an 18-year-old male during the course of a robbery. Since its abolition in Canada in 1976, there have been recurring calls from members of the public and politicians to bring back the death penalty.

It seems to stand to reason that if severity of punishment can deter crime, then fear of the death penalty, the ultimate legal deterrent, should significantly reduce murder rates. Failure of the death penalty to deter violent crime jeopardizes the validity of the entire deterrence concept.

Various studies have tested the assumption that capital punishment deters violent crime. The research can be divided into three types: immediate impact studies, comparative research, and time-series analysis.

Immediate Impact

If capital punishment is a deterrent, the reasoning goes, then its impact should be greatest after a well-publicized execution. Robert Dann began testing this assumption in the United States in 1935, when he chose five highly publicized executions of convicted murderers in different years and determined the number of homicides in the 60 days before and after each execution.[72] Dann's study revealed that an average of 4.4 more homicides occurred during the 60 days following an execution than during those preceding it, suggesting that the overall impact of executions might actually be to increase the incidence of homicide.

The fact that executions may actually increase the likelihood of murders being committed is a consequence referred to as the **brutalization effect**. The basis of this theory is that potential criminals may

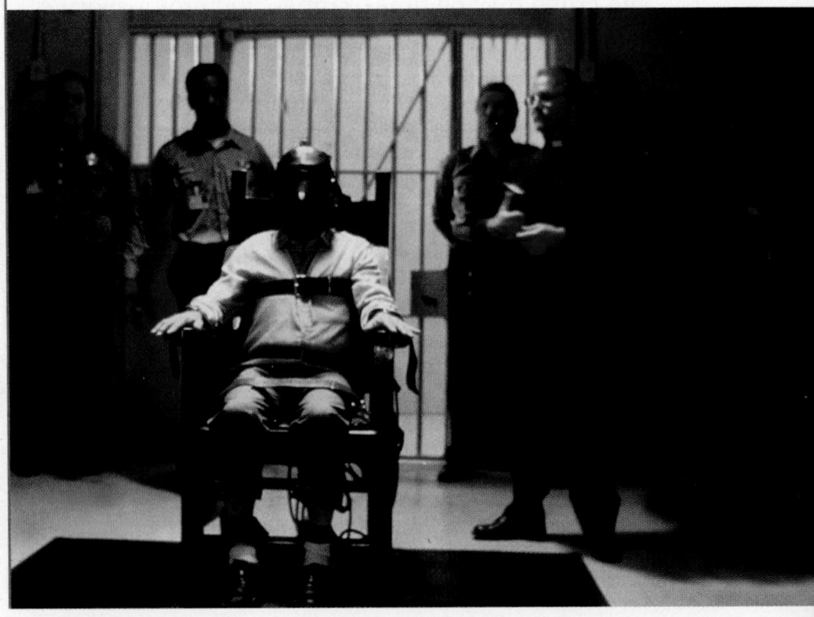
© AF archive/Alamy

begin to model their behaviour after state authorities: If the government can kill its enemies, so can they.[73] The brutalization effect means that after an execution murders may increase, causing even more deaths of innocent victims.

Although many criminologists question the utility of capital punishment, claiming that it causes more harm than it prevents, others believe that in the short run, executing criminals can bring the murder rate down.[74] Steven Stack's analysis of 16 well-publicized executions in the United States concluded that they may have saved 480 lives by immediately deterring potential murderers.[75] In sum, a number of criminologists find that executions actually increase murder rates, whereas others argue that their immediate impact is to lower murder rates.

Comparative Research

Another type of research compares the murder rates in jurisdictions that have abolished the death penalty with the rates in those that employ the death penalty.[76] Two pioneering studies, one by Thorsten Sellin (1959) and the other by Walter Reckless (1969), showed little difference in the murder rates of adjacent states, regardless of their use of the death penalty; capital punishment did not appear to influence the reported rate of homicide.[77] Similar research carried out by Canadian criminologist Ezzat Fattah in the 1970s arrived at the same conclusion.[78] More recent research gives little reason to believe that executions deter homicide.[79] Studies have compared murder rates in jurisdictions having a death penalty statute with those that don't and have also taken into account the number of people actually executed. These comparisons indicate that the death penalty—whether on the books or actually used—does not deter violent crime.[80]

AP Photo/Matt Cilley

Marion Rivera's daughter Lori was among the victims of Washington sniper John Allen Muhammed, who was executed in 2009 for the murders.

In addition, research conducted in 14 nations around the world found little evidence that countries with a death penalty have lower violence rates than those without. In fact, homicide rates decline after capital punishment is abolished, a direct contradiction to its supposed deterrent effect.[81]

Time-Series Analysis

Statistical analysis has allowed researchers to gauge whether the murder rate changes when death penalty statutes are created or eliminated. The most widely cited study is Isaac Ehrlich's 1975 work, in which he used U.S. crime and execution data to reach the conclusion that each execution in the United States would save seven or eight people from being murdered.[82] Ehrlich's research has been widely cited by advocates of the death penalty as empirical proof of the deterrent effect of capital punishment. However, subsequent research that attempted to replicate Ehrlich's analysis showed that his approach was flawed and that capital punishment is no more effective as a deterrent than life imprisonment.[83] For example, a recent test of the deterrent effect of the death penalty during the years 1984–1997 in Texas found no association between the frequency of execution and murder rates.[84]

Why Capital Punishment Fails

In sum, studies that have attempted to show the deterrent effect of capital punishment on the murder rate indicate that executing convicted criminals has relatively little influence on behaviour.[85] Although it is still uncertain why the threat of capital punishment has failed as a deterrent, the cause may lie in the nature of homicide itself. Murder is often an expressive "crime of passion" involving people who know each other and who may be under the influence of drugs or alcohol. Murder is also a byproduct of the criminal activity of people who suffer from the burdens of poverty and income inequality.[86] These factors may either prevent or inhibit rational evaluation of the long-term consequences of an immediate violent act.

The failure of the "ultimate deterrent" to deter the "ultimate crime" has been used by critics to question the validity of the general deterrence hypothesis that severe punishment will lower crime rates. In general, there is little direct evidence that severity of punishment alone can reduce or eliminate crime.

Swiftness of Punishment

A core element of general deterrence theory is that people who believe that they will be swiftly punished if they break the law will abstain from crime.[87]

Again, the evidence on the association between perceived punishment risk and crime has been mixed. Some research efforts have found a relationship,[88] while others have not.[89]

The threat of swift retaliation seems to work best when would-be criminals believe they will be subjected to very harsh punishments.[90] However, even this fear may be negated or overcome by the belief that a crime gives them a significant chance for large profit. When interviewed by criminologists Alex Piquero and George Rengert, active burglars reported that fear of a quick capture was in fact a deterrent, but one that could be overcome by the promise of a "big score." In short, greed overcomes fear.[91]

Informal Sanctions

Although the threat of even the most severe punishment may not have a deterrent effect, evidence is accumulating that the fear of informal sanctions may in fact reduce crime.[92] **Informal sanctions** occur when significant others—such as parents, peers, neighbours, and teachers—direct their disapproval, stigma, anger, and indignation toward an offender. If this happens, law violators run the risk of feeling shame, being embarrassed, and suffering a loss of respect.[93] Can the fear of public humiliation deter crime?

Research efforts have in fact established that the threat of informal sanctions can be a more effective deterrent than the threat of formal sanctions.[94] Fear of shame and embarrassment can be a powerful deterrent to crime. Those who fear being rejected by family and peers are reluctant to engage in deviant behaviour.[95] These factors manifest themselves in two ways: (1) personal shame over violating the law and (2) the fear of public humiliation if the deviant behaviour becomes public knowledge. People who say that their involvement in crime would cause them to feel ashamed are less likely to commit theft, fraud, motor vehicular, and other offences than people who report they would not feel ashamed.[96]

Anti-crime campaigns have been designed to play on this fear of shame. They are most effective when they convince the general public that being accused of crime will make them feel ashamed or embarrassed.[97] For example, spouse abusers report they are more afraid of the social costs of crime (loss of friends and family disapproval) than they are of legal punishment (going to jail). Women are more likely to fear shame and embarrassment than men, a finding that may help explain gender differences in the crime rate.[98]

informal sanctions
Disapproval, stigma, or anger directed toward an offender by significant others (parents, peers, neighbours, teachers), resulting in shame, embarrassment, and loss of respect.

Christina Xu/Flickr

The effect of informal sanctions may vary according to the cohesiveness of community structure and the type of crime. Not surprisingly, informal sanctions may be most effective in highly unified areas where everyone knows one another and the crime cannot be hidden from public view.[99]

Critique of General Deterrence

Some experts believe that the purpose of the law and justice system is to create a "threat system."[100] The threat of legal punishment should, on the face of it, deter lawbreakers through fear. Nonetheless, the relationship between crime rates and deterrent measures is far less than choice theorists might expect. Despite efforts to punish criminals and make them fear crime, there is little evidence that the fear of apprehension and punishment alone can reduce crime rates. How can this discrepancy be explained?

Rationality

Deterrence theory assumes a rational offender who weighs the costs and benefits of a criminal act before deciding on a course of action. However, criminals may be desperate people who choose crime because they believe there is no reasonable alternative. Some may suffer from personality disorders that impair their judgment and render them incapable of making truly rational decisions. Psychologists believe that chronic offenders suffer from an emotional state that renders them both incapable of fearing punishment and less likely to appreciate the consequences of crime.[101] For example, research on repeat sex offenders finds that they suffer from an elevated emotional state that negates the deterrent effect of the law.[102]

Certainty, Severity, and Speed

As Beccaria's famous equation tells us, the threat of punishment involves not only its severity, but its certainty and speed. The Canadian legal system is not very effective. Less than half (about 40 percent) of all crimes are reported to police, and police make arrests in only about 20 percent of reported crimes. Even when offenders are detected, police officers may choose to warn rather than arrest.[103] The odds of receiving a prison term are only about 20 per 1000 crimes committed. As a result, some offenders believe that they will not be severely punished for their acts and consequently have little regard for the law's deterrent power. Even those accused of murder are often convicted of lesser offences and spend what seem to be relatively short amounts of time behind bars.[104] In making their "rational choice," offenders may be aware that the deterrent effect of the law is minimal.

Choice

Among some groups of high-risk offenders, such as youth living in economically depressed neighbourhoods, the threat of formal sanctions is irrelevant. Young people in these areas may believe they have little to lose if arrested, because their opportunities are few and they have little attachment to social institutions such as school or family. Even if they truly fear the consequences of the law, they must commit crime to survive in a hostile environment.

To recap, studies measuring the perception of punishment agree with studies using aggregate criminal justice data that the certainty of punishment has a greater deterrent effect than its severity. Nonetheless, neither the perception nor the reality of punishment can deter most crimes.

LO4 Specific Deterrence

The theory of **specific deterrence** (also called special or particular deterrence) holds that criminal sanctions should be so powerful that known criminals will never repeat their criminal acts. According to this view, the drunk driver whose sentence is a substantial fine and a one-year licence suspension should be convinced that the price to be paid for drinking and driving is too great to consider future violations. Similarly, burglars who spend ten years in a tough, maximum-security prison should find their enthusiasm for theft dampened.[105] In principle, punishment works if a connection can be established between the planned action and memories of its consequence; if these recollections are adequately intense, the action will be unlikely to occur again.[106]

Does Specific Deterrence Deter Crime?

specific deterrence The view that criminal sanctions should be so powerful that offenders will never repeat their criminal acts.

incarceration Confinement in jail or prison.

recidivism Repetition of criminal behaviour.

probation Sentence served in the community under the supervision of a probation officer and subject to certain conditions.

At first glance, specific deterrence does not seem to work, because a majority of known criminals are not deterred by their punishment. Research on chronic offenders indicates that arrest and punishment seem to have little effect on experienced criminals and may even increase the likelihood that first-time offenders will commit new crimes.[107] Nearly two-thirds of all convicted offenders are re-arrested within three years of their release from prison, and those who have been punished in the past are the most likely to commit a new offence.[108] **Incarceration** may sometimes slow down or delay **recidivism** in the short term, but the overall probability of re-arrest does not change following incarceration.[109] On the other hand, recidivism rates are generally lower (in the 30–50 percent range) for those who have received a sentence of **probation**, suggesting that for some offenders, rehabilitation and ongoing integration in the community may be a more effective deterrent than punishment.[110]

Some research efforts have shown that, rather than reducing the frequency of crime, severe punishment actually increases reoffending rates.[111] Punishment may bring defiance rather than deterrence, while the stigma of apprehension may help lock offenders into a criminal career.

Stigmatization versus Reintegrative Shaming

In his book *Crime, Shame, and Reintegration*, John Braithwaite helps explain why specific deterrence measures may be doomed to failure.[112] In most Western societies, punishment stigmatizes offenders and sets them, resentful, outside the mainstream. Law violators view themselves as victims of the justice system, punished by strangers, such as police and judges, who are being paid to act. In contrast, Braithwaite notes that countries such as Japan, in which conviction for crimes brings an inordinate amount of personal shame, have extremely low crime rates.

Braithwaite divides the concept of shame into two distinct types. In North American society, shaming typically involves **stigmatization**—an ongoing process of degradation in which the offender is branded

stigmatization
Ongoing degradation or humiliation, in which the offender is branded as an evil person and cast out of society.

reintegrative shaming
Brief and controlled shaming that is followed by forgiveness, apology, repentance, and reconnection with the community.

incapacitation effect
The idea that keeping offenders in confinement will eliminate the risk of their committing further offences.

as an evil person and cast out of society. Shaming can occur at a school disciplinary hearing or a criminal court trial. As a specific deterrent, stigma is doomed to failure. People who suffer humiliation at the hands of the justice system "reject their rejectors" by joining a deviant subculture of like-minded people who collectively resist social control. Despite these dangers, there has been an ongoing effort to brand offenders and make their "shame" both public and permanent. For example, most American states and some Canadian provinces have passed sex offender registry and notification laws that make public the names of those convicted of sex offences and warn neighbours of their presence in the community.[113]

Braithwaite argues that crime control can be better achieved through a policy of **reintegrative shaming**. In this approach, the offenders' evil deeds are condemned while, at the same time, efforts are made to reconnect them to their neighbours, friends, and family. A critical element of reintegrative shaming is an effort to help offenders understand and recognize their wrongdoing and feel ashamed of their actions. To be reintegrative, shaming must be brief and controlled and then followed by ceremonies of forgiveness, apology, and repentance.

An important part of reintegrative shaming is bringing offenders together with victims so that the offenders can learn to understand the impact of their actions. Close family members and peers are also present to help the offender reintegrate back into society. Efforts like these can humanize a system of justice that today relies on repression, rather than forgiveness, as the basis of specific deterrence.

LO5 Incapacitation

It stands to reason that if more criminals are sent to prison, the crime rate should go down. Because most people age out of crime, the duration of a criminal career is limited. Placing offenders behind bars during their prime crime years should lessen their lifetime opportunity to commit crime. The shorter the span of opportunity, the fewer offences they can commit during their lives; hence crime is reduced. This theory, known as the **incapacitation effect**, seems logical, but does it work?

The past 20 years have witnessed significant growth in the number and percentage of the population held in prisons and jails. Today, on any given day, more than 32 000 Canadians are incarcerated. Advocates of incapacitation suggest that this effort has been responsible for the decade-long decline in crime rates. However, critics counter that what appears to be an incapacitation effect may actually reflect the effect of some other legal or social phenomenon. The economy has improved, the huge cohort of baby boomers is now entering their 50s and 60s and has aged out of committing many types of crime, and police may simply be more effective. Crime rates could also be dropping because potential criminals fear tough sentencing laws that provide long mandatory prison sentences for serious violent crimes. What appears to be an incapacitation effect may actually be an effect of general deterrence.[114]

Can Incapacitation Reduce Crime?

Research on the direct benefits of incapacitation has been inconclusive. A number of studies have set out to measure the precise effect of incarceration rates on crime rates, and the results have not supported a strict incarceration policy.[115] Gendreau, Goggin, Cullen, and Andrews report that, in fact, incarceration results in as much as a 3 percent increase in the likelihood that those imprisoned will reoffend when they are released, thereby increasing the crime rate.[116] On the other hand, Gendreau and colleagues report that community-based correctional programs such as probation and parole reduce the likelihood of reoffending by as much as 10 percent. Looking at the relationship from another perspective, if the prison population were reduced and community correctional programs were used more, we could reduce the crime rate by at least 3 percent and possibly more.

While these findings are problematic, a few studies have found an inverse relationship between incarceration rates and crime rates. In a frequently cited study, Reuel Shinnar and Shlomo Shinnar's research on incapacitation in New York led them to conclude that mandatory prison sentences of five years for violent crime and three for property offences could reduce the reported crime rate by a factor of four or five.[117] Other research studies also claim that a strict incarceration policy can reduce the level of violent crime.[118]

The Logic behind Incarceration

Considering that the criminals are unable to continue their illegal activities while housed in a prison or jail, incapacitation should in fact be an excellent crime control strategy. For example, a study of 201 heroin abusers in New York City found that, if given a one-year jail sentence, they would not have been able to commit their yearly haul of crimes: 1000 robberies, 4000 burglaries, 10 000 shopliftings, and more than 3000 other property crimes.[119]

Nonetheless, evaluations of incarceration strategies reveal that their impact is less than expected. For one thing, there is little evidence that incapacitating criminals will deter them from future criminality and even more reason to believe that they may be more inclined to commit crimes upon release. Prison has few specific deterrent effects: The more prior incarceration experiences inmates have, the more likely they are to reoffend (and return to prison) within 12 months of their release.[120] The short-term crime reduction effect of incapacitating criminals is negated if the prison experience has the long-term effect of escalating the frequency of criminal behaviour upon release. By its nature, the prison experience exposes young, first-time offenders to higher-risk, more experienced inmates who can influence their lifestyle and help shape their attitudes. Novice inmates also run an increased risk of becoming infected with HIV/AIDS and other health hazards, and that exposure reduces their life chances after release.[121]

Furthermore, the economics of crime suggest that if money can be made from criminal activity, there will always be someone to take the place of the incarcerated offender. New criminals will be recruited and trained, offsetting any benefit accrued by incarceration. Imprisoning established offenders may likewise open new opportunities for competitors who were suppressed by the more experienced criminals. For example, incarcerating organized crime members may open drug markets to new gangs. The flow of narcotics may actually increase after the more experienced organized crime leaders are imprisoned, because newcomers are willing to take greater risks.

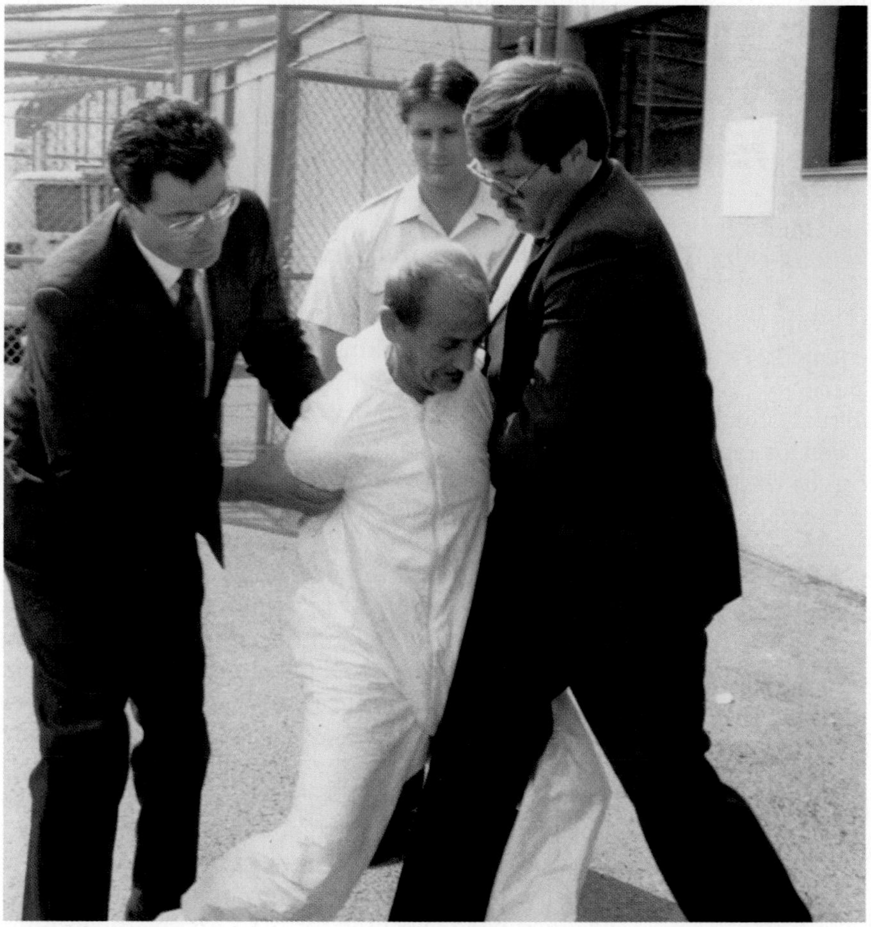

Another reason that incarceration may not work is that most criminal offences are committed by teens and very young adult offenders, who are unlikely to be sent to prison for a single conviction. At the same time, many incarcerated criminals, aging behind bars, are already past the age when they are likely to commit crime. As a result, a strict incarceration policy may keep people in prison beyond the time they are a threat to society while a new cohort of high-risk adolescents is on the street. It is possible that the most serious criminals are already behind bars and that adding less dangerous offenders to the population will have little appreciable effect while adding tremendous costs to the correctional system.[122]

An incapacitation strategy is very expensive. The prison system costs billions of dollars

Toronto Star Archives

If dangerous criminals were incapacitated, they would never again have the opportunity to prey upon others. One of the most dramatic Canadian examples of the utility of incapacitation is the case of Joseph Fredericks. Fredericks was a known sadistic pedophile who was released under "mandatory supervision" into the community of Brampton, Ontario, in 1988 to serve out the balance of his sentence for the violent sexual assault of an Ottawa-area boy. Three months into his release, Fredericks abducted, sexually assaulted, and murdered 11-year-old Christopher Stephenson. Fredericks himself was later murdered in prison. Should dangerous predators such as Fredericks ever be released from incapacitation? Is rehabilitation even a remote possibility?

three strikes and you're out
American policy whereby people convicted of three felony offences receive a mandatory life sentence.

just desert
The principle that those who violate the rights of others deserve punishment commensurate with the seriousness of the crime, without regard for their personal characteristics or circumstances.

each year. Even if incarceration could reduce the crime rate, the costs would be enormous. Are Canadian taxpayers willing to spend millions, even billions, more on new prison construction and annual maintenance fees? A strict incarceration policy would result in a growing number of elderly inmates whose maintenance costs, estimated at as much as $80 000–$100 000 per year, ar two to three times higher than those of younger inmates. In 2000, inmates 50 years and older comprised 12 percent of the federal correctional population; 38 percent of those serving life terms will be 55 or older before they are eligible for parole, raising fears of a "geriatric overload" of the prison system and prison costs.[123]

Three Strikes and You're Out

Some experts maintain that incapacitation can work if it is focused on the most serious chronic offenders. For example, in the United States, the **three strikes and you're out** policy, giving people convicted of three felony offences a mandatory life sentence, has received widespread publicity. Many American states already employ habitual offender laws that provide long (or life) sentences for repeat offenders. In Canada, an individual can be declared a "dangerous offender" and sentenced to an indeterminate period in prison if the prosecution can show evidence of a continuing pattern of aggressive or sexual behaviour that is not likely to be deterred by a traditional sentence.[124] Criminologists retort that although such strategies are politically compelling, they will not work, for several reasons:

- Most three-time offenders are at the verge of aging out of crime anyway.
- Current sentences for violent crimes are already quite severe.
- An expanding prison population will drive up already high prison costs.
- There would be racial disparity in sentencing.
- The police would be in danger because two-time offenders would violently resist a third arrest, knowing they face a life sentence.[125]
- The prison population probably already contains the highest-frequency criminals.

Those who support a selective incapacitation strategy argue that criminals who are already in prison (high-rate offenders) commit significantly more crimes each year than the average criminal who is on the outside (low-rate offenders). If a broad policy of incarceration were employed, requiring mandatory prison sentences for all those convicted of crimes, more low-rate criminals would be placed behind bars.[126] It would be both costly and nonproductive to incarcerate large groups of people who commit relatively few crimes. It makes more economic sense to focus incarceration efforts on known high-rate offenders by lengthening their sentences.

LO6 Policy Implications of Choice Theory

From the origins of classical theory to the development of modern rational choice views, the belief that criminals choose to commit crime has influenced the relationship among law, punishment, and crime. Although research on the core principles of choice theory and deterrence theories has produced mixed results, these models have had an important impact on crime prevention strategies.

When police patrol in well-marked cars, it is assumed that their presence will deter would-be criminals. When the harsh realities of prison life are portrayed in movies and TV shows, the lesson is not lost on potential criminals. Nowhere is the idea that the threat of punishment can control crime more evident than in the implementation of tough mandatory criminal sentences to control violent crime and drug trafficking.

Despite its questionable deterrent effect, some advocates argue that the death penalty can effectively restrict criminality; at least it ensures that convicted criminals never again get the opportunity to kill. Many observers are dismayed because people who are convicted of murder sometimes kill again when released on parole or mandatory supervision. One study of 52 000 incarcerated murderers in the United States found that 810 had been previously convicted of murder and had killed 821 people following their previous release from prison.[127] About 9 percent of all inmates on death row in the United States have had prior convictions for homicide. Death penalty advocates argue that if these criminals had been executed for their first offences, hundreds of people would be alive today.[128]

The concept of criminal choice has also prompted the development of justice policies that treat all offenders equally, without regard for their background or personal characteristics. This is referred to as the concept of **just desert**, or what has become known as the "justice model" philosophy of criminal justice. The justice model position has been most clearly spelled out by criminologist Andrew Von

Hirsch in his book *Doing Justice*.[129] Von Hirsch argues that while punishment is needed to preserve the social equity disturbed by crime, it should be commensurate with the seriousness of the crime.[130] Von Hirsch's views can be summarized as follows:

1. Those who violate others' rights deserve to be punished.
2. We should not deliberately add to human suffering; punishment makes those punished suffer.
3. Punishment may prevent more misery than it inflicts, which justifies the need for desert-based punishment.†

The justice model is also concerned with the rights of the accused. It alleges that the rights of the person being punished should not be unduly sacrificed for the good of others (as with deterrence). The offender should not be treated as more (or less) blameworthy than is warranted by the character of his or her offence. For example, Von Hirsch asks the following question: If two crimes, A and B, are equally serious, but if severe penalties are shown to have a deterrent effect only with respect to A, would it be fair to punish the person who has committed crime A more harshly simply to deter others from committing the crime? Conversely, it is unfair for a merciful judge to impose a light sentence on a teenage criminal, because in so doing he or she arbitrarily makes the younger offender less blameworthy than an older criminal who commits the same act. All offenders must be treated the same on the basis of what they did, not who they are.

In sum, the justice model suggests that retribution justifies punishment because people deserve what they get for past deeds. Punishment based on deterrence or incapacitation is wrong because it involves an offender's future actions, which cannot be accurately predicted. Punishment should be the same for all people who commit the same crime. Criminal sentences based on individual needs or characteristics are inherently unfair because all people are equally blameworthy for their misdeeds. The influence of Von Hirsch's views can be seen in mandatory sentencing models that give the same punishment to all people who commit the same type of crime.

†Excerpt from DOING JUSTICE: THE CHOICE OF PUNISHMENTS by Andrew von Hirsch.

Thinking Like a Criminologist

Visit icancrim2.com to find the resources you need today!

Located at the back of the textbook are rip-out Chapter in Review cards. Make sure you also go online to check out other tools that CRIM offers to help you successfully pass your course.

- Flashcards
- Glossary
- Test Yourself
- Videos
- Games
- Interactive Quizzing
- Audio Chapter Reviews

CHAPTER 5

Trait Theory: It's in Their Blood

Learning Outcomes

LO1 Explain the basic premises of trait theory.

LO2 Explain how fetal alcohol spectrum disorder (FASD) and criminality may be linked.

LO3 Explain the relationship between genetics and criminality.

LO4 Describe the major varieties of psychological trait theories.

LO5 Describe the relationship between mental illness and criminality.

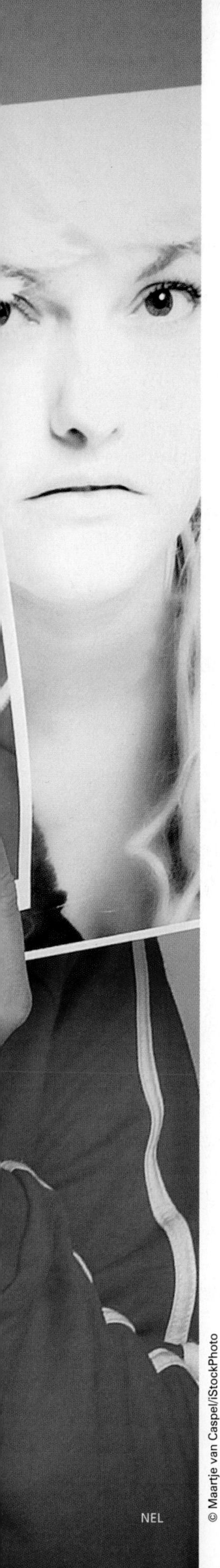
© Maartje van Caspel/iStockPhoto

Gamil Rodrigue Gharbi was born in Montreal in 1964 to Algerian Muslim Liess Gharbi and former Catholic nun Monique Lepine. The family was financially well off, and the early years were good. However, Liess is reported to have been an incessant womanizer who showed little respect for women. By 1972 Monique had had enough and left the marriage, reporting at the divorce hearing that her husband had been physically abusive to her and a stern disciplinarian with Gamil and younger sister Nadia. Monique was granted custody of the two children. A year later, Gamil changed his name to Marc Lepine. Though bright and generally a good student, the course of Marc Lepine's life through his teenage years and young adulthood appears to have been one of increasing frustration and failure—rejected by the Canadian military as "unsuitable," failing out of community college, rejected by the engineering program at l'École Polytechnique in Montreal. Lepine grew isolated and withdrawn, and increasingly blamed "feminists" for his troubles. On December 6, 1989, Lepine interrupted a student presentation in Room 230 at l'École Polytechnique and ordered all of the males to leave the room. He told the nine remaining female engineering students, "I'm here to fight against feminism." Lepine then emptied the magazine of a semi-automatic Sturm Ruger Mini-14 rifle into the women, seriously wounding three and killing six. He left the classroom and proceeded to move about the building in search of women. Before the 20-minute rampage was over, 14 women lay dead and 13 others wounded. Lepine then killed himself at the scene. He left a suicide note blaming feminists for wanting to "retain the advantages of being women ... while trying to grab those of the men."[1]

DID YOU KNOW?

- Early criminologists such as Cesare Lombroso suggested that some people had crime-producing biological traits.
- Some contemporary criminologists believe that human traits interact with environmental factors to produce criminal behaviours.
- No single trait is responsible for all crime. Suspected crime-producing traits include neurological problems, blood chemistry disorders, and personality disorders.
- All people are not born physically and psychologically equal; if they were, all people living in the same environment would act in a similar fashion.

CBC TV Archive Sales

Marc Lepine's violent shooting spree at l'École Polytechnique in Montreal on December 6, 1989, seemed to be the product of a deranged mind. Can people such as Lepine who go on murderous rampages ever be considered "normal" or "sane"?

© AF archive/Alamy (t, b); © Photos 12/Alamy (r)

Lepine's case provides the public with an image of the criminal offender as a deeply disturbed individual who suffers from some sort of mental abnormality. The image of a disturbed, mentally ill offender seems plausible because a generation of North Americans has grown up on films and TV shows that portray violent criminals as mentally deranged and physically abnormal. Lurking out there are deranged roommates (*Single White Female*), abnormal partners (*Sleeping with the Enemy*), and lunatic high school friends (*Scream*), who evolve into even crazier college classmates (*Scream II*) and then grow up to become nutty young adults (*Scream III*). No one is safe when the psychologists and psychiatrists who are hired to treat these disturbed people turn out to be demonic murderers themselves (*Silence of the Lambs; Hannibal*). Is it any wonder that we respond to a particularly horrible crime by saying of the perpetrator, "That guy must be crazy" or "She is a monster"?

This chapter reviews those criminological theories that suggest that criminality is a matter of abnormal human traits. These **trait theories** can be subdivided into two major categories: one stressing biological makeup and the other stressing psychological functioning. Although these views often overlap (e.g., brain function may have a biological basis), each branch has unique characteristics and will be discussed separately.

trait theory
The view that criminality is a product of abnormal biological and/or psychological traits.

sociobiology
View that human behaviour is motivated by inborn biological urges to survive and preserve the species.

LO1 The Development of Trait Theory

The view that criminals have physical or mental traits that make them different and abnormal is not restricted to movie viewers, but began with the Italian physician and criminologist Cesare Lombroso.

The early research of Lombroso and his contemporaries is today regarded as historical curiosity, not scientific fact. The research methodology they used has since been brought into question, and many of the traits they assumed to be inherited are not really genetically determined but caused by environment and diet. As criticism of their work mounted, biological explanations of crime fell out of favour and were abandoned in the early 20th century.[2]

In the early 1970s, spurred by the publication of *Sociobiology* by Edmund O. Wilson, biological explanations of crime once again emerged.[3] **Sociobiology** differs from earlier theories of behaviour in that it stresses that biological and genetic conditions affect how social behaviours are learned and perceived. It suggests that both animal and human behaviour is determined in part by the need to ensure survival of offspring and replenishment of the gene pool. These perceptions, in turn, are linked to existing environmental structures.

CONNECTIONS

As you may recall from Chapter 1, Lombroso's work on the born criminal was a direct offshoot of applying the scientific method to the study of crime. His identification of primitive, atavistic anomalies was based on what he believed to be sound empirical research using established scientific methods.

Sociobiologists view biology, environment, and learning as mutually interdependent factors. These views revived interest in finding a biological and/or psychological basis for crime and delinquency. It prompted some criminologists to conclude that personal traits must separate the deviant members of society from the nondeviant. Possessing these traits may help explain why, when faced with the same life situations, one person commits crime, whereas another obeys the law. Put another way, living in a disadvantaged neighbourhood may not cause a well-adjusted person to commit crime; living in an affluent area may not stop a maladapted person from offending.[4] All people may be aware of and even fear the sanctioning power of the law, but some are unable to control their urges and passions.

Contemporary Trait Theory

Contemporary trait theorists do not suggest that a single biological or psychological attribute adequately explains all criminality. Rather, each offender is considered physically and mentally unique; consequently, there must be different explanations for each person's behaviour. Some may have inherited criminal tendencies; others may be suffering from neurological problems; still others may have blood chemistry disorders that heighten their antisocial activity. Criminologists who focus on the individual see many explanations for crime because, in fact, there are many differences among criminal offenders.

Contemporary trait theorists focus on basic human behaviour and drives that are linked to antisocial behaviour patterns.

Trait theorists today recognize that having a particular physical characteristic does not, in itself, produce criminality. Crime-producing interactions involve both personal traits (such as defective intelligence, impulsive personality, and abnormal brain chemistry) and environmental factors (such as family life, educational attainment, socioeconomic status, and neighbourhood conditions). People may develop physical or mental traits at birth or soon after that affect their social functioning over the life course and influence their behaviour choices. For example, low-birth-weight babies have been found to suffer poor educational achievement later in life; academic deficiency, in turn, has been linked to delinquency and drug abuse.[5] A condition present at birth or soon after can thus affect behaviour across the life span. In their national longitudinal study adolescent health, Beaver et al. (2010) noted that postnatal exposure to cigarette smoke, duration of breastfeeding, maternal involvement, and household income are all good predictors of adolescent and adulthood levels of neuropsychological functioning,[6] and a large body of research that has revealed that neuropsychological functioning is one of the most consistent predictors of antisocial behaviour.

Jupiter Images

Older males who pursue younger females as partners are said to be more reproductively successful.
© Image Source/Alamy

Although some people may have a predisposition toward aggression, that does not mean that they will necessarily or automatically engage in violent behaviours; environmental stimuli can either suppress or trigger antisocial acts.[7]

Trait theories have gained prominence recently because of what is now known about chronic recidivism and the development of criminal careers. If only a few offenders become persistent repeaters, then what sets them apart from the rest of the criminal population may be an abnormal biochemical makeup, brain structure, genetic constitution, or some other human trait.[8] Even if crime is a choice, the fact that some people make that choice repeatedly could be linked to their physical and mental makeup. According to this view, biological makeup contributes significantly to human behaviour.

Biological Trait Theories

One branch of contemporary trait theory focuses on the biological conditions that control human behaviour. Criminologists who work in this area typically refer to themselves as biocriminologists, biosocial criminologists, or biologically oriented criminologists; the terms are used here interchangeably.

The following sections examine some important subareas within biological criminology (see Figure 5.1). First we review the biochemical factors that are believed to affect how proper behaviour patterns are learned. Then we consider the relationship between brain function and crime. Next we analyze current ideas about the association between genetic factors and crime. Finally, we evaluate evolutionary views of crime causation.

Biochemical Conditions and Crime

Some trait theorists believe that biochemical conditions, including both those that are genetically predetermined and those that are acquired through diet and environment, influence antisocial behaviour. This view of crime received widespread attention in 1979 when Dan White, who confessed to killing San Francisco Mayor George Moscone and City Councilman Harvey Milk, claimed that his behaviour was precipitated by an addiction to sugar-laden junk foods.[9]

White's successful "Twinkie defence" prompted a California jury to find him guilty of the lesser offence of diminished-capacity manslaughter rather than first-degree murder. (White committed suicide after serving his prison sentence.) Some of the biochemical factors that have been linked to criminality are set out in detail here.

FIGURE 5.1

Biosocial Perspectives on Criminality

Perspective	Cause
BIOCHEMICAL	• Diet • Hormones • Contaminants
NEUROPHYSIOLOGICAL	• Brain structure • Brain damage • Brain chemicals
GENETIC	• Inherited aggressive predisposition • Inherited condition associated with crime such as impulsive personality
EVOLUTIONARY	• Aggression evolves over time • Aggressive males produce more offspring

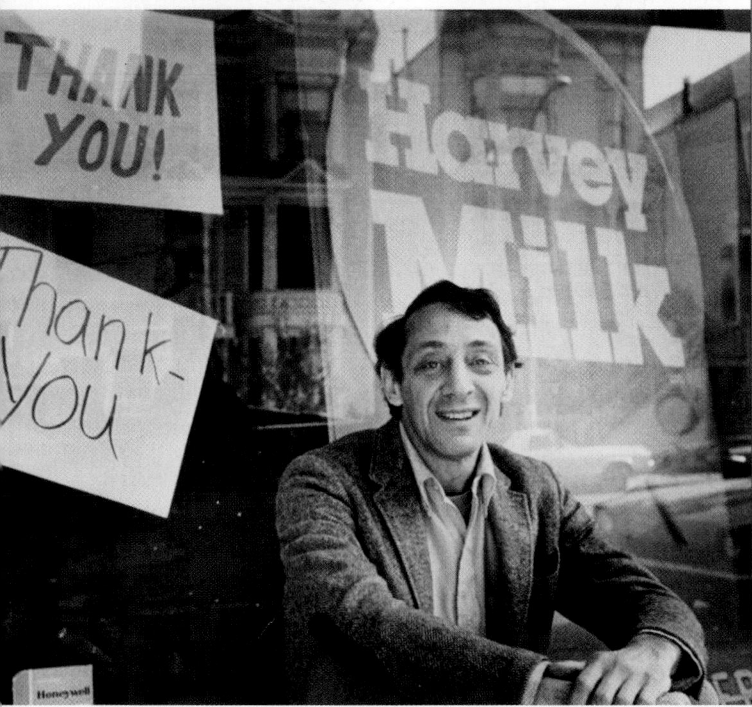

© Bettmann/CORBIS

San Francisco City Councilman Harvey Milk (pictured) was murdered by Dan White, whose defence was that his actions were the result of his addiction to junk foods.

Chemical and Mineral Influences

Biocriminologists maintain that minimal levels of minerals and chemicals are needed for normal brain functioning and growth, especially in the early years of life.

Research conducted over the past decade shows that dietary inadequacy of certain chemicals and minerals, including sodium, potassium, calcium, amino acids, monoamines, and peptides, can lead to depression, mania, cognitive problems, memory loss, and abnormal sexual activity.[10] Research studies examining the relationship between crime and vitamin deficiency and dependency have identified a close link between antisocial behaviour and insufficient quantities of some B vitamins and vitamin C. In addition, studies have purported to show that a major proportion of all schizophrenics and

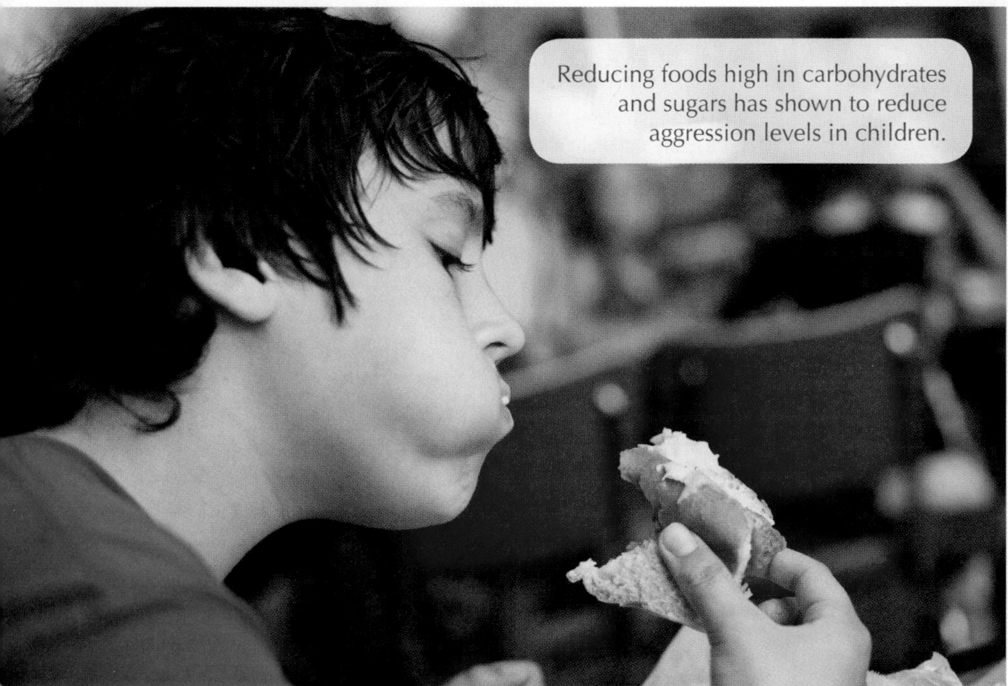

Reducing foods high in carbohydrates and sugars has shown to reduce aggression levels in children.

© Juanmonino/iStockPhoto

children with learning and behaviour disorders have abnormal levels of vitamins B3 and B6.[11]

Another suspected nutritional influence on aggressive behaviour is a diet especially high in carbohydrates and sugar.[12] Experiments have altered children's diets so that sweet drinks were replaced with unsweetened fruit juices, table sugar was replaced with honey, and so on. Results indicate that these changes can reduce aggression levels.[13]

Although these results are impressive, some recent research efforts have failed to find a link between sugar consumption and violence.[14] In one important study, a group of researchers had 25 preschool children and 23 school-age children described as sensitive to sugar follow a different diet for three consecutive three-week periods. One diet was high in sucrose, the second substituted aspartame (Nutrasweet) as a sweetener, and the third relied on saccharin. Careful measurement of the subjects found little evidence of cognitive or behavioural differences that could be linked to diet. If anything, sugar seemed to calm the children.[15] In some cases, in fact, sugar intake has been found to possibly reduce or curtail violent tendencies.[16]

While this research damages the suspected link between diet and aggression, some recent research indicates that it may be premature to dismiss the suspected association between the two factors.

Hormonal Influences

Biosocial theorists note that males are biologically and naturally more aggressive than females, whereas women are more nurturing toward the young.[17] This discrepancy has been linked to gender-based hormonal differences. Hormones cause areas of the brain to become less sensitive to environmental stimuli. Abnormally high hormone levels require people to seek excess stimulation and to be willing to tolerate pain in their quest for thrills. Hormones are linked to brain seizures that, under stressful conditions, can result in emotional volatility. Hormones also affect the brain structure itself: They influence the left hemisphere of the neocortex, the part of the brain that controls sympathetic feelings toward others.[18] These effects promote violence and other serious crimes by causing people to seek greater levels of environmental stimulation and to tolerate more punishment, and by increasing impulsivity, emotional volatility, and antisocial emotions.[19]

Biosocial research has found that abnormal levels of male sex hormones (**androgens**) do in fact produce aggressive behaviour.[20] Other androgen-related male traits include sensation seeking, impulsivity, dominance, and reduced verbal skills; all of these androgen-related traits are also related to antisocial behaviour.[21] A growing body of evidence suggests that hormonal changes are also related to mood and behaviour. Adolescents experience more intense mood swings, anxiety, and restlessness than their elders, explaining in part the high violence rates found among teenage males.[22]

Testosterone, the most abundant androgen, which controls secondary sex characteristics such as facial hair and voice timbre, has been linked to criminality.[23] Research conducted on both human and animal subjects has found that prenatal exposure to unnaturally high levels of testosterone permanently alters behaviour. Girls who were unintentionally exposed to elevated amounts of testosterone during their fetal development display an unusually high, long-term tendency toward aggression. Conversely, boys who were prenatally exposed to steroids that decrease testosterone levels display decreased aggressiveness.[24] Gender differences in the crime rate, therefore, may be explained by the relative difference in testosterone and other androgens between the two sexes.

androgens
Male sex hormones.

testosterone
The principal male hormone.

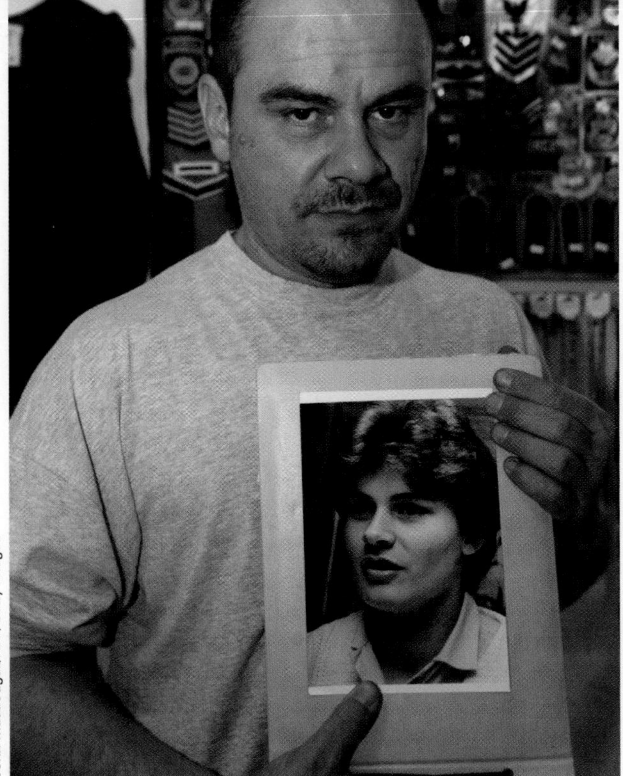

John Macdougall/AFP/Getty Images

Steroids, drugs that mimic the effect of testosterone on the body, gave this German athlete, born female, masculine traits.

premenstrual syndrome (PMS)
The hypothesis that several days prior to and during menstruation, excessive amounts of female sex hormones stimulate antisocial, aggressive behaviour.

Females may be biologically protected from deviant behaviour in the same way they are immune from some diseases that strike males.[25] Hormone levels also help explain the aging-out process. Levels of testosterone decline during the life cycle, which may explain why violence rates diminish over time.[26]

Premenstrual Syndrome

The suspicion has long existed that the onset of the menstrual cycle triggers excessive amounts of the female sex hormones, which stimulate antisocial, aggressive behaviour. This condition is commonly referred to as **premenstrual syndrome (PMS)**.[27] The link between PMS and delinquency was first popularized more than 30 years ago by Katharina Dalton, whose studies of English women indicated that females are more likely to commit suicide and to be aggressive and otherwise antisocial just before or during menstruation.[28]

Although the Dalton research is often cited as evidence of the link between PMS and crime, methodological problems make it impossible to accept her findings at face value. There is still significant debate over any link between PMS and aggression. Some doubters argue that the relationship is spurious; it is equally likely that the psychological and physical stress of aggression brings on menstruation and not vice versa.[29] However, Diana Fishbein, a noted expert on biosocial theory, concludes that there is in fact an association between elevated levels of female aggression and menstruation. Research efforts, she argues, show that (1) a significant number of incarcerated females committed their crimes during the premenstrual phase and (2) at least a small percentage of women appear vulnerable to cyclical hormonal changes that make them more prone to anxiety and hostility.[30]

The debate is ongoing, but the overwhelming majority of females who suffer anxiety and hostility before and during menstruation do not engage in violent criminal behaviour. Thus, any link between PMS and crime is tenuous at best.[31]

DID YOU KNOW?

- Brain chemistry and hormonal differences are related to aggression and violence.
- Most evidence suggests that there is no relationship between sugar intake and crime.
- The male hormone testosterone is linked to criminality.
- Neurological impairments have been linked to crime.
- Genetic theory holds that violence-producing traits are passed on from generation to generation.
- According to evolutionary theory, instinctual drives control behaviour. The urge to procreate influences male violence.
- Biological explanations fail to account for the geographic, social, and temporal patterns in the crime rate; critics question the methodology used.

Environmental Contaminants

Dangerous amounts of copper, cadmium, mercury, and inorganic gases, such as chlorine and nitrogen dioxide, are found in the ecosystem. Research indicates that these environmental contaminants can influence behaviour. At high levels, these substances can cause severe illness or death; at more moderate levels, they have been linked to emotional and behavioural disorders.[32] Some studies have linked the ingestion of food dyes and artificial colours and flavours to hostile, impulsive, and otherwise antisocial behaviour in youths.[33] Lighting may be another important environmental influence on antisocial behaviour. Research projects have suggested that radiation from artificial light sources, such as fluorescent tubes and television sets, may produce antisocial, aggressive behaviour.[34]

A number of recent research studies have linked lead ingestion to problem behaviour. Ingestion of lead may help explain why hyperactive children manifest conduct problems and antisocial behaviour.[35] Criminologist Deborah Denno investigated the behaviour of more than 900 black youths and found that lead poisoning was one of the most significant predictors of male delinquency and persistent adult criminality.[36]

Neurophysiological Conditions and Crime

Some researchers focus their attention on **neurophysiology**, or the study of brain activity.[37] They believe that neurological and physical abnormalities, acquired as early as the fetal or perinatal stage or through birth delivery trauma, control behaviour throughout the life span.[38]

The relationship between neurological dysfunction and crime first received a great deal of attention in 1968 following a tragic incident in Texas. Charles Whitman killed his wife and mother, and then barricaded himself in a tower at the University of Texas with a high-powered rifle; he killed 14 people and wounded 24 others before he was killed by police. An autopsy revealed that Whitman suffered from a malignant infiltrating brain tumour. He had previously experienced uncontrollable urges to kill and had gone to a psychiatrist seeking help for his problems. He kept careful notes documenting his feelings and his inability to control his homicidal urges, and he left instructions for his estate to be given to a mental health foundation to study mental problems such as his own.[39]

Since the Whitman case, a great deal of attention has been focused on the association between neurological impairment and crime. Studies have shown a significant relationship between impairment in executive brain functions (such as abstract reasoning, problem solving, and motor skills) and aggressive behaviour.[40] Research using memorization and visual awareness tests, short-term auditory memory tests, and verbal IQ tests indicates that this relationship can be detected quite early and that children who suffer measurable neurological deficits at birth or in adolescence are more likely to become criminals later in life.[41]

Studies using an electroencephalogram (EEG)—a device that records electrical impulses in the brain—have found far higher levels of abnormal EEG recordings in violent criminals than in nonviolent or one-time offenders.[42] Although about 5 percent of the general population show abnormal EEG readings, about 50 to 60 percent of adolescents with known behaviour disorders display abnormal recordings.[43] Behaviours highly correlated with abnormal EEG readings include poor impulse control, inadequate social adaptation, hostility, temper tantrums, and destructiveness.[44]

neurophysiology The study of brain activity.

minimal brain dysfunction (MBD) An abruptly appearing, maladaptive behaviour, such as episodic periods of explosive rage.

Newer brain-scanning techniques using electronic imaging, such as positron emission tomography (PET), brain electrical activity mapping (BEAM), and superconducting interference device (SQUID), have made it possible to assess which areas of the brain are directly linked to antisocial behaviour.[45] Both violent criminals and substance abusers have been found to have impairment in the prefrontal lobes, thalamus, medial temporal lobe, and superior parietal and left angular gyrus areas of the brain.[46] Chronic violent criminals have far higher levels of brain dysfunction than the general population; murderers exhibit brain pathology at a rate 32 times greater than in the general population.[47]

Minimal Brain Dysfunction (MBD)

Related to abnormal cerebral structure, **minimal brain dysfunction (MBD)** has been defined as an abruptly appearing, maladaptive behaviour that interrupts an individual's lifestyle and life flow. One type of minimal brain dysfunction is manifested in episodic periods of explosive rage. This form of the disorder is considered an important cause of behaviours such as spouse and child abuse, suicide, aggressiveness, and motiveless homicide. One perplexing feature of this syndrome is that people who are afflicted with it often maintain warm, pleasant personalities between episodes of violence. Studies measuring the presence of minimal brain dysfunction in offender populations have found that up to 60 percent exhibit brain dysfunction on psychological tests.[48] More sophisticated brain-scanning techniques, such as PET, have also shown that brain abnormality is linked to violent crime.[49]

Attention Deficit/Hyperactivity Disorder (ADHD)

Many parents have noticed that their children do not pay attention to them—they run around and do things in their own way. Sometimes this inattention is a function of age; in other instances it is a symptom of **attention deficit/hyperactivity disorder (ADHD)**, in which a child shows a developmentally inappropriate lack of attention, impulsivity, and hyperactivity. The various symptoms of ADHD are listed in Table 5.1. About 3 percent of children, most often boys, are believed to suffer from this disorder,

TABLE 5.1

Symptoms of Attention Deficit/Hyperactivity Disorder

Lack of Attention	Impulsivity	Hyperactivity
Frequently fails to finish projects	Frequently acts without thinking	Constantly runs around and climbs on things
Does not seem to pay attention	Often "calls out" in class	Shows excessive motor activity while asleep
Does not sustain interest in play activities	Does not want to wait his or her turn in lines or games	Cannot sit still; is constantly fidgeting
Cannot sustain concentration on schoolwork or related tasks	Shifts from activity to activity	Does not remain in his or her seat in class
Is easily distracted	Cannot organize tasks or work	Is constantly on the go like a "motor"
	Requires constant supervision	

Source: Reprinted with permission from *The Diagnostic and Statistical Manual of Mental Disorders*, Fourth Edition, Text Revision, Copyright 2000. American Psychiatric Association.

attention deficit/hyperactivity disorder (ADHD) A developmentally inappropriate lack of attention, along with impulsivity and hyperactivity.

and it is the most common reason children are referred to mental health clinics. The condition has been associated with poor school performance, grade retention, placement in special needs classes, bullying, stubbornness, and lack of response to discipline.[50] Although the origin of ADHD is still unknown, suspected causes include neurological damage, prenatal stress, and even reactions to food additives and chemical allergies. Recent research has suggested a genetic link.[51] There are also links to family turmoil: mothers of ADHD children are more likely to be divorced or separated, and ADHD children are much more likely to move to new locales than non-ADHD children.[52] It may be possible that emotional turmoil either produces symptoms of ADHD or, if they already exist, causes them to intensify.

The nearby scan compares a normal brain (left) and an ADHD brain (right). Differing shades contrast normal and abnormally low metabolic rates. Why is ADHD so prevalent in North America today? Some experts believe that our immigrant forebears, risk takers who impulsively left their homelands for life in a new world, may have brought with them a genetic predisposition for ADHD.

Research studies now link ADHD to the onset and maintenance of a delinquent career.[53] Children diagnosed as having ADHD are more likely to be suspended from school and to engage in criminal behaviour as adults. This ADHD–crime association is important because symptoms of ADHD seem stable through adolescence into adulthood[54]; therefore, early diagnosis and treatment of children with ADHD may enhance their life chances. Today the most typical treatment is doses of stimulants, such as Ritalin, which ironically help control emotional and behavioural outbursts. The relationship between chronic delinquency and attention disorders may also be mediated by school performance. Children who are poor readers are the most prone to antisocial behaviour; many poor readers also have attention problems.[55] Early school-based intervention programs may thus benefit children with ADHD.

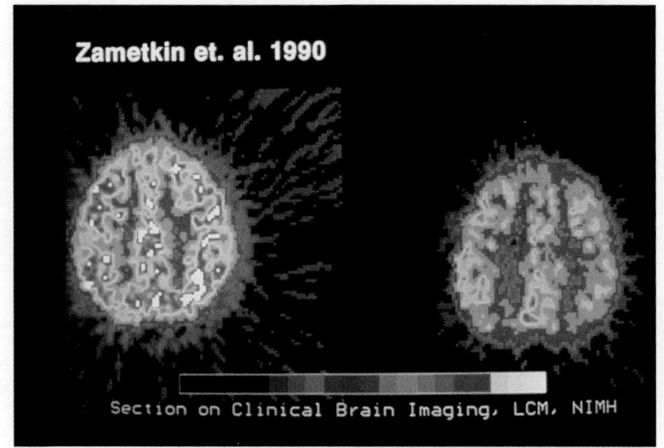

Dr. Alan Zametkin/Clinical Brain Imaging, Courtesy of Office of Scientific Information, NIMH.

© VStock/Alamy

LO2 Fetal Alcohol Spectrum Disorder (FASD)

In 1970, while doing research for her thesis on infants who were hospitalized because they failed to thrive after birth, University of Washington medical student Christine Ulleland found that nearly half of the mothers of the at-risk infants she studied had a history of alcoholism. When other medical researchers began to look more closely at the link between alcohol and pre- and postnatal health problems, they began to notice a distinctive pattern of physical and behavioural characteristics in the infants and children of alcoholic mothers. In 1973, medical researchers Kenneth Lyon Jones and David Smith coined the term *Fetal Alcohol Syndrome*. Though there are as yet no firm guidelines for diagnosing FAS, scientists believe that a range or spectrum of physical characteristics (small eyes; flat face; thin, flat upper lip; poor walking coordination) and neurological problems (lower intelligence, language deficits, short attention span, lack of impulse control, problems with memory and thinking) are characteristic of individuals who have what has come to be known as Fetal Alcohol Spectrum Disorder (FASD).[56]

In recent years, increasing attention has been paid to possible links between what has come to be known as FASD and involvement in crime, in particular the link between FASD, lower intelligence, and a lack of impulse control.[57] According to Chapman (2008), as many as half of inmates in the federal correctional system may have prenatal alcohol-related physical and neurological impairments, and as many as 300 000 Canadians currently have symptoms of FAS with a disproportionate number of these cases found among Aboriginal people.[58] According to research conducted by Streissguth and colleagues (2004), 60 percent of the individuals with FASD they studied had trouble with the law, nearly half had engaged in inappropriate sexual behaviour, 35 percent had a drug or alcohol problem, and 80 percent had not been raised by their biological parents. For individuals with FASD, lower intelligence, inability to understand and predict the consequences of their actions, and lack of impulse control are factors that make it more likely they will engage in actions that will bring them into contact with the legal system.[59] The suspected relationship between FASD and involvement in crime prompted the Department of Justice Canada in 2004 to commission a special study of the problem titled "Fetal Alcohol Syndrome and the Youth Criminal Justice System: A Discussion Paper"; websites providing information about the links between alcohol consumption, pregnancy, FASD and physical, neurological, and behavioural problems (including involvement with the justice system) have sprung up across Canada. Still, Verbrugge points out that there are many questions to be answered about the relationship between FASD and criminal behaviour, including (1) how many offenders in the youth and adult justice system have FASD, (2) what are the legal implications of having FASD (e.g., fit to stand trial), and (3) how do we provide treatment to individuals with FASD and how effective will these treatments be in reducing their likelihood of getting in trouble with the law?[60]

neurotransmitters
Chemical compounds that influence or activate brain functions.

Brain Chemistry

Neurotransmitters are chemical compounds that influence or activate brain functions. Those studied in relation to aggression include dopamine, norepinephrine, serotonin, monoamine oxidase, and GABA.[61] Evidence exists that abnormal levels of these chemicals are associated with aggression. Studies of habitually violent Finnish criminals show that low serotonin (5-hydroxytryptamine; 5-HT) levels are associated with poor impulse control and hyperactivity. In addition, a relatively low concentration of 5-hydroxyindoleacetic acid (5-HIAA) predicts increased irritability, sensation seeking, and impaired impulse control.[62]

What is the link between brain chemistry and crime? Prenatal exposure of the brain to high levels of androgens can result in a brain structure that is less sensitive to environmental inputs. Affected individuals seek more intense and varied stimulation and are willing to tolerate more adverse consequences than individuals not so affected.[63] It has also been suggested that individuals with a low supply of the

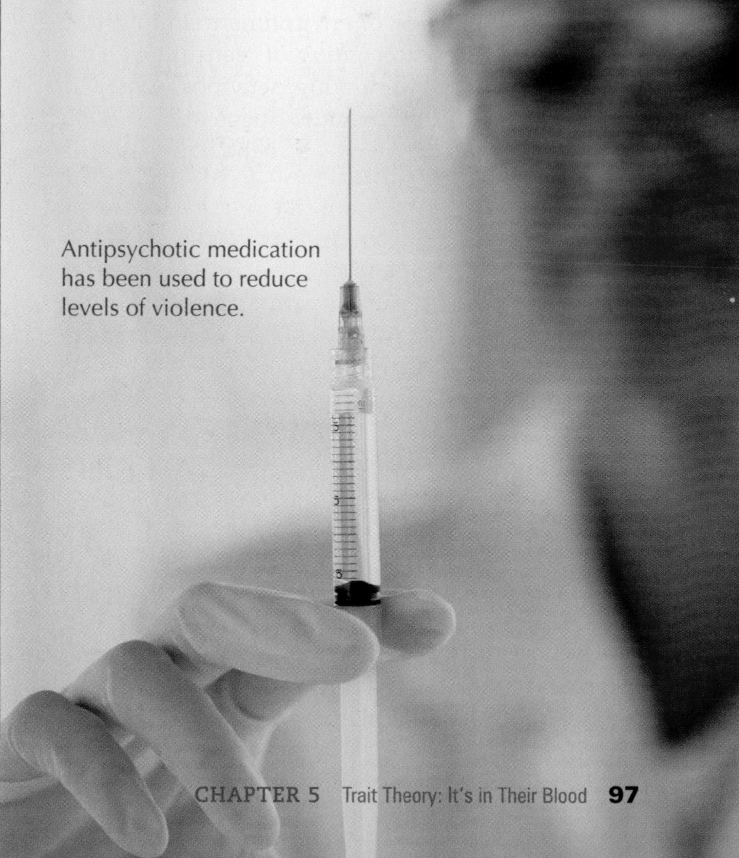
Antipsychotic medication has been used to reduce levels of violence.

arousal theory
The view that people seek to maintain a preferred level of arousal, but vary in how they process sensory input. A need for high levels of environmental stimulation may lead to aggressive, violent behaviour patterns.

enzyme monoamine oxidase (MAO) engage in behaviours linked with violence and property crime, including defiance of punishment, impulsivity, hyperactivity, poor academic performance, sensation seeking and risk taking, and recreational drug use. Abnormal MAO levels may explain both individual and group differences in the crime rate. For example, females have higher MAO levels than males, which may explain gender differences in the crime rate.[64]

Because this linkage has been found, it is not uncommon for violence-prone people to be treated with antipsychotic drugs, such as Haldol, Stelazine, Prolixin, and Risperdal. These drugs, which help control levels of neurotransmitters (such as serotonin or dopamine), are sometimes referred to as chemical restraints or chemical straitjackets.

Arousal Theory

According to **arousal theory**, for a variety of genetic and environmental reasons, people's brains function differently in response to environmental stimuli. All of us seek to maintain a preferred or optimal level of arousal: too much stimulation leaves us anxious and stressed, whereas too little makes us feel bored and weary. However, people vary in the way their brains process sensory input. Some nearly always feel comfortable with little stimulation, whereas others require a high degree of environmental input to feel comfortable. The latter group of "sensation seekers" look for stimulating activities, which may include aggressive, violent behaviour patterns.[65]

Although the factors that determine a person's level of arousal are not fully understood, suspected sources include brain chemistry (such as serotonin levels) and brain structure. Some brains have many more nerve cells with receptor sites for neurotransmitters than others. Another view is that people with low heart rates are more likely to commit crime because they seek stimulation to increase their arousal to normal levels.[66]

LO3 Genetics and Crime

Another biosocial theme is that the human traits associated with criminality have a genetic basis.[67] This line of reasoning was spotlighted in the 1970s when genetic testing of Richard Speck, the convicted killer of eight Chicago nurses, allegedly found that he had an abnormal XYY chromosomal structure (XY is normal in males). There was much public concern that all people with XYY chromosomes were potential killers and should be closely controlled. Civil libertarians expressed fear that all XYY males could be labelled dangerous and violent regardless of whether they had engaged in violent activities.[68] When it was disclosed that neither Speck nor most violent offenders actually had an extra Y chromosome, interest in the XYY theory dissipated.[69] However, the Speck case drew researchers' attention to looking for a genetic basis of crime.

Researchers have carefully explored the heritability of criminal tendencies by looking at a variety of factors. Some of the most important are described here.

Parental Deviance

If criminal tendencies are inherited, then the children of criminal parents should be more likely to become law violators than the offspring of conventional parents. A number of studies have found that parental criminality and deviance do, in fact, powerfully influence delinquent behaviour.[70] Some of the most important data on parental deviance were gathered by Donald J. West and David P. Farrington as part of the long-term Cambridge Youth Survey. These cohort data indicate that a significant number of delinquent youths have criminal fathers.[71] Whereas 8.4 percent of the sons of noncriminal fathers eventually became chronic offenders, about 37 percent of youths with

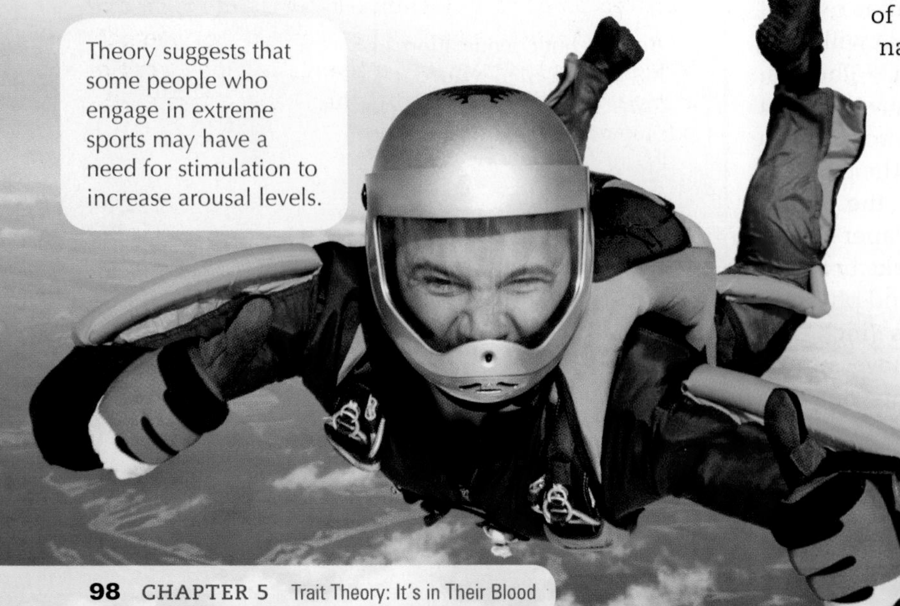
2happy/Shutterstock.com

Theory suggests that some people who engage in extreme sports may have a need for stimulation to increase arousal levels.

criminal fathers were multiple offenders.[72] In another important analysis, Farrington found that one type of parental deviance, schoolyard aggression or bullying, may be both inter- and intragenerational. Bullies have children who bully others, and these second-generation bullies grow up to father children who are also bullies, in a never-ending cycle.[73]

Although there is no certainty about the relationship between parental and child deviance, recent evidence indicates that at least part of the association is genetic.[74]

Twin Behaviour

If, in fact, inherited traits cause criminal behaviour, we might expect that twins would be quite similar in their antisocial activities. However, because twins are usually brought up in the same household and exposed to the same social conditions, determining whether their behaviour is a result of biological, sociological, or psychological conditions is difficult. Trait theorists have tried to overcome this dilemma by comparing identical, **monozygotic (MZ) twins** with fraternal, **dizygotic (DZ) twins**.[75] MZ twins are genetically identical, whereas DZ twins have only half their genes in common. If heredity determines criminal behaviour, we should expect that MZ twins would be much more similar in their antisocial activities than DZ twins.

The earliest studies conducted on twin behaviour detected a significant relationship between the criminal activities of MZ twins and a much lower association between those of DZ twins. A review of relevant studies found that 60 percent of MZ twins shared criminal behaviour patterns (if one twin was criminal, so was the other), whereas only 30 percent of DZ twins were similarly related.[76] These findings may be viewed as powerful evidence of a genetic basis for criminality. Similarly, criminologists David Rowe and D. Wayne Osgood analyzed the factors that influence self-reported delinquency in a sample of twin pairs and concluded that genetic influences have significant explanatory power.[77] Genetic effects significantly predict problem behaviours in children as young as three years old.[78] Although the behaviour of some twin pairs seems to be influenced by their environment, others display behaviour disturbances that can be explained only by their genetic similarity.[79]

Not all research efforts have found that MZ twin pairs are more closely related in their criminal behaviour than DZ or ordinary sibling pairs, and some have found an association that is at best modest.[80] On the other hand, some experts conclude that individuals who share genes are alike in personality regardless of how they are reared; environment, they argue, induces little or no personality resemblance in twin pairs.[81]

monozygotic (MZ) twins
Identical twins.

dizygotic (DZ) twins
Fraternal (nonidentical) twins.

Adoption Studies

It seems logical that if the behaviour of adopted children is more closely aligned to that of their biological parents than to that of their adoptive parents, then the idea of a genetic basis for criminality would be supported. If, on the other hand, adoptees' behaviour is more closely aligned to the behaviour of their adoptive parents than of their biological parents, an environmental basis for crime would seem more valid.

Several studies indicate that some relationship exists between biological parents' behaviour and the behaviour of their children, even when they have had no contact.[82] In what is considered the most significant study in this area, Barry Hutchings and Sarnoff Mednick analyzed 1145 male adoptees born in Copenhagen, Denmark, between 1927 and 1941. Of these, 185 had criminal records.[83] After following up on 143 of the criminal adoptees and matching them with a control group of 143 noncriminal adoptees, Hutchings and Mednick found that the biological father's criminality strongly predicted the child's criminal behaviour. When both the biological and the adoptive fathers were criminal, the probability that the youth would engage in criminal behaviour greatly increased. Of the boys whose adoptive and biological fathers were both criminals, 24.5 percent had been convicted of a criminal law violation. Only 13.5 percent of those whose biological and adoptive fathers were not criminals had similar conviction records.[84]

The findings of the twin and adoption studies tentatively support a genetic basis for criminality. However, those who dispute the genes–crime relationship point to inadequate research designs and weak methodologies in the supporting research. Newer, better-designed research studies, critics charge, provide less support than earlier, less methodologically sound studies.[85]

Evolutionary Views of Crime

Some criminologists believe that the human traits that produce violence and aggression have been advanced by the long process of human evolution.[86] According to this evolutionary view, the competition for scarce resources has influenced and shaped the human species.[87] Over the course of human existence, people whose personal characteristics allowed them to accumulate more than others were the most likely to breed and dominate the species. People have been shaped to engage in actions that promote their well-being and ensure the survival and reproduction of their genetic line. Males who are impulsive risk takers may be able to father more children because they are reckless in their social relationships and have sexual encounters with numerous partners. If, according to evolutionary theories, such behaviour patterns are inherited, impulsive behaviour becomes intergenerational, passed down from parents to children. It is therefore not surprising that human history has been marked by war, violence, and aggression.

The Evolution of Gender and Crime

Evolutionary concepts that have been linked to gender differences in violence rates are based loosely on mammalian mating patterns. To ensure survival of the gene pool (and the species), it is beneficial for a male of any species to mate with as many suitable females as possible, because each can bear his offspring. In contrast, because of the long period of gestation, females require a secure home and a single, stable, nurturing partner to ensure their survival. Because of these differences in mating patterns, the most aggressive males mate most often and have the greatest number of offspring. Therefore, over the history of the human species, aggressive males have had the greatest impact on the gene pool. The descendants of these aggressive males now account for the disproportionate amount of male aggression and violence.[88]

CONNECTIONS

The relationship between evolutionary factors and crime has just begun to be studied. Criminologists are now exploring how social organizations and institutions interact with biological traits to influence personal decision making, including criminal strategies. See the discussion of latent trait theories in Chapter 9 for more about the integration of biological and environmental factors.

Crime rate differences between the genders, then, may be less a matter of socialization than of inherent differences in mating patterns that have developed over time.[89] Among young men, reckless, life-threatening risk proneness is especially likely to evolve in cultures that force them to find suitable mates to ensure their ability to reproduce. Unless they are aggressive with potential mates and potential rivals for those suitable mates, they will remain childless.[90] High rates of spouse abuse in modern society may be a function of aggressive men seeking to control and possess mates. (See Figure 5.2.) Men who feel most threatened over the potential of losing mates to rivals are the most likely to engage in sexual violence. Research shows that women in common-law marriages, especially those who are much younger than their husbands, are at greater risk of abuse than older, married women. Abusive males may fear the potential loss of their younger mates, especially if

FIGURE 5.2

Impact of Spousal Violence for Victims

According to the 2004 General Social Survey (GSS), 7 percent of women living with a spouse, in either a common-law or marital relationship, reported being physically or sexually assaulted by their partner at least once during the previous five years.

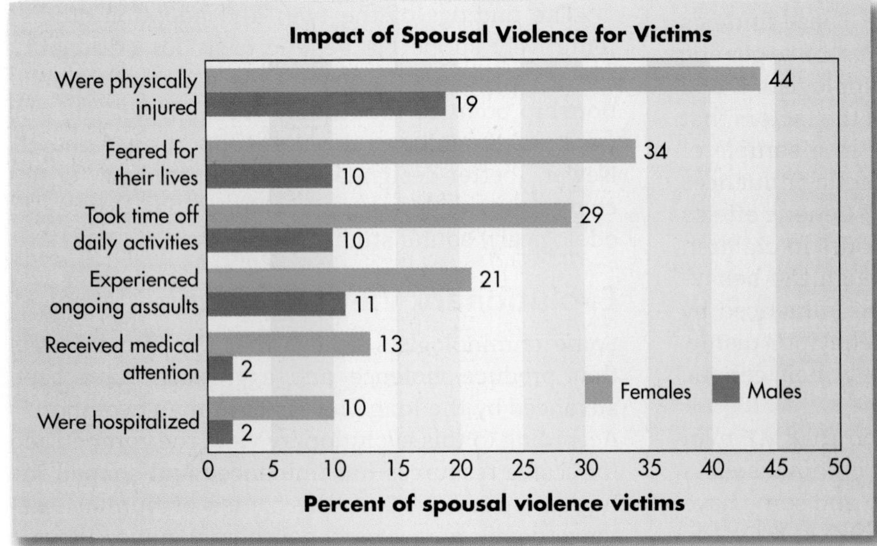

Note: Figures may not add up to 100 percent due to multiple responses.

Adapted from Statistics Canada publication "Measuring Violence Against Women, Statistical Trends 2006," Catalogue 85-570-XIE2006001 (http://www.statcan.gc.ca/pub/85-570-x/85-570-x2006001-eng.pdf).

they are not bound by a marriage contract, and may use force for purposes of control and possession.[91]

"Cheater" Theory

According to **cheater theory**, a subpopulation of men has evolved with genes that incline them toward extremely low parental involvement. They are sexually aggressive and use cunning to achieve sexual conquest of as many females as possible. Because females would not willingly choose them as mates, they use stealth to gain sexual access, including tactics such as mimicking the behaviour of more stable males. These deceptive reproductive tactics spill over into other endeavours, where their irresponsible, opportunistic behaviour supports their antisocial activities. Deceptive reproductive strategies, then, are linked to a deceitful lifestyle.[92]

Psychologist Byron Roth notes that cheater-type males may be especially attractive to younger, less intelligent women who begin having children at a very early age. Government-sponsored welfare, claims Roth, removes the need for potential mates to have the resources required of stable providers and family caretakers.[93] With the government meeting their financial needs, these women are drawn to men who are physically attractive and flamboyant. Their fleeting courtship produces children with low IQ scores, aggressive personalities, and little chance of proper socialization in father-absent families. According to Roth, over time, these children will grow up to be cheaters who are both antisocial and sexually aggressive.

CONNECTIONS

Biosocial theory focuses on the violent crimes of the lower classes while ignoring the white-collar crimes of the upper and middle classes. That is, although it may seem logical to believe there is a biological basis to aggression and violence, it is more difficult to explain how insider trading and fraud are biologically related. For the causes of white-collar crime, see Chapter 12.

Evaluation of the Biological Branch of Trait Theory

cheater theory
A theory suggesting that a subpopulation of men has evolved with genes that incline them toward extremely low parental involvement. Sexually aggressive, they use deceit for sexual conquest of as many females as possible.

Biosocial perspectives on crime have raised some challenging questions. Critics find some of these theories racist and dysfunctional. If there are biological explanations for street crimes such as assault, murder, or rape, the argument goes, and if, as official crime statistics suggest, the poor and minority-group members commit a disproportionate number of such acts, then by implication biological theory says that members of these groups are biologically different, flawed, or inferior.

Biological explanations for the geographic, social, and temporal patterns in the crime rate are also problematic. Is it possible that more people are genetically predisposed to crime in the West and North than in Central and Eastern Canada? Furthermore, biological theory seems to divide people into criminals and noncriminals on the basis of their genetic and physical makeup, ignoring self-reports that indicate almost everyone has engaged in some type of illegal activity.

Biosocial theorists counter that their views should not be confused with Lombrosian, deterministic biology. Rather than suggesting that there are born criminals and noncriminals, they maintain that some people carry the potential to be violent or antisocial and that environmental conditions can sometimes trigger antisocial responses.[94] This would explain why some otherwise law-abiding citizens perform a single, seemingly unexplainable antisocial act and, conversely, why some people with long criminal careers often behave conventionally. The most significant criticism of biosocial theory has been the lack of adequate empirical testing. Most research samples are relatively small and nonrepresentative. A great deal of biosocial research is conducted with samples of adjudicated offenders who have been placed in clinical treatment settings. Methodological problems make it impossible to determine whether findings apply only to offenders who have been convicted of crimes and placed in treatment or to all criminals.[95] More research is needed to clarify the relationships proposed by biosocial researchers and to silence critics.

LO4 Psychological Trait Theories

The second branch of trait theory focuses on the psychological aspects of crime, including the associations

psychodynamic (psychoanalytic)
Theory originated by Freud that the human personality is controlled by unconscious mental processes developed early in childhood, involving the interaction of id, ego, and superego.

id
The primitive part of people's mental makeup, present at birth, that represents unconscious biological drives for food, sex, and other life-sustaining necessities. The id seeks instant gratification without concern for the rights of others.

ego
The part of the personality, developed in early childhood, that helps control the id and keep people's actions within the boundaries of social convention.

superego
Incorporation within the personality of the moral standards and values of parents, community, and significant others.

among intelligence, personality, learning, and criminal behaviour. This view has a long history, and psychologists, psychiatrists, and other mental health professionals have long played an active role in formulating criminological theory.

Among 19th-century pioneers in this area were Charles Goring (1870–1919) and Gabriel Tarde (1843–1904). Goring studied 3000 English convicts and found little difference in the physical characteristics of criminals and noncriminals. However, he uncovered a significant relationship between crime and a condition he referred to as "defective intelligence," which involved traits such as feeblemindedness, epilepsy, insanity, and defective social instinct.[96] Tarde was the forerunner of modern learning theorists, who hold that people learn from one another through imitation.[97]

In their quest to understand and treat all varieties of abnormal mental conditions, psychologists have encountered clients whose behaviour falls within the categories that society has labelled as criminal, deviant, violent, and antisocial. A number of different psychological views have been associated with criminal behaviour causation (see Figure 5.3). The most important of these perspectives are discussed in the following sections.

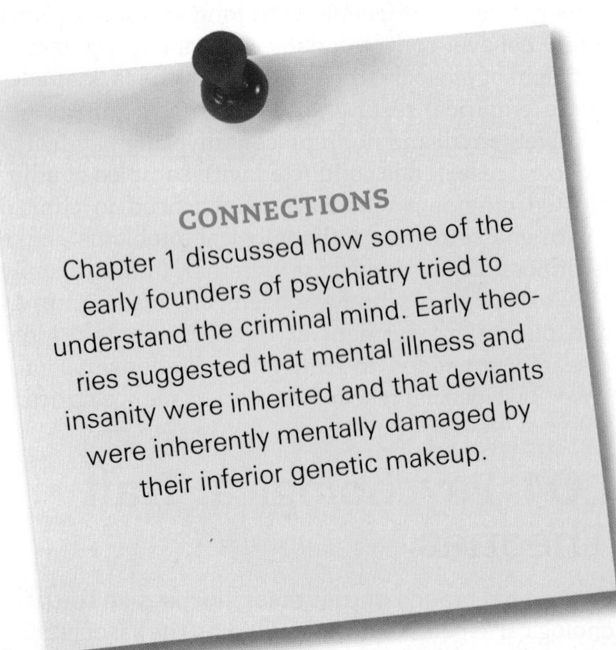

CONNECTIONS
Chapter 1 discussed how some of the early founders of psychiatry tried to understand the criminal mind. Early theories suggested that mental illness and insanity were inherited and that deviants were inherently mentally damaged by their inferior genetic makeup.

Sigmund Freud (1856–1939)

The Psychodynamic Perspective

Psychodynamic (or **psychoanalytic**) psychology was originated by Viennese psychiatrist Sigmund Freud (1856–1939) and has remained a prominent segment of psychological theory ever since.[98] Freud believed that we all carry with us residue of the most significant emotional attachments of our childhood, which then guides our future interpersonal relationships.

According to Freud's version of psychodynamic theory, the human personality has a three-part structure. The **id** is the primitive part of people's mental makeup, present at birth, that represents unconscious biological drives for food, sex, and other life-sustaining necessities. The id seeks instant gratification without concern for the rights of others. The **ego** develops early in life, when a child begins to learn that his or her wishes cannot be instantly gratified. The ego is the part of the personality that compensates for the demands of the id by helping the individual guide his or her actions to remain within the boundaries of social convention. The **superego** develops as a result of incorporating within the personality the moral standards and values of parents, community, and significant others. It is the moral aspect of people's personalities; it judges their behaviour.

FIGURE 5.3

Psychological Perspectives on Criminology

Theory	Cause
PSYCHODYNAMIC (psychoanalytic)	**Intrapsychic processes** • Unconscious conflicts • Defences • Tendencies • Anger • Sexuality
BEHAVIOURAL	**Learning processes** • Past experiences • Stimulus • Rewards and punishments
COGNITIVE	**Information processing** • Thinking • Planning • Memory • Perspective • Ethical values
Trait	**Cause**
PERSONALITY	**Personality processes** • Antisocial personality • Sociopath/psychopath temperament • Abnormal affect, lack of emotional depth
INTELLIGENCE	**Intellectual processes** • Low IQ • Poor school performance • Bad decision making

Psychodynamics of Abnormal Behaviour

Psychodynamic theory originally used the term **neurotic** to refer to people who experienced feelings of mental anguish and feared that they were losing control of their personalities. People who had completely lost control and who were dominated by their primitive id were referred to as **psychotic**. Today these terms have, for the most part, been replaced by the term **disorder**, as in *anxiety disorders, mood disorders*, and *conduct disorders*. The most serious disorder is **schizophrenia**, marked by hearing nonexistent voices, seeing hallucinations, and exhibiting inappropriate responses.

People with schizophrenia have illogical, incoherent thought processes and lack insight into their behaviour. They may experience delusions and hallucinate. For example, they may see themselves as agents of the devil, avenging angels, or the

Accused of beheading a fellow Greyhound bus passenger, Vincent Li is escorted by police.

THE CANADIAN PRESS/John Woods

recipients of messages from animals and plants. Serial killer David Berkowitz, dubbed "Son of Sam" or the "44-calibre killer," claimed that his 1976–1977 killing spree began after he received messages from a neighbour's dog. People with paranoid schizophrenia, such as Aaron Millar, who used a ceremonial sword to kill his mother in her Victoria, B.C., home in 1997, suffer complex behavioural delusions involving wrongdoing or persecution—they think everyone is out to get them.[99]

Psychodynamics of Criminal Behaviour

Since Freud's original research, psychoanalysts have continued to view criminals as id-dominated persons who suffer from one or more disorders that render them incapable of controlling impulsive, pleasure-seeking drives.[100] The psychoanalyst whose work is most closely associated with criminality is August Aichorn.[101] After examining many delinquent youths, Aichorn concluded that societal stress, though damaging, could not in itself cause a life of crime unless a predisposition existed that psychologically prepared youths for antisocial acts. This mental state, which he

neurotic
In Freudian psychology, a personality marked by mental anguish and feared loss of control.

psychotic
In Freudian psychology, a personality marked by complete loss of control over the id, characterized by delusions, hallucinations, and sudden mood shifts.

disorder
Any type of psychological problem (formerly labelled neurotic or psychotic), such as anxiety disorders, mood disorders, and conduct disorders.

schizophrenia
A severe disorder marked by hearing nonexistent voices, seeing hallucinations, and exhibiting inappropriate responses.

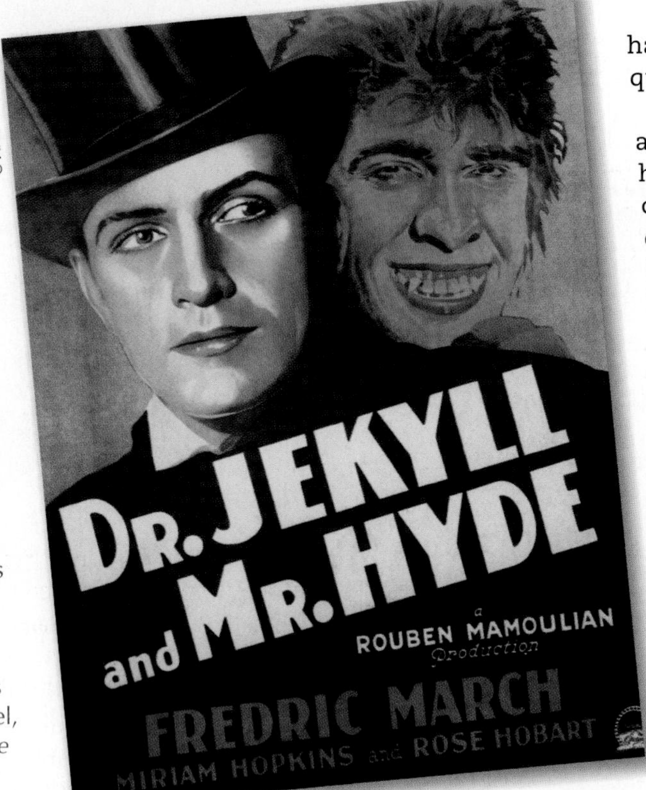

Famous writer Robert Louis Stevenson was heavily influenced by Freud's concept of the id-controlled personality as evidenced in his best-selling novel, *The Strange Case of Dr. Jekyll and Mr. Hyde*.

labelled **latent delinquency**, is found in youngsters whose personality requires them to:

- Seek immediate gratification (act impulsively)
- Consider satisfying their personal needs to be more important than relating to others
- Satisfy instinctual urges without considering right and wrong (i.e., they lack guilt)

The psychodynamic model of the criminal offender depicts an aggressive, frustrated person dominated by events that occurred early in childhood. Perhaps as a result of unhappy experiences in childhood or families that could not provide proper love and care, criminals suffer from weak or damaged egos that make them unable to cope with conventional society. Weak egos are associated with immaturity, poor social skills, and excessive dependence on others. People with weak egos may be easily led into crime by antisocial peers and drug abuse. Some offenders have underdeveloped superegos and consequently lack internalized representations of those behaviours that are punished in conventional society. They commit crimes because they have difficulty understanding the consequences of their actions.[102]

latent delinquency
A psychological predisposition to commit antisocial acts because of an id-dominated personality that renders an individual incapable of controlling impulsive, pleasure-seeking drives.

bipolar disorder
An emotional disturbance in which moods alternate between periods of wild elation and deep depression.

Offenders, then, have various mood and behaviour disorders. They may be histrionic, depressed, antisocial, or narcissistic.[103] They may exhibit conduct disorders (long histories of antisocial behaviour) or mood disorders (disturbance in expressed emotions). Among the latter is **bipolar disorder**, in which moods alternate between periods of wild elation and deep depression.[104] Some offenders are driven by an unconscious desire to be punished for prior sins, either real or imaginary. They may violate the law to gain attention or punish their parents.

From this perspective, then, crime is a manifestation of feelings of oppression and people's inability to develop the proper psychological defences and rationales to keep these feelings under control. Criminality allows troubled people to survive by producing positive psychic results: It helps them feel free and independent, and it gives them the possibility of excitement and the chance to use their skills and imagination. In addition, it allows them to blame others for their predicament (e.g., the police), and it gives them a chance to rationalize their sense of failure ("If I hadn't gotten into trouble, I could have been a success").[105]

LO5 Crime and Mental Illness

In the early evening of July 30, 2008, a horrific scene unfolded on the side of the Trans-Canada Highway near Portage la Prairie, Manitoba. Vincent Li, 40, a passenger on a Greyhound bus travelling east from Edmonton to Thunder Bay, attacked and repeatedly stabbed fellow passenger Tim McLean, 22, as panicked passengers called out for the bus driver to stop the bus and scrambled to get off. Horrified passengers stood at the side of the highway as Li proceeded to decapitate the victim. Li was arrested at the scene by RCMP officers as he attempted to escape out a bus window. According to the court-appointed forensic psychiatrist who later examined Li, he had heard voices earlier that day telling him to use an assumed name and get on a bus. He chose to sit next to the victim, because Tim McLean had made a "friendly gesture" to him. The voices told Li that McLean was "a force of evil" who would kill him if Li did not strike first.[106] Li was deemed by the court unfit to stand trial as he was suffering from schizophrenia, and sent to Selkirk Mental Health Centre in Winnipeg, Manitoba for further assessment and treatment. In March 2009, he was found not criminally responsible.[107]

Psychodynamic theory suggests a linkage between mental illness and crime. Although the association appears clear-cut, empirical evidence has been contradictory.

Many early research efforts found that offenders who engage in serious, violent crimes suffer from some sort of mental disturbance. Studies of adolescent males accused of murder found that 75 percent could be classified as having some mental illness, including schizophrenia.[108] Abusive mothers have been found to have mood and personality disorders and a history of psychiatric diagnoses.[109] The diagnosed mentally ill appear in arrest and court statistics at a rate disproportionate to their presence in the population.[110]

Despite this evidence, questions remain as to whether the mentally ill population has a greater inclination toward criminal behaviour than the mentally sound. The mentally ill may in fact be more likely to withdraw or harm themselves or be victimized than to act aggressively toward others.[111] Research shows that after release, prisoners with prior histories of hospitalization for mental disorders are less likely to be rearrested than those who have never been hospitalized.[112] Even research that finds a mental illness–crime association indicates that the great majority of known criminals are not mentally ill and that the relationship is modest at best. And if there is a statistically significant association between mental illness and crime, the fact remains that most mentally ill people are not criminals.

There has been much recent research regarding an association between mental illness and violence. The conventional view was that there was little evidence to support a strong association between mental illness and violence. As Monahan and Steadman (1983) concluded, "... the relation between crime and mental disorder can be accounted for largely by demographic and historical characteristics that the two groups share" (p. 152).[113] As Douglas (2009) noted, by the early 1990s, a shift could be detected in the conventional view as studies began to emerge suggesting that although the majority of people with serious mental illness are not violent, the probability of committing violence was greater for people with a serious mental illness than for those in the general population.[114] According to Douglas, the strongest evidence in favour of a link comes from those investigations that have moved beyond the broad categorization of mental illness to an examination of the relationship between subcategories such as psychosis (e.g., schizophrenia) and specific symptoms (e.g., hallucinations and delusions).[115] Recently, support for the existence of a relationship between psychosis and violence has come from two **meta-analytic studies**. Investigating the association between violence and schizophrenia and other psychoses in the general population, Fazel, Gulati, Linsell, Geddes, and Grann (2009) conducted a meta-analysis on 20 studies reporting data from 18 423 individuals with schizophrenia and other psychoses. The investigators found that the risk of violent outcomes for those having a schizophrenic disorder was 4 to 5 times greater than the general population, and between 14 and 25 times greater for homicide.[116] Also, they found that the presence of substance use disorders in addition to schizophrenia substantially increased the risk, which was estimated to be four times higher compared to individuals with schizophrenia without substance use disorders.[117] The second meta-analytic study, which was conducted by Canadian criminologist Steven Douglas et al. (2009), published in the same year, examined 204 studies and found that psychosis was reliably associated with a 49 percent to 68 percent increased likelihood of violence. Like Fazel et al. (2009), Douglas et al. (2009) found that comorbid psychosis and substance-related diagnoses substantially increased the risk of violence.[118]

meta-analytic studies
A systematic method of evaluating statistical data based on results of several independent studies of the same problem. In effect, it is a "study of studies" on the same subject.

behaviour theory
The view that all human behaviour is learned through a process of social reinforcement (rewards and punishment).

The Behavioural Perspective

Behaviour theory maintains that human actions are developed through learning experiences. The major

DID YOU KNOW?

- According to psychodynamic theory, unconscious motivations developed early in childhood propel some people into destructive or illegal behaviour.
- Behaviourists view aggression as a learned behaviour.
- Learning may be either direct and experiential or observational, such as watching TV and movies.
- Cognitive theory stresses knowing and perception. Some people have a warped view of the world.
- There is evidence that people with abnormal or antisocial personalities are crime-prone.
- While some criminologists find a link between intelligence and crime, others dispute any linkage between IQ level and law-violating behaviours.

social learning theory
The view that people learn to be aggressive by observing others acting aggressively to achieve some goal or being rewarded for violent acts.

behaviour modelling
Process of learning behaviour (notably aggression) by observing others. Aggressive models may be parents, criminals in the neighbourhood, or characters on television or in movies.

premise of behaviour theory is that people alter their behaviour according to the reactions it receives from others: Behaviour is supported by rewards and extinguished by negative reactions or punishments. The behaviourist views crimes, especially violent acts, as learned responses to life situations that do not necessarily represent abnormality or moral immaturity.

The branch of behaviour theory most relevant to criminology is **social learning theory**.[119] Social learning theorists, most notably Albert Bandura, argue that people are not actually born with the ability to act violently, but that they learn to be aggressive through their life experiences. These experiences include personally observing others acting aggressively to achieve some goal or watching people being rewarded for violent acts on television or in movies. People learn to act aggressively when, as children, they model their behaviour after the violent acts of adults. Later in life, these violent behaviour patterns persist in social relationships. For example, the boy who sees his father repeatedly strike his mother with impunity is likely to become a battering parent and husband.

Although social learning theorists agree that mental or physical traits may predispose a person toward violence, they believe that a person's violent tendencies are activated by factors in the environment. The specific form of aggressive behaviour, the frequency with which it is expressed, the situations in which it is displayed, and the specific targets selected for attack are largely determined by social learning. However, people are also self-aware and engage in purposeful learning. Their interpretations of behaviour outcomes and situations influence the way they learn from experiences. One adolescent who spends a weekend in jail for drunk driving may find it the most awful experience of her life—one that teaches her never to drink and drive again. Another person, however, may find it an exciting experience about which he can brag to his friends.

Social learning theorists view violence as something learned through a process called **behaviour modelling**. In modern society, aggressive acts are usually modelled after three principal sources:

1. *Family interaction.* Studies of family life show that aggressive children have parents who use similar tactics when dealing with others.

2. *Environmental experiences.* People who reside in areas where violence occurs daily are more likely to act violently than those who dwell in low-crime areas whose norms stress conventional behaviour.

3. *Mass media.* Films and television shows commonly depict violence graphically. Moreover, violence is often portrayed as acceptable, especially for heroes who never have to face legal consequences for their actions.[120] Viewing violence is believed to influence behaviour in a number of ways:

- Media violence can provide aggressive scripts that children store in memory. Repeated exposure to these scripts can increase their retention and change attitudes.
- Children learn from what they observe. In the same way they learn cognitive and social skills from their parents and friends, children learn to be violent by watching television.
- Television violence increases the arousal levels of viewers and makes them more prone to act aggressively. Studies measuring the galvanic skin response of subjects—a physical indication of arousal based on the amount of electricity conducted across the palm of the hand—show that viewing violent television shows increases arousal levels in young children.
- Watching television violence promotes negative attitudes such as suspiciousness and the expectation that the viewer will become involved in violence. Those who watch television frequently view aggression and violence as common, socially acceptable behaviour.

Dmitriy Shironosov/Shutterstock.com

- Television violence allows aggressive youths to justify their behaviour. Rather than causing violence, television may help violent youths rationalize their behaviour as socially acceptable.
- Television violence may disinhibit aggressive behaviour, which is normally controlled by other learning processes. Disinhibition takes place when adults are viewed as being rewarded for violence and when violence is seen as socially acceptable. This contradicts previous learning experiences in which violent behaviour was viewed as wrong.[121]

Social learning theorists have tried to determine what triggers violent acts. One position is that a direct, pain-producing, physical assault will usually trigger a violent response. Yet the relationship between painful attacks and aggressive responses has been found to be inconsistent. Whether people counterattack depends, in part, on their fighting skill and their perception of the strength of their attackers. Verbal taunts and insults have also been linked to aggressive responses. People who are predisposed to aggression by their learning experiences are likely to view insults from others as a challenge to their social status and to react violently.

In summary, social learning theorists suggest that the following four factors may contribute to violent or aggressive behaviour:

1. *An event that heightens arousal*—such as a person's frustrating or provoking another through physical assault or verbal abuse.
2. *Aggressive skills*—learned aggressive responses picked up from observing others, either personally or through the media.
3. *Expected outcomes*—the belief that aggression will somehow be rewarded. Rewards can come in the form of reducing tension or anger, gaining some financial reward, building self-esteem, or gaining the praise of others.
4. *Consistency of behaviour with values*—the belief, gained from observing others, that aggression is justified and appropriate, given the circumstances of the current situation.

The Cognitive Perspective

One area of psychology that has received increasing recognition in recent years is **cognitive theory**. Psychologists with a cognitive perspective focus on mental processes—how people perceive and mentally represent the world around them and solve problems. The pioneers of this school were Wilhelm Wundt (1832–1920), Edward Titchener (1867–1927), and William James (1842–1910). Today the cognitive area includes several subdisciplines. The moral development branch is concerned with how people morally represent and reason about the world. Humanistic psychology stresses self-awareness and getting in touch with feelings. **Information-processing theory** focuses on how people process, store, encode, retrieve, and manipulate information to make decisions and solve problems.

When cognitive theorists who study information processing try to explain antisocial behaviour, they do so in terms of mental perception and how people use information to understand their environment. When people make decisions, they engage in a sequence of cognitive thought processes:

1. First, they encode information so that it can be interpreted.
2. Next, they search for a proper response and decide on the most appropriate action.
3. Finally, they act on their decision.[122]

cognitive theory
Psychological perspective that focuses on mental processes—how people perceive and mentally represent the world around them and solve problems.

information-processing theory
Theory that focuses on how people process, store, encode, retrieve, and manipulate information to make decisions and solve problems.

personality
The reasonably stable patterns of behaviour, including thoughts and emotions, that distinguish one person from another.

According to this cognitive approach, people who use information properly, who are better conditioned to make reasoned judgments, and who can make quick and reasoned decisions when facing emotion-laden events are best able to avoid antisocial behaviour choices.[123] In contrast, violence-prone people may use information incorrectly when they make decisions. One reason is that they may be relying on mental scripts learned in childhood that tell them how to interpret events, what to expect, how they should react, and what the outcome of the interaction should be.[124] Hostile children may have learned improper scripts by observing how others react to events; their own parents' aggressive, inappropriate behaviour would have considerable impact. Some may have had early, prolonged exposure to violence (such as child abuse), which increases their sensitivity to slights and maltreatment. Oversensitivity to rejection by their peers is a continuation of sensitivity to rejection by their parents.[125] Violence becomes a stable behaviour because the scripts that emphasize aggressive responses are repeatedly rehearsed as the child matures.

Information-processing theory has been used to explain the occurrence of date rape. Sexually violent males believe that when their dates refuse sexual advances, the women are really playing games and actually want to be taken forcefully.[126]

The Personality and Crime Perspective

Personality can be defined as the reasonably stable patterns of behaviour, including thoughts and emotions, that distinguish one person from another.[127] One's personality reflects a characteristic way of

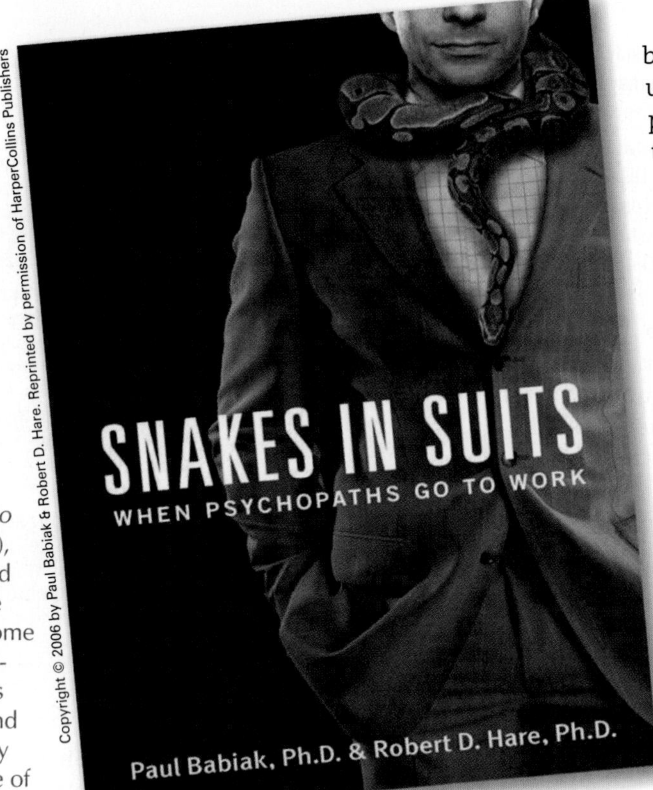

In their book *Snakes in Suits: When Psychopaths Go To Work* (2006), Paul Babiak and Robert D. Hare explain how some successful business executives exhibit traits and behaviours very similar to those of a psychopath.

antisocial personality
Combination of traits, such as hyperactivity, impulsivity, hedonism, and inability to empathize with others, that make a person prone to deviant behaviour and violence; also referred to as sociopathic or psychopathic personality.

adapting to life's demands and problems. The way we behave is a function of how our personality enables us to interpret life events and make appropriate behavioural choices. Can the cause of crime be linked to personality?

Several research efforts have attempted to identify criminal personality traits.[128] Suspected traits include impulsivity, hostility, and aggression.[129] For example, Hans Eysenck associates two personality traits with antisocial behaviour: extraversion-introversion and stability-instability. Extreme introverts are overaroused and avoid sources of stimulation; extreme extroverts are underaroused and seek sensation. Introverts are slow to learn and be conditioned; extroverts are impulsive individuals who lack the ability to examine their own motives and behaviours. Those who are unstable, a condition that Eysenck calls neuroticism, are anxious, tense, and emotionally unstable.[130] People who are both neurotic and extroverted lack self-insight and are impulsive and emotionally unstable; they are unlikely to have reasoned judgments of life events. Whereas extroverted neurotics may act self-destructively, for example, by abusing drugs, more stable people will be able to reason that such behaviour is ultimately harmful. Eysenck believes that personality is controlled by genetic factors and is heritable.

A number of other personality deficits have been identified in the criminal population. A common theme is that criminals are hyperactive, impulsive individuals with short attention spans (attention deficit disorder), conduct disorders, anxiety disorders, and depression.[131] They lack affect, cannot empathize with others, and are shortsighted and hedonistic. These traits make them prone to problems ranging from psychopathology to drug abuse, sexual promiscuity, and violence.[132] As a group, people who share these traits are believed to have a character defect referred to as sociopathic, psychopathic, or **antisocial personality**. Although these terms are often used interchangeably, some psychologists distinguish between sociopaths and psychopaths by suggesting that the former are a product of a destructive home environment, whereas the latter are a product of a defect or aberration within themselves.[133]

Studies of the antisocial personality have been conducted worldwide.[134] There is evidence that offenders with an antisocial personality are crime-prone, respond to frustrating events with strong negative emotions, feel stressed and harassed, and are adversarial in their interpersonal relationships. They maintain "negative emotionality"—a tendency to experience aversive affective states such as anger, anxiety, and irritability. They also are predisposed to weak personal constraints and have difficulty controlling impulsive behaviour urges. Because they are both impulsive and aggressive, crime-prone people are quick to act against perceived threats.

Evidence that personality traits predict crime and violence suggests that the root cause of crime can be found in the forces that influence early human development. If these results are valid, rather than focus on job creation and neighbourhood improvement, crime control efforts might be better focused on helping families raise reasoned, reflective children who enjoy a safe environment.

The Intelligence and Crime Perspective

Early criminologists maintained that many delinquents and criminals have below-average intelligence and that low IQ causes their criminality.

Criminals were believed to have inherently substandard intelligence and thus seemed naturally inclined to commit more crimes than more intelligent persons. Furthermore, it was thought that if authorities could determine which individuals had low IQs, they might identify potential criminals before they committed socially harmful acts. These ideas led to the nature-versus-nurture controversy that continues to rage today.

Nature Theory

Proponents of **nature theory** argue that intelligence is largely determined genetically, that ancestry determines IQ, and that low intelligence, as demonstrated by low IQ, is linked to criminal behaviour. When newly developed IQ tests were administered to inmates of prisons and juvenile training schools in the first decades of the 20th century, the nature position gained support because most of the inmates scored low on the tests.[135] In 1926, William Healy and Augusta Bronner tested groups of delinquent boys in Chicago and Boston and found that 37 percent were subnormal in intelligence. They concluded that delinquents were 5 to 10 times more likely to be mentally deficient than normal boys.[136] These and other early studies were embraced as proof that low IQ scores indicated potentially delinquent children and that a correlation existed between innate low intelligence and deviant behaviour. IQ tests were believed to measure the inborn genetic makeup of individuals, and many criminologists accepted the idea that individuals with substandard IQs were predisposed toward delinquency and adult criminality.

Nurture Theory

Proponents of **nurture theory** argue that intelligence is not inherited and that low-IQ parents do not necessarily produce low-IQ children.[137] Intelligence must be viewed as partly biological but primarily sociological. Nurture theorists discredit the notion that persons commit crimes because they have low IQs. Instead, they postulate that environmental stimulation from parents, relatives, social contacts, schools, peer groups, and innumerable others account for a child's IQ level and that low IQs may result from an environment that also encourages delinquent and criminal behaviour. Thus, if low IQ scores are recorded among criminals, these scores may reflect the criminals' cultural background, not their mental ability.

In 1931, Edwin Sutherland evaluated IQ studies of criminals and delinquents and questioned whether criminals in fact have low IQs.[138] Sutherland's research all but put an end to the belief that crime was caused by feeblemindedness; the IQ–crime link was almost forgotten in criminological literature.

IQ and Criminality

nature theory
The view that intelligence is largely determined genetically and that low intelligence is linked to criminal behaviour.

nurture theory
The view that intelligence is not inherited, but is largely a product of environment. Low IQ scores do not cause crime, but may result from the same environmental factors.

Although the alleged IQ–crime link was dismissed by mainstream criminologists, it once again became an important area of study when respected criminologists Travis Hirschi and Michael Hindelang published a widely read 1977 article linking the two variables.[139] They proposed the idea that low IQ increases the likelihood of criminal behaviour through its effect on school performance. That is, youths with low IQs do poorly in school, and school failure and academic incompetence are highly related to delinquency and later to adult criminality.

Hirschi and Hindelang's inferences have been supported by research worldwide.[140] In their influential book *Crime and Human Nature*, James Q. Wilson and Richard Herrnstein also agreed that the IQ–crime link is indirect: Low intelligence leads to poor school performance, which enhances the chances of criminality.[141] They conclude, "A child who chronically loses standing in the competition of the classroom may feel justified in settling the score outside, by violence, theft, and other forms of defiant illegality."[142]

IQ and Crime Reconsidered

In their controversial 1994 book, *The Bell Curve*, Richard Herrnstein and Charles Murray firmly advocate an IQ–crime link. Their extensive review of the available literature shows that adolescents with low IQs are more likely to commit crime, get caught, and be sent to prison. Conversely, at-risk kids with higher IQs seem to be protected from becoming criminals by their superior ability to succeed in school and in social relationships. Herrnstein and Murray conclude that criminal offenders have an average IQ of 92, about 8 points below the mean; chronic offenders score even lower than the average criminal. To those who suggest that the IQ–crime relationship can be explained by the fact that only low-IQ criminals get caught, they counter with data showing little difference in IQ scores between self-reported and official criminals.[143] This means that even criminals whose activities go undetected have lower IQs than the general public; the IQ–crime relationship cannot be explained away by the fact that slow-witted criminals are the ones most likely to be apprehended.

Although Herrnstein and Murray's review of the literature was extensive, a number of recent studies have found that IQ has negligible influence on

primary prevention programs
Programs, such as substance abuse clinics and mental health associations, that seek to treat personal problems before they manifest themselves as crime.

secondary prevention programs
Programs that provide treatment such as psychological counselling to youths and adults after they have violated the law.

criminal behaviour.[144] Also, a recent evaluation of research on intelligence conducted by the American Psychological Association concludes that the strength of an IQ–crime link is "very low."[145]

It is unlikely that the IQ–criminality debate will be settled soon. Measurement is beset by many methodological problems. The well-documented criticisms suggesting that IQ tests are race and class biased would certainly influence the testing of the criminal population, which is besieged with a multitude of social and economic problems. Even if it can be shown that known offenders have lower IQs than the general population, it is difficult to explain many patterns in the crime rate: Why are there more male than female criminals? Why do crime rates vary by region, time of year, and even weather patterns? Why does aging out occur? IQ does not increase with age, so why should crime rates fall?

Social Policy Implications

For most of the 20th century, biological and psychological views of criminality have influenced crime control and prevention policy. The result has been front-end or **primary prevention programs** that seek to treat personal problems before they manifest themselves as crime. To this end, thousands of family therapy organizations, substance abuse clinics, and mental health associations operate throughout North America. Teachers, employers, courts, welfare agencies, and others make referrals to these facilities. These services are based on the premise that if a person's problems can be treated before they become overwhelming, some future crimes will be prevented. **Secondary prevention programs** provide treatment such as psychological counselling to youths and adults after they have violated the law. Attendance at such programs may be a requirement of a probation order, part of a diversionary sentence, or aftercare at the end of a prison sentence.

Biologically oriented therapy is also being used in the criminal justice system. Programs have altered diets, changed lighting, compensated for learning disabilities, treated allergies, and so on.[146] More controversial has been the use of mood-altering chemicals, such as lithium, pemoline, imipramine, phenytoin, and benzodiazepines, to control behaviour. Another practice that has elicited concern is the use of psychosurgery (brain surgery) to control antisocial behaviour. Surgical procedures have been used to alter the brain structure of convicted sex offenders in an effort to eliminate or control their sex drives. Results are still preliminary, but some critics argue that these procedures are without scientific merit.[147]

Numerous psychologically based treatment methods range from individual counselling to behaviour modification. For example, treatment based on how people process information takes into account that people are more likely to respond aggressively to provocation if thoughts intensify the insult or otherwise stir feelings of anger. Cognitive therapists attempt to teach explosive people to control aggressive impulses by viewing social provocations as problems demanding a solution rather than retaliation. Programs are aimed at teaching problem-solving skills that may include self-disclosure, role-playing, listening, following instructions, joining in, and using self-control.[148] Therapeutic interventions designed to make people better problem solvers may involve measures that enhance[149]

- Coping and problem-solving skills
- Relationships with peers, parents, and other adults
- Conflict resolution and communication skills, and methods for resisting peer pressure related to drug use and violence
- Consequential thinking and decision-making abilities
- Prosocial behaviours, including cooperation with others, self-responsibility, respecting others, and public speaking efficacy
- Empathy*

71% The percentage of students who go online to study for a class.
© Anderson Ross/Getty Images
GET ONLINE

The easy-to-navigate website for **CRIM** offers guidance on key topics in **criminology** in a variety of engaging formats. You have the opportunity to refine and check your understanding via interactive quizzes and flashcards. Videos provide inspiration for your own further exploration. And, in order to make **CRIM** an even better learning tool, we invite you to speak up about your experience with **CRIM** by completing a survey form and sending us your comments.

Get online and discover the following resources:

- Printable and Audio Flashcards
- Videos
- Interactive Quizzing
- Crossword Puzzles
- Discipline-specific activities

"I think this book is awesome for students of all ages. It is a much simpler way to study."

—Yasmine Al-Hashimi, Fanshawe College

Visit **www.icancrim2.com** to find the resources you need today!

CHAPTER 6

Social Structure Theories

Learning Outcomes

LO1 Explain why sociology has been the main orientation of criminologists.

LO2 Explain why social structure theory supports the idea that those living in poverty are more likely to commit crimes.

LO3 State the three branches of social structure theories.

LO4 Explain the concept of "collective efficacy."

LO5 Discuss how strain theories interpret crime.

LO6 Explain the concept of "differential opportunity."

LO1 Introduction

On Friday, January 11, 2002, at 3:30 A.M., Montreal police responded to a report of a disturbance outside a downtown bar. When police arrived, they found a savagely beaten man lying unconscious on the sidewalk outside the bar. Witnesses reported that three youths had repeatedly beaten the homeless man, who had been panhandling outside the bar. Alerted by patrons, bouncers from the bar intervened and managed to subdue one of the attackers. The other two fled the scene. An ambulance transported the unconscious and bleeding victim to the hospital where, despite having suffered serious facial injuries and fractures, he recovered. Police later arrested the other two youths involved in the attack.

DID YOU KNOW?

- Because crime rates are higher in lower-class areas, many criminologists believe that the causes of crime are rooted in socioeconomic factors.
- Despite economic headway, there are still more than 5 million indigent Canadians. Visible-minority groups and Aboriginal Canadians are more likely than the white majority to be poor.
- Some criminologists believe that destructive social forces in poor areas are responsible for high crime rates.
- The strain and frustration caused by poverty is a suspected cause of crime.
- Indigents may become involved in a deviant subculture that sustains and supports criminality.

The attack was just another in a series of assaults, robberies, and even murders of homeless people, another example of the plight of the growing number of homeless in Canadian cities.[1] Although the United Nations has ranked Canada as one of the best places on earth to live, still many Canadians—particularly women, Aboriginal people, and youth—cannot afford decent housing, do not have the education or skills for employment, or are suffering from illness or addiction. As the number of homeless grows in Canadian cities, crime and victimization will increase.

The Montreal beating of a homeless man outside a "seedy" downtown bar exemplifies the belief of many criminologists that crime and violence are endemic in poor, deteriorated neighbourhoods. Because these neighbourhoods have substantially higher crime rates than more affluent areas, the majority of criminologists believe it would be a mistake to ignore social and environmental factors in trying to understand the cause of criminal behaviour.[2] Most criminals are indigent and desperate, not calculating or evil. Many were raised in deteriorated parts of town and lack the social support and economic resources familiar to more affluent members of society. Understanding criminal behaviour, then, requires analyzing the influence of these destructive social forces on human behaviour.

Criminologists have long attempted to discover why certain neighbourhoods and geographic locations are more prone to criminal activity than others. Explanations of crime as an individual-level phenomenon, with its locus in either destructive

Martin Poole/The Image Bank/Getty Images

CONNECTIONS

Concern about the ecological distribution of crime, the effect of social change, and the interactive nature of crime itself has made sociology the foundation of modern criminology. This chapter reviews sociological theories that emphasize the relationship between social status and criminal behaviour. In Chapter 7 the focus shifts to theories that emphasize socialization and its influence on crime and deviance; Chapter 8 covers theories based on the concept of social conflict.

personal choices or deviant traits, fail to account for these consistent crime rate patterns. If violence, as some criminologists suggest, is related to chemical or chromosome abnormality, then how can ecological differences in crime rates be explained? It is unlikely that all people with physical anomalies live in one section of town or in one area of the country. There is an ongoing public debate over the effects of violent TV shows on adolescent aggression. Yet adolescents in cities and towns with widely disparate crime rates may all watch the same shows and movies; so how can crime rate differences in these areas be explained? If violence has a biological or psychological origin, should it not be distributed more evenly throughout the social structure rather than concentrated in certain areas?

Because of these issues, many criminologists believe that understanding the dynamics of interactions between individuals and important social institutions, such as families, peers, schools, jobs, and criminal justice agencies, is important for understanding the cause of crime.[3] The relationship of one social class or group to another or to the power structure that controls a country's legal and economic system may also be closely related to criminality. It seems logical that people on the lowest rung of the economic ladder will have the greatest incentive to commit crime. They may be either enraged by their lack of economic success or simply financially desperate and disillusioned. In either case, crime, despite its inherent dangers, may be an attractive alternative to a life of indigence.

stratification
Grouping based on economic or social class and characterized by the unequal distribution of wealth, power, and prestige.

social class
Segment of the population whose members are at a relatively similar economic level and who share attitudes, values, norms, and an identifiable lifestyle.

LO2 Economic Structure and Crime

All societies are characterized by some measure of social **stratification**. Social strata are created by unequal distribution of wealth, power, and prestige. **Social classes** are segments of the population whose members have a relatively similar portion of desirable things and who share attitudes, values, norms, and an identifiable lifestyle. In Canadian society, it is common to identify people as upper, middle, working, or lower class, with a broad range of economic variations within each group.

The upper-upper class consists of a small number (around 5 percent) of exceptionally well-to-do families who control enormous financial and social resources. In contrast, those in the lower class (about 20 percent of the population) have scant, if any, resources and suffer socially and economically as a result. In Canada, the most common measure of poverty is the "low income cut-offs" used by Statistics Canada. For example, in 2009, the low-income cut-off line for an individual living in a large city (over 500 000) was about $22 229, and for a family of four it was around $41 307. About 10 percent of Canadians, or roughly 3.5 million people, live below these low-income cut-offs.[4]

Children are hit especially hard by poverty. While Canada is widely considered one of the best countries to live in, one out of every ten children in Canada (about 637 000 children) were living in poverty in 2007; even more shocking, 1 out of every 4 Aboriginal children live in poverty.[5] Hundreds of studies have documented the association between family poverty and children's health, achievement, and behaviour impairments.[6] Children who grow up in low-income homes are less likely to achieve in school and are less likely to complete their schooling than children with more affluent parents.[7] Poor children are also more likely to suffer from health problems and to receive inadequate health care. Children who live in extreme poverty or who remain poor for multiple years appear to suffer the worst outcomes. The timing of poverty also seems to be relevant. Findings suggest that poverty during early childhood may have a more severe impact than poverty during adolescence.[8]

Besides their increased chance of physical illness, poor children are much more likely than wealthy children to suffer various social and physical ills, ranging from low birth weight to limited educational achievement. The social problems found in poverty-plagued neighbourhoods have been described as an "epidemic" that spreads like a contagious disease, destroying the inner workings that enable neighbourhoods to survive; they become "hollowed out."[9] As neighbourhood quality decreases, the probability that residents will develop problems sharply increases. Adolescents in the worst neighbourhoods have the greatest risks of dropping out of school and of becoming teenage parents.

Rates of child poverty vary by race and ethnicity. In Canada child poverty is highest among recent immigrants, especially those who are a visible minority, and among Aboriginal people. It is estimated that more than 50 percent of Aboriginal children live in poverty.[10]

Inequality and Culture

Lower-class slum areas are scenes of inadequate housing and health care, disrupted family lives, underemployment, and despair. Members of the lower class also suffer in other ways. They are more prone to depression, less likely to have achievement motivation, and less likely to put off immediate gratification for future gain. For example, they may be less willing to stay in school because the rewards for educational achievement are in the distant future. Some are driven to desperate measures to cope with their economic plight.[11]

Members of the lower class are constantly bombarded by advertisements linking material possessions to self-worth, but they are often unable to attain desired goods and services through conventional means. Although they are members of a society that extols material success above any other form, they are unable to satisfactorily compete for such success with members of the upper classes. As a result, they may turn to illegal solutions to their economic plight. They may deal drugs for profit or steal cars and sell them to chop shops; they may even commit armed robberies for desperately needed funds. They may become so depressed that they take alcohol and drugs as a form of self-tranquillization; because of their poverty, they acquire the drugs and alcohol through illegal channels.

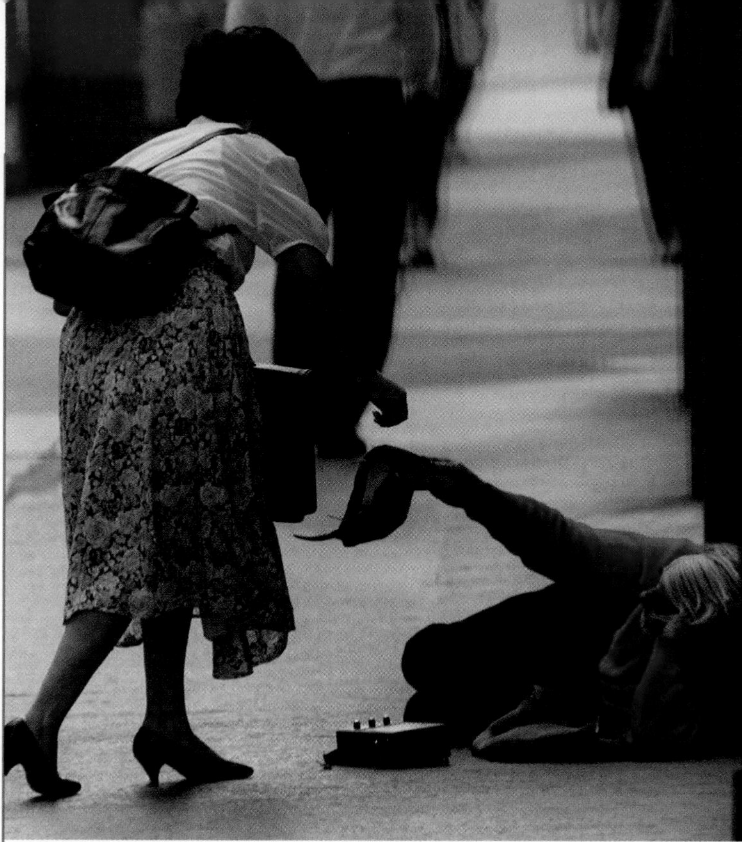
Hans Deryk/CP PHOTO

In 1966 sociologist Oscar Lewis argued that the crushing lifestyle of slum areas produces a **culture of poverty** passed from one generation to the next.[12] Apathy, cynicism, helplessness, and mistrust of social institutions, such as schools, government agencies, and the police, mark the culture of poverty. This mistrust prevents slum dwellers from taking advantage of the meagre opportunities available to them. Lewis's work was the first of a group of studies that described the plight of at-risk children and adults. In 1970 Swedish

culture of poverty
A separate lower-class culture, characterized by apathy, cynicism, helplessness, and mistrust of social institutions, such as schools, government agencies, and the police, that is passed from one generation to the next.

underclass
The lowest social stratum in any country, whose members lack the education and skills needed to function successfully in modern society.

DID YOU KNOW?

First Nation(s)

The term *First Nations* came into common usage in the 1970s to replace *band* or *Indian*, which some people found offensive. The term is distinct from *Aboriginal peoples* because it doesn't include Inuit or Métis and it applies to both Status and Non-Status Indians.

First Peoples

First peoples is a term used to describe the original peoples of Canada and their descendants. It is used less frequently than terms such as *Aboriginal peoples* and *Native peoples*.

Indian

The term *Indian* collectively describes all the *Indigenous people* in Canada who are not Inuit or Métis. Indian peoples are one of three peoples recognized as Aboriginal in the Constitution Act of 1982 along with Inuit and Métis. In addition, three categories apply to Indians in Canada: Status Indians, Non-Status Indians, and Treaty Indians. The term *Indian* is considered outdated by many people, and there is much debate over whether to continue using this term.

Status Indians

Status Indians are people who are entitled to have their names included on the Indian Register, an official list maintained by the federal government. Only Status Indians are recognized as Indians under the Indian Act and are entitled to certain rights and benefits under the law.

Non-Status Indians

Non-Status Indians are people who consider themselves Indians or members of a First Nation but whom the Government of Canada does not recognize as Indians under the Indian Act, either because they are unable to prove their Indian status or have lost their status rights. Non-Status Indians are not entitled to the same rights and benefits available to Status Indians.

Treaty Indians

Treaty Indians are descendants of Indians who signed treaties with Canada and who have a contemporary connection with a treaty band.

Indigenous

Indigenous means "native to the area." In this sense, Aboriginal peoples are indigenous to North America. The meaning of *Indigenous* is similar to Aboriginal peoples, Native peoples, or First peoples. Currently, the term is rarely used and, when it is, it usually refers to Aboriginal people internationally. However, the term is gaining acceptance, particularly among some Aboriginal scholars to recognize the place of Aboriginal peoples in Canada's late-colonial era and implies land tenure. The term is also used by the United Nations in its working groups and in its Decade of the World's Indigenous People.

Innu

Innu are the Naskapi and Montagnais First Nations peoples who live in Quebec and Labrador. They are not to be confused with Inuit or Inuk.

Inuit

Inuit live primarily in the Northwest Territories, Nunavut, northern parts of Quebec, and most of Labrador. They are the Aboriginal people of the Arctic. The word *Inuit* means "the people" in Inuktitut and is the term by which Inuit refer to themselves. *Inuk* is the singular form of Inuit. When referring to two people, the correct term is *Inuuk*, while three or more takes *Inuit*. Since Inuit have never lived on reserves, the terms *on-reserve* and *off-reserve* do not apply.

Métis

The word *Métis* is French for "mixed blood." The Constitution Act of 1982 recognizes Métis as one of the three Aboriginal peoples. Today, the term is used broadly to describe people with mixed First Nations and European ancestry who identify themselves as Métis. Métis organizations in Canada have differing criteria about who qualifies as a Métis person.

Native

Native is a word similar in meaning to *Aboriginal*. *Native peoples* is a collective term to describe the descendants of the original peoples of North America. The term is increasingly seen as outdated (particularly when used as a noun) and is starting to lose acceptance.

Native American

This commonly used term in the United States describes the descendants of the original peoples of North America. The term has not caught on in Canada because of the apparent reference to U.S. citizenship. However, some Aboriginal peoples in Canada have argued that because they are descendants of the original peoples of the Americas, the term *Native American* should apply to them regardless of their citizenship. *Native North American* has been used to identify the original peoples of Canada and the United States.

economist Gunnar Myrdal described a worldwide **underclass** that was cut off from society, its members lacking the education and skills needed to function successfully in modern society.[13]

The burdens of underclass life are most often felt by minority group members. In Canada, this is especially true for Aboriginal people. Among "registered Indians" (those the government officially recognizes as Aboriginal), the average yearly income is less than one-half what other Canadians earn ($12 000 versus $25 000); employment rates are 60 percent lower than for non-Aboriginals; and rates of infant mortality, respiratory diseases, diabetes, and suicide are at least three times higher than for other Canadians.[14] More than half of Aboriginal people in Canada live in poverty. Overall, visible minorities are almost twice as likely as nonminorities to fall below the poverty line.[15] See Figure 6.1.

Economic disparity continually haunts members of the underclass and their children. Even if they value education and other middle-class norms, their desperate life circumstances (including high unemployment, crowded and dilapidated housing, poor diet, lack of access to technology such as computers) may prevent them from developing the skills, and habits, that lead first to educational success and

FIGURE 6.1

Aboriginal, Visible Minority Children, and Children with Disabilities Most Likely to Be Poor

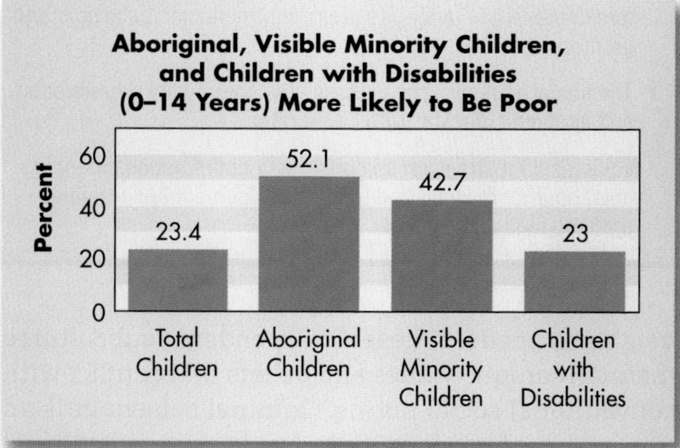

Source: Reprinted by permission of Canadian Council on Social Development.

later to success in the workplace. Both of these factors have been linked to crime and drug abuse.[16]

Community effects may particularly damage children. Adolescents residing in areas of concentrated poverty are more likely to suffer in their cognitive development, sexual understanding, school attendance habits, and transition to employment.[17] Lack of education and family instability make them poor candidates for employment or for the eventual formation of their own cohesive families. These findings suggest that the poor confront obstacles far greater than the mere lack of financial resources. The social problems they face render them unprepared to take advantage of employment opportunities even in tight labour markets.[18] The fact that many of the underclass are visible minorities and Aboriginal children who can expect to spend all their lives in poverty is an important problem facing our society today.[19]

LO3 Social Structure Theories

Many criminologists view disadvantaged economic-class position as a primary cause of crime. This view is referred to as **social structure theory**. As a group, social structure theories suggest that social and economic forces operating in deteriorated lower-class areas push many of their residents into criminal behaviour patterns. These theories consider the existence of unsupervised teenage gangs, high crime rates, and social disorder in slum areas as major social problems.

social structure theory The view that disadvantaged economic-class position is a primary cause of crime.

Lower-class crime is often the violent, destructive product of youth gangs and marginally employed or underemployed young adults. Underemployment means that many working adults earn relatively low wages and have few benefits such as vacation time, medical or dental plans, and retirement programs. Their ability to accumulate capital for home ownership is restricted and so, consequently, is their stake in society.

Although members of the middle and upper classes also engage in crime, social structure theorists view middle-class and white-collar crime as being of relatively lower frequency, seriousness, and danger to the general public. The real crime problem is essentially a lower-class phenomenon that breeds criminal behaviour, begins in youth, and continues into young adulthood. Because crime rates are higher in lower-class urban centres than in middle-class suburbs, social forces must influence or control behaviour.[20] We will examine some specific structure theories that support this perspective.

The social structure perspective encompasses three independent yet overlapping branches: social disorganization theory, strain theory, and cultural deviance theory. These three branches are summarized in Figure 6.2.

FIGURE 6.2

The Three Branches of Social Structure Theory

Social disorganization theory focuses on conditions in the environment:
- Deteriorated neighbourhoods
- Inadequate social control
- Law-violating gangs and groups
- Conflicting social values

Strain theory focuses on conflict between goals and means:
- Unequal distribution of wealth and power
- Frustration
- Alternative methods of achievement

Cultural deviance theory combines the other two:
- Development of subcultures as a result of disorganization and stress
- Subcultural values in opposition to conventional values

CRIME

social disorganization theory
Branch of social structure theory that focuses on the breakdown of institutions such as the family, school, and employment in inner-city neighbourhoods.

strain theory
Branch of social structure theory that sees crime as a function of the conflict between people's goals and the means available to obtain them.

strain
The anger, frustration, and resentment experienced by people who believe they cannot achieve their goals through legitimate means.

cultural deviance theory
Branch of social structure theory that sees strain and social disorganization together resulting in a unique lower-class culture that conflicts with conventional social norms.

subculture
A set of values, beliefs, and traditions unique to a particular social class or group within a larger society.

cultural transmission
Process whereby values, beliefs, and traditions are handed down from one generation to the next.

Social Disorganization Theory

Social disorganization theory focuses on the urban conditions that affect crime rates. A disorganized area is one in which institutions of social control, such as the family, commercial establishments, and schools, have broken down and can no longer perform their expected or stated functions. Indicators of social disorganization include high unemployment and school dropout rates, deteriorated housing, low income levels, and large numbers of single-parent households. Residents in these areas experience conflict and despair, and, as a result, antisocial behaviour flourishes.

Strain Theory

Strain theory holds that crime is a function of the conflict between people's goals and the means they can use to obtain them. Strain theorists argue that although social and economic goals are common to people in all economic strata, the ability to obtain these goals is class-dependent. Most people in Canada desire wealth, material possessions, power, prestige, and other life comforts. Members of the lower class are unable to achieve these symbols of success through conventional means. Consequently, they feel anger, frustration, and resentment, referred to collectively as **strain**. Lower-class citizens can either accept their condition and live as socially responsible if unrewarded citizens, or they can choose an alternative means of achieving success, such as theft, violence, or drug trafficking.

Cultural Deviance Theory

Cultural deviance theory combines elements of both strain and social disorganization theories. According to this view, because of strain and social isolation, a unique lower-class culture develops in disorganized neighbourhoods. These independent **subcultures** maintain unique values and beliefs that conflict with conventional social norms. Criminal behaviour is an expression of conformity to lower-class subcultural values and traditions, not a rebellion from conventional society. Subcultural values are handed down from one generation to the next in a process called **cultural transmission**.

Although each of these theories is distinct in critical aspects, each approach has at its core the view that socially isolated people, living in disorganized neighbourhoods, are likely to experience crime-producing social forces. In the remainder of this chapter, each branch of social structure theory will be discussed in some detail.

DID YOU KNOW?

- Social disorganization theory holds that destructive social forces present in inner-city areas control human behaviour and promote crime.
- The social ecology school associates community deterioration and economic decline with crime rates.
- Ecological factors such as community deterioration, changing neighbourhoods, fear, and lack of employment opportunities produce high crime rates.

Social Disorganization Theory

Social disorganization theory links crime rates to neighbourhood ecological characteristics. Crime rates are elevated in highly transient, mixed-use (where residential and commercial property exist side by side), and changing neighbourhoods in which the fabric of social life has become frayed. These localities are unable to provide essential services, such as education, health care, and proper housing, and, as a result, they experience significant levels of unemployment, single-parent families, and families on welfare.

Social disorganization theory views crime-ridden neighbourhoods as those in which residents are trying to leave at the earliest opportunity. Residents are uninterested in community matters, so the common sources of control—the family, school, business community, social service agencies—are weak and disorganized. Personal relationships are strained because neighbours are constantly moving. Constant resident turnover weakens communications and blocks attempts at solving neighbourhood problems or establishing common goals (see Figure 6.3).[21]

FIGURE 6.3

Social Disorganization Theory

Poverty
- Development of isolated slums
- Lack of conventional social opportunities
- Racial and ethnic discrimination

Social disorganization
- Breakdown of social institutions and organizations such as school and family
- Lack of informal social control

Breakdown of social control
- Development of gangs, groups
- Peer group replaces family and social institutions

Criminal areas
- Neighbourhood becomes crime-prone
- Stable pockets of delinquency develop
- Lack of external support and investment

Cultural transmission
Older youths pass norms (focal concerns) to younger generation, creating stable slum culture.

Criminal careers
Most youths "age out" of delinquency, marry, and raise families, but some remain in life of crime.

The Work of Shaw and McKay

Social disorganization theory was popularized by the work of two Chicago sociologists, Clifford R. Shaw and Henry McKay, who linked life in transitional slum areas to the inclination to commit crime. Shaw and McKay began their pioneering work on Chicago crime during the early 1920s while working as researchers for a state-supported social service agency.[22]

Shaw and McKay explained crime and delinquency within the context of the changing urban environment and ecological development of the city. They saw that Chicago had developed into distinct neighbourhoods (natural areas), some affluent and others wracked by extreme poverty. These poverty-ridden **transitional neighbourhoods** suffered high rates of population turnover and were incapable of inducing residents to remain and defend the neighbourhoods against criminal groups.

transitional neighbourhood
An area undergoing a shift in population and structure, usually from middle-class residential to lower-class mixed use.

In transitional areas, successive changes in the population composition, the disintegration of the traditional cultures, the diffusion of divergent cultural standards, and the gradual industrialization of the area dissolve neighbourhood culture and organization. The continuity of conventional neighbourhood traditions and institutions is broken, leaving children feeling displaced and without a strong or definitive set of values.

Concentric Zones

Shaw and McKay identified the areas in Chicago that had excessive crime rates. They noted that distinct ecological areas had developed in the city, forming a series of nine concentric circles, or zones, and that there were stable and significant interzone differences in crime rates (see Figure 6.4). The areas of heaviest crime concentration appeared to be the transitional inner-city zones, where large numbers of foreign-born citizens had recently settled.[23] The zones farthest from the city's centre had correspondingly lower crime rates.

Analysis of these data indicated a surprisingly stable pattern of criminal activity in the nine ecological zones over 65 years. Shaw and McKay concluded that in the transitional neighbourhoods, multiple cultures and diverse values, both conventional and deviant, coexist. Children growing up in the street culture often find that adults who have adopted a deviant lifestyle (gamblers, pimps, drug dealers) are the most financially successful people in the neighbourhood. Forced to choose between conventional and deviant lifestyles, many slum kids opt for the latter. They join other like-minded youths and form law-violating gangs and cliques. The development of teenage law-violating groups is an essential element of youthful misbehaviour in slum areas. The values that slum youths adopt often conflict with existing middle-class norms, which demand strict obedience to the legal code. Consequently, a value conflict further separates the delinquent youth and his or her peer group from conventional society; the result is a more solid embrace of deviant goals and behaviour. To further justify their choice of goals, these youths seek support for their choice by recruiting new members and passing on the delinquent tradition.

Shaw and McKay's statistical analysis confirmed that even though crime rates changed, the highest rates were always in zones I and II (the central city and a transitional area). The areas with the highest crime rates retained high rates even when their ethnic composition changed (the areas Shaw and McKay examined shifted from German and Irish to Italian and Polish).[24]

The Legacy of Shaw and McKay

Social disorganization concepts articulated by Shaw and McKay have remained prominent within criminology for more than 80 years. The most important of Shaw and McKay's findings were that crime rates correspond to neighbourhood structure and that crime is created by the destructive ecological conditions in urban slums. They contended that criminals are not, as some criminologists of the time believed, biologically inferior, intellectually impaired, or psychologically damaged. Their research supported their belief that crime is a constant fixture in areas of poverty, regardless of residents' racial or ethnic identity. Because the basis of their theory was that neighbourhood disintegration and slum conditions are the primary causes of criminal behaviour, Shaw and McKay paved the way for many community action and treatment programs developed in the last half-century.

FIGURE 6.4

Shaw and McKay's Concentric Zones Map of Chicago

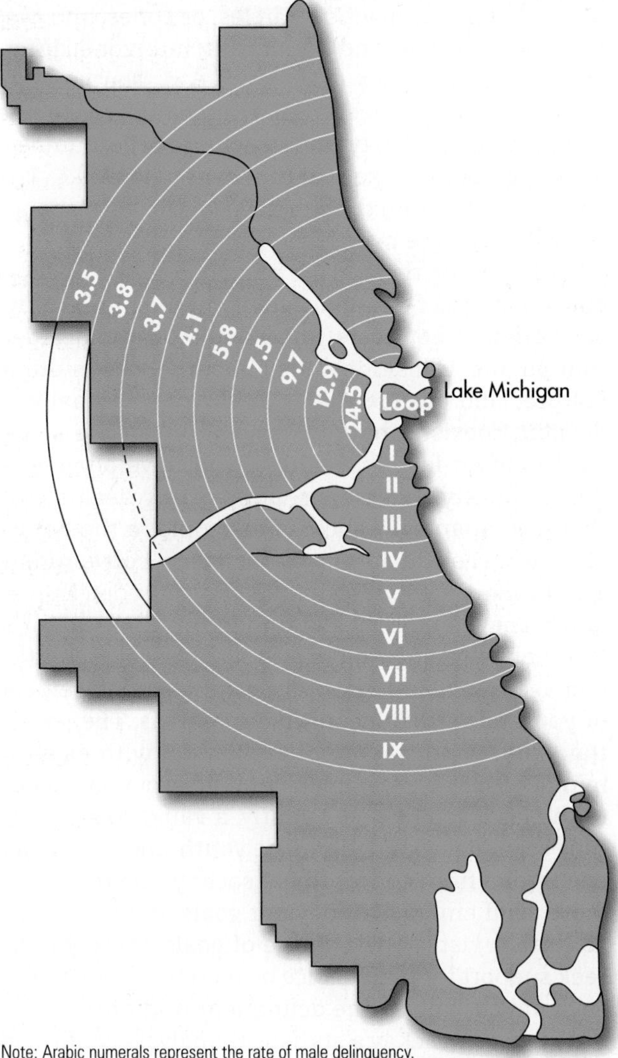

Note: Arabic numerals represent the rate of male delinquency.

Source: Clifford R. Shaw et al., *Delinquency Areas* (Chicago: University of Chicago Press, 1929), p. 99. Copyright 1929 by the University of Chicago. Reprinted with permission of The University of Chicago Press.

CBC TV Archive Sales

When neighbourhoods are under stress, people are reluctant to cooperate with the police, who they believe have little chance of addressing community problems. Police may find it difficult to be effective without community cooperation. In March 2004 RCMP officers were pelted with rocks and forced to flee the Labrador community of Sheshatsui when a peaceful protest by Innu community members, designed to draw attention to the lack of decent housing, turned violent. In many Aboriginal communities, the lack of adequate housing has been linked to a host of serious social ills, including gas sniffing, alcoholism, violence, and suicide.

The Social Ecology School

During the 1970s, criminologists were influenced by several critical analyses of social disorganization theory that challenged its validity.[25] The criminological literature of the period was dominated by theories with a social–psychological orientation, stressing offender socialization within the family, school, and peer group.

In the 1980s, a group of criminologists continued studying ecological conditions, reviving concern about the effects of social disorganization.[26] These contemporary social ecologists developed a purer form of structural theory that emphasizes the association of community deterioration and economic decline with criminality but places less emphasis on value conflict. The following sections discuss some of the more recent social ecological research.

Community Disorganization

Crime rates and the need for police services are associated with community deterioration: disorder, poverty, alienation, disassociation, and fear of crime.[27] Even in rural areas, which normally have low crime rates, increased levels of crime and violence are associated with indicators of social disorganization such as residential instability (a large number of people moving in and out), family disruption, and changing ethnic composition.[28]

In larger cities, neighbourhoods with a high percentage of deserted houses and apartments experience high crime rates; abandoned buildings serve as a "magnet for crime."[29] Areas in which houses are in poor repair, boarded up, and burned out, whose owners are best described as slumlords, are also the location of the highest violence rates and gun crime.[30] These neighbourhoods, in which retail establishments often go bankrupt, are abandoned and deteriorate physically.[31]

Poverty and Unemployment

The percentage of people living in poverty and the percentage of broken homes are strongly related to neighbourhood crime rates.[32] Violent crime rates are associated with variables such as the percentage of the neighbourhood living below the poverty line, the lack of mortgage investment in a neighbourhood, the unemployment rate, and the influx of new immigrants; these factors are usually found in disorganized areas.[33] The influence of these economic disadvantages is felt by both male and female residents. Though female crime rates may be lower than male rates, women living in deteriorated areas also feel the effects of poverty.[34]

Shaw and McKay claimed that areas continually wracked by poverty also experience social disorganization.[35] Research indicates that neighbourhoods with few employment opportunities for youth and adults are the most vulnerable to predatory crime such as armed robbery and mugging.[36] Unemployment destabilizes households, and unstable families are likely to breed children who use violence and aggression to deal with limited opportunity. This lack of opportunity perpetuates higher crime rates, especially when large groups or cohorts of people of the same age compete for relatively scant resources.[37]

CONNECTIONS

If social disorganization causes crime, why are most low-income people law abiding? To explain this anomaly, some sociologists have devised theoretical models suggesting that individual socialization experiences mediate environmental influences. These theories will be discussed in Chapter 7.

Community Fear

Disorganized neighbourhoods suffer social and physical incivilities—rowdy youth, trash and litter, graffiti, abandoned storefronts, burned-out buildings, littered lots, strangers, drunks, vagabonds, loiterers, prostitutes, noise, congestion, angry words, dirt, and stench. The presence of such incivilities makes residents of disorganized areas believe that their neighbourhood is dangerous and that they face a considerable chance of becoming crime victims. Therefore, when crime rates are actually high in these disorganized areas, fear levels increase dramatically.[38] Perceptions of crime and victimization produce neighbourhood fear.[39]

Fear can be contagious. People tell others when they have been victimized, thus spreading the word that the neighbourhood is getting dangerous and that the chance of future victimization is high.[40] As a result, people dread leaving their homes at night and withdraw from community life. Not surprisingly, people who have already been victimized fear the future more than those who have escaped crime.[41]

Fear is a powerful influence. When it grips a neighbourhood, business conditions begin to deteriorate, population mobility increases, and a "criminal element" begins to drift into the area.[42] In essence, the presence of fear incites more crime, increasing the chances of victimization and producing even more fear in a never-ending loop.[43]

Community Change

Communities undergoing rapid structural changes in racial and economic composition also seem to experience the greatest change in crime rates. Recent studies recognize that change, not stability, is the hallmark of many inner-city areas. A neighbourhood's

concentration effect
As working- and middle-class families flee inner-city poor areas, the most disadvantaged population is consolidated in urban ghettos.

collective efficacy
Social control exerted by cohesive communities, based on mutual trust, including intervention in the supervision of children and maintenance of public order.

residents, wealth, density, and purpose are constantly evolving. Even disorganized neighbourhoods acquire new identifying features. Some may become multiracial, while others become racially homogeneous. Some areas become stable and family-oriented, while in others, mobile, never-married people predominate.[44]

As areas decline, residents flee to safer, more stable locales. Those who cannot afford to leave for more affluent communities face an increased risk of victimization. Because of racial differences in economic well-being, those left behind are often minority citizens.[45] Those who cannot move find themselves surrounded by new residents. High population turnover can devastate community culture because it thwarts communication and information flow.[46] In response to this turnover, a culture may develop that dictates to neighbourhood youth standards of dress, language, and behaviour that are opposite to those of conventional society. All these factors are likely to increase crime rates.[47]

As communities change, neighbourhood deterioration precedes increasing rates of crime and delinquency.[48] Neighbourhoods most at risk for increased crime contain large numbers of single-parent families and unrelated people living together, have changed from owner-occupied to renter-occupied units, and have lost semiskilled and unskilled jobs (indicating a growing residue of discouraged workers who are no longer seeking employment).[49] These ecological disruptions strain existing social control mechanisms and inhibit their ability to control crime and delinquency.

Poverty Concentration

One aspect of community change may be the concentration of poverty in deteriorated neighbourhoods. William Julius Wilson describes how working- and middle-class families flee inner-city poverty areas, resulting in a **concentration effect** in which the most disadvantaged population is consolidated in urban ghettos. As the working and middle classes move out, they take with them their financial and institutional resources and support. Businesses are disinclined to locate in poor areas; banks become reluctant to lend money for new housing or businesses.[50] Areas marked by concentrated poverty become isolated and insulated from the social mainstream and more

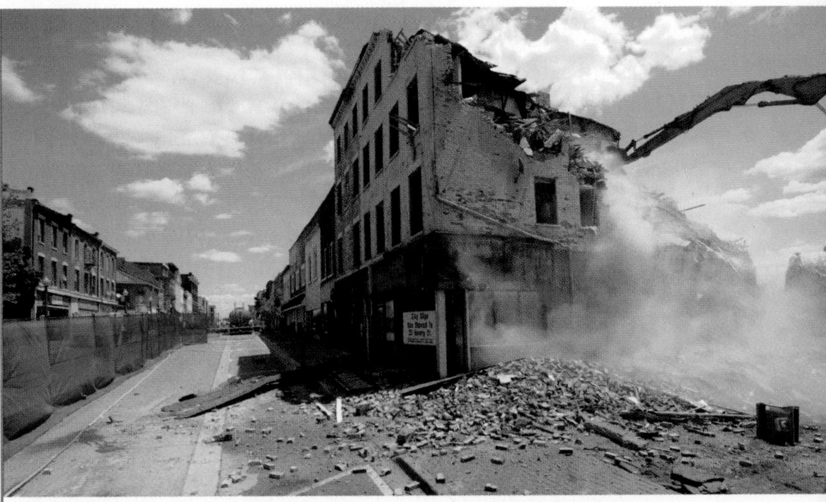
Tony Bock/GetStock.com

prone to criminal activity. Ethnically and racially isolated areas maintain the highest crime rates.[51] Minority-group members living in these areas also suffer race-based inequality, including income inequality and institutional racism.[52] Gangs may also concentrate in these areas, bringing with them a significant increase in criminal activity.[53]

LO4 Collective Efficacy

Cohesive communities with high levels of social control develop **collective efficacy**: mutual trust, a willingness to intervene in the supervision of children, and the maintenance of public order.[54] In contrast, socially disorganized neighbourhoods find that efforts at social control are weak and attenuated. When community social control efforts are blunted crime rates increase, further weakening neighbourhood cohesiveness.

In October 2010 the Ontario Association of Chiefs of Police unveiled a new model and direction for community policing in Ontario (see Figure 6.5). The new model incorporates virtually all of the features of social disorganization theory we talked about above—including the relationship between poverty, substandard housing, addictions, and social disorder—along with the need to identify and assess the extent to which each community has the resources to demonstrate "collective efficacy" in organizing and mobilizing community resources to address crime and disorder problems.

Neighbourhoods maintain a variety of agencies and institutions of social control. Some operate on the primary or private level, involving the control placed on people by their peers and families. These sources exert informal control by either awarding or withholding approval, respect, and admiration. Informal control mechanisms include direct criticism, ridicule, ostracism, desertion, or physical punishment.[55]

FIGURE 6.5

Ontario's Mobilization & Engagement Model of Community Policing

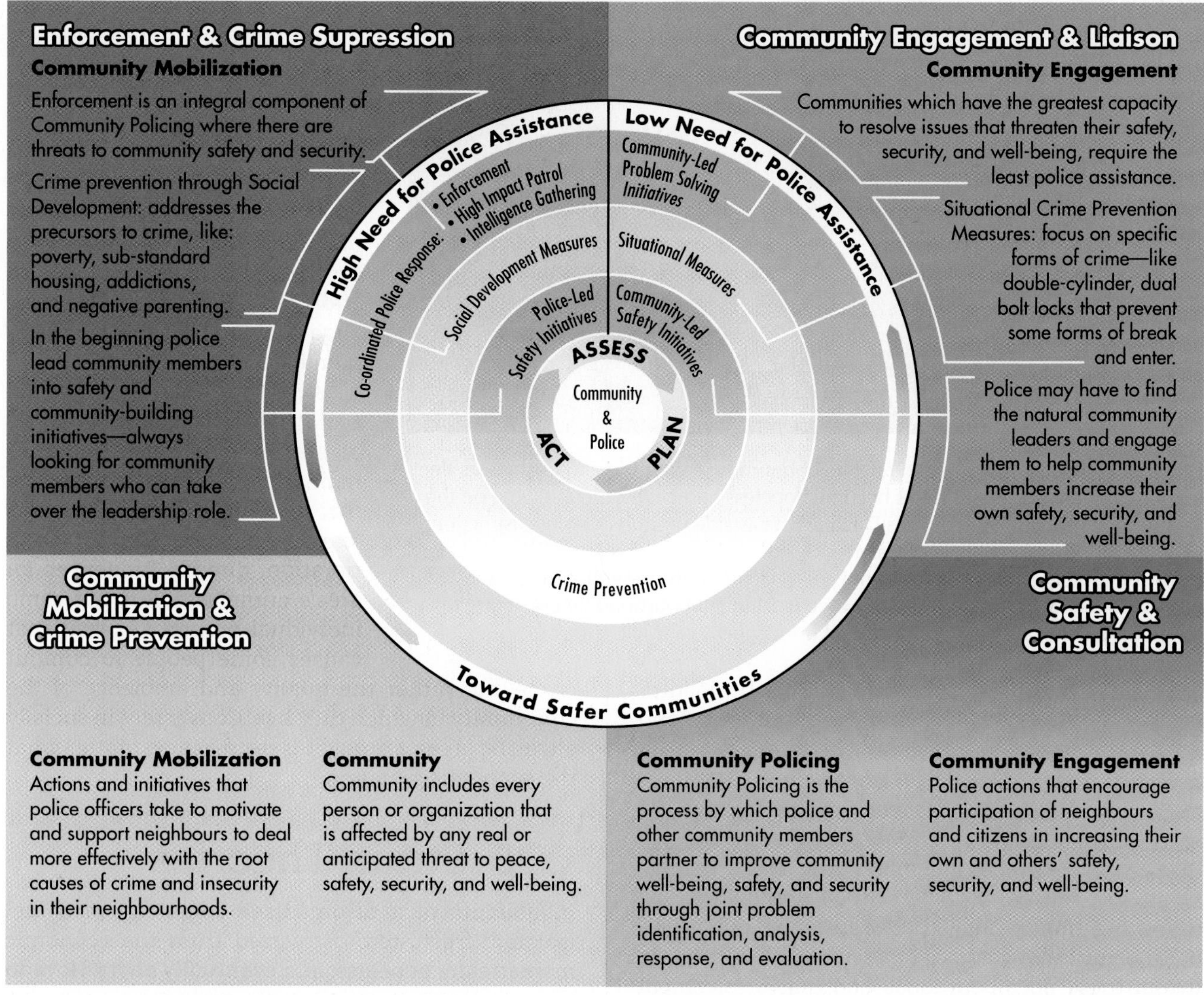

Enforcement & Crime Supression
Community Mobilization
Enforcement is an integral component of Community Policing where there are threats to community safety and security.
Crime prevention through Social Development: addresses the precursors to crime, like: poverty, sub-standard housing, addictions, and negative parenting.
In the beginning police lead community members into safety and community-building initiatives—always looking for community members who can take over the leadership role.
Community Engagement & Liaison
Community Engagement
Communities which have the greatest capacity to resolve issues that threaten their safety, security, and well-being, require the least police assistance.
Situational Crime Prevention Measures: focus on specific forms of crime—like double-cylinder, dual bolt locks that prevent some forms of break and enter.
Police may have to find the natural community leaders and engage them to help community members increase their own safety, security, and well-being.
High Need for Police Assistance
Low Need for Police Assistance
Co-ordinated Police Response:
• Enforcement
• High Impact Patrol
• Intelligence Gathering
Community-Led Problem Solving Initiatives
Social Development Measures
Situational Measures
Police-Led Safety Initiatives
Community-Led Safety Initiatives
ASSESS
PLAN
ACT
Community & Police
Crime Prevention
Toward Safer Communities
Community Mobilization & Crime Prevention
Community Safety & Consultation
Community Mobilization
Actions and initiatives that police officers take to motivate and support neighbours to deal more effectively with the root causes of crime and insecurity in their neighbourhoods.
Community
Community includes every person or organization that is affected by any real or anticipated threat to peace, safety, security, and well-being.
Community Policing
Community Policing is the process by which police and other community members partner to improve community well-being, safety, and security through joint problem identification, analysis, response, and evaluation.
Community Engagement
Police actions that encourage participation of neighbours and citizens in increasing their own and others' safety, security, and well-being.

Source: Ontario's Mobilization & Engagement Model of Community Policing, used by permission of the Ontario Association of Chiefs of Police.

For example, families may exert control by corporal punishment, withholding privileges, or ridiculing lazy or disrespectful children. Communities also use internal networks and local institutions to control crime. Sources of institutional social control include businesses, schools, religious institutions, and social service and volunteer organizations.[56]

Stable neighbourhoods can arrange for external sources of social control. The level of policing, an important source of neighbourhood stability, may vary among neighbourhoods. Police officers patrolling in stable, low-crime areas may have the resources and motivation to respond vigorously to crime, preventing criminal groups from gaining a toehold in the neighbourhood.[57] Community organizations and local leaders may have sufficient political clout to get funding for additional law enforcement personnel. The presence of police sends a message that the area will not tolerate deviant behaviour. Criminals and drug dealers avoid such areas and relocate to easier and more appealing targets.[58] In more disorganized areas, police officers are less motivated, and their resources are stretched more tightly. These communities cannot mount an effective social control effort because as neighbourhood disadvantage increases, informal social control decreases.[59]

The ramifications of having adequate controls are critical. In areas where collective efficacy remains high, children are less likely to become involved with deviant peers and engage in problem behaviours.[60] In disorganized areas, however, the population is transient, so interpersonal relationships remain

Andy Clark/Reuters/Landov

When poverty begins to concentrate, neighbourhoods crumble and businesses flee to more affluent areas. Residents become hopeless and bewildered, relying on the government for help. Vancouver's Downtown Eastside has the dubious distinction of being the "heroin capital" of Canada. Residents in the Downtown Eastside have called on the government (and the police) to clean up the neighbourhood and make it safe. The Downtown Eastside area is the neighbourhood where accused serial murderer Robert Pickton recruited his victims.

anomie
A lack of norms or clear social standards. Because of rapidly shifting moral values, the individual has few guides to what is socially acceptable.

superficial. Social institutions such as schools and religious institutions cannot work effectively in a climate of alienation and mistrust. In these areas, the absence of political power brokers limits access to external funding and protection; without outside money, the neighbourhood cannot get back on its feet.[61] Children who live in these neighbourhoods find that involvement with conventional social institutions, such as schools and afternoon programs, is blocked; they are instead at risk for involvement in delinquent behaviour, or recruitment into gangs.[62] These problems are stubborn and difficult to overcome. And even when an attempt is made to revitalize a disorganized neighbourhood by creating institutional support programs such as community centres and better schools, the effort may be countered by the ongoing drain of deep-rooted economic and social deprivation.[63]

According to the social ecology school, then, social disorganization produces criminality. The quality of community life, including levels of change, fear, incivility, poverty, and deterioration, directly influences an area's crime rate. It is not some individual property or trait that causes some people to commit crime, but rather the quality and ambience of the community in which they live. Conversely, in socially altruistic areas, crime rates decrease no matter what the economic situation.

DID YOU KNOW?

- Shaw and McKay first identified the concepts central to social disorganization. They found stable patterns of crime in the central city.
- Strain theories hold that economic deprivation causes frustration, which leads to crime.
- According to Merton's anomie theory, many people who desire material goods and other forms of economic success lack the means to achieve their goals. Some may turn to crime.
- Messner and Rosenfeld's institutional anomie theory argues that the goal of success at all costs has invaded every aspect of North American life.
- Agnew's general theory of strain suggests that there is more than one source of anomie.

LO5 Strain Theories

Inhabitants of a disorganized inner-city area feel isolated, frustrated, ostracized from the economic mainstream, hopeless, and eventually angry. How do these feelings affect criminal activities?

Strain theorists view crime as a direct result of lower-class frustration and anger. They believe that although most people share similar values and goals, the ability to achieve personal goals is stratified by socioeconomic class. Strain is limited in affluent areas because educational and vocational opportunities are available. In disorganized areas, strain occurs because legitimate avenues for success are all but closed. To relieve strain, indigent people may achieve their goals through deviant methods, such as theft or drug trafficking, or they may reject socially accepted goals and substitute more deviant goals, such as being tough and aggressive (see Figure 6.6).

Theory of Anomie

Sociologist Robert Merton applied the sociological concepts first identified by Emile Durkheim to criminology in his theory of **anomie**.[64]

FIGURE 6.6

The Basic Compounds of Strain Theory

Poverty
- Development of isolated lower-class culture
- Lack of conventional social opportunities
- Racial and ethnic discrimination

Maintenance of conventional rules and norms
Lower-class citizens remain loyal to conventional values and rules of dominant middle-class culture.

Strain
Lack of opportunity coupled with desire for conventional success produces strain and frustration.

Formation of gangs and groups
Youths form law-violating groups to seek alternative means of achieving success.

Crime and delinquency
Methods of groups—theft, violence, substance abuse—are defined as illegal by dominant culture.

Criminal careers
Most youthful gang members "age out" of crime, but some continue as adult criminals.

Merton found that two elements of culture interact to produce potentially anomic conditions: culturally defined goals and socially approved means for obtaining them. For example, modern societies stress the goals of acquiring wealth, success, and power. Socially permissible means include hard work, education, and thrift.

Merton argues that the legitimate means to acquire wealth are stratified across class and status lines. Those with little formal education and few economic resources soon find that they are denied the ability to legally acquire wealth—the preeminent success symbol. When socially mandated goals are uniform throughout society and access to legitimate means is bound by class and status, the resulting strain produces anomie among those who are locked out of the legitimate opportunity structure. Consequently, they may develop criminal or delinquent solutions to the problem of attaining goals.

CONNECTIONS

As you may recall from Chapter 1, the roots of strain theories can be traced to Emile Durkheim's notion of anomie (from the Greek *a nomos*, without norms). According to Durkheim, an anomic society is one in which rules of behaviour—norms—have broken down or become inoperative during periods of rapid social change or social crisis such as war or famine.

Social Adaptations

Merton argues that each person has his or her own concept of society's goals and means to attain them. Some people have inadequate means of attaining success; others who have the means reject societal goals. The result is a variety of social adaptations:

1. *Conformity.* Conformity occurs when individuals embrace conventional social goals and also have the means to attain them. They remain law abiding.
2. *Innovation.* Innovation occurs when individuals accept the goals of society but are unable or unwilling to attain them through legitimate means. The resulting conflict forces them to adopt innovative solutions to their dilemma: they steal, sell drugs, or extort money. Of the five adaptations, innovation is most closely associated with criminal behaviour.
3. *Ritualism.* Ritualists gain pleasure from practising traditional ceremonies, regardless of whether they have a real purpose or a goal. The strict customs in religious orders, feudal societies, clubs, and university fraternities encourage and appeal to ritualists. Ritualists should have the lowest level of criminal behaviour because they have abandoned the success goal, which is at the root of criminal activity.
4. *Retreatism.* Retreatists reject both the goals and the means of society. They attempt to escape their lack of success by withdrawing, either mentally or physically, by taking drugs or becoming drifters.
5. *Rebellion.* Rebellion involves substituting an alternative set of goals and means for conventional ones. Revolutionaries who wish to promote radical change in the existing social structure and who call for alternative lifestyles, goals, and beliefs are engaging in rebellion. Rebellion may be a reaction against a corrupt, hated government or an effort to create alternative opportunities and lifestyles within the existing system.

anomie theory
View that anomie results when socially defined goals (such as wealth and power) are universally mandated but access to legitimate means (such as education and job opportunities) is stratified by class and status.

institutional anomie theory
The view that anomie pervades modern culture because the drive for material wealth dominates and undermines social and community values.

"American Dream"
The goal of accumulating material goods and wealth through individual competition; the process of being socialized to pursue material success and to believe it is achievable.

Evaluation of Anomie Theory

According to **anomie theory**, social inequality leads to perceptions of anomie. To resolve the goals–means conflict and relieve their sense of strain, some people innovate by stealing or extorting money; others retreat into drugs and alcohol; some rebel by joining revolutionary groups; and still others get involved in ritualistic behaviour by joining a religious cult.

Merton's view of anomie has been one of the most enduring and influential sociological theories of criminality. By linking deviant behaviour to the success goals that control social behaviour, anomie theory attempts to pinpoint the cause of the conflict that produces personal frustration and consequent criminality. By acknowledging that society unfairly distributes the legitimate means to achieving success, anomie theory helps explain the existence of high-crime areas and the apparent predominance of delinquent and criminal behaviour in the lower class. By suggesting that social conditions, not individual personalities, produce crime, Merton greatly influenced the directions taken to reduce and control criminality during the latter half of the 20th century.

A number of questions are left unanswered by anomie theory.[65] Merton does not explain why people choose to commit certain types of crime. For example, why does one anomic person become a mugger while another deals drugs? Anomie may explain differences in crime rates, but it cannot explain why most young criminals desist from crime as adults. Does this mean that perceptions of anomie dwindle with age? Is anomie short lived?

Institutional Anomie Theory

Steven Messner and Richard Rosenfeld's **institutional anomie theory** is an updating of Merton's work.[66]

Messner and Rosenfeld agree with Merton that the success goal is pervasive in North American culture. For them, the **"American Dream"** refers to both a goal and a process. As a goal, it involves accumulating material goods and wealth via open individual competition. As a process, it involves both being socialized to pursue material success and believing that prosperity is achievable. Anomic conditions arise because the desire to succeed at any cost drives people apart, weakens the collective sense of community, fosters ambition, and restricts the desire to achieve anything other than material wealth. Achieving respect, for example, is not sufficient.

Why does anomie pervade modern culture? According to Messner and Rosenfeld, it is because institutions that might otherwise control the exaggerated emphasis on financial success, such as religious or charitable institutions, have been rendered powerless or obsolete. These social institutions have been undermined in three ways:

1. *Noneconomic functions and roles have been devalued.* Performance in other institutional settings—the family, school, or community—is assigned a lower priority than the goal of financial success.
2. *When conflicts emerge, noneconomic roles become subordinate to and must accommodate economic roles.* The schedules, routines, and demands of the workplace take priority over those of the home, the school, the community, and other aspects of social life.
3. *Economic language, standards, and norms penetrate into noneconomic realms.* Economic terms become part of the

Owning your own home is still an integral part of the American (or Canadian) dream.

Vacclav/Shutterstock.com

common vernacular: People want to get to the "bottom line." Spouses view themselves as "partners" who "manage" the household. Retired people say they want to "downsize" their household. We "outsource" home repairs instead of doing them ourselves. Corporate leaders run for public office promising to "run the country like a business."

According to Messner and Rosenfeld, the relatively high crime rates in many modern societies can be explained by the interrelationship between culture and institutions. At the cultural level, the dominance of the "American Dream" mythology ensures that many people will develop desires for material goods that cannot be satisfied by legitimate means. Anomie becomes a norm, and extralegal means become a strategy for attaining material wealth. At the institutional level, the dominance of economic concerns weakens the informal social control exerted by family, religious institutions, and school. These institutions have lost their ability to regulate behaviour and have instead become a conduit for promoting material success. For example, schools are evaluated not for imparting knowledge but for their ability to train students to get high-paying jobs. Social conditions reinforce each other: Culture determines institutions, and institutional change influences culture. Crime rates may rise in a healthy economy because national prosperity heightens the attractiveness of monetary rewards, encouraging people to gain financial success by any means possible, including illegal ones. In this culture of competition, self-interest prevails and generates amorality, acceptance of inequality, and disdain for the less fortunate.[67]

General Strain Theory (GST)

Sociologist Robert Agnew's **general strain theory (GST)** helps identify the micro- or individual-level influences of strain. Whereas Merton and Messner and Rosenfeld try to explain social class differences in the crime rate, Agnew tries to explain why individuals who feel stress and strain are likely to commit crimes. Agnew also attempts to offer a more general explanation of criminal activity among all elements of society rather than restrict his views to lower-class crime.[68]

Multiple Sources of Strain

Agnew suggests that criminality is the direct result of **negative affective states**—the anger, frustration, and adverse emotions that emerge in the wake of destructive social relationships. He finds that negative affective states are produced by a variety of sources of strain (see Figure 6.7):

general strain theory (GST)
The view that multiple sources of strain interact with an individual's emotional traits and responses to produce criminality.

negative affective states
Anger, frustration, and adverse emotions produced by a variety of sources of strain.

- *Failure to achieve positively valued goals.* This cause of strain, similar to what Merton speaks of in his theory of anomie, is a result of the disjunction between aspirations and expectations. This type of strain occurs when a youth aspires to wealth and fame but, lacking financial and educational resources, assumes that such goals are impossible to achieve; he then turns to crime and drug dealing.
- *Disjunction of expectations and achievements.* Strain can also be produced by a disjunction between expectations and achievements. When people compare themselves to peers who seem to be doing a lot better financially or socially (such as making more money or getting better grades), even those doing relatively well feel strain. For example, when a student graduating high school is accepted at a good college or university but not a prestige school, like some of her friends, she will feel strain. Perhaps she is not being treated fairly because the playing field is tilted against her: "Other kids have connections," she may say. Perceptions of inequity may result in many adverse reactions, ranging from running away from its source to lowering others' benefits through physical attacks or property vandalism.
- *Removal of positively valued stimuli.* Strain may occur because of the actual or anticipated loss of positively valued stimuli.[69] For example, the loss of a girl- or boyfriend can produce strain, as can the death of a loved one, moving to a new neighbourhood or school, or the divorce or separation of parents. The loss of positive stimuli may lead to delinquency as the adolescent tries to prevent the loss, retrieve what has been lost, obtain substitutes, or seek revenge against those responsible for the loss.
- *Presentation of negative stimuli.* Strain may also be caused by negative or noxious stimuli, such as child abuse or neglect, crime

FIGURE 6.7

Elements of General Strain Theory (GST)

Sources of strain
- Failure to achieve goals
- Disjunction of expectations and achievements
- Removal of positive stimuli
- Presentation of negative stimuli

Negative affective states
- Anger
- Frustration
- Disappointment
- Depression
- Fear

Antisocial behaviour
- Drug abuse
- Delinquency
- Violence
- Dropping out

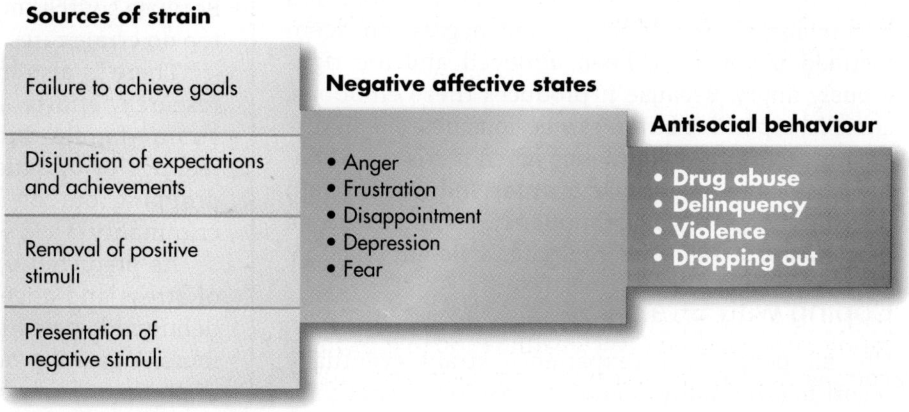

victimization, physical punishment, family or peer conflict, school failure, or stressful life events ranging from verbal threats to air pollution. For example, adolescent delinquency has been linked to maltreatment through the rage and anger it generates. Children who are abused at home may take out their rage on younger children at school or become involved in violent delinquency.[70]

CONNECTIONS

The GST is not solely a cultural deviance theory since it recognizes non-class-related sources of strain. In this regard it is similar to the social process theories discussed in Chapter 7. It is included here because it incorporates the view that social class position can be an important source of strain, thus following in the tradition of Merton's theory of anomie.

Although these sources of strain are independent of one another, they may overlap. For example, if a teacher insults a student, it may be viewed as an unfair application of negative stimuli that interferes with a student's academic aspirations. The greater the intensity and frequency of strain experiences, the greater their impact and the more likely they are to cause delinquency.

According to Agnew, each type of strain increases the likelihood of experiencing negative emotions such as disappointment, depression, fear, and most important, anger. Anger increases perceptions of injury and of being wronged. It produces a desire for revenge, energizes individuals to take action, and lowers inhibitions. Violence and aggression seem justified if you have been wronged and are righteously angry. Because it produces these emotions, chronic, repetitive strain can be considered a predisposing factor for delinquency when it creates a hostile, suspicious, aggressive attitude. Individual strain episodes may trigger delinquency, such as when a particularly stressful event ignites a violent reaction.

Coping with Strain

Not all people who experience strain eventually resort to criminality. Some are able to marshal their emotional, mental, and behavioural resources to cope with the anger and frustration produced by strain. Some individuals may be able to rationalize frustrating circumstances: Getting a good job is "just not that important"; they may be poor, but the "next guy is worse off"; if things didn't work out, they "got what [they] deserved." Others seek behavioural solutions, running away from adverse conditions or seeking revenge against those who caused the strain. Some try to regain emotional equilibrium with techniques ranging from physical exercise to drug abuse.

However, some people cannot cope with strain because they have traits that make them particularly sensitive to strain. These include an explosive temperament, low tolerance for adversity, poor problem-solving skills, and being overly sensitive or emotional. Although these traits, which are linked to aggressive, antisocial behaviour, seem to be stable over the life cycle, they may peak during adolescence.[71] This is a period of social stress caused by weakening parental supervision and the development of relationships with a diverse peer group. Many adolescents going through the trauma of family breakup and frequent changes in family structure feel a high degree of strain. They may react by becoming involved in precocious sexuality or by turning to substance abuse to mask the strain.[72]

As children mature, their expectations increase. Some are unable to meet academic and social demands. Adolescents are very concerned about their standing with peers. Teenagers who are deficient in these areas may find they are social outcasts, another source of strain. In adulthood, crime rates may drop because these sources of strain are reduced. New sources of self-esteem emerge, and adults seem more likely to align their goals with reality.

Evaluating GST

Agnew's important work both clarifies the concept of strain and directs future research agendas. It also adds to the body of literature describing how social and life history events influence offending patterns. Because sources of strain vary over the life course, so too do crime rates.

There is also empirical support for GST.[73] Some research efforts have shown that indicators of strain—family breakup, unemployment, moving, feelings of dissatisfaction with friends and school, dropping out of school—are positively related to criminality.[74]

As predicted by GST, people who report feelings of stress and anger are more likely to interact with delinquent peers and to engage in criminal behaviours.[75] Lashing out at others may reduce feelings of strain, as may stealing or vandalizing property.[76]

There is also evidence that, as predicted by the GST, people who fail to meet success goals are more likely to engage in criminal activities.[77]

Cultural Deviance Theory

The third branch of social structure theory combines the effects of social disorganization and strain to explain how people living in deteriorated neighbourhoods react to social isolation and economic deprivation. Because their lifestyle is draining, frustrating, and dispiriting, members of the lower class create an independent subculture with its own set of rules and values. Whereas middle-class culture stresses hard work, delayed gratification, formal education, and being cautious, the lower-class subculture stresses excitement, toughness, taking risks, fearlessness, immediate gratification, and street smarts.

FIGURE 6.8

Elements of Cultural Deviance Theory

Poverty
- Lack of opportunity
- Feeling of oppression

Socialization
Lower-class youths are socialized to value middle-class goals and ideas. However, their environment inhibits proper socialization.

Subculture
Blocked opportunities prompt formation of groups with alternative lifestyles and values.

Success goal
Gangs provide alternative methods of gaining success for some, venting anger for others.

Crime and delinquency
New methods of gaining success involve law-violating behaviour.

Criminal careers
Some gang boys can parlay their status into criminal careers; others become drug users or violent assaulters.

focal concerns
Values, such as toughness and street smarts, that have evolved specifically to fit conditions in lower-class environments.

delinquent subculture
A value system adopted by lower-class youths that is directly opposed to that of the larger society.

status frustration
A form of culture conflict experienced by lower-class youths because social conditions prevent them from achieving success as defined by the larger society.

The lower-class subculture is an attractive alternative because the urban poor find it impossible to meet the behavioural demands of middle-class society. However, subcultural norms often clash with conventional values. Urban dwellers are forced to violate the law because they obey the rules of the deviant culture with which they are in immediate contact (see Figure 6.8).

More than 40 years ago, sociologist Walter Miller identified the unique conduct norms that help define lower-class culture.[78] Miller referred to them as **focal concerns**, values that have evolved specifically to fit conditions in lower-class environments. The major lower-class focal concerns are set out in Table 6.1.[79]

According to Miller, clinging to lower-class focal concerns promotes illegal or violent behaviour. Toughness may mean displaying fighting prowess; street smarts may lead to drug deals; excitement may result in drinking, gambling, or drug abuse.[80] To illustrate, consider a study of violent young men in New York, conducted by sociologist Jeffrey Fagan. He found that the most compelling function that violence served was to develop status as a "tough," an identity that helps young men acquire social power while at the same time insulating them from becoming victims. Violence was also seen as a means to acquire the trappings of wealth (such as nice clothes, flashy cars, or access to clubs), control or humiliate another person, defy authority, settle drug-related disputes, attain retribution, satisfy the need for thrills or risk taking, and respond to challenges to one's manhood.[81] Lower-class focal concerns seem as relevant today as when they were first identified by Miller more than 40 years ago!

Theory of Delinquent Subcultures

Albert Cohen first articulated the theory of **delinquent subcultures** in his classic 1955 book, *Delinquent Boys*.[82] Cohen's central position was that delinquent behaviour of lower-class youths is actually a protest against the norms and values of modern middle-class culture. Because social conditions prevent them from achieving success legitimately, lower-class youths experience a form of culture conflict that Cohen labels **status frustration**.[83] As a result, many of them join

TABLE 6.1

Miller's Lower-Class Focal Concerns

Trouble	In lower-class communities, people are evaluated by their actual or potential involvement in making trouble. Getting into trouble includes such behaviours as fighting, drinking, and sexual misconduct. Dealing with trouble can confer prestige—for example, when a man establishes a reputation for being able to handle himself well in a fight. Not being able to handle trouble, and having to pay the consequences, can make a person look foolish and incompetent.
Toughness	Lower-class males want local recognition of their physical and spiritual toughness. They refuse to be sentimental or soft and instead value physical strength, fighting ability, and athletic skill. Those who cannot meet these standards risk getting a reputation for being weak, inept, and effeminate.
Smartness	Members of the lower-class culture want to maintain an image of being streetwise and savvy, using their street smarts, and having the ability to outfox and out-con the opponent. Although formal education is not admired, knowing essential survival techniques, such as gambling, conning, and outsmarting the law, is a requirement.
Excitement	Members of the lower class search for fun and excitement to enliven an otherwise drab existence. The search for excitement may lead to gambling, fighting, getting drunk, and sexual adventures. In between, the lower-class citizen may simply "hang out" and "be cool."
Fate	Lower-class citizens believe their lives are in the hands of strong spiritual forces that guide their destinies. Getting lucky, finding good fortune, and hitting the jackpot are all daily dreams.
Autonomy	Being independent of authority figures, such as the police, teachers, and parents, is required; losing control is an unacceptable weakness, incompatible with toughness.

Source: Walter Miller, "Lower-Class Culture as a Generating Milieu of Gang Delinquency," *Journal of Social Issues* 14 (1958): 5–19. Reprinted by permission of John Wiley and Sons via Rightslink.

middle-class measuring rods
The standards by which authority figures, such as teachers and employers, evaluate lower-class youngsters and often prejudge them negatively.

gangs and engage in behaviour that is "non-utilitarian, malicious, and negativistic."[84]

Cohen viewed the delinquent gang as a separate subculture, possessing a value system directly opposed to that of the larger society. He described the subculture as one that "takes its norms from the larger culture, but turns them upside down. The delinquent's conduct is right by the standards of his subculture precisely because it is wrong by the norms of the larger culture."[85]

According to Cohen, the development of the delinquent subculture is a consequence of socialization practices in lower-class environments. Here children lack the basic skills necessary to achieve social and economic success, including a proper education, which renders them incapable of developing the skills to succeed in society. Lower-class parents are incapable of teaching children the necessary techniques for entering the dominant middle-class culture. The consequences of this deprivation include developmental handicaps, poor speech and communication skills, and inability to delay gratification.

Middle-Class Measuring Rods

One significant handicap that lower-class children face is the inability to positively impress authority figures, such as teachers, employers, or supervisors. In North American society, these positions tend to be held by members of the middle class, who have difficulty relating to the lower-class youngster. Cohen calls the standards set by these authority figures **middle-class measuring rods**.

The conflict and frustration lower-class youths experience when they fail to meet these standards is a primary cause of delinquency. They may find themselves prejudged by others and not measuring up in the final analysis. Negative evaluations become part of a permanent file that follows an individual for the rest of his or her life. When he or she wants to improve, evidence of prior failures is used to discourage advancement.

The Formation of Deviant Subcultures

Cohen believes that lower-class boys rejected by middle-class decision makers usually join one of three existing subcultures: the corner boy, the college boy, or the delinquent boy.

The corner boy role is the most common response to middle-class rejection. The corner boy is not a chronic delinquent but may be a truant who engages in petty or status offences, such as precocious sex and recreational drug abuse. His main loyalty is to his peer group, on which he depends for support, motivation, and interest. His values, therefore, are those of the group with which he is in close contact. The corner boy, well aware of his failure to achieve the standards of the "American Dream," retreats into the comforting world of his lower-class peers and eventually becomes a stable member of his neighbourhood, holding a menial job, marrying, and remaining in the community.

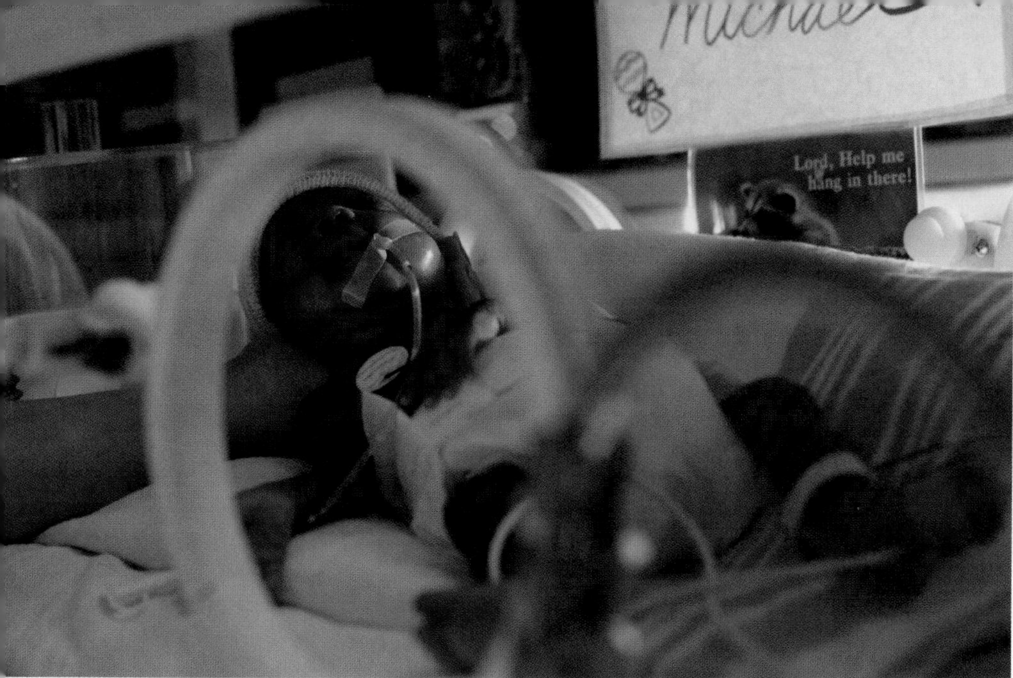

© PHOTOTAKE Inc./Alamy

Deviant subcultures feature social problems that are handed down from one generation to the next. Health Canada estimates that every day in Canada, at least one child is born with fetal alcohol syndrome (FAS). FAS has been linked to a variety of neurological problems, including hyperactivity, memory deficits, and inability to control anger. Here, a premature infant affected by FAS is monitored in an incubator.

The college boy embraces the cultural and social values of the middle class. Rather than scorning middle-class measuring rods, he actively strives to succeed by those standards. Cohen views this type of youth as one who is embarking on an almost hopeless path because he is ill equipped academically, socially, and linguistically to achieve the rewards of middle-class life.

The delinquent boy adopts a set of norms and principles that directly oppose middle-class values. He engages in *short-run hedonism*, living for today and letting "tomorrow take care of itself."[86] Delinquent boys strive for group autonomy. They resist efforts by family, school, or other sources of authority to control their behaviour. Frustrated by their inability to succeed, these boys resort to a process Cohen calls **reaction formation**, including overly intense responses that seem disproportionate to the stimuli that trigger them. For the delinquent boy, this takes the form of irrational, malicious, and unaccountable hostility to the enemy, which in this case is "the norms of respectable middle-class society."[87]

Cohen's approach skillfully integrates strain and social disorganization theories and has become an enduring element of criminological literature.

LO6 Theory of Differential Opportunity

In their classic work *Delinquency and Opportunity*, written more than 40 years ago, Richard Cloward and Lloyd Ohlin combined strain and social disorganization principles to portray a gang-sustaining criminal subculture.[88]

The centrepiece of the Cloward and Ohlin theory is the concept of **differential opportunity**. According to this concept, people in all strata of society share the same success goals; however, those in the lower class have limited means of achieving them. People who perceive themselves as failures within conventional society will seek alternative or innovative ways to succeed. People who conclude that there is little hope for legitimate advancement may join like-minded peers to form a gang, which can provide them with emotional support. The youth who is considered a failure at school and is qualified for only a menial job at a minimum wage can earn thousands of dollars plus the respect of his or her peers by joining a gang and engaging in drug deals or armed robberies.

Cloward and Ohlin recognize that the opportunity for success in both conventional and criminal careers is limited. In stable areas, adolescents may be recruited by professional criminals, drug traffickers, or organized crime groups. Unstable areas, however, cannot support flourishing criminal opportunities. In these socially disorganized neighbourhoods, adult role models are absent, and young criminals have few opportunities to join established gangs or learn the fine points of professional crime. Cloward and Ohlin's most important finding, then, is that all opportunities for success, both illegal and conventional, are closed for the most disadvantaged youths.

Because of differential opportunity, young people are likely to join one of three types of gangs:

1. *Criminal gangs.* Criminal gangs exist in stable neighbourhoods where close connections among adolescent, young adult, and adult offenders create an environment for successful criminal enterprise.[89] Youths are recruited into established criminal gangs that provide training for a successful criminal career. Gang membership is a learning experience in which the knowledge

reaction formation
Irrational hostility evidenced by young delinquents, who adopt norms directly opposed to middle-class goals and standards that seem impossible to achieve.

differential opportunity
The view that lower-class youths, whose legitimate opportunities are limited, join gangs and pursue criminal careers as alternative means to achieve universal success goals.

and skills needed for success in crime are acquired. During this apprenticeship, older, more experienced members of the criminal subculture hold youthful trainees on tight reins, limiting activities that might jeopardize the gang's profits (e.g., engaging in nonfunctional, irrational violence).

2. *Conflict gangs.* Conflict gangs develop in communities unable to provide either legitimate or illegitimate opportunities.[90] These gangs attract tough adolescents who fight with weapons to win respect from rivals and engage in unpredictable and destructive assaults on people and property. Conflict gang members must be ready to fight to protect their own and their gang's integrity and honour. By doing so, they acquire a "rep," which gains admiration from their peers and consequently helps them develop their self-image.

3. *Retreatist gangs.* Retreatists are double failures, unable to gain success through legitimate means and unwilling to do so through illegal ones. Members of the retreatist subculture constantly search for ways of getting high—alcohol, pot, heroin, unusual sexual experiences, music. To feed their habits, retreatists develop a "hustle"—pimping, conning, selling drugs, or committing petty crimes. Personal status in the retreatist subculture is derived from peer approval.

Cloward and Ohlin's theory integrates cultural deviance and social disorganization variables and recognizes different modes of criminal adaptation. The fact that criminal cultures can be supportive, rational, and profitable seems to more realistically reflect the actual world of the delinquent than Cohen's original view of purely negativistic, destructive delinquent youths who oppose all social values.

Social Structure Theory and Social Policy

Social structure theory has significantly influenced social policy. If the cause of criminality is viewed as a schism between lower-class individuals and conventional goals, norms, and rules, it seems logical that alternatives to criminal behaviour can be provided by giving inner-city youth opportunities to share in the rewards of conventional society.

One approach is to give indigent people direct financial aid through public assistance or welfare. Although welfare has been curtailed under many provincial governments in Canada, U.S. research shows that crime rates decrease when families receive supplemental income through public assistance payments.[91]

Efforts have also been made to reduce crime by improving the community structure in high-crime neighbourhoods. Crime prevention efforts based on social structure precepts can be traced back to the Chicago Area Project supervised by Clifford R. Shaw. This program attempted to organize existing community structures to develop social stability in otherwise disorganized slums. The project sponsored recreation programs for neighbourhood children, including summer camping. It campaigned for community improvements in areas such as education, sanitation, traffic safety, resource conservation, and law enforcement. Project members also worked with police and court agencies to supervise and treat gang youth and adult offenders. Today, Shaw's legacy continues on in ambitious projects like Hamilton, Ontario's "Neighbourhood Safety Project," where police officers and community development staff work with neighbourhood associations to address the whole gamut of neighbourhood problems, including crime and public order issues.[92]

Social structure concepts, especially Cloward and Ohlin's views, were a critical ingredient in "War on Poverty" initiatives begun in the United States in the early 1960s. Similar programs in both the United States and Canada—including Head Start, Neighbourhood Legal Services, the Community Action Program, breakfast clubs for school-age children, and after-school homework and recreation programs—have continued to help people.

CHAPTER 7

Socialization and Crime

Learning Outcomes

LO1 Explain how social process theories view criminality.

LO2 Identify major family factors predictive of behaviour.

LO3 Explain how the educational process and adolescent school achievement have been linked to criminality.

LO4 Explain how peer relationships have been linked to delinquency.

LO5 Explain the difference between social learning theory and social control theory.

LO6 Explain the difference between the most prominent forms of social learning theory: differential association theory and neutralization theory.

LO7 Describe how Travis Hirschi's contemporary social control theory explains why people obey the law.

LO8 Discuss why critics have charged that labelling theory lacks credibility.

LO1 Socialization and Crime

Some criminologists focus their attention on social–psychological processes and interactions common to people in all segments of the social structure, not just the lower class. They believe that criminality is a function of individual **socialization** and the interactions people have with various organizations, institutions, and processes of society. Most people are influenced by their family relationships, peer group associations, educational experiences, and interactions with authority figures, including teachers, employers, and agents of the justice system. If these relationships are positive and supportive, people can succeed within the rules of society; if these relationships are dysfunctional and destructive, conventional success may be impossible, and criminal solutions may become a feasible alternative. Taken together, this view of crime is referred to as **social process theory**.

Social process theories share one basic concept: All people, regardless of their race, class, or gender, have the potential to become delinquents or criminals. Although members of the lower class may have the added burdens of poverty, racism, poor schools, and disrupted family lives, these social forces can be counteracted by positive peer relations, a supportive family, and educational success. In contrast, even the most affluent members of society may turn to antisocial behaviour if their life experiences are intolerable or destructive.

Social process theories have endured because the relationship between social class and crime is still uncertain. Most residents of inner-city areas refrain from criminal activity, and few of those who commit crimes persist into adulthood. If poverty were the sole cause of crime, then indigent adults would be as criminal as indigent teenagers. But we know that, regardless of class position, most people age out of crime. The association between economic status and crime is problematic because class position alone cannot explain crime rates.[1]

Criminologists have long studied the critical elements of socialization to determine how they contribute to a burgeoning criminal career. Prominent

DID YOU KNOW?

- Social process theories say that the way people are socialized controls their behaviour choices.
- There is strong evidence that social relations influence behaviour.
- Children growing up with conflict, abuse, and neglect are at risk for crime and delinquency.
- Educational failure has been linked to criminality.
- Adolescents who associate with deviant peers are more likely to engage in crime than those who maintain conventional peer group relations.
- Some criminologists maintain that crime is a learned behaviour.
- Other criminologists view criminals as people whose behaviour has not been controlled.
- Some view criminality as a function of labelling and stigma.

socialization
Process of human development and enculturation. Socialization is influenced by key social processes and institutions.

social process theory
The view that criminality is a function of people's interactions with various organizations, institutions, and processes in society.

CONNECTIONS

Chapter 2's analysis of the class–crime relationship showed why this relationship is still a hotly debated topic. Although serious criminals may be found disproportionately in lower-class areas, self-report studies show that criminality cuts across class lines. The discussion of drug use in Chapter 13, which shows that members of the middle class use and abuse recreational substances, suggests that law violators are not necessarily economically motivated.

among these elements are family, school, peer group, and church.

LO2 Family Relations

Family relationships are considered a major determinant of behaviour.[2] In fact, parenting factors, such as the ability to communicate and provide proper discipline, may play a critical role in determining whether people misbehave as children and even later as adults. This is one of the most replicated findings in the criminological literature.[3]

Youths who grow up in a household characterized by conflict and tension, where parents are absent or separated, or where there is a lack of familial love and support, are susceptible to crime-promoting forces in the environment.[4]

Even children living in high-crime areas will be better able to resist the temptations of the streets if they receive fair discipline, care, and support from parents who provide them with strong, positive role models.[5] Nonetheless, living in a disadvantaged neighbourhood places terrific strain on family functioning, especially in lone-parent families that are socially isolated from relatives, friends, and neighbours. Children raised within such distressed families are at risk for delinquency.[6]

At one time, growing up in a lone-parent home was considered a primary cause of criminal behaviour. However, many criminologists today discount the association between family structure and the onset of criminality, claiming that family conflict and discord determine behaviour more than family structure.[7] Not all experts, though, discount the effects of family structure on crime. Even if lone parents can make up for the loss of a second parent, the argument goes, it is simply more difficult to do so, and the chances of failure increase.[8] Lone parents may find it difficult to provide adequate supervision, and children who live with lone parents receive less encouragement and less help with schoolwork. Poor school achievement and limited educational aspirations have been associated with delinquent behaviour. Also, because they are receiving less attention as a result of having just one parent, these children may be more prone to rebellious acts, such as running away and truancy.[9] Children in two-parent households are more likely to want to attend college or university than those raised in lone-parent homes.[10]

Other family factors that have predictive value include the following:

1. Inconsistent discipline, poor supervision, and the lack of a warm, loving, supportive parent–child relationship are all associated with delinquency.[11] Children who grow up in homes where parents use severe discipline yet lack warmth and involvement in their lives are prone to antisocial behaviour.[12]
2. Children who have affectionate ties to their parents report greater levels of self-esteem beginning in adolescence and extending into adulthood; high self-esteem is inversely related to criminal behaviour.[13] Children growing up in homes where a parent suffers mental impairment are also at risk for delinquency.[14]
3. Children as young as two whose parents are drug abusers exhibit personality defects such as excessive anger and negativity.[15] These children, as well as older children of drug abusers, are more likely to become persistent substance abusers than the children of nonabusers.[16]

© Judy Barranco/iStockPhoto

Children who have a warm, loving, and supportive relationship with their parents are less likely to be involved in criminal activity.

Jupiter Images

Children who grow up in homes with parents who have mental health problems, who abuse substances, or who are abusive are at risk of becoming delinquent.

4. Children who experience abuse, neglect, or sexual abuse are believed to be more crime prone.[17] Links have been found among corporal punishment, delinquency, anger, spousal abuse, depression, and adult crime.[18]

LO3 Educational Experience

The educational process and adolescent school achievement have been linked to criminality. Children who do poorly in school, lack educational motivation, and feel alienated are the most likely to engage in criminal acts.[19] Children who fail in school offend more frequently than those who succeed. These children commit more serious and violent offences and persist in crime into adulthood.[20]

Schools contribute to criminality by labelling problem youths, which sets them apart from conventional society. One way in which schools perpetuate this stigmatization is through "streaming," which identifies some students as college or university bound and others as academic underachievers or potential dropouts.[21] Research findings over the past two decades indicate that many school dropouts, especially those who have been expelled, face a significant chance of entering a criminal career.[22]

LO4 Peer Relations

Psychologists have long recognized that peer groups powerfully affect human conduct and can dramatically influence decision making and behaviour choices.[23] Children who are rejected by their peers are more likely to display aggressive behaviour and disrupt group activities through bickering, bullying, or other antisocial behaviour.[24] Research shows that adolescents who report inadequate or strained peer relations, and who say they are not popular with the opposite sex, are most likely to become delinquent.[25]

Negative or inadequate peer relationships have been tied to delinquency.

SW Productions/Photolibrary

Delinquent peers often exert tremendous influence on behaviour, attitudes, and beliefs.[26] In every level of the social structure, youths who fall in with a bad crowd become more susceptible to criminal behaviour patterns.[27] Deviant peers provide friendship networks that support delinquency and drug use.[28] Activities such as riding around, staying out late, and partying with deviant peers give these youths the opportunity to commit deviant acts.[29] Because delinquent friends tend to be, as criminologist Mark Warr puts it, "sticky" (once acquired, they are not easily lost), peer influence may continue through the life span.[30] The more antisocial the peer group, the more likely its members are to engage in delinquency. Nondelinquent friends help to moderate delinquency.[31]

As children grow and move forward, friends influence their behaviour, and their behaviour influences their friends.[32] Antisocial friends guide delinquent careers so they withstand the aging-out process.[33] Chronic offenders surround themselves with peers who share their antisocial activities, and these relationships seem quite stable over time. People who maintain close relations with antisocial peers will sustain their own criminal behaviour into adulthood. If peer influence diminishes, so too does criminal activity.[34]

Institutional Involvement and Belief

Logic would dictate that people who hold high moral values and beliefs, who have learned to distinguish right from wrong, and who regularly attend religious services, should also eschew crime and other antisocial behaviours. Religion binds people together and forces them to confront the consequences of their behaviour. Committing crimes would violate the principles of all organized religions.

However, an often-cited study by sociologists Travis Hirschi and Rodney Stark found that, contrary to expectations, the association between religious attendance or belief and delinquent behaviour patterns was negligible.[35] However, some recent research efforts have reached an opposing conclusion: Attending religious services significantly reduces crime. Interestingly, this type of participation seems to inhibit crime more than merely having religious beliefs and values.[36] Cross-national research shows that countries with high rates of church membership and attendance have lower crime rates.[37]

FIGURE 7.1

The Complex Web of Social Processes that Controls Human Behaviour

Social learning theory
Criminal behaviour is learned through human interaction.

Social control theory
Human behaviour is controlled through close associations with institutions and individuals.

Social reaction theory
Some people are labelled "criminal" by police and court authorities; people so labelled, shunned by conventional society, adopt the labelled identity.

LO5 The Effects of Socialization on Crime

According to the social process view, people living in even the most deteriorated urban areas can successfully resist inducements to crime if they have a positive self-image, strong moral values, and support from their parents, peers, teachers, and neighbours. The girl with a positive self-image who is chosen for a university scholarship; has the warm, loving support of her parents; and is viewed as someone "going places" by friends and neighbours is less likely to adopt a criminal way of life than another young woman who is abused at home, who lives with criminal parents, and whose bond to her school and peer group is shattered because she is labelled a "troublemaker." The more social problems encountered during the socialization process, the greater the likelihood that youths will encounter difficulties and obstacles as they mature, such as being unemployed or becoming teenage parents.

social learning theory
The view that people learn to be aggressive by observing others acting aggressively to achieve some goal or being rewarded for violent acts.

social control theory
The view that people commit crime when the forces that bind them to society are weakened or broken.

social reaction theory (labelling theory)
The view that people become criminals when labelled as such and they accept the label as a personal identity.

The social process approach has several independent branches (see Figure 7.1). The first branch, **social learning theory**, suggests that people learn the techniques and attitudes of crime from close relationships with criminal peers: Crime is a learned behaviour. The second branch, **social control theory**, maintains that everyone has the potential to become a criminal, but most people are controlled by their bonds to society. Crime occurs when the forces that bind people to society are weakened or broken. The third branch, **social reaction theory (labelling theory)**, says that people become

© Photos 12/Alamy

The central theme of William Golding's *Lord of the Flies* reflects the concept of social control theory where young boys who are deserted on an island return to a "natural" state characterized by savagery, which highlights the need for rules of civilization to control it.

criminals when significant members of society label them as such and they accept those labels as a personal identity.

Put another way, social learning theories assume that people are born good and learn to be bad; social control theory assumes that people are born bad and must be controlled in order to be good; and social reaction theory assumes that whether good or bad, people are controlled by the evaluations of others. Each of these independent branches will be discussed separately.

LO6 Social Learning Theories

Social learning theorists believe that crime is a product of learning the norms, values, and behaviours associated with criminal activity. Social learning can involve the actual techniques of crime (how to hot-wire a car or roll a joint) as well as the psychological aspects of criminality (how to deal with the guilt or shame associated with illegal activities). This section briefly reviews two of the most prominent forms of social learning theory: differential association theory and neutralization theory.

Differential Association Theory

One of the most prominent social learning theories is Edwin H. Sutherland's **differential association theory**. Often considered the preeminent U.S. criminologist, Sutherland first put forth his theory in 1939 in his text *Principles of Criminology*.[38] The final version of the theory appeared in 1947. When Sutherland died in 1950, his long-time associate Donald Cressey continued his work. Cressey was so successful in explaining and popularizing his mentor's efforts that differential association theory remains one of the most enduring explanations of criminal behaviour.

Sutherland's research on white-collar crime, professional theft, and intelligence led him to dispute the notion that crime was a function of the inadequacy of people in the lower classes.[39] He believed crime was a function of a learning process that could affect any individual in any culture. Acquiring a behaviour is a socialization process, not a political or legal process. Skills and motives conducive to crime are learned as a result of contact with pro-crime values, attitudes, and definitions and other patterns of criminal behaviour.

Principles of Differential Association

Sutherland and Cressey explain the basic principles of differential association as follows:[40]

differential association theory
The view that people commit crime when their social learning leads them to perceive more definitions favouring crime than favouring conventional behaviour.

1. *Criminal behaviour is learned.* This statement differentiates Sutherland's theory from prior attempts to classify criminal behaviour as an inherent characteristic of criminals. Sutherland implies that criminality is learned in the same manner as any other learned behaviour, such as writing, painting, or reading.

2. *Criminal behaviour is learned as a byproduct of interacting with others.* An individual does not start violating the law simply by living in a criminogenic environment or by manifesting personal characteristics, such as low IQ or family problems, associated with criminality. People actively learn as they are socialized and interact with other individuals who serve as teachers and guides to crime. Thus, criminality cannot occur without the aid of others.

3. *Learning criminal behaviour occurs within intimate personal groups.* People's contacts with their most intimate social companions—family, friends, peers—have the greatest influence on their deviant behaviour and attitude development. Relationships with these influential individuals colour and control the way individuals interpret everyday events. For example, children who grow up in homes where parents abuse alcohol are more likely to view drinking as socially and physically beneficial.[41]

4. *Learning criminal behaviour involves assimilating the techniques of committing crime, including motives, drives, rationalizations, and attitudes.* Young delinquents learn from their associates the proper way to pick a lock, shoplift, and obtain and use narcotics. In addition, novice criminals learn the proper terminology for their acts and acquire approved reactions to law violations. Criminals must learn how to react properly to their illegal acts, such as when to defend them, rationalize them, or show remorse for them.

© Moviestore collection Ltd/Alamy

Oliver Twist learns the fine art of how to pickpocket from a gang of criminals who take him in after a miserable existence in a workhouse.

© Bettmann/CORBIS

One of the best examples of culture conflict comes from the sporting world. Canada's Ben Johnson was disqualified after winning the 100-metre race at the Seoul Olympics when he tested positive for anabolic steroids. Some believe that it was not so much that he used them, but that he and his coach had apparently been so careless as to be detected, reflecting a cultural norm in the sporting world that still persists today.

© Photos 12/Alamy

Martin Scorsese's *Goodfellas* (1990) shows us both the romantic side of the gangster lifestyle but also the reality of life in the underworld. Characters in the film extol the lifestyle of criminals who "boldly take what they want" in contrast to the "rest of us ... suckers in our nine-to-five jobs ..."

culture conflict
Result of exposure to opposing norms, attitudes, and definitions of right and wrong, moral and immoral.

5. *The specific direction of motives and drives is learned from perceptions of various aspects of the legal code as favourable or unfavourable.* Because the reaction to social rules and laws is not uniform across society, people constantly meet others who hold different views on the utility of obeying the legal code. Some people they admire may openly disdain or flout the law or ignore its substance. People experience what Sutherland calls **culture conflict** when they are exposed to opposing attitudes toward right and wrong or moral and immoral. The conflict of social attitudes and cultural norms is the basis for the concept of differential association.

6. *A person becomes a criminal when he or she perceives more favourable than unfavourable consequences to violating the law.* According to Sutherland's theory, individuals become law violators when they are in contact with persons, groups, or events that produce an excess of definitions favourable toward criminality and are isolated from counteracting forces (see Figure 7.2). A definition favourable toward criminality occurs, for example, when a person hears friends talking about the virtues of getting high on drugs. A definition unfavourable toward crime occurs when friends or parents demonstrate their disapproval of crime.

7. *Differential associations may vary in frequency, duration, priority, and intensity.* Whether a person learns to obey the law or to disregard it is influenced by the quality of social interactions. Those of lasting duration have greater influence than those that are brief. Similarly, frequent contacts have greater effect than rare, haphazard contacts. *Priority* means the age of children when they first encounter definitions of criminality. Contacts made early in life probably have more influence than those developed later on. Finally, *intensity* is generally interpreted to mean the

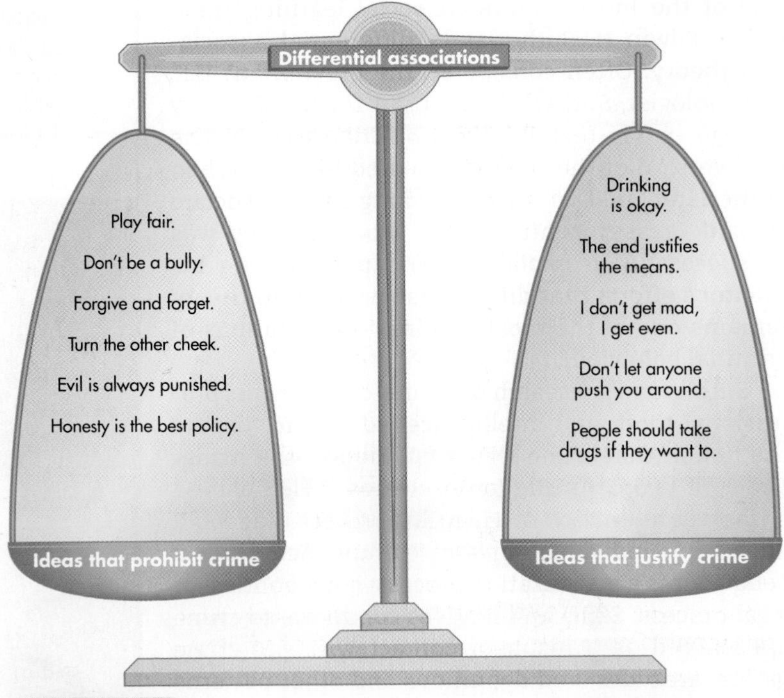
Differential associations
Play fair.
Don't be a bully.
Forgive and forget.
Turn the other cheek.
Evil is always punished.
Honesty is the best policy.
Ideas that prohibit crime
Drinking is okay.
The end justifies the means.
I don't get mad, I get even.
Don't let anyone push you around.
People should take drugs if they want to.
Ideas that justify crime

FIGURE 7.2

Differential Associations

Differential association theory suggests that criminal behaviour will occur when the definitions favourable toward crime outweigh the unfavourable definitions.

importance and prestige attributed to the individual or groups from whom the definitions are learned. For example, the influence of a father, mother, or trusted friend far outweighs the effect of more socially distant figures.

8. *The process of learning criminal behaviour by association with criminal and anticriminal patterns involves all of the mechanisms that are involved in any other learning process.* Learning criminal behaviour patterns is similar to learning nearly all other patterns and is not a matter of mere imitation.

9. *Although criminal behaviour expresses general needs and values, it is not excused by those general needs and values because noncriminal behaviour also expresses the same needs and values.* This principle suggests that the motives for criminal behaviour cannot logically be the same as those for conventional behaviour. Sutherland rules out such motives as desire to accumulate money or social status, personal frustration, or low self-concept as causes of crime because they are just as likely to produce noncriminal behaviour, such as getting a better education or working harder on a job. Only the learning of deviant norms through contact with an excess of definitions favourable toward criminality produces illegal behaviour.

In sum, differential association theory holds that people learn criminal attitudes and behaviour during their adolescence from close, trusted friends or relatives. A criminal career develops if learned antisocial values and behaviours are not matched or exceeded by conventional attitudes and behaviours. Criminal behaviour, then, is learned in a process that is similar to learning any other human behaviour.

Analysis of Differential Association Theory

Differential association theory is important because it does not specify that criminals come from a disorganized area or are members of the lower class. Outwardly law-abiding, middle-class parents can encourage delinquent behaviour by their own drinking, drug use, or family violence. The influence of differential associations is affected by social class; deviant learning experiences can affect youths in all classes.[42]

There are, however, a number of valid criticisms of Sutherland's work.[43] It fails to account for the origin of criminal definitions. How did the first "teacher" learn criminal attitudes and definitions in order to pass them on? Another criticism of differential association theory is that it assumes criminal and delinquent acts to be rational and systematic. This ignores spontaneous, wanton acts of violence and damage that appear to have little utility or purpose, such as many alcohol or drug-related outbursts of domestic violence, the isolated psychopathic killing that is virtually unsolvable because of the killer's anonymity and lack of delinquent associations.

The most serious criticism of differential association theory concerns the vagueness of its terms, which makes its assumptions difficult to test. What constitutes an excess of definitions favourable toward criminality? How can we determine whether an individual actually has a crime-supporting imbalance of these deviant or antisocial definitions? Must we assume that, by definition, all criminals have experienced a majority of definitions toward crime and all noncriminals, a minority of them? Unless the theory's terms can be defined more precisely, its validity remains a matter of guesswork.

neutralization theory
The view that law violators learn to neutralize conventional values and attitudes, enabling them to drift back and forth between criminal and conventional behaviour.

drift
Movement in and out of delinquency, shifting between conventional and deviant values.

neutralization techniques
Methods of rationalizing deviant behaviour, such as denying responsibility or blaming the victim.

Neutralization Theory

Neutralization theory is identified with the writings of Gresham Sykes and David Matza.[44] These criminologists also view the process of becoming a criminal as a learning experience. They theorize that law violators must learn and master techniques that enable them to neutralize conventional values and attitudes, thus allowing them to drift back and forth between illegitimate and conventional behaviour.

Neutralization theory points out that even the most committed criminals and delinquents are not involved in criminality all the time; they also attend schools, family functions, and religious services. Thus, their behaviour falls along a continuum between total freedom and total restraint. This process of **drift**, or movement from one extreme to another, produces behaviour that is sometimes unconventional or deviant and at other times constrained and sober.[45] Learning **neutralization techniques** allows a person to temporarily drift away from conventional behaviour and become involved in antisocial behaviours, including crime and drug abuse.[46]

Neutralization Techniques

Individuals who engage in criminal behavior have grown up in the same society as the rest of us—and, just like the rest of us, they know right from wrong, they have the same values and beliefs that we have, they even feel guilty over the crimes they commit—but somehow, they manage to put their conventional, law-abiding life aside and engage in criminal activities. Sykes and Matza suggest that many criminals develop a distinct set of excuses or "neutralizations" for their law violating that make it appear as though they are not really to blame for what they have done.[47]

Through their research, Sykes and Matza identified the following techniques of neutralization:

- *Denial of responsibility.* Young offenders sometimes claim that their unlawful acts are not their fault—that they result from forces beyond their control or are accidents.
- *Denial of injury.* By denying the injury caused by their acts, criminals neutralize illegal behaviour. For example, stealing is viewed as borrowing; vandalism is considered mischief that has gotten out of hand. Offenders may find that their parents and friends support their denial of injury. In fact, parents and friends may claim that the behaviour was merely a prank, helping affirm the offender's perception that crime can be socially acceptable.
- *Denial of the victim.* Criminals sometimes neutralize wrongdoing by maintaining that the crime victim "had it coming." Vandalism may be directed against a disliked teacher or neighbour, or a gang may beat up gays because their behaviour is considered offensive.
- *Condemnation of the condemners.* An offender views the world as a corrupt place with a dog-eat-dog code. Because police and judges are on the take, teachers show favouritism, and parents take out their frustrations on their children, offenders claim it is ironic and unfair for these authorities to condemn criminal misconduct. By shifting the blame to others, criminals repress the feeling that their own acts are wrong.
- *Appeal to higher loyalties.* Novice criminals often argue that they are caught in the dilemma of being loyal to their peer group while attempting to abide by the rules of society. The needs of the group take precedence because group demands are immediate and localized (see Figure 7.3).

CONNECTIONS

Denial of the victim may help explain hate crimes, in which people are victimized simply because they belong to the "wrong" race, religion, or ethnic group or because of their sexual orientation. Hate crimes are discussed in Chapter 10.

In sum, neutralization theory states that people neutralize conventional norms and values by using excuses that allow them to drift into crime.

Analyzing Neutralization Theory

Although the existing research findings are ambiguous,[48] the weight of the evidence shows that most adolescents generally disapprove of deviant behaviours such as violence, and that neutralizations do in fact enable youths to engage in socially disapproved behaviour.[49] And, as Matza predicted, people seem to drift in and out of antisocial behaviour rather than being committed solely to a criminal way of life.[50]

FIGURE 7.3

Techniques of Neutralization

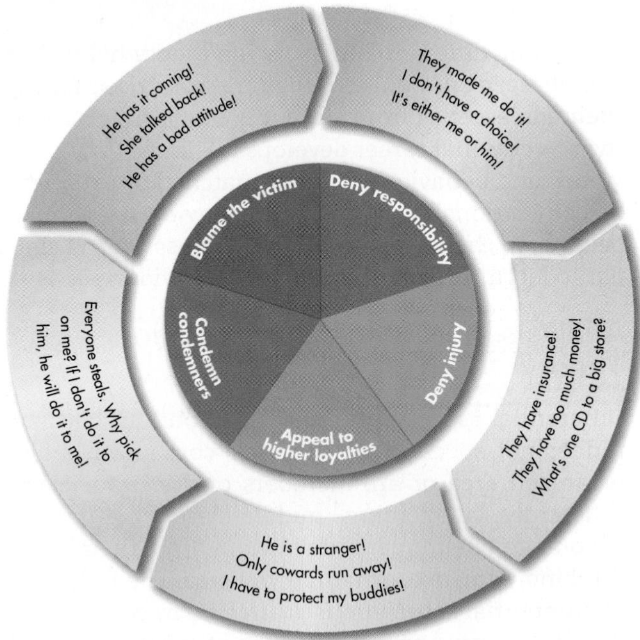

Are Learning Theories Valid?

Learning theories imply that people systematically learn techniques that allow them to be active, successful criminals. However, learning theories fail to adequately explain spontaneous, wanton acts of violence, damage, and other expressive crimes that appear to have little utility or purpose. Although principles of differential association can easily explain shoplifting, is it possible that a random shooting is caused by excessive deviant definitions? It is estimated that more than 50 percent of those who commit crimes are under the influence of drugs or alcohol when they commit the act.[51] Do "crackheads" pause to neutralize their moral inhibitions

DID YOU KNOW?

- Social control theories maintain that behaviour is a function of the attachment that people feel toward society. People who have a weak commitment to conformity are free to commit crime.
- A strong self-image may insulate people from crime.
- According to Hirschi, social control is measured by a person's attachment, commitment, involvement, and belief.

before mugging a victim? Do drug-involved kids stop to consider what they have learned about moral values?[52]

Despite these criticisms, learning theories have an important place in the study of delinquent and criminal behaviour. Unlike social structure theories, these theories are not limited to explaining a single facet of antisocial activity; they explain criminality across all class structures. Even corporate executives may be exposed to pro-criminal definitions and learn to neutralize moral constraints. Learning theories can thus be applied to a wide assortment of criminal activity.

LO7 Social Control Theory

Social control theorists maintain that all people have the potential to violate the law and that modern society presents many opportunities for illegal activity. Criminal activities, such as drug abuse and car theft, are often exciting pastimes that hold the promise of immediate reward and gratification.

Considering the attractions of crime, social control theorists question why people obey the rules of society. They argue that people obey the law because behaviour and passions are controlled by internal and external forces. Some individuals have **self-control**—a strong moral sense that renders them incapable of hurting others and violating social norms. Other people have been socialized to have a **commitment to conformity**. They have developed a real, present, and logical reason to obey the rules of society, and they instinctively avoid behaviour that will jeopardize their reputation and achievements.[53] The stronger people's commitment to conventional institutions, individuals, and processes, the less likely they are to commit crime. If that commitment is absent, there is little to lose, and people are free to violate the law.[54]

Self-Concept and Crime

Early versions of control theory speculated that criminality was a product of weak self-concept and poor self-esteem: youths who are socialized to feel good about themselves and maintain a positive attitude are able to resist the temptations of the streets.

As early as 1951, sociologist Albert Reiss described delinquents as having weak egos and lacking the self-control to produce conforming behaviour.[55] Pioneering control theorist Walter Reckless argued that a strong self-image insulates a youth from the pressures of criminogenic influences in the environment.[56] In studies conducted within the school setting, Reckless and his colleagues found that students who were able to maintain a positive self-image were insulated from delinquency.[57]

These early social control theorists suggested that people who have a weak self-image and damaged ego are crime prone. They are immune from efforts to apply social control: Why obey the rules of society when you have no stake in the future and little to lose?

self-control
A strong moral sense that renders a person incapable of hurting others or violating social norms.

commitment to conformity
A strong personal investment in conventional institutions, individuals, and processes that prevents people from engaging in behaviour that might jeopardize their reputation and achievements.

social bonds
The ties that bind people to society, including relationships with friends, family, neighbours, teachers, and employers. Elements of the social bond include commitment, attachment, involvement, and belief.

Contemporary Social Control Theory

The version of control theory articulated by Travis Hirschi in his influential 1969 book *Causes of Delinquency* is today the dominant version of control theories.[58] Hirschi links the onset of criminality to the weakening of the ties that bind people to society. He assumes that all individuals are potential law violators, but most are kept under control because they fear that illegal behaviour will damage their relationships with friends, family, neighbours, teachers, and employers. Without these **social bonds** or ties, a person is free to commit criminal acts. Among all ethnic, religious, racial, and social groups, people whose bond to society is weak may fall prey to criminogenic behaviour patterns.

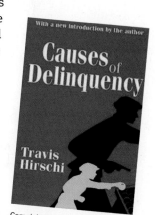

Hirschi argues that the social bond a person maintains with society is divided into four main elements: attachment, commitment, involvement, and belief (see Figure 7.4).

© Robert Churchill/iStockPhoto

According to Hirschi, heavy involvement in conventional activities such as schooling leaves little time for criminal activity.

1. *Attachment.* Attachment refers to a person's sensitivity to and interest in others.[59] Hirschi views parents, peers, and schools as the important social institutions with which a person should maintain ties. Attachment to parents is the most important. Even if a family is shattered by divorce or separation, a child must retain a strong attachment to one or both parents. Without this attachment, it is unlikely that respect for other authorities will develop.

2. *Commitment.* Commitment involves the time, energy, and effort expended in conventional actions such as getting an education and saving money for the future. If people build a strong commitment to conventional society, they will be less likely to engage in acts that jeopardize their hard-won position. Conversely, the lack of commitment to conventional values may foreshadow a condition in which risk-taking behaviour, such as crime, becomes a reasonable behaviour alternative.

3. *Involvement.* Heavy involvement in conventional activities leaves little time for illegal behaviour. Hirschi believes that involvement in school, recreation, and family insulates people from the potential lure of criminal behaviour. Idleness, on the other hand, enhances that lure.

4. *Belief.* People who live in the same social setting often share common moral beliefs; they may adhere to such values as sharing, sensitivity to the rights of others, and admiration for the legal code. If these beliefs are absent or weakened, individuals are more likely to participate in antisocial or illegal acts.

Hirschi further suggests that the interrelationship of social bond elements controls subsequent behaviour. For example, people who feel kinship and sensitivity to parents and friends should be more likely to adopt and work toward legitimate goals. On the other hand, a person who rejects such social relationships is more likely to lack commitment to conventional goals. Similarly, people who are highly committed to conventional acts and beliefs are more likely to be involved in conventional activities.

FIGURE 7.4

Elements of the Social Bond

Testing Social Control Theory

One of Hirschi's most significant contributions was his attempt to test the principal hypotheses of social control theory. He administered a detailed self-report survey to a sample of more than 4000 junior and senior high school students in Contra Costa County, California.[60] In a detailed analysis of the data, Hirschi found considerable evidence to support the control theory model. Among Hirschi's more important findings are the following:

- Youths who were strongly attached to their parents were less likely to commit criminal acts.
- Youths involved in conventional activity, such as homework, were less likely to engage in criminal behaviour.
- Youths involved in unconventional behaviour, such as smoking and drinking, were more prone to delinquency.

CONNECTIONS

Hirschi, along with his colleague Michael Gottfredson, restructured his concept of control by integrating biosocial, psychological, and rational choice theory ideas into a general theory of crime; They claim that the essential element of criminality is the absence of self-control. Because this theory is essentially integrated, it will be discussed more fully in Chapter 9

- Youths who maintained weak, distant relationships with people tended toward delinquency.
- Those who shunned unconventional acts were attached to their peers.
- Delinquents and nondelinquents shared similar beliefs about society.

Hirschi's data gave important support to the validity of social control theory. Even when the statistical significance of his findings was less than he expected, the direction of his research data was notably consistent. Only rarely did his findings contradict the theory's most critical assumptions.

Supporting Research

Hirschi's version of social control theory has been corroborated by numerous research studies showing that delinquent youths often feel detached from society.[61] Supporting research indicates that both male and female delinquents experience attachments to the family, peer group, and school that are strained and weakened.[62] In contrast, positive attachments help control delinquency.[63] For example, youths who fail at school and are detached from the educational experience are at risk of criminality; those who do well and are committed to school are less likely to engage in delinquent acts.[64]

Opposing Views

More than 70 published attempts have been made to corroborate social control theory by replicating Hirschi's original survey techniques.[65] Though providing significant empirical support for Hirschi's work, these studies have also raised a number of questions.

- *Friendship.* One significant criticism concerns Hirschi's contention that delinquents are detached loners whose bond to family and friends has been broken. In fact, delinquents seem not to be "lone wolves" whose only personal relationships are exploitative; their friendship patterns seem quite close to those of conventional youth.[66] Some types of offenders, such as drug abusers, may maintain even more intimate relations with their peers than nonabusers.[67]
- *Failure to achieve.* Hirschi argues that commitment to career and economic advancement reduces criminal involvement. However, research indicates that people who are committed to success but fail to achieve it may be crime prone.[68]
- *Involvement negates supervision.* Adolescents who report high levels of involvement, which Hirschi suggests should reduce delinquency, actually report high levels of criminal behaviour. Perhaps adolescents who are involved in activities outside the home have less contact with parental supervision and greater opportunity to commit crime.[69]
- *Deviant peers and parents.* Hirschi's conclusion that any form of social attachment is beneficial, even to deviant peers and parents, has also been disputed. Rather than deter delinquency, attachment to deviant peers may support and nurture antisocial behaviour.[70] A number of research efforts have found that youths attached to drug-abusing parents are more likely to use drugs themselves.[71] Attachment to deviant family members, peers, and associates may help motivate youths to commit crime and facilitate their antisocial acts.[72]

REUTERS/Lyle Stafford

Hirschi maintains that delinquents are not attached to their peers. Even if teens join to form criminal gangs, within-group relationships are actually strained and remote. For example, at 22, Kelly Ellard was found guilty in 2005 of second-degree murder in the death of teen Reena Virk, found beaten and drowned in Victoria, B.C. in 1997. Ellard was part of a group of teens who assaulted Virk, but acting outside the group she committed the murder. After spending over a decade in jail, she is now eligible to apply for parole.

Hirschi's theory proposes that a weakened bond leads to delinquency, but Robert Agnew suggests that the chain of events may flow in the opposite direction: Perhaps youngsters who break the law find that their bonds to parents, schools, and society eventually become weak. Other studies have also found that criminal behaviour weakens social bonds and not vice versa.[73]

While these criticisms are important, Hirschi's views still constitute one of the preeminent theories in criminology.[74] Many criminologists consider social control theory the most important way of understanding the onset of youthful misbehaviour.

DID YOU KNOW?

- According to labelling theory, stigma helps lock people into a deviant career.
- Labels amplify deviant behaviour rather than deter future criminality.
- Primary deviants view themselves as good people who have done a bad thing; secondary deviants accept a negative label as an identity.
- Labels are bestowed in a biased fashion. The poor and minority-group members are more likely to receive labels.

LO8 Social Reaction (Labelling) Theory

Social reaction theory, or labelling theory (the two terms are used interchangeably here), explains criminal careers in terms of destructive social interactions and stigma-producing encounters.

According to this view, people are given a variety of symbolic labels that help define not only one trait, but also the whole person. Valued labels, such as "smart," "honest," and "hard working," suggest overall competence. Sometimes the labels are symbolic, such as being named "most likely to succeed" or class valedictorian. People who hold these titles are automatically assumed to be leaders who are well on their way to success. Without meeting them, we know that they are hard working, industrious, and bright. These positive labels can improve self-image and social standing. Research shows that people who are labelled with one positive trait, such as being physically attractive, are assumed to have other positive traits, such as being intelligent and competent.[75]

stigmatize
To apply negative labelling with enduring effects on a person's self-image and social interactions.

FRAN
HE'S OBVIOUSLY DEPRESSED, LET'S LABEL HIM AND SEE IF SEVERAL YEARS OF UNEMPLOYMENT AND POOR RELATIONSHIPS HELPS HIS CONDITION!

www.CartoonStock.com

In contrast, some people are given negative labels, such as "troublemaker," "mentally ill," and "stupid," that **stigmatize** them and reduce their self-image. For example, people labelled "insane" are also assumed to be dangerous, dishonest, unstable, violent, strange, and otherwise unsound.

Both positive and negative labels involve subjective interpretation of behaviour: A "troublemaker" is merely someone whom people label as "troublesome." There need not be any objective proof or

AP Photo/John Miller

The Scary Guy (now his legal name) is covered from head to toe in tattoos. What do you think he is like? What are his personality traits? Would you want him to meet your family? Are you labelling him?

FIGURE 7.5

The Labelling Process

Initial criminal act	**Detection by the justice system**	**Decision to label**	**Creation of a new identity**	**Acceptance of labels**	**Deviance amplification**
People commit crimes for a number of reasons.	Arrest is influenced by racial, economic, and power relations.	Some are labelled "official" criminals by police and court authorities.	Those labelled are known as troublemakers, criminals, etc., and shunned by conventional society.	Labelled people begin to see themselves as outsiders (secondary deviance, self-labelling).	Stigmatized offenders are now locked into criminal careers.

measure indicating that the person is actually a troublemaker. Although a label may be a function of rumour, innuendo, or unfounded suspicion, its adverse impact can be immense.

If a devalued status is conferred by a significant other—teacher, police officer, parent, or valued peer—the negative label may permanently harm the target. The degree to which a person is perceived as a social deviant may affect his or her treatment at home, at work, at school, and in other social situations. Children may find that their parents consider them a bad influence on younger brothers and sisters. School officials may limit them to classes reserved for people with behavioural problems. Likewise, when adults are labelled as "criminal," "ex-con," or "drug addict," they may find their eligibility for employment severely restricted. If the label is bestowed as the result of conviction for a criminal offence, the labelled person may also be subjected to official sanctions ranging from a mild reprimand to incarceration. The simultaneous effects of labels and sanctions reinforce feelings of isolation and detachment.

According to labelling theory, depending on the visibility of the label and the manner and severity with which it is applied, negatively labelled individuals will become increasingly committed to a deviant career. They may be watched, suspected, and excluded more and more from legitimate opportunities.[76] Labelled persons may find themselves turning to others similarly stigmatized for support and companionship. Isolated from conventional society, they may identify themselves as members of an outcast group and become locked into deviance. Figure 7.5 above illustrates this process.

Because the process of becoming stigmatized is essentially interactive, labelling theorists blame the establishment of criminal careers on the social agencies originally designed for crime control, such as police, courts, and correctional agencies. It is these institutions, labelling theorists claim, that produce the stigma that harms the people they are trying to help, treat, or correct. As a result, they actually help to maintain and amplify criminal behaviour.

Crime and Labelling Theory

According to the social reaction approach, crime and deviance are defined by the social audience's reaction to people and their behaviour and the subsequent effects of that reaction; they are not defined by the moral content of the illegal act itself. In a famous statement, Howard Becker sums up the importance of the audience's reaction:

> Social groups create deviance by making rules whose infractions constitute deviance, and by applying those rules to particular people and labeling them as outsiders. From this point of view, deviance is not a quality of the act a person commits, but rather a consequence of the application by others of rules and sanctions to an "offender." The deviant is one to whom the label has successfully been applied; deviant behavior is behavior that people so label.[77]

In its purest form, social reaction theory argues that even crimes such as murder, sexual assault,

THE CANADIAN PRESS/ Toronto Star-Rene Johnston

The government of Canada has been ordered to fix the medical marijuana program or face the prospect of legalizing possession and production of cannabis after an Ontario Superior Court judge's ruling that the medical marijuana program is unconstitutional. The order is under appeal.

moral entrepreneur
A person who creates moral rules, which thus reflect the values of those in power rather than any objective, universal standards of right and wrong.

reflective role taking
Assuming an identity based on the actual or perceived appraisals of others.

and theft are bad or evil only because people label them as such. After all, the difference between an excusable act and a criminal one is often a matter of changing legal definition. Acts such as performing an abortion, using marijuana, possessing a handgun, and gambling have been legal at some times and places and illegal at others.

Justice Donald Taliano found that sick people are forced to resort to crime because they cannot get access to medical marijuana through appropriate means, branding them as criminals. The judgment came in the case of a seriously ill young man, Matthew Mernagh, who used medical marijuana to help manage the symptoms from a variety of ailments including fibromyalgia, scoliosis, and seizures. Mernagh was charged by Niagara Regional Police in 2008 when police seized 70 marijuana plants in his apartment in St. Catharines, Ontario.

Even if some acts are labelled as bad or evil, those who participate in them can be spared a negative label. For example, it is possible to take another person's life but not be considered a "murderer" because the killing was considered self-defence or even an accident. Acts have negative consequences for the killer only when they are labelled wrong or evil by others.

A social reaction theorist views crime as a subjective concept whose definition depends entirely on the viewing audience. An act that is considered criminal by one person may be perfectly acceptable behaviour to another. Because crime is defined by those in power, the shape of criminal law is defined by the values of those who rule, not an objective standard of moral conduct. Howard Becker refers to people who create rules as **moral entrepreneurs**. An example of a moral entrepreneur today might be a member of an ultra-orthodox religious group who targets the gay lifestyle and campaigns to prevent gays from adopting children or marrying their same-sex partners.[78]

Differential Enforcement

An important principle of social reaction theory is that the law is differentially applied, benefiting those who hold economic and social power and penalizing the powerless. The probability of being brought under the control of legal authority is a function of a person's race, wealth, gender, and social standing. A core concept of social reaction theory is that police officers are more likely to formally arrest males, minority-group members, and those in the lower class, and to use their discretionary powers to give beneficial treatment to more favoured groups.[79] Minorities and the poor are more likely to be prosecuted for criminal offences and receive harsher punishment when convicted.[80] Judges may sympathize with white defendants and help them avoid criminal labels, especially if they seem to come from "good families," whereas minority youths are not afforded that luxury.[81] This helps to explain why there are significant racial and economic differences in the crime rate.

In sum, a major premise of social reaction theory is that the law is differentially constructed and applied, depending on the offender. It favours powerful members of society, who direct its content, and penalizes people whose actions threaten those in control, such as minority-group members and the poor who demand equal rights.[82]

Consequences of Labelling

Negative labels stigmatize people and alter their self-image. The labelled person is transformed into a social outcast who is prevented from enjoying higher education, well-paying jobs, and other social benefits.

Public denunciation plays an important part in the labelling process. Condemnation is often carried out in "ceremonies" in which the individual's identity is officially transformed. Examples of such re-identification ceremonies are a competency hearing in which a person is declared to be "mentally ill" or a public trial in which a person is found to be a "rapist" or "child molester." During the process, a permanent record is produced, such as an arrest or conviction record, so that the denounced person is ritually separated from a place in the legitimate order and placed outside the world occupied by citizens of good standing. Harold Garfinkle has called transactions that produce irreversible, permanent labels "successful degradation ceremonies."[83]

Changing Self-Image

Successful labelling produces a re-evaluation of the self that reflects actual or perceived appraisals made by others. Children who view themselves as delinquents after being labelled as such are giving an inner voice to their perceptions of how parents, teachers, peers, and neighbours view them. When they believe that others view them as antisocial or troublemakers, they take on attitudes and roles that reflect this assumption. They expect to become suspects and then to be rejected.[84]

Tempering or enhancing the effect of this **reflective role taking** are the people and institutions with whom the labelled person comes in contact.

For example, an understanding teacher can help overcome the negative label of a low-track student and encourage an adolescent to excel in school. However, when these groups are dysfunctional, such as when parents use drugs, they encourage rather than control antisocial behaviour.[85]

Joining Deviant Cliques

People who are labelled as deviant may join with similarly outcast peers who facilitate their behaviour. Eventually, antisocial behaviour becomes habitual and automatic.[86] The desire to join deviant cliques and groups may stem from self-rejecting attitudes ("At times, I think I am no good at all") that eventually weaken commitment to conventional values and behaviours. In turn, stigmatized individuals may acquire motives to deviate from social norms because they now share a common bond with similarly labelled social outcasts.[87] They may join cliques like the "Trenchcoat Mafia" whose members were involved in the 1999 Littleton, Colorado, school massacre. Membership in a deviant subculture often involves conforming to group norms that conflict with those of conventional society, further enhancing the effects of the labelling process.

© Saed Hindash/Star Ledger/Corbis

Ex-con Andre Latallade's appearance fits the preconceived notion of an "ex-con"; however, looks can be deceiving. After spending eight years of his life locked up, Latallade turned his life around after doing time on drug and aggravated assault charges. He built a name for himself as an activist for prisoners' rights and fighting capital punishment. "When I was in prison, everyone forgot about me," says Latallade, a rapper whose stage name is Capital X. "I want to show inmates on death row that I won't forget about them." In July 2011, Latallade began a 2735-kilometre walk from his home in Trenton, New Jersey, to Texas, the state with the most executions and where more than 3000 prisoners are on death row.

Retrospective Reading

Beyond any immediate results, labels tend to redefine the whole person. For example, the label "ex-con" may create in people's imaginations a whole series of behaviour descriptions—tough, mean, dangerous, aggressive, dishonest, sneaky—that may or may not apply to a person who has been in prison. People react to the label description and what it signifies, instead of reacting to the actual behaviour of the person who bears it. The labelled person's past is reviewed and re-evaluated to fit his or her current status—a process known as **retrospective reading**. For example, boyhood friends of an assassin or serial killer, interviewed by the media, report that the suspect was withdrawn, suspicious, and negativistic as a youth; they were always suspicious but never thought to report their concerns to the authorities. According to this retrospective reading, we can now understand what prompted his current behaviour; therefore, the label must be accurate.[88]

retrospective reading
The reassessment of a person's past to fit a current generalized label.

Labels, then, become the basis of personal identity. As the negative feedback of law enforcement agencies, parents, friends, teachers, and other figures amplifies the force of the original label, stigmatized offenders may begin to re-evaluate their own identities. If they are not really evil or bad, they may ask themselves, why is everyone making such a fuss? This process has been referred to as the "dramatization of evil."[89]

primary deviance A norm violation or crime with little or no long-term influence on the violator.

secondary deviance A norm violation or crime that comes to the attention of significant others or social control agents, who apply a negative label with long-term consequences for the violator's self-identity and social interactions.

deviance amplification Process whereby secondary deviance pushes offenders out of the mainstream of society and locks them into an escalating cycle of deviance apprehension, labelling, and criminal self-identity.

Primary and Secondary Deviance

One of the better-known views of the labelling process is Edwin Lemert's concept of primary deviance and secondary deviance.[90] According to Lemert, **primary deviance** involves norm violations or crimes that have little influence on the actor and can be quickly forgotten. For example, a university student successfully steals a textbook at the campus bookstore, gets an A in the course, graduates, is admitted to law school, and later becomes a famous judge. Because his shoplifting goes unnoticed, it is a relatively unimportant event that has little bearing on his future life.

In contrast, **secondary deviance** occurs when a deviant event comes to the attention of significant others or social control agents, who apply a negative label. The newly labelled offender then reorganizes his or her behaviour and personality around the consequences of the deviant act. The shoplifting student is caught by a security guard and expelled from university. With his law school dreams dashed and future cloudy, his options are limited; people say he lacks character, and he begins to share their opinion. He eventually becomes a drug dealer and winds up in prison (see Figure 7.6).

Secondary deviance involves resocialization into a deviant role. The labelled person is transformed into one who, according to Lemert, "employs his behavior or a role based upon it as a means of defense, attack, or adjustment to the overt and covert problems created by the consequent social reaction to him."[91] Secondary deviance produces a **deviance amplification** effect: Offenders feel isolated from the mainstream of society and become locked within their deviant role. They may seek others similarly labelled to form deviant groups. Ever more firmly enmeshed in their deviant role, they are trapped in an escalating cycle of deviance, apprehension, more powerful labels, and identity transformation. Lemert's concept of secondary deviance expresses the core of social reaction theory: Deviance is a process in which one's identity is transformed. Efforts to control offenders, whether by treatment or punishment, simply help to lock them in their deviant role.

FIGURE 7.6

Primary and Secondary Deviance

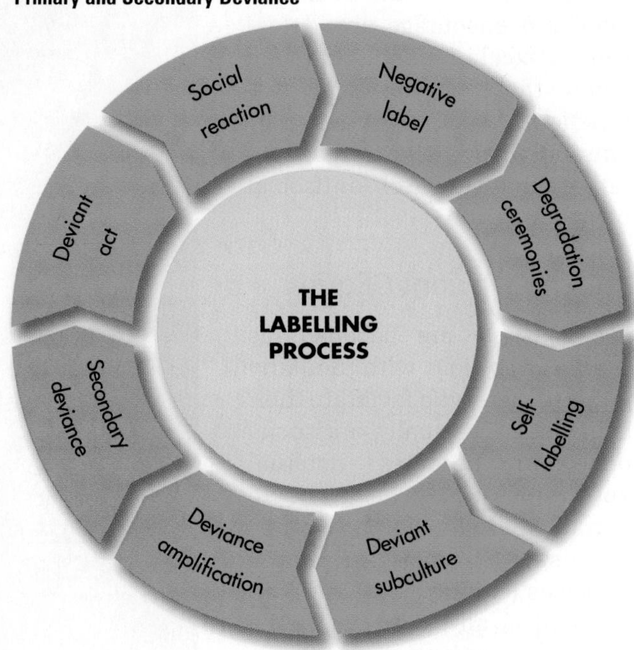

Research on Social Reaction Theory

Research on social reaction theory can be classified into two distinct categories. The first focuses on the characteristics of those offenders who are chosen for labelling. The theory predicts that they will be relatively powerless people who are unable to defend themselves against the negative labelling. The second type of research attempts to discover the effects of being labelled. Labelling theorists predict that people who are negatively labelled will view themselves as deviant and commit increasing amounts of crime.

Victims of Labelling

There is evidence that, as predicted by labelling theory, poor and powerless people are victimized by the law and justice system. Labels are not equally distributed across class and racial lines. From the police officer's decision on whom to arrest, to the prosecutor's decisions on whom to charge and how many and what kinds of charges to bring, to the court's decision on whom to release or grant bail, to the judge's decision on sentence length, discretion works to the detriment of minorities.[92] For example, in a study of the Ontario criminal justice system researchers found that blacks were more likely than other groups to be denied bail, to be convicted in court, and to receive harsher sentences.[93] Judges may also be more likely to impose prison sentences on racial minorities in borderline cases for which whites get probation.

Effects of Labelling

Empirical evidence shows that negative labels dramatically influence the self-image of offenders. Considerable evidence indicates that social sanctions lead to self-labelling and deviance amplification.[94] For example, children negatively labelled by their parents routinely suffer a variety of problems, including antisocial behaviour and school failure.[95] This process is important because once they are labelled as troublemakers, adolescents begin to reassess their self-image. Parents who label their children as troublemakers promote deviance amplification. Labelling alienates parents from their children, and negative labels reduce children's self-image and increase delinquency.[96]

As they mature, children are in danger of receiving repeated, intensive, official labelling, which has been shown to produce self-labelling and damage identities.[97] Youngsters labelled as troublemakers in school are the most likely to drop out; dropping out has been linked to delinquent behaviour.[98] Even in adults, the labelling process can take its toll. Male drug users labelled as addicts by social control agencies eventually become self-labelled and increase their drug use.[99] People arrested in domestic violence cases, especially those with a low stake in conformity (e.g., those who are jobless and unmarried), often increase offending after being given official labels.[100]

Empirical evidence supports the view that labelling plays an important role in persistent offending.[101] Although labels may not cause adolescents to initiate criminal behaviours, experienced delinquents are significantly more likely to continue offending if they believe that their parents and peers view them in a negative light.[102] Labelling, then, may help sustain criminality over time.

CONNECTIONS

Fear of stigma has prompted efforts to reduce the impact of criminal labels through programs such as pretrial diversion and community treatment. In Canada, under the terms of the Youth Criminal Justice Act (YCJA), youth under the age of 18 who are charged with a criminal offence cannot be publicly identified, except when the crime is a very serious violent crime.

Is Labelling Theory Valid?

Criminologists Raymond Paternoster and Leeann Iovanni have identified features of the labelling perspective that are important contributions to the study of criminality:[103]

- The labelling perspective identifies the role played by social control agents in crime causation. Criminal behaviour cannot be fully understood if the agencies and individuals empowered to control and treat it are neglected.
- Labelling theory recognizes that criminality is not a disease or pathological behaviour. It focuses attention on the social interactions and reactions that shape individuals and their behaviour.
- Labelling theory distinguishes between criminal acts (primary deviance) and criminal careers (secondary deviance) and shows that these concepts must be interpreted and treated differently.

Labelling theory is also important because of its focus on interaction as well as the situation surrounding the crime. Rather than viewing the criminal as a robot-like creature whose actions are predetermined, it recognizes that crime often results from complex interactions and processes. The decision to commit crime involves actions of a variety of people, including peers, victim, police, and other key characters. Labels may foster crime by guiding the actions of all parties involved in these criminal interactions. Actions deemed innocent when performed by one person are considered provocative when engaged in by someone who has been labelled as deviant. Similarly, labelled people may be quick to judge, take offence, or misinterpret others' behaviour because of past experience.

An Evaluation of Social Process Theory

The branches of social process theory—social learning, social control, and social reaction—are compatible because they all suggest that criminal behaviour is part of the socialization process. Criminals are people whose interactions with critically important social institutions and processes—the family, schools, the justice system, peer groups, employers, and neighbours—are troubled. Although some disagree about the relative importance of those influences and the form they take, there is little question that social interactions shape the behaviour, beliefs, values, and self-image of the offender. People who have learned deviant social values, find themselves detached from conventional social relationships, or are the subject of stigma and labels from significant others are the most likely to commit crime. These negative influences can influence anyone, beginning in youth and continuing through adulthood. The major strength of the social process view is the vast body of empirical data showing that delinquents and criminals are people who grew up in dysfunctional families, who had troubled childhoods, and who failed at school, at work, and in marriage. Prison data show that these characteristics are typical of inmates.

Although persuasive, these theories do not always account for some of the patterns and fluctuations in the crime rate. If social process theories are valid, for example, people in Western Canada must be socialized differently from those in Central or Eastern Canada, where crime rates are generally lower. How can seasonal crime rate variations be explained if crime is a function of learning or control? How can social processes explain why criminals escalate their activity or why they desist from crime? Once a social bond is broken, how can it be reattached? Once crime is learned, how can it be unlearned? These are questions that must still be answered by social process theorists.

CP PHOTO/ap-fls

During the 1960s and 1970s George Chuvalo was Canada's heavyweight boxing champion and was regularly ranked in the top ten in the world, fighting Muhammad Ali, Joe Frazier, George Foreman, and Jerry Quarry. Chuvalo was never knocked to the mat in his 93 professional fights, and is considered by many to have the toughest chin in boxing history. Chuvalo's personal life also took a beating when after retiring he lost three of his four sons and his wife to drugs. He now gives talks to high school and elementary school children about the consequences of drug abuse.

Social Process Theory and Social Policy

Social process theories have had a major influence on social policies since the 1950s. Learning theories have greatly influenced the way criminal offenders are treated. The effect of these theories has been felt mainly by young offenders, who are viewed as being more salvageable than hardened criminals. Advocates of the social learning approach argue that if people become criminal by learning definitions and attitudes favouring criminality, they can unlearn them by being exposed to definitions favouring conventional behaviour.

This philosophy has been used in numerous treatment facilities based in part on two early, pioneering efforts: the Highfields Project in New Jersey and the Silverlake Program in Los Angeles. These were residential treatment programs, geared toward young male offenders, that used group interaction sessions to attack criminal behaviour orientations while promoting conventional lines of behaviour. It is common today for residential and nonresidential programs in both the United States and Canada to offer similar treatment, teaching children and adolescents to refuse drugs, to forgo delinquent behaviour, and to stay in school. It is even common for celebrities such as former Canadian heavyweight boxing champion George Chuvalo to publicly urge young people to stay in school or off drugs. If learning did not affect behaviour, such exercises would be futile.

Control theories have also influenced criminal justice and other social policies. Programs have been developed to increase people's commitment to conventional lines of action. Some work at creating and strengthening bonds early in life before the onset of criminality. The educational system has hosted numerous programs designed to improve basic skills and create an atmosphere in which youths will develop a bond to their schools. The accompanying Policy and Practice in Criminology feature discusses the Head Start program, perhaps the largest and most successful attempt to solidify social bonds.

Control theory's focus on the family has played a key role in programs designed to strengthen the bond between parent and child. Others attempt to repair bonds that have been broken or frayed.

POLICY AND PRACTICE IN CRIMINOLOGY

HEAD START

Head Start is probably the best-known effort to help young children achieve proper socialization and, in so doing, reduce their potential for future criminality. Head Start programs were instituted in the United States in the 1960s as part of President Lyndon Johnson's War on Poverty. In the beginning, Head Start was a two-month summer program for children who were about to enter school. Aimed at embracing the "whole child," it offered comprehensive programming designed to enhance physical health, mental processes, social and emotional development, self-image, and interpersonal relationships. Preschoolers were provided with an enriched educational environment to develop their learning and cognitive skills. They were given the opportunity to use pegs and pegboards, puzzles, toy animals, dolls, letters and numbers, and other materials that middle-class children take for granted. These opportunities provided these children a leg up in the educational process.

Head Start teachers strive to provide a variety of learning experiences appropriate to the child's age and development. These experiences allow children to read books, to understand cultural diversity, to express feelings, and to play with and relate to their peers in an appropriate fashion. Students are guided in developing gross and fine motor skills and self-confidence. Health care is also an issue, and most children enrolled in the program receive comprehensive health screenings, physical and dental examinations, and appropriate follow-up. Many programs provide meals, helping children receive proper nourishment.

Head Start programs now serve parents in addition to their preschoolers. Some programs allow parents to enroll in classes, which cover parenting, literacy, nutrition/weight loss, domestic violence prevention, and other social issues; social services, health, and education services are also available.

Considerable controversy has surrounded the success of the Head Start program. In 1970, the Westinghouse Learning Corporation issued a definitive evaluation of the Head Start effort and concluded that there was no evidence of lasting cognitive gains on the part of the participating children. Initial gains seemed to evaporate during the elementary school years, and by grade 3, the performance of the Head Start children was no different from that of their peers. Though disappointing, this evaluation focused on IQ levels and gave short shrift to improvement in social competence and other survival skills.

More recent research has produced dramatically different results. One report found that by age five, children who had experienced the enriched daycare offered by Head Start averaged more than ten points higher on their IQ scores than their peers who did not participate in the program. Other research that carefully compared Head Start children to similar children who did not attend the program found that the former made significant intellectual gains. Head Start children were less likely to have been retained in a grade or placed in classes for slow learners, they outperformed peers on achievement tests, and they were more likely to graduate from high school.

Head Start children have also made strides in nonacademic areas. They appear to have better health, higher immunization rates, improved nutrition, and enhanced emotional characteristics after leaving the program. Research also shows that the Head Start program can have important psychological benefits for the mothers of participants, such as decreasing depression and anxiety and increasing feelings of life satisfaction. While findings in some areas may be tentative, they are all in the same direction: Head Start enhances school readiness and has enduring effects on social competence.

If, as many experts believe, there is a close link between school performance, family life, and crime, programs such as Head Start can help some potentially criminal young people avoid problems with the law. By implication, their success indicates that programs that help socialize youngsters can be used to combat urban criminality. Although some problems have been identified in individual centres, the U.S. government has shown its faith in Head Start as a socialization agent. The current budget of more than US$4.2 billion is used to serve more than 820 000 children.

Aboriginal Head Start (AHS) in urban and northern communities is a Health Canada–funded early childhood development program for First Nations, Inuit, and Métis children and their families. Started in 1995 with an annual budget of about $23 million, and modelled on the U.S. Head Start program, AHS programs have been implemented in 114 Aboriginal communities across Canada. Evaluations of the programs show substantial gains in all areas of child development, and improved parenting skills.

CRITICAL THINKING

1. Does a program such as Head Start substitute one type of negative label (special-needs child) for another (slow starter)?
2. What do you think are some benefits that children who participate in Head Start will carry with them throughout their childhood and adolescence?

Sources: Personal contact, Head Start Program, 2000; Edward Zigler and Sally Styfco, "Head Start: Criticisms in a Constructive Context," *American Psychologist* 49 (1994): 127–132; Nancy Kassebaum, "Head Start: Only the Best for America's Children," *American Psychologist* 49 (1994): 123–126; Faith Lamb Parker, Chaya Piorkowski, and Lenore Peay, "Head Start as Social Support for Mothers: The Psychological Benefits of Involvement," *American Journal of Orthopsychiatry* 57 (1987): 220–233; Health Canada, Division of Childhood and Adolescence, "Program Overview: Aboriginal Head Start (AHS) in Urban and Northern Communities," http://www.hc-sc.gc.ca/dca-dea/programs.

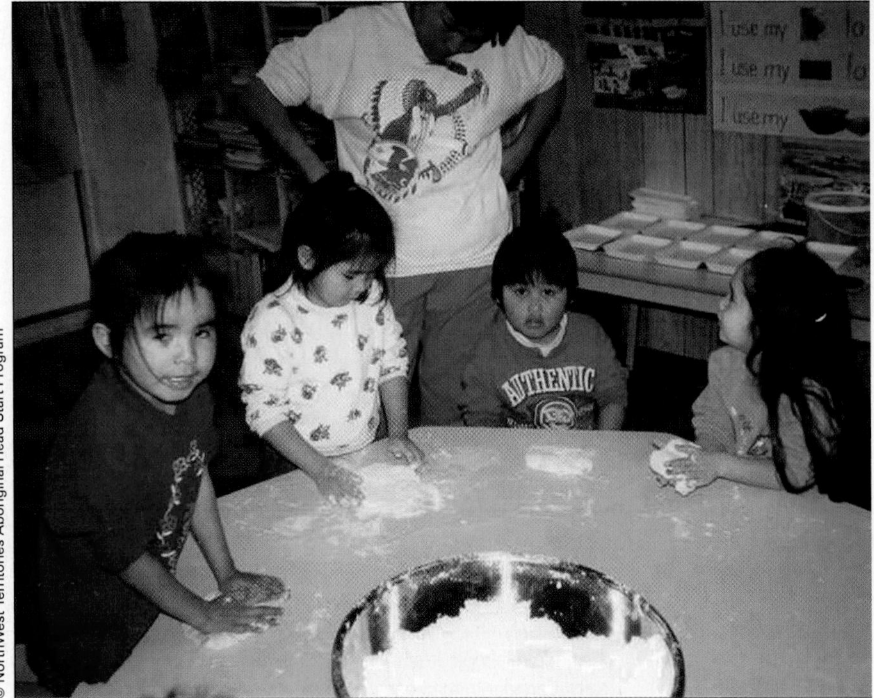

© NorthWest Territories Aboriginal Head Start Program

Social process theories suggest that people can be helped by social programs that help them become committed and attached to society. Using the U.S. Head Start program as a model, in 1995 the Canadian government established the Aboriginal Head Start (AHS) program to promote child development and school readiness for First Nations, Métis, and Inuit children. AHS programs stress Aboriginal culture, involvement of parents in building pride in one's heritage, a positive social environment, and acquiring skills for later success.

diversion programs
Programs of rehabilitation that remove offenders from the normal channels of the criminal justice process, thus avoiding the stigma of a criminal label.

restitution
Permitting an offender to repay the victim or do useful work in the community rather than face the stigma of a formal trial and a court-ordered sentence.

Examples of this approach are the employment skills and educational opportunity programs that are in place in Canada's prisons. These programs are designed to help inmates maintain a stake in society so they will be less willing to resort to criminal activity after their release.

Labelling theorists caution against too much intervention. Rather than ask social agencies to attempt to rehabilitate people having problems with the law, they argue, less is better. Put another way, the more institutions try to help people, the more these people will be stigmatized and labelled. For example, a special education program designed to help problem readers may cause them to label themselves and others as slow or stupid. Similarly, a mental health rehabilitation program created with the best intentions may cause clients to be labelled as crazy or dangerous.

The influence of labelling theory can be seen in diversion and restitution programs. **Diversion programs** remove both juvenile and adult offenders from the normal channels of the criminal justice process by placing them in rehabilitation programs. For example, a university student whose drunken driving hurts a pedestrian may, before trial, be placed for six months in an alcohol treatment program. If he successfully completes the program, charges against him will be dismissed; thus he avoids the stigma of a criminal label. Such programs are common throughout Canada and the United States. Often they offer counselling, medical advice, and vocational, educational, and family services.

Another popular label-avoiding innovation is **restitution**. Rather than face the stigma of a formal trial, an offender is asked either to pay back the victim of the crime for any loss incurred or to do some useful work in the community, in lieu of receiving a court-ordered sentence.

Despite their good intentions, stigma-reducing programs have not met with great success. Critics charge that they substitute one kind of stigma for another—for instance, attending a mental health program in lieu of a criminal trial. In addition, diversion and restitution programs usually screen out violent and repeat offenders. Finally, there is little hard evidence that these alternative programs improve recidivism rates.

71% The percentage of students who go online to study for a class.

CRIM was designed for students just like you—busy people who want choices, flexibility, and multiple learning options.

CRIM delivers concise, electronic resources such as discipline-specific activities, flashcards, test yourself questions, crossword puzzles and more!

At **www.icancrim2.com**, you'll find electronic resources such as **printable interactive flashcards, downloadable study aids, games, quizzes, and videos** to test your knowledge of key concepts. These resources will help supplement your understanding of core **criminology** concepts in a format that fits your busy lifestyle.

"I really like how you use students' opinions on how to study and made a website that encompasses everything we find useful. Seeing this website makes me excited to study!"

—Abby Boston, Fanshawe College

Visit **www.icancrim2.com** to find the resources you need today!

CHAPTER 8

Social Conflict Theory: It's a Dog-Eat-Dog *World*

STOP WAR

Learning Outcomes

LO1 Discuss how social conflict theorists explain the existence of crime in a society.

LO2 Explain the purpose of the legal system according to conflict theorists.

LO3 Explain why Marxist criminologists view the justice system as an army.

LO4 Describe how Marxist criminologists explain crime.

LO5 Explain how restorative justice is meant to prevent and control crime.

LO6 Explain why social conflict theorists feel the legal system is biased.

It would be unusual to pick up the morning paper and not see headlines loudly proclaiming renewed strife in the Middle East, between union negotiators and management lawyers, between citizens and police authorities, or between rival political parties. The world is filled with conflict. Conflict can be destructive when it leads to war, violence, and death; it can be functional when it results in positive social change.

Criminologists who view crime as a function of social conflict and economic rivalry are aligned with a number of schools of thought. These are referred to as conflict, critical, Marxist, and radical schools of criminology. Among their affiliated branches are peacemaking, left realism, radical feminism, and postmodernism (also called deconstructionism).

Social conflict theory tries to explain crime within economic and social contexts and to express the connection between social class, crime, and social control.[1] Conflict theorists are concerned with issues such as

- Social conflict theory
- The view that crime is a function of class conflict and power relations; laws are created and enforced by those in power to protect their own interests
- The role that government plays in creating a criminogenic environment
- The relationship between personal or group power and the shaping of criminal law
- The prevalence of bias in justice system operations
- The relationship between a capitalist, free enterprise economy and crime rates

Conflict promotes crime by creating a social atmosphere in which the law is a mechanism for controlling dissatisfied, have-not members of society while the wealthy maintain their power. This is why crimes that are the province of the wealthy, such as illegal corporate activities, are sanctioned much more leniently than those, such as burglary, that are considered lower-class activities. As you may recall (see Chapter 1), Karl Marx identified the economic structures in society that control all human relations. In so doing, he sowed the seeds of social conflict theory.

DID YOU KNOW?

- Social conflict theory is aimed at identifying "real" crimes in society such as profiteering, sexism, and racism.
- It seeks to evaluate how criminal law is used as a mechanism of social control.
- It describes how power relations create inequities in society.
- The idea of the social reality of crime is that those who hold power in society define those who oppose their values as criminals.
- Racism and classism pervade the contemporary justice system and shape crime rates.

© Peter Turnley/Corbis

Despite attempts to block social media sites, protesters effectively used them to communicate, inform, and organize demonstrations in the 2011 uprising in Egypt.

radical criminology The view that crime is a product of the capitalist system; Marxist criminology.

Marxist criminology The view that crime is a product of the capitalist system; radical criminology.

Those criminologists who gain their inspiration from Marx reject the notion that law is designed to maintain a tranquil, fair society and that criminals are malevolent people who wish to trample the rights of others. Conflict theorists consider acts of racism, sexism, imperialism, unsafe working conditions, inadequate child care, substandard housing, pollution of the environment, and poverty to be the most serious crimes because they create the conditions in society that lead many people to desperation, drug and alcohol abuse, and violence. The crimes of the poor and disadvantaged—drugs, burglary, robbery, and assault—are therefore often seen as reactions to and expressions of rage over unjust social conditions.[2] By focusing on how the capitalist state uses law to control the lower classes, Marxist thought serves as the basis for all social conflict theory.

This chapter reviews criminological theories that see criminal behaviour as a function of conflict, a reaction to the unfair distribution of wealth and power in society. The social conflict perspective has several independent branches. One, generally referred to as "pure" conflict theory, maintains that intergroup conflict and rivalry cause crime in any society, regardless of its economic structure. A second branch focuses on the crime-producing traits of capitalist society; included here are critical, radical, and Marxist criminology.[3] In general, the terms **radical criminology** and **Marxist criminology** will be used interchangeably; where appropriate, distinctions will be made between the various schools of thought they contain. Finally, emerging forms of social conflict theory include feminist, new realist, peacemaking, and postmodern thought (see Figure 8.1).

LO1 The Conflict Theory of Crime

Conflict theory came into criminological prominence during the 1960s, when self-report studies began to yield data suggesting that the class–crime correlation found in official crime data was spurious. The self-reports showed that crime and delinquency were distributed much more evenly through the social structure than indicated by official statistics, which reported more crime in lower-class environments.[4] If these self-reports were accurate, middle-class participation in crime was going unrecorded while the lower class was subjected to discriminatory law enforcement practices.[5]

The theme that dominated much of this scholarship was the contention that criminal legislation was determined by the relative power of groups determined to use criminal law to advance their own special interests or to impose their own moral preferences on others.[6] This movement was aided by the widespread social and political upheaval of the late 1960s and early 1970s. These social forces included anti–Vietnam War demonstrations, counterculture movements, and various forms of political protest, including the formation of the terrorist group the Front de Libération du Québec (FLQ), which was responsible for bombings, kidnappings, and even the murder of a provincial cabinet minister during the

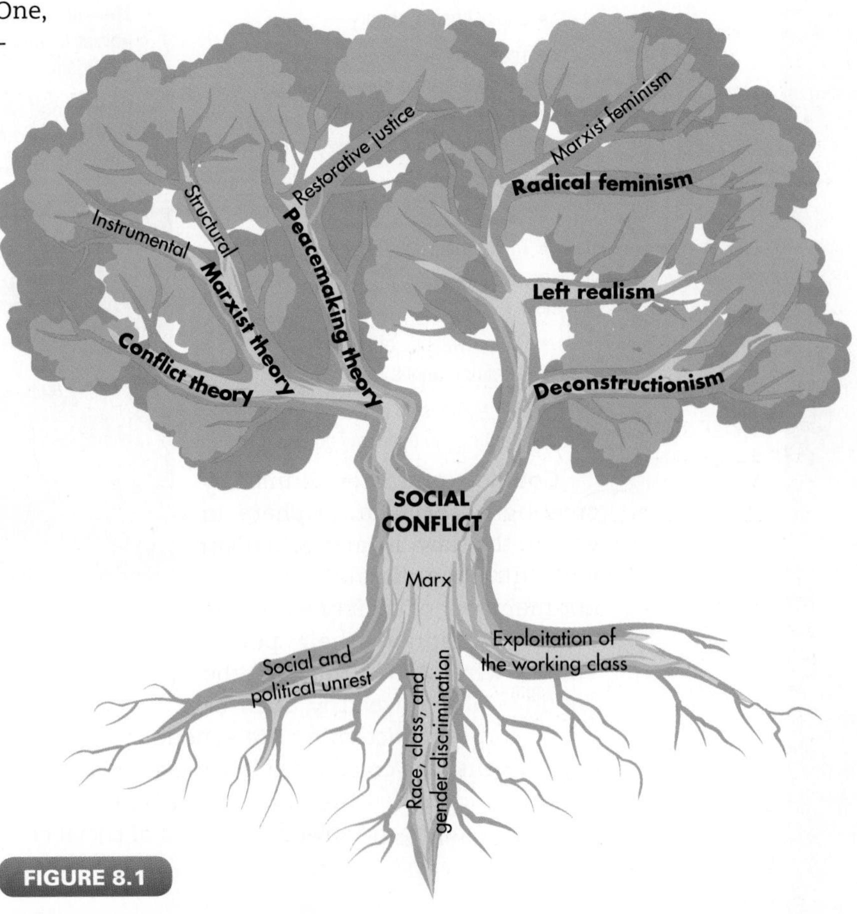

FIGURE 8.1

The Branches of Social Conflict Theory

CP PHOTO/Ryan Remiorz

The Front de Libération du Québec (FLQ) was responsible for a series of bombings, kidnappings, and murders in the late 1960s. The kidnapping and murder of the British Trade Commissioner in 1970 led to Prime Minister Pierre Trudeau's implementation of the War Measures Act and the suspension of civil liberties in Quebec.

1960s and 1970s.[7] Conflict theory flourished within this framework because it provided a systematic basis for challenging the legitimacy of the government's creation and application of law. Government crackdowns on political dissidents seemed designed to maintain control in the hands of the status quo.

As conflict theory began to influence criminological study, several influential scholars embraced its ideas. William Chambliss and Robert Seidman wrote the well-respected treatise *Law, Order and Power*, which documented how the justice system protects the rich and powerful. After closely observing its operations, Chambliss and Seidman concluded:

> In America, it is frequently argued that to have "freedom" is to have a system which allows one group to make a profit over another. To maintain the existing legal system requires a choice. That choice is between maintaining a legal system that serves to support the existing economic system with its power structure and developing an equitable legal system accompanied by the loss of "personal freedom." But the old question comes back to plague us: Freedom for whom? Is the black man who provides such a ready source of cases for the welfare workers, the mental hospitals, and the prisons "free"? Are the slum dwellers who are arrested night after night for "loitering," "drunkenness," or being "suspicious" free? The freedom protected by the system of law is the freedom of those who can afford it. The law serves their interests, but they are not "society"; they are one element of society. They may in some complex societies even be a majority (though this is very rare), but the myth that the law serves the interests of "society" misrepresents the facts.[8]

According to Chambliss and Seidman, the law serves the interests of those who can afford it.

© Natalia Lukiyanova/iStockPhoto

Some common objectives of conflict criminology that appear in Chambliss and Seidman's writing include

- Describing how control of the political and economic system affects the way criminal justice is administered
- Showing how definitions of crime favour those who control the justice system
- Analyzing the role of conflict in contemporary society

Their scholarship also reflects another major objective of conflict theory: to show how justice is skewed. Those who deserve the most severe sanctions (wealthy white-collar criminals whose crimes cost society millions of dollars) are actually

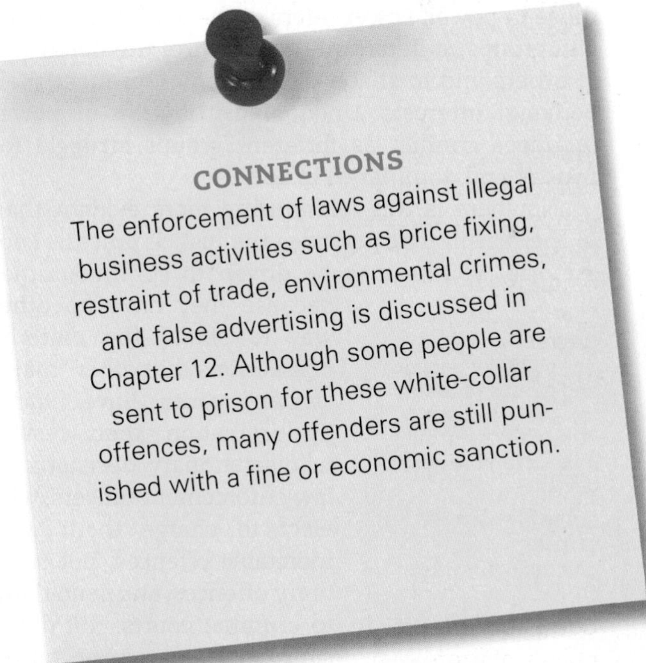
CONNECTIONS

The enforcement of laws against illegal business activities such as price fixing, restraint of trade, environmental crimes, and false advertising is discussed in Chapter 12. Although some people are sent to prison for these white-collar offences, many offenders are still punished with a fine or economic sanction.

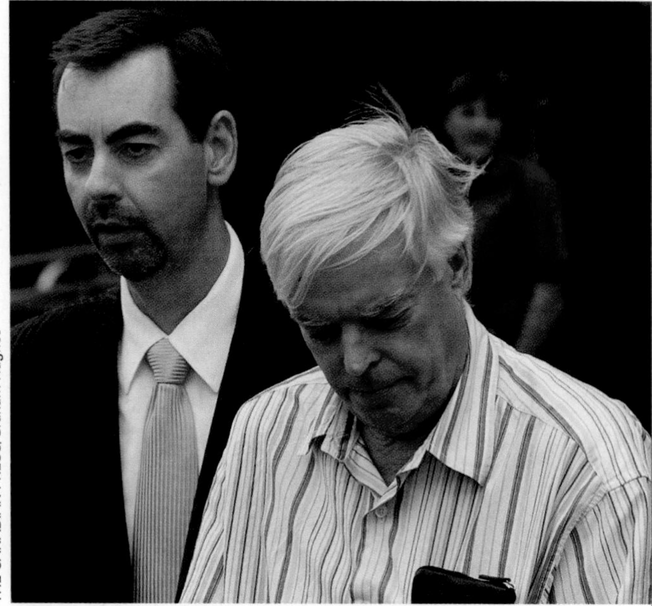

THE CANADIAN PRESS/Graham Hughes

On Monday, February 15, 2010, Montreal investment financier Earl Jones was sentenced to 11 years in prison for defrauding 158 investors out of more than $50 million. Many of those Jones defrauded were friends, elderly couples, even his own brother. Because white-collar crime is nonviolent, Jones could be out of prison after serving only 22 months of the sentence.

punished the least, whereas those whose relatively minor crimes are committed out of economic necessity (petty thieves and drug dealers) receive stricter penalties.[9]

Power Relations

According to the conflict view, crime is defined by those in power. **Power** refers to the ability of persons and groups to determine and control the behaviour of others and to shape public opinion to meet their personal interests. Unequal distribution of power produces conflict as different groups struggle for control and dominance in society.

Nowhere is this relationship more evident than in the racism that pervades the justice process. Poor minority youths may be driven to commit crimes because they have no other way to obtain the material possessions that other "mainstream" youth have. Racial discrimination then results in discretionary decisions by law enforcement officers, who elect to charge them with indictable offences, not summary offences, and send them to criminal courts, not diversion programs. Busy public defenders often pressure their clients into plea bargains that ensure early criminal records. Health-care workers and teachers are quick to report suspected violent acts to the police; this results in frequent, early arrests of minority youths and adults. Police routinely search, question, and detain all black males in an area if a violent criminal has been described as "looking or sounding black"; this is called "racial profiling." By creating the image of pervasive black criminality and coupling it with unfair treatment, those in power further alienate this population from the mainstream, perpetuating a class- and race-divided society. Surveys in both the United States and Canada show that blacks are much more likely to perceive criminal injustice than whites.[10] Other research shows that Aboriginal people are both more likely to be arrested and imprisoned than other Canadians.[11]

power
The ability of persons and groups to control the behaviour of others, to shape public opinion, and to define deviance.

social reality of crime
The main purpose of criminology is to promote a peaceful, just society.

The Social Reality of Crime

Richard Quinney, one of the more influential conflict theorists of the time, integrated these beliefs about power, society, and criminality into a theory he referred to as the **social reality of crime**. According to Quinney, criminal definitions (law) represent the interests of those who hold power in society. Where there is conflict between social groups—for example, the wealthy

arindambanerjee/Shutterstock.com

Conflict theory views power as the ability of persons or groups to control the behaviour of others. Toronto police were accused of abusing their powers and the law to arrest hundreds of peaceful protesters and even members of the media during the G-20 world leaders' summit, held in Toronto in June 2010. Police claimed to have the authority to search and demand identification from anyone coming within five metres of the security fence surrounding the G20 site but the Ontario government was forced to admit after the summit ended that the police were never granted that authority. Most of those arrested during the summit were held in temporary detention centres only to discover that all charges were dropped following the summit. Protesters, civil libertarians, and unions have called for a public inquiry into the treatment of protesters at the summit.[12]

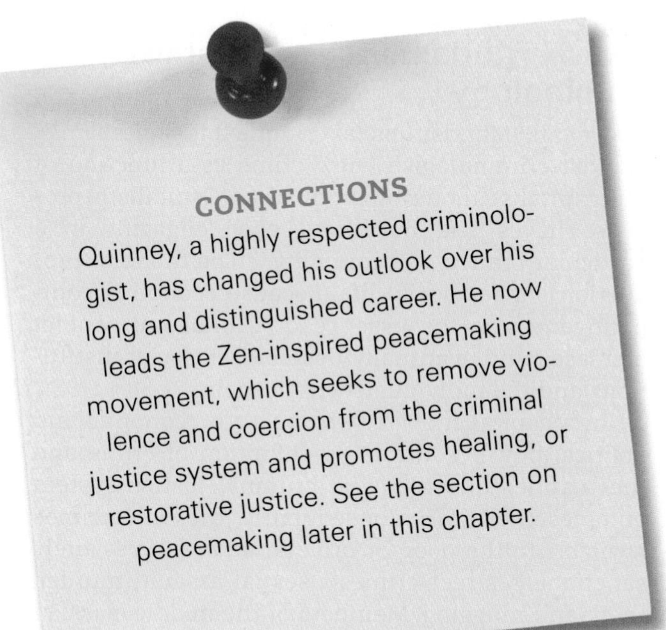

and the poor—those who hold power create laws that benefit themselves and hold their rivals in check.

CONNECTIONS
Quinney, a highly respected criminologist, has changed his outlook over his long and distinguished career. He now leads the Zen-inspired peacemaking movement, which seeks to remove violence and coercion from the criminal justice system and promotes healing, or restorative justice. See the section on peacemaking later in this chapter.

According to Quinney, law is not an abstract body of rules that represents an absolute moral code; rather, law is an integral part of society, a force that represents a way of life and a method of doing things. Crime is a function of power relations and an inevitable result of social conflict. Criminals are not simply social misfits, but people who have come up short in the struggle for success and are seeking alternative means of achieving wealth, status, or even survival.[13] Consequently, law violations can be viewed as political or even quasi-revolutionary acts.[14]

LO2 Research on Conflict Theory

Conflict theorists maintain that social inequality forces people to commit some crimes, such as break and enter and theft, as a means of social and economic survival, whereas other crimes, such as assault, homicide, and drug use, are a means of expressing rage, frustration, and anger. Data show that crime rates vary according to indicators of poverty and need. For example, infant mortality rates have been associated with homicide rates, which shows that a society that cannot care for its young is also prone to social unrest and violence.[15] Crime rates seem strongly related to measures of social inequality such as income level, deteriorated living conditions, and relative economic deprivation.[16]

Another area of conflict-oriented research involves examining the criminal justice system to see if it operates as an instrument of class oppression or as a fair, even-handed social control agency. Some conflict researchers have found evidence of class bias. Legal jurisdictions with significant levels of economic disparity are also the most likely to have large numbers of people killed by police officers. Police may act more forcefully in areas where class conflict creates the perception that extreme forms of social control are needed to maintain order.[17] It is not surprising to conflict theorists that police brutality complaints are highest in minority neighbourhoods, especially those that experience relative deprivation (minority residents earn significantly less money than the white majority).[18]

Criminal courts are also more likely to punish members of powerless, disenfranchised groups.[19] When criminals are convicted, both white and black offenders have been found to receive stricter sentences if their personal characteristics (single, young, urban, male) show them to be members of the "dangerous classes."[20] The unemployed, especially racial minorities, may be perceived as "social dynamite" who present a real threat to society and must be controlled and incapacitated.[21]

Conflict theorists also point to studies showing that the criminal justice system is quick to act when a crime victim is wealthy, white, and male but is disinterested when the victim is poor, black or Aboriginal, and female.[22] Analysis of population trends and imprisonment rates shows that as the percentage of minority-group members increases in a population, the imprisonment rate does likewise.[23] As minority populations increase, the majority may become less tolerant or feel more threatened.

One reason for such displays of discrimination may be the overt or covert racist attitudes of decision makers. Justice professionals who express racist values (such as stating that race-based trait differences actually exist) are also more punitive, believe that courts should be stricter, and are likely to let race affect their judgments.[24] Critical theorists argue that there must be a thorough rethinking of the role and purpose of the criminal justice system, giving the powerless a greater voice to express their needs and concerns, if these inequities are to be addressed.[25]

Radical Criminology

The writings of Karl Marx and Friedrich Engels greatly influenced the development of social conflict thinking. Although Marx himself did not write much on the topic of crime, his views on the relationship between the economic structure and social behaviour deeply influenced other thinkers.

In the 1960s, theories that focused on the relationship between crime and conflict in any society began to be supplanted by more radical, Marxist-oriented theories that examined the specific role of capitalism in law and criminality.

In 1973, radical theory was given a powerful academic boost when British scholars Ian Taylor, Paul Walton, and Jock Young published *The New Criminology*.[26] This brilliant, thorough, and well-constructed critique of existing concepts in criminology called for the development of new methods of criminological analysis and critique. *The New Criminology* became the standard resource for scholars critical of both the field of criminology and the existing legal process.

During the same period, a small group of scholars in the United States and Canada also began to follow a new, radical approach to criminology. In the United States, the locus of the radical school was the criminology program at the University of California at Berkeley. The most noted Marxist scholars at that institution were Anthony Platt, Paul Takagi, Herman Schwendinger, and Julia Schwendinger. Radical scholars at other American academic institutions included Richard Quinney, William Chambliss, Steven Spitzer, and Barry Krisberg. In Canada, radical criminology took root at a number of universities across the country, and includes scholarly work by Ronald Hinch, Walter DeKeseredy, John Hagan, Thomas O'Reilly-Fleming, Brian Maclean, Neil Boyd, Christine Boyle, and others.

The North American radicals were influenced by the widespread social ferment during the late 1960s and early 1970s. The war in Vietnam, prison struggles, the Quiet Revolution in Quebec, and broad-based civil rights and feminist movements in both Canada and the United States produced a climate in which criticism of the ruling class seemed a natural byproduct. Mainstream, positivist criminology was criticized as being overtly conservative, pro-government, and antihuman. Critical criminologists scoffed when their fellow scholars used statistical analysis of computerized data to describe criminal and delinquent behaviour.

In the following years, new branches of a radical criminology developed in North America and abroad. In the early 1980s, the left realism school was started by scholars affiliated with the Middlesex Polytechnic and the University of Edinburgh in Great Britain. In the United States, scholars influenced in part by the pioneering work of Dennis Sullivan and Larry Tifft laid the foundation for what eventually became known as the peacemaking movement, which calls for a humanist vision of justice.[27] At the same time, feminist scholars began to critically analyze the relationship between gender, power, and criminality. These movements have coalesced into a rich and complex criminological tradition.

LO3 Fundamentals of Marxist Criminology

Above all, Marxism is a critique of capitalism.[28] Marxist criminologists view crime as a function of the capitalist mode of production. Capitalism produces haves and have-nots, each engaging in a particular branch of criminality.[29] The mode of production shapes social life. Because economic competitiveness is the essence of capitalism, conflict increases and eventually destabilizes social institutions and the individuals within them.[30]

In a capitalist society, those with economic and political power control the definition of crime and the manner in which the criminal justice system enforces the law.[31] Consequently, the only crimes available to the poor, or proletariat, are the severely sanctioned "street crimes": sexual assault, murder, theft, and mugging. Members of the middle class, or petit bourgeoisie, cheat on their taxes and engage in petty corporate crime (employee theft), acts that generate social disapproval but are rarely punished severely. The wealthy bourgeoisie are involved in acts that should be described as crimes but are not, such as racism, sexism, and profiteering.

Although regulatory laws control illegal business activities, these are rarely enforced, and violations are lightly punished. Laws regulating corporate crime are actually designed to impress the working class with how fair the justice system is. In reality, the justice system is the equivalent of an army that defends the owners of property in their ongoing struggle against the workers.[32]

The rich are insulated from street crimes because they live in areas far removed from crime. Those in power use the fear of crime as a tool to maintain their control over society. The poor are controlled through incarceration, and the middle class is diverted from

"And here's when Mr.Kimbel, the company accountant, went on his extended holiday to Brazil."

caring about the crimes of the powerful by their fear of the crimes of the powerless.[33] Ironically, they may have more to lose from the economic crimes committed by the rich than the street crimes of the poor. Stock market swindles and price fixing cost the public billions of dollars but are typically settled with fines and probationary sentences.

Because private ownership of property is the true measure of success in capitalism (as opposed to being, say, a worthy person), the state becomes an ally of the wealthy in protecting their property interests. As a result, theft-related crimes are often punished more severely than are acts of violence because while the former may be interclass, the latter are typically intraclass.

LO4 Defining Crime

Marxists use the conflict definition of crime: Crime is a political concept designed to protect the power and position of the upper classes at the expense of the poor. Some, but not all, Marxists would include in a list of "real" crimes acts such as violations of human rights due to racism, sexism, and imperialism, and other violations of human dignity, physical needs, and necessities. Part of the radical agenda, argues criminologist Robert Bohm, is to make the public aware that these behaviours "are crimes just as much as burglary and robbery."[34]

The nature of a society controls the direction of its criminality; criminals are not social misfits, but products of the society and its economic system. "Capitalism," claims Bohm, "as a mode of production, has always produced a relatively high level of crime and violence."[35] According to Michael Lynch and W. Byron Groves, three implications follow from this view:

1. Each society produces its own types and amounts of crime.
2. Each society has its own distinctive ways of dealing with criminal behaviour.
3. Each society gets the amount and type of crime that it deserves.[36]

This analysis tells us that criminals are not a group of outsiders who can be controlled by increased law enforcement. Criminality, instead, is a function of social and economic organization. To control crime and reduce criminality is to end the social conditions that promote crime.

Economic Structure and Surplus Value

Although no single view or theory defines Marxist criminology today, its general theme is the relationship between crime and the ownership and control of private property in a capitalist society.[37] That ownership and control is the principal basis of power in capitalist societies such as Canada and the United States.[38] Social conflict is fundamentally related to the historical and social distribution of productive private property. Destructive social conflicts inherent

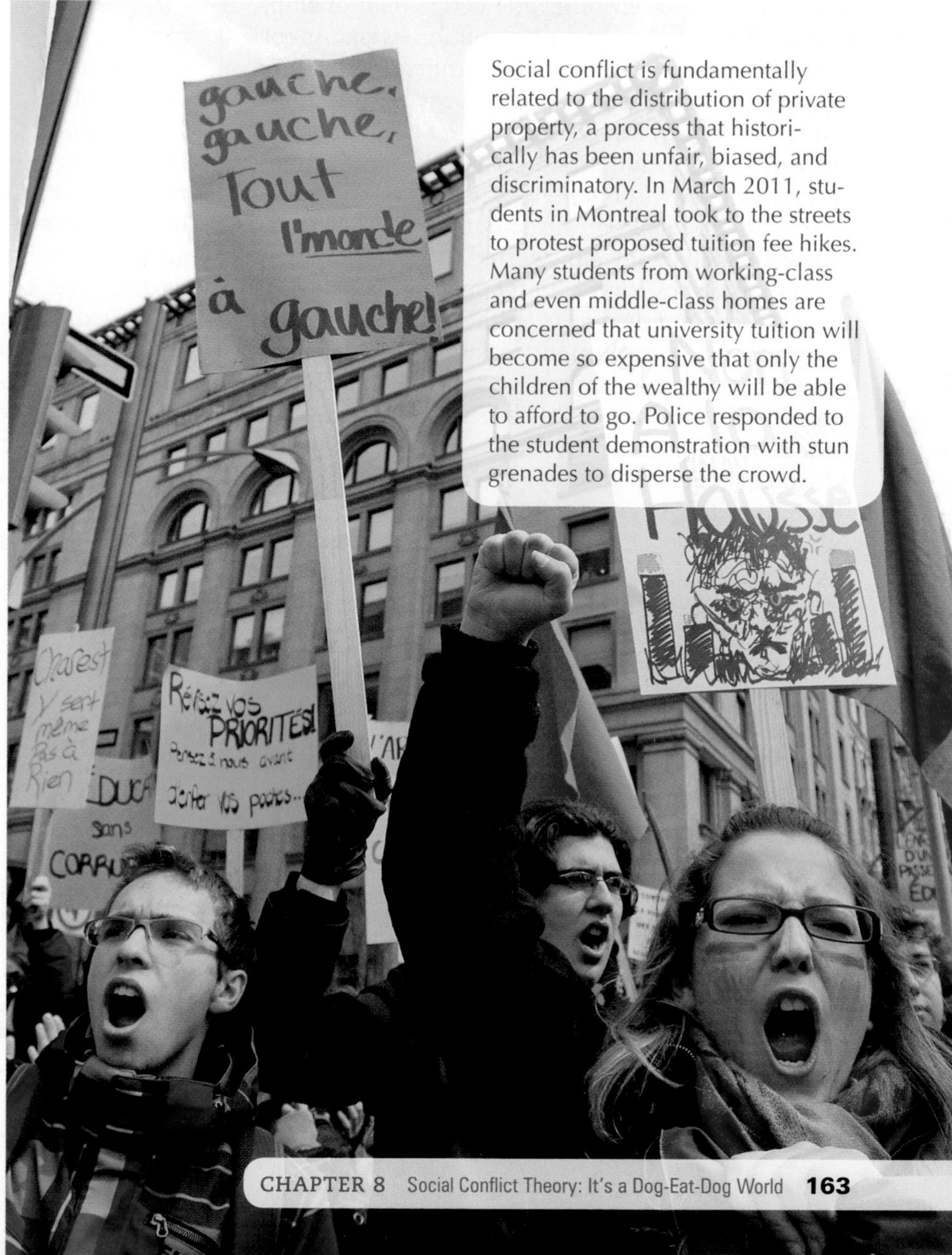

The CANADIAN PRESS/Graham Hughes

Social conflict is fundamentally related to the distribution of private property, a process that historically has been unfair, biased, and discriminatory. In March 2011, students in Montreal took to the streets to protest proposed tuition fee hikes. Many students from working-class and even middle-class homes are concerned that university tuition will become so expensive that only the children of the wealthy will be able to afford to go. Police responded to the student demonstration with stun grenades to disperse the crowd.

surplus value The difference between what workers produce and what they are paid, which goes to business owners as profits.

marginalization Displacement of workers, pushing them outside the economic and social mainstream.

within the capitalist system cannot be resolved unless that system is destroyed or ended.

One important aspect of the capitalist economic system is the effect of **surplus value**—the profits produced by the labouring classes that are accrued by business owners. Surplus value can be either reinvested or used to enrich the owners. To increase the rate of surplus value, workers can be made to work harder for less pay, be made more efficient, or be replaced by machines or technology. Therefore, economic growth does not benefit all elements of the population, and in the long run it may produce the same effect as a depression or recession.

As the rate of surplus value increases, more people are displaced from productive relationships, and the size of the marginal population swells. As corporations downsize to increase profits, high-paying labour and managerial jobs are lost to computer-driven machinery. Displaced workers are forced into service jobs at minimum wage. Many become temporary employees without benefits or a secure position.

As more people are thrust outside the economic mainstream, a condition referred to as **marginalization**, a larger portion of the population is forced to live in areas conducive to crime. Once people are marginalized, commitment to the system declines, producing another criminogenic force: a weakened bond to society.[39] This process is illustrated in Figure 8.2.

The government may be quick to respond during periods of economic decline because those in power assume that poor economic conditions breed crime and social disorder. When unemployment is increasing, public officials assume the worst and devote greater attention to the criminal justice system, perhaps building new prisons to prepare for the coming "crime wave."[40] Empirical research confirms that economic downturns are indeed linked to both crime rate increases and government activities such as passing anticrime legislation.[41] For example, as the level of surplus value increases, so too do police expenditures, most likely because of the perceived or real need for the state to control those on the economic margin.[42]

Although these themes can be found throughout Marxist writing, a number of different schools of thought have arisen within the radical literature. Among these various approaches are instrumental Marxism and structural Marxism.

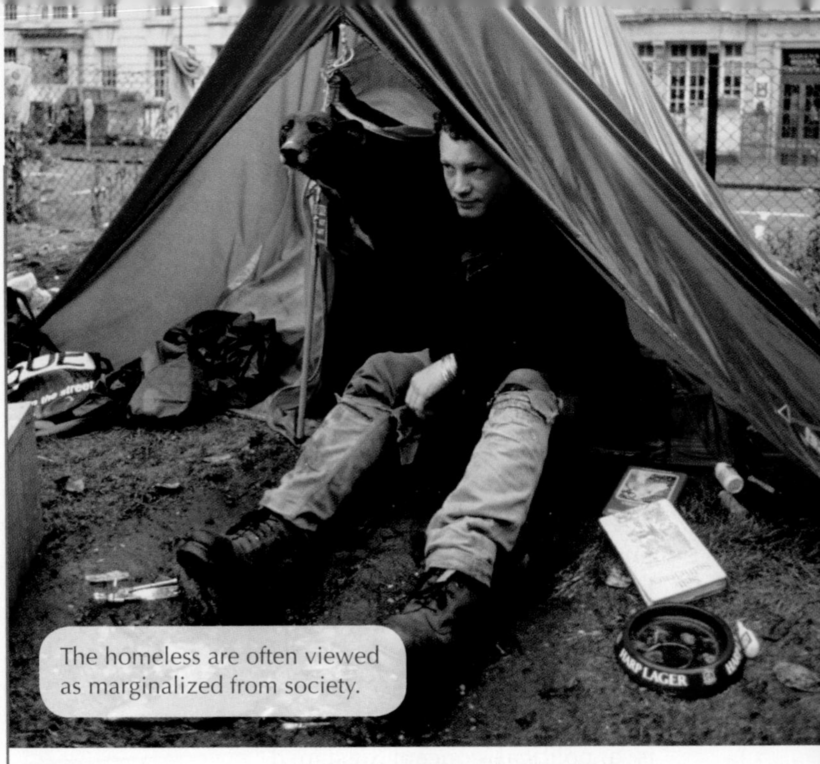
HARP LAGER
The homeless are often viewed as marginalized from society.

FIGURE 8.2

Surplus Value and Crime

Worker produces goods that exceed wages in value
Profit
Capitalist keeps profits
Uses profits to buy machines and replace workers
Workers are marginalized
Crime rates increase

Instrumental Marxism

Instrumental Marxists view criminal law and the criminal justice system solely as instruments for controlling the poor, have-not members of society. They see the state as the tool of capitalists.

According to the instrumental view, capitalist justice serves the powerful and rich and enables them to impose their morality and standards of behaviour on the entire society. Under capitalism, those who wield economic power are able to extend their self-serving definition of illegal or criminal behaviour to encompass those who might threaten the status quo or interfere with their quest for ever-increasing profits.[43] For example, the concentration of economic assets in the nation's largest industrial firms translates into the political power needed to control tax laws to limit the firms' tax liabilities.[44] Some have the economic clout to hire top lawyers to defend themselves against antitrust actions, making them almost immune to regulation.

The poor, according to this branch of Marxist theory, may or may not commit more crimes than the rich, but they certainly are arrested and punished more often. Under the capitalist system, the poor are driven to crime because a natural frustration exists in a society in which affluence is well publicized but unattainable. When class conflict becomes unbearable, frustration can spill out in riots, such as the one that occurred in June 2000 when a large crowd of antipoverty protesters clashed with police at the Ontario legislature.[45] Because of class conflict, a deep-rooted hostility is generated among members of the lower class toward a social order they are not allowed to shape and whose benefits are unobtainable.[46]

Instrumental Marxists consider it essential to **demystify** law and justice—that is, to unmask its true purpose. Criminological theories that focus on family structure, intelligence, peer relations, and school performance keep the lower classes servile by showing why they are more criminal, less intelligent, and more prone to school failure and family problems than the middle class. Demystification involves identifying the destructive intent of capitalist-inspired and capitalist-funded criminology. Instrumental Marxists' goal for criminology is to show how capitalist law preserves ruling-class power.[47]

instrumental Marxist
One who sees criminal law and the criminal justice system as capitalist instruments for controlling the lower class.

demystify
To unmask the true purpose of law, justice, or other social institutions.

structural Marxist
One who sees criminal law and the criminal justice system as means of defending and preserving the capitalist system.

Structural Marxism

Structural Marxists disagree with the view that the relationship between law and capitalism is unidirectional, always working for the rich and against the poor.[48] Law is not the exclusive domain of the rich, but rather is used to maintain the long-term interests of the capitalist system and control members of any class who threaten its existence. If law and justice were purely instruments of the capitalist class, why would laws controlling corporate crimes, such as price-fixing, false advertising, and illegal restraint of trade, have been created and enforced?

To a structuralist, the law is designed to keep the capitalist system operating efficiently, and anyone, capitalist or proletarian, who rocks the boat is targeted for sanction. For example, antitrust legislation is designed to prevent any single capitalist from dominating the system. If the capitalist system is to

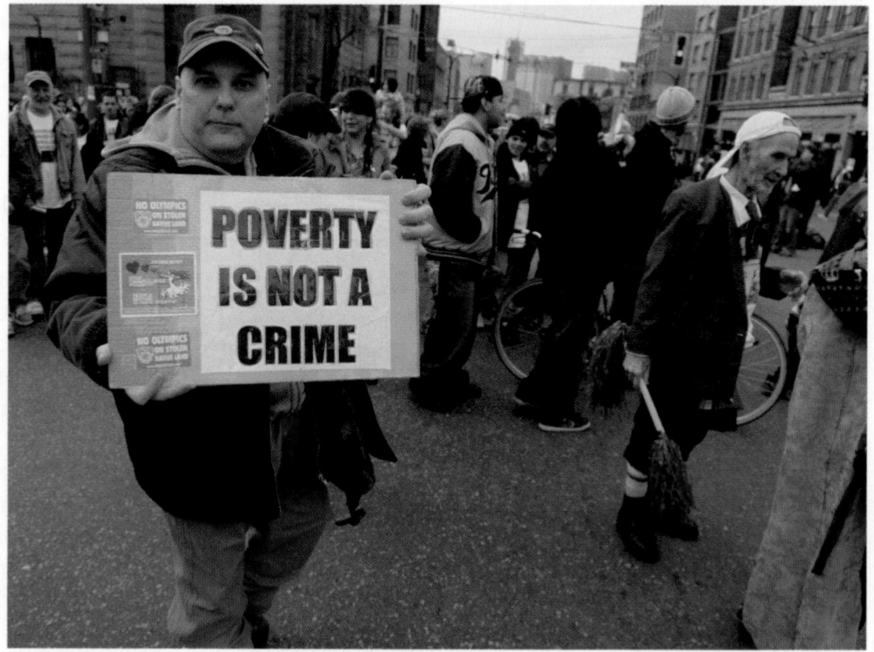

© ryan koopmans/Alamy

Antipoverty groups in Lower Mainland Vancouver demonstrated following the decision to host the 2010 Winter Olympics in the city. The groups claimed that while homelessness in Vancouver had doubled since 2003, the city introduced new bylaws making it illegal to ask for money or sleep outdoors. Also, far from being green or sustainable, the Olympic venues could cause a great deal of ecological damage.

function, no single person can become too powerful at the expense of the economic system as a whole. Structuralists would regard the decision of the U.S. government to break up Microsoft, and recent efforts to regulate the dominance of Apple in the online music industry, as an example of capitalists controlling capitalists to keep the system on an even keel.

Research on Marxist Criminology

Marxist criminologists rarely use standard social science methodologies to test their views because many believe the traditional approach of measuring research subjects is antihuman and insensitive.[49] Marxists believe that the research conducted by mainstream liberal and positivist criminologists is designed to unmask weak, powerless members of society so they can be better dealt with by the legal system. They are particularly offended by purely empirical studies, such as those designed to show that minority-group members have lower IQs than whites or that the inner city is the site of the most serious crime whereas middle-class areas are relatively crime-free.

Empirical research, however, is not considered totally incompatible with Marxist criminology, and there have been some important efforts to test its fundamental assumptions quantitatively.[50] For example, research has shown that the property crime rate reflects a change in the level of surplus value; the capitalist system's emphasis on excessive profits accounts for the need of the working class to commit property crime.[51] Nonetheless, Marxist research tends to be historical and analytical, not quantitative and empirical. Social trends are interpreted with regard to how capitalism has affected human interaction. Marxists investigate both macro-level issues, such as how the accumulation of wealth affects crime rates, and micro-level issues, such as the effect of criminal interactions on the lives of individuals living in a capitalist society. Of particular importance to Marxist critical thinkers is analyzing the historical development of capitalist social control institutions, such as criminal law, police agencies, courts, and prison systems.

© GL Archive/Alamy

Karl Marx

Crime, the Individual, and the State

Marxists devote considerable attention to the relationships among crime, the victims, the criminal, and the state. Two common themes emerge: (1) crime and its control are a function of capitalism; and (2) the justice system is biased against the working class and favours upper-class interests.

Marxist analysis of the criminal justice system is designed to identify the often-hidden processes that control people's lives. It takes into account how conditions, processes, and structures evolved into what they are today. One issue considered is the process by which deviant behaviour is defined as criminal or delinquent in society.[52] Another issue is the degree to which class affects the justice system's decision-making process.[53] Also subject to analysis is how power relationships help undermine any benefit the lower class receives from sentencing reforms.[54] In general, Marxist research efforts have yielded evidence linking operations of the justice system to class bias.[55] In addition, some researchers have attempted to show how capitalism intervenes across the entire spectrum of crime-related phenomena.

Historical Analysis

Another type of Marxist research focuses on the historical background of commonly held institutional beliefs and practices. One goal is to show how changes in criminal law correspond to the development of the capitalist economy. The second goal is to investigate the development of modern police agencies.

To examine the changes in criminal law, historian Michael Rustigan analyzed historical records to show that law reform in 19th-century England was largely a response to pressure from the business community to increase punishment for property law violations in order to protect their rapidly increasing wealth.[56] Other research has focused on topics such as how the relationship between convict work and capitalism evolved during the 19th century. During this period, prisons became a profitable method of centralized state control over lower-class criminals, whose labour was exploited by commercial concerns.

These criminals were forced to labour in order to pay off wardens and correctional administrators.[57]

Critique of Marxist Criminology

Marxist criminology has been sharply criticized by some members of the criminological mainstream, who charge that its contribution has been "hot air, heat, but no real light."[58] In turn, radicals have accused mainstream criminologists of being culprits in developing state control over individual lives and selling out their ideals for the chance to receive government funding.

Mainstream criminologists have also attacked the substance of Marxist thought. Some argue that Marxist theory simply rehashes the old tradition of helping the underdog, in which the poor steal from the rich to survive.[59] In reality, most theft is for luxury, not survival. While the wealthy do commit their share of illegal acts, these are nonviolent and leave no permanent injuries.[60] People do not live in fear of corrupt businessmen and stock traders; they fear muggers and rapists.

Other critics suggest that Marxists unfairly neglect the capitalist system's efforts to regulate itself—for example, by instituting antitrust regulations and putting violators in jail. Similarly, they ignore efforts to institute social reforms aimed at helping the poor.[61] There seems to be no logic in condemning a system that helps the poor and empowers them to take on corporate interests in a court of law. Some argue that Marxists refuse to address the problems and conflicts that exist in socialist countries, such as the gulags and purges of the Soviet Union under Stalin. Similarly, they fail to explain why some highly capitalist countries, such as Japan, have extremely low crime rates. Marxists are too quick to blame capitalism for every human vice without adequate explanation or regard for other social and environmental factors.[62] In so doing, they ignore objective reality and refuse to acknowledge that members of the lower classes tend to victimize one another. They ignore the plight of the lower classes, who must live in crime-ridden neighbourhoods, while condemning the capitalist system from the security of the "ivory tower."

Marxist scholars criticize their critics for relying on "traditional" variables, such as class and poverty, in their analysis of radical thought. Although important, these do not reflect the key issues in the structural and economic process. In fact, like crime, they too may be the outcome of the capitalist system.[63] Marxists also point out that although other capitalist nations may have lower crime rates, this does not mean they are crime-free. Even Japan has significant problems with teen prostitution and organized crime.

DID YOU KNOW?

- Marxist criminology tries to explain how the workings of the capitalist system produce inequality and crime.
- In this view, the state serves the interests of the ruling capitalist class. Criminal law is an instrument of economic oppression. Capitalism demands that the subordinate classes remain oppressed.
- Instrumental Marxists believe that the legal system supports the owners at the expense of the workers.
- Structural Marxists believe that the law also ensures that no capitalist becomes too powerful. The law is used to maintain the long-term interests of the capitalist system.
- Marxist research is designed to show how capitalism creates the people who turn to crime for survival.

Emerging Forms of Social Conflict Theory

Although radical criminologists dispute criticisms, they have also responded by creating new theoretical models that innovatively incorporate Marxist ideas. The following sections discuss in detail some recent forms of radical theory.

Left Realism

Some radical scholars are now addressing the need for the left wing to respond to the increasing power of right-wing conservatives. They are troubled by the emergence of a strict "law and order" philosophy, which has as its centrepiece a policy of punishing juveniles severely in adult court. At the same time, they find the focus of most left-wing scholarship—the abuse of power by the ruling elite—too narrow. It is wrong, they argue, to ignore inner-city gang crime and violence, which often target indigent people.[64] The approach of scholars who share these concerns is referred to as **left realism**.[65]

Left realism is most often connected to the writings of British scholars John Lea and Jock Young. In their well-respected 1984 work, *What Is to Be Done About Law and Order?* they reject the utopian views of "idealistic" Marxists who portray street criminals as revolutionaries.[66] They take the more "realistic" approach that street criminals prey on the poor and disenfranchised, thus making the poor doubly abused, first by the capitalist system and then by members of their own class.

left realism
Approach that sees crime as a function of relative deprivation under capitalism and favours pragmatic, community-based crime prevention and control.

Lea and Young's view of crime causation borrows

preemptive deterrence Efforts to prevent crime through community organization and youth involvement.

Marxist feminism Approach that explains both victimization and criminality among women in terms of gender inequality, patriarchy, and the exploitation of women under capitalism

patriarchal Male-dominated.

from conventional sociological theory and closely resembles the relative deprivation approach, which posits that experiencing poverty in the midst of plenty creates discontent and breeds crime. As they put it, "The equation is simple: relative deprivation equals discontent; discontent plus lack of political solution equals crime."[67]

Left realists argue that crime victims in all classes need and deserve protection; crime control reflects community needs. They do not view police and the courts as inherently evil tools of capitalism whose tough tactics alienate the lower classes. In fact, they recognize that these institutions offer life-saving public services. The left realists wish, however, that police would reduce their use of force and increase their sensitivity to the public.[68]

Preemptive deterrence is an approach in which community organization efforts eliminate or reduce crime before police involvement becomes necessary. The reasoning behind this approach is that if the number of marginalized youths (those who feel they are not part of society and have nothing to lose by committing crime) could be reduced, then delinquency rates would decline.[69]

Although implementing a socialist economy might help eliminate the crime problem, left realists recognize that something must be done to control crime under the existing capitalist system. To develop crime control policies, left realists not only welcome radical ideas but also build on the work of strain theorists, social ecologists, and other mainstream views. Community-based efforts seem to hold the greatest promise of crime control.

Left realism has been criticized by radical thinkers as legitimizing the existing power structure: By supporting existing definitions of law and justice, it suggests that the "deviant" and not the capitalist system causes society's problems. Critics question whether left realists advocate the very institutions that "currently imprison us and our patterns of thought and action."[70] In rebuttal, left realists would say that it is unrealistic to speak of a socialist state lacking a police force or a system of laws and justice. They believe that the criminal code does, in fact, represent public opinion.

Radical Feminist Theory

Like so many theories in criminology, most of the efforts of radical theorists have been devoted to explaining male criminality.[71] To remedy this theoretical lapse, a number of feminist writers have attempted to explain the cause of crime, gender differences in crime rates, and the exploitation of female victims from a radical feminist perspective.

Marxist feminism views gender inequality as stemming from the unequal power of men and women in a capitalist society, which leads to the exploitation of women by fathers and husbands. Under this system, women are considered a commodity worth possessing, like land or money.[72]

The origin of gender differences can be traced to the development of private property and male domination of the laws of inheritance, which led to male control over property and power.[73] A **patriarchal** system developed in which men's work was valued and women's work was devalued. As capitalism prevailed, the division of labour by gender made women responsible for the unpaid maintenance and reproduction of the current and future labour force, which was derisively called "domestic work." Although this unpaid work done by women is crucial and profitable for capitalists, who reap these free benefits, such labour is exploitative and oppressive for women.[74] Even when women gained the right to work for pay, they were exploited as cheap labour. The dual exploitation of women within the household and in the labour market means that women produce far greater surplus value for capitalists than men.

Patriarchy, or male supremacy, has been and continues to be supported by capitalists. This system sustains female oppression at home and in the workplace.[75] Although the number of traditional patriarchal families is in steep decline, in those that still exist, a wife's economic dependence ties men more securely to wage-earning jobs, further serving the interests of capitalists by undermining potential rebellion against the system.

Patriarchy and Crime

Marxist feminists link criminal behaviour patterns to the gender conflict created by the economic and social struggles common in postindustrial societies. In his book *Capitalism, Patriarchy, and Crime*, James Messerschmidt argues that capitalist society is marked by both patriarchy and class conflict. Capitalists control the labour of workers, while men control women both economically and biologically.[76] This "double marginality" explains why females in a capitalist society commit fewer crimes than males. Because they are isolated in the family, they have fewer opportunities to engage in elite deviance (white-collar and economic crimes). Although powerful females as well as males will commit white-collar crimes, the female crime rate is restricted because of the patriarchal nature of the capitalist system.[77] Women are also denied access to male-dominated street crimes. Because capitalism renders lower-class women powerless, they are forced to commit less serious, nonviolent, self-destructive crimes, such as abusing drugs.

Powerlessness also increases the likelihood that women will become targets of violent acts.[78] When lower-class males are shut out of the economic opportunity structure, they try to build their self-image through acts of machismo; such acts may involve violent abuse of women. This type of reaction accounts for a significant percentage of female victims who are attacked by a spouse or intimate partner.

In *Masculinities and Crime*, Messerschmidt expands on these themes.[79] He suggests that in every culture, males try to emulate "ideal" masculine behaviours. In Western culture, this means being authoritative, in charge, combative, and controlling. Failure to adopt these roles leaves men feeling effeminate and unmanly. Their struggle to dominate women in order to prove their manliness is called "doing gender." Crime is a vehicle for men to "do gender" because it separates them from the weak and allows them to demonstrate physical bravery. Violence directed toward women is an especially economical way to demonstrate manhood. Would a weak, effeminate male ever attack a woman?

Exploitation and Criminality

Radical feminists also focus on the social forces that shape women's lives and experiences to explain female criminality.[80] For example, they attempt to show how the sexual victimization of girls is a function of male socialization because so many young males learn to be aggressive and to exploit women. Males seek out same-sex peer groups for social support; these groups encourage members to exploit and sexually abuse women. On college and university campuses, peers encourage sexual violence against women who are considered "teasers," "bar pickups," or "loose women." These derogatory labels allow the males to justify their actions; a code of secrecy then protects the aggressors from retribution.[81]

According to the radical feminist view, exploitation triggers the onset of female delinquent and deviant behaviour. When female victims run away and abuse substances, they may be reacting to abuse they have suffered at home or at school. Their attempts at survival are labelled as deviant or delinquent behaviour.[82] In a sense, the female criminal is herself a victim.

Research shows that a significant number of girls who are sent to hospital emergency rooms to be treated for sexual abuse later report engaging in physical fighting as a teen or as an adult. Many of these abused girls later form romantic attachments with abusive partners. Clearly many girls involved in delinquency, crime, and violence have themselves been the victims of violence in their youth and later as adults.[83]

Radical feminist opinions differ on certain issues. For example, some feminist scholars charge that the movement focuses on the problems and viewpoints of white, middle-class, heterosexual women without taking into account the special interests of lesbians and visible-minority women.[84]

How the Justice System Penalizes Women

Radical feminists have indicted the justice system and its patriarchal hierarchy as contributing to the onset of female delinquency. Some have studied the early history of the justice system and uncovered an enduring pattern of discrimination. From its inception, the juvenile justice system has viewed most female delinquents as sexually precocious girls who have to be brought under control. Writing about the "girl problem," Ruth Alexander has described how working-class young women desiring autonomy and freedom in the 1920s were considered delinquents and placed in reformatories. Lacking the ability to protect themselves from the authorities, these young girls were considered outlaws in a male-dominated society because they flouted the very narrow rules of appropriate behaviour that were applied to females. Girls who rebelled against parental authority or who engaged in sexual behaviour deemed inappropriate were incarcerated in order to protect them from a career in prostitution.[85]

Using court records, training school files, government documents, and other publications, Joan Sangster investigated the "social construction"

DID YOU KNOW?

- Left realists are conflict scholars who believe the lower classes must be protected from predatory criminals until the social system changes and makes crime obsolete.
- Radical feminists study patriarchy and the oppression of women. They link female criminality to gender inequality.
- Power–control theory shows how family structure, women's economic status, and gender inequity interact to produce male/female differences in crime rate.
- Postmodernists think language controls thought and behaviour.
- Peacemaking criminologists seek nonviolent, humane alternatives to coercive punishment.

power–control theory
The view that gender differences in crime are a function of economic power (class position, one-versus two-earner families), and parental control (paternalistic versus egalitarian families).

postmodernist
Approach that focuses on the use of language by those in power to define crime based on their own values and biases; also called deconstructionist.

deconstructionist
Approach that focuses on the use of language by those in power to define crime based on their own values and biases; also called postmodernist.

semiotics
The use of language elements as signs or symbols beyond their literal meaning.

of female delinquency in Ontario from 1940 to 1960, and found that sexual activity, real or presumed, was often the "lightning rod" that resulted in girls being incarcerated in a training school. Young girls were routinely subjected to gynecological exams to obtain evidence of wrongdoing. Sometimes, girls were even incarcerated in training school as a preventive measure, to avert contact with boys. In some cases, if officials deemed a girl's family "immoral," that was enough to prompt her removal from the home and incarceration. Sangster concludes that in the 1940–1960 period, the criminal justice system was one designed to "punish, rather than to aid, working-class girls" who were somehow perceived as threats to middle-class notions of proper upbringing and behaviour.[86]

Meda Chesney-Lind has also written extensively about the victimization of female delinquents by agents of the juvenile justice system.[87] She suggests that because female adolescents have a much narrower range of acceptable behaviour than male adolescents, any sign of misbehaviour in girls is seen as a substantial challenge to authority and to the viability of the double standard of sexual inequality. Female delinquency is viewed as relatively more serious than male delinquency and therefore is more likely to be severely sanctioned.

Power–Control Theory

Canadian criminologist John Hagan and his associates have created a radical feminist model that uses gender differences to explain the onset of criminality.[88] Hagan's view is that crime and delinquency rates are a function of two factors: (1) class position (power) and (2) family functions (control).[89] The link between these two variables is that, within the family, parents reproduce the power relationships they hold in the workplace; a position of dominance at work is equated with control in the household. As a result, parents' work experiences and class position influence the criminality of children.

In paternalistic families, fathers assume the traditional role of breadwinners, while mothers tend to have menial jobs or remain at home to supervise domestic matters. Within the paternalistic home, mothers are expected to control the behaviour of their daughters while granting greater freedom to sons. In such a home, the parent–daughter relationship can be viewed as a preparation for the "cult of domesticity," which makes girls' involvement in delinquency unlikely, whereas boys are freer to deviate because they are not subject to maternal control. Girls growing up in patriarchal families are socialized to fear legal sanctions more than are males; consequently, boys in these families exhibit more delinquent behaviour than their sisters.

In egalitarian families—those in which the husband and wife share similar positions of power at home and in the workplace—daughters gain a kind of freedom that reflects reduced parental control. These families produce daughters whose law-violating behaviour mirrors their brothers'. Ironically, these relationships also occur in female-headed households with absent fathers. Hagan and his associates found that when fathers and mothers hold equally valued managerial positions, the similarity between the rates of their daughters' and sons' delinquency is greatest. By implication, middle-class girls are the most likely to violate the law because they are less closely controlled than their lower-class counterparts. In homes in which both parents hold positions of power, girls are more likely to have the same expectations of career success as their brothers. Consequently, siblings of both sexes will be socialized to take risks and engage in other behaviour related to delinquency.

This **power–control theory** has received a great deal of attention in the criminological community because it encourages a new approach to the study of criminality, one that includes gender differences, class position, and the structure of the family. Empirical analysis of its premises has generally been supportive. For example, Brenda Sims Blackwell's research supports a key element of power–control theory: Females in paternalistic households have learned to fear legal sanctions more than have their brothers.[90]

Postmodern Theory

A number of radical thinkers, referred to as **postmodernists** or **deconstructionists**, have embraced semiotics as a method of understanding all human relations, including criminal behaviour. **Semiotics** refers to the use of language elements as signs or symbols beyond their literal meaning. Thus, deconstructionists critically analyze communication and language in legal codes to determine whether they contain language and content that institutionalizes racism or sexism.[91]

Postmodernists rely on semiotics to conduct their research efforts. For example, the term *special-needs children* is designed to describe these youngsters' learning needs, but it may also characterize the children themselves as mentally challenged, dangerous, or uncontrollable. Similarly, application of the term *young offender* to a young person carries with it much more than a legal consequence; in the public mind, the term has been constructed to be associated with threat, unpredictability, violence, and the need for strong control. Though the youth crime rate in Canada has been in decline for more than ten years, and though only a very small number of youth commit serious violent crimes (usually against other youth) still, as postmodernist criminologists such as Moore and Padavic (2010) observe, we continue to use language to "demonize" young persons who come into conflict with the law, including using subtle notions of race and "good girl/bad girl" stereotypes in judges' sentencing decisions.[92]

Postmodernists believe that value-laden language can promote inequities. Truth, identity, justice, and power are all concepts whose meaning is derived from the language dictated by those in power.[93] Laws, legal skill, and justice are commodities that can be bought and sold like any other service or product.[94] For example, the O.J. Simpson case is vivid proof that the affluent can purchase a different brand of justice than the indigent.[95]

Postmodernists go further to assert that there are different languages and ways of knowing, depending on time and position that one is looking at the issue from. For example, prior to the implementation of the new legislation on sexual assault implemented in 1986, many male Canadians (including politicians) could not conceive of a sexual assault being committed by a husband against his wife—though women had long pointed to this problem.

deezign/Shutterstock.com

Postmodernists rely on semiotics, or the study of signs and symbols, to conduct their research efforts.

peacemaking
Approach that considers punitive crime control strategies to be counterproductive and favours the use of humanistic conflict resolution to prevent and control crime.

Those in power can use their own language to define crime and law while excluding or dismissing those who oppose their control, such as prisoners and the poor. By dismissing these oppositional languages, certain versions of how to think, feel, or act are devalued and excluded. This exclusion is seen as the source of conflict in society.

Allen studied the narratives of women survivors of abuse in an attempt to explore how women's resistance develops and unfolds as a survival mechanism and, perhaps, as a movement toward exit from the abusive situation—in contrast to "official" or "governmental" theories, laws, and treatment approaches to domestic violence. For postmodernist criminologists, research such as Allen's challenges, and ultimately improves upon and make more relevant, current approaches to addressing domestic violence.[96]

LO5 Peacemaking Criminology

One of the newer movements in radical theory is **peacemaking** criminology. To members of the peacemaking movement, the main purpose of criminology is to promote a peaceful, just society. Rather than standing on empirical analysis of data, peacemaking draws its inspiration from religious and philosophical teachings ranging from traditional North American Aboriginal to Zen.

Peacemakers view the efforts of the state to punish and control as crime encouraging rather than crime discouraging. These views were first articulated in a series of books with an anarchist theme written by criminologists Larry Tifft and Dennis Sullivan in 1980.[97] Tifft argues, "The violent punishing acts of the state and its controlling professions are of the same genre as the violent acts of individuals. In each instance these acts reflect an attempt to monopolize human interaction."[98]

Sullivan stresses the futility of correcting and punishing criminals in the context of our conflict-ridden society: "The reality we must grasp is that we live in a culture of severed relationships, where every available institution provides a form of banishment but no place or means for people to become connected, to be responsible to and for each other."[99] Sullivan suggests that mutual aid rather than coercive punishment is the key to a harmonious society.

Today, advocates of the peacemaking movement, such as Harold Pepinsky and Richard Quinney (who has shifted his theoretical orientation from conflict theory to Marxism and now to peacemaking), try to find humanist solutions to crime and other social problems.[100] Rather than punishment and prison, they advocate policies such as mediation and conflict resolution.

LO6 Social Conflict Theory and Social Policy

At the core of all the various branches of social conflict theory is the premise that conflict causes crime. If conflict and competition in society could somehow be reduced, crime rates would fall. Some critical theorists believe that this goal can be accomplished only by thoroughly reordering society so that capitalism is destroyed and a socialist state is created. Others call for a more practical application of conflict principles. Nowhere has this been more successful than in applying peacemaking principles in the criminal justice system.

There has been an ongoing effort to reduce the conflict created by the criminal justice system when it harshly punishes offenders, many of whom are powerless social outcasts. Rather than cast them aside, peacemakers have found a way to bring them back into the community. This peacemaking movement has applied nonviolent methods through what is known as **restorative justice**. Springing from both academia and justice system personnel, the restorative approach relies on nonpunitive strategies to prevent and control crime.[101] The principles of restorative justice are outlined in Figure 8.3.

restorative justice
Using humanistic, nonpunitive strategies to right wrongs and restore social harmony.

Restoration turns the justice system into a healing process rather than a distributor of retribution and revenge. Most people involved in offender–victim relationships know one another or were related in some way before the crime took place. According to restorative justice advocates, instead of treating one involved party as a victim deserving sympathy and the other as a criminal deserving punishment, it is

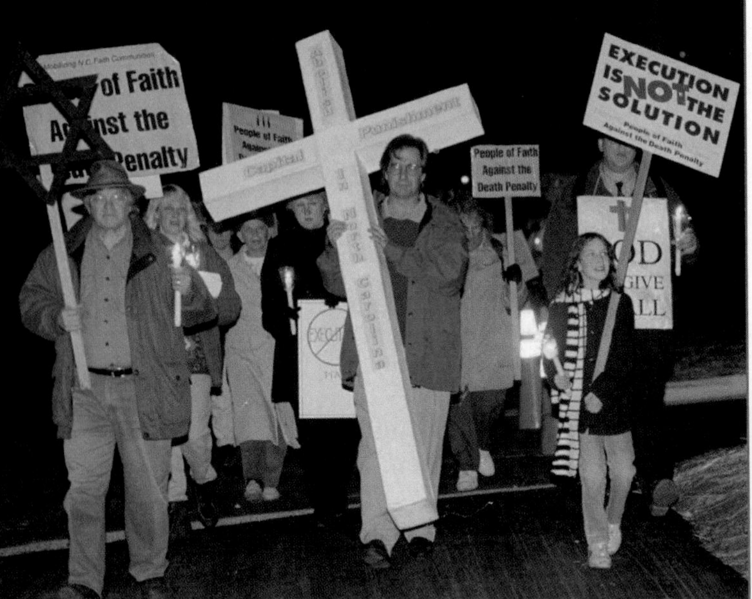

Restorative justice advocates argue that if the goal of the criminal justice system is to create long-term peace in communities, then we need to identify strategies that focus less on punishment of offenders, and more on bringing together victims, offenders, and the community to agree on solutions. But is it possible to reintegrate all offenders back into their communities, even those who have taken another's life?

AP Photo/Karen Tam

FIGURE 8.3

Principles of Restorative Justice

1. Crime is fundamentally a violation of people and interpersonal relationships.
   a. Victims and the community have been harmed and need restoration. Victims include the target of the offence, family members, witnesses, and the community at large.
   b. Victims, offenders, and the affected communities are the key stakeholders in justice. The state must investigate crime and ensure safety, but it is not the centre of the justice process. Victims are the key, and they must help in the search for restoration, healing, responsibility, and prevention.

2. Violations create obligations and liabilities.
   a. Offenders have the obligation to make things right as much as possible. They must understand the harm they have caused. Their participation should be as voluntary as possible; coercion is to be minimized.
   b. The community's obligations are to victims, to offenders, and to the general welfare of its members. This includes the obligation to reintegrate offenders back into the community and to ensure them the opportunity to make amends.

3. Restorative justice seeks to heal and put right the wrongs.
   a. Victims' needs are the focal concern of the justice process. Safety is a top priority, and victims should be empowered to participate in determining their needs and case outcomes.
   b. The exchange of information between victim and offender should be encouraged; when possible, face-to-face meetings might be undertaken. There should be mutual agreement over imposed outcomes.
   c. Offenders' needs and competencies need to be addressed. Healing and reintegration are emphasized; isolation and removal from the community are restricted.
   d. The justice process belongs to the community; members are encouraged to "do justice." The justice process should be sensitive to community needs and geared toward preventing similar harm in the future. Early interventions are encouraged.
   e. Justice is mindful of the outcomes, intended and unintended, of its responses to crime and victimization. It should monitor case outcome and provide necessary support and opportunity to all involved. The least restrictive intervention should be used, and overt social control should be avoided.

Source: "Fundamental Concepts of Restorative Justice" by Howard Zehr and Harry Mika, *Contemporary Justice Review* (1998), vol. 1, pp. 47-55. Reprinted by permisison of Taylor & Francis Ltd. (http://www.tandf.co.uk/journals).

POLICY AND PRACTICE IN CRIMINOLOGY

RESTORATIVE JUSTICE IN THE COMMUNITY

There are now more than 100 different restorative justice programs operating in Canada. In 1996 the Criminal Code was amended to recognize restorative justice principles in sentencing, and in 1999 the Law Commission of Canada formally endorsed restorative justice as a practice. In line with the principles on which they are based, restorative justice programs have a built-in flexibility to allow them to deal with different circumstances. Referrals to make use of restorative programs may come from the police, Crown attorneys, offenders themselves, or correctional services. The point at which referrals are made can be precharge, postcharge, presentence, or postsentence. Recommended solutions for restoring peace can range from victim–offender mediation and restitution, through public apologies and community service, to incarceration or community probation. Most programs offer training for volunteers and local justice personnel who are involved in the programs, and a national website (http://www.restorativejustice.ca) has been established to provide information about the operations of the different programs.

Services offered by restorative justice include facilitating dispute resolution/mediation between offenders and victims; family/community group conferencing to provide opportunities for victims, offenders, and the community to express their feelings and to renew their faith in the community; and sentencing circles, where all come together to agree on appropriate measures to address the behaviour of the offender in a way that will restore peace in the community.

Restorative justice programs can be found operating in large cities, towns, rural areas, and on First Nations reserves across Canada. Programs typically serve both adults and youth but, with the Youth Criminal Justice Act's emphasis on alternative measures for young offenders, programs for youth are growing much more rapidly. Programs deal with a wide variety of criminal offences from simple shoplifting through physical assault and domestic abuse.

Because traditional Aboriginal justice systems were based on the same principles, restorative justice programs are a natural fit in Aboriginal communities. In fact, peacemaking circles have been held in Aboriginal communities in Yukon since the late 1980s.

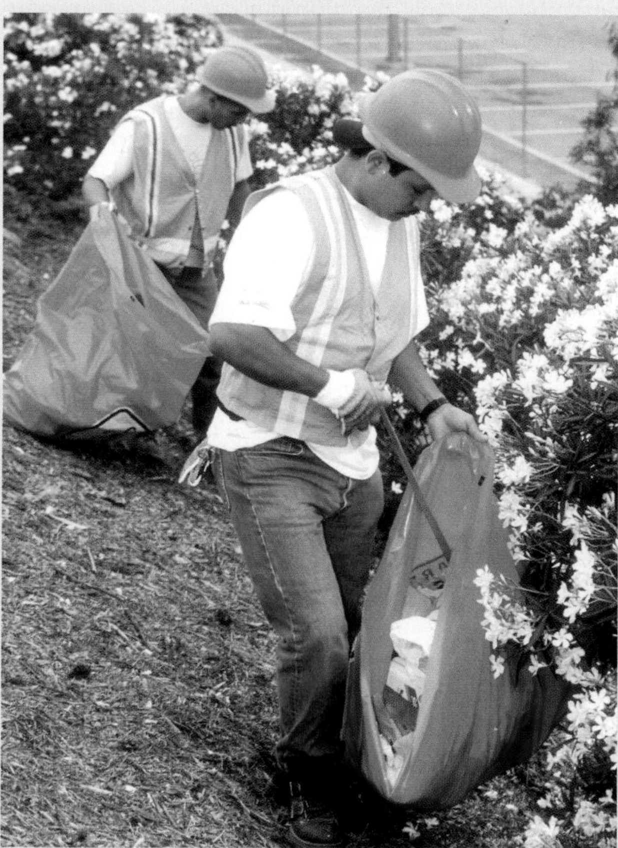

Gilles Mingasson/Getty Images

DUI offenders pick up trash on the side of a road for community service in Los Angeles, California.

CRITICAL THINKING

Restorative justice may be the model that best serves alternative sanctions. How can this essentially humanistic approach be sold to the general public, which now supports more punitive sanctions? For example, would it be feasible to argue that using restoration with nonviolent offenders frees up resources for the relatively few dangerous people in the criminal population?

Sources: Canadian Restorative Justice, http://www.restorativejustice.ca; Department of Justice Restorative Justice in Canada, 2003, http://canada.justice.gc.ca/en/news/conf/rst/rj.html.

sentencing circle A peacemaking technique in which offenders, victims, and other community members are brought together in an effort to formulate a sanction that addresses the needs of all.

more productive to address the issues that produced conflict between these people. Rather than take sides and choose whom to isolate and punish, society should try to reconcile the parties involved in conflict.[102]

Restorative programs typically divert cases away from the formal court process. Instead, these programs encourage reconciling the conflicts between offenders and victims through victim advocacy, mediation programs, and **sentencing circles**, in which crime victims and their families are brought together with offenders and their families in an effort to formulate a sanction that addresses the needs of each party.[103]

Negotiation, mediation, consensus building, and peacemaking have been part of the dispute resolution process in European and Asian communities for centuries.[104] North American Aboriginal people have long used the type of community participation in the adjudication process (e.g., sentencing circles, sentencing panels, and elders panels) that restorative justice advocates now embrace.[105] In some First Nations communities, people accused of breaking the law will meet with community members, victims, village elders, and agents of the justice system in a sentencing circle. Each member of the circle expresses his or her feelings about the act that was committed and raises questions or concerns. The accused can express regret about his or her actions and a desire to change the harmful behaviour. People may suggest ways the offender can make things up to the community and those he or she has harmed. A treatment program such as Alcoholics Anonymous may be suggested, if appropriate. The purpose of this process is to reduce the conflict and harm and restore rather than punish.[106] The accompanying Policy and Practice in Criminology feature reviews restorative justice programs now being used in Canada.

Thinking Like a *Criminologist*

Visit icancrim2.com to find the resources you need today!

Located at the back of the textbook are rip-out Chapter in Review cards. Make sure you also go online to check out other tools that CRIM offers to help you successfully pass your course.

- Flashcards
- Glossary
- Test Yourself
- Videos
- Games
- Interactive Quizzing
- Audio Chapter Reviews

CRIM has it all, and you can, too. Between the text and our online offerings, you have everything at your fingertips. Make sure you check out all that **CRIM** has to offer:

- Printable and Audio Flashcards
- Interactive Quizzing
- Crossword Puzzles
- Discipline-specific activities

"I really like how you use student's opinions on how to study and made a website that encompasses everything we find useful. Seeing this website makes me excited to study!"

—Abby Boston, Fanshawe College

Visit **www.icancrim2.com** to find the resources you need today!

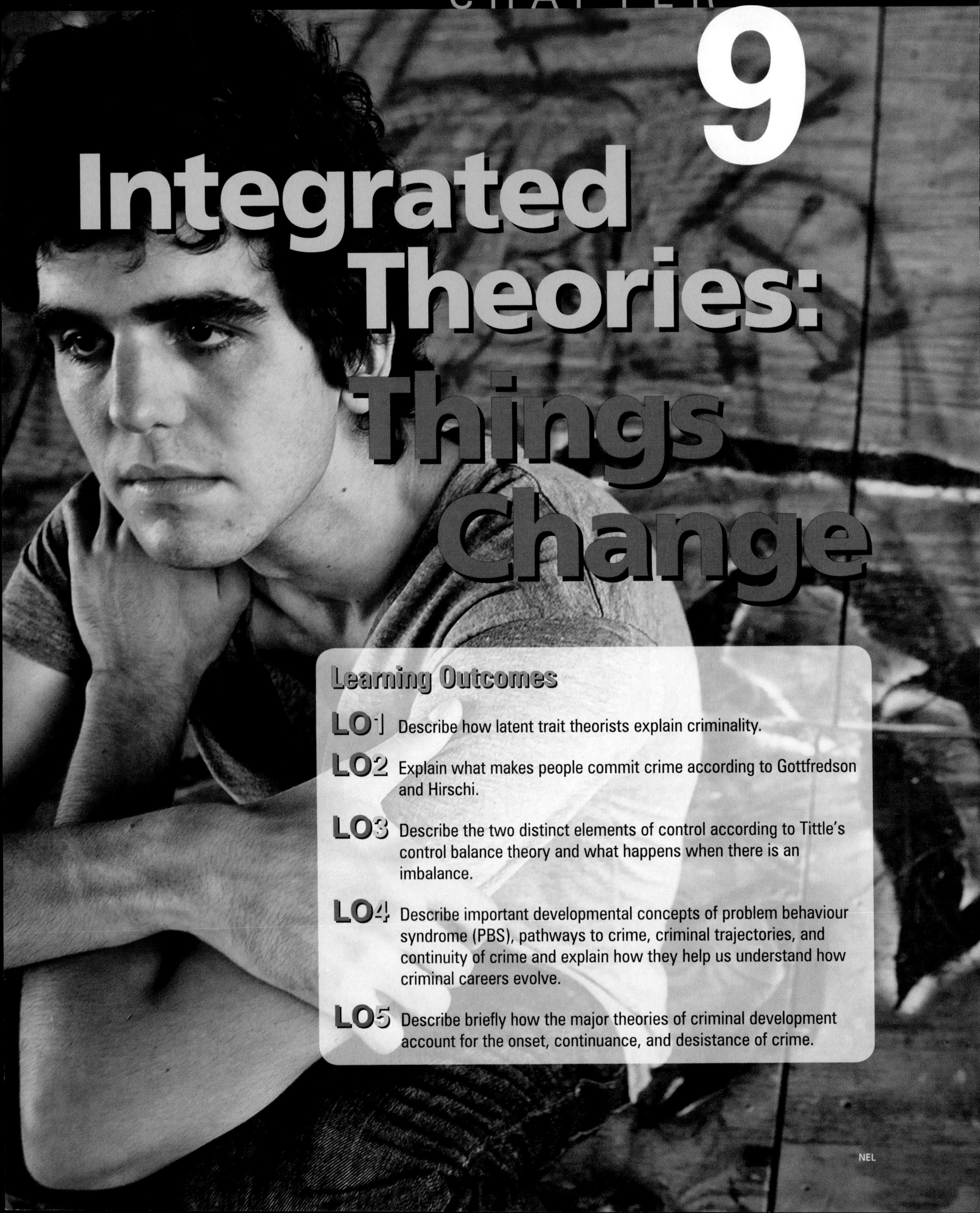

CHAPTER 9

Integrated Theories: Things Change

Learning Outcomes

LO1 Describe how latent trait theorists explain criminality.

LO2 Explain what makes people commit crime according to Gottfredson and Hirschi.

LO3 Describe the two distinct elements of control according to Tittle's control balance theory and what happens when there is an imbalance.

LO4 Describe important developmental concepts of problem behaviour syndrome (PBS), pathways to crime, criminal trajectories, and continuity of crime and explain how they help us understand how criminal careers evolve.

LO5 Describe briefly how the major theories of criminal development account for the onset, continuance, and desistance of crime.

Andrea Gingerich/Vetta/The Image Bank/Getty Images

To derive more powerful explanations of crime, some criminologists have begun integrating individual factors into complex multifactor theories. These **integrated theories** attempt to blend seemingly independent concepts into coherent explanations of criminality.

integrated theory
A complex, multifactor theory that attempts to blend seemingly independent concepts into a coherent explanation of criminality.

Integrated theories seek to avoid the shortcomings of single-factor theories, which focus on the onset of crime and tend to divide the world into criminals and noncriminals—those who have a crime-producing condition and those who do not. For example, people with high testosterone levels are violent; people with low levels are not.

The view that people can be classified as either criminals or noncriminals, with this status being stable for life, is now being challenged. Criminologists today are concerned not only with the onset of criminality but also with its termination as well. Why do people age out of crime? If, for example, criminality is a function of lower intelligence, as some criminologists claim, why do most delinquents fail to become adult criminals? It seems unlikely that intelligence increases as young offenders mature. If the onset of criminality can be explained by low intelligence, then some other factor must explain its termination.

It has also become important to chart the natural history of a criminal career. Why do some offenders escalate their criminal activities while others decrease or limit their law violations? Why do some offenders specialize in a particular crime while others become generalists? Why do some criminals reduce criminal activity and then resume it once again? Research now shows that some offenders begin their criminal

DID YOU KNOW?

- Latent trait theories assume a physical or psychological trait makes some people crime-prone.
- Opportunity to commit crime varies; latent traits remain stable.
- The general theory of crime says an impulsive personality is key.
- Impulsive people have low self-control, and a weak bond to society.
- Impulsive people often cannot resist criminal opportunities.
- According to Tittle, crime may be a function of efforts to maintain control and avoid restraint.

raluca teodorescu/Shutterstock.com

Do violent men have higher levels of testosterone? The latest research indicates that there's only a weak connection between the two; and when aggression is defined as simple physical violence, the connection all but disappears. Castration experiments demonstrate that testosterone is necessary for violence, but other research has shown that testosterone by itself is not sufficient.

CONNECTIONS

The issues of age and crime desistance were discussed in Chapter 2. As you may recall, crime rates peak in the teenage and young adult years and then decline. Explaining this decline has become an important focus of criminology.

Trailer Park Boys was a popular Canadian television series focusing on the misadventures of a group of career criminals living in the fictional Sunnyvale Trailer Park, located near Cole Harbour, Nova Scotia. The show premiered in April 2001 and has become a hit with audiences worldwide.

careers at a very early age, whereas others begin later. How can early- and late-onset criminality be explained?[I] This view of the nature of crime is referred to as **developmental criminology**.

Integrated theories focus attention on the chronic or persistent offender. Although the concept of chronic offenders, who begin their offending careers as children and persist into adulthood, is now an accepted fact, criminologists are still struggling to understand why this is so. They do not fully understand why, when faced with a similar set of life circumstances, such as poverty and family dysfunction, one youth becomes a chronic offender while another may commit an occasional illegal act but later desists from crime. Single-factor theories, such as social structure and social process theories, have trouble explaining why only a relatively few of the many individuals exposed to criminogenic influences in the environment actually become chronic offenders.

By integrating a variety of ecological, social, psychological, biological, and economic factors into a coherent structure, criminologists are attempting to answer the complex questions listed above.

developmental criminology
A branch of criminology that examines changes in criminal careers over the life course.

latent trait theory
The view that criminal behaviour is controlled by a "master trait," present at birth or soon after, that remains stable and unchanging throughout a person's lifetime.

developmental theory
The view that criminality is a dynamic process, influenced by social experiences as well as individual characteristics.

Recent attempts at creating integrated theories can be divided into two distinct groups. **Latent trait theories** hold that criminal behaviour is controlled by a "master trait," present at birth or soon after, that remains stable and unchanging throughout a person's lifetime. Latent trait theorists believe that "people don't change, opportunities do." **Developmental theories** view criminality

CONNECTIONS

As you may recall from Chapter 2, the Philadelphia cohort studies conducted by Wolfgang and his associates identified a relatively small group of chronic offenders who committed a significant amount of all serious crimes and persisted in criminal careers into their adulthood.

as a dynamic process, influenced by individual characteristics as well as social experiences. Thus, developmental theorists hope for personal change and growth. These two positions are summarized in Figure 9.1 and discussed in detail in the following sections.

LO1 Latent Trait Theories

In a popular 1985 book, *Crime and Human Nature*, two prominent social scientists, James Q. Wilson and Richard Herrnstein, argued that personal traits, such as genetic makeup, intelligence, and body build, operate in tandem with social variables such as poverty and family function. Together these factors influence people to "choose crime" over noncriminal behavioural alternatives.[2]

Following their lead, David Rowe, D. Wayne Osgood, and W. Alan Nicewander proposed the concept of **latent traits**. Their model assumes that a number of people in the population have a personal attribute or characteristic that controls their inclination or propensity to commit crimes.[3] This disposition, or latent trait, is either present at birth or established early in life, and it remains stable over time. Suspected latent traits include defective intelligence, impulsive personality, genetic abnormalities, the physical–chemical functioning of the brain, and environmental influences on brain function such as drugs, chemicals, and injuries.[4] Those who carry one of these latent traits are in danger of becoming career criminals; those who lack the traits have a much lower risk. Latent traits should affect the behavioural choices of all people equally, regardless of their gender or personal characteristics.[5]

FIGURE 9.1

Latent Trait versus Developmental Theories

Latent trait theory
- Master trait
  - Personality
  - Intelligence
  - Genetic makeup
- People do not change, criminal opportunities change; maturity brings fewer opportunities
- Early social control and proper parenting can reduce criminal propensity
- Criminal careers are a passage
- Personal and structural factors influence crime
- Change affects crime
- Personal versus situational

Developmental theory
- Multiple traits: social, psychological, economic
- People change over the life course
- Family, job, peers influence behaviour

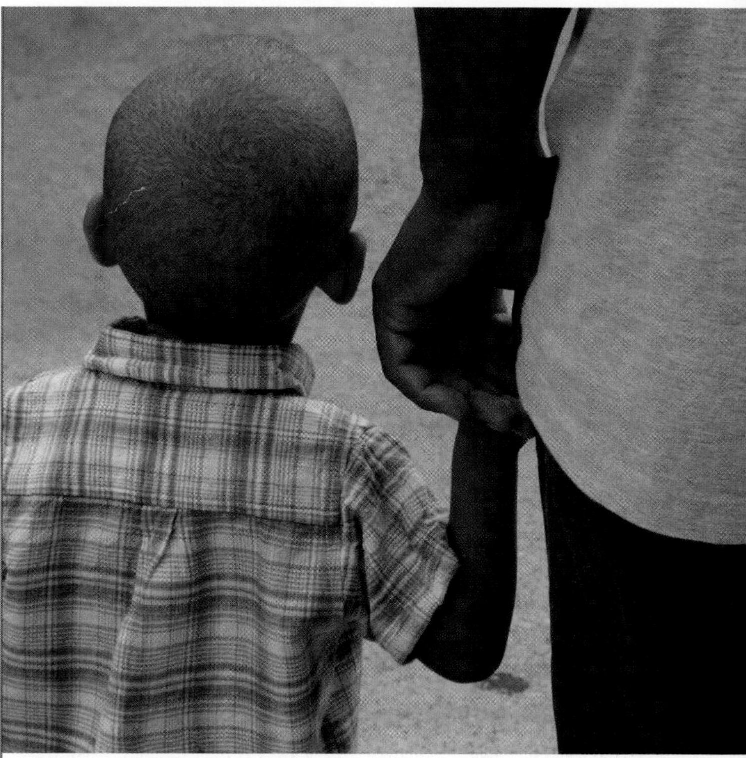

© Steve Debenport/iStockPhoto

According to this emerging latent trait view, the *propensity* to commit crime is stable, but the *opportunity* to commit crime fluctuates over time. People age out of crime because, as they mature, there are simply fewer opportunities to commit crime and greater inducements to remain "straight." They may marry, have children, and obtain jobs. The former delinquents' newfound adult responsibilities leave them little time to hang with their friends, abuse substances, and get into scrapes with the law.

Assume, for example, that a stable latent trait such as low IQ causes some people to commit crime. Teenagers have more opportunity to commit crime than adults, so at every level of intelligence, adolescent crime rates will be higher. As they mature, however, teens with both high and low IQs will commit less crime because their adult responsibilities provide them with fewer criminal opportunities. Thus, latent trait theories integrate concepts usually associated with trait theories (such as personality and temperament) and concepts associated with rational choice theories (such as criminal opportunity and suitable targets).

latent trait
A stable feature, characteristic, property, or condition, such as defective intelligence or impulsive personality, that makes some people crime-prone over the life course.

general theory of crime (GTC) A developmental theory that modifies social control theory by integrating concepts from biosocial, psychological, routine activities, and rational choice theories.

LO2 General Theory of Crime

Michael Gottfredson and Travis Hirschi's **general theory of crime** (GTC) modifies and redefines some of the principles articulated in Hirschi's social control theory (Chapter 7) by integrating the concepts of control with those of biosocial, psychological, routine activities, and rational choice theories.[6]

The Act and the Offender

In their general theory of crime, Gottfredson and Hirschi consider the criminal offender and the criminal act as separate concepts.

Criminal acts, such as robberies or break and enter, are illegal events or deeds that people engage in when they perceive them to be advantageous. For example, break and enter is typically committed by young males looking for cash, liquor, and entertainment; the crime provides "easy, short-term gratification."[7] Crime is rational and predictable: People commit crime when it promises rewards with minimal threat of pain. The threat of punishment can deter crime: If targets are well guarded, crime rates diminish.

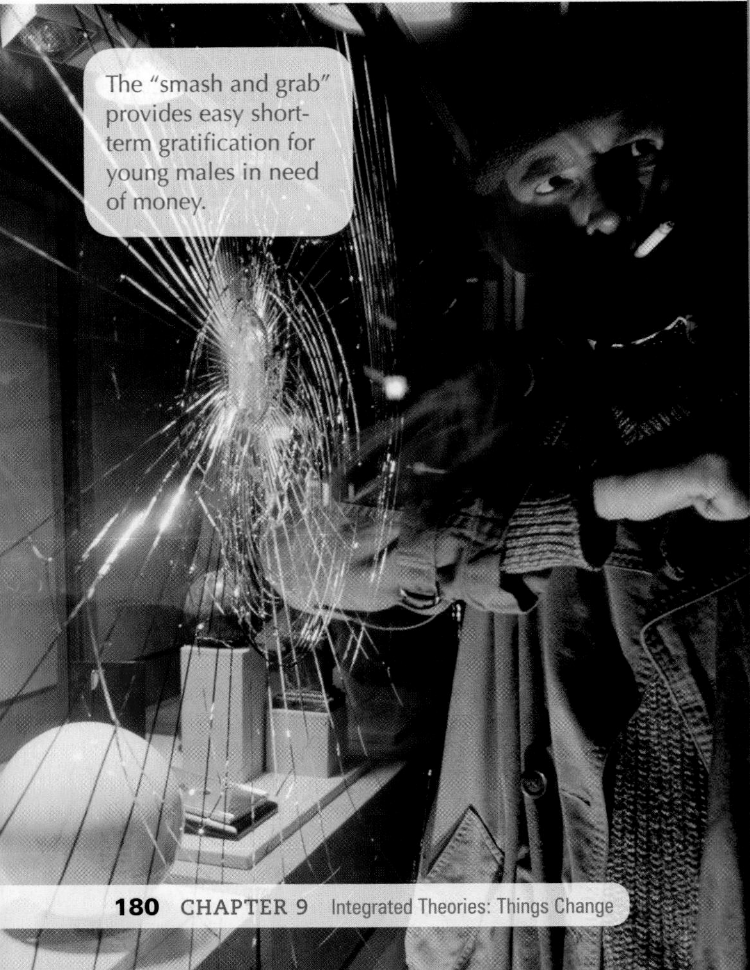

The "smash and grab" provides easy short-term gratification for young males in need of money.

FIGURE 9.2

The General Theory of Crime

Impulsive personality
- Physical
- Insensitive
- Risk taking
- Shortsighted
- Nonverbal

Low self-control
- Poor parenting
- Deviant parents
- Lack of supervision
- Active
- Self-centred

Weakening of social bonds
- Attachment
- Involvement
- Commitment
- Belief

Criminal opportunity
- Gangs
- Free time
- Drugs
- Suitable targets

Crime and deviance
- Delinquency
- Smoking
- Drinking
- Sex
- Crime

Criminal offenders are individuals predisposed to commit crimes. They are not robots who commit crime without restraint; their days are also filled with conventional behaviours, such as going to school, parties, concerts, and places of worship. But given the same set of criminal opportunities, such as having a lot of free time for mischief and living in a neighbourhood with unguarded homes containing valuable merchandise, crime-prone people have a much higher probability of violating the law than do noncriminals. The propensity to commit crimes remains stable throughout a person's life. Change in the frequency of criminal activity is purely a function of change in criminal opportunity.

By recognizing that there are stable differences in people's propensity to commit crime, the GTC adds a biosocial element to the concept of social control. The biological and psychological factors that make people impulsive and crime-prone may be inherited or may develop through incompetent or absent parenting. (See Figure 9.2 above.)

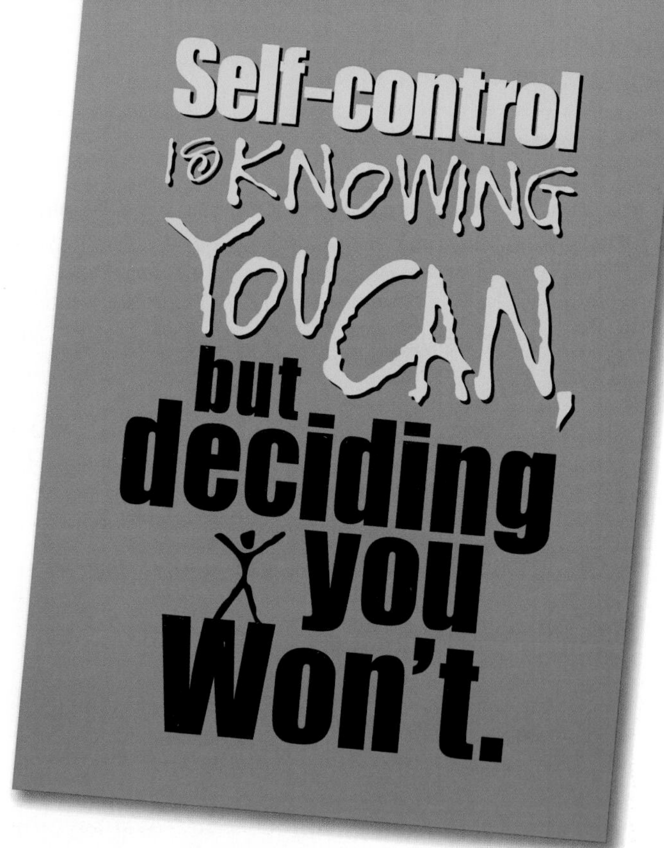

What Makes People Crime-Prone?

What, then, causes people to become excessively crime-prone? Gottfredson and Hirschi attribute the tendency to commit crimes to a person's level of self-control. People with limited self-control tend to be impulsive; they are insensitive to other people's feelings, physical (rather than mental), risk takers, shortsighted, and nonverbal.[8] They have a "here and now" orientation and refuse to work for distant goals; they lack diligence, tenacity, and persistence. People lacking self-control tend to be adventuresome, active, physical, and self-centred. As they mature, they often have unstable marriages, jobs, and friendships.[9] People lacking self-control are less likely to feel shame if they engage in deviant acts and are more likely to find them pleasurable.[10] They are also more likely to engage in dangerous behaviours such as drinking, smoking, and reckless driving; all of these behaviours are associated with criminality.[11] (See Figure 9.2.)

Because those with low self-control enjoy risky, exciting, or thrilling behaviours with immediate gratification, they are more likely to enjoy criminal acts, which require stealth, agility, speed, and power, than conventional acts, which demand long-term study and cognitive and verbal skills. Because they enjoy taking risks, they are more likely to get involved in accidents and suffer injuries than people who maintain self-control.[12] As Gottfredson and Hirschi put it, they derive satisfaction from "money without work, sex without courtship, revenge without court delays."[13] Many of these individuals who have a propensity for committing crime also engage in other behaviours such as smoking, drinking, gambling, and illicit sexuality.[14] Although these acts are not illegal, they too provide immediate, short-term gratification. Figure 9.3 lists the elements of impulsivity, or low self-control.

Gottfredson and Hirschi trace the root cause of poor self-control to inadequate childrearing practices (Figure 9.3). Parents who are unwilling or unable to monitor a child's behaviour, to recognize deviant behaviour when it occurs, and to punish that behaviour, will produce children who lack self-control.

CONNECTIONS

In his original version of control theory, discussed in Chapter 7, Hirschi focused on the social controls that attract people to conventional society and insulate them from criminality. In this newer work, he concentrates on self-control as a stabilizing force. The two views are connected, however, because both social control (or social bonds) and self-control are acquired through early experiences with effective parenting.

Baloo
"I fell in with a bad crowd when I was young — my parents."
www.CartoonStock.com

FIGURE 9.3

The Elements of Impulsivity: Signs that a Person has Low Self-Control

- Insensitive
- Physical
- Shortsighted
- Nonverbal
- Here-and-now orientation
- Unstable social relations
- Enjoys deviant behaviours
- Risk taker
- Refuses to work for distant goals
- Lacks diligence
- Lacks tenacity
- Adventuresome
- Self-centred
- Shameless
- Imprudent
- Lacks cognitive and verbal skills
- Enjoys danger and excitement

Children who are not attached to their parents, who are poorly supervised, and whose parents are criminal or deviant themselves are the most likely to develop poor self-control. In a sense, lack of self-control occurs naturally when steps are not taken to stop its development.[15] Low self-control develops early in life and remains stable into and through adulthood.[16]

Self-Control and Crime

Gottfredson and Hirschi claim that the principles of self-control theory can explain all varieties of criminal behaviour and all the social and behavioural correlates of crime. That is, such widely disparate crimes as break and enter, robbery, embezzlement, drug dealing, murder, sexual assault, and insider trading all stem from a deficiency of self-control. Likewise, gender, racial, and ecological differences in crime rates can be explained by discrepancies in self-control. Put another way, the male crime rate is higher than the female crime rate because males have lower levels of self-control.

Unlike other theoretical models that explain only narrow segments of criminal behaviour (such as theories of teenage gang formation), Gottfredson and Hirschi argue that self-control applies equally to all crimes, ranging from murder to corporate theft. For example, Gottfredson and Hirschi maintain that white-collar crime rates remain low because people who lack self-control rarely attain the positions necessary to commit those crimes. However, the relatively few white-collar criminals lack self-control to the same degree and in the same manner as criminals such as rapists and burglars. Although the criminal activity of individuals with low self-control also declines as those individuals mature, they maintain an offence rate that remains consistently higher than for those with strong self-control.

POOL/INFphoto.com/CP PHOTO

According to the general theory of crime, people who have low self-control are crime-prone even if they are born into affluent families. One example is Hollywood actress and celebrity Lindsay Lohan, 24, who was charged in February 2011 with one count of felony grand theft for allegedly stealing a $2500 necklace from a jewellery store in Venice, California. On probation at the time for failing a court-ordered drug test related to a previous 2007 conviction for impaired driving, the young actress has a history of low self-control and impulsivity.

Supporting Evidence for the GTC

Following the publication of *A General Theory of Crime*, dozens of research efforts tested the validity of Gottfredson and Hirschi's theoretical views. One approach involved identifying indicators of impulsiveness and self-control to determine whether scales measuring these factors correlate with measures of criminal activity. A number of studies have successfully shown this type of association.[17] Some of the most important findings are summarized in Figure 9.4.

Analyzing the GTC

By integrating the concepts of socialization and criminality, Gottfredson and Hirschi help explain why some people who lack self-control can escape criminality, and, conversely, why some people who have self-control might not escape criminality. People who are at risk because they have impulsive personalities may forgo criminal careers because there are no criminal opportunities that satisfy their impulsive needs; instead they may find other outlets for their impulsive personalities. In contrast, if the opportunity is strong enough, even people with relatively strong self-control may be tempted to violate the law; the incentives to commit crime may overwhelm self-control.

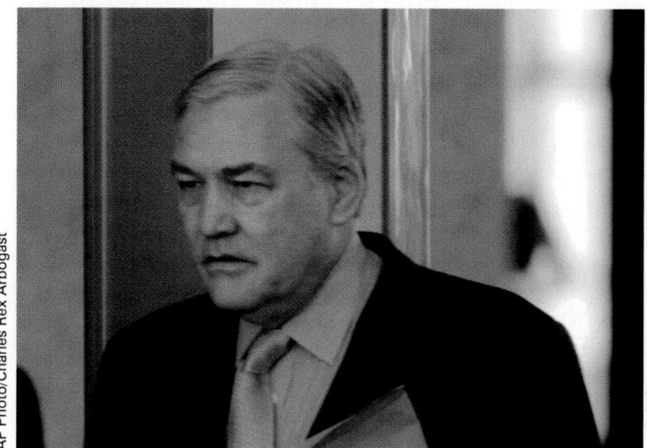

AP Photo/Charles Rex Arbogast

In November 2005, Conrad Black, media mogul, member of the British House of Lords and (former) Canadian citizen was charged by U.S. authorities with more than a dozen counts of fraud related to the operations of his media company, Hollinger International. Convicted in 2007 on four counts, Black was sentenced to six and one half years in federal prison. In July 2010 Black was released on bail from a Florida prison pending an appeal of the sentence on the grounds that the jury that convicted Black had not been properly instructed on the law used to convict him. Two of the fraud counts were overturned in October 2010, leaving one fraud and one obstruction of justice conviction; in June 2011 he was resentenced. Given time already served, Black will serve at least a further 13 months at a low-security federal prison in Florida.

FIGURE 9.4

Empirical Evidence Supporting the General Theory of Crime

- Novice offenders, lacking in self-control, commit a garden variety of criminal acts.[18]
- More mature and experienced criminals become more specialized in their choice of crime (e.g., robbers, burglars, drug dealers).[19]
- Male and female drunk drivers are impulsive individuals who manifest low self-control.[20]
- Repeat violent offenders are more impulsive than their less violent peers.[21]
- Incarcerated youth enjoy risk-taking behaviour and hold values and attitudes that suggest impulsivity.[22]
- Kids who take drugs and commit crime are impulsive and enjoy engaging in risky behaviours.[23]
- Measures of self-control can predict deviant and antisocial behaviour across age groups ranging from teens to adults age 50.[24]
- People who commit white-collar and workplace crime have lower levels of self-control than nonoffenders.[25]
- Gang members have lower levels of self-control than the general population; gang members report lower levels of parental management, a factor associated with lower self-control.[26]
- Low self-control shapes perceptions of criminal opportunity and consequently conditions the decision to commit crimes.[27]
- People who lack self-control expect to commit crime in the future.[28]
- Kids whose problems develop early in life are the most resistant to change in treatment and rehabilitation programs.[29]
- Gender differences in self-control are responsible for crime rate differences. Females who lack self-control are as crime-prone as males with similar personalities.[30]
- Parents who manage their children's behaviour increase their self-control, which helps reduce their delinquent activities.[31]
- Having parents (or stepparents) available to control behaviour may reduce the opportunity to commit crime.[32]
- Victims have lower self-control than nonvictims. Impulsivity predicts both the likelihood that a person will engage in criminal behaviour and the likelihood that the person will become a victim of crime.[33]

control balance theory
A developmental theory that attributes deviant and criminal behaviours to imbalances between the amount of control that the individual has over others and that others have over him or her.

Integrating criminal propensity and criminal opportunity can explain why some children enter into chronic offending while others living in similar environments are able to resist criminal activity. It can also help us understand why the corporate executive with a spotless record gets caught up in business fraud. Even a successful executive may find self-control inadequate if the potential for illegal gain is large. The driven executive, used to both academic and financial success, may find that the fear of failure can overwhelm self-control. During tough economic times, the impulsive manager who fears dismissal may be tempted to circumvent the law to improve the bottom line.[34]

Although the general theory seems persuasive, several questions and criticisms remain unanswered. Among the most important are the following:

1. *Tautological.* Some critics argue that the theory is tautological—that is, it involves circular reasoning. How do we know when people are impulsive? When they commit crimes. Are all criminals impulsive? Of course, or else they would not have broken the law![35]

2. *Personality disorder.* Saying someone lacks self-control implies a personality defect that makes him or her impulsive and rash. There is still no conclusive proof that criminals can be distinguished from noncriminals on the basis of personality alone.

3. *Ecological/individual differences.* The GTC also fails to address individual and ecological patterns in the crime rate. For example, if crime rates are higher in Hamilton, Ontario, than in Edmonton, Alberta, can it be assumed that residents of Hamilton are more impulsive than residents of Edmonton?

4. *Racial and gender differences.* Although distinct gender differences in the crime rate exist, there is little evidence that males are more impulsive than females (although females and males differ in many other personality traits).[36] Similarly, Gottfredson and Hirschi explain racial differences in the crime rate as a failure of childrearing practices in the black community.[37] In so doing, they overlook issues of institutional racism, poverty, and relative deprivation, which have been shown to have a significant impact on crime rate differentials.

5. *People change.* The general theory assumes that criminal propensity does not change; opportunities change. A number of research efforts show that factors that help control criminal behaviour, such as peer relations and school performance, vary over time. Social influences, which are dominant in early adolescence, may fade and be replaced by others in adulthood.[38] This finding contradicts the GTC, which suggests that the influence of friends should be stable and unchanging.

   Gottfredson and Hirschi assume that low self-control varies little with age and that low self-control is almost exclusively a product of early childhood rearing; but research shows that self-control may vary with age. As people mature, they may be better able to control their impulsive behaviour.[39] These findings contradict the GTC, which assumes that levels of self-control and therefore criminal propensity are constant and independent of personal relationships. However, it is uncertain whether life changes affect the propensity to commit crime or merely the opportunity, as Gottfredson and Hirschi suggest.

6. *Modest relationship.* Some research results support the proposition that self-control is a causal factor in criminal and other forms of deviant behaviour, but that the association is quite modest.[40] This would indicate that other forces influence criminal behaviour and that low self-control alone cannot predict the onset of a criminal or deviant career.

7. *Cross-cultural differences.* Evidence shows that criminals in other parts of the world do not lack self-control, indicating that the GTC may be culturally limited.[41] Behaviour that may be considered imprudent in one culture may be socially acceptable in another and therefore cannot be viewed as "lack of self-control."[42]

Although questions like these remain, the strength of the general theory lies in its scope and breadth; it attempts to explain all forms of crime and deviance, from lower-class gang delinquency to sexual harassment in the business community.[43] By integrating concepts of criminal choice, criminal opportunity, socialization, and personality, Gottfredson and Hirschi make a plausible argument that all deviant behaviours may originate at the same source. Continued efforts are needed to test the GTC and establish the validity of its core concepts. It remains one of the key developments of modern criminological theory.

LO3 Control Balance Theory

Charles Tittle's **control balance theory** expands on the concept of personal control as a predisposing element for criminality.[44]

According to Tittle, the concept of control has two distinct elements: the amount of control one is subject to by others and the amount of control one can exercise over others. Conformity results when these two elements are in balance; control imbalances produce deviant and criminal behaviours.

Tittle envisions control as a continuous variable (see Figure 9.5), ranging from a control deficit, which occurs when a person's desires or impulses are limited by other people's ability to regulate or punish their behaviour, to a control surplus, which occurs when the amount of control one can exercise over others exceeds the ability others have to control or modify one's own behaviour.

People who sense a deficit of control turn to three types of behaviour to restore balance: *predation*, *defiance*, and *submission*. Predation involves direct forms of physical violence, such as robbery or sexual assault. Defiance is designed to challenge control

FIGURE 9.5

Tittle's Control Balance Theory

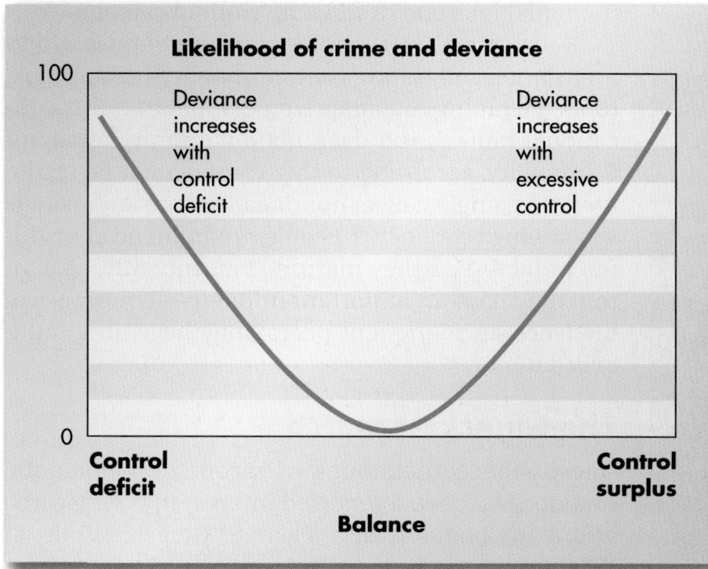

mechanisms but stops short of physical harm, such as vandalism, curfew violations, or unconventional sex. Submission involves passive obedience to the demands of others, such as submitting to physical or sexual abuse without response.

According to Tittle, an excess of control can also lead to deviance and crime—a contention that contradicts Hirschi and Gottfredson's view that only low control leads to crime. Those who have an excess of control engage in three types of behaviour: exploitation, plunder, and decadence. Exploitation involves using others to commit crime—for example, as contract killers or drug runners. Plunder involves using power without regard for others, such as committing a hate crime or polluting the environment. Decadence involves spur-of-the-moment, irrational acts such as child molesting.

Control imbalance represents a potential to commit crime and deviance. That is, possessing deficient or excessive control increases the likelihood that when presented with situational motivations a person will react in an antisocial manner. Deviant motivations emerge when a person suffering from control imbalance believes that engaging in some antisocial act will alter his or her control ratio in a favourable way. For example, when a person who has a surplus of control is insulted, he may tell his friends to attack the instigator; a student with a control deficit may vandalize a school after getting a bad grade on her report card.

Even if people are motivated to commit crime, they may be constrained by their perceptions of external forces of control. Even highly motivated individuals may be constrained if they believe that their deviant behaviour is very serious and likely to be discovered by those who can exert control, such as the police. Tittle also recognizes that opportunity shapes antisocial behaviour. No matter how great the motivation or how little the restraint, the actual likelihood of a crime occurring depends on the opportunity.

Tittle's view is essentially integrated because, like Hirschi and Gottfredson before him, he incorporates external or social concepts such as opportunity and restraint with internal or individual variables such as degree of control.

LO4 Developmental Theory

The second integrated approach that has emerged is developmental theory. According to this view, even as toddlers, people begin relationships and behaviours that will determine their adult life course. At first they must learn to conform to social rules and function effectively in society. Later they are expected to begin thinking about careers, leave their parental homes, find permanent relationships, and eventually marry and begin their own families.[45] These transitions are expected to take place in order, beginning with finishing school, entering the workforce, getting married, and having children.

Some individuals, however, are incapable of maturing in a reasonable and timely fashion because of family, environmental, or personal problems. In some cases transitions can occur too early—for example, when adolescents engage in precocious sex. In other cases transitions may occur too late, as when a student fails to graduate on time because of bad grades or too many incomplete classes. Sometimes disruption of one trajectory can harm another. For example, teenage childbirth will most likely disrupt educational and career development. Because developmental theories focus on the associations between life events and deviant behaviours, they are sometimes referred to as **life-course theories**.

Disruptions in life's major transitions can be destructive and ultimately can promote criminality. Those who are already at risk because of socioeconomic problems or family dysfunction are the most susceptible to these awkward transitions. The cumulative impact of

life-course theory Theory that focuses on changes in criminality over the life course; developmental theory.

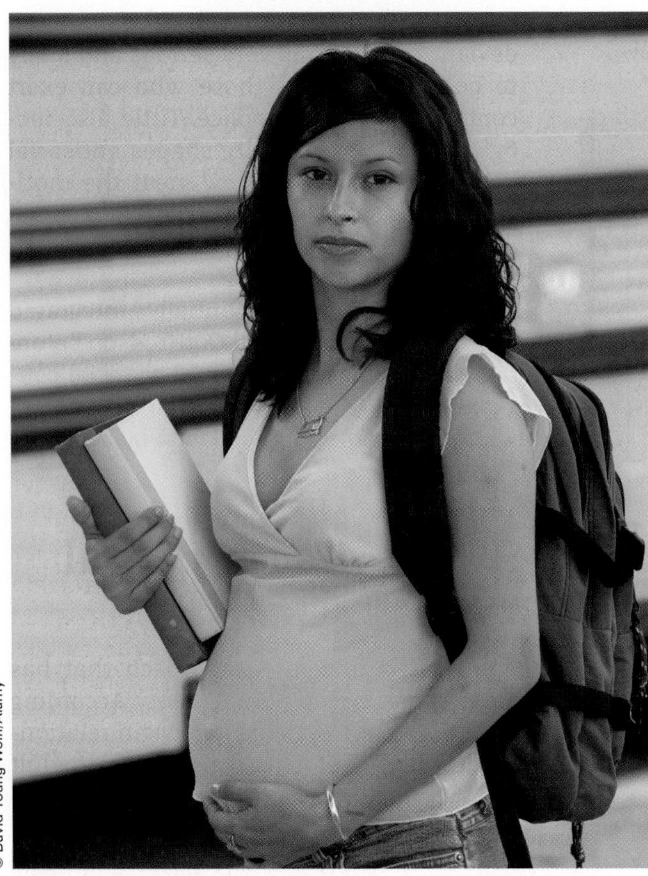

© David Young-Wolff/Alamy

Teenage childbirth has been known to disrupt educational and career development.

these disruptions sustains criminality from childhood into adulthood.

Because a transition from one stage of life to another can be a bumpy ride, the propensity to commit crimes is neither stable nor constant; it is a developmental process. A positive life experience may help some criminals desist from crime for a while, whereas a negative one may cause them to resume their activities. Criminal careers are also said to be interactional because people are influenced by the behaviour of those around them and, in turn, influence others' behaviour. For example, a youth's antisocial behaviour may turn his or her more conventional friends against him; their rejection solidifies and escalates the antisocial behaviour.

Developmental theories also recognize that as people mature, the factors that influence their behaviour change.[46] At first, family relations may be most influential; in later adolescence, school and peer relations predominate; in adulthood, vocational achievement and marital relations may be the most critical influences. For example, some antisocial children who are in trouble throughout their adolescence may manage to find stable work and maintain intact marriages as adults; these life events help them desist from crime. In contrast, the less fortunate adolescents who develop arrest records and get involved with the wrong crowd may find themselves limited to menial jobs and at risk for criminal careers.

Developmental theories are inherently multidimensional, suggesting that criminality has multiple roots, including maladaptive personality traits, educational failure, and dysfunctional family relations. Criminality, according to this view, cannot be attributed to a single cause, nor does it represent a single underlying tendency.[47] People are influenced by different factors as they mature. Consequently, a factor that may have an important influence at one stage of life (such as delinquent peers) may have little influence later on.[48]

The Glueck Research

One of the cornerstones of recent developmental theories has been a renewed interest in the research efforts of Sheldon and Eleanor Glueck. While at Harvard University in the 1930s, the Gluecks popularized research on the life cycle of delinquent careers. In a series of longitudinal research studies, they followed the careers of known delinquents to determine the factors that predicted persistent offending.[49] The Gluecks made extensive use of interviews and records in their elaborate comparisons of delinquents and nondelinquents.[50]

The Gluecks' research focused on early onset of delinquency as a harbinger of a criminal career: "The deeper the roots of childhood maladjustment, the smaller the chance of adult adjustment."[51] They also noted the stability of offending careers: Children who are antisocial early in life are the most likely to continue their offending careers into adulthood.

The Gluecks identified a number of personal and social factors related to persistent offending. The most important of these factors was family relations, considered in terms of quality of discipline and emotional ties with parents. The adolescent raised in a large, single-parent family of limited economic means and educational achievement was the most vulnerable to delinquency.

The Gluecks did not restrict their analysis to social variables. When they measured biological and psychological traits such as body type, intelligence, and personality, they found that physical and mental factors also played a role in determining behaviour. Children with low intelligence, a background of mental disease, and a powerful (mesomorph) physique were the most likely to become persistent offenders.

Developmental Concepts

A 1990 review paper (revised in 1998) by Rolf Loeber and Marc LeBlanc was an important event in popularizing developmental theory.[52] In their landmark work, Loeber and LeBlanc proposed that criminologists should devote time and effort to understanding some basic questions about the evolution of criminal careers: Why do people begin committing antisocial acts? Why do some stop while others continue? Why do some escalate the severity of their criminality (that is, go from shoplifting to drug dealing to armed robbery) while others de-escalate and commit less serious crimes as they mature? If some terminate their criminal activity, what, if anything, causes them to begin again? Why do some criminals specialize in certain types of crime, whereas others are generalists engaging in a variety of antisocial behaviours? According to Loeber and LeBlanc's developmental view, criminologists must pay attention to how a criminal career unfolds.

Consequently, a view of crime has emerged that both incorporates personal change and growth and recognizes that the factors that produce crime and delinquency at one point in the life cycle may not be relevant at another.[53] People may show a propensity to offend early in their lives, but the nature and frequency of their activities are affected by outside forces beyond their control, such as the likelihood of getting arrested and being punished for crime.[54]

In this section, we review some of the more important concepts associated with the developmental perspective. In the remainder of the chapter, we discuss some prominent developmental theories.

FIGURE 9.6

Problem Behaviours

Social
- Family dysfunction
- Unemployment
- Educational underachievement
- School misconduct

Personal
- Substance abuse
- Suicide attempts
- Early sexuality
- Sensation seeking
- Early parenthood
- Accident-proneness
- Medical problems
- Mental disease
- Anxiety
- Eating disorders (bulimia, anorexia)

Environmental
- High-crime area
- Disorganized area
- Racism
- Exposure to poverty

problem behaviour syndrome (PBS) A cluster of antisocial behaviours that may include family dysfunction, substance abuse, smoking, precocious sexuality and early pregnancy, educational underachievement, suicide attempts, sensation seeking, and unemployment, as well as crime.

Problem Behaviour Syndrome

The developmental view is that criminality can best be understood as one of many social problems faced by at-risk youth. Crime is just one among a group of antisocial behaviours that cluster together, referred to collectively as **problem behaviour syndrome (PBS)**. PBS typically involves family dysfunction, substance abuse, smoking, precocious sexuality and early pregnancy, educational underachievement, suicide attempts, sensation seeking, and unemployment as well as crime (see Figure 9.6).[55] People who exhibit one of these conditions typically exhibit many of the others.[56] All varieties of criminal behaviour, including violence, theft, and drug offences, may be part of a generalized PBS, indicating that all forms of antisocial behaviour have similar developmental patterns.[57]

Those who exhibit PBS are prone to more difficulties than the general population.[58] They face a range of personal dilemmas ranging from drug abuse, to being accident-prone, to requiring more health care and hospitalization, to becoming teenage parents. PBS has been linked to personality problems (such as rebelliousness and low ego), family problems (such as intrafamily conflict and parental mental disorder), and educational failure.[59] Multisite research has shown that PBS is not unique to any single geographical area, and that children who exhibit PBS, including drug use, delinquency, and precocious sexuality, display symptoms at an early age.[60]

LO5 Pathways to Crime

Developmental theorists recognize that career criminals may travel more than a single road. Some may specialize in violence and extortion; some may be involved in theft and fraud; others may engage in a variety of criminal acts. Some offenders may begin their careers early in life, whereas others are late bloomers who begin committing crime when most people desist.

Are there different pathways to crime? Using data from a longitudinal cohort study conducted in Pittsburgh, Pennsylvania, Rolf Loeber and his associates have identified three distinct paths to a criminal career (see Figure 9.7):[61]

FIGURE 9.7

Loeber's Pathways to Crime

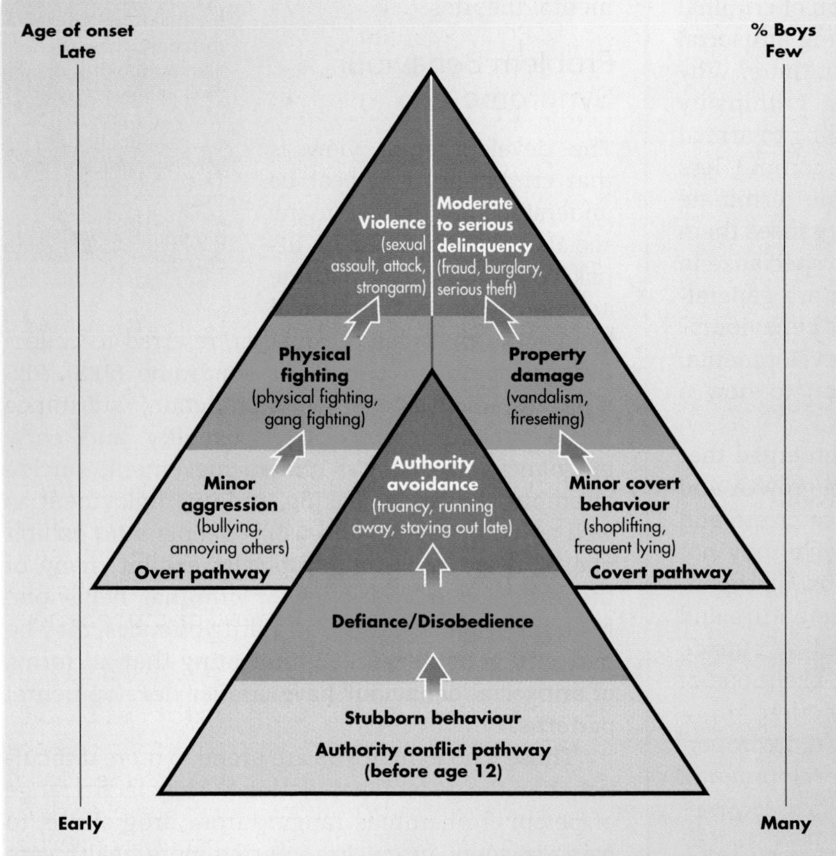

Source: Barbara Tatem Kelley, Rolf Loeber, Kate Keenan, and Mary DeLamatre, "Developmental Pathways in Boys' Disruptive and Delinquent Behavior," *Juvenile Justice Bulletin* (November 1997), p. 3. Originally published by the Office of Juvenile Justice and Delinquency Prevention, Office of Justice Programs, U.S. Department of Justice.

authority conflict pathway
Pathway to criminal deviance that begins at an early age with stubborn behaviour and leads to defiance and then to authority avoidance.

covert pathway
Pathway to a criminal career that begins with minor underhanded behaviour, leads to property damage, and eventually escalates to more serious forms of theft and fraud.

overt pathway
Pathway to a criminal career that begins with minor aggression, leads to physical fighting, and eventually escalates to violent crime.

1. The **authority conflict pathway** begins at an early age with stubborn behaviour. This leads to defiance (doing things one's own way, disobedience) and then to authority avoidance (staying out late, truancy, running away).

2. The **covert pathway** begins with minor, underhanded behaviour (lying, shoplifting) that leads to property damage (setting nuisance fires, damaging property). This behaviour eventually escalates to more serious forms of criminality, ranging from joyriding, pocket picking, larceny, and fencing to passing bad cheques, using stolen credit cards, stealing cars, dealing drugs, and breaking and entering.

3. The **overt pathway** escalates to aggressive acts beginning with aggression (annoying others, bullying), leading to physical (and gang) fighting and then to violence (attacking someone, forced theft).

The Loeber research indicates that each of these paths may lead to a sustained deviant career. Some people enter two or even three paths simultaneously: They are stubborn, lie to teachers and parents, are bullies, and commit petty thefts. These adolescents are the most likely to become persistent offenders as they mature. Although some persistent offenders may specialize in one type of behaviour, others engage in varied criminal acts and antisocial behaviours as they mature. For example, they cheat on tests, bully others in the schoolyard, take drugs, commit burglary, steal a car, and shoplift from a store.

Criminal Trajectories

In addition to taking different paths to criminality, people may begin their journey at different times. Some are precocious, beginning their criminal careers early; others stay out of trouble until their teenage years. Some offenders may peak at an early age, whereas others persist into adulthood.

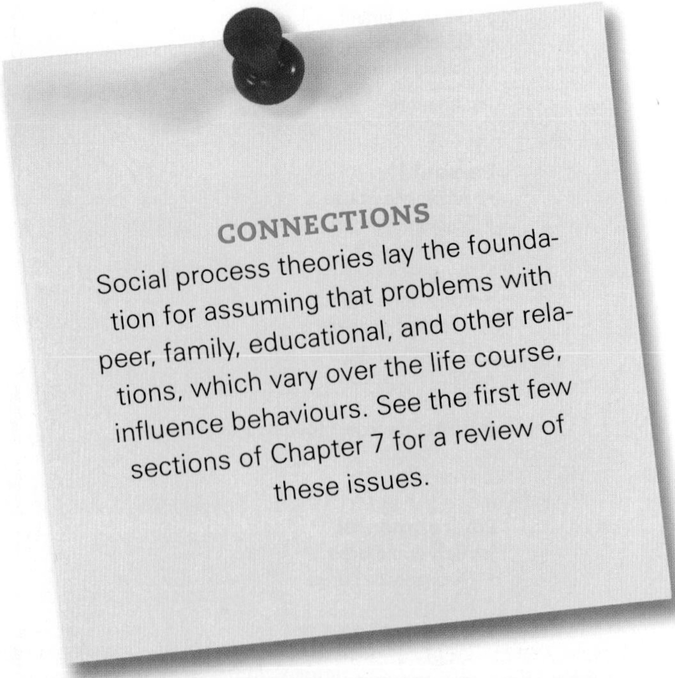

CONNECTIONS
Social process theories lay the foundation for assuming that problems with peer, family, educational, and other relations, which vary over the life course, influence behaviours. See the first few sections of Chapter 7 for a review of these issues.

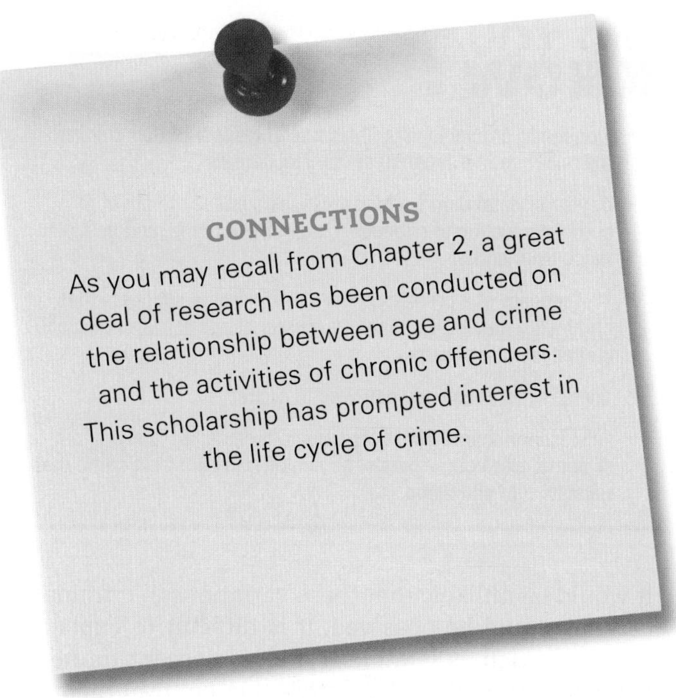

CONNECTIONS
As you may recall from Chapter 2, a great deal of research has been conducted on the relationship between age and crime and the activities of chronic offenders. This scholarship has prompted interest in the life cycle of crime.

Research indicates a number of different classes of criminal careers that seem to reflect changes in the life course. Some adolescents maximize their offending rate at a relatively early age and then reduce their criminal activity; others persist into their 20s. Some are high-rate offenders, whereas others offend at relatively low rates.[62] According to psychologist Terrie Moffitt, although the prevalence and frequency of antisocial behaviour peak in adolescence and then diminish for most offenders (she labels these **adolescent-limiteds**), a small group of **life-course persisters** who offends well into adulthood.[63]

Life-course persisters combine family dysfunction with severe neurological problems that predispose them to antisocial behaviour patterns. These problems can be the result of maternal drug abuse, poor nutrition, or exposure to toxic agents such as lead. Life-course persisters may have lower verbal ability, which inhibits reasoning skills, learning ability, and school achievement. They seem to mature faster and engage in early sexuality and drug use, referred to as **pseudomaturity**.[64] There may be more than one subset of life-course persisters. One group begins acting out during the preschool years; these children show signs of ADHD and do not outgrow the levels of disobedience typical of the preschool years. The second group shows few symptoms of ADHD but, from an early age, is aggressive, underhanded, and in constant opposition to authority.[65]

Adolescent-limited delinquents mimic the behaviour of these more troubled teens, but reduce the frequency of their offending as they mature to around age 18.[66] They are deeply influenced by the misbehaviour of their friends and peers up to around age 16, when peer group influence begins to decline. Peer influence, then, has a significant influence on their law-violating behaviour.[67] This group tends to focus on a specific type of misbehaviour such as drug abuse.

Why do some people enter a "path to crime" later rather than sooner? Early starters, who begin offending before age 14, follow a path from (1) poor parenting to (2) deviant behaviours and then to (3) involvement with delinquent groups. Late starters, who begin offending after age 14, follow a somewhat different path: (1) Poor parenting leads to (2) identification with delinquent groups and then to (3) deviant

adolescent-limited Offender who follows the most common criminal trajectory, in which antisocial behaviour peaks in adolescence and then diminishes.

life-course persister One of the small group of offenders whose criminal career continues well into adulthood.

pseudomaturity Characteristic of life-course persisters, who tend to engage in early sexuality and drug use.

© AF archive/Alamy

Scene from *Wassup Rockers,* a 2005 film about teenagers in South Central Los Angeles who would rather skateboard and listen to punk rock than get involved in the hip-hop culture of their neighbourhood.

behaviours. By implication, adolescents who suffer poor parenting and are at risk for deviant careers can avoid criminality if they can bypass involvement with delinquent peers.[68]

Continuity of Crime

Another aspect of developmental theory is the continuity of crime: The best predictor of future criminality is past criminality. Children who are repeatedly in trouble during early adolescence generally will still be antisocial in their middle and late teens and as adults.[69] Early criminal activity is likely to be sustained because these offenders seem to lack the social survival skills necessary to find work or to develop the interpersonal relationships needed to allow them to drop out of crime.[70]

One explanation for this phenomenon suggests that criminal propensity may be "contagious." Children at risk to commit crime may be located in families and neighbourhoods in which they are constantly exposed to deviant behaviour. As they mature, having brothers, fathers, neighbours, and friends who engage in and support their activities reinforces their deviance.[71]

social development model (SDM) A developmental theory that attributes criminal behaviour patterns to childhood socialization and pro- or antisocial attachments over the life course.

The discovery that people begin their criminal careers at different ages and follow different criminal paths and trajectories provides strong support for developmental theory. If all criminals possessed a singular latent trait that made them crime-prone, it would be unlikely that these variations in criminal careers would be observed. It is difficult to explain concepts such as late-onset and adolescent-limited behaviour from the perspective of latent trait theory.

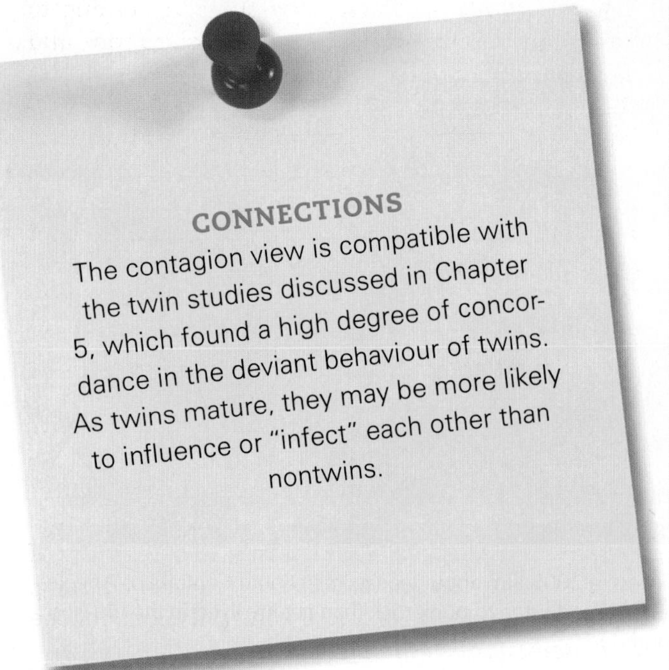

CONNECTIONS
The contagion view is compatible with the twin studies discussed in Chapter 5, which found a high degree of concordance in the deviant behaviour of twins. As twins mature, they may be more likely to influence or "infect" each other than nontwins.

DID YOU KNOW?

- Pioneering criminologists Sheldon and Eleanor Glueck tracked the onset and termination of criminal careers.
- Developmental theories look at issues such as the onset of crime, escalation of offences, continuity of crime, and desistance from crime.
- The concept of a problem behaviour syndrome suggests that criminality may be just one of a cluster of social, psychological, and physical problems.
- There is more than one pathway to crime.
- Adolescent-limited offenders begin offending late and age out of crime. Life-course persisters exhibit early onset of crime that persists into adulthood.

Theories of Criminal Development

An ongoing effort has been made to track persistent offenders over their life course.[72] The early data seem to support what is already known about delinquent and criminal career patterns: Juvenile offenders are likely to become adult criminals; early onset predicts more lasting crime; and chronic offenders commit a significant portion of all crimes.[73] Based on these findings, criminologists have formulated a number of systematic theories that account for the onset, continuance, and desistance from crime.

The Social Development Model

In their **social development model (SDM)**, Joseph Weis, Richard Catalano, J. David Hawkins, and their associates show how different factors affecting a child's social development over the life course influence criminal behaviour patterns.[74] As children mature within their environment, elements of socialization control their developmental process. Children are socialized and develop bonds to their families through four distinct interactions and processes:

1. Perceived opportunities for involvement in activities and interactions with others
2. The degree of involvement and interaction with parents
3. The children's ability to participate in these interactions
4. The reinforcement (such as feedback) they perceive for their participation

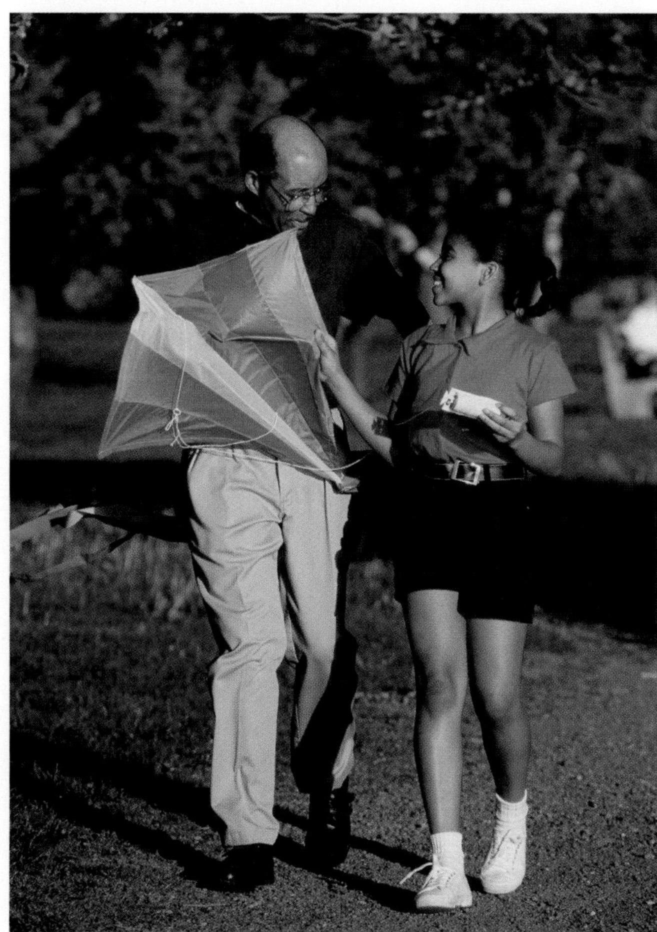

© Kindra Clineff/Index Stock Imagery/Photolibrary

According to the social development model, children must develop prosocial bonds in order to control the risk of antisocial behaviour. These bonds are usually formed within the context of the family.

To control the risk of antisocial behaviour, a child must maintain **prosocial bonds**. These are developed within the context of family life, which not only provides prosocial opportunities but also reinforces them by consistent, positive feedback. Parental attachment affects a child's behaviour for life, determining both school experiences and personal beliefs and values. For those with strong family relationships, school will be a meaningful experience marked by academic success and commitment to education. Young people in this category are likely to develop conventional beliefs and values, become committed to conventional activities, and form attachments to conventional others.

Children's antisocial behaviour also depends on the quality of their attachments to parents and other influential relations. If they remain unattached or develop attachments to deviant others, their behaviour may become deviant as well. Unlike Hirschi's control theory, which assumes that all attachments are beneficial, the SDM suggests that interaction with antisocial peers and adults promotes participation in delinquency and substance abuse.[75]

prosocial bonds
Socialized attachment to conventional institutions, activities, and beliefs.

interactional theory
A developmental theory that attributes criminal trajectories to mutual reinforcement between delinquents and significant others over the life course—family in early adolescence, school and friends in mid-adolescence, and social peers and one's own nuclear family in adulthood.

Interactional Theory

Terence Thornberry has proposed an age-graded view of crime that he calls **interactional theory** (see Figure 9.8).[76] He too finds that the onset of crime can be traced to a deterioration of the social bond during adolescence, marked by weakened attachment to parents, commitment to school, and belief in conventional values.

Interactional theory holds that seriously delinquent youths form belief systems that are consistent with their deviant lifestyle. They seek out the company of other adolescents who share their interests and who are likely to reinforce their beliefs about the world and support their delinquent behaviour. According to interactional theory, delinquents find a criminal peer group in the same way that chess buffs look for others who share their passion for the game; hanging out with other chess players helps improve their game. Similarly, deviant peers do not turn an otherwise innocent boy into a delinquent; they support and amplify the behaviour of those who have already accepted a delinquent way of life.[77]

Thornberry suggests that criminality is a developmental process that takes on different meanings and forms as a person matures. According to Thornberry, the causal process is a dynamic one and develops over a person's life.[78] During early adolescence, attachment to the family is the single most important determinant of whether a youth will adjust to conventional society and be shielded from delinquency. By mid-adolescence, the influence of the family is replaced by the "world of friends, school and youth culture."[79] In adulthood, a person's behavioural choices are shaped by his or her place in conventional society and his or her own nuclear family.

In sum, interactional theory suggests that criminality is part of a dynamic social process and not just an outcome of that process. Although crime is influenced by social forces, it also influences these processes and associations to create behavioural trajectories toward increasing law violations for some people.[80] Interactional theory integrates elements of social disorganization, social control, social learning, and cognitive theories into a powerful model of the development of a criminal career.

turning points Critical life events, such as career and marriage, that may enable adult offenders to desist from crime.

social capital Positive relations with individuals and institutions, as in a successful marriage or a successful career, that support conventional behaviour and inhibit deviant behaviour.

Sampson and Laub: Age-Graded Theory

If there are various pathways to crime and delinquency, are there trails back to conformity? In an important 1993 work, *Crime in the Making*, Robert Sampson and John Laub identify **turning points** in a criminal career.[81] Reanalyzing the original Glueck data, they found that the stability of delinquent behaviour can be affected by events that occur later in life, even after a chronic delinquent career has been established. They agree with Hirschi and Gottfredson that formal and informal social controls restrict criminality and that crime begins early in life and continues over the life course; they disagree that once this course is set, nothing can impede its progress.

Turning Points

Sampson and Laub's most important contribution is identifying the life events that enable adult offenders to desist from crime. Two critical turning points are career and marriage.

FIGURE 9.8

Overview of the Interactional Theory of Delinquency

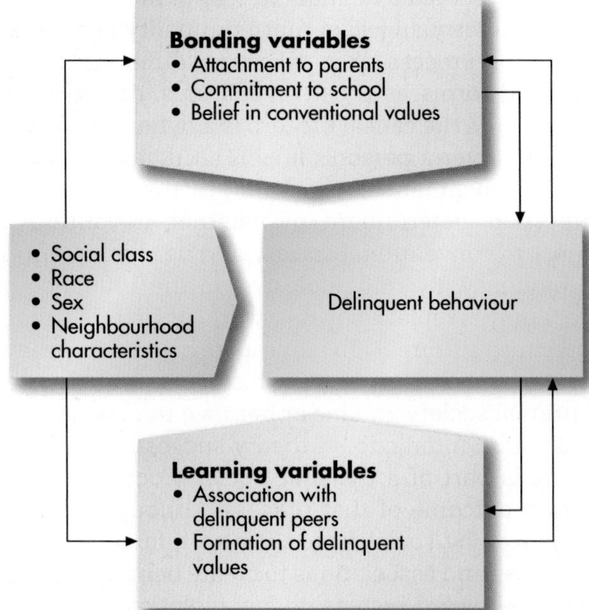

Source: Terence Thornberry, Margaret Farnworth, Alan Lizotte, and Susan Stern, "A Longitudinal Examination of the Causes and Correlates of Delinquency," working paper No. 1, Rochester Youth Development Study (Albany, NY: Hindelang Criminal Justice Research Center, 1987), p. 11. Reprinted by permission of the Hindelang Criminal Justice Research Center.

Adolescents who are at risk for crime can live conventional lives if they can find good jobs or achieve successful careers. Their success may hinge on a lucky break. Even those who have been in trouble with the law may turn from crime if employers are willing to give them a chance despite their records.

Adolescents who have had significant problems with the law are also able to desist from crime if, as adults, they become attached to a spouse who supports and sustains them even when the spouse knows they have been in trouble in the past. Happy marriages are life sustaining, and marital quality improves over time (as people work less and have fewer parental responsibilities).[82] Spending time in marital and family activities also reduces exposure to deviant peers, which in turn reduces the opportunity to become involved in delinquent activities.[83] People who cannot sustain secure marital relations are less likely to desist from crime.

Sampson and Laub's age-graded theory is supported by research that shows that children who grow up in two-parent families are more likely to have happier marriages than children whose parents were divorced or never married.[84] This finding suggests that the marriage–crime association may be intergenerational: If people with marital problems are more crime-prone, their children will also suffer a greater long-term risk of marital failure and antisocial activity.

Social Capital

Social scientists recognize that people build **social capital**—positive relations with individuals and institutions that are life sustaining. In the same manner that building financial capital improves the chances for economic success, building social capital supports conventional behaviour and inhibits deviant behaviour. A successful marriage creates social capital when it improves a person's stature, creates feelings of self-worth, and encourages others to trust the person. A successful career inhibits crime by creating a stake in conformity: Why commit crime when you are doing well at your job? The relationship is reciprocal. If people are chosen to be employees, they return the favour by doing the best job possible; if they are chosen as spouses, they blossom into devoted partners. In contrast, moving to a new city reduces social capital by closing people off from long-term relationships.[85]

Sampson and Laub's research indicates that building social capital and strong social bonds reduces the likelihood of long-term deviance. This finding suggests that, in contrast to latent trait theories, events that occur in later adolescence and adulthood do, in fact, influence the direction

FIGURE 9.9

Sampson and Laub's Age-Graded Theory

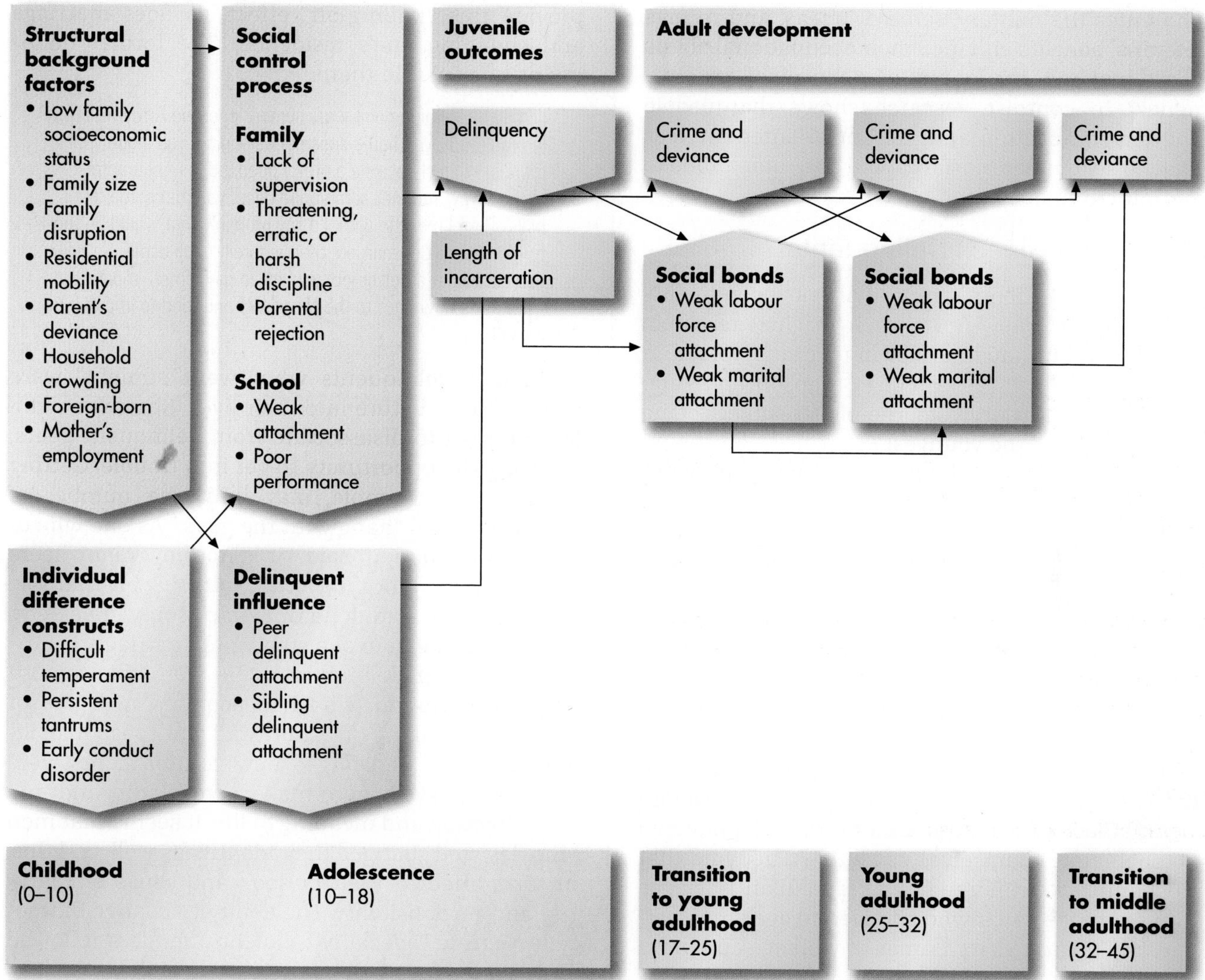

Source: Reprinted by permission of the publisher from CRIME IN THE MAKING: PATHWAYS AND TURNING POINTS THROUGH LIFE by Robert Sampson and John Laub, pp. 244-245, Cambridge, Mass.: Harvard University Press, Copyright © 1993 by the President and Fellows of Harvard College. All rights reserved.

of delinquent and criminal careers. Life events can help either terminate or sustain deviant careers. For example, getting arrested and punished may have little direct effect on future criminality, but it can help sustain a criminal career because it reduces the chances of employment and job stability, two factors that are directly related to crime (see Figure 9.9).[86]

Testing Age-Graded Theory

Several indicators support the validity of age-graded theory.[87] Evidence now shows that once begun, criminal career trajectories can be reversed if life conditions improve, an outcome predicted by age-graded theory.[88] For example, employment status affects behaviour. Men who are unemployed or underemployed report higher criminal participation rates than employed men. Similarly, men released from prison on parole who obtain jobs are less likely to reoffend than those who lack or lose employment.[89]

Research has been directed at identifying the sources of social capital and determining whether and how it is related to crime. For example, youths who accumulate social capital in childhood (e.g., by doing well in school or having a tightly knit family) are also the most likely to maintain steady work as adults; employment may help insulate them from crime.[90] Also, people who maintain a successful marriage in their 20s and become parents themselves are the most likely to mature out of crime.[91] Although it is possible that marriage stabilizes people and helps them build social capital, it is also likely that marriage may discourage crime by reducing contact with criminal peers.[92]

A number of research efforts have supported Sampson and Laub's proposed association between social capital and crime. For example, delinquents who enter the military, serve overseas, and receive veterans' benefits enhance their occupational status (social capital) while reducing criminal involvement.[93] In contrast, research shows that people who are self-centred and present oriented are less likely to accumulate social capital and more prone to commit criminal acts.[94]

Finding the Glueck Delinquents

John Laub and Robert Sampson are now conducting an important follow-up to their original research: They are finding and interviewing the survivors from the original Glueck research.[95] Sampson and Laub have located the survivors, the oldest subject being 70 years old and the youngest 62.

Their preliminary findings suggest that delinquency and other forms of antisocial conduct in childhood are strongly related to adult crime and drug and alcohol abuse. Former delinquents also suffer consequences in other areas of social life, such as school, work, and family life. For example, delinquents are far less likely to finish high school than nondelinquents and subsequently are more likely to be unemployed, receive welfare, and experience separation or divorce as adults.

In their latest research, Laub and Sampson address one of the key questions posed by developmental theories: Is it possible for former delinquents to rehabilitate themselves as adults? They find that most antisocial children do not remain antisocial as adults. Of those men who survived to age 50, 24 percent had no arrests for crimes of violence and property after age 17 (6 percent had no arrests for any crime); 48 percent had no arrests for these predatory crimes after age 25 (19 percent for total crime); 60 percent had no arrests for predatory crimes after age 31 (33 percent for total crime); and 79 percent had no arrests for predatory crimes after age 40 (57 percent for total crime). They conclude that desistance from crime is the norm and that most, if not all, serious delinquents later desist from crime.[96]

Why Do Delinquents Desist?

Laub and Sampson's earlier research had already indicated that marriage and job, as means of building social capital, were key components of desistance from crime. In this new round of research, Laub and Sampson were able to find out more about long-term desistance by interviewing 52 men as they approached age 70. Drawing on the men's own words, they found that one important element for "going straight" is the "knifing off" of individuals from their immediate environment, offering them a new "script" for the future. Joining the military can provide this "knifing-off" effect, as does marriage and changing one's residence. One former delinquent (age 69) told them:

> I'd say the turning point was, number one, the Army. You get into an outfit, you had a sense of belonging, you made your friends. I think I became a pretty good judge of character. In the Army, you met some good ones, you met some foul balls. Then I met the wife. I'd say probably that would be the turning point. Got married, then naturally, kids come. So now you got to get a better job, you got to make more money. And that's how I got to the Navy Yard and tried to improve myself.*

Former delinquents who "went straight" were able to put structure into their lives. Structure often led the men to disassociate from delinquent peers, reducing the opportunity to get into trouble. Getting married, for example, may limit the number of nights men can "hang with the guys." As one wife of a former delinquent said, "It is not how many beers you have, it's who you drink with." Even multiple offenders who had done time in prison were able to desist with the help of a stabilizing marriage.

The former delinquents who were able to turn their lives around, who had acquired a degree of maturity by taking on family and work responsibilities, and who had forged new commitments were the ones most likely to make a fresh start and find new direction and meaning in life. It seems that men who desisted changed their identity as well, and this, in turn, affected their outlook and sense of maturity and responsibility. The ability to change did not reflect crime "specialty"; violent offenders followed the same path as property offenders.

Policy Implications

Laub and Sampson found that youth problems—delinquency, substance abuse, violence, dropping out, teen pregnancy—often share common risk characteristics. Intervention strategies, therefore, should consider a broad array of antisocial, criminal, and deviant behaviours, and not limit their focus to one subgroup or crime type. Because delinquency and other social problems are linked (problem behaviour syndrome), early prevention efforts that reduce crime will probably also reduce alcohol abuse, drunk driving, drug abuse, sexual promiscuity, and family violence, as well as school failure, unemployment, marital disharmony, and divorce.

*John Laub, "Crime Over the Life Course," *Poverty Research News*, Newsletter of the Northwestern University/University of Chicago Joint Center for Poverty Research, vol. 4, no. 3 (May -June 2000). Reprinted with permission.

The best way to achieve these goals is through four significant life-changing events: marriage, joining the military, getting a job, and changing one's environment or neighbourhood. What appears to be important about these processes is that they all involve, to varying degrees, the following items: a "knifing off" of the past from the present, new situations that provide supervision and monitoring as well as new opportunities for social support and growth, and new situations that provide the opportunity for transforming identity. Prevention of crime must therefore be a policy at all times and at all stages of life.

DID YOU KNOW?

- The social development model (SDM) integrates social control, social learning, and structural models.
- According to interactional theory, the causes of crime are bidirectional. Weak bonds lead to deviant peer relations and delinquency; delinquency weakens conventional bonds and strengthens relations with deviant peers.
- According to age-graded theory, building social capital and strong social bonds reduces the likelihood of long-term deviance.
- Many delinquents desist as adults. Building social capital helps people desist.

Thinking Like a *Criminologist*

Visit icancrim2.com to find the resources you need today!

Located at the back of the textbook are rip-out Chapter in Review cards. Make sure you also go online to check out other tools that CRIM offers to help you successfully pass your course.

- Flashcards
- Glossary
- Test Yourself
- Videos
- Games
- Interactive Quizzing
- Audio Chapter Reviews

10

Violent Crime

Learning Outcomes

LO1 Identify the different types of interpersonal violent crime.

LO2 Name the various explanations for violent crimes.

LO3 Explain the nature of the changes in Canadian law in regard to rape.

LO4 Identify the different degrees of murder.

LO5 Explain the prevalence of assault that occurs in the family home.

LO6 Explain why robbery is considered a violent crime.

LO7 Identify emerging forms of violent crime.

LO8 Identify the forms of political violence.

LO1 Introduction

An early morning robbery at a Concordia Avenue pizza shop on May 15, 2011, left a 54-year-old Winnipeg man clinging to life after he was savagely beaten by two male suspects. People working in the strip mall where the shop was located expressed shock at the brutality of the crime. "We shake our heads, we don't understand how these things can happen, but, unfortunately, they do in the world we live in today," claimed one store owner. "It was senseless, what they did to him," said another woman who worked in the strip mall. While Winnipeg Police Service forensics officers continued to collect evidence at the crime scene, detectives are reviewing video surveillance tapes in an attempt to identify the suspects.[1]

DID YOU KNOW?

- There are a number of suspected causes of violence.
- Some violent criminals have personal traits that make them violence prone, including mental impairment and intellectual dysfunction.
- Victims of severe child abuse and neglect may become violence-prone adults.
- Violence may have its roots in human evolution, being almost instinctual in some instances.
- Drug and alcohol abuse has been linked to violence, through either a psychopharmacological relationship, economic compulsive behaviour, or a systemic link.
- Although guns do not cause violence, their presence can escalate its severity.

The Winnipeg robbery and savage beating is a shocking reminder that violence is all too common in North American life. "Violence is the primal problem of American history," writes social historian David Courtwright, "… the dark reverse of its coin of freedom and abundance."[2] Although the violent crime rate has recently declined, people are continually bombarded with news stories featuring grisly accounts of mass murder, child sexual abuse, and serial rape. Many people have personally experienced violence and almost everyone knows someone who has been robbed, beaten, or killed. Riots and mass disturbances have ravaged urban areas; racial attacks plague schools and university and college campuses; and assassination has claimed the lives of political, religious, and social leaders all over the world.[3]

instrumental violence
Violence designed to improve the financial or social position of the criminal.

expressive violence
Violence that vents rage, anger, or frustration.

When violence is designed to improve the financial or social position of the criminal, as in an armed robbery, it is referred to as **instrumental violence**. Crimes that vent rage, anger, or frustration are known as **expressive violence**. An extreme example of expressive violence occurred on July 22, 2011, when a 32-year-old Norwegian, Anders Behring Breivik, went on a bombing and shooting rampage that killed 77 people. Breivik posted a 1500-page document on the Internet calling for a war against multiculturalism and Islam just hours before he set off a

Reuters TV/Reuters /Landov

Anders Behring Breivik: Can we ever know why some individuals commit such acts of extreme violence?

bomb in the Norwegian capital, Oslo, killing 8 people. Breivik then drove 50 kilometres to Lake Tyrifjorden, where he took a boat over to a youth camp located on Utoeya Island. Dressed in a police uniform and toting an automatic rifle and pistol, Breivik moved through the island camp shooting everyone in his path, even pursuing the fleeing teenagers and adult supervisors as they leapt off cliffs into the water in an attempt to flee. Breivik surrendered to police at the scene.[4] A similar event occurred at Dawson College in Montreal in September 2006 when 25-year-old Kimveer Gill arrived at the college at lunchtime armed with a rifle, a shotgun, and a 9 mm handgun. Referring to himself on his personal website as "Trench," the goth-looking Gill shot one student outside the building before entering and heading to the crowded cafeteria area, where he shot another 19 students. Wounded in the arm by Montreal police officer Denis Côté, who happened to be visiting the college that day and had rushed to the cafeteria after hearing the gunfire, Gill killed himself with a gunshot to the head. Anastasia De Sousa, 18, a business student at Dawson, died at the scene. The other 19 students who were shot recovered from their wounds. Police investigators later discovered pictures on Gill's personal website of him dressed in combat gear with a Beretta CX4 Storm semi-automatic rifle in his grip, and a caption reading "Ready for Action."[5]

This chapter surveys the nature and extent of violent crime. First, it briefly reviews some possible causes of violence. Then, it focuses on specific types of interpersonal violence—rape, homicide, assault (including domestic violence), and robbery. Finally, it briefly examines political violence, including terrorism.

LO2 The Roots of Violence

What causes people to behave violently? A number of competing explanations have been offered for violent behaviour. A few of the most prominent are discussed here.

Personal Traits

On December 6, 1989, Marc Lepine burst into a classroom at l'École Polytechnique Montréal with an automatic gun in his hand. First, he ordered the male students to leave the room; then, shouting a few incoherent curses against feminists, Lepine opened fire into the crowd of terrified women students. Lepine claimed 14 lives before turning the gun on himself. This horrific crime shocked Canadians into implementing strict controls on all guns in the form of Bill C-68, which was proclaimed on December 5, 1995, in time for the sixth anniversary of the Montreal murders.[6]

Bizarre outbursts such as Lepine's support a link between violence and personal traits and personality disorders. Violent offenders often display abnormal personality structures marked by psychopathic tendencies such as impulsivity, aggression, dishonesty, pathological lying, and lack of remorse.[7]

American psychologist Dorothy Otnow Lewis and her associates found that murderous youths show signs of major neurological impairment, such as abnormal EEGs, multiple psychomotor impairment, and severe seizures; low intelligence as measured on standard IQ tests; psychotic close relatives; and psychotic symptoms such as paranoia, illogical

CONNECTIONS

As you may recall from Chapter 5, biosocial theorists link violence to a number of biological irregularities, including (but not limited to) genetic influences and inheritance, the action of hormones, the functioning of neurotransmitters, brain structure, and diet. Psychologists link violent behaviour to observational learning from violent TV shows, traumatic childhood experiences, low intelligence, mental illness, impaired cognitive processes, and abnormal (psychopathic) personality structure.

thinking, and hallucinations.[8] In her 1998 book *Guilty by Reason of Insanity*, Lewis reports that American death-row inmates have a history of mental impairment and intellectual dysfunction.[9] It comes as no surprise, then, that many murderers kill themselves shortly after committing their crime. Even more bizarre are the cases of people who commit murder with the expectation that they will be executed for their crimes, a form of "suicide-murder."[10]

Abnormal personality structure, including depression, borderline personality syndrome, and psychopathology, have been associated with various forms of spousal and family abuse.[11] A high proportion of serial rapists and repeat sexual offenders exhibit psychopathic personality structures.[12] Although this evidence indicates that violent offenders may be more prone to psychological disorders than other people, no single clinical diagnosis can characterize their behaviour.[13]

Ineffective Families

Much research traces violence to rejecting, ineffective, or abusive parenting.[14] Absent or deviant parents, inconsistent discipline, and lack of supervision have all been linked to persistent violent offending.[15]

A number of research studies have found that children who are clinically diagnosed as abused later engage in delinquent behaviours, including violence, at a rate significantly greater than that of unabused children.[16] Samples of convicted murderers reveal a high percentage of seriously abused youth.[17] The abuse–violence association has been established in many cases in which parents have been killed by their children; sexual abuse is also a constant factor in father (patricide) and mother (matricide) killings.[18] Dorothy Otnow Lewis found in her study of juvenile death row inmates that all had long histories of intense child abuse.[19]

Evolutionary Factors/Human Instinct

Perhaps violent responses and emotions are actually inherent in all humans, easily triggered by the right spark. Sigmund Freud believed that human aggression and violence are produced by two instinctual drives: *eros*, the life instinct, which drives people toward self-fulfillment and enjoyment; and *thanatos*, the death instinct, which produces self-destruction. Thanatos can be expressed externally (as violence and sadism) or internally (as suicide, alcoholism, or other self-destructive behaviours). Because aggression is instinctual, Freud saw little hope for its treatment.[20] A number of biologists and anthropologists have also speculated that instinctual violence-promoting traits may be common in the human species. One view is that aggression and violence are the results of instincts inborn in all animals, including human beings.[21]

Exposure to Violence

People who are constantly exposed to violence at home, at school, or in the environment may adopt violent methods themselves.[22] In a study of Chicago youth, social scientist Felton Earls found that between 30 and 40 percent of the children who reported exposure to violence also displayed significant violent behaviour themselves.[23] Exposure to violence may also have an effect on adults, even police officers. Research indicates that police officers' use of deadly force is much higher in areas with high violence and murder rates. The perception of danger may contribute to the use of violent means for self-protection, even among people trained in the use of force.[24]

subculture of violence
Norms and customs that, in contrast to society's dominant value system, legitimize and expect the use of violence to resolve social conflicts.

Cultural Values

The various sources of crime statistics tell us that interpersonal violence is more common in urban areas than in rural areas.[25] It is unlikely that violent crime rates would be so high in these socially disorganized areas, however, unless other social forces encouraged violent crime.[26]

Criminologists Marvin Wolfgang and Franco Ferracuti have attributed these disproportionately high violence rates in urban areas to a **subculture of violence**.[27] The norms of this subculture are separate from society's central, dominant value system. In this

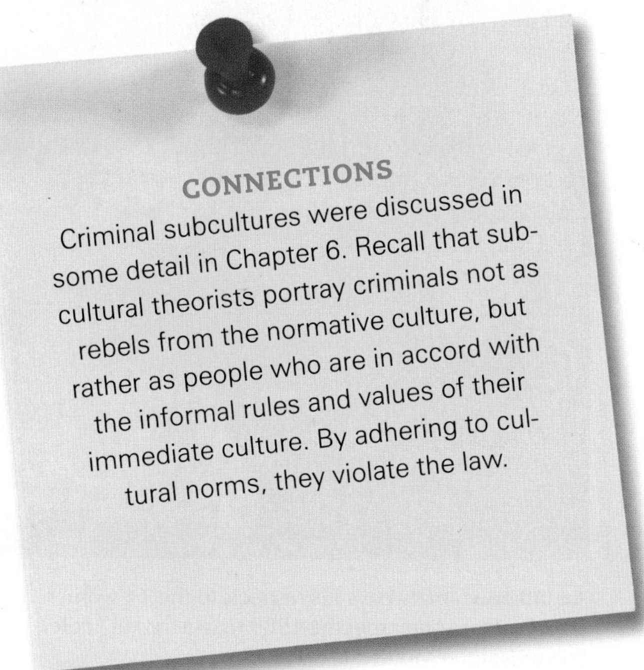
CONNECTIONS
Criminal subcultures were discussed in some detail in Chapter 6. Recall that subcultural theorists portray criminals not as rebels from the normative culture, but rather as people who are in accord with the informal rules and values of their immediate culture. By adhering to cultural norms, they violate the law.

subculture, a potent theme of violence influences lifestyles, the socialization process, and interpersonal relationships. Its members expect that violence will be used to solve social conflicts and dilemmas, and violence is legitimized by custom and norms. It is considered appropriate behaviour within culturally defined conflict situations, in which an individual who has been offended by a negative outcome in a dispute seeks reparations through violent means.[28]

Substance Abuse

It has become common to link violence to substance abuse. In fact, substance abuse, particularly of alcohol, influences violence in three ways:[29]

1. *Psychopharmacological relationship.* Violence may be a direct consequence of ingesting mood-altering substances. Experimental evidence shows that high doses of drugs such as PCP and amphetamines may produce violent, aggressive behaviour.[30] Alcohol abuse has long been associated with all forms of violence. A direct alcohol–violence link may occur because drinking reduces cognitive ability, making miscommunication more likely, while at the same time limiting the capacity for rational dialogue and compromise.[31]
2. *Economic compulsive behaviour.* Drug users may resort to violence to support their habit.
3. *Systemic link.* Violence may be a function of rival gangs' battling over drug markets and territories. Drug trafficking activities can lead to personal vendettas and a perceived need for violent self-protection.[32]

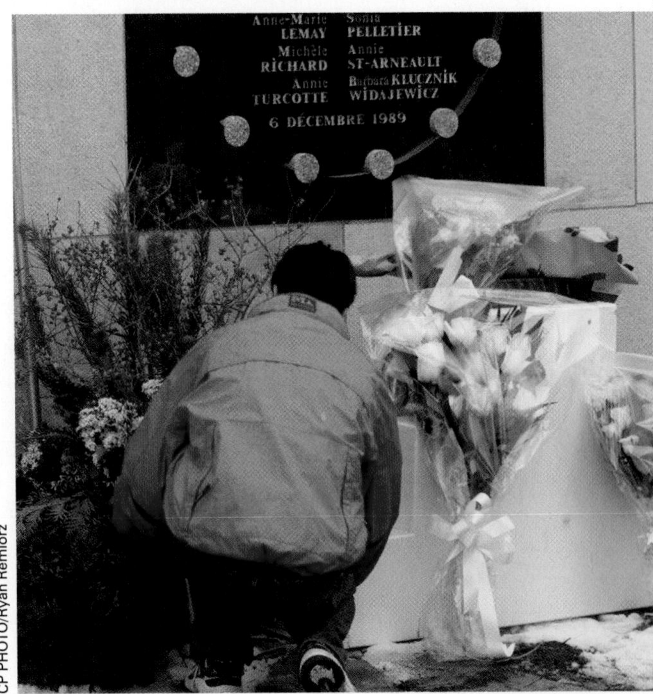

CP PHOTO/Ryan Remiorz

An unknown male pays his respects to the 14 women slain by Marc Lepine in the 1989 massacre at l'École Polytechnique Montréal.

Drug testing of arrestees in major American cities consistently shows that criminals are also drug abusers; almost three-quarters of all people incarcerated in American jails and prisons have a substance abuse or substance dependency problem.[33] Canadian crime statistics show that in about half of all cases of homicide, the accused had consumed drugs or alcohol at the time of the murder.[34] Surveys of prison inmates show that a significant majority report being under the influence of drugs or alcohol when they committed their last criminal offence.[35]

Firearm Availability

Although firearm availability does not cause violence, it is certainly a facilitating factor. A petty argument can escalate into a fatal encounter if one party has a handgun. In Canada, handguns account for over half of all homicides involving a firearm. In 2009, 29 percent of all homicides involved firearms.[36] It may not be a coincidence that the United States, which has a huge surplus of guns and in which most firearms (80 percent) used in crimes are stolen or obtained through illegal or unregulated transactions, also has one of the world's highest violence rates.[37] Figure 10.1 lists some facts about weapons and violent crime.

FIGURE 10.1

Quick Facts about Weapons and Violent Crime in Canada

- Physical force or threats are the methods used in 75% of violent crimes.[38]
- Weapons are used against victims of violent crime only 18% of the time.[39]
- Knives are the most common weapon used to commit violent crime.[40]
- Homicide and attempted murder are the violent crimes most likely to involve the use of a weapon.[41]
- Stabbings accounted for nearly 41% of spousal homicides between 2000 and 2009; shootings accounted for 23% of spousal homicides over the same period.[42]
- Violent crime, including homicide and attempted murder, has been in decline since the early 1990s.[43]
- Three-quarters of firearms deaths are suicides.[44]

DID YOU KNOW?

- Rape and sexual assault have occurred throughout history and are often linked with war and violence.
- Types of sexual assault include date rape, marital rape, and sexual interference; types of rapists include serial rapists and sadists.
- Suspected causes of sexual assault include male socialization, hypermasculinity, and biological determinism.
- Murder can involve either strangers or acquaintances.
- Mass murder refers to the killing of numerous victims in a single outburst; serial killing involves numerous victims over an extended period of time.
- Patterns of assault are quite similar to those for homicide.
- There are millions of cases of child abuse and spouse abuse each year.
- Robbers use force to steal. Some are opportunists looking for ready cash; others are professionals who have a long-term commitment to crime.

JUST BECAUSE YOU HELP HER HOME...
DOESN'T MEAN YOU GET TO HELP YOURSELF.
sex without consent = sexual assault
DON'T BE THAT GUY.
sexualassaultvoices.com

Sexual Assault Voices of Edmonton

"Don't Be That Guy," an edgy anti-rape campaign released in Edmonton targets young men aged 18–24. While anti-rape ads have commonly focused on the victims of the crime, this new focus puts the spotlight on potential perpetrators.

Each of these factors is believed to influence violent crimes, including both traditional common-law crimes, such as sexual assault, murder, assault, and robbery, and newly recognized problems, such as workplace violence, hate crimes, and biker gangs. Each of these forms of violent behaviour is discussed in some detail later in this chapter.

LO3 Rape and Sexual Assault

Rape (from the Latin *rapere*, to take by force) is defined in common law as "the carnal knowledge of a female forcibly and against her will."[45] It is one of the most loathed, misunderstood, and frightening of crimes. Under traditional common-law definitions, rape involves nonconsensual sexual intercourse that a male performs against a female whom he is neither married to nor cohabitating with. Before the 1980s, husbands were immune from prosecution for raping their wives. However, in 1983 the government of Canada reformed the laws pertaining to rape and this immunity was removed. Further, because rape is viewed as a violent, coercive act of aggression, the term *rape* was replaced with *sexual assault*, which refers to any form of sexual contact that is without voluntary consent.

There have been various national campaigns to alert the public to the seriousness of sexual assault and, in particular, the impact it has on victims. Such efforts have made significant progress in revising rape laws and developing a vast social service network to aid victims.

Rape versus Sexual Assault

As previously noted, the term *rape* is no longer used in a legal sense in Canada. After the 1983 revisions to the Criminal Code of Canada, "rape" was replaced with "sexual assault." Part of the rationale underlying the change was to recognize the violent, aggressive nature of the act. **Sexual assault** can be anything from unwanted touching to rape. The Criminal Code identifies numerous types of sexual assault, some of which include descriptions of specific acts (e.g., using a weapon, causing bodily harm) as well as types of relationships (e.g., where the aggressor is in a position of authority). Further, there are three levels of sexual assault:

- Level I—simple sexual assault
- Level II—sexual assault with a weapon or resulting in bodily harm
- Level III—aggravated sexual assault

sexual assault
Anything from unwanted touching to rape.

Luca Giordano 1634 Italy - 1705 The rape of the Sabine women (Il ratto delle Sabine) c.1672-74 oil on canvas 257.2 x 314.6 cm National Gallery of Australia, Canberra Purchased with the assistance of Philip Bacon AM 2000,

For the purposes of the present text, the term *rape* will be used in a colloquial sense, whereas *sexual assault* will refer to the Criminal Code definition.

History of Rape and Sexual Assault

Rape has been a recognized crime throughout history. It has been the subject of art, literature, film, and theatre. Paintings such as the *Rape of the Sabine Women* by Nicolas Poussin (see above), novels such as *Clarissa* by Samuel Richardson, poems such as *The Rape of Lucrece* by William Shakespeare, and films such as *The Accused* have sexual violence as their central theme.

In early civilization, rape was common. Men staked a claim of ownership on women by forcibly abducting and raping them. This practice led to males' solidification of power and their historical domination of women.[46] During the Middle Ages, it was common for ambitious men to abduct and rape wealthy women in an effort to force them into marriage. The practice of "heiress stealing" illustrates how feudal law gave little thought or protection to women and equated them with property.[47] Only in the late 15th century was forcible sex outlawed, and then only if the victim was of the nobility. Peasant women and married women were not considered rape victims until well into the 16th century.

Sexual Assault and War

The link between military conflicts and sexual assault is inescapable. Throughout recorded history, sexual assault has been associated with armies and warfare. Soldiers of conquering armies have considered sexual possession of their enemies' women one of the spoils of war. Among the ancient Greeks, rape was socially acceptable within the rules of warfare. During the Crusades, even knights and pilgrims, ostensibly bound by vows of chivalry and Christian piety, took time to rape as they marched toward Constantinople.

The belief that women are part of the spoils of war has continued. During World War II, the Japanese army forced as many as 200 000 Korean women into frontline brothels, where they were repeatedly assaulted. In a 1998 Japanese ruling, the surviving Korean women were awarded the equivalent of US$2300 each in compensation.[48] The systematic rape of Bosnian and Kosovar women by Serbian army officers during the civil war in the former Yugoslavia horrified the world during the 1990s. These crimes seemed particularly atrocious because they were part of an official policy of genocide: rape was deliberately used to impregnate Bosnian women with Serbian children.[49] Human rights groups have estimated that more than 30 000 women and young girls were sexually abused in the Balkan fighting. In Congo, where a decades-long war rages, it is estimated in the population of 70 million more than 1000 women are raped every day.[50]

Incidence of Sexual Assault

According to the Canadian Centre for Justice Statistics, between 1993 and 2007 the rate of police-reported sexual assaults in Canada declined from a historical high of 136 per 100 000, to 73 per 100 000. Police-reported statistics show that females are more than five times more likely to be a victim of a sexual assault.[51]

These data must be interpreted with caution, because many cases of sexual assault go unreported. For example, it is estimated that only 10 percent of sexual assaults are reported to police.[52] Many people fail to report sexual assaults because they are embarrassed, believe nothing can be done, or blame themselves. Because other victim surveys indicate that at least 20 percent of women, 15 percent of university and college-age women, and 12 percent of adolescent girls have experienced sexual abuse or assault sometime during their lives, it is evident that both official and victimization statistics significantly undercount the incidence of sexual assault.[53]

Population density influences the sexual assault rate. Metropolitan areas today have sexual assault rates significantly higher than rural areas; nonetheless, urban areas have experienced a much greater drop in sexual assault reports than rural areas. Sexual assault is also a warm-weather crime. Most incidents occur during July and August, with the lowest rates reported for December, January, and February.

Types of Sexual Assault

Some rapes are planned; others are spontaneous. Some focus on a particular victim, while in others the victim appears to be chosen at random.[54] Some sexual assaults involve a single offender; others, called **gang rapes**, involve multiple attackers. Compared to individual assaults, gang rapes are more likely to involve alcohol and drugs, to occur at night, and to include other types of sexual assault such as penetration with objects.[55]

Whereas some sexual assaults involve strangers, others involve people who are acquainted with one another. Included within **acquaintance rapes** are the subcategories of **date rape**, which involves a sexual attack during a courting relationship, and **marital rape**, which is forcible sex between people who are legally married to each other. More than 50 percent of all rapes involve acquaintances.[56] According to the Canadian Centre for Justice Statistics, only 19 percent of police-reported sexual assaults are committed by a stranger.[57]

Some rapists are one-time offenders, but others engage in multiple or serial rapes. Some serial rapists constantly increase their use of force; others do not.[58] Some rapists commit "blitz" rapes, in which they attack their victims without warning; others try to "capture" their victims by striking up a conversation or offering them a ride; still others use personal relationships to gain access to their targets.[59]

gang rape
Forcible sex involving multiple attackers.

acquaintance rape
Forcible sex in which offender and victim are acquainted with one another.

date rape
Forcible sex during a courting relationship.

marital rape
Forcible sex between people who are legally married to each other.

One of the best-known attempts to classify the personalities of rapists was made by psychologist A. Nicholas Groth, an expert on classifying and treating sex offenders. According to Groth, every sexual assault contains three elements: anger, power, and sexuality.[60] Consequently, rapists can be classified according to one of the dimensions described in Table 10.1. In treating rape offenders, Groth found that about 55 percent were of the power type; about 40 percent, the anger type; and about 5 percent, the sadistic type. Groth's major contribution has been his recognition that rape is generally a crime of violence, not a sexual act. In all of these circumstances, sexual assault involves a violent criminal offence in which a predatory criminal chooses to attack a victim.[61]

Date Rape

One disturbing trend is the increase in sexual assault involving people who are in some form of courting relationship. There is no single form of date rape. Some sexual assaults occur on first dates; others after a relationship has been developing; still others after the couple has been involved for some time. In

TABLE 10.1

Varieties of Sexual Assault

Anger rape	occurs when sexuality becomes a means of expressing and discharging pent-up anger and rage. The rapist uses far more brutality than would have been necessary if his real objective had been simply to have sex with his victim. His aim is to hurt his victim as much as possible; the sexual aspect of rape may be an afterthought. Often the anger rapist acts on the spur of the moment after an upsetting incident has caused him conflict, irritation, or aggravation. Surprisingly, anger rapes are less psychologically traumatic for the victim than might be expected. Because a woman is usually physically beaten during an anger rape, she is more likely to receive sympathy from her peers, relatives, and the justice system and consequently be immune from any suggestion that she complied with the attack.
Power rape	involves an attacker who does not want to harm his victim as much as he wants to possess her sexually. His goal is sexual conquest, and he uses only the amount of force necessary to achieve his objective. The power rapist wants to be in control, to be able to dominate women and have them at his mercy. Yet it is not sexual gratification that drives the power rapist; in fact, he often has a consenting relationship with his wife or girlfriend. Sexual assault is instead a way of putting personal insecurities to rest, asserting heterosexuality, and preserving a sense of manhood. The power rapist's victim usually is a woman equal in age to or younger than the rapist. The lack of physical violence may reduce the support given the victim by family and friends. Therefore, the victim's personal guilt over her rape experience is increased—perhaps, she thinks, she could have done something to get away.
Sadistic rape	involves both sexuality and aggression. The sadistic rapist is bound up in ritual—he may torment his victim, bind her, or torture her. Victims are usually related, in the rapist's view, to a personal characteristic that he wants to harm or destroy. The rape experience is intensely exciting to the sadist; he gets satisfaction from abusing, degrading, or humiliating his captive. This type of rape is particularly traumatic for the victim. Victims of such crimes need psychiatric care long after their physical wounds have healed.

Source: *From Men Who Rape* by A. Nicholas Groth and Jean Birnbaum. Copyright © 2001 A. Nicholas Groth. Reprinted by permission of Basic Books, a member of the Perseus Books Group.

marital exemption Traditional legal doctrine that a legally married husband could not be charged with raping his wife.

sexual interference Touching the body of a person who is under 16 years of age for a sexual purpose.

invitation to sexual touching Inviting, counselling, or inciting someone under age 16 to touch the body of someone else for a sexual purpose.

sexual exploitation Sexual contact, even if consensual, between a person aged 16 to 18 and someone in a position of trust or authority, such as a minister, coach, employer, or teacher.

long-term or close relationships, the male partner may feel he has invested so much time and money in his partner that he is "owed" sexual relations or that sexual intimacy is an expression that the involvement is progressing. He may make comparisons to other couples who have dated as long and are sexually active.[62] Males who use force in their dating relationships are more likely to be angry, jealous, and stressed; have poor communication skills; act irrationally; use alcohol; and report more efforts to control their partners than those men who never use force in dating relationships.[63]

Date rape is believed to be frequent on university and college campuses. It has been estimated that 15 to 20 percent of all college women are victims of rape or attempted rape.[64] The incidence of date rape may be even higher than surveys indicate because many victims blame themselves and do not recognize the incident as a sexual assault, saying, for example, "I should have fought back harder" or "I shouldn't have gotten drunk."[65] Thus, despite their seriousness and prevalence, fewer than one in ten date rapes may be reported to police.[66] Another disturbing issue is the increasing use of date rape drugs such as rohypnol, gamma hydroxybutyrate (GHB), ecstasy (MDMA), and ketamine hydrochloride ("K"). In response to calls from victims, police, and the public, in September 2011 the Canadian government tabled new legislation introducing tough new penalties for trafficking in date rape drugs.[67]

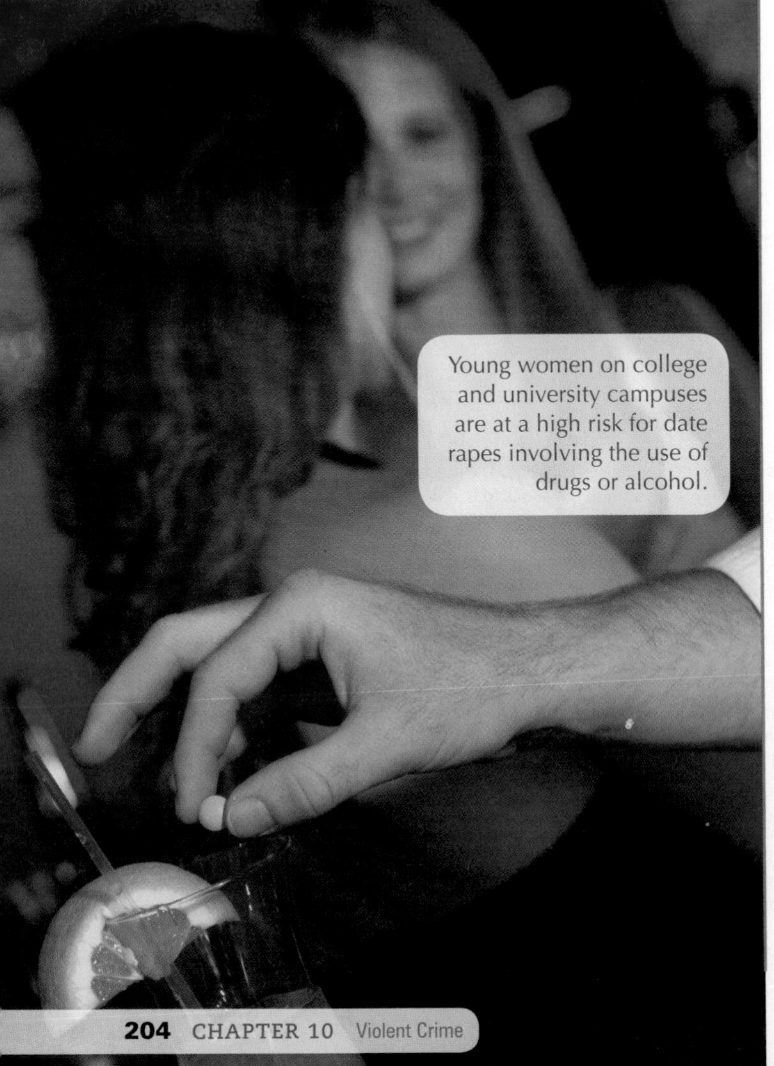

Young women on college and university campuses are at a high risk for date rapes involving the use of drugs or alcohol.

Monkey Business Images/Shutterstock.com

Marital Rape

In 1978, Greta Rideout filed rape charges against her husband John. This Oregon case grabbed headlines because it was one of the first in which a husband was prosecuted for raping his wife while sharing a residence with her. John was acquitted, and the couple briefly reconciled; later, continued violent episodes culminated in divorce and a jail term for John.[68]

Traditionally, in Canada and the United States a legally married husband could not be charged with raping his wife; this legal doctrine was referred to as the **marital exemption**. The origin of this doctrine can be traced to the 16th-century pronouncement of Matthew Hale, England's chief justice, who wrote:

> But the husband cannot be guilty of rape committed by himself upon his lawful wife, for by their mutual matrimonial consent and contract the wife hath given up herself in this kind unto the husband which she cannot retract.[69]

However, research indicates that many women are raped each year by their husbands as part of an overall pattern of spousal abuse. Many spousal rapes are accompanied by brutal, sadistic beatings and have little to do with normal sexual interests.[70] As noted earlier, the marital exemption was removed from the Canadian Criminal Code in 1983. Doing away with the marital exemption is not unique to Canada; it has also been abolished in many American states, and in Australia, Belgium, Denmark, Israel, Scotland, New Zealand and in more than 60 other countries around the world.[71]

Sexual Assault and Persons Under the Age of Consent

In Canada, traditional statutory rape laws were replaced in 1988 with laws against a variety of sexual offences, including **sexual interference**, **invitation to sexual touching**, and **sexual exploitation**. Anyone who for sexual purposes touches any part of the body of someone under the age of 16 is guilty of the offence of sexual interference. Consent by the minor or mistake concerning the age of the victim cannot be used as a defence. However, there is no crime if the accused person is between the ages of 12 and 14 and the victim is less than two years younger than the accused and consented to the activity. Anyone who invites a person under the age of 16 years to touch them or another person for a sexual purpose is guilty of the crime of invitation to sexual touching. Similarly, consent by the minor or mistake concerning the age of the victim cannot be used as a defence. However, there is no crime if the accused person is between the ages of 12 and 14 and the victim is less than two years younger than the accused and consented to the activity; or, if the victim is between the ages of 14 and 16, and the accused is less than 5 years older than the complainant, or is married to the complainant.

Sexual exploitation also makes it an offence for an adult to have any sexual contact with boys and girls between 16 and 18, where a relationship of trust or authority exists between the adult and the child.

The Causes of Sexual Assault

What factors predispose some men to commit sexual assault? Criminologists' responses to this question are almost as varied as the crime itself. However, most explanations can be grouped into a few consistent categories.

Evolutionary/Biological Factors

One explanation for sexual assault focuses on the evolutionary, biological aspects of the male sexual drive. This perspective suggests that sexual assault may be instinctual, developed over the ages as a means of perpetuating the species. In more primitive times, forcible sexual contact may have helped spread genes and maximize offspring. Some believe that these prehistoric drives remain: Males still have a natural sexual drive that encourages them to have intimate relations with as many women as possible.[72] The evolutionary view is that the sexual urge corresponds to the unconscious need to preserve the species by spreading one's genes as widely as possible. Men who are sexually aggressive will have a reproductive edge over their more passive peers.[73]

Male Socialization

In contrast to the evolutionary biological view, some researchers argue that sexual assault is a function of modern male socialization.[74] According to this view, from an early age, boys are taught to be aggressive,

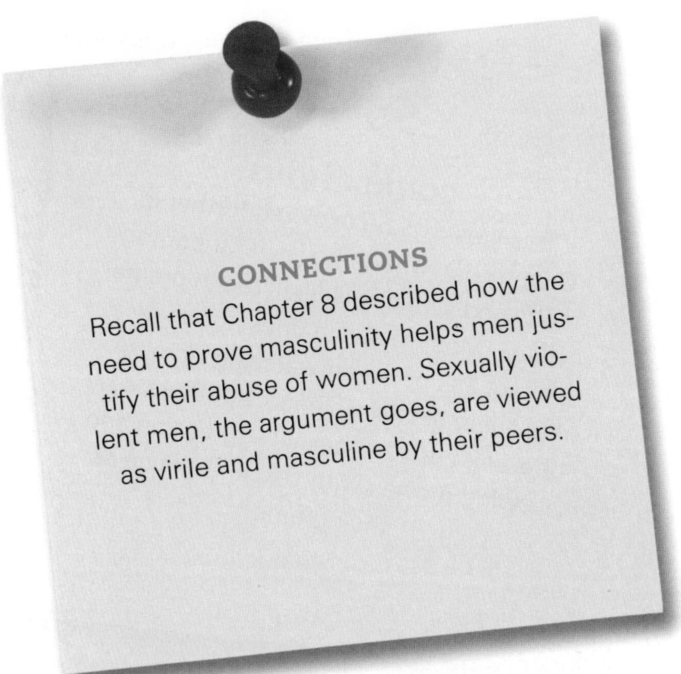

forceful, tough, and dominating and are led to believe that women want to be dominated. This "virility mystique" dictates that males must separate their sexual feelings from needs for love, respect, and affection. Men are socialized to be the aggressors and expect to be sexually active with many women; consequently, male virginity and sexual inexperience are shameful. Conversely, sexually aggressive women frighten some men and cause them to doubt their own masculinity. Sexual insecurity may lead some men to commit sexual assault to bolster their self-image and masculine identity.

CONNECTIONS
Recall that Chapter 8 described how the need to prove masculinity helps men justify their abuse of women. Sexually violent men, the argument goes, are viewed as virile and masculine by their peers.

Hypermasculinity

If rape is an expression of male anger and devaluation of women and not an act motivated by sexual desire, it follows that men who hold so-called macho attitudes will be more likely to engage in sexual violence. Hypermasculine men typically have a callous sexual attitude and believe that violence is manly. They perceive danger as exciting and are overly sensitive to insult and ridicule. They are also impulsive, more apt to brag about sexual conquests, and more likely to lose control, especially when using alcohol.[75] These men are quicker to anger and more likely to be sexually aggressive. In fact, the sexually aggressive male may view almost any female as a likely victim for sexual violence.

Violent Experiences

Another view is that men learn to commit sexual assaults much as they learn any other behaviour. Groth found that 40 percent of the rapists he studied

CONNECTIONS

This view will be explored further in Chapter 13, where the issue of pornography and violence is analyzed in greater detail. Most research does not show a direct link between watching pornography and sexual violence, but there may be a link between sexual aggression and viewing movies with sexual violence as their theme.

had been sexually victimized as adolescents.[76] A growing body of literature links personal sexual trauma with the desire to inflict sexual trauma on others.[77] Watching violent or pornographic films featuring women who are beaten, raped, or tortured has been linked to sexually aggressive behaviour in men.[78]

Sexual Motivation

American research reveals that sexual assault victims tend to be young and that rapists prefer younger, presumably more attractive victims. Data show an association between the ages of rapists and their victims, indicating that men choose sexual assault targets of approximately the same age as consensual sex partners. And, despite the fact that younger criminals are usually the most violent, older rapists tend to harm their victims more than younger rapists. This pattern suggests that older criminals may rape for motives of power and control, whereas younger offenders may be seeking sexual gratification and may therefore be less likely to harm their victims.[79]

In sum, criminologists are still at odds over the precise cause of sexual assault, but there is evidence that it is the product of a number of social, cultural, and psychological forces.[80] Although some experts view it as a normal response to an abnormal environment, others view it as the product of a disturbed mind and deviant life experiences.

Sexual Assault and the Law

Of all violent crimes, none has created such conflict in the legal system as rape. Even if women choose to report a sexual assault to police, they may be initially reluctant because of the discriminatory provisions built into many rape laws. Historically, the sexist fashion in which rape victims are treated by police, prosecutors, and court personnel, and the legal technicalities that can authorize invasion of women's privacy when a sexual assault case is tried in court can devastate the victim.

While the prosecution of sexual assault cases has always been a problem, police and courts are now more sensitive to the plight of victims. High-profile cases, such as the Jane Doe sexual assault case in Toronto and several well-publicized coroner's inquests, have forced the justice system to take sexual assault cases more seriously.[81]

Law Reform

In 1983, the Canadian government introduced Bill C-127 containing a series of sweeping amendments to the Criminal Code, which completely eliminated the term "rape," introducing instead a three-stepped ladder of sexual assault offences. The goal of the amendments was to eliminate long-standing misconceptions and biases in the way in which the public and even criminal justice officials themselves viewed the crime of rape; namely, as an act of forced vaginal penetration only; as an act committed only against women; and an act protected by "spousal immunity." Instead, pushed by women's rights lobby groups such as the Women's Legal Education and Action Fund, the National Action Committee on the Status of Women, the National Association of Women and the Law, along with women's shelter and rape crisis centre organizations, the 1983 amendments introduced the legal position that unwanted touching or grabbing, or the use of threats or force to get any form of sexual gratification (ranging from unwanted kissing or touching through to forced penetration) is an assault, and should be treated as such in law. A sexual assault can occur against a male as well as a female and a spousal or partner relationship does not mean that threats or force can be used to obtain sexual gratification—there is no spousal immunity from sexual assault. In addition, Bill C-127 abolished the provisions that a complaint of a sexual assault must have been recent, that there must be corroboration of the assault by a witness, and that the previous "reputation" of the victim can be taken into account as a factor in determining the "degree of guilt" of the accused.[82]

In 1992, Bill C-49 introduced additional amendments to the Criminal Code clarifying in law the meaning of "consent" with respect to sexual acts, eliminating the defence of "mistaken belief," placing the onus on both of the partners to ensure that consent to a sexual act is freely given; and further clarifying the legal parameters under which evidence about a victim's sexual past can be introduced as evidence in court.[83]

Still, with nearly half a million police-recorded sexual assaults against women each year (males account for about 85 000 each year), representing possibly only 10 percent of actual cases, it is clear that much more needs to be done to deal with the crime of sexual assault.[84] Critics observe that, beyond any ongoing changes in law, education in contemporary knowledge about male and female sexuality and gender roles and confronting male use of aggression in relationships will go much further in addressing the problem of sexual assault.[85]

LO4 Murder and Homicide

Murder is defined in common law as "the unlawful killing of a human being with malice aforethought."[86] It is the most serious of all common-law crimes and the only one that is still punishable by death in some American states. Of course, the death penalty was abolished in Canada in 1976 after a 98-hour parliamentary debate. The last two people to be executed in Canada were Arthur Lucas and Robert Turpin, who were hanged on December 10, 1962. Before capital punishment was abolished in Canada, 1481 people were sentenced to death, and 710 of these were executed, of whom 697 were men and 13 were women.

Murder is divided into first-degree murder and second-degree murder. **First-degree murder** is the killing of another person that is planned and deliberate, the killing of a law enforcement agent, or a killing that is related to committing or attempting to commit other crimes that are particularly offensive to society (e.g., hostage taking, sexual assault, hijacking an airplane, etc.). **Second-degree murder** is intentional homicide that does not fit under the definition of first-degree murder. Western society's abhorrence of murderers is illustrated by the fact that there is no statute of limitations in murder cases. Accused killers can be brought to justice at any time after their crimes were committed.

A **homicide** may be either culpable or nonculpable. Culpable homicide is where the person who caused the death is blameworthy, accountable, and responsible for the death, which includes murder, **manslaughter**, and **infanticide**. It is a wrongful act, but does not involve malice. Nonculpable homicide is not an offence because no one is held responsible. Culpable homicide that does not qualify as murder is, by definition, manslaughter. The punishment for murder is life imprisonment with no parole eligibility for periods that range from 10 to 25 years. The punishment for manslaughter ranges from a suspended sentence to life imprisonment.

One issue that has received national attention is whether a fetus can be a murder victim. In some instances, fetal harm involves a mother whose behaviour endangers an unborn child; in other cases, feticide results from the harmful action of a third party. Canada adheres to the traditional common-law rule that only persons have rights and that the fetus, whatever its stage of gestation, is not a person. According to section 223(1) of the Criminal Code of Canada, "A child becomes a human being within the meaning of this Act when it has completely proceeded, in a living state, from the body of its mother whether or not (a) it has breathed, (b) it has an independent circulation, or (c) the navel string is severed."

The Nature and Extent of Murder

It is possible to track murder rate trends with the aid of Uniform Crime Report (UCR) data. For example, the Canadian homicide rate decreased by 42 percent between 1975 and 1998, and since 1999 the homicide rate in Canada has hovered around 1.8 per 100 000. There were 610 homicides in Canada in 2009, a decrease of 1.4 percent from the previous year.[87]

In the United States, the homicide rate peaked in 1980, at 10.2 per 100 000 population, and then fell to 7.9 per 100 000 in 1985. It rose again in the late 1980s and early 1990s, to a peak of 9.8 per 100 000 in 1991. Since then, the rate has declined, to 5.7 per 100 000 by 1999. Although this decline is an extremely positive development, more than 15 241 American citizens were killed in 2009.[88]

What else do official crime statistics tell us about murder today? Murder victims tend to be males over

murder
Intentional killing of another person; recognized as having two classes: first- and second-degree murder.

first-degree murder
The killing of another person that is planned and deliberate, the killing of a law enforcement agent, or killing that is related to committing or attempting other crimes that are particularly offensive to society (e.g., hostage taking, sexual assault, hijacking an airplane, etc.).

second-degree murder
Intentional killing of another person that is not first-degree murder.

homicide
First-degree murder, second-degree murder, manslaughter, or infanticide. Deaths caused by criminal negligence, suicide, and accidental or justifiable homicide are not included.

manslaughter
Homicide, or the killing of another person, by committing an unlawful act with only a general intent (e.g., speeding and killing a pedestrian, giving a lethal punch in a sudden, provoked brawl).

infanticide
The killing of an infant shortly after birth by the mother because she is not fully recovered from the effects of giving birth (e.g., in the case of postpartum depression) and her mind is disturbed.

18 years of age. Most victims of homicide knew their killer. In Canada in 2009, about one-third of all solved homicides were committed by a family member, one-half by an acquaintance, and the remaining 18 percent by a stranger, an increase of 17 percent over 2008 figures. Stabbings accounted for 34 percent of all homicides in 2009. Though the use of firearms in homicide had been on the increase since 2002, the trend was reversed in 2009, with firearms homicides decreasing to 179 from 200 in 2008, a 12 percent decline. Firearms were used in 29 percent of homicides, with handguns accounting for two-thirds of all firearms homicides. Two-thirds of the firearms used to commit homicide were unregistered. Beatings accounted for another 19 percent of homicides, and strangulation or suffocation another 7 percent.[89]

Though spousal homicides increased slightly in 2009 over the previous year, there has been a long-term decline since the mid-1970s in spousal and other family homicides. Thirty-one percent of female victims in 2009 were killed by a current or former spouse, compared to 3 percent of male victims. The year 2009 marked the second lowest proportion (26 percent) of homicide victims ever recorded in Canadian data.

Though on the increase in recent years, gang-related killings decreased by 10 percent in 2009, down to 124 from 138 in 2008. The number of youth accused of homicide increased by 42 percent between 2008 and 2009, from 55 to 78, the second highest number and rate in over 30 years.[90]

There were 11 persons killed on the job in 2009. The most common occupations at risk were taxi drivers and police officers.[91] As is the case historically, homicide rates were generally higher in the West than in the East in 2009. Among the provinces, Manitoba recorded the highest rate (4.66 homicides per 100 000 population), followed by Saskatchewan (3.49 per 100 000). The lowest rates were found in Prince Edward Island (0.0 per 100 000), Newfoundland (0.20 per 100 000), and Quebec (1.12 per 100 000). Among the ten largest metropolitan areas with more than 500 000 population in 2009, Abbotsford-Mission, B.C. reported the highest homicide rate per 100 000 (5.2) for the second year in a row. Thunder Bay, Ontario (5.0) and Winnipeg, Manitoba (4.1) followed. Vancouver (2.62), Toronto (1.61), and Montreal (1.15) recorded lower rates, though Quebec City (0.27) was lowest among large cities. Overall, the Canadian homicide rate continues to remain at a low level compared to the peak levels in the 1960s and 1970s, and is only one-third the rate found in the United States.[92]

Murderous Relations

One factor that has received a great deal of attention from criminologists is the relationship between the murderer and the victim.[93] Most criminologists agree that murders can generally be separated into those involving strangers, typically involving an indictable offence such as a robbery or a crime involving drugs, and acquaintance homicides involving disputes between family members, friends, and acquaintances.[94] The quality of relationships and interpersonal interactions, then, may influence murder.

Acquaintance Homicide

Killing someone you know or interact with is actually the most common form of murder. Social change has influenced this phenomenon. For example, the rate of homicide among married couples has declined significantly during the past two decades, a finding that can be attributed to the shift away from marriage in modern society. There are, however, significant gender differences in spousal homicide. Women are more likely to be murdered by a legally married spouse, while men are at greater risk for homicide from a common-law partner. Females are at a much greater risk of being murdered by a former spouse or intimate partner, with 28 percent of spousal homicides of females committed by a separated or divorced ex-partner.

Research indicates that females who kill their mates most often do so after suffering repeated violent attacks.[95] Perhaps the number of males killed by their partners has declined because alternatives to abusive relationships, such as women's shelters, are becoming more prevalent. Regions that provide greater social support for physically abused women and that have passed legislation to protect abuse victims also have lower rates of homicide committed by females.[96]

It is possible that men kill their spouses or partners because they fear losing control and power. Some people kill their mates because they find themselves involved in a love triangle.[97] Interestingly, women who kill out of jealousy aim their aggression at their partners; in contrast, men are more likely to kill their mates' suitors. Love triangles tend to become lethal when the offenders believe they have been lied to or betrayed. Lethal violence is more common when (1) the rival initiated the affair, (2) the killer knew the spouse was in a steady relationship outside the marriage, and (3) the killer was repeatedly lied to or betrayed.[98]

Stranger Homicides

Most stranger homicides occur in the aftermath of a common-law crime, such as break and enter or robbery. However, stranger homicides take various forms.

Photographs of missing or murdered women from British Columbia displayed at a Sisters in Spirit vigil, Vancouver, B.C., October 2009.

THE CANADIAN PRESS/Darryl Dyck

Thrill killing involves the deliberate slaying of a stranger as an act of daring or recklessness. For example, in April 2011 an aspiring filmmaker, Mark Twitchell, 31, was convicted of murdering and dismembering Johnny Altinger, 38, in an Edmonton garage in an apparent attempt to mimic the exploits of the television character *Dexter*. Twitchell lured the victim to the garage by posing as a woman on the Internet, and made arrangements to meet Altinger for a date at the address. A 42-page document titled "SKconfessions," found by police on Twitchell's computer hard drive, detailed the narrator's progression to becoming a serial killer, including the description of a successful attack on a man who is killed, dismembered, and dumped in a city sewer, and another attack on a man who escaped. Though Twitchell claimed at trial that the SKconfessions document was mainly a fictionalized account of his life, witnesses called by the Crown testified that most of the document was true, including the appearance and testimony in court of Gilles Tetreault, the man who escaped the attack described in the document. Twitchell was convicted of first-degree murder and sentenced to life in prison with no chance of parole for 25 years. Twitchell has appealed the conviction.[99]

Police reported that one in every five homicides in 2009 involved organized crime or street gangs. There were 124 victims of gang-related homicide, over half of which occurred in the ten largest cities in Canada. Toronto had the most gang-related homicides, with 30; followed by Vancouver (23) and Montreal (12). Most gang-related homicides involved young adults. The average age of those accused of committing a gang-related homicide was 23 years; the age of victims was 28 years.[100]

Serial Murder

thrill killing
Impulsive slaying of a stranger as an act of daring or recklessness.

serial killer
One who kills a series of victims, usually over an extended period of time.

mass murderer
One who kills many victims in a single, violent outburst.

According to a 2010 report by the Native Women's Association of Canada, there were at least 582 Aboriginal women in Canada who were currently missing or murdered. The report found that Aboriginal women were more likely than non-Aboriginal women to be murdered by a stranger. Most of the Aboriginal women who go missing or are murdered are under the age of 31, and more than two-thirds were living in cities. Almost half of the murders of Aboriginal women remain unsolved, compared to an 84 percent clearance rate for murders of non-Aboriginal women. In October 2010, the murdered body of Cynthia Maas, a 35-year-old Aboriginal woman, one of three recent disappearances of women in the Prince George area, was discovered in a wooded area off Highway 16, the infamous "Highway of Tears" in northern B.C. Over the years, dozens of mostly Aboriginal women, many of them sex-trade workers, have gone missing along Highway 16. Most of the cases remain unsolved, though police suspect that a serial killer or killers targeting sex trade workers may be travelling regularly along the highway.[101]

Most **serial killers** operate over an extended period of months and even years, and can be distinguished from **mass murderers**, who kill many victims in a single, violent outburst. While most serial killers are males, an estimated 10 to 15 percent of serial killers are women. (See Table 10.2.)

Frank Gunn/CP PHOTO

Serial killer Paul Bernardo was charged and convicted for three murders that occurred between December 1990 and April 1992. Like Bernardo, most serial killers are men.

TABLE 10.2

Explanation for Multiple Murder

Motivation for Multiple Murder	Type of Multiple Murder	
	Serial Murder	***Mass Murder***
Power	Inspired by sadistic fantasies, a man tortures and kills a series of strangers to satisfy his need for control and dominance.	A pseudo-commando, dressed in battle fatigues and armed with a semiautomatic, turns a shopping mall into a "war zone."
Revenge	Grossly mistreated as a child, a man avenges his past by slaying women who remind him of his mother.	After being fired from his job, a gunman returns to the worksite and opens fire on his former boss and co-workers.
Loyalty	A team of killers turn murder into a ritual for proving their dedication and commitment to one another.	A depressed husband/father kills his entire family and himself to remove them from their miserable existence to a better life in the hereafter.
Profit	A woman poisons to death a series of husbands in order to collect on their life insurance.	A band of armed robbers executes the employees of a store to eliminate all witnesses to their crime.
Terror	A profoundly paranoid man commits a series of bombings to warn the world of impending doom.	A group of antigovernment extremists blows up a train to send a political message.

Sources: James Alan Fox and Jack Levin, "Multiple Homicide: Patterns of Serial and Mass Murder," *Crime and Justice: An Annual Edition*, vol. 23, ed. Michael Tonry (Chicago: University of Chicago Press,1998): 407–455,Table A, p. 444; James Alan Fox and Jack Levin, *Overkill: Mass Murder and Serial Killing Exposed* (New York: Plenum,1994); James Alan Fox and Jack Levin, "A Psycho-Social Analysis of Mass Murder," in *Serial and Mass Murder: Theory, Policy, and Research*, ed. Thomas O'Reilly-Fleming and Steven Egger (Toronto: University of Toronto Press,1993); James Alan Fox and Jack Levin, "Serial Murder: A Survey," in *Serial and Mass Murder: Theory, Policy, and Research*, ed. Thomas O'Reilly-Fleming and Steven Egger (Toronto: University of Toronto Press,1993); Jack Levin and James Alan Fox, *Mass Murder* (New York: Plenum,1985).

Criminologists Belea Keeney and Kathleen Heide, who investigated the characteristics of a sample of 14 female serial killers, found some striking differences between the way male and female killers carried out their crimes.[102] Males were much more likely than females to use extreme violence and torture. Whereas males used a "hands-on" approach, including beating, bludgeoning, and strangling their victims, females were more likely to poison or smother their victims. Men tracked or stalked their victims, but women were more likely to lure victims to their death.

To date, law enforcement officials have been at a loss to control random killers who leave few clues, constantly move, and have little connection to their victims. Serial killers come from diverse backgrounds and catching them is often a matter of luck. In Canada, the RCMP coordinates the Violent Crime Linkage Analysis System (ViCLAS) for all police agencies in Canada; it links crimes to determine if they appear to be the work of a single culprit. In addition, the RCMP makes available the services of trained criminal profilers to all police agencies, and other large police services, such as the Ontario Provincial Police, have now added trained criminal profilers to their agencies.

assault level 1
Applying, attempting to apply, or threatening to apply force, with intent and without consent, against another person, or openly wearing a weapon (or an imitation) and accosting or impeding another person.

assault level 2
Assault with a weapon, threatening to use a weapon (or an imitation), or assault causing bodily harm.

assault level 3
Aggravated assault involving wounding, maiming, disfiguring, or endangering the life of another person.

LO5 Assault

The word *assault* is used to describe different kinds of incidents with different levels of seriousness. Contrary to popular belief, assault does not necessarily have to involve a physical act; however, it must involve more than words alone. That is, there must be a gesture or some other act that leads to harm or the threat of harm. According to the Criminal Code of Canada, an assault is the intentional application of force, directly or indirectly, to another person without that person's consent. There are three levels of assault. **Assault level 1**, or common assault, can include situations when there is intentional application of force without consent, when there is an attempt or threatening to apply force to another person, or openly wearing a weapon (or an imitation) and accosting or impeding another person. Assault with a weapon or causing bodily harm is known as **assault level 2**. It comprises assault with a weapon, threats to use a weapon (or an imitation), or assault causing bodily harm. Aggravated **assault level 3** involves wounding, maiming, disfiguring, or endangering the life of another person.[103]

In addition, each of the Level 1, 2, 3 categories of assault committed against a peace officer (including police officers, correctional officers, and others as defined in the Criminal Code), along with "**disarming a peace officer**," are outlined as distinct categories of crime in the Criminal Code.

The Nature and Patterns of Assault

The pattern of criminal assault is quite similar to that of homicide; one could say that the only difference between the two is that the victim survives.[104] Assaults may be common in our society simply because of common life stresses. Motorists who assault each other have become such a familiar occurrence that the term "road rage" has been coined. There have even been frequent incidents of violent assault among frustrated airline passengers who lose control while travelling. In 2004, the United Nations International Civil Aeronautical Organization met in Montreal to revise and call for the implementation of new laws to address the growing problem of "air rage" assaults by passengers on flight crews.[105]

In 2009, Canadian police reported 3619 aggravated assaults (Level 3), 53 481 assaults with a weapon or causing bodily harm (Level 2), and 181 570 "common assaults" (Level 1). Between 1998 and 2009, police-reported Level 3 assaults increased by 38 percent and Level 2 assaults by 43 percent; Level I assaults decreased slightly by 1.3 percent. Assaults against a police officer increased nearly 44 percent between 1998 and 2009.[106]

© Chris Ryan/Alamy

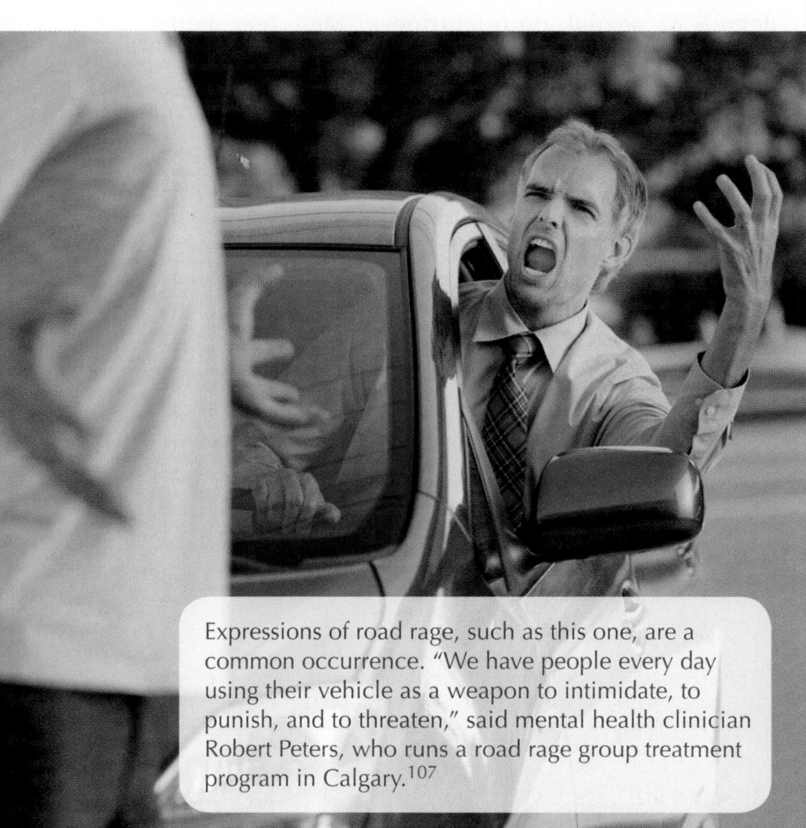

Expressions of road rage, such as this one, are a common occurrence. "We have people every day using their vehicle as a weapon to intimidate, to punish, and to threaten," said mental health clinician Robert Peters, who runs a road rage group treatment program in Calgary.[107]

Assault in the Home

Among the most frightening types of assault are violent attacks within the home. Criminologists recognize that intrafamily violence is an enduring social problem in our society.

disarming a peace officer
Taking or attempting to take a weapon without consent from a peace officer engaged in the execution of his or her duties.

child abuse
Physical, sexual, or emotional maltreatment or neglect that a child or adolescent may experience while in the care of someone he or she either trusts or depends on, such as a parent, sibling, other relative, caregiver, or guardian.

child neglect
Failing to provide what a child needs for his or her physical, psychological, or emotional development and well-being.

sexual abuse
The exploitation of a child through rape, incest, or molestation by a parent or other adult.

Child Abuse

One area of intrafamily violence that has received a great deal of media attention is **child abuse**.[108] This term describes any physical, sexual, or emotional trauma or neglect to a child for which no reasonable explanation, such as an accident or ordinary parental or disciplinary practices, can be found.[109] Abuse may take place anywhere and may occur, for example, within the child's home or that of someone known to the child.

Child abuse can result from physical beatings administered to a child by hands, feet, weapons, belts, sticks, burning, and so on. Another form of abuse results from **child neglect**—not providing a child with the care and shelter to which he or she is entitled. For example, neglect includes failing to provide a child with food, clothing, shelter, cleanliness, medical care, or protection from harm. Emotional neglect includes failing to provide a child with love, safety, and a sense of worth.

A third form is **sexual abuse**—the exploitation of a child through rape, incest, or molestation by a parent or other adult. Examples of child sexual abuse include fondling, inviting a child to touch or be touched sexually, intercourse, sodomy, exhibitionism, or involving a child in prostitution or pornography.

According to Statistics Canada, nearly 55 000 children and youth were the victims of a sexual offence or physical assault in 2009, 27 percent of which (14 833) were perpetrated by a family member. In six out of every ten cases in which a child or youth was victimized by a family member, the perpetrator was a parent. Of the 14 833 child and youth victims of family-related violence in 2009, the majority (67 percent) were physically assaulted, with most assaults (81 percent) categorized as Level 1. Child victims under the age of three were the most likely to be victimized by a parent.[110]

Why do parents physically assault their children? Such maltreatment is a highly complex problem with neither a single cause nor a readily available solution. It cuts across ethnic, religious, and socioeconomic lines. Abusive parents cannot be categorized by sex, age, or educational level; they come from all walks of life.[111]

Three factors have been linked to abuse and neglect. First, a pattern of family violence seems to be perpetuated from one generation to the next within families. Evidence indicates that many abused and neglected children grow into adolescence and adulthood with a tendency to engage in violent behaviour. The behaviour of abusive parents can often be traced to negative experiences in their own childhood—physical abuse, lack of love, emotional neglect, incest, and so on. These parents become unable to separate their own childhood traumas from their relationships with their children; they also often have unrealistic perceptions of the appropriate stages of childhood development.[112]

Second, blended families, in which children live with an unrelated adult such as a stepparent or another unrelated co-resident, have also been linked to abuse. For example, children who live with a mother's boyfriend are at much greater risk for abuse than children living with two genetic parents. According to sociologists Martin Daly and Margo Wilson, some stepparents do not have strong emotional ties to their nongenetic children, nor do they reap emotional benefits from the parent–child relationship.[113]

Third, parents may become abusive if they are isolated from friends, neighbours, or relatives who can help in times of crisis.[114] Many abusive and neglectful parents describe themselves as highly alienated from their families and lacking close relationships with people who could provide support in stressful situations. These people are unable to cope effectively with life crises such as divorce, financial problems, alcohol and drug abuse, or poor housing conditions, and excessive stress leads them to maltreat their children.[115]

Spouse Abuse

Spouse abuse has occurred throughout recorded history. Roman men had the legal right to beat their wives for attending public games without permission, drinking wine, or walking outdoors with their faces uncovered.[116] More serious transgressions, such as adultery, were punishable by death.[117] During the early Middle Ages, a husband was expected to beat his wife for "misbehaviours" and might himself be punished by neighbours if he failed to do so.[118] Between 1400 and 1900, there was little community objection to a man's using force against his wife as long as the assaults did not exceed certain limits, usually construed as death or disfigurement. By the mid-19th century, severe wife beating fell into disfavour, and accused wife beaters were subject to public ridicule. Yet the long history of husbands' domination of their wives has made physical coercion hard to control.

There is still some debate over the cause of spouse abuse. One view is that people who physically abuse their spouses are damaged individuals who suffer a variety of neuropsychological disorders and cognitive deficits; many suffered brain injuries in youth.[119] Psychologists Neil Jacobson and John Mordechai Gottman studied 200 couples and found that batterers tend to fall into one of two categories, which they call "Pit Bulls" and "Cobras."[120] Pit Bulls, whose emotions are quick to erupt, are driven by deep insecurity and a dependence on the wives and partners they abuse. They tend to become stalkers, unable to let go of relationships once they have ended. In contrast, Cobras coolly and methodically inflict pain and humiliation on their spouses. Many Cobras were physically or sexually abused in childhood and, as a consequence, see violence as an unavoidable part of life.

Some experts view spousal abuse from an evolutionary standpoint: Males are aggressive toward their mates because they have evolved with a high degree of sexual proprietariness. Men fear both losing a valued reproductive resource to a rival and making a paternal investment in a child that is not their own. Violence serves as a coercive social tool to dissuade interest in other males and to lash out in jealousy if threats are not taken seriously (that is, if the woman leaves). This explains why men often kill or injure their ex-wives; threats lose their effectiveness if they are merely a bluff.[121]

DID YOU KNOW?

Data from the 2009 GSS indicate that there is a greater risk of experiencing spousal violence for the following:

- Younger Canadians 25 to 34, especially women
- Persons living in common-law relationships
- Persons living in gay, lesbian, or bisexual relationships
- Aboriginal persons, especially women
- Persons living with a partner who is emotionally abusive
- Persons living with a partner who is very controlling, including one committing financial abuse

Source: Adapted from the Statistics Canada publication "Family Violence in Canada: A Statistical Profile," 2011, Minister of Industry, 2011, Catalogue no. 85-224-X.

This group of criminals, known as the "Boyd Gang," was notorious in Toronto in the early 1950s for exploits that included bank robbery and breaking out of jail. Public interest in the gangsters was high, and they became a popular story for the media.

Some personal attributes and characteristics of spouse abusers are listed in the previous Did You Know? box.[122]

Both women and men experience spousal abuse. GSS data from 2009 indicate that 6.4 percent of women (601 000) and 6 percent of men (585 000) reported experiencing at least one incident of violence by a current or previous partner during the preceding five-year period. Overall, this amounts to 6.2 percent of adult Canadians. Among Aboriginal peoples, the rate jumps to 10 percent.

There have been other notable patterns related to the nature and severity of violence experienced by victims. Women, for example, experienced more severe forms of violence, and were twice as likely as men to report being physically injured (42 percent versus 18 percent), including having broken bones (just under 10 percent). Male victims were more likely to report suffering cuts, scratches, and burns (53 percent, versus 30 percent of female victims). Bruising was the most common injury for both female (95 percent) and male victims (75 percent), and 13 percent of victims reported having been hospitalized due to spousal violence.

Women in common-law relationships seem to be at much greater risk of domestic violence than legally married or single women. A possible cause may be that domestic relationships among unmarried people tend to be less stable and more short lived.[123] Nonetheless, the rate of domestic violence appears to be declining among both married couples and single cohabitants. One reason is that females now find it easier to get high-paying jobs, to obtain legal divorces, and to receive domestic violence counselling. Financial independence and emotional support allow women to leave a bad relationship before interspousal conflict leads to violence and death. And even if partners stay together in troubled relationships, newly emerging social interventions empower women to end male partner violence.[124]

LO6 Robbery

The common-law definition of **robbery** is "taking or attempting to take anything of value from the care, custody or control of a person or persons by force or threat of force or violence and/or by putting the victim in fear."[125] A robbery is considered a violent crime because it involves the use of force to obtain money or goods. Robbery is punished severely because the victim's life is put in jeopardy. In fact, the severity of punishment is based on the amount of force used during the crime, not the value of the items taken.

Robberies accounted for just over 7 percent of violent crimes in 2009. The rate of robberies has declined by 2 percent since 1998 and has generally been dropping since 1991. The use of firearms during the commission of a robbery has declined significantly in the last 20 years. In 2006, some 14 percent of all robberies were committed with a firearm, compared with 25 percent in 1988 and 37 percent in 1978.

Robberies are much more likely than all other violent crimes to involve youths aged 12 to 17. In 2008, 35 percent of all those charged with robbery were youths, although they accounted for only 12 percent of assaults and 12 percent of homicides.[126]

Robbery rates are almost three times higher in the United States than in Canada. Further, a larger proportion of robberies in the United States involve firearms. Firearm robbery rates in the United States are four times higher than in Canada. In the United States

robbery
Taking or attempting to take something of value by force or threat of force and/or by putting the victim in fear.

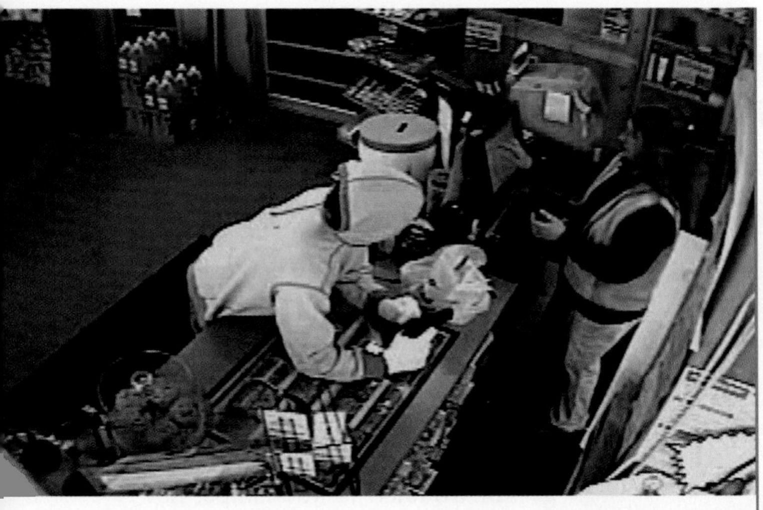
AP Photo

the average firearm robbery rate is 60 per 100 000 population, compared to 14 per 100 000 population in Canada. Both the American and Canadian robbery rates have declined in recent years.[127]

Robbery is most often a street crime; that is, fewer robberies occur in the home than in public places, such as parks, streets, and alleys. The U.S. Bureau of Justice Statistics analyzed more than 14 million robbery victimizations to provide a more complete picture of the nature and extent of robbery. It found that about two-thirds of victims had property stolen, one-third were injured in the crime, and one-quarter suffered both personal injury and property loss.[128]

While most robberies involve strangers, about one-third involve acquaintances. Richard Felson and his associates found that when robbers target someone they know, they choose victims who are least likely to call police. Targets may be people with whom the robber has a pre-existing grievance, so that the robbery is a form of "payback." Robbers may also have "inside information" that the victims are carrying valuables, making them a hard target to resist.[129]

Attempts have been made to classify and explain the nature and dynamics of robbery. One approach is to characterize robberies (see Table 10.3); another is to characterize types of robbers based on their specialties (see Table 10.4).

As these typologies indicate, the typical armed robber is unlikely to be a professional who carefully studies targets while planning a crime. Convenience stores, gas stations, and people walking along the street are much more likely robbery targets than banks or other highly secure environments. Robbers seem to be diverted by modest defensive measures, such as having more than one clerk in a store or locating stores in strip malls; they are more likely to try an isolated store.[130]

TABLE 10.3

Types of Robberies

Robbery of persons who, as part of their employment, are in charge of money or goods.	This category includes robberies in jewellery stores, banks, offices, and other places in which money changes hands.
Robbery in an open area.	These robberies include street muggings, purse snatchings, and other attacks. Street robberies are the most common type, especially in urban areas, where this type of robbery constitutes about 60 percent of reported totals. Street robbery is most closely associated with mugging or yoking, which refers to grabbing victims from behind and threatening them with a weapon. Street muggers often target unsavoury characters such as drug dealers or pimps who carry large amounts of cash, because these victims would find it awkward to report the crime to the police. Most commit their robberies within a short distance of their homes.
Commercial robbery.	This type of robbery occurs in businesses ranging from banks to liquor stores. Banks are among the most difficult targets to rob, usually because they have more personnel and a higher level of security.
Robbery on private premises.	In Canada there were 865 residential robberies recorded, a rate of 5 per 100 000 population.
Robbery after a short, preliminary association.	This type of robbery comes after a chance meeting—in a bar, at a party, or after a sexual encounter.
Robbery after a longer association between the victim and offender.	An example of this type of robbery would be an intimate acquaintance robbing his paramour and then fleeing the jurisdiction.
Carjacking.	Carjacking is a completed or attempted theft of a motor vehicle by force or threat of force. On average, there are about 49 000 completed or attempted carjackings in the United States each year. In Canada, newspaper accounts demonstrate an increasing number of carjackings in large Canadian cities.

Sources: Patsy Klaus, *Carjackings in the United States*, 1992–96 (Washington, DC: Bureau of Justice Statistics, 1999); Peter J. van Koppen and Robert Jansen, "The Road to the Robbery: Travel Patterns in Commercial Robberies," *British Journal of Criminology* 38 (1998): 230–247; F. H. McClintock and Evelyn Gibson, *Robbery in London* (London: Macmillan, 1961), p. 15; Orest Fedorowycz, *Breaking and Entering in Canada*—2002, Canadian Centre for Justice Statistics, Statistics Canada, Cat. 85-002-XPE, vol. 24, no. 5; Marnie Wallace, *Motor Vehicle Theft in Canada*—2001, Statistics Canada, Canadian Centre for Justice Statistics, Cat. 85-002-XPE vol. 23, no. 1, p. 5.

TABLE 10.4

Types of Robbers

Professional robbers	have a long-term commitment to crime as a source of livelihood. This type of robber plans and organizes crimes prior to committing them and seeks money to support a hedonistic lifestyle. Some professionals are exclusively robbers, whereas others engage in additional types of crimes. Professionals are committed to robbing because it is direct, fast, and profitable. They hold no other steady job and plan three or four "big scores" a year to support themselves. Planning and skill are the trademarks of professional robbers, who usually operate in groups with assigned roles. Professionals usually steal large amounts from commercial establishments. After a score, they may stop for a few weeks until "things cool off."
Opportunist robbers	steal to obtain small amounts of money when an accessible target presents itself. They are not committed to robbery but will steal from cab drivers, drunks, the elderly, and other vulnerable persons if they need some extra spending money. Opportunists are usually young minority-group members who do not plan their crimes. Although they operate within the milieu of the juvenile gang, they are seldom organized and spend little time discussing weapon use, getaway plans, or other strategies.
Addict robbers	steal to support their drug habits. They have a low commitment to robbery because of its danger but a high commitment to theft because it supplies needed funds. The addict is less likely to plan crime or use weapons than the professional robber but is more cautious than the opportunist. Addicts choose targets that present minimal risk; however, when desperate for funds, they are sometimes careless in selecting the victim and executing the crime. They rarely think in terms of the big score; they just want enough money to get their next fix.
Alcoholic robbers	steal for reasons related to their excessive consumption of alcohol. Alcoholic robbers steal (1) when, in a disoriented state, they attempt to get some money to buy liquor or (2) when their condition makes them unemployable and they need funds. Alcoholic robbers have no real commitment to robbery as a way of life. They plan their crimes randomly and give little thought to their victim, circumstance, or escape. For that reason, they are the most likely to be caught.

Source: *Robbery and the Criminal Justice System* by John Conklin, p. 1-80. © 1972 by J.B. Lippincott. Reprinted by permission.

© Allstar Picture Library/Alamy

In 2009, Canadian actress Carly Pope was injured in a Vancouver carjacking.

While most robbers may be opportunistic rather than professional, the patterns of robbery suggest that it is not merely a random act committed by an alcoholic or drug abuser. Though most crime rates are higher in the summer, robberies seem to peak during the winter months. One reason may be that the cold weather allows for greater disguise. Another is that robbers may be attracted to the large amounts of cash people and merchants carry during the holiday shopping season.[131] Robbers may also be more active during the winter because the days are shorter, affording them greater concealment in the dark.

CONNECTIONS

Chapter 4 discussed the rationality of street robbery. Even when robbers are stealing to support a drug habit, their acts do not seem haphazard or irrational. Only the most inebriated might fail to take precautions. The fact that robbery is gender-specific is also evidence that robbers are rational decision makers.

LO7 Emerging Forms of Violent Crime

Assault, sexual assault, robbery, and murder are traditional forms of interpersonal violence. As more data become available, criminologists have recognized relatively new subcategories within these crime types, such as serial murder and date rape. Additional categories of interpersonal violence are now receiving attention in criminological literature; the following

stalking
An offence of criminal harassment, which is behaviour that causes another person to fear for his or her safety or for another person's safety: for example, repeatedly following a person, repeatedly communicating with a person, or watching a person's workplace or home.

sections describe some of these newer forms of violent crime.

Stalking

In Wes Craven's popular movies *Scream* 1–3, the heroine Sydney (played by Neve Campbell) is stalked by a mysterious adversary who scares her half to death while killing off most of her peer group. While obviously extreme even by Hollywood standards, the *Scream* movies focus on a newly recognized form of long-term and repeat victimization: **stalking.**[132]

Stalking is defined in the Criminal Code under a general heading of "Criminal Harassment," which prohibits the following conduct:

> (a) repeatedly following from place to place the other person or anyone known to them;
> (b) repeatedly communicating with, either directly or indirectly, the other person or anyone known to them;
> (c) besetting or watching the dwelling-house, or place where the other person, or anyone known to them, resides, works, carries on business or happens to be; or
> (d) engaging in threatening conduct directed at the other person or any member of their family.[133]

Prior to 1993, stalking was not against the law in Canada. The Criminal Code was amended to include section 264, which deals with criminal harassment. In it are sections prohibiting trespassing on another's property at night, uttering threats, indecent or harassing phone calls, intimidation, and mischief to another person's property. It is possible to get a restraining order or a peace bond against a person to prevent contact.

A key requirement of section 264 of the Criminal Code is that the "following" or "communicating" be "repeated," which means that it must happen more than once for it to be criminal harassment. However, if the behaviour is severe enough and is threatening, one incident may be sufficient to get a conviction. Some facts about stalking include the following:

- In 2009 there were 20 007 police-reported criminal harassment (stalking) incidents in Canada, representing about 5 percent of all violent crimes.[134] Nearly 70 percent of stalking incidents occur at the victim's home.[135]
- Seventy-six percent of the stalking victims in Canada were women. One-half of the female victims were criminally harassed (stalked) by a current or former intimate partner.[136]
- Eighty-six percent of persons accused of stalking in these cases were male.[137]
- Male victims of stalking are more likely (37 percent) to be criminally harassed by a casual acquaintance.[138]

Home Invasions

The term "home invasion" is used to describe a robbery or break and enter of a private residence where someone uses force to enter another's home, and uses or threatens to use violence against the occupants. There is no specific section of the Criminal Code that deals with home invasions. However, in 2002 the Criminal Code was amended (Bill C-15A) to make home invasion an aggravating circumstance that a judge must take into consideration at the time of sentencing. The amendment makes it clear that home invasion is viewed as a serious crime that should be met with significant penalties. Under Part IX, "Offences Against Rights of Property—Breaking and Entering," it states:

> Aggravating circumstance—home invasion
> 348.1. If a person is convicted of an offence under any of subsection 279(2) or sections 343, 346 and 348 in relation to a dwelling-house, the court imposing the sentence on the person shall consider as an aggravating circumstance the fact that the dwelling-house was occupied at the time of the commission of the offence and that the person, in committing the offence,
> (a) knew that or was reckless as to whether the dwelling-house was occupied; and
> (b) used violence or threats of violence to a person or property.[139]

Because there is currently no specific offence in the Criminal Code called "home invasion," the police do not record it in the UCR Survey. According to the Canadian Centre for Justice Statistics, examples of incidents that could be considered as "home invasions" include the following:

- A homeowner returns home unexpectedly while a break and enter is in progress and there is a confrontation.
- A person breaks into a home believing that no one is home and someone is, or believing that the occupants are all asleep and they wake up, and there is confrontation.
- Someone forcibly enters the home of a person known to him or her to "settle a score."[140]
- Since 1998, the rate of "home invasions" of this sort has increased by 24 percent, to a total of 865 in Canada in 2002, or 5 per 100 000 population.[141]

Three general categories of home invasions have been identified: residential robberies, those committed by criminals against other criminals, and those targeting the elderly. Home invasions account for a very small proportion of robberies, but they have prompted public concern and fear because of the unique predatory nature of these crimes and the often-devastating psychological effect that they have on their victims.[142]

Hate Crimes

A **hate crime** is a violent act directed toward a particular person or group because of a discernible

DID YOU KNOW?

- Hate crime are violent acts against targets selected because of their religion, race, ethnic background, status, or sexual orientation.
- Some hate criminals are thrill seekers; others are motivated by hatred of outsiders; still others believe they are on a mission.
- Workplace violence has become commonplace. It is believed to be related to a number of factors, including job stress and insensitive management style.
- Political crimes are committed when people believe that violence is the only means available to produce political change.
- Revolutionary terrorists seek to overthrow those in power; political terrorists oppose government policies; nationalist terrorists are minority-group members who want to carve out a homeland; cause-based terrorists use violence to address their grievances; environmental terrorists aim at frightening off developers; state-sponsored terrorism is aimed at political dissenters or minority groups.

colour, race, religion, or ethnic origin. References to "hate" can be found in sections 318 and 319 of the Criminal Code of Canada. Section 318 describes the criminal act of "advocating genocide" by supporting or arguing for the killing of members of an "identifiable group"—persons distinguished by their colour, race, religion, or ethnic origin. The intention or motivation would be the destruction of members of the targeted group. Any person who promotes genocide is guilty of an indictable offence, and liable to imprisonment for a term not exceeding five years. To obtain a conviction, there must be factual proof that it occurred, but also that it was a deliberate act with intent and motivation. Amendments to the Criminal Code, made under the Anti-Terrorism Act in December 2001, identify offences in relation to Internet hate crimes.

Section 319(1) refers to the crime of "publicly inciting hatred," which involves four elements:

- Communicating (by telephone, broadcasting, or other audible or visible means) statements (spoken, written, or recorded) or gestures, and signs or other visible representations.
- Doing so in a public place (one to which the public has access by right or invitation).
- Inciting hatred against an identifiable group.
- Doing so in such a way that there will likely be a breach of the peace.

All the above elements must be proven for a court to find an accused guilty of either an indictable offence, for which the punishment is imprisonment for a term not exceeding two years; or an offence punishable on summary conviction. Section 320 permits the seizure and forfeiture of physical hate propaganda material kept on any premises for distribution or sale. Section 320.1 was added under the Anti-Terrorism Bill in 2001; it allows hate propaganda to be deleted from computer systems and websites.

hate crime
A violent act directed toward a particular person or group because of a discernible colour, race, religion, or ethnic origin.

If hate, bias, or prejudice was involved while committing other offences such as assault, damage to property, threatening, or harassment, the courts may view them as aggravating circumstances, which could result in a more severe punishment.

The Roots of Hate

Why do people commit hate crimes? Research by sociologist Jack McDevitt shows that hate crimes are generally spontaneous incidents motivated by the victims' walking, driving, shopping, or socializing in an area in which their attackers believe they "do not belong."[143] Other factors that motivate bias attacks include a victim's moving into an ethnically distinct neighbourhood or dating a member of a different race or ethnic group. Although hate crimes are often unplanned, McDevitt finds that most of these crimes are serious incidents that involve assaults and robberies.[144] In their book *Hate Crimes*, McDevitt and Jack Levin note that hate crimes are typically one of three types that reflect different motives:

1. *Thrill-seeking hate crimes.* In the same way some kids like to get together to shoot hoops, hate-mongers join forces to have fun by assaulting minorities or destroying property. Inflicting pain on others gives them a sadistic thrill.
2. *Reactive hate crimes.* Perpetrators of these crimes rationalize their behaviour as a defensive stand taken against outsiders who they believe are threatening their community or way of life. A gang of teens that attacks a new family in the neighbourhood because they are the "wrong" race is committing a reactive hate crime.
3. *Mission hate crimes.* Some disturbed individuals see it as their duty to rid the world of evil. Those on a "mission"—skinheads, the Ku Klux Klan (KKK), white supremacist groups—may seek to eliminate people who threaten their religious beliefs because they are members of a different faith or threaten "racial purity" because they are of a different race.[145]

Extent of Hate Crime

Canadian police services reported a total of 892 hate crime incidents in 2006. Sixty-one percent were motivated by race or ethnicity, 27 percent were motivated by religion, and sexual orientation was the motivation in about 10 percent of the incidents [146] (see Figure 10.2). Half of all racially motivated hate crimes targeted blacks, and two-thirds of religious-based hate crimes targeted members of the Jewish

FIGURE 10.2

Hate Crime in Canada[1]

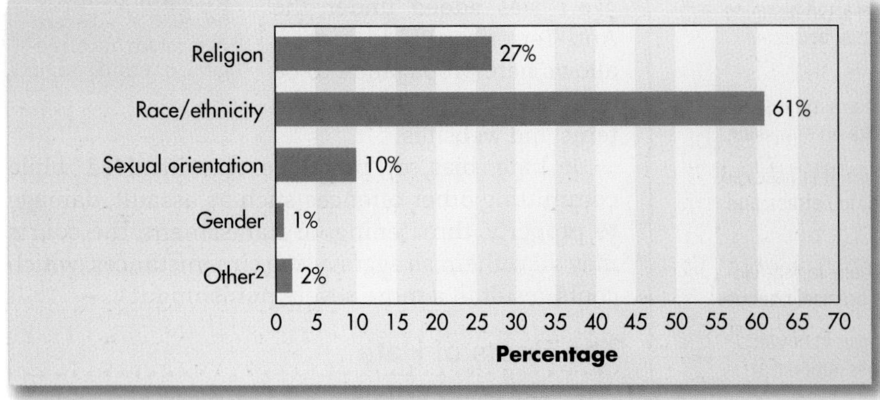

Notes:

1. Police-reported hate crime.
2. Includes hate crimes motivated by language, disability, or other similar factors, such as profession or political beliefs.

Source: Canadian Centre for Justice Statistics Profile Series, *Hate Crime in Canada 2006*, Mia Dauvergne, Katie Scrim and Shannon Brennan, Catalogue no. 85F0033M—No. 17.

faith. Young people are more likely to be involved in hate crime incidents, both as victims and perpetrators. Males are more likely to be victims of hate crimes (1.8 per 100 000) compared to females (0.7 per 100 000).[147]

The most common types of hate crimes included mischief or vandalism (29 percent), assault (25 percent), uttering threats (20 percent), and spreading hate propaganda (13 percent). Those targeted because of their sexual orientation were more likely than other groups to suffer violent crimes, including assault and uttering threats. Identifying a suspect is often difficult, particularly in cases of graffiti, other acts of vandalism, or incidents involving anonymous hate messages.[148]

Just over one-half of the 892 hate crime incidents reported in this survey were property offences, the majority of which (two-thirds) were mischief. Thirty-seven percent were offences against the person, most commonly assaults Level 1. There was one homicide and two attempted hate crime–related murders reported in 2006.[149] The remaining hate crime incidents were classified as "other violations," including offences against a person's reputation and criminal harassment. According to the 2004 General Social Survey, about 40 percent of victims of hate crimes reported them to the police.

Workplace Violence

On April 6, 1999, a former employee of OC Transpo in Ottawa stunned the country when he went on a shooting rampage that left four employees dead, before turning the gun on himself. The subsequent coroner's inquest identified the killer as being a victim of workplace harassment. Among the inquest recommendations was that the definition of workplace violence include both physical and psychological violence such as bullying, mobbing, teasing, ridicule, or any other act or words that could psychologically hurt or isolate a person in the workplace. The jury also recommended that the federal and provincial governments enact legislation to prevent workplace violence and that employers develop policies to address violence and harassment.

According to the 2004 GSS, 17 percent of all self-reported incidents of violent victimization occurred in the workplace, with men and women equally likely to report being victimized. People who work in the health-care or social services employment sectors are at highest risk, with 33 percent of workplace violence taking place there. Fourteen percent of workplace violence incidents took place in the hotel and food services sector, and 11 percent in educational services. Most incidents took place inside a building such as a store, office, hospital, or school, and in two-thirds of cases the perpetrator was known to the victim.[150]

Most workplace violent incidents are physical assaults (71 percent), followed by sexual assault (24 percent). Alcohol or drugs were believed to be involved in almost half of the incidents (46 percent), and males were identified as the perpetrator in more than 90 percent of the incidents.

Who engages in workplace violence? The typical offender is a middle-aged white male who faces termination in a worsening economy. The fear of economic ruin is especially strong in many traditional workplaces, where long-term employees fear job loss because of automation and reorganization. Repeated incidents have generated the term *going postal* as a synonym for a violent workplace incident. On September 1, 2000, the U.S. Postal Service, stung by this bad publicity, was forced to issue a statement claiming that there is far less on-the-job homicide in the postal service than at other workplaces, and that the term *going postal* is unjustified and unfair.[151]

A number of factors precipitate workplace violence. One may simply be the conflict caused by economic restructuring. As corporations cut their staffs due to recent trends such as office automation and company buyouts, long-term employees who had never thought of themselves losing a job are suddenly unemployed. There is often a correlation between sudden, unexpected layoffs and violent reactions.[152] Another trigger may be leadership styles. Some companies have authoritarian management styles that demand performance, above all else, from employees. Unsympathetic, unsupportive managers may help trigger workplace violence.

Not all workplace violence is triggered by management-induced injustice. In some incidents, co-workers have been killed because they refused romantic relationships with the assailants or reported them for sexual harassment. Others have been killed because they got a job the assailant coveted. Irate clients and customers have also killed because of poor service or perceived slights. For example, in one Los Angeles incident, a former patient shot and critically wounded three doctors because his demands for painkillers had gone unheeded.[153]

There is a variety of responses to workplace provocations. Some people take out their anger and aggression by attacking their supervisors in an effort to punish the company that dismissed them; this is a form of murder by proxy.[154] Disgruntled employees may also attack family members or friends, misdirecting the rage and frustration caused by their work situation. Others are content with sabotaging company equipment; computer data banks are particularly vulnerable to tampering. The aggrieved party may do nothing to rectify the situation; this inaction is referred to as sufferance. Over time, the unresolved conflict may be compounded by other events that cause an eventual eruption.

A number of efforts have been made to control workplace violence. One approach is to use third parties to mediate disputes before they escalate into violence. Another idea involves a human resources approach, with aggressive job retraining and extended medical coverage after layoffs. It is also important to hold objective, fair hearings to thwart unfair or biased terminations. Perhaps rigorous screening tests can help identify violence-prone workers so that they can be given anger management training.

LO8 Political Violence

In addition to interpersonal violence and street crime, another category of violence is politically motivated acts, including terrorism. Political crime has been with us throughout history. It is virtually impossible to find a society without political criminals, who have been described as "those craftsmen of dreams who possess a gigantic reservoir of creative energy as well as destructive force."[155]

terrorism
The illegal use of force against innocent people to achieve a political objective.

Terrorism

One aspect of political violence that greatly concerns criminologists is **terrorism**.[156] Because of its complexity, an all-encompassing definition of terrorism is difficult to formulate. However, most experts agree that it generally involves the illegal use of force against innocent people to achieve a political objective.[157]

One U.S. commission defined terrorism as "a tactic or technique by means of which a violent act or the threat thereof is used for the prime purpose of creating overwhelming fear for coercive purposes."[158] In Canada, "terrorism" is defined in law by section 83.01 of the Criminal Code. Terrorism is generally defined as a type of political crime that emphasizes violence as a mechanism to promote change. Whereas some political criminals may demonstrate, counterfeit, sell secrets, or spy, terrorists systematically murder and destroy or threaten such violence to terrorize individuals, groups, communities, or governments into conceding to the terrorists' political demands.[159] However, it may be erroneous to equate terrorism with political goals because not all terrorist actions are aimed at political change; some terrorists may try to bring about economic or social reform, for example, by attacking women wearing fur coats or sabotaging property during a labour dispute. Terrorism must also be distinguished from conventional warfare because it requires secrecy and clandestine operations to exert social control over large populations.[160]

Forms of Terrorism

Today the term *terrorism* describes many different behaviours and goals. Some of the more common forms are briefly described here.[161]

Revolutionary Terrorists

Revolutionary terrorists use violence against a regime that they consider to have unjustly taken control of their land either by force or coercion. In the Middle East, terrorist activities were first linked to Jewish groups such as the Irgun and Stern Gang, which were successful in driving the British out of Palestine in the 1940s leading to the creation of Israel, and today to Muslim groups such as Hamas and Hezbollah, which seek to do the same to Israel.

Political Terrorists

Political terrorism is directed at people or institutions who oppose the terrorists' political ideology.

North American political terrorists tend to be heavily armed groups organized around themes such as white supremacy, militant tax resistance, and religious revisionism. Identified groups have included the Aryan Nation, the Posse Comitatus, and the Ku Klux Klan.

Recently, right-wing political extremists have engaged in a pattern of uncoordinated violence motivated by hate, rage, and the inability of more coordinated groups to either bring down the U.S. government or gain public support.[162] Although unlikely to topple the government, these individualistic acts of terror are difficult to predict or control. On April 19, 1995, 168 people were killed during the Oklahoma City bombing, and on September 11, 2001, over 3000 people perished in the World Trade Center towers in New York City and the Pentagon in Washington, D.C. These were the most extreme examples of political terrorism in North America.

Nationalist Terrorism

Nationalist terrorism promotes the interests of a minority ethnic or religious group that believes it has been persecuted under majority rule in an effort to secure a homeland within the country. In Spain, Basque terrorists have assassinated Spanish officials in order to convince the government to create a separate Basque homeland in northern Spain. In December 2006, Pakistani political leader Benazir Bhutto was assassinated in front of thousands of supporters while attending a rally in a public park. Bhutto died in an explosion that also killed those responsible for detonating the bomb. It is believed that Islamist terrorists, or perhaps even Pakistan's own secret intelligence service, may have been behind the assassination, with the goal of destabilizing the Pakistan People's Party (PPP) that Bhutto led, and that was poised to return the popular leader to power.[163]

Cause-Based Terrorism

When the U.S. embassies in Kenya and Tanzania were bombed in 1998, killing more than 250 people, Osama bin Laden's Al Qaeda movement was quickly identified as the culprit. In a 1997 interview with CNN, bin Laden said his *jihad*, or holy war, against the United States was started because American forces were still operating in Saudi Arabia. He demanded that the United States end its "aggressive intervention against Muslims in the whole world."[164] On September 11, 2001, bin Laden continued the jihad by bringing the holy war onto American soil, with the attacks on the World Trade Center and the Pentagon. Thus began a ten-year-long search by U.S. authorities for the terrorist, which ended in the early morning hours of Sunday, May 1, 2011, when U.S. Navy Seals shot and killed bin Laden at a residential compound in Pakistan, where he had been living in hiding for some months.

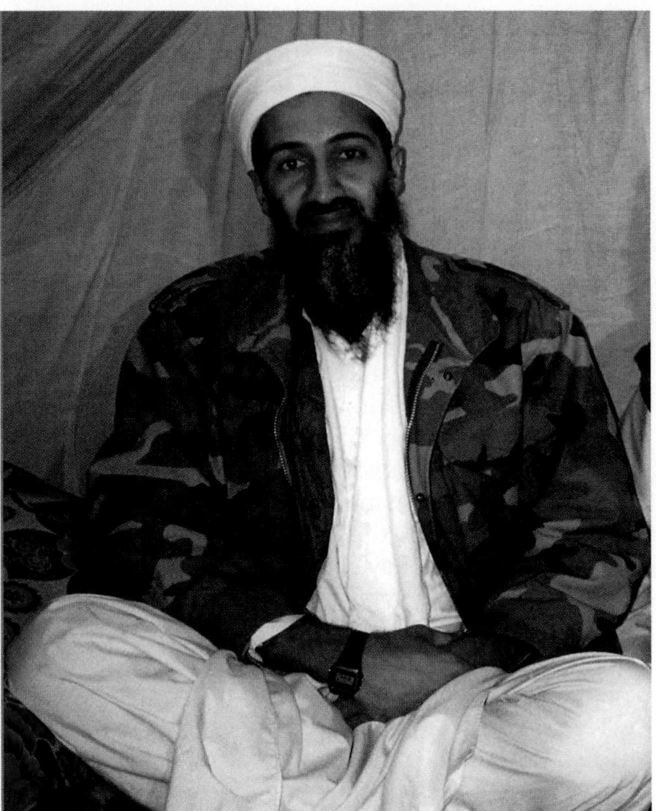
AP Photo

After a ten-year-long search for the terrorist leader, U.S. Navy Seals shot and killed Osama bin Laden at a residential compound in Pakistan.

Osama bin Laden's brand of terrorist activity is one of many conducted by groups that espouse a particular social or religious cause and use violence to address their grievances.[165] For example, anti-abortion groups have demonstrated at abortion clinics, and some members have attacked clients, bombed offices, and killed doctors who perform abortions. On May 31, 2009, Dr. George Tiller was shot and killed while serving as an usher for Sunday services at the Reformation Lutheran Church in Wichita, Kansas, one of a growing number of abortion providers believed to be the victims of terrorists who ironically claim to be "pro-life."[166]

Environmental Terrorism

In January 2010, Alberta farmer and eco-activist Wiebo Ludwig was arrested by RCMP officers at his home in connection with a rash of recent bombings of EnCana pipelines in northeastern B.C. near the Alberta border. Ludwig had been convicted in 2000 of five offences related to the blowing up and vandalizing of gas and oil wells near his Alberta farm. Ludwig claimed that the "sour gas" produced by the wells was responsible for a host of health problems among members of his family, including miscarriages and the stillbirth of one of his children. Despite his convictions, a 28-month jail sentence and intensive, ongoing investigations and periodic arrests by the RCMP, the Alberta farmer and former Christian Reform minister remains unapologetic, pointing out that, while he admits no involvement in any of the incidents for which he has been accused, all conventional forms of protest aimed at forcing the oil and gas well companies to close or clean up the polluting gases escaping from their wells have failed. According to the *National Post*, "the Ludwig name has become synonymous with alleged environmental extremism."[167] Following a brief investigation, the RCMP released Mr. Ludwig in January 2010 for lack of evidence.

State-Sponsored Terrorism

State-sponsored terrorism occurs when a repressive governmental regime forces its citizens into obedience, oppresses minorities, and stifles political dissent.[168]

Much of what we know about state-sponsored terrorism comes from the efforts of human rights groups. London-based Amnesty International maintains that tens of thousands of people continue to become victims of security operations that result in disappearances and executions.[169] Political prisoners are now being tortured in about 100 countries; people have disappeared or are being held in secret detention in about 20; and government-sponsored death squads have been operating in more than 35. Countries known for encouraging violent control of dissidents include Brazil, Colombia, Guatemala, Honduras, Peru, Sudan, Libya, and, most notably, Iraq, where the United States waged an all-out war against Saddam Hussein's state-sponsored terrorism. When Tupac Amaru rebels seized and held hostages at the Japanese ambassador's villa in Peru on December 17, 1996, Amnesty International charged that the action came in response to a decade-long campaign of human rights violations by national security forces and extensive abuses against opposition groups.[170]

genocide
The attempt by a government to wipe out a minority group within its jurisdiction.

The most extreme form of state-sponsored terrorism occurs when a government seeks to wipe out a minority group within its jurisdiction. This atrocity is referred to as **genocide**. The World War II Holocaust is the most extreme example of genocide to date, but more recent occurrences have taken place in Cambodia, Rwanda, Sudan, the Democratic Republic of the Congo, Bosnia, and Somalia, among others.

Responses to Terrorism

Governments have tried numerous responses to terrorism. The attacks on September 11, 2001, changed these responses from being largely passive to more active steps. Across the world, governments have implemented tough new security measures at border checkpoints and in airports and at seaports. In Canada, the Anti-Terrorism Act was implemented in 2001 to give the government more powers to investigate and arrest suspected terrorists and sympathizers providing support and financial resources to terrorist groups, along with other measures designed to strengthen Canada's border security. In the United States, the Department of Homeland Security was created to coordinate all efforts to protect citizens at home in the United States. In addition, the U.S. government went to war with Iraq to end Saddam Hussein's campaign of state-sponsored terrorism. Law enforcement agencies have infiltrated terrorist groups and turned members over to police.[171] Rewards are often offered for information leading to the arrest of terrorists. "Democratic" elections have been held to discredit terrorists' complaints that the state is oppressive. Counterterrorism laws have increased penalties and decreased political rights afforded known terrorists.

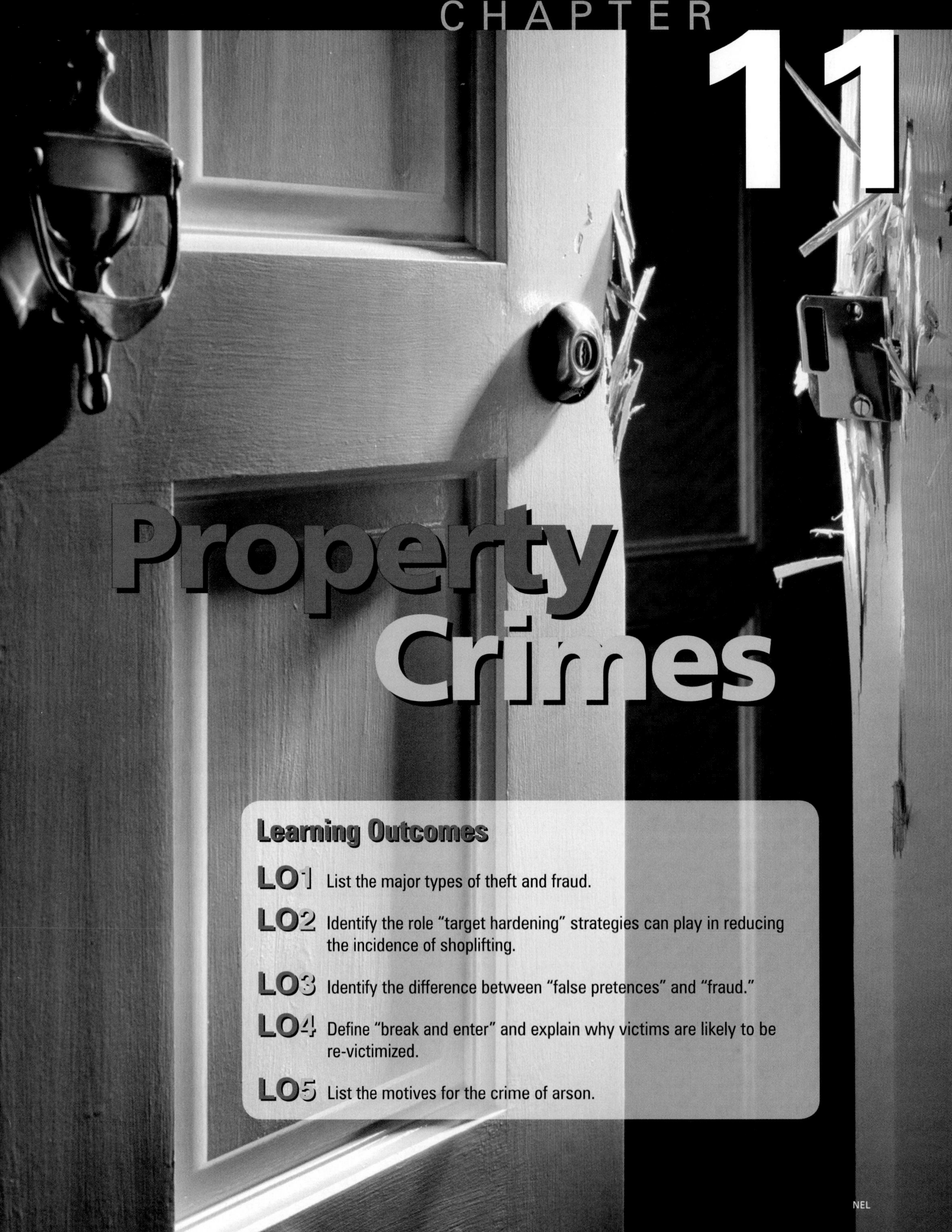

CHAPTER 11

Property Crimes

Learning Outcomes

LO1 List the major types of theft and fraud.

LO2 Identify the role "target hardening" strategies can play in reducing the incidence of shoplifting.

LO3 Identify the difference between "false pretences" and "fraud."

LO4 Define "break and enter" and explain why victims are likely to be re-victimized.

LO5 List the motives for the crime of arson.

As a group, economic crimes can be defined as acts that violate criminal law and are designed to bring financial reward to an offender. The range and scope of Canadian criminal activity motivated by financial gain are tremendous. Self-report studies show that property crime is widespread among the young in every social class. National surveys of criminal behaviour indicate that almost 1.1 million personal and household thefts occur annually; corporate and other white-collar crimes are accepted as commonplace; and political scandals, ranging from the convictions of 14 Conservative Saskatchewan MPPs in the 1980s for fraud, to the recent resignation of Canadian Senator Raymond Lavigne, who was convicted of defrauding the government and breach of trust, indicate that even high government officials may be suspected of criminal acts.

This chapter is the first of two that review the nature and extent of economic crime in Canada. It begins with some background information on the history and nature of theft as a crime. It then discusses theft and related offences, including shoplifting, credit card theft, motor vehicle theft, fraud, confidence games, and embezzlement. Next the discussion turns to a more serious form of theft, "burglary" or break and enter, which involves forcible entry into a person's home or workplace for the purpose of theft. Finally, the crime of arson is discussed briefly. The next chapter is devoted to white-collar crimes and economic crimes that involve criminal organizations.

DID YOU KNOW?

- Theft offences have been common throughout recorded history.
- During the Middle Ages, poachers stole game, smugglers avoided taxes, and thieves worked as pickpockets and forgers.
- Occasional thieves are opportunistic amateurs who steal because of situational inducements.
- Professional thieves learn their trade and develop skills that help them avoid capture.

History of Theft

Theft is not unique to modern times; the theft of personal property has been known throughout recorded history. The Crusades of the 11th century inspired peasants and downtrodden noblemen to leave the shelter of their estates to prey upon passing pilgrims.[1] Crusaders felt it within their rights to appropriate the possessions of any infidels—Greeks, Jews, or Muslims—they happened to encounter during their travels. By the 13th century, returning pilgrims, not content to live as serfs on feudal estates, gathered in the forests of England and the European continent to poach game that was the rightful property of their lord or king and, when possible, to steal from passing strangers. By the 14th century, many such highwaymen and poachers were full-time livestock thieves, stealing great numbers of cattle and sheep.[2]

The 15th and 16th centuries brought hostilities between England and France in the Hundred Years' War. Foreign mercenary troops fighting for both sides roamed the countryside; loot and pillage were viewed as a rightful part of their pay. As cities developed and a permanent class of propertyless urban poor[3] was established, theft

Stuart McClymont/Stone/Getty Images

An Exact Representation of MACLAINE the Highwayman Robbing LORD EGLINGTON on Hounslow Heath on the 26th of June 1750.
(From a Contemporary Engraving.)

Mary Evans Picture Library

Early in the 18th century, there are well-documented cases of gentlemen who engaged in highway robbery and other violent property crimes.

occasional criminals
Offenders who do not define themselves by a criminal role or view themselves as committed career criminals.

situational inducement
Short-term influence on a person's behaviour, such as financial problems or peer pressure, that increases risk taking.

became more professional. By the 18th century, three separate groups of property criminals were active:

- Skilled thieves typically worked in the larger cities, such as London and Paris. This group included pickpockets, forgers, and counterfeiters, who operated freely. They congregated in flash houses—public meeting places, often taverns, that served as headquarters for gangs. Here, deals were made, crimes were plotted, and the sale of stolen goods was negotiated.[4]
- Smugglers moved freely in sparsely populated areas and transported goods, such as spirits, gems, gold, and spices, without paying tax or duty.
- Poachers typically lived in the country and supplemented their diet and income with game that belonged to a landlord.

At the same time, professional thieves in the larger cities had banded together into gangs to protect themselves, increase the scope of their activities, and help dispose of stolen goods. Jonathan Wild, perhaps London's most famous thief, perfected the process of buying and selling stolen goods and gave himself the title of "Thief-Taker General of Great Britain & Ireland." Before he was hanged, Wild controlled numerous gangs and dealt harshly with any thief who violated his strict code of conduct.[5]

© Mary Evans Picture Library/Alamy

During this period, individual theft-related crimes began to be defined by common law. The most important of these categories are still used today.

Contemporary Thieves

Of the millions of property and theft-related crimes that occur each year, most are committed by **occasional criminals** who do not define themselves by a criminal role or view themselves as committed career criminals. Other thefts are committed by skilled professional criminals.

Criminologists suspect that most economic crimes are the work of amateur occasional criminals, whose decision to steal is spontaneous and whose acts are unskilled, unplanned, and haphazard. Millions of thefts occur each year, and most are not reported to police agencies. Many of these theft offences are committed by school-age youths who are unlikely to enter criminal careers and who drift between conventional and criminal behaviour. Added to the pool of amateur thieves are the millions of adults whose behaviour may occasionally violate the law—shoplifters, pilferers, tax cheats—but whose main source of income is conventional and whose self-identity is noncriminal. Added together, their behaviours form the bulk of theft crimes.

Occasional property crime occurs when there is an opportunity or **situational inducement** to commit crime.[6] Members of the upper class have the opportunity to engage in lucrative business-related crimes such as price-fixing, bribery, and embezzlement; lower-class individuals, lacking such opportunities, are overrepresented in street crime. Situational inducements are short-term influences on a person's behaviour that increase risk taking. They include psychological factors, such as financial problems, and social factors, such as peer pressure.

Occasional criminals may deny their criminality and instead view their transgressions as out of character. For example, they were only "borrowing" the car the police caught them with; they were going to pay—eventually—for the merchandise that they stole from the store. Because of their lack of commitment to a criminal lifestyle, occasional

FIGURE 11.1

Categories of Professional Theft

Pickpocket (cannon)
Sneak thief from stores, banks, and offices (heel)
Shoplifter (booster)
Jewel thief who substitutes fake gems for real ones (pennyweighter)
Thief who steals from hotel rooms (hotel prowl)
Confidence game artist (con artist)
Thief in rackets related to confidence games
Forger
Extortionist from those engaging in illegal acts (shakedown artist)

Source: Edwin Sutherland and Chic Conwell, *The Professional Thief* (Chicago: University of Chicago Press, 1937). Copyright 1937 by the University of Chicago. Reprinted with permission of The University of Chicago Press.

offenders may be the most likely to respond to the general deterrent effect of the law.

In contrast to occasional criminals, **professional criminals** make a significant portion of their income from crime. Professionals do not delude themselves with the belief that their acts are impulsive, one-time efforts, nor do they use elaborate rationalizations to excuse the harmfulness of their actions ("shoplifting doesn't really hurt anyone"). Consequently, professionals pursue their craft with vigour, attempting to learn from older, experienced criminals the techniques that will earn the most money with the least risk. Although their numbers are relatively few, professionals engage in crimes that produce the greater losses to society and perhaps cause the more significant social harm.

Zurijeta/Shutterstock.com

professional criminals
Offenders who make a significant portion of their income from crime.

theft
Taking for one's own use the property of another, by means other than force or threats on the victim or forcibly breaking into a person's home or workplace.

Professional theft traditionally refers to nonviolent forms of criminal behaviour that are undertaken with a high degree of skill for monetary gain and that maximize financial opportunities and minimize the possibilities of apprehension. The most typical forms include pocket picking, break and enter, shoplifting, forgery, counterfeiting, extortion, sneak theft, and confidence swindling (see Figure 11.1).[7]

The following sections discuss some of the more important contemporary theft categories in some detail.

LO1 Theft

Theft was one of the earliest common-law crimes created by English judges to define acts in which one person took for his or her own use the property of another.[8] According to common law, theft was defined as "the trespassory taking and carrying away of the personal property of another with intent to steal."[9] Contemporary definitions of theft often include familiar acts such as shoplifting, passing bad cheques, and other theft offences that do not involve using force or threats on the victim or forcibly breaking into a person's home or workplace. (The former is robbery; the latter, break and enter.)

As originally construed, theft involved taking property that was in the possession of the rightful owner. For example, it would have been considered theft for someone to sneak into a farmer's field and steal a cow. Thus, the original common-law definition required a "trespass in the taking"; that is, for an act to be considered theft, goods must have been taken from the physical possession of the rightful owner. In creating this definition of theft, English judges were more concerned with disturbance of the peace than with theft itself. They reasoned that if someone tried to steal property from another's possession, the act could eventually lead to a physical confrontation and possibly the death of one party or the other. Consequently, the original definition of theft did not

constructive possession
A legal fiction that applies to situations in which persons voluntarily give up physical custody of their property but still retain legal ownership.

theft under $5000
Theft where the value of the property stolen does not exceed $5000; treated as a hybrid offence for which the Crown can proceed by way of summary conviction or indictment.

theft over $5000
Theft where the value of property stolen exceeds $5000; treated as an indictable offence.

include crimes in which the thief had taken the property by trickery or deceit. For example, if someone entrusted with another person's property decided to keep it, it was not considered theft.

The growth of manufacturing and the development of the free enterprise system required greater protection for private property. The pursuit of commercial enterprise often required that one person's legal property be entrusted to a second party; therefore, larceny evolved to include the theft of goods that had come into the thief's possession through legitimate means.

To get around the element of "trespass in the taking," English judges created the concept of **constructive possession**. This legal fiction applies to situations in which persons voluntarily, temporarily give up custody of their property, but still believe that the property is legally theirs. For example, if a person gives a jeweller her watch for repair, she still believes she owns the watch, although she has handed it over to the jeweller. Similarly, when a person misplaces his wallet and someone else finds it and keeps it (although identification of the owner can be plainly seen), the concept of constructive possession makes the person who has kept the wallet guilty of theft.

The Criminal Code separates theft into two categories—**theft under $5000** and **theft over $5000**—for the purposes of trial and sentencing. Theft under $5000 is treated as a "hybrid offence" for which the Crown attorney can choose to proceed by way of a summary conviction offence (maximum penalty six months in jail and $2000 fine) or by way of indictment (maximum two years' imprisonment). Theft over $5000 is automatically treated as an indictable offence, and carries with it a maximum sentence of ten years' imprisonment.

Theft is probably the most common of all crimes. Self-report studies indicate that a significant number of youths have engaged in theft. Based on police-reported UCR data, the Canadian Centre for Justice Statistics recorded almost 570 000 thefts in 2009, a rate of approximately 1700 per 100 000 persons. Theft rates declined nearly 30 percent between 1999 and 2009.[10]

There are many different varieties of theft. Some involve small items of little value. Many of these go

© Jimmy Anderson/iStockPhoto

unreported, especially if the victims are business owners who do not want to take the time to get involved with police; they simply write off losses as a cost of doing business. For example, hotel owners in the United States estimate that each year guests filch US$100 million worth of towels, bathrobes, ashtrays, bedspreads, showerheads, flatware, and even television sets and wall paintings.[11]

Other thefts can involve complex schemes involving many different people. For example, in 144 break-ins at convenience stores and gas bars, a gang of ten thieves operating in the Port Hope–Cobourg area northeast of Toronto netted more than $1 million in cigarettes.[12] Satellite service providers claim to lose millions every year in lost revenues due to the sale of "pirated" decoder chips produced illegally by "homebrew" operations. Every year, employees steal more than $2 billion from Canadian employers in the retail section, half of it out of the cash register.[13]

In Laval, Quebec, theft of four computers from a Canada Revenue Agency office in 2003 represented the biggest loss of personal information in Canadian history; the computers contained the names, dates of birth, home addresses, and social insurance numbers of thousands of Canadians, information that could be sold on the black market and used to construct new identities for criminals or terrorists. In May 2011, Sony Corporation was hit with a series of hacker attacks in which the personal information of more than 2000 Canadian users of Sony Ericsson brand cellphones was stolen, on the heels of a previous hacker attack that shut down Sony's PlayStation Network system, affecting more than 100 million users worldwide.[14]

Identity theft is one of the fastest-growing crimes in North America. The Canadian Anti-Fraud Centre, an antifraud call centre jointly operated by the RCMP Ontario Provincial Police and the Competition Bureau Canada, reported that in 2010 18 146 people were victims of identity fraud, with losses totalling nearly $9.5 million.[15]

There is growing evidence that identity theft is being used by organized crime and to further the aims of other crimes such as terrorism.[16]

LO2 Shoplifting

Shoplifting is a common form of theft involving the taking of goods from retail stores. Usually shoplifters try to snatch goods—such as jewellery, clothes, CDs, and appliances—when store personnel are otherwise occupied and hide the goods on their bodies. The "five-finger discount" is an extremely common crime, and retailers lose an estimated $760 million annually to inventory shrinkage; on average, stores small and large lose at least 2 percent of total sales to thieves.[17] Retail security measures add to the already high cost of this crime, all of which is passed on to the consumer. The Retail Council of Canada estimates that Canadian retailers lose as much as $8 million a day to retail theft, most of it due to shoplifting.[18] Some studies estimate that about one in every nine shoppers steals from department stores. Moreover, the increasingly popular discount stores, such as Zellers and Walmart, have minimal sales help and depend on highly visible merchandise displays to attract purchasers, all of which makes them particularly vulnerable to shoplifters.

shoplifting
The taking of goods from retail stores.

booster
Professional shoplifter who steals with the intention of reselling stolen merchandise.

fence
A receiver of stolen goods.

snitch
Amateur shoplifter who does not self-identify as a thief but who systematically steals merchandise for personal use.

The Shoplifter

In the early 1960s, Mary Owen Cameron conducted a classic study of shoplifting.[19] In her pioneering effort, Cameron found that about 10 percent of all shoplifters were professionals who derived the majority of their income from shoplifting. Sometimes called **boosters**, or heels, professional shoplifters steal with the intention of reselling stolen merchandise to pawnshops or **fences** (people who buy stolen property), usually at half the original price.[20]

Cameron found that the majority of shoplifters are amateur pilferers, called **snitches** in thieves' argot. Snitches are otherwise respectable persons who do not conceive of themselves as thieves but systematically steal merchandise for their own use. They are not simply taken by an uncontrollable urge to snatch something that attracts them; they come equipped to steal. Usually snitches who are arrested have never been apprehended before. For the most part, they lack the kinds of criminal experience that suggest extensive association with a criminal subculture.

DID YOU KNOW?

- Theft is the taking and carrying away of the constructive possessions of another.
- Shoplifting involves theft from a retail establishment by stealth and deception. Some shoplifters are impulsive; others are professionals who use elaborate means and devices.
- Passing bad cheques without adequate funds is a crime of fraud.
- The use of stolen credit cards and account numbers results in annual losses of more than $200 million.
- Auto theft adds up to more than $1 billion each year.
- Embezzlement or criminal breach of trust occurs when trusted persons or employees take someone else's property for their own use.

© Pinto/Corbis

arrest by owner of property The right of the owner or designate to arrest without warrant anyone found committing a criminal offence on or in relation to the owner's property.

target removal strategy Displaying dummy or disabled goods as a means of preventing shoplifting.

target hardening strategy Locking goods into place or using electronic tags and sensing devices as means of preventing shoplifting.

Criminologists view shoplifters as people who are likely to reform if apprehended. Cameron reasoned that because snitches are not part of a criminal subculture and do not think of themselves as criminals, they are deterred by initial contact with the law. Getting arrested traumatizes them, and they will not risk a second offence.[21] Although this argument seems plausible, some criminologists suggest that apprehension may in fact have a labelling effect that inhibits deterrence and results in repeated offending.[22]

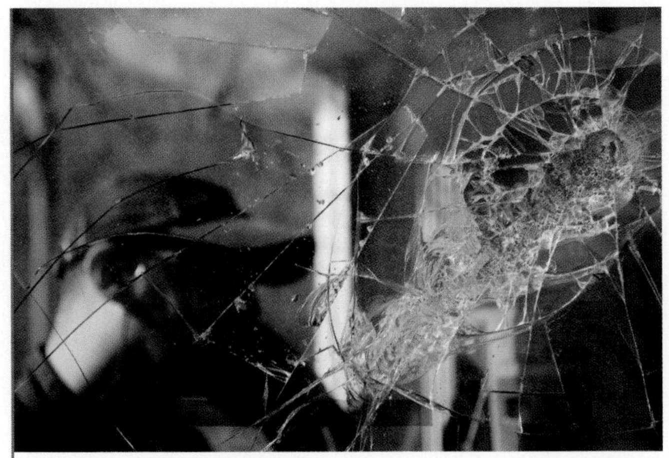

© magicinfoto/iStockPhoto

"Target hardening" involves making a home or business more resistant to burglars. For example, when thieves try to smash glass where "security film" has been applied, the glass will break but the transparent film will hold the shards in place, making entry very difficult.

Controlling Shoplifting

Fewer than 10 percent of shoplifting incidents are detected by store employees; customers who notice boosters are unwilling to report even serious cases to managers.[23]

Section 494(2) of the Criminal Code allows for **arrest by owner of property**—that is, business owners and their employees are permitted by law to arrest without a warrant anyone found committing an offence on or in relation to the owner's property. The law requires that arrests be made on reasonable and probable grounds, that detention be short, and that store employees or security guards conduct themselves reasonably and in accordance with the law.

Retail stores are now initiating a number of strategies designed to reduce or eliminate shoplifting. **Target removal strategies** involve displaying dummy or disabled goods while the "real" merchandise is locked up. For example, audio equipment is displayed with parts missing, and only after items are purchased are the necessary components installed. Some stores sell from catalogues, keeping the merchandise in stockrooms.

Target hardening strategies involve locking goods into place or having them monitored by electronic systems. Clothing stores may use racks designed to prevent large quantities of garments from being slipped off easily. Store owners also rely on electronic article surveillance (EAS) systems, featuring tags with small electronic sensors that trip alarms if not removed by employees before the item leaves the store. Security systems now feature source tagging, a process by which manufacturers embed the tag in the packaging or in the product itself. Thieves have trouble removing or defeating such tags, and retailers save on the time and labour needed to attach the tags at the store.

Here are some of the steps retail insurers recommend to reduce the incidence of shoplifting:

- Train employees to watch for suspicious behaviour such as a shopper loitering over a trivial item. Have them keep an eye out for shoppers wearing baggy clothes,

© Tannis Toohey/ZUMA Press/Corbis

In October 2010, Toronto grocery store owner David Chen was acquitted on charges of assault and forcible confinement stemming from an incident in May 2010 when Chen chased down and tied up a man who had stolen a plant from his store.

carrying their own bag, or using some other method to conceal products taken from the shelf.

- Develop a call code. When employees suspect that a customer is shoplifting, they can use the call to bring store management or security to the area.
- Because products on lower floors face the greatest risk, relocate the most tempting targets to upper floors.
- Use smaller exits, and avoid placing the most expensive merchandise near these exits.
- Design routes within stores to make theft less tempting and funnel customers toward cashiers.
- Place service departments (credit and packaging) near areas where shoplifters are likely to stash goods. Extra supervision reduces the problem.
- Avoid creating corners where there are no supervision sight lines in areas of stores favoured by young males. Restrict and supervise areas where electronic tags can be removed.[24]

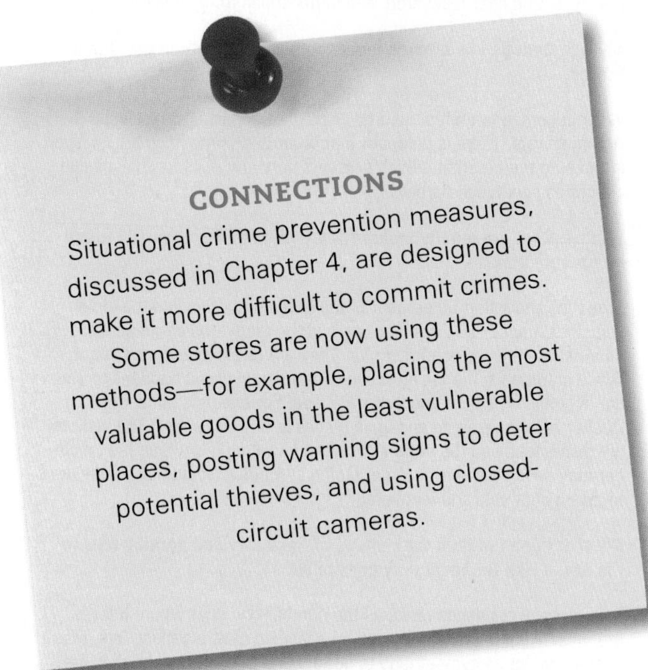

CONNECTIONS
Situational crime prevention measures, discussed in Chapter 4, are designed to make it more difficult to commit crimes. Some stores are now using these methods—for example, placing the most valuable goods in the least vulnerable places, posting warning signs to deter potential thieves, and using closed-circuit cameras.

Credit and Bank Card Theft

The use of stolen credit cards has become a major problem in North America. Most credit card abuse is the work of amateurs who acquire stolen cards through theft or mugging and then use them for two or three days. However, professional credit card rings have gotten into the act. In January 2007 Montreal police arrested five men in raids on two high-tech fake credit card operations, seizing sophisticated colour printers, hologram-producing machines, computers, credit card blanks, and a $30 000 embossing machine used to imprint the fake cards. "Obviously with that kind of equipment, you're able to produce cards a lot quicker than you were with older equipment," said a Montreal police spokesperson.[25]

It is a criminal offence to steal or forge or falsify a credit card, or to knowingly use a credit card that has been revoked or cancelled. According to the RCMP, credit and bank card fraud losses topped $360 million in 2010.[26]

The problem of credit card misuse is being compounded by thieves who set up bogus Internet sites to trick people into giving them their credit card numbers, which they then use for their own gain. This problem is growing so rapidly that a number of new technologies are being prepared to combat credit card number theft over the Internet. One method incorporates digital signatures into computer operating systems, which can be accessed with a digital key that comes with each computer. Owners of new systems can present three forms of identification to a notary public and trade a notarized copy of their key for a program that will sign files. The basis of the digital signature is a digital certificate, a small block of data that contains a person's "public key." This certificate is signed, in turn, by a certificate authority. The digital certificate acts like a credit card with a hologram and a photograph; it identifies the user to the distant website.[27]

Motor Vehicle Theft

Under section 355(1) of the Criminal Code, auto theft is defined as "Taking motor vehicle or vessel or found therein without consent." Nearly 110 000 vehicles were stolen in Canada in 2009, down 15.5 percent from the previous year, and a 40 percent decrease since 1999.[28] The Insurance Bureau of Canada estimates that motor vehicle thefts cost Canadians $1 billion annually.[29] (See Table 11.1.)

Though almost all motor vehicle thefts are reported to police (as every province requires owners to insure their vehicles), 2007 data show that fully 40 percent of all vehicles stolen are never recovered. In recent years, organized crime groups have become increasingly involved in motor vehicle theft, shipping stolen vehicles to foreign countries for resale at high profits. Canada ranks in the top one-third of industrialized countries for car thefts. Canada's car theft rate is higher than the American rate.[30]

Types of Motor Vehicle Theft

A number of attempts have been made to categorize the various forms of motor vehicle theft. Typically, distinctions are made between theft for temporary personal use, for resale, and for chopping or stripping cars for parts. One of the most detailed of these typologies was developed by Charles McCaghy and his associates after examining data from police and court files in several American states.[31]

The researchers uncovered five categories of auto theft transactions:

1. *Joyriding.* Many motor vehicle thefts are motivated by teenagers' desire to acquire the power, prestige, sexual potency, and recognition associated with an automobile. Joyriders steal cars not for profit or gain but to experience, even briefly, the benefits associated with owning an automobile.

2. *Short-term transportation.* Motor vehicle theft for short-term transportation is similar to joyriding. It involves the theft of a car, an SUV, or other motor vehicle simply to go from one place to another. In more serious cases, the thief may drive to another city and then steal another vehicle to continue the journey.

3. *Long-term transportation.* Thieves who steal motor vehicles for long-term transportation intend to keep the cars for their personal use. Usually older than joyriders and from a lower-class background, these thieves may repaint and otherwise disguise vehicles to avoid detection.

4. *Profit.* Motor vehicle theft for profit is motivated by the hope of monetary gain. At one extreme are highly organized professionals who resell expensive cars after altering their identification numbers and falsifying their registration papers. At the other end of the scale are amateur auto strippers who steal batteries, tires, and wheel covers to sell them or re-equip their own cars.

5. *Commission of another crime.* A few motor vehicle thieves steal vehicles to use in other crimes, such as robberies and thefts. This type of thief desires both mobility and anonymity.

According to police, joyriding remains a primary motive for motor vehicle theft. Youth aged 12–17 account for 28 percent of vehicle thefts. However, the clearance rate for motor vehicle theft continues to decline, with police identifying an accused in only 12.5 percent of incidents. The low clearance rate, coupled with declining recovery rates for stolen vehicles, suggests to many that there may be increased involvement by professional car thieves linked to chop shops, export rings, or both. Exporting stolen vehicles has become a global problem, and the emergence of capitalism in Eastern Europe has increased the demand for North American–made cars.[32]

DID YOU KNOW?

Tips for Preventing Theft

Several automobile manufacturers have introduced features designed to reduce the incidence of vehicle theft (e.g., alarms and ultrasonic devices, the etching of parts and accessories, fuel cut-off systems, etc.). Ask your local police and motorists' associations for advice on which vehicles are the most difficult for thieves to steal. Here are some tips on how to discourage car thieves:

- Don't leave your car unlocked or with the key in the ignition. Always pocket the keys.
- Keep your house keys separate from your car keys.
- Park your car in a busy, well-lit area.
- Do not leave valuable items or packages in sight in your car.
- Keep your vehicle registration in your wallet or purse.
- Etch or mark some of the more expensive parts on your car in an inconspicuous place with an engraving tool, using your car's Vehicle Identification Number (VIN). On metal parts, cover the number with rust-inhibitor.
- Install safety door-lock buttons.
- Always keep your car trunk locked.

Source: http://www.docstoc.com/docs/79656613/Myths-About-Car-Theft.

TABLE 11.1

Myths About Car Theft

Automobile theft is often thought of as a minor crime but in reality it's a serious problem in our society. Let's dispel some of the more common myths around this growing problem.

Myth 1: Only sports cars or deluxe models are stolen. Who would want a two- or three-year-old ordinary car?
Authorities report that the most popular makes are the most likely stolen and the least likely to be recovered. Ordinary sedans are the backbone of the lucrative stolen used-parts market and therefore are the least frequently recovered.
Myth 2: Car theft is not really a big issue and everything is usually covered under insurance anyway.
In Canada, thieves steal a vehicle every 5 1/4 minutes and a vehicle is broken into every 30 seconds. Auto theft is a crime that everyone pays for. Car theft costs Canadian consumers about $470 million a year in insurance premiums for unrecovered vehicles, damage to vehicles that are stolen and later recovered, and items stolen from vehicles.
Myth 3: Canada has a much lower auto theft rate than the United States.
When it comes to theft of insured cars, the Canadian rate exceeds the American rate. There is no doubt that organized crime rings are involved in the auto theft market, which presents very low risks for thieves and generates spectacular profits.
Myth 4: Cars are mostly stolen for joy rides and are usually found intact very quickly.
Statistics show that 60 percent of the time authorities find the stolen vehicles within 2–10 days. The state of the recovered car depends on what the thieves used them for. They are rarely abandoned intact. While automobile theft is an urban phenomenon, what happens to your car depends on where you live in Canada. For example, a car stolen in Quebec is quite likely to end up in pieces in a "chop shop." The vehicles are dismantled and the parts sold, often for much more than the whole car may have been worth. A car stolen in Alberta would more likely be taken on a joy ride and recovered.
Myth 5: I don't park in dark alleys or unsupervised parking lots so I'm not at risk for having my car stolen.
Your place of residence ranks as the number-one spot where thieves are most likely to strike, followed by shopping centre parking lots. Most people are not as sympathetic to automobile theft victims as they are to victims of burglary. Because they are viewed as nonviolent crimes, automobile thefts hardly cause a ripple. Usually the victim is not injured and if they are insured, they will be reimbursed and everything will soon be back to normal. But the reality includes the emotional upset of victims and the loss of irreplaceable personal belongings.

Source: http://www.docstoc.com/docs/79656613/Myths-About-Car-Theft. Reprinted with permission of The Co-operators.

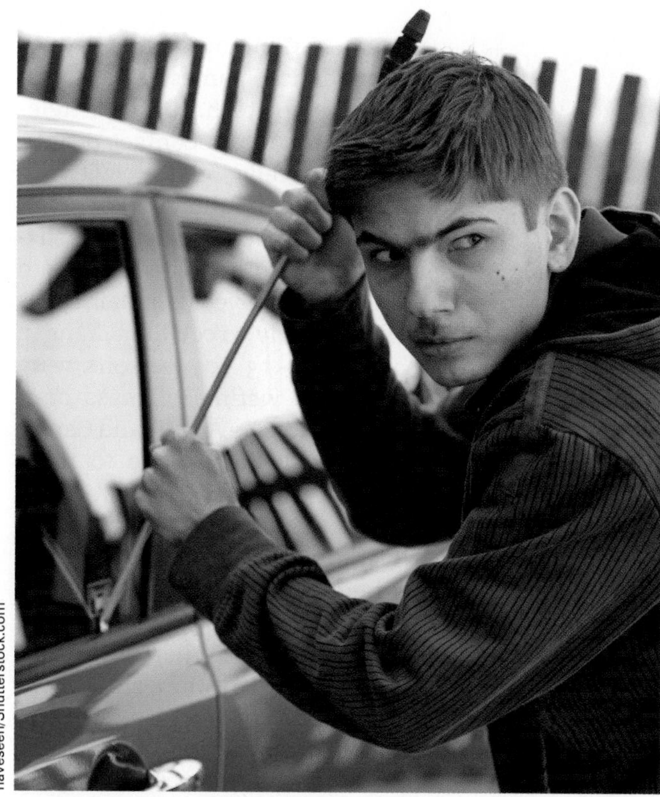
haveseen/Shutterstock.com

Each year millions of thefts from cars, homes, and schools are reported to police. Some are the work of professionals, while others are the spontaneous acts of occasional or amateur thieves.

Combating Motor Vehicle Theft

Motor vehicle theft is a significant target of situational crime prevention efforts. One approach to theft deterrence has been to increase the risks of apprehension. Information hotlines offer rewards for information leading to the arrest of car thieves. A British Columbia–based antitheft program known as IMPACT (Integrated Municipal Provincial Auto Crime Team) is credited with recovering more than 1150 vehicles, worth $18 million, and resulting in the arrest of 531 people. Another approach has been to place fluorescent decals on windows indicating that the car is never used between 1:00 and 5:00 A.M.; if police spot a car with the decal being operated during this period, they know it is stolen.[33]

The "Boomerang" system installs a hidden tracking device in cars; the device gives off a signal enabling the police to pinpoint its location. Research evaluating the effectiveness of these types of devices finds that they significantly reduce crime.[34] Other prevention efforts involve making it more difficult to steal cars. Publicity campaigns have been directed at encouraging people to lock their cars. Parking lots have been equipped with theft-deterring closed-circuit TV cameras and barriers. Manufacturers have installed more sophisticated steering-column locking devices and other security systems that complicate theft.

A study by the Highway Loss Data Institute (HLDI) in the United States found that most car-theft prevention methods, especially alarms, have little effect on theft rates. The most effective methods appear to be devices that immobilize a vehicle by cutting off the electrical power needed to start the engine when a theft is detected.[35]

LO3 False Pretences and Fraud

Unlike theft, the crime of **false pretences** involves deliberate misrepresentation of facts to obtain money or property. In 1757, the English Parliament defined false pretences in order to cover an area of law left untouched by theft statutes. The first false pretences law punished people who "knowingly and designedly by false pretence or pretences, [obtained] from any person or persons, money, goods, wares or merchandise with intent to cheat or defraud any person or persons of the same."[36]

False pretence differs from traditional theft because the victims willingly give their possessions to the offender, and the crime does not, as does theft, involve a "trespass in the taking." Examples of false pretences would be an unscrupulous merchant selling someone a chair by claiming it was an antique, knowing that it was a cheap copy, or a phony healer selling coloured sugar water as an "elixir" that would cure a disease.

Fraud is a broader offence than false pretences that involves the use of deceit or falsehood, whether or not it is a false pretence, to obtain property, money, or other valuables from a person or the public. An example of a fraud is using the mail or the Internet to distribute information about get-rich-quick schemes that require an initial down payment by investors, money that is then pocketed by the fraud artist. Another example would be defrauding someone of his or her money by convincing the person that you are in contact with the spirit world, and a payment must be made to appease the spirits. So-called confidence games are another common type of fraud.

false pretences
Misrepresenting a fact in a way that causes a deceived victim to give money or property to the offender.

fraud
Use of deceit or falsehood, whether or not it is a false pretence, to obtain property, money, or other valuables from a person or the public.

Bad Cheques

Writing bad cheques is probably the most common example of the crime of fraud. The cheques are intentionally drawn on a nonexistent or underfunded bank account. In general, for a person to be guilty of passing a bad cheque, the bank the cheque is drawn on must refuse payment and the cheque casher must fail to make the cheque good within ten days after finding out the cheque was not honoured.

Edwin Lemert conducted the best-known study of cheque forgers more than 50 years ago.[37] Lemert found that the majority of cheque forgers—he calls them **naïve cheque forgers**—are amateurs who do not believe their actions will hurt anyone. Most naïve cheque forgers come from middle-class backgrounds and have little identification with a criminal subculture. They cash bad cheques because of a financial crisis that demands an immediate resolution—perhaps they have lost money at the horse track and have some pressing bills to pay. Naïve cheque forgers are often socially isolated people who have been unsuccessful in their personal relationships. They are risk-prone when faced with a situation that is unusually stressful for them. The willingness of stores and other commercial establishments to cash cheques with a minimum of fuss to promote business encourages the cheque forger to risk committing a criminal act.

Lemert found that a few professionals, whom he calls **systematic forgers**, make a substantial living by passing bad cheques. It is difficult to estimate the number of such forgeries committed each year or the amounts involved. Stores and banks may choose not to press charges because the effort to collect the money due them is often not worth their while. It is also difficult to separate the true cheque forger from the neglectful shopper.

Fotoline/Shutterstock.com

naïve cheque forgers
Amateurs who cash bad cheques because of some financial crisis but have little identification with a criminal subculture.

systematic forgers
Professionals who make a living by passing bad cheques.

confidence game
A swindle, usually involving a get-rich-quick scheme, often with illegal overtones, so that the victim will be too afraid or too embarrassed to call the police.

Confidence Games

Confidence games are a good example of the crime of fraud, run by swindlers who aspire to separate a victim from his or her hard-earned money. These con games usually involve getting a mark (target) interested in some get-rich-quick scheme, which may have illegal overtones. The criminal's hope is that when victims lose their money, they will be either too embarrassed or too afraid to call the police. There are hundreds of varieties of con games.

Contemporary confidence games have gone high tech. Corrupt telemarketers contact people, typically elderly victims, over the phone in order to bilk them out of their savings. The Canadian Anti-Fraud Centre received complaint calls from nearly 50 000 Canadians in 2010, and 13 603 persons were confirmed victims of mass marketing fraud. The Anti-Fraud Centre estimates the losses due to mass marketing fraud in 2010 at more than $50 million. One popular scam is known as the "Nigerian letter" scam, where individuals are asked to help out a Nigerian millionaire by allowing him to temporarily deposit $25–$50 million in their bank account, for which they will receive 10–15 percent of the amount as a reward; all the contacted individuals have to do is forward their complete bank account information to the letter writer, and the transaction will take place electronically.[38]

The RCMP estimates that Canadians have lost nearly $10 million since 1994 to the Nigerian letter scam.[39] In June 2007, the *Toronto Star* reported that the "Wish Kids Foundation," a charitable foundation claiming to be raising money to give dying children their final wish, was in fact using the funds raised to buy an airplane; in another scam, the executive director of "Canadians Against Child Abuse" was accused of using the funds raised to pay for his own home and vacations.[40]

© Moviestore collection Ltd/Alamy

The movie *The Sting* (1973) was a classic depiction of the confidence game where a young con man seeking revenge for his murdered partner teams up with a master of the big con to win a fortune from a criminal banker.

DID YOU KNOW?

Types of Scams

Fraudulent websites claiming to sell expensive, luxury items such as "Coach"' purses and "Canada Goose" coats are a growing problem; once your credit card information is obtained you are billed for purchases you will never receive. More information about this scam, and others listed below, can be obtained by visiting the Canadian AntiFraud website at http://www.antifraudcentre.ca/english/recognizeit.html.

- 900 Scams
- Advanced Fee Letter Fraud (419/Nigerian Letters)
- Advanced Fee Loans
- Bomb Threat
- Cheque Overpayment Fraud
- Dead Air Calls
- Emergency Scam
- False Charities
- Hitman Email
- Identity Theft
- Inheritance
- Internet 101
- Lottery Emails
- Office Supplies/Directory
- Phishing
- Phone Number Spoofing
- Prize Pitch
- Puppy Scam
- Pyramid Schemes
- Recovery Pitch
- Travel
- Vacation
- Vehicle Warranty Package
- Service Scam

Source: © Copyright 2011, Her Majesty the Queen in Right of Canada as represented by the Royal Canadian Mounted Police.

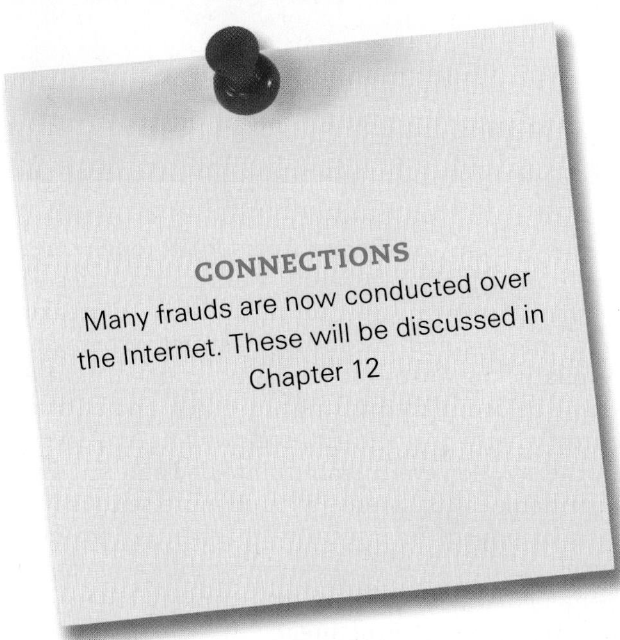

CONNECTIONS
Many frauds are now conducted over the Internet. These will be discussed in Chapter 12

With the growth of direct-mail marketing and "900" telephone numbers that charge callers per minute for conversations with what are promised to be beautiful, willing sex partners, a flood of new confidence games may be about to descend on the public.

Embezzlement/Breach of Trust

Embezzlement (breach of trust) goes back at least to ancient Greece; the writings of Aristotle allude to theft by road commissioners and other government officials.[41]

embezzlement (breach of trust) Taking and keeping the property of others, such as clients or employers, with which one has been entrusted.

The crime of embezzlement was first codified into law by the English Parliament during the 16th century.[42] Until then, to be guilty of theft, a person had to take goods from the physical possession of another (trespass in the taking). However, as explained earlier, this definition did not cover instances in which one person trusted another and willingly gave that person temporary custody of his or her property. For example, in everyday commerce, store clerks, bank tellers, brokers, and merchants gain lawful possession but not legal ownership of other people's money. Embezzlement occurs when someone who is trusted with property fraudulently converts it—that is, keeps it for his or her own use or for the use of others. In Canada, embezzlement is defined in section 336 of the Criminal Code as the offence of "criminal breach of trust," which carries with it a penalty of up to 14 years' imprisonment. An example of criminal breach of trust is collecting funds from the sale of raffle tickets and "converting" them to one's own use, perhaps to buy a car or pay a debt.

Due to their relatively small number, the Canadian Centre for Justice Statistics does not report arrests for criminal breach of trust as a separate category. In the United States, the FBI found that only 17 000 people

© Dave Henrys/Alamy

DID YOU KNOW?

- Burglary/break and enter is the breaking into and entering of a structure in order to commit an indictable offence, typically theft.
- Some burglars specialize in residential theft; others steal from commercial establishments.
- Some burglars repeatedly attack the same target, mainly because they are familiar with the layout and protective measures.
- Professional burglars have careers in which they learn the tricks of the trade from older, more experienced pros.

were arrested for embezzlement in 1999—probably an extremely small percentage of all embezzlers. However, the number of people arrested for embezzlement has increased in the past two decades, indicating that (1) more employees are willing to steal from their employers, (2) more employers are willing to report instances of embezzlement, or (3) law enforcement officials are more willing to prosecute embezzlers.

LO4 Burglary/Break and Enter

Common law defines the crime of **burglary (break and enter)** as "the breaking and entering of a dwelling house of another in the nighttime with the intent to commit an indictable offence within."[43] Burglary is considered a much more serious crime than theft because it involves entering another's home, which threatens occupants. Even though the home may be unoccupied at the time of the break and enter, the potential for harm to the occupants is so significant that break and enter is punished as an indictable offence.

The legal definition of burglary has undergone considerable change since its common-law origins. When first created by English judges during the late Middle Ages, laws against burglary were designed to protect people whose home might be set upon by wandering criminals. Including the phrase "breaking and entering" in the definition protected people from unwarranted intrusions; if an invited guest stole something, it would not be considered a burglary. Similarly, the requirement that the crime be committed at nighttime was added because evening was considered the time when honest people might fall prey to criminals.[44]

burglary (break and enter) Breaking into and entering a place with the intent to commit an indictable offence.

Recent Canadian criminal laws do not require forced entry. Entry through deceit (e.g., by posing as a delivery person), through threat, or through conspiracy with others such as guests or servants is deemed legally equivalent to breaking and entering and is called "constructive breaking." Similarly, there is no longer a requirement that the crime be committed during nighttime, and all structures, whether or not a private dwelling, are covered by the law. However, breaking into and entering a private home is considered a much more serious invasion of privacy and security than entry into other types of structures, and carries with it a maximum penalty of life imprisonment (compared to ten years for other types of structures).

The Nature and Extent of Break and Enter

The Criminal Code definition of break and enter includes three different categories of the offence: (1) break and enter with intent to commit an indictable offence; (2) break and enter and committing an indictable offence; and (3) break out of a place and intending or actually committing an indictable offence.

DavidEwingPhotography/Shutterstock.com

The need to get money to buy drugs is a common motive for break and enter crimes. One example is that of Richard Seguin, the Ottawa-area burglar called "Spiderman" because of his heroin-induced spider-like powers to scale tall buildings and break into apartments in search of money and valuables. Once arrested, he pleaded guilty to 20 counts of break and enter.

According to Statistics Canada, 205 710 police-reported break and enters were recorded in 2009. The break and enter rate has dropped by 42 percent since 1999 (see Figure 11.2).

FIGURE 11.2

Break and Enter Rate, 1999–2009

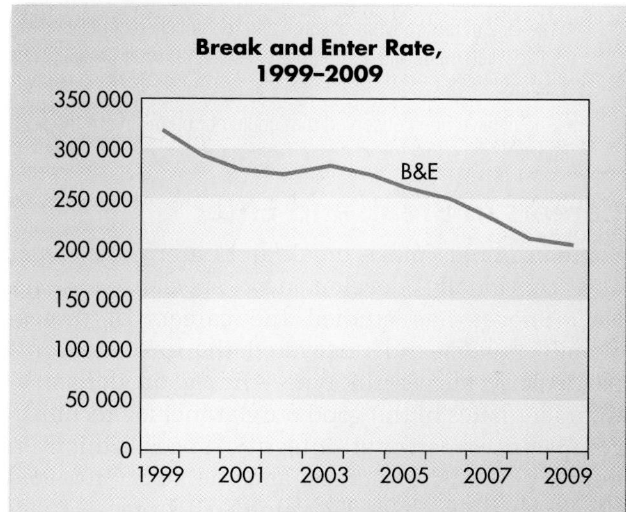

Source: Adapted from Statistics Canada CANSIM Database (http://www5.statcan.gc.ca/cansim/home-accueil?lang=eng, Table 252-0051).

Overall, the average loss for a burglary is about $1500 per victim, for a total of about $3 billion.[45] On the other hand, self-reported data collected as part of the 2009 GSS-PRVS reveals that about 630 000 residential break and enters were either attempted or completed in 2009, a 20 percent increase from 2004. Only slightly more than 50 percent of these were reported to police.[46]

According to the PRVS, those most likely to be victims of break and enter live in cities and in households earning over $60 000 per year. Owner-occupied and single-family residences had lower break and enter rates than renter-occupied and multiple-family dwellings.

Types of Break and Enter

Though some burglars are crude thieves who smash a window and enter a vacant home or structure with minimal preparation, others plan a strategy. Because it involves planning, risk, and skill, break and enter has long been associated with professional thieves who carefully learn their craft.[47]

Burglars must master the skills of their trade, learning to spot environmental cues that nonprofessionals fail to notice.[48] In an important book called *Burglars on the Job*, Richard Wright and Scott Decker describe the working conditions of active burglars.[49] Most are motivated by the need for cash in order to get high; they want to enjoy the good life, "keep the party going," without having to work. They approach their job in a rational, businesslike fashion; still, their lives are controlled by their culture and environment. Unskilled and uneducated, urban burglars choose crime because they have few conventional opportunities for success. (See Figure 11.3.)

Some burglars prefer to victimize commercial property rather than private homes. Of all business establishments, retail stores are the favourite target. Because they display merchandise, burglars know exactly what to look for, where it can be found, and, because the prices are also displayed, how much they can hope to gain from resale to a fence. Burglars can legitimately enter a retail store during business hours and see what the store contains and where it is stored; they can also check for security alarms and devices. Commercial burglars perceive retail establishments as ready sources of merchandise that can be easily sold.[50]

Other commercial establishments, such as service centres, warehouses, and factories, are less attractive targets because it is more difficult to gain legitimate access to plan the theft. The burglar must use guile to scope out these places, perhaps posing as a delivery person. In addition, the merchandise is more likely to be used or more difficult to fence at

FIGURE 11.3

How Burglars Approach Their "Job"

- Targets are often acquaintances.
- Drug dealers are a favoured target because they have lots of cash and drugs, and victims aren't going to call police.
- Tipsters help the burglars select attractive targets.
- Some stake out residences to learn the occupants' routine.
- Many burglars approach a target masquerading as workers, such as carpenters or housepainters.
- Most avoid occupied residences, considering them high-risk targets.
- Alarms and elaborate locks do not deter burglars but tell them there is something inside worth stealing.
- Some call the occupants from a pay phone; if the phone is still ringing when they arrive, they know no one is home.
- After entering a residence, their anxiety turns to calm as they first turn to the master bedroom for money and drugs. They also search kitchens, believing that some people keep money in the mayonnaise jar!
- Most work in groups, one serving as a lookout while the other(s) ransack the place.
- Some dispose of goods through a professional fence; others try to pawn the goods, exchange the goods for drugs, or sell them to friends and relatives. A few keep the stolen items for themselves, especially guns and jewellery.

Sources: Richard Wright and Scott Decker, *Burglars on the Job: Streetlife and Residential Break-ins* (Boston: Northeastern University Press, 1994). Reprinted by permission of University Press of New England; and Manne Laukkanen, Pekka Santtila, Patrick Jern, and Kenneth Sandnabba, "Predicting Offender Home Location in Urban Burglary Series," *Forensic Science International*, vol. 176, iss. 2–3, 7 April 2008, pp. 224–35.

a premium price. If burglars choose to attack factories, warehouses, or service centres, the most vulnerable properties are those located far from major roads and away from pedestrian traffic. In remote areas, burglar alarms are less effective because it takes police longer to respond than on more heavily

CONNECTIONS

According to the rational choice approach discussed in Chapter 4, burglars make rational, calculating decisions before committing crimes. If circumstances and culture dictate their activities, their decisions must be considered a matter of choice.

patrolled thoroughfares, and an alarm is less likely to be heard by a pedestrian who would be able to call for help. Even in the most remote areas, however, burglars are wary of alarms, though their presence suggests that there is something worth stealing.

Whether residential or commercial, some burglars strike the same victim more than once.[51] Graham Farrell, Coretta Phillips, and Ken Pease have articulated some reasons that burglars might want to hit the same target more than once:

- It takes less effort to break and enter a home or apartment known to be a suitable target than an unknown or unsuitable one.
- The burglar is already aware of the target's layout.
- The ease of entry of the target has probably not changed, and escape routes are known.
- The lack of protective measures and the absence of nosy neighbours, which made the first burglary a success, have probably not changed.
- Goods have been observed that could not be taken out the first time.[52]

Careers in Break and Enter

Some criminals make break and enter their career and continually develop new specialized skills. Neal Shover has studied the careers of professional burglars and uncovered the existence of a particularly successful type—the "good burglar."[53] Characteristics of the good burglar include technical competence, personal integrity, specialization in burglary, financial success, and the ability to avoid prison sentences. Shover found that to receive recognition as good burglars, novices must develop four key requirements of the trade:

1. *They must learn the many skills needed to commit lucrative break and enters.* These skills may include gaining entry into homes and apartments; selecting targets with high potential payoffs; choosing items with a high resale value; opening safes properly without damaging their contents; and using the proper equipment, including cutting torches, electric saws, explosives, and metal bars.
2. *The good burglar must be able to team up to form a criminal gang.* Choosing trustworthy companions is essential if the obstacles to completing a successful job—police, alarms, secure safes—are to be overcome.
3. *The good burglar must have inside information.* Without knowledge of what awaits them inside, burglars can spend a tremendous amount of time and effort on empty safes and jewellery boxes.
4. *The good burglar must cultivate fences or buyers for stolen wares.* Once the burglar gains access to people who buy and sell stolen goods, he or she must also learn how to successfully sell these goods for a reasonable profit.

According to Shover, a person becomes a good burglar by learning the techniques of the trade from older, more experienced burglars. During this process, the older burglar teaches the novice how to handle requirements of the trade such as dealing with defence lawyers, bail bond agents, and other agents of the justice system. Apprentices must be known to have the appropriate character before they are accepted for training. Usually the opportunity to learn burglary comes as a reward for being a highly respected juvenile gang member; from knowing someone in the neighbourhood who has made a living at burglary; or, more often, from having built a reputation for being solid while serving time in prison. Consequently, the opportunity to become a good burglar is not open to everyone.

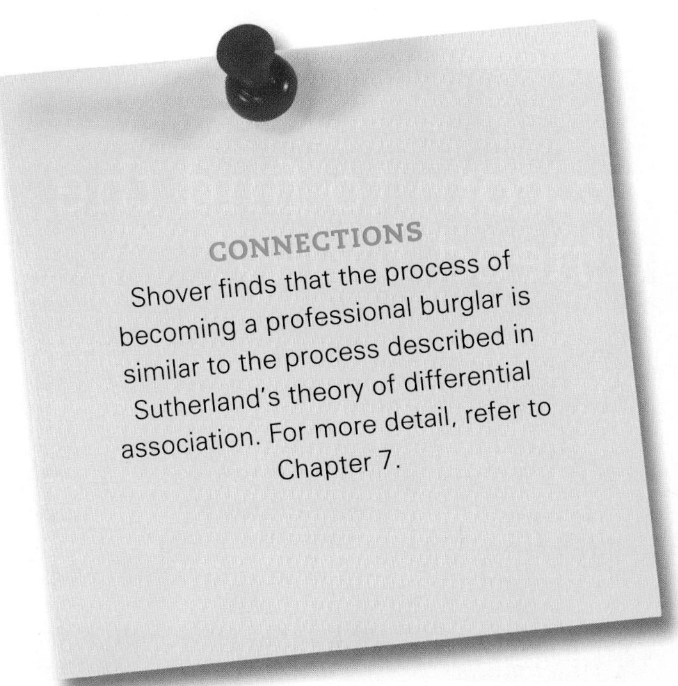
CONNECTIONS
Shover finds that the process of becoming a professional burglar is similar to the process described in Sutherland's theory of differential association. For more detail, refer to Chapter 7.

arson
The intentional or reckless damage by fire or explosion to property.

The "good burglar" concept is supported by the interviews Paul Cromwell, James Olson, and D'Aunn Wester Avary conducted with 30 active burglars in Texas. They found that burglars go through stages of career development, beginning as young novices who learn the trade from older, more experienced burglars, frequently siblings or relatives. Novices continue to get this tutoring as long as they can develop their own markets (fences) for stolen goods. After their education is over, novices enter the journeyman stage, characterized by forays in search of lucrative targets and by careful planning. At this point they develop reputations as experienced, reliable criminals. They become professional burglars when they have developed advanced skills and organizational abilities that give them the highest esteem among their peers.[54] Cromwell, Olson, and Avary also found that many burglars had serious drug habits and that their criminal activity was, in part, aimed at supporting their substance abuse.

LO5 Arson

Arson is the intentional or reckless damage by fire or explosion to property, and includes damage to one's own property, bodily harm to another as a consequence of the arson, possession of incendiary devices, negligence, and fraudulent burning of property.

About 45 percent of those charged with arson in Canada are youth 12 to 17 years of age. Canadian Centre for Justice Statistics data show that juveniles are arrested for a greater share of this crime than any other.[55]

There are several motives for arson. Adult arsonists may be motivated by severe emotional turmoil. Some psychologists view fire starting as a function of a disturbed personality and claim that arson should be viewed as a mental health problem, not a criminal act.[56] It is alleged that arsonists often experience sexual pleasure from starting fires and then observing their destructive effects. Although some arsonists may be aroused sexually by their activities, there is little evidence that most arsonists are psychosexually motivated.[57] It is equally likely that fires are started by angry people looking for revenge against property owners or by teenagers out to vandalize property.

Juveniles, who are the most prolific fire starters, may get involved in arson for a variety of reasons

© Oleksiy Maksymenko/Alamy

as they mature. Other fires are set by professionals, who engage in arson for profit. People looking to collect insurance money, but who are afraid or unable to set the fires themselves, hire professional arsonists who know how to set fires yet make the cause seem accidental (such as an electrical short). Another form is arson fraud, which involves a business owner burning his or her property, or hiring someone to do it, to escape financial problems.[58] Over the years, investigators have found that businesspeople are willing to become involved in arson to collect fire insurance or for various other reasons, such as

- Obtaining money during a period of financial crisis
- Getting rid of outdated or slow-moving inventory
- Destroying outmoded machines and technology
- Paying off legal and illegal debts
- Relocating or remodelling a business—for example, a theme restaurant that has not been accepted by customers
- Taking advantage of government funds available for redevelopment
- Applying for government-funded energy conservation or retrofitting construction grants, pocketing the money without making any repairs, and then claiming that fire destroyed the "rehabilitated" building
- Planning bankruptcies to eliminate debts after the merchandise supposedly destroyed was secretly sold before the fire
- Eliminating business competition by burning out rivals
- Employing extortion schemes that demand that victims pay up or the rest of their holdings will be burned
- Solving labour–management problems (this type of arson may be committed by a disgruntled employee)
- Concealing another crime, such as embezzlement

During the past decade, a variety of programs across Canada have been established to address the growing concern about juvenile fire setting. Housed primarily within the fire service, these programs are designed to identify, evaluate, and treat juvenile fire setters to prevent the recurrence of fire-setting behaviours.

12

White-Collar Crime *and* Organized Crime

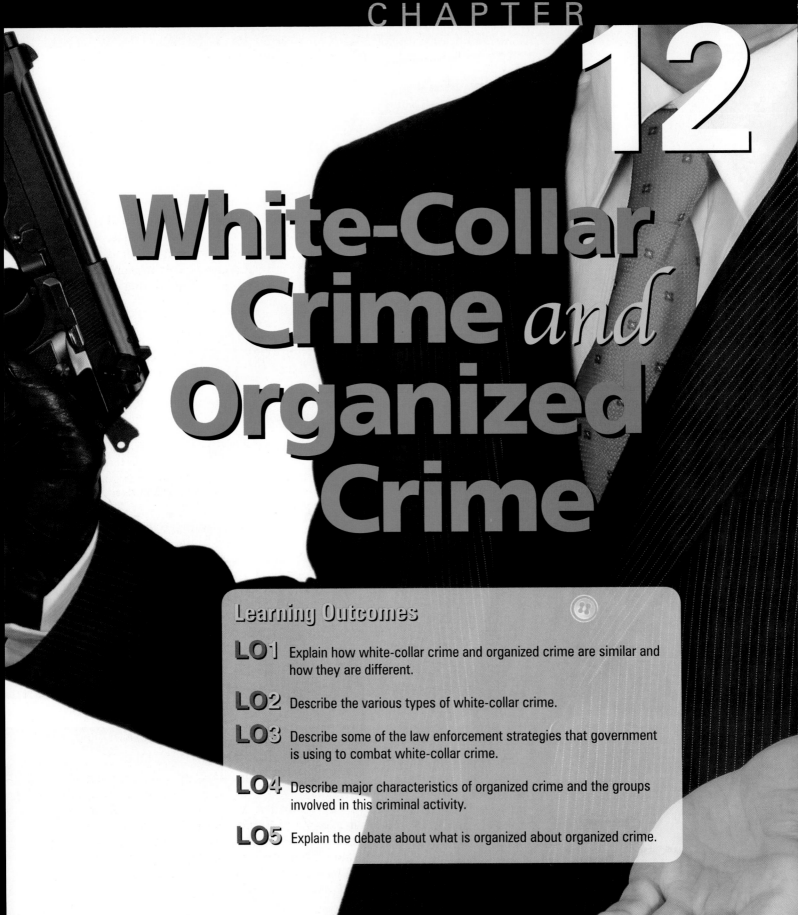

Learning Outcomes

LO1 Explain how white-collar crime and organized crime are similar and how they are different.

LO2 Describe the various types of white-collar crime.

LO3 Describe some of the law enforcement strategies that government is using to combat white-collar crime.

LO4 Describe major characteristics of organized crime and the groups involved in this criminal activity.

LO5 Explain the debate about what is organized about organized crime.

LO1 Introduction

In 1999, fifteen Canadian men were charged in a complex fraud scheme that bilked taxpayers out of more than $20 million in GST tax rebate cheques. The scheme involved the men setting up fake companies that purchased and sold thousands of automobiles for the sole purpose of obtaining GST rebates. The cars, however, existed only on paper. According to Paul Stunt, one of the prosecutors involved in the case, "This is really the high end. This is the Cadillac of GST frauds." The masterminds of the scheme, Ewaryst Prokofiew, 44, of Mississauga, and Joseph Rothe, 51, of Aurora, were each convicted and sentenced to four years in jail, and ordered to pay $500 000 in restitution to taxpayers. Prokofiew's conviction was appealed, and is scheduled to be heard by the Supreme Court of Canada in 2012. Similarly, in February 2011 Adolf Schiel, 74, of Surrey, B.C. was sentenced to four years in jail for defrauding taxpayers of nearly $2 million in false GST tax rebate claims. His daughter Sandy, 43, was sentenced to five years in jail for her part in the scheme. The Schiels claimed to have spent $26 million in purchases of equipment, supplies, and services to develop two properties they owned on Vancouver Island, for which they submitted $1 959 910 in GST rebate claims to the government. Judge Gregory Bowden of the Vancouver Provincial Court found that the $26 million in expenses claimed by the Schiels was bogus. In addition to serving the jail sentence, the Schiels were ordered to pay back the $1 959 910 once they are released from jail. The Schiels have been released on bail pending appeals.

DID YOU KNOW?

- White-collar crime involves the illegal distribution of legal material.
- Organized crime involves the illegal distribution of illegal material.
- White-collar and organized crime are linked together because they involve entrepreneurship.
- The definition of white-collar crime has expanded to include all forms of corrupt business practices by individuals as well as corporations.
- Losses from white-collar crime may far outstrip any other type of crime.

In what has become known as the "GST scam," fake companies are set up, usually dealing in items such as automobiles, and false claims are made for the rebate based on nonexistent sales. To keep Canadian companies competitive in the international market, the government reimburses the 7 percent Goods and Services Tax (GST) to those companies that sell to foreign countries. Because not all sales are validated, some unscrupulous individuals capitalize on the situation by submitting false claims in order to get the GST rebate. Many cases of GST fraud have come to light since the introduction of

white-collar crime Illegal acts that may include theft, embezzlement, fraud, market manipulation, restraint of trade, and false advertising; also known as commercial/business crime or economic offences.

organized crime Illegal activities of people and organizations whose acknowledged purpose is profit through illegitimate business enterprise.

enterprise Taking risks for profit in the marketplace.

the GST, including the "phony lumber company scam" in British Columbia and a scam involving automobiles in Ontario.

Experts estimate that fraud involving the GST amounts to as much as $1 billion annually. Moreover, it is almost impossible to track and reclaim the money or to ascertain exactly how much money was lost.[1]

Typically, business-related crimes involve efforts to bend the rules of enterprise and commerce in order to make a profit or gain an illegal advantage over competitors. In this chapter, we divide these crimes of illicit entrepreneurship into two distinct categories: white-collar crime and organized crime. **White-collar crime** involves illegal activities of people and institutions whose acknowledged purpose is profit through legitimate business transactions. **Organized crime** involves illegal activities of people and organizations whose acknowledged purpose is profit through illegitimate business enterprise. Organized crime and white-collar crime are linked here because **enterprise**, the goal of making money through criminal means, is the governing characteristic of both phenomena.[2]

According to criminologist Dwight Smith, business enterprise can be viewed as flowing through a spectrum of acts ranging from the most "saintly" to the most "sinful."[3] Although "sinful" organizational practices may be desirable to many consumers (such as the sale of narcotics) or an efficient way of doing business (such as the dumping of hazardous wastes), society has regulated or outlawed these behaviours. Organized crime and business crimes are the results of a process by which "political, value-based constraints are based on economic activity."[4]

White-collar crime and organized crime share some striking similarities. Mark Haller has coined the phrase "illegal enterprise crimes" to signify the sale of illegal goods and services to customers who know they are illegal. Haller's analysis also shows the overlap between criminal and business enterprise. For example, he compares the Mafia crime family to a chamber of commerce, as an association of businesspeople who join to further their business careers. Joining a crime syndicate allows one to cultivate contacts and be in a position to take advantage of good deals offered by more experienced players. The criminal group settles disputes between members, who, after all, cannot take their problems to court.[5]

Both organized crime and white-collar crime taint and corrupt the free market system; they involve all phases of illegal entrepreneurial activity. Organized crime involves individuals or groups whose marketing techniques (threat, extortion, smuggling) and product lines (drugs, prostitution, gambling, loansharking) have been outlawed. White-collar crimes include the use of illegal business practices (theft, embezzlement, price-fixing, bribery) to merchandise what are ordinarily legitimate commercial products.

Surprisingly to some, both forms of crime can involve violence. Although the use of force and coercion by organized crime members has been popularized in the media and therefore comes as no shock, that white-collar crimes may inflict pain and suffering seems more astonishing. Yet experts claim that the number of occupational deaths that occur each year is on the rise and that "corporate violence" annually kills and injures more people than all street crimes combined.[6]

It is also possible to link organized crime and white-collar crime because some criminal enterprises involve both forms of activity. Organized criminals may seek legitimate enterprises to launder money, diversify their source of income, increase their power and influence, and gain and enhance respectability.[7] Otherwise legitimate businesspeople may turn to organized criminals to help them with

DID YOU KNOW?

- White-collar crime has a number of different subcategories.
- Stings and swindles involve long-term efforts to cheat people out of their money.
- Chiselling involves regular cheating of an organization or its customers.
- People who engage in exploitation demand that victims pay for services they are entitled to by threatening consequences if they refuse. The victim here is the client.
- Influence peddling and bribery occur when a person in authority demands payment for a service to which the payer is clearly not entitled. The victim here is the organization.
- Embezzlement and employee fraud occur when a person uses a position of trust to steal from an organization.
- Client fraud involves theft from an organization that advances credit, covers losses, or reimburses for services.
- Corporate crime involves various illegal business practices such as price-fixing, restraint of trade, and false advertising.
- High-tech crimes are a new form of white-collar crime involving computer and Internet fraud.

economic problems (such as breaking up a strike or dumping hazardous waste products), stifle or threaten competition, and increase their influence. The distinction between organized crime and white-collar criminals may often become blurred.[8]

Some forms of white-collar crime may be more like organized crime than others.[9] Whereas some corporate executives cheat to improve their company's position in the business world, others are motivated purely for personal gain. It is this latter group, people who engage in ongoing criminal conspiracies for their own profit, that most resembles organized crime.[10]

Jupiter Images

Much white-collar crime takes place in the boardroom, behind closed doors, making it difficult for police to investigate this crime and lay charges.

LO2 White-Collar Crime

In the late 1930s, the distinguished criminologist Edwin Sutherland first used the phrase "white-collar crime" to describe the criminal activities of the rich and powerful. He defined white-collar crime as "a crime committed by a person of respectability and high social status in the course of his occupation."[11] As Sutherland saw it, white-collar crime involved conspiracies by members of the wealthy classes to use their position in commerce and industry for personal gain without regard to the law. Often these actions were handled by civil courts, because injured parties were more concerned with recovering their losses than seeing the offenders punished criminally. Yet the cost of white-collar crime is probably several times greater than all the crimes that are customarily regarded as the "crime problem." And, in contrast to street crimes, white-collar offences breed distrust in economic and social institutions, lowering public morale and undermining faith in business and government.[12]

© Andrew Rubtsov/Alamy

Double-charging customers for a purchase they have made with their credit card is a common credit card scam. It is up to credit card holders to check their statements to make sure they are accurate.

corporate crime
A legal offence, such as price-fixing, restraint of trade, or hazardous waste dumping, committed by a corporate entity to improve its market share or profitability.

Although Sutherland's work is considered a milestone in criminological history, his focus was on corporate criminality, including the crimes of the rich and powerful. Contemporary definitions of white-collar crime are typically much broader, including both middle-income earners and corporate executives who use the marketplace for their criminal activity.[13] Included within recent views of white-collar crime are such middle-class acts as income tax evasion, credit card fraud, and mortgage fraud. Other white-collar criminals use their positions of trust in business or government to commit crimes. Their activities might include pilfering, soliciting bribes or kickbacks, and embezzlement. Some white-collar criminals set up business for the sole purpose of victimizing the general public.

In addition to acting as individuals, some white-collar criminals become involved in criminal conspiracies designed to improve the market share or profitability of their corporations. This type of white-collar crime, which includes antitrust violations, price-fixing, and false advertising, is known as **corporate crime**.[14]

It is difficult to estimate the extent and influence of white-collar crime on victims because all too often those who suffer the consequences of white-collar crime are ignored by victimologists.[15] According to the PricewaterhouseCoopers' 2009 Global Economic Crime Survey, which was based on over 3000 respondents from 54 countries, 30 percent of companies worldwide reported being a victim of an economic crime in the previous 12 months. More than 50 percent of Canadian companies were victims of economic crime, and in more than half of cases the losses were reported to be in excess of $500 000.[16]

Beyond their monetary cost, white-collar crimes often damage property and kill people. Violations of safety standards, pollution of the environment, and industrial accidents due to negligence can be classified as corporate violence. White-collar crime also destroys confidence, saps the integrity of commercial life, and has the potential for devastating destruction. Think of the possible results if nuclear regulatory rules are flouted or if toxic wastes are dumped into a community's drinking water supply.[17]

Nor is white-collar crime a uniquely Western phenomenon. It occurs in other parts of the world as well, often in the form of corruption by government agents. In China, corruption by public officials accounts for a high percentage of all cases of economic crime, despite the fact that the penalty for corruption is death.[18] China is not alone in experiencing organizational crimes. In Thailand, crime and corruption are skyrocketing; top executives of the Bangkok Bank of Commerce are believed to have absconded with billions of dollars worth of depositors' money.[19] Western companies are also the targets of white-collar criminals. Agents have been inserted into North American companies abroad to steal trade secrets and confidential procedures, including intellectual property such as computer programs and technology. The cost is somewhere between a conservative US$50 billion and an astounding US$240 billion a year.[20]

Types of White-Collar Crime

White-collar crimes today represent a range of behaviours involving individuals acting alone and within the context of a business structure. The victims of white-collar crime can be the general public, the organization that employs the offender, or a competing organization. Numerous attempts have been made to create subcategories or typologies of white-collar criminality.[21]

This text adopts a typology created by criminologist Mark Moore to organize the analysis of white-collar crime.[22] Moore's typology contains seven elements, ranging from an individual's using a business enterprise to commit theft-related crimes, to an individual's using his or her place within a business enterprise for illegal gain, to business enterprises collectively engaging in illegitimate activity. Because no single typology of white-collar crime may sufficiently encompass the complex array of acts that the term usually denotes, Moore's typology has been expanded to include newly emerging high-tech crimes such as Internet fraud.[23] Figure 12.1 shows that Internet fraud is one of the most frequently reported types of fraud.

Stings and Swindles

The first category of white-collar crime involves stealing through deception by individuals who use their institutional or business position to bilk people out of their money. Offences in this category range from the door-to-door selling of faulty merchandise to the passing of millions of dollars in counterfeit stock certificates to an established brokerage firm. If caught, white-collar swindlers are usually charged with theft or fraud.

In February 2011 the RCMP's Integrated Market Enforcement Team (IMET) charged 11 Montreal and Toronto residents for fraud and fraudulent manipulation of stock exchange transactions, estimated to have netted the men in excess of $3 million. According to police, the men emptied the RRSP accounts of victims by manipulating a series of false stock market transactions to make it appear

FIGURE 12.1

Percentage of Frauds Reported by Crime Type

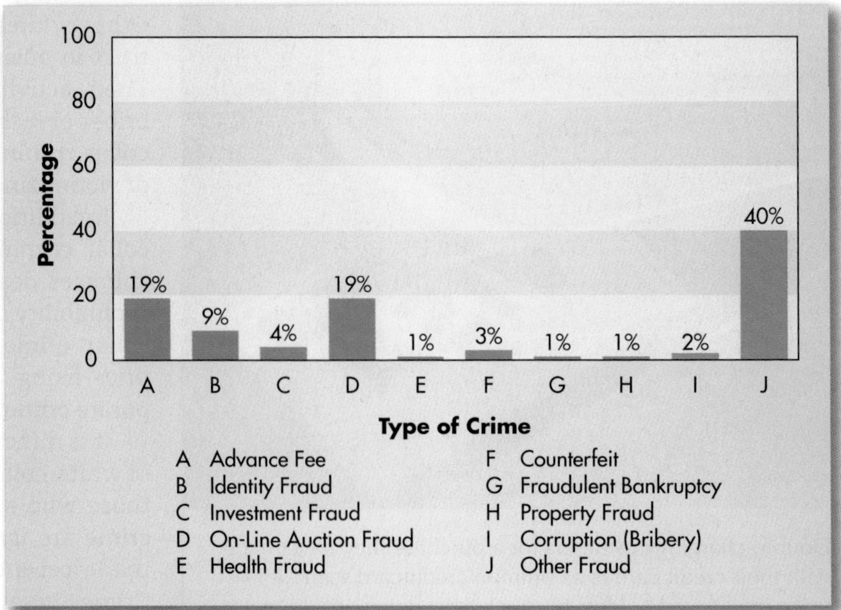

Source: Courtesy of the National White Collar Crime Centre of Canada.

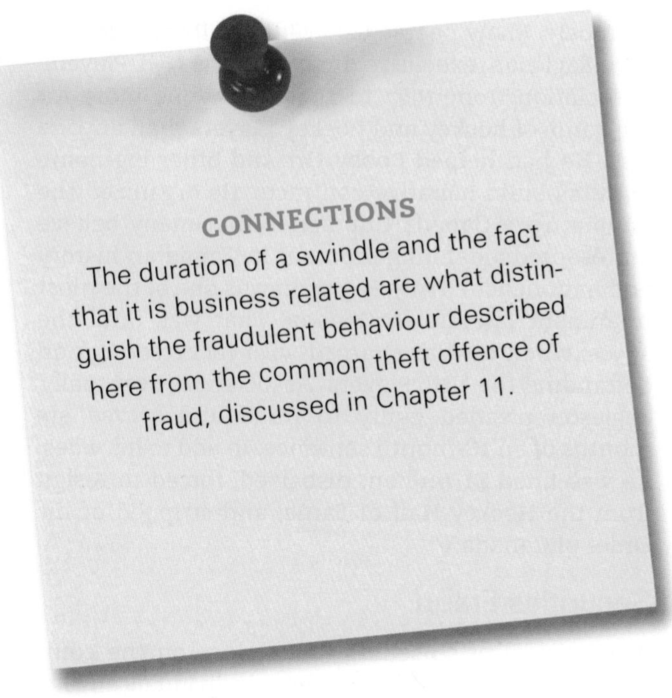
CONNECTIONS
The duration of a swindle and the fact that it is business related are what distinguish the fraudulent behaviour described here from the common theft offence of fraud, discussed in Chapter 11.

as though the victims' investments had been lost in downturns in the market, when in fact the accused had pocketed the money.[24]

Another case involves Albert Walker, a small-town Ontario businessman who specialized in financial services. Walker, his wife, and their four children were regular churchgoers and respected members of their community. Partly because of his solid standing in the community, Walker gained the trust of many in his congregation, including seniors, and convinced them to invest heavily in his company. In 1990, his congregation was stunned after it was revealed that both Walker and his daughter Sheena mysteriously disappeared while on a trip to London, England, along with much of his clients' money. Subsequent investigations revealed that Walker had deposited millions in various European banks.

chiselling
Regularly cheating an organization, its customers, or both.

In an attempt to change their identities, Walker befriended Englishman Ronald Platt, who had a keen interest in visiting Canada. He convinced Platt to give him his birth certificate and driver's licence in exchange for a plane ticket to Canada. With new identities, Walker and his daughter, the new "Mrs. Platt," moved to southeast England, where they lived for the next six years and where Sheena had two children.

Unfortunately, Platt decided to return to England and look up his old friend, Albert Walker. The investigation revealed that Walker subsequently murdered Platt and dumped his weighted, battered body into the sea. Shortly afterward, fishermen pulled a body out of the water that was identified as that of Platt through a serial number on the Rolex watch still strapped to his wrist. When apprehended by police, Walker and his daughter were planning a quick getaway with over £67 000 of gold bullion. In the bizarre aftermath, Sheena testified against her father, claiming he had hypnotized her. Walker was eventually convicted of embezzlement and murder and sent to jail for life.[25]

In 1999, small-town businessman Albert Walker and his daughter gained worldwide notoriety after absconding with millions of dollars of his clients' money. In a plot out of Hollywood, the case involved embezzlement, stolen identity, and murder, culminating in a life sentence for Walker.

Chiselling

Chiselling, the second category of white-collar crime, involves regularly cheating an organization, its customers, or both. Chisellers may be individuals looking to make quick profits in their own businesses or employees of large organizations who decide to cheat on obligations to their own company or its clients by doing something contrary to either the law or company policy.

Chiselling may involve charging for bogus auto repairs, cheating customers on home repairs, or short-weighting (intentionally tampering with the accuracy of scales used to weigh products) in supermarkets or dairies. Chiselling may even involve illegal use of information

churning
A form of stockbroker chiselling involving repeated, excessive, and unnecessary buying and selling of stock.

front running
A form of stockbroker chiselling in which brokers place personal orders ahead of a large customer's order to profit from the market effects of the trade.

bucketing
A form of stockbroker chiselling in which brokers skim customer trading profits by falsifying trade information.

insider trading
Buying and selling securities based on business information derived from a position of trust and not available to the general public.

about company policies that have not been disclosed to the public. The secret information can be sold to speculators or used to make money in the stock market. Use of the information violates the obligation to keep company policy secret.

Professional Chiselling

It is not uncommon for professionals to use their positions to chisel clients. Pharmacists have been known to alter prescriptions or substitute low-cost generic drugs for more expensive name brands. One study found that pharmacists who were business oriented—those who stressed merchandising, inventory turnover, and the pursuit of profit at the expense of professional ethics—were the ones most inclined to chisel customers.[26]

The legal profession has also come under fire because of the unscrupulous behaviour of some of its members. Many people believed that Toronto lawyer Alan Eagleson, executive director of the NHL Players' Association from 1967 to 1990, had done more for the game of hockey and hockey players than anyone else. He had helped Bobby Orr and other big-name players obtain lucrative contracts. He organized the famous 1972 Canada Cup series that many believe represented a defining moment in Canadian history and nationalism. Truly, Eagleson was one of the most prominent lawyers in Canada. That was until the 1990s, when he was charged with racketeering and defrauding the NHL Players' Association. Eventually, Eagleson pleaded guilty to fraud and served six months of an 18-month sentence. To add to his woes, he was fined $1 million, disbarred, forced to resign from the Hockey Hall of Fame, and stripped of his Order of Canada.[27]

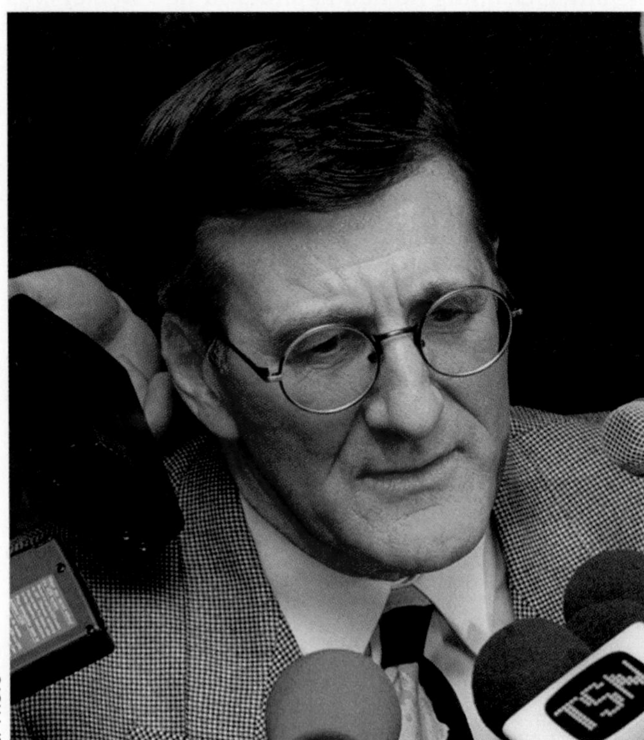

CP PHOTO

Fall of the czar: Alan Eagleson, organizer of the famous Canada–Russia Summit Series of 1972.

Securities Fraud

A great deal of chiselling takes place on the commodity and stock markets, where individuals engage in deceptive practices that are prohibited by law. Some brokers will use their positions to cheat individual clients, for example, by **churning** the client's account through repeated, excessive, and unnecessary buying and selling of stock.[28] Other broker fraud includes **front running**, in which brokers place personal orders ahead of a large customer's order to profit from the market effects of the trade, and **bucketing**, which is skimming customer trading profits by falsifying trade information.[29]

Securities chiselling can also involve using one's position of trust to profit from inside business information, referred to as **insider trading**. The information can then be used to buy and sell securities, giving the trader an unfair advantage over the general public, which lacks this inside information.

Traders and even company executives can use insider information about what will happen to a company to buy or sell stock shares, and make huge profits. The big losers are honest citizens who can lose thousands of dollars.

Insider trading violations can occur in a variety of situations. As originally conceived, it was illegal for corporate employees with direct knowledge of market-sensitive information to use that information for their own benefit—for example, by buying stock in a company that they learn will be taken over by the larger organization for which they work. In recent years, the definition of insider trading has been expanded to include employees of financial institutions, such as law or banking firms, who misappropriate confidential information on pending corporate actions to purchase stock or give the information to a third party so that party may buy shares in the company. Courts have ruled that such actions are deceptive and violate security trading codes.

One interesting Canadian case concerns Bre-X, a small Calgary mining company. The company's investors were made overnight millionaires as the stock skyrocketed from pennies in 1994 to $240 in less than a year. Bre-X had reportedly discovered one of the world's largest deposits of gold in Indonesia. But all was not as it appeared. After further tests, it was reported that the original core samples had been "salted" in order to increase the gold content. Shortly thereafter, the geologist employed by Bre-X, Michael de Guzman, died after jumping from a helicopter, in what many believe was a suicide. Trading in the company's stock on the Toronto Stock Exchange came to a halt, and the price of the stock dropped from $15.80 to $2.50. An estimated 40 000 investors in Canada lost over $3 billion.[30]

In March 2004, Bill C-13 received royal assent. Investor confidence had been seriously undermined by such well-publicized scandals as that involving Bre-X in Canada, and Enron, WorldCom, and ImClone in the United States. Bill C-13 established the criminal offences of insider trading, tipping, and whistle-blowing retaliation. Maximum sentences for corporate criminal offences were increased and judges were given the discretion to impose harsher penalties in cases where there were aggravating factors, such as where a crime had eroded the confidence of the public. Integrated market enforcement teams (comprising RCMP investigators, lawyers, and forensic accountants) were also established to respond quickly to major capital markets fraud and other market-related crimes.

Individual Exploitation of Institutional Position

Another type of white-collar crime involves individuals' exploiting their power or position in an organization by extorting money from people who do business with that organization by threatening to withhold services that the victim has a clear right to expect. For example, a fire inspector who threatens to cause trouble or find phantom fire code violations unless a business owner pays him is abusing his institutional position. Here the victim is the person who is being extorted.

Influence Peddling and Bribery

Sometimes individuals holding important institutional positions will sell power, influence, and information to outsiders who hold no legitimate interest in the institution or who hope to gain a favourable position by influencing the activities of the institution. Offences within this category include government employees' taking of kickbacks from contractors in return for awarding them contracts they could not have won on merit or outsiders' bribing of government officials who might sell information about future government activities.

© Alex Slobodkin/iStockPhoto

One major difference distinguishes influence peddling from the previously discussed exploitation of an institutional position. Exploitation involves forcing victims to pay for services to which they have a clear right. In contrast, influence peddlers and bribe takers use their institutional positions to grant favours and sell information to which their co-conspirators are not entitled. In sum, in crimes of institutional exploitation, the victim is the person forced to pay for services he or she deserves, whereas the victim of influence peddling is the organization compromised by its employees for their own interests.

Influence Peddling in Government

In March 2011, Prime Minister Stephen Harper called in the RCMP to investigate one of his own former top advisers, Bruce Carson, for allegedly promising privileged access to Conservative government ministers in return for money. The Aboriginal Peoples Television Network (APTN) first uncovered the alleged influence peddling when investigating complaints that Carson had used his connections in the Conservative government to illegally lobby Indian Affairs Minister John Duncan on behalf of a company seeking to sell water filtration systems to remote First Nations communities. APTN claimed to have in its possession an email written to the water filtration company in which Carson boasted about having insider knowledge that Duncan was about to be appointed Minister of Indian Affairs, his insider connections to the newly appointed minister, and that he would be "calling the new Minister this morning—so it is full steam ahead." Carson

pilferage
Employee theft of company property.

responded to the APTN allegations and the RCMP investigation by announcing that he was taking a leave of absence from his professional activities with the government, effective immediately. Carson, a long-time Conservative party insider, had been disbarred in the 1980s for defrauding his clients.[31]

Corruption in the Criminal Justice System

Agents of the criminal justice system have also gotten caught up in official corruption, a circumstance that is particularly disturbing because society expects a higher standard of moral integrity from people empowered to uphold the law and judge their fellow citizens. Police officers have been particularly vulnerable to charges of corruption.

One of the largest *police corruption* investigations in Canadian history was sparked by a 2003 RCMP wiretap in a Toronto bar, where names of Toronto police officers were overheard in connection to loans and organized crime. A special RCMP-led task force was established to investigate organized crime and the Toronto Police Force. The investigation identified three major areas of concern: (1) the Toronto drug squad was accused of physically assaulting informants, stealing from drug dealers, falsifying documents, and conducting illegal searches; (2) the 52 Division plainclothes unit was alleged to have been engaged in a protection racket with bar owners in the entertainment area of the city; and (3) there were allegations over an inappropriate relationship between some officers and a car-leasing salesman who reportedly had connections with organized crime.[32]

After three years of investigation and a cost of millions, over 20 Toronto officers were charged with 135 criminal and Police Services Act charges. Then-Toronto Police Chief Julian Fantino stated, "I will not tolerate any unprofessional behaviour, corrupt practices, compromises to the moral and ethical code of conduct demanded of the policing profession, abuses of power and authority, racial intolerance or discriminating conduct on or off the job."[33] Later, other allegations were made against a second police narcotics squad by Milos Markovic, a suspected drug dealer, who claimed that officers had stolen money from his safety deposit boxes during an investigation. Markovic's lawyer, Julian Falconer, alleges that Toronto police chose to ignore his client's claims in their investigation in an attempt to mask the full extent of the corruption.[34]

Influence Peddling in Business

Politicians and government officials are not the only ones accused of bribery; business has had its share of scandals. The 1970s witnessed revelations that multinational corporations regularly made payoffs to foreign officials and businesspeople to secure business contracts. Gulf Oil executives admitted paying US$4 million to the South Korean ruling party; Burroughs Corporation admitted paying US$1.5 million to foreign officials; and Lockheed Aircraft admitted paying US$202 million to Japanese politicians in return for an agreement to buy new aircraft. McDonnell–Douglas Aircraft Corporation was indicted for paying US$1 million in bribes to officials of Pakistani International Airlines to secure orders.[35]

Theft and Employee Fraud

The fifth type of white-collar crime involves individuals' use of their positions to embezzle or steal company funds or appropriate company property for themselves. Here the company or organization that employs the criminal, rather than an outsider, is the victim of white-collar crime. Employee theft can reach all levels of the organizational structure.

Blue-collar employees have been involved in systematic theft of company property, commonly called **pilferage**.[36] Employee theft is most accurately explained by factors relevant to the work setting,

Peter Dazeley/Photographer's Choice/Getty Images

Employee thefts can extend to stealing company information for sale to unscrupulous competitors, or to organized crime gangs engaged in identity theft.

such as job dissatisfaction and the workers' belief that they are being exploited by employers or supervisors; economic problems play a relatively small role in the decision to pilfer. Although employers attribute employee fraud to economic conditions and declining personal values, workers themselves say they steal because of strain and conflict. It is difficult to determine the value of goods taken by employees, but it has been estimated that pilferage accounts for 30 to 75 percent of all shrinkage.[37]

Blue-collar workers are not the only employees who commit corporate theft. Management-level fraud is also quite common. Such acts include (1) converting company assets for personal benefit; (2) fraudulently receiving increases in compensation (such as raises or bonuses); (3) fraudulently increasing personal holdings of company stock; (4) retaining one's present position within the company by manipulating accounts to show success; and (5) concealing unacceptable performance from stockholders.[38]

Alex Tavshunsky

In 2009 Dr. Lorne Sokol, a Toronto doctor, was found guilty of fraud and money laundering and agreed to repay $3.5 million he fraudulently billed the Ontario Health Insurance Plan (OHIP). Between March 2003 and February 2007, Sokol, a pain specialist, submitted billings for services that were never provided.

Client Fraud

A sixth component of white-collar crime is theft from an organization that advances credit to its clients or reimburses them for services rendered. These offences are linked because they involve cheating an organization (such as a government agency or insurance company) with many individual clients that the organization supports financially (such as welfare clients), reimburses for services provided (such as health-care providers), covers losses of (such as insurance policyholders), or extends credit to (such as bank clients or taxpayers). Included in this category are insurance fraud, credit card fraud, fraud related to the health-care system, and tax evasion.

Health-Care Fraud

Client fraud may be common even among upper-income people.[39] Some physicians have been caught cheating the government out of government-sponsored health-care payments.

In 1998, Ontario established a health-care fraud squad run by Ontario Provincial Police officers to crack down on fraud in relation to the Ontario Health Insurance Plan (OHIP). Since the establishment of the unit, more than 500 cases have been investigated, the majority of which involved people attempting to defraud OHIP. Examples of this form of fraud include "double doctoring" to obtain multiple prescriptions, using someone else's card, or illegally obtaining health services. Those found guilty can face prison terms of up to ten years, plus fines.

Medical health professionals, including doctors, account for only about 12 percent of frauds, such as billing for unnecessary services, billing for services that were not performed, billing for unnecessary medical referrals, or billing for a more expensive service. Some of the cases investigated by the unit have included that of 62-year-old Stephen Kai Yiu Chung of Hamilton, who posed as a physician for 15 years and allegedly defrauded OHIP of $4.5 million; Dr. Alexander Scott of Kingston, who received 30 months in a penitentiary after defrauding OHIP of $600 000; and Dr. Donald MacDiarmid of Ajax, who received an 18-month conditional sentence and was fined $100 000 for defrauding OHIP of $150 000. One of the most complex cases to date involves 12 doctors at a Mississauga walk-in clinic who were charged with defrauding OHIP of about $2 million in 1997.[40]

Bank Fraud

Bank fraud can encompass such diverse schemes as cheque kiting, cheque forgery, false statements on loan applications, sale of stolen cheques, bank credit card fraud, unauthorized use of automated teller machines (ATMs), auto title fraud, and illegal transactions with offshore banks. To be found guilty of **bank fraud**, one must knowingly execute or attempt to execute a scheme to fraudulently obtain money or property from a financial institution. For example, a car dealer would commit bank fraud by securing loans on titles to cars it no longer owned. A real estate owner would be guilty of bank fraud if he or she obtained a false appraisal on a piece of

bank fraud
To obtain money or property from a financial institution by false pretences, as by forgery or misrepresentation.

Edmonton Sun/Walter Tychnowicz

Bank employees who steal from their employers commit bank fraud. In 2002, Nick Lysyk of Edmonton pled guilty to 63 counts of fraud over $5000 in what was the largest bank fraud case to date in Canadian history. By falsifying a steady stream of loans dating back to the late 1990s, he defrauded his employer, the Bank of Montreal, out of an estimated $16 million, $10 million of which still remains unaccounted for. Lysyk used the money to bankroll a lavish lifestyle that included 40 vehicles, expensive jewellery, 17 homes, and home furnishings, not to mention a family and two girlfriends. For his crime, Lysyk was sentenced to just over seven years in prison.[41]

restraint of trade A contract or conspiracy designed to stifle competition, create a monopoly, artificially maintain prices, or otherwise interfere with free market competition.

property with the intention of obtaining a bank loan in excess of the property's real worth.

In 2003, two Toronto women, Marina Kachin and Ioulia Rovenskaya, were found guilty and sentenced to 20 months in jail for their role in one of the most significant attacks on the ATM network in Canada. The investigation revealed that ten people from Vancouver to Sudbury were involved in a scam using independent ATMs set up in stores. The machines were equipped to record user card information and personal identification numbers that were later used to make counterfeit cards. Approximately $1.2 million has been recovered from funds illegally withdrawn from customers' accounts.[42] In a similar case in November 2010, Winnipeg police arrested a health centre employee for fraudulently withdrawing over $1 million over a ten-year period from an ATM at the site.[43]

Tax Evasion

Another important aspect of client fraud is tax evasion. Here the victim, the government, is cheated by one of its clients, the errant taxpayer to whom it has extended credit by allowing the taxpayer to delay paying taxes on money he or she has already earned. Tax fraud is a particularly challenging area for criminological study because (1) so many citizens regularly underreport their income, and (2) it is often difficult to separate honest error from deliberate tax evasion.

The Canada Revenue Agency (CRA) regularly reviews taxes submitted by businesses and individuals. When fraudulent activity is discovered, the CRA is responsible for enforcement through its Special Investigations Section. If it is determined that reasonable and probable grounds exist, then the investigators apply for a search warrant and prepare the case for prosecution in the courts under section 239 of the Income Tax Act. Convictions are made public in the hope of deterring others from evading taxes.

Corporate Crime

Yet another component of white-collar crime involves situations in which powerful institutions or their representatives wilfully violate the laws that restrain these institutions from doing social harm or require them to do social good. This is also known as corporate crime.

Corporate crimes are socially injurious acts committed by people who control companies to further their business interests. The target of their crimes can be the general public, the environment, or even their companies' workers. What makes these crimes unique is that the perpetrator is a legal fiction—a corporation—and not an individual. In reality, it is company employees or owners who commit corporate crimes and who ultimately benefit through career advancement or greater profits.

Some of the acts included within corporate crime are price-fixing and illegal restraint of trade, false advertising, and the use of company practices that violate environmental protection statutes. The variety of crimes contained within this category is great, and they cause vast damage. The following subsections examine some of the most important offences.

Illegal Restraint of Trade and Price-Fixing

A **restraint of trade** involves a contract or conspiracy designed to stifle competition, create a monopoly, artificially maintain prices, or otherwise interfere with free market competition.

Price-fixing is an example of restraint of trade, and it has several variations. In one variation, large companies agree among themselves to sell their product at a price below market value, so weaker companies are then pushed out of business. In another type of price-fixing, companies agree beforehand to submit identical inflated bids for a contract. Rotational bidding, a third variation, occurs when companies decide beforehand who will put in a low bid. Of course, the other bids are inflated, making the "low bid" not necessarily as low as it would have been if the companies had not conspired.[44]

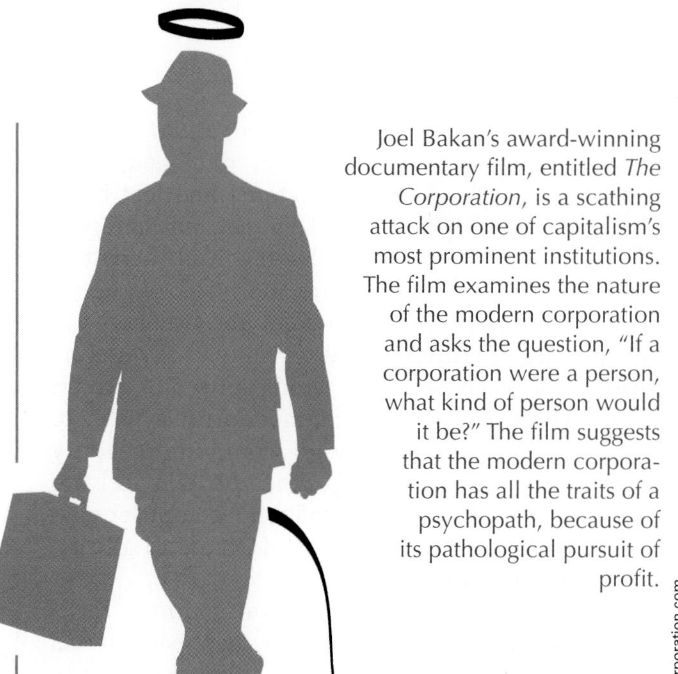

Joel Bakan's award-winning documentary film, entitled *The Corporation*, is a scathing attack on one of capitalism's most prominent institutions. The film examines the nature of the modern corporation and asks the question, "If a corporation were a person, what kind of person would it be?" The film suggests that the modern corporation has all the traits of a psychopath, because of its pathological pursuit of profit.

Image courtesy of TheCorporation.com

Deceptive Pricing

Even the largest corporations commonly use deceptive pricing schemes when they respond to contract solicitations. Deceptive pricing occurs when contractors provide the government or other corporations with incomplete or misleading information on how much it will actually cost to fulfill the contracts they are bidding on or use mischarges once the contracts are signed.[45] For example, defence contractors have been prosecuted for charging the government for costs incurred on work they are doing for private firms or shifting the costs on fixed-price contracts to ones in which the government reimburses the contractor for all expenses ("cost-plus" contracts).

False Claims and Advertising

Executives in even the largest corporations sometimes face stockholders' expectations of ever-increasing company profits, which seem to demand that sales be increased at any cost. Executives sometimes respond to this challenge by making claims about their products that cannot be justified by actual performance. However, the line between clever, aggressive sales techniques and fraudulent claims is a fine one. It is traditional to show a product in its best light, even if that involves resorting to fantasy. It is not fraudulent to show a delivery service vehicle taking off into outer space or to imply that taking one sip of iced tea will make people feel they have just jumped into a swimming pool. However, it is illegal to knowingly and purposely advertise a product as possessing qualities that the manufacturer realizes it does not have.

Environmental Crimes

Much attention has been paid to intentional or negligent environmental pollution caused by many large corporations. The numerous allegations in this area involve almost every aspect of business.

There are many different types of environmental crimes. Some corporations have endangered the lives of their own workers by maintaining unsafe conditions in their plants and mines. According to one report of fatal on-the-job accidents occurring annually in Canada, more than half were the result of unsafe working conditions. It was estimated that annual workplace deaths approximate those for street homicides, without including the number of "lingering deaths." Studies conducted in Ontario indicate that over 100 000 employees were often needlessly exposed to dangerous pollutants found in the workplace.[46]

price-fixing
A conspiracy to set and control the price of a necessary commodity.

High-Tech Crime

Computer Crimes

There is an ongoing debate among experts on what exactly constitutes a computer crime (or "cyber crime"). According to Public Safety and Emergency Preparedness Canada, high-tech crime falls into two broad categories: (1) "traditional crimes" that are committed with the aid of a computer, such as money laundering, distributing child pornography, illegal gambling, Internet fraud, and hate propaganda; and (2) "pure" high-tech crimes, which include crimes directed against a computer or a computer network such as "hacking" (unauthorized use of computer systems) and spreading viruses. It has been estimated that these types of crimes cost the world

virus
A computer program that disrupts or destroys existing programs and networks.

economy over US$1 trillion per year in damaged computer systems and lost business. This second category typically involves activities that are motivated more by malice than by profit. When computers themselves are the target, criminals are typically motivated by revenge for some perceived wrong, a need to exhibit their technical prowess and superiority, a wish to highlight the vulnerability of computer security systems, a desire to spy on other peoples' private financial and personal information ("computer voyeurism"), or a philosophy of open access to all systems and programs.[47]

Computer criminals use several common techniques. In fact, computer theft has become so common that experts have created their own jargon to describe theft styles and methods:

- *The Trojan horse.* One computer is used to reprogram another for illicit purposes. In one incident, two high school–age computer users reprogrammed the computer at DePaul University, preventing that institution from using its own processing facilities.
- *The salami slice.* An employee sets up a dummy account in the company's computerized records. A small amount—even a few pennies—is subtracted from each customer's account and added to the thief's account. Even if they detect the loss, the customers don't complain, because a few cents is an insignificant amount to them. The pennies picked up here and there eventually amount to thousands of dollars in losses.
- *"Super-zapping."* Most computer programs used in business have built-in antitheft safeguards. However, employees can use a repair or maintenance program to supersede the antitheft program. Some tinkering with the program is required, but the "super-zapper" is soon able to order the system to issue cheques to the thief's private account.
- *The logic bomb.* A program is secretly attached to the company's computer system. The new program monitors the company's work and waits for a sign of error to appear, some illogic that was designed for the computer to follow. Illogic causes the logic bomb to kick into action and exploit the weakness. The way the thief exploits the situation depends on his or her original intent—theft of money or defence secrets, sabotage, or whatever.
- *Impersonation.* An unauthorized person uses the identity of an authorized computer user to access the computer system.
- *Data leakage.* A person illegally obtains data from a computer system by leaking it out in small amounts.

A different type of computer crime involves installing a virus in a computer system. A **virus** is a program that disrupts or destroys existing programs and networks.[48] All too often, this high-tech vandalism is the work of hackers, who consider their efforts to be pranks.

An accurate accounting of computer crime will probably never be made because so many offences go unreported. Sometimes company managers refuse to report the crime to police lest they display their incompetence and vulnerability to stockholders and competitors.[49] In other instances, computer crimes go unreported because they involve low-visibility acts such as copying computer software in violation of copyright laws.[50]

This category of crime is of utmost concern for the future, given society's increasing reliance on vital computerized services and the threat to national security that a disruption in these services might entail. Hackers pose one type of problem, but a disruption caused by organized criminal groups or political extremists might pose yet-unforeseen consequences.[51]

Controlling Internet Crime

The Canadian government recognized the threat posed by cyber crime in a 2007 report entitled *Overview of the National Agenda to Combat Organized Crime 2000–2006* that recommended that the government pay particular attention to high-tech crime. In the same year, the federal government passed the Personal Information Protection and Electronic Documents Act to protect e-commerce transactions in Canada. The legislation was designed to protect and ensure the safety of Internet-based commerce both nationally and internationally.[52]

Other legislation has been aimed at particular aspects of high-tech crime; for example, Bill C-15A, passed in 2002, created the offence of "luring" or exploiting children through the Internet. It is now an offence to transmit, make available, export, and access child pornography on the Internet. Tougher penalties for other related crimes have also been included.

Also in 2002, the Office of Critical Infrastructure Protection and Emergency Preparedness (OCIPEP) was established to provide national leadership in protecting Canada's infrastructure, both from external physical threats and those emanating from cyber crime. A comprehensive website (http://www.psepc.gc.ca) was created that includes information on subjects ranging from cyber crime to emergency procedures in the advent of natural catastrophes.[53]

A number of agencies have been created to deal with telemarketing fraud and cyber crime. For example, since 1993, the Canadian Anti-Fraud Centre has been operated jointly by the RCMP and the Ontario Provincial Police as a national anti-fraud call centre that collects information on organized telemarketing crime throughout Canada and disseminates the information to the appropriate enforcement agencies. A toll-free telephone number provides an avenue for complaints to be registered and, more importantly, to be used for prosecution and education purposes. In 1997, Senior Busters was established to educate seniors about telemarketing fraud, to provide support for victims, and to collect information on the latest scams.[54] In December 2010, the Government of Canada passed the Canadian Anti-Spam Law (CASL) making it illegal to send unsolicited commercial electronic messages to non-consenting recipients, and a national anti-spam investigation and enforcement centre will be established in 2012.[55]

RECOL (Reporting Economic Crime On-Line), another national Web-based crime-reporting centre, was established in 2000 by the RCMP. Complaints can be made by phone, fax, or Internet concerning any frauds (traditional or Internet based), and clients will be referred to the appropriate agency for possible investigation and follow-up. RECOL is also involved with consumer education. The RECOL Centre links the RCMP, the Ontario Provincial Police, the U.S. Federal Bureau of Investigation and other international police agencies. The RCMP is working with the Law Enforcement Working Group of the G8 nations to establish similar complaint-distribution systems in each country. Canadian Eagle is yet another joint law enforcement effort between the RCMP and the FBI that investigates organized crime where fraudulent cross-border telemarketing activity is involved.[56]

- There are numerous explanations for white-collar crime.
- Some offenders are motivated by greed; others offend due to personal problems.
- Corporate culture theory suggests that some businesses encourage employees to cheat or cut corners.
- The self-control view is that white-collar criminals are like any other law violators: impulsive people who lack self-control.
- White-collar enforcement may encourage self-regulation. Organizations that violate the law are given civil fines.
- Deterrence systems punish individuals with prison sentences.

Some of the latest frauds, scams, or "pitches" are listed in Table 12.1.

The Cause of White-Collar Crime

When Wall Street financial whiz Ivan Boesky pled guilty to one count of securities fraud, he agreed to pay a civil fine of US$100 million, the largest at that time in the history of the U.S. Securities and Exchange

TABLE 12.1

High-Tech Frauds and Scams

The number and complexity of frauds and scams now operating means that enforcement agencies are always playing catch-up. Below are examples of some frauds and scams now being used:

Advanced fee loans	A company guarantees you a loan even if you have bad credit or no credit and requests an up-front fee.
Travel scams	These can take the form of filling out a ballot to win a dream vacation. Later someone calls by phone requesting your credit card number and other personal information in order to hold the vacation for you.
False charities	Fraudulent charities often use names that are very close to legitimate charities.
Pyramid schemes	These are based on recruiting more and more investors with those at the peak of the pyramid, those who got in early, making the most profit. Sooner or later, the number of investors dries up and those at the bottom stand to lose the most.
900 scams	These scams usually start with an offer in the mail to call a 1-900 number in order to collect a prize. When the number is dialed, the caller is charged by the minute and a voice-response system is used so that the call cannot be speeded up. The cost of the call is inevitably more than the prize.
Advance fee fraud	This fraud requires that you make a payment up front before you receive an item or a service; however, you will not receive either.
Identity theft	A very prevalent crime usually involving the illegal acquisition and use of personal information such as credit card numbers or a social insurance number to commit fraud.
"Phishing"	Using email lures to "fish" for passwords and financial data from the sea of Internet users.
Auto-dial programs	These programs use your modem to dial long-distance telephone numbers and bill your phone account.
Telephone fraud	Selling fraudulent services or products over the telephone.
Counterfeit	Frauds associated with counterfeit currency or debit or credit cards.[57]

Source: © Copyright 2011, Her Majesty the Queen in Right of Canada as represented by the Royal Canadian Mounted Police

Commission. Boesky's fine was later surpassed by financier Michael Milken's fine of more than US$1 billion. In June 2009, Wall Street financier Bernard Madoff was sentenced by a U.S. court to 150 years in prison. Madoff was accused of running the world's biggest "Ponzi scheme," a fake investment scam, that bilked his investment clients, many of them members of high society or Hollywood celebrities, out of more than $13 billion.[58] How, people asked, can people with so much disposable wealth get involved in a risky scheme to produce even more?

There probably are as many explanations for white-collar crime as there are white-collar crimes. Many offenders feel free to engage in business crime because they can easily rationalize its effects; they are convinced that their actions are not really crimes because the acts involved do not resemble street crimes. For example, a banker who uses his position of trust to lend his institution's assets to a company he secretly controls may see himself as a shrewd businessman, not as a criminal. Some businesspeople feel justified in committing white-collar crime because they believe that government regulators do not really understand the business world or the problems of competing in the free enterprise system. Even when caught, many white-collar criminals cannot see the error of their ways. For example, one offender convicted in a major electrical industry price-fixing conspiracy categorically denied the illegality of his actions. "We did not fix prices," he said; "I am telling you that all we did was recover costs."[59] Some white-collar criminals believe that everyone violates business laws, so it is not so bad if they do so themselves. Rationalizing greed is a common trait of white-collar criminals.

Greed is not the only motivation for white-collar crime; need also plays an important role. Executives may tamper with company books because they feel the need to keep or improve their jobs, satisfy their egos, or support their children. Blue-collar workers may pilfer because they want to keep pace with inflation or buy a new car.[60]

A well-known study of embezzlers by Donald Cressey illustrates the important role need plays in white-collar crime.[61] According to Cressey, embezzlement is caused by what he calls a "nonshareable financial problem." This condition may be the result of offenders' living beyond their means, perhaps piling up gambling debts; offenders feel they cannot let anyone know about such financial problems without ruining their reputations. Cressey claims that the door to solving personal financial problems through criminal means is opened by the rationalizations society has developed for white-collar crime: "Some of our most respectable citizens got their start in life by using other people's money temporarily"; "in the real estate business, there is nothing wrong about using deposits before the deal is closed"; "all people steal when they get in a tight spot."[62] Offenders use these and other rationalizations to resolve the conflict they experience over engaging in illegal behaviour. Rationalizations allow offenders' financial needs to be met without compromising their values.

corporate culture view
The view that some business organizations promote white-collar crime by maintaining a business climate that stresses profit over fair play.

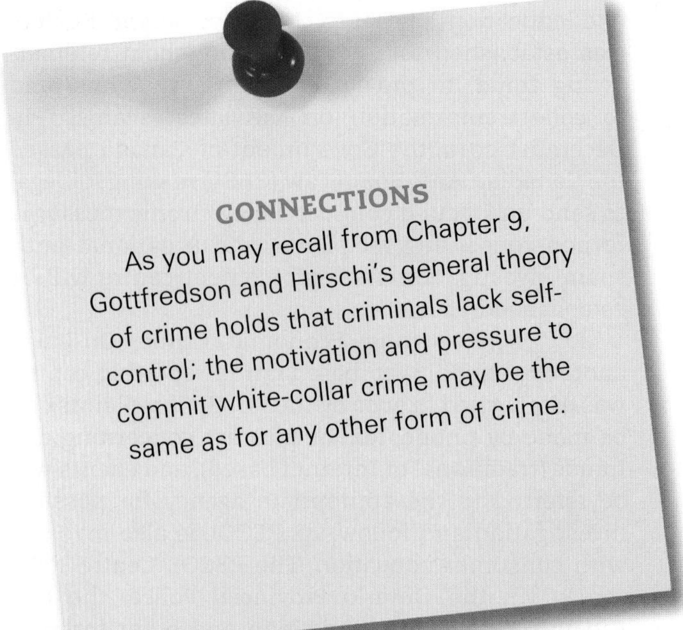

CONNECTIONS
As you may recall from Chapter 9, Gottfredson and Hirschi's general theory of crime holds that criminals lack self-control; the motivation and pressure to commit white-collar crime may be the same as for any other form of crime.

There are a number of more formal theories of white-collar crime. The **corporate culture view** is that some business organizations promote white-collar criminality in the same way that lower-class culture encourages the development of juvenile gangs and street crime. According to this view, some business enterprises cause crime by placing excessive demands on employees while at the same time maintaining a business climate tolerant of employee deviance. New employees acquire the attitudes and techniques needed to commit white-collar crime from their business peers through a learning process. Those holding the corporate culture view would see the savings and loan and insider trading scandals as prime examples of what happens when people work in organizations whose cultural values stress profit over fair play, in which government scrutiny is limited and regulators are viewed as the enemy, and in which senior members encourage newcomers to believe that "greed is good."

According to the **self-control view**, the motives that produce white-collar crimes are the same as those that produce any other criminal behaviours: "the desire for relatively quick, relatively certain benefit, with minimal effort."[63] According to this view, white-collar criminals have low self-control and are inclined to follow momentary impulses without considering the long-term costs of such behaviour.[64] White-collar crime is relatively rare because, as a matter of course, business executives tend to hire people with self-control, thereby limiting the number of potential white-collar criminals.

LO3 Controlling White-Collar Crime

The prevailing wisdom is that unlike lower-class street criminals, white-collar criminals are rarely prosecuted and, when convicted, receive relatively light sentences. In years past, it was rare for a corporate or white-collar criminal to receive a serious criminal penalty.[65]

What efforts have been made to bring violators of the public trust to justice? White-collar criminal enforcement typically involves two strategies designed to control organizational deviance: compliance and deterrence.[66]

Compliance Strategies

Compliance strategies aim for law conformity without the necessity of detecting, processing, or penalizing individual violators. At a minimum, they ask for cooperation and self-policing from the business community. Compliance systems attempt to create conformity by giving companies economic incentives to obey the law. They rely on administrative efforts to prevent unwanted conditions before they occur. Compliance systems depend on the threat of economic sanctions or civil penalties to control corporate violators.

Deterrence Strategies

Deterrence strategies involve detecting criminal violations, determining who is responsible, and penalizing the offenders to deter future violations.[67] Deterrence systems are oriented toward apprehending violators and punishing them rather than creating conditions that induce conformity to the law.

Deterrence strategies should work—and they have in the past—because white-collar crime by its nature is a rational act whose perpetrators are extremely sensitive to the threat of criminal sanctions. Perceptions of detection and punishment for white-collar crimes should be a powerful deterrent to future law violations.[68] However, the recent evidence about the effectiveness of deterrence strategies is mixed—too often, the crimes go undetected or the laws are poorly enforced.[69] At the same time, courts have traditionally been reluctant to throw corporate executives in jail. As mentioned earlier, recent amendments to the Criminal Code brought about by Bill C-13 created the criminal offences of insider trading, tipping, and whistle-blowing retaliation. The bill increased maximum sentences and provides some guidance to judges on sentencing for corporate criminal offences, even allowing for harsher penalties where there are aggravating factors. Senior executives should no longer be able to avoid a jail term by using their status, reputation, or good standing in the community to mitigate the sentence. Bill C-13 is viewed as a step in the right direction, with Canadian corporations increasingly become the subjects of criminal investigation and prosecution in the courts.[70] In November 2009, Toronto lawyer Stan Grmovsek pleaded guilty to illegal insider trading, marking Canada's first conviction under the new law.[71]

Because white-collar crime is rarely a one-time event, the identification of white-collar criminals is certainly less difficult than it is for street criminals.[72] Deterrence strategies have gone so far as charging business executives with murder in incidents where employees have died because of business-related injuries or illness. This issue is discussed in the accompanying Policy and Practice in Criminology feature.

self-control view
The view that white-collar crime, like all crime, is a product of low self-control.

compliance strategies
Fostering law conformity, cooperation, and self-policing in the business community through the use of economic incentives and administrative agencies.

deterrence strategies
Detecting criminal violations, determining who is responsible, and penalizing the offenders to deter future violations.

LO4 Organized Crime

The second branch of organizational criminality involves organized crime—the ongoing criminal enterprise groups whose ultimate purpose is personal economic gain through illegitimate means. Here, a structured enterprise system is set up to supply consumers with merchandise and services banned by criminal law but for which a ready market exists: prostitution, pornography, gambling, and narcotics. The system may resemble a legitimate business run by an ambitious chief executive officer, his or her assistants, staff lawyers, and accountants, with thorough, efficient accounts receivable and complaint departments.[73]

POLICY AND PRACTICE IN CRIMINOLOGY

CAN CORPORATIONS COMMIT MURDER?

One of the most controversial issues surrounding the punishment of white-collar criminals involves prosecuting corporate executives who work for companies that manufacture products believed to have killed workers or consumers. Are the executives guilty of manslaughter, or even murder? This issue is especially relevant when we consider the number of deaths caused by the negligence of some corporations. How should corporate executives whose products or services cause death or whose business practices result in fatal harm to their employees be treated?

EDHAR/Shutterstock.com

About 800 000 Canadians are hurt on the job each year, but successful prosecution of corporations for wrongdoing has been rare. Criminal negligence used to be something that mainly applied to accidents involving vehicles, but a new law makes it easier to convict a corporation or individual of criminal negligence due to a workplace accident.

In 1992, 26 coal miners died at the Westray mine in Plymouth, Nova Scotia, the result of an explosion caused by a buildup of methane gas and coal dust. Charges were laid against the company, Curragh Inc., and two managers under provincial health-and-safety regulations and under the federal Criminal Code. When all charges were eventually dropped, a public inquiry was called that resulted in 74 recommendations, including one that would make corporate executives and directors responsible for workplace safety.

In the fall of 2003, almost 11 years after the accident at Westray, the government of Canada passed Bill C-45, which was designed to improve workplace safety and to modernize the Criminal Code regarding the criminal liability of corporations. Bill C-45 complemented recent changes to the Canada Labour Code, which gave new rights for workers—for example, the right to be informed about hazards in the workplace, the right to participate in correcting those hazards, and the right to refuse dangerous work. Fines of up to $1 000 000 are provided for breach of the Canada Labour Code.

Under Bill C-45, not only is proving negligence made easier but also the consequences of being found guilty are more substantial. There is now a legal duty on employers and those who direct work to take reasonable measures to protect employee and public safety. If it is demonstrated that this duty is wantonly or recklessly disregarded and bodily harm or death results, an organization could be charged with criminal negligence.

The penalty for individuals convicted of criminal negligence is ten years of jail time for an accident resulting in injury; if someone dies, those responsible could face life imprisonment. The organization could also be placed under probation, which could include publicly acknowledging the conviction, the sentence, and any health-and-safety reforms imposed.

CRITICAL THINKING

1. Should corporate executives be found guilty of murder if they fail to take reasonable measures to protect their staff and an employee subsequently dies?
2. Is it fair to blame a single executive for the activities of a company that has thousands of employees?

Sources: H. Glasbeek, "Westray Bill Doesn't Make Shareholders Accountable," *Daily News* (Halifax, NS), November 28, 2004, p.17. Reprinted by permission of the *Daily News*, Halifax; Andrew Sharpe and Jill Hardt, *Five Deaths a Day: Workplace Fatalities in Canada*, 1993–2005, CSLS Research Paper 2006-04, December 2006, http://odin.pragmatic-solutions.com/drupal/sites/default/files/images/pdf/Five%20Deaths%20a%20Day%20Workplace%20Fatalities%20in%20Canada.pdf (accessed August 3, 2011).

© Moviestore collection Ltd/Alamy

A popular depiction of an organized crime family was the award-winning series *The Sopranos*.

Because of its secrecy, power, and fabulous wealth, a great mystique has grown up about organized crime. Its legendary leaders—Al Capone, Meyer Lansky, Lucky Luciano—have been the subjects of books and films. The famous *Godfather* films popularized and humanized organized crime figures; the media often glamorize organized crime figures.[74] Most citizens believe that organized criminals are capable of taking over legitimate business enterprises if given the opportunity. Almost everyone is familiar with terms such as *mob, underworld, Mafia, wise guys, syndicate*, or *La Cosa Nostra*, all of which refer to organized crime. Although most of us have neither met nor seen members of organized crime families, we feel sure that they exist, and we fear them. This section briefly defines organized crime, reviews its activities, and discusses its economic effect and control.

AP Photo/Adriana Sapone

In 2011 police conducted a major crackdown on the 'Ndrangheta crime syndicate, arresting scores of suspects in Italy and Germany, and one person in Toronto and seven in Thunder Bay. It was reported that the connection between the 'Ndrangheta and Canada dates back to the 1950s. The Canadian branch, known as the Siderno Group, is believed to have many members in Canada because the country's banking system is seen as secretive and an ideal place to launder money, and also because Canada is thought of as a useful drug smuggling entry point into North America.

Characteristics of Organized Crime

A precise description of the characteristics of organized crime is difficult to formulate, but here are some of its general traits:[75]

- Organized crime is a conspiratorial activity, involving the coordination of numerous persons in the planning and execution of illegal acts or in the pursuit of a legitimate objective by unlawful means (e.g., threatening a legitimate business to get a stake in it). Organized crime involves continuous commitment by primary members, although individuals with specialized skills may be brought in as needed. Organized crime is usually structured along hierarchical lines—a chieftain supported by close advisers, several ranks of subordinates, and so on.
- Organized crime has economic gain as its primary goal, although power and status may also be motivating factors. Economic gain is achieved through maintenance of a near-monopoly on illegal goods and services, including drugs, gambling, pornography, and prostitution.
- Organized crime activities are not limited to providing illicit services. They include sophisticated activities such as laundering illegal money through legitimate businesses, land fraud, and computer crimes.
- Organized crime employs predatory tactics, such as intimidation, violence, and corruption. It appeals to greed to accomplish its objectives and preserve its gains.
- By experience, custom, and practice, organized crime's conspiratorial groups are usually very quick and effective in controlling and disciplining their members, associates, and victims. The individuals involved know that any deviation from the rules of the organization will evoke a prompt response from the other participants. This response may range from a reduction in rank and responsibility to a death sentence.
- Organized crime is not synonymous with the Mafia—the most experienced, most diversified, and possibly best-disciplined of these groups. The Mafia is actually a common stereotype of organized crime. Although several families in the organization called the Mafia are important components of organized crime activities, they do not hold a monopoly on underworld activities.
- Organized crime does not include terrorists dedicated to political change. Although violent acts are a major tactic of organized crime, the use of violence does not mean that a group is part of a confederacy of organized criminals.

Major Organized Crime Groups and Their Activities

There are an estimated 18 organized crime groups operating in Canada who are mainly engaged in

Alex Tavshunsky

A member of the Bandidos Motorcycle Club spat on his lawyer after he and five other club members were each convicted of multiple counts of first-degree murder for the ambush and execution-style slayings of eight Greater Toronto Area bikers in the biggest mass murder in modern Ontario history. Marcelo Aravena, 33, of Winnipeg, exploded in anger in the prisoners' dock after hearing he had been convicted of seven counts of first-degree murder and another of manslaughter for the massacre of the bikers in tiny Iona Station, west of London, on the night of April 7–8, 2006. "F---ing goofs," Aravena, a 127-kilogram pro fighter said, glaring at the jury and making obscene gestures with both hands.

smuggling cigarettes, alcohol, and drugs; luxury car theft; credit card fraud; extortion; and smuggling of immigrants.[76]

Canada's Criminal Intelligence Service (CISC) is mandated to report annually on organized crime, including the activities of Asian-based and Eastern European–based organized crime groups; Aboriginal-based organized crime; organized crime at marine ports, airports, and land border areas; outlaw motorcycle gangs; and traditional (Italian-based) crime groups. Asian-based criminal organizations continue to be involved in credit card fraud, illegal gaming, loan-sharking, prostitution and human smuggling/trafficking, importation, and production and distribution of a variety of illicit drugs. Vietnamese-based criminal groups are involved in residential marijuana grow operations, with distribution within Canada and to the United States. Eastern European–based criminal organizations are particularly noted for involvement in payment frauds, stolen luxury vehicles, drug importation and trafficking, extortion, prostitution, money laundering, and the smuggling of humans and contraband.[77]

Mafia
A criminal society that originated in Sicily, Italy, and is believed to control racketeering in the United States.

alien conspiracy theory
The view that organized crime in the United States is controlled by the Mafia, centrally coordinated by a national committee that settles disputes, dictates policy, and assigns territory.

La Cosa Nostra
A U.S. syndicate of 25 or so Italian-dominated crime families who control crime in distinct geographic areas.

There are three main Italian-based criminal organizations in Canada: the Sicilian Mafia, the 'Ndrangheta, and La Cosa Nostra. The Sicilian Mafia based in Montreal remains the most influential group in Canada and has international connections. Traditional crime groups continue to be involved in the drug trade, illegal gaming, bookmaking, loan sharking, prostitution, money laundering, and extortion.[78]

Outlaw motorcycle gangs are involved in a range of illegal activities, including prostitution, fraud, extortion, drug trafficking (particularly cocaine, marijuana, and methamphetamine), telemarketing, and possessing and trafficking illegal weapons, stolen goods, and contraband. The Hell's Angels are the largest and most powerful outlaw motorcycle gang in Canada, with 460 members and 34 chapters.[79] There continues to be tension between the Hell's Angels and the Bandidos in Quebec, and between the Outlaws and the Hell's Angels in Ontario, mainly over the drug trade.

Aboriginal-based criminal organizations are almost exclusively composed of street gangs; however, those in Ontario and Quebec are involved in criminal activities related to cross-border smuggling.[80]

LO5 The Concept of Organized Crime

One view of organized crime is that it is a direct offshoot of a criminal society—the **Mafia**—that first originated in Sicily, Italy, and now controls racketeering in major North American cities. A major premise of this **alien conspiracy theory** is that the Mafia is centrally coordinated by a committee that settles disputes, dictates policy, and assigns territory.[81] According to the alien conspiracy theory, organized crime is made up of a syndicate of Italian-dominated crime families that call themselves **La Cosa Nostra**, which is based in the United States and has branches in Canada. The major families have a core group of what has been referred to as "made men," who have been inducted into organized crime families, and another 17 000 "associates," who are criminally involved with syndicate members.[82] The families control crime in distinct geographic areas. New York City, the most important organized crime area, alone contains five families—the Gambino, Columbo, Lucchese, Bonnano, and Genovese families—named after their founding "godfathers"; in contrast, Chicago contains a single mob organization called the "outfit," which also influences racketeering in cities such as Milwaukee, Kansas City, and Phoenix (see Figure 12.2).

FIGURE 12.2

Traditional Organization of the Mafia "Family"

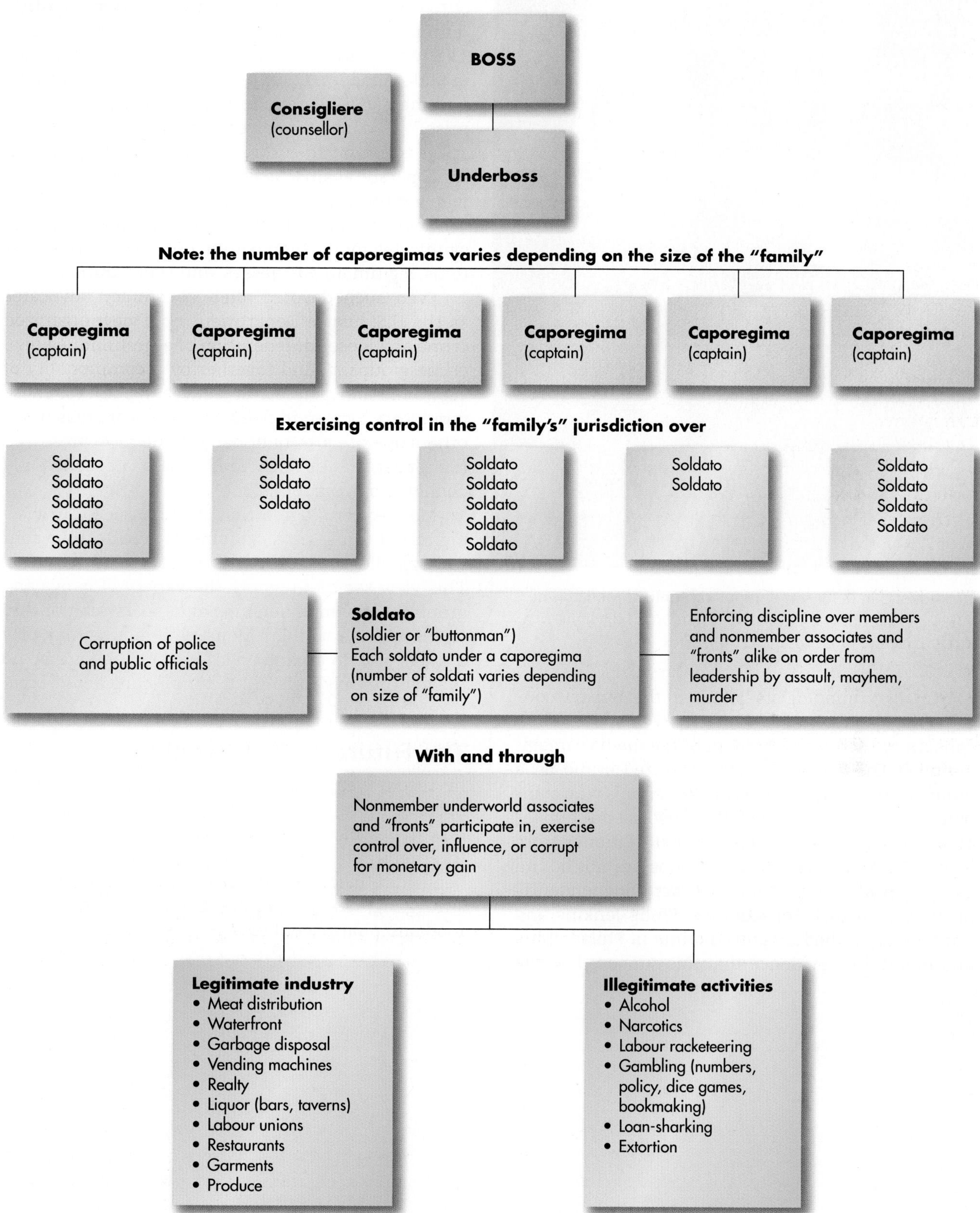

Source: U.S. Senate, Permanent Subcommittee on Investigations, Committee on Government Affairs, Hearings on Organized Crime and Use of Violence, 96th Cong., 2d Sess., April 1980, p.117.

CP PHOTO/Ian Barrett

Nick Rizutto Jr. (left), son of reputed Montreal Mafia crime boss Vito Rizutto, was gunned down in broad daylight on a Montreal street in December 2009.

Not all criminologists believe in this narrow concept of organized crime, and many view the alien conspiracy theory as a figment of the media's imagination.[83] Their view depicts organized crime as a group of ethnically diverse gangs or groups who compete for profit in the sale of illegal goods and services or who use force and violence to extort money from legitimate enterprises. These groups are not bound by a central organization but act independently on their own turf. For example, Philip Jenkins and Gary Potter studied organized crime in Philadelphia and found little evidence that this supposed "Mafia stronghold" was controlled by an Italian-dominated crime family.[84]

Sociologist Alan Block finds that independent crime organizations can be characterized as either "enterprise syndicates" or "power syndicates."[85] The former are involved in providing services; they include madams, drug distributors, bookmakers, and the like—"workers in the world of illegal enterprise." In contrast, power syndicates perform no set task except to extort or terrorize. Their leaders can operate against legitimate business or against fellow criminals who operate enterprise syndicates. Through coercion, buyouts, and other means, power syndicates graft themselves onto enterprise systems, legitimate businesses, and trade unions.

Even such devoted alien conspiracy advocates as the U.S. Justice Department now view organized crime as a loose confederation of ethnic and regional crime groups, bound together by a commonality of economic and political objectives.[86] Some of these groups are located in fixed geographical areas while others operate internationally. Some have preserved their past identity, whereas others are constantly changing organizations.

Most experts agree that it is simplistic to view organized crime as a national syndicate that controls all illegitimate rackets in an orderly fashion. This view seems to ignore the variety of gangs and groups, their membership, and their relationship to the outside world.[87] Mafia-type groups may play a major role in organized crime, but they are by no means the only ones that can be considered organized criminals.[88]

The Future of Organized Crime

In recent years, organized criminal groups have become more complex and sophisticated, as have new types of crime, such as cyber terrorism and Internet fraud. Areas of emerging concerns have also been identified, including mortgage fraud, human smuggling, heavy equipment theft, and counterfeit food and pharmaceuticals distribution.[89]

71% The percentage of students who go online to study for a class.
© Anderson Ross/Getty Images
GET ONLINE

CHAPTER 13

Public Order Crimes

Learning Outcomes

LO1 Define a *public order crime*.

LO2 Define prostitution according to the law and think critically about whether prostitution should be legalized.

LO3 Evaluate how we decide what is pornographic and understand how the law has changed to support police in dealing with child pornography.

LO4 Know the impact, the good and the bad, of legal gambling in Canada.

LO5 Understand the role that substance abuse plays in criminal behavior.

LO6 Think critically about whether Canada should decriminalize the possession of cannabis for personal use.

Introduction

In 1993, Toronto artist Eli Langer, 27, was charged under Bill C-128, which introduced for the first time a definition of "child pornography" into the Criminal Code (now known as section 163.1). Some of the individuals in the sexually explicit painting that Langer was exhibiting appeared to be under the age of 18. In one particular piece, a small naked girl is sitting on an older adult male's lap, and in another a naked girl is sitting across the neck of an adult male who has an erection. There were also images of children having oral and anal sex with each other. In the well-publicized court case, Judge David McCombs upheld the child pornography law. He accepted the defence of "artistic merit" and recognized that the artwork did not pose "a realistic risk of harm to children." However, he concluded, "society's interest in protecting its children is paramount, and where the safety of children is concerned, community standards of tolerance based on the risk of harm are more important than freedom of expression, no matter how fundamental." Although the charges were dropped, the Ontario government seized the work as child porn with the intention of destroying it, but in the end, it was returned to Langer. The argument was made that the child pornography law restricts an artist's freedom under the Canadian Charter of Rights and Freedoms, and the Supreme Court of Canada was asked to hear the case. The court, however, refused to hear the case.[1]

- Societies can ban behaviours that lawmakers consider offensive. Critics question whether this amounts to censorship.
- The line between behaviours that are merely immoral and those that are criminal is often blurred.
- People who seek to control or criminalize deviant behaviours are called moral entrepreneurs.

Should politicians and the courts have the right to censor public art exhibitions they find offensive or immoral? After all, many of the great works of Western art depict nude males and females, some quite young. Should a politician be able to ban Michelangelo's *David*, one of the world's most famous sculptures, because he or she considers the nude statue "pornographic"? And does the fact that a show's backers stand to profit from the notoriety make it fair game for political censors?

Societies have long banned or limited behaviours that are believed to run contrary to social norms, customs, and values. These behaviours are often referred to as **public order crimes** or victimless crimes, although the latter term can be misleading.[2] Public order crimes involve acts that interfere with the operations of society and the ability of people to function efficiently. Put another way, whereas common-law crimes such as sexual assault or robbery are considered inherently wrong and damaging, other behaviours are

public order crime
Behaviour that is outlawed because it threatens the general well-being of society and challenges its accepted moral principles.

Peter Cade/The Image Bank/Getty Images

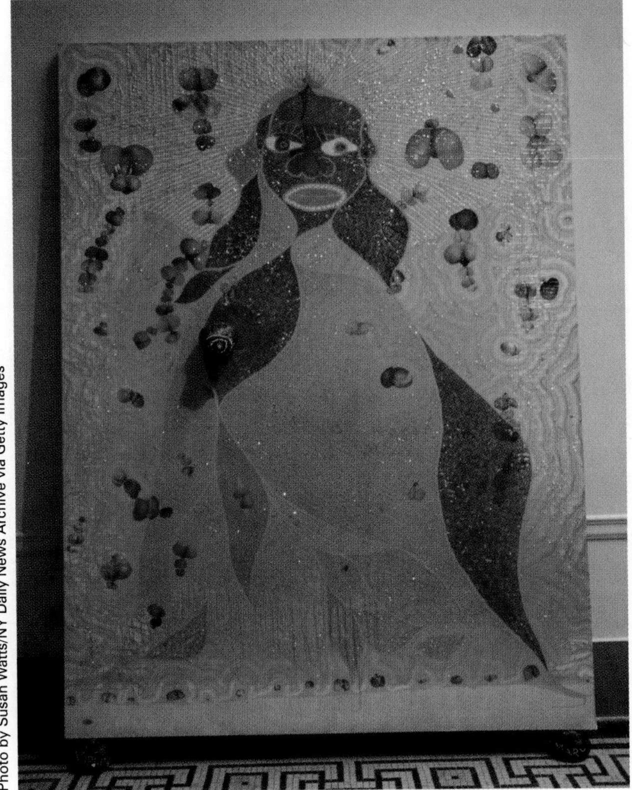

Photo by Susan Watts/NY Daily News Archive via Getty Images

The Holy Virgin Mary, a painting by Chris Ofili, a British artist of Nigerian descent, at the Brooklyn Museum in New York City. Declaring the work "sick stuff," New York's mayor threatened to withhold the museum's funding and evict it from its city-owned building. Should a politician's moral values dictate what can be shown at a metropolitan museum? Who is to say what is offensive and what is "art"?

victimless crime
Public order crime that violates the moral order but has no specific victim other than society as a whole.

outlawed because they conflict with social policy, prevailing moral standards, and current public opinion.

Statutes designed to uphold public order usually prohibit the manufacture and distribution of morally questionable goods and services such as erotic material, commercial sex, and mood-altering drugs. Such statutes are controversial in part because millions of otherwise law-abiding citizens often engage in these outlawed activities and consequently become criminal. These statutes are also controversial because they selectively prohibit desired goods, services, and behaviours; in other words, they outlaw sin and vice.

This chapter covers these public order crimes. It first briefly discusses the relationship between law and morality. Next the chapter addresses public order crimes of a sexual nature: pornography and prostitution. Gambling is discussed as another example of a public order crime, and the chapter concludes by focusing on the abuse of drugs and alcohol.

LO1 Law and Morality

Legislation of moral values has continually frustrated lawmakers. There is little debate that the purpose of criminal law is to protect society and reduce social harm. When a store is robbed or a child assaulted, it is relatively easy to see and condemn the harm done the victim. It is, however, more difficult to sympathize with or even identify the victims of immoral acts, such as pornography or prostitution, where the parties involved may be willing participants. If there is no victim, can there be a crime? Should acts be made illegal merely because they violate prevailing moral standards? If so, who defines morality?

To answer these questions, we might first consider whether there is actually a victim in so-called **victimless crimes**. Some participants may have been coerced into their acts; if so, then they are victims. Opponents of pornography, such as Andrea Dworkin, charge that women involved in adult films, far from being highly paid stars, are "dehumanized—turned into objects and commodities."[3] Research on prostitution shows that many young runaways and abandoned children are coerced into prostitution where they are cruelly treated and held as virtual captives.[4]

Some scholars argue that pornography, prostitution, and drug use erode the moral fabric of society and therefore should be prohibited and punished. They are crimes, according to the great legal scholar Morris Cohen, because "it is one of the functions of the criminal law to give expression to the collective feeling of revulsion toward certain acts, even when they are not very dangerous."[5]

According to this view, so-called victimless crimes are prohibited because one of the functions of criminal law is to express a shared sense of public

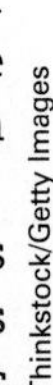

Proliferation of Internet porn may have far-reaching effects particularly on the young.

Thinkstock/Getty Images

morality.[6] However, basing criminal definitions on moral beliefs is often an impossible task. Who defines morality? Are we not punishing differences rather than social harm? As U.S. Supreme Court Justice William O. Douglas so succinctly put it, "What may be trash to me may be prized by others."[7] Would not any attempt to control or limit "objectionable" material eventually lead to the suppression of free speech and political dissent? Is this not a veiled form of censorship? Not so, according to social commentator Irving Kristol:

> If we start censoring pornography and obscenity, shall we not inevitably end up censoring political opinion? A lot of people seem to think this would be the case—which only shows the power of doctrinaire thinking over reality. We had censorship of pornography and obscenity for 150 years, until almost yesterday, and I am not aware that freedom of opinion in this country was in any way diminished as a consequence of this fact.[8]

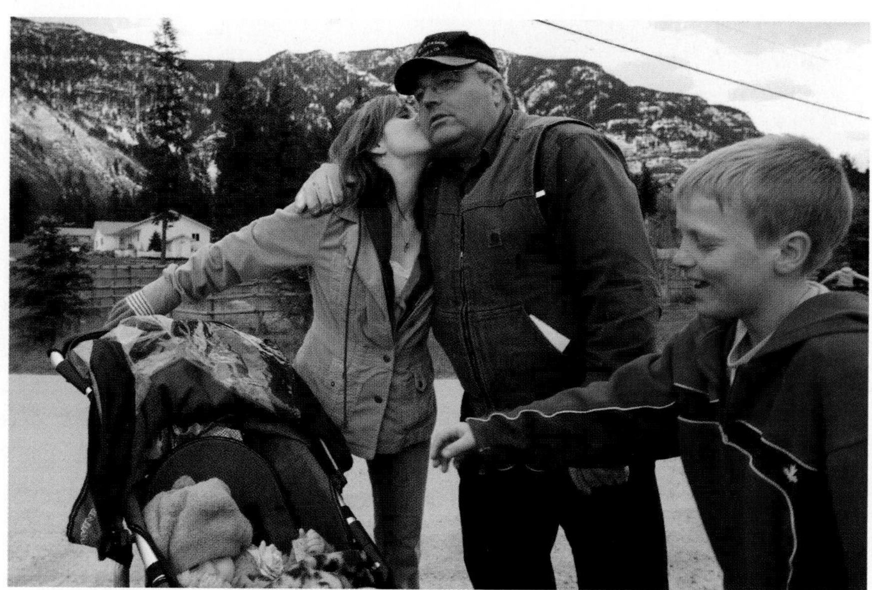
THE CANADIAN PRESS/Jonathan Hayward

In April 2011, final arguments wrapped up in a B.C. Supreme Court hearing on the legality of polygamous marriage. Male members of a fundamentalist Mormon sect located in Bountiful, B.C., such as religious leader Winston Blackmore (above), have pursued the practice of having more than one wife since the 1940s. Under pressure from critics of the practice, the B.C. government has sought a ruling from the court on the legality of the practice.

Criminal or Immoral?

Acts that most of us deem highly immoral are not criminal. There is no law against lust, gluttony, avarice, spite, or envy, although they are considered some of the "seven deadly sins." Nor is it a crime in most jurisdictions to ignore the pleas of a drowning person, even though such callous behaviour is surely immoral.

Some acts that seem both well intentioned and moral are nonetheless considered criminal. It is a crime (euthanasia) to kill a loved one who is suffering from an incurable disease to spare him or her further pain. Stealing a rich person's money to feed a poor family is considered theft. Marrying more than one woman is considered a crime (bigamy), even though multiple marriage may conform to religious beliefs.[9]

As legal experts Wayne LaFave and Austin Scott, Jr., state, "A good motive will not normally prevent what is otherwise criminal from being a crime."[10]

Generally, immoral acts can be distinguished from crimes on the basis of the social harm they cause: Acts that harm the public are usually outlawed. Yet this perspective does not always hold sway. Some acts that cause enormous amounts of social harm are perfectly legal. All of us are aware of the illness and death associated with the consumption of tobacco and alcohol, but they remain legal to produce and sell. Governments, charities, and sports organizations run lotteries and charity casinos. Manufacturers continue to sell sports cars and motorcycles that can accelerate to more than 200 km/hour, although the legal speed limit on major Canadian highways is usually 100 km/hour. More people die each year from alcohol-, tobacco-, and auto-related deaths than from all illegal drugs combined. Should drugs be legalized and fast cars outlawed?

moral entrepreneur
A person who creates moral rules, which thus reflect the values of those in power rather than any objective, universal standards of right and wrong.

Moral Crusaders

Public order crimes often trace their origin to moral crusaders who seek to shape the law toward their own way of thinking; Howard Becker calls them **moral entrepreneurs**. These rule creators, argues Becker, operate with an absolute certainty that their way is right and that any means are justified to get their way; "the crusader is fervent and righteous, often self-righteous."[11] Today's moral crusaders take on issues such as the right to legal abortions, Internet pornography, polygamous marriage and the elimination of the long-gun registry.

Moral crusades are often directed against people clearly defined as evil by one segment of

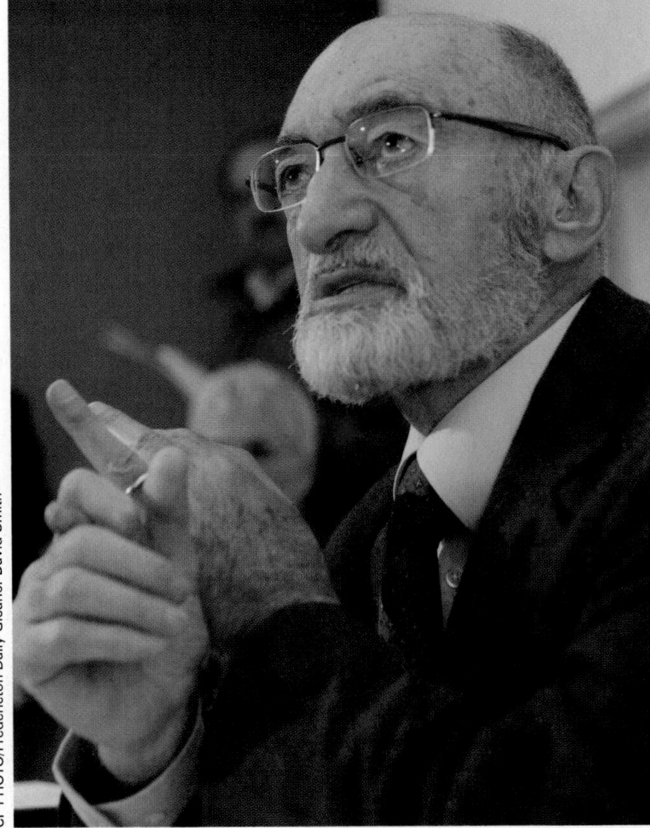

CP PHOTO/Fredericton Daily Gleaner-David Smith

Canada's most controversial abortion crusader, Dr. Henry Morgentaler, fought for nearly four decades to ensure women across the country have the right to legally end unwanted pregnancies. His efforts ultimately led to the 1988 Supreme Court of Canada decision to strike down the anti-abortion law in the Criminal Code, ruling that it violated Canada's Charter of Rights. Morgentaler was named a member of the Order of Canada on July 1, 2008 "for his commitment to women's health care, influence on public policy, and participation in civil liberties organizations."

the population, even though they may be admired by others. For example, antismut campaigns may attempt to ban the books of a popular author from the school library or prevent a controversial figure from speaking at the local university. One way for moral crusaders to accomplish their goal is to prove to all who will listen that some unseen or hidden trait makes their target truly evil and unworthy of a public audience—for example, the Bible condemns their behaviour. This polarization of good and evil creates a climate where those categorized as "good" are deified while the "bad" are demonized and become objects suitable for control.

Moral crusaders seek to rid society of people whose behaviour falls outside their personal standards of right and wrong.

The public order crimes discussed in this chapter are divided into two broad areas. The first relates to what conventional society considers deviant sexual practices: pornography and prostitution. The second area concerns practices that have been outlawed or controlled because of the alleged harm they cause: gambling, drugs, and alcohol.

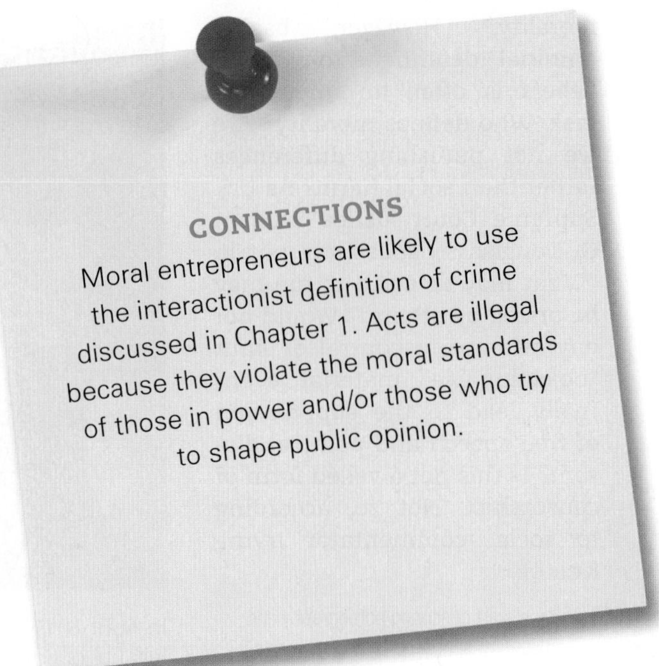

CONNECTIONS
Moral entrepreneurs are likely to use the interactionist definition of crime discussed in Chapter 1. Acts are illegal because they violate the moral standards of those in power and/or those who try to shape public opinion.

Brian Gavriloff/Edmonton Journal

Gloria Meldrum, 38 of Calgary, a survivor of child sexual abuse, launched a campaign designed to educate adults about how to recognize and prevent child abuse. A successful business owner, Meldrum used her business savvy to fund the campaign and to found Little Warriors, a cross-country organization that facilitates child sexual abuse awareness training.

DID YOU KNOW?

- Prostitution has been common throughout recorded history. There are many kinds of prostitutes, including streetwalkers, bar girls, call girls, brothel prostitutes, and circuit travellers.
- It is feared that some girls are forced or tricked into prostitution against their will.
- Pornography is a billion-dollar industry that is growing through technological advances such as the Internet.
- There is great debate whether obscene materials are harmful and are related to violence.
- The Supreme Court of Canada has ruled that material is obscene if it links sex with undue exploitation, violence, or degrading or dehumanizing treatment, and has no redeeming social value.

In Canada, the act of prostitution is not illegal; rather, the illegal act is the means used to practise it, such as "soliciting" for the purpose of prostitution.

LO2 Prostitution

Prostitution has been known for thousands of years. The term derives from the Latin *prostituere*, which means "to cause to stand in front of." The prostitute is viewed as publicly offering his or her body for sale. The earliest record of prostitution appears in ancient Mesopotamia, where priests engaged in sex to promote fertility in the community. All women were required to do temple duty, and passing strangers were expected to make donations to the temple after enjoying its services.[12]

Modern commercial sex appears to have its roots in ancient Greece, where Solon established licensed brothels in 500 B.C. The earnings of Greek prostitutes helped pay for the temple of Aphrodite. Famous men openly went to prostitutes to enjoy intellectual, aesthetic, and sexual stimulation; prostitutes, however, were prevented from marrying.[13]

The act of **prostitution** can be defined as the consensual exchange of sex for money, established by mutual agreement of the prostitutes, their clients, and their employers. However, in Canada, the act of prostitution itself is not illegal; instead, according to sections 210–213 of the Criminal Code, what is illegal are the means used to practise prostitution—"keeping a common bawdy house," "procurement," and "solicitation."

Why doesn't the law just make the act of prostitution itself illegal? Beginning with the 1981 report of the Committee on Sexual Offences Against Children and Youth (known as the Badgley Report) and the 1983 report of the Special Committee on Pornography and Prostitution (known as the Fraser Report), Canadian policy makers recognized that traditional laws against prostitution end up further victimizing prostitutes, who too often are already victims of abuse, poverty, broken homes, and addiction. Revisions to the Criminal Code have attempted to recognize that prostitution is equally an illegal act for those soliciting the services of a prostitute (section 213), those procuring individuals to work as prostitutes (section 212), and those operating premises for this purpose (section 210).

Criminologist Scot Wortley conducted a study of the Toronto "John School" Diversion Program, a one-day education program used as an alternative to jail time for males who have pled guilty to solicitation. Wortley found that although the education program was effective in increasing males' awareness of the laws regarding prostitution, and understanding that it is not a crime without victims, still, only a minority of males identified the prostitute as a primary victim, and one out of ten males reported they would use the services of a prostitute again in the future, despite the information provided by the education program.[14] Sociologist Monica Prasad reports that most customers who become

prostitution
The consensual exchange of sex for money.

"regulars" view prostitution as a service occupation not different from other service occupations, ignoring the criminal nature of the act and its consequences for victims.[15]

Incidence of Prostitution

It is impossible to assess the number of prostitutes operating in Canada. What we do know is that in 2009, only 3534 prostitution-related offences were recorded in the country. The offence rate per 100 000 population has decreased by 39 percent since 1999, similar to trends in the United States. Most of the arrests (about 85 percent) are for the related offence of "stopping or impeding" vehicles or pedestrians for the purpose of engaging in prostitution.[16] Typically, recorded offences are for so-called street prostitution—little is known about other forms of prostitution, such as "call girl" operations and escort services.[17]

Even less is known about the customers, almost exclusively male, who use prostitutes. One study conducted in British Columbia found the average age of men frequenting prostitutes was 34, most (53 percent) were white, and "blue collar" (36 percent) was the most common occupational group.[18] Men may be less likely to use prostitutes now than in the past because legitimate alternatives for sexuality are more open to them. In addition, the prevalence of sexually transmitted diseases has caused many men to avoid visiting prostitutes for fear of irreversible health hazards.[19]

Types of Prostitutes

Several different types of prostitutes operate in Canada.

Streetwalkers

Prostitutes who work the streets in plain sight of police, citizens, and customers are referred to as hustlers, hookers, or streetwalkers. Although glamorized by the Julia Roberts character in the film *Pretty Woman* (who winds up with multimillionaire Richard Gere), streetwalkers are considered the least-attractive, lowest-paid, most vulnerable men and women in the profession. Streetwalkers wear bright clothing, makeup, and jewellery to attract customers; they take their customers to hotels. The term *hooker*, however, is not derived from the ability of streetwalkers to hook clients on their charms. It actually stems from the popular name given women who followed Union General "Fighting Joe" Hooker's army during the U.S. Civil War.[20] Studies indicate they are most likely to be impoverished members of ethnic or racial minorities. Many are young runaways who gravitate to major cities to find a new, exciting life and escape from sexual and physical abuse at home.[21] Of all prostitutes, streetwalkers have the highest incidence of drug abuse.[22]

Bar Girls

B-girls, as they are also called, spend their time in bars, drinking and waiting to be picked up by customers. Although alcoholism may be a problem, B-girls usually work out an arrangement with the bartender so they are served diluted drinks or water coloured with dye or tea, for which the customer is charged an exorbitant price. In some bars, the B-girl is given a credit for each drink she gets the customer to buy. It is common to find B-girls in towns with military bases and large transient populations.[23]

Brothel Prostitutes

Also called bordellos, cathouses, sporting houses, and houses of ill repute, brothels flourished in the 19th and early 20th centuries. They were large establishments, usually run by madams, that housed several prostitutes. A madam is a woman who employs prostitutes, supervises their behaviour, and receives a fee for her services; her cut is usually 40 to 60 percent of the prostitutes' earnings. The madam's role may include recruiting women into prostitution and socializing them in the trade.[24]

Brothels declined in importance following World War II. The closing of the last brothel in Texas is chronicled in the play and movie *The Best Little Whorehouse in Texas*. Today the best-known brothels in North America exist in Nevada, where prostitution is legal outside large population centres.

Call Girls

The aristocrats of prostitution are call girls. They charge customers up to $1500 per night and may net more than $100 000 per year. Some gain clients through employment in escort services, while others develop independent customer lists. Many call girls come from middle-class backgrounds and service upper-class customers. Attempting to dispel the notion that their service is simply sex for money, they concentrate on making their clients feel important and attractive. Working exclusively via telephone "dates," call girls get their clients by word of mouth or by making arrangements with bellhops, cab drivers, and so on. They either entertain clients in their own apartments or visit clients' hotels and apartments. Upon retiring, a call girl can sell her datebook listing client names and sexual preferences for thousands of dollars. Despite the lucrative nature of their business, call girls suffer considerable risk by being alone

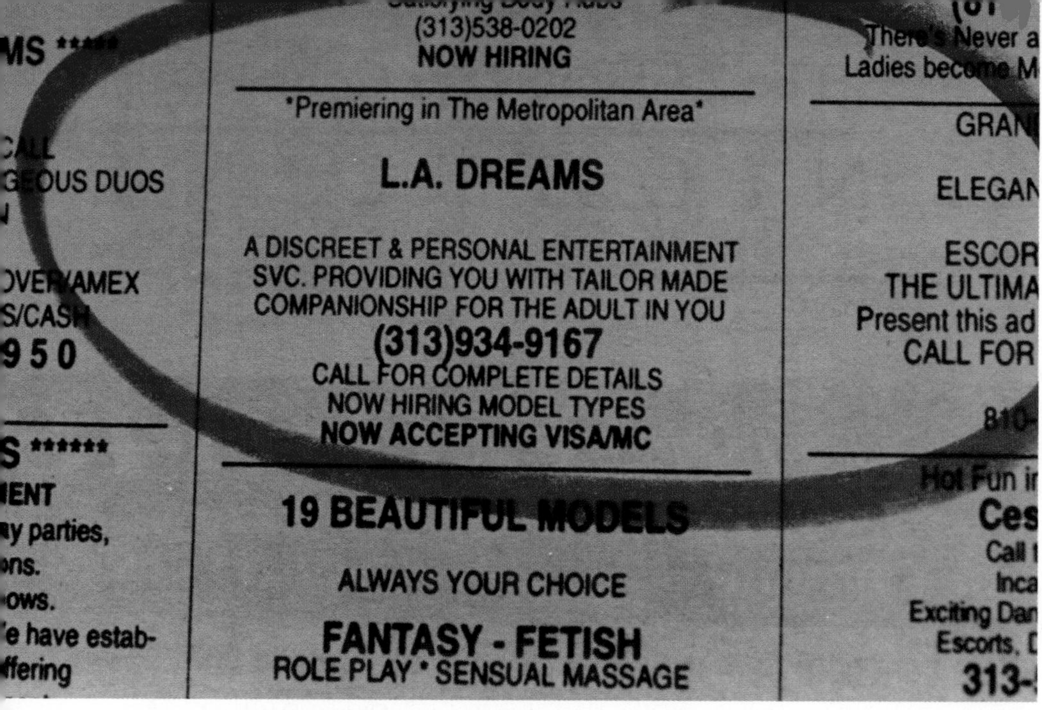

Time & Life Pictures/Getty Images

and unprotected with strangers. They often request the business cards of their clients to make sure they are dealing with "upstanding citizens."

Escort Services/Call Houses

Some escort services are fronts for prostitution rings. Increasingly, the Internet is used to advertise escort services, where female or male escorts can be hired by "discerning" professionals in search of "desirable companions." Both male and female sex workers can be sent out after the client responds on the Internet or calls an ad in the Yellow Pages. In Toronto and other large cities, dozens of escort service websites and page after page in the phone book are dedicated to such services, with costs ranging from $50 per half hour to more than $200 per hour.[25]

Circuit Travellers

Prostitutes known as circuit travellers move around in groups of two or three to lumber, labour, and agricultural camps. They ask the foreman for permission to ply their trade, service the whole crew in an evening, and then move on. Some circuit travellers seek clients at truck stops and rest areas.

Sometimes young girls are forced to become circuit travellers by unscrupulous pimps. In 1998, 16 people were charged with enslaving at least 20 women, some as young as 14, and forcing them to work for months as prostitutes in agricultural migrant camps in Florida and South Carolina. The young women were lured from Mexico with offers of jobs in landscaping, health care, housecleaning, and restaurants. During their captivity, the young women were raped, beaten, and forced to have abortions. Those who tried to escape were tracked down, brought back, beaten, and raped.[26]

Becoming a Prostitute

Why does someone turn to prostitution? While women and men may become prostitutes for different reasons, there are some commonalities. Both often come from troubled homes marked by extreme conflict and hostility, and from poor urban areas or rural communities. Divorce, separation, or death splits the family; most prostitutes grew up in homes without fathers.[27] Many prostitutes were initiated into sex by family members at ages as young as 10 to 12 years; they have long histories of sexual exploitation and abuse.[28] The early experiences with sex help teach them that their bodies have value and that sexual encounters can be used to obtain affection, power, or money. Lower-class girls who get into "the life" report conflict with school authorities, poor grades, and an overly regimented school experience.[29] Drug abuse, including heroin and cocaine addiction, is often a factor in the prostitute's life.[30] However, there is no evidence that people become prostitutes because of psychological problems or personality disturbances. Money, drugs, and survival seem to be greater motivations.

Legalize Prostitution?

In September 2010, a Toronto judge struck down Canada's prostitution laws, ruling that Criminal Code provisions against keeping a common bawdy house, living on the avails of prostitution, and communicating for the purposes of prostitution violated Charter rights both to freedom of expression and to security of the person by forcing sex workers to ply their trade in the street in risky, frequently dangerous circumstances.[31]

Valerie Scott, one of the sex workers who brought the legal challenge to Canada's prostitution laws to court, claimed that "the decision means sex workers no longer have to worry about being raped, robbed or murdered." Almost immediately following the court decision, federal Justice Minister Rob Nicholson announced the government's intention to appeal the ruling. Until the court renders its decision, expected sometime in late 2011 or early 2012, the prostitution laws will remain in effect.

Feminists have staked out conflicting views of prostitution. One position is that women must become emancipated from male oppression and reach sexual equality. The sexual equality view considers the prostitute a victim of male dominance. In patriarchal societies, male power is predicated on female subjugation, and prostitution is a clear example of this gender exploitation.[32] In contrast, for some feminists, the fight for equality depends on controlling all attempts by men or women to impose their will on women. The free choice view is that prostitution, if freely chosen, expresses women's equality and is not a symptom of subjugation.[33]

Advocates of both positions argue that the penalties for prostitution and prostitution-related offences should be reduced (decriminalized), and all agree that the law itself and health, education, and employment services should be put in place to provide support for those who want to get out of prostitution.[34]

Canadian Bishop Raymond Lahey arrives at a police station in Ottawa, October 1, 2009, to face child pornography charges. The Vatican condemned Lahey and said it planned to take disciplinary action against him. In May 2011 he pleaded guilty and is currently awaiting sentencing.

Chris Wattie/Reuters /Landov

Decriminalization would relieve already desperate women of the additional burden of severe legal punishment. However, legalization might be coupled with regulation by male-dominated justice agencies. For example, required medical examinations would mean increased male control over women's bodies. Although both sides advocate change in the criminal status of prostitution, few communities (except Winnipeg and Edmonton) have openly debated or voted on its legalization.[35]

LO3 Pornography

The term **pornography** derives from the Greek *porne*, meaning "prostitute," and *graphein*, meaning "to write." In the heart of many major cities are stores that display and sell books, magazines, and DVDs explicitly depicting every imaginable sex act. Though some materials depicting nudity and sex are legal in Canada, the Criminal Code prohibits the production, display, and sale of material that is deemed "obscene" as per section 163(8), which states that "For the purpose of this Act, any publication a dominant characteristic of which is the undue exploitation of sex, or of sex and any one or more of the following subjects, namely, crime, horror, cruelty and violence, shall be deemed to be obscene."

pornography
Books, magazines, films, tapes, pictures, or videos that graphically exploit sex or depict sex in combination with crime, horror, cruelty, or violence; includes any and all sexual exploitation of children.

obscenity
Material that links sex with undue exploitation, violence, or degrading or dehumanizing treatment, and has no redeeming social value.

Obscenity, derived from the Latin *caenum* for "filth," is defined by Webster's dictionary as "deeply offensive to morality or decency ... designed to incite to lust or depravity."[36] The problem of controlling pornography centres on this definition of obscenity. Police and law enforcement officials can legally seize only material that is judged obscene. "But who," critics ask, "is to judge what is obscene?" At one time, novels such as *Tropic of Cancer* by Henry Miller, *Ulysses* by James Joyce, *Lady Chatterley's Lover* by D. H. Lawrence, and even Margaret Laurence's *Stone Angel* were prohibited because they were considered obscene; today they are considered works of great literary value. In the past, the definition of what was obscene usually relied almost exclusively on the "community standards" test; what "crosses the line" or is intolerable to members of a community at the time defines obscenity. However, such an approach to defining obscenity opens the door to all sorts of different interpretations of community standards. Consequently, the Supreme Court of Canada has ruled that what is "obscene" and therefore harmful to society is any media that link sex with undue exploitation, violence, or degrading or dehumanizing treatment, and have no redeeming social value.[37]

Is Pornography Harmful?

Opponents of pornography argue that it degrades both the people who are photographed and members of the public who are sometimes forced to see obscene material. Pornographers exploit their models, who often include the poor and disadvantaged, along with underage children. In the United States, the Attorney General's Commission on Pornography, set up by the Reagan administration to review the sale and distribution of sexually explicit material, concluded that many performers and models are victims of physical and psychological coercion.[38]

One uncontested danger of pornography is "kiddie porn." ECPAT International, a child welfare and children's rights group, estimates that on any given day there are more than 1 million child pornographic images cycling through the Internet, and somewhere between 50 000 and 100 000 individuals, mostly white males living in Western countries, involved in swapping and sharing child pornographic images and videos.[39] Ann Wolbert Burgess studied 55 child pornography rings and found that they typically contain between 3 and 11 children, predominantly males, some of nursery-school age. The adults who control the ring use positions of trust to recruit the children and then continue to exploit them through a combination of material and psychological rewards. Burgess found different types of child pornography rings. Solo sex rings involve several children and a single adult, usually male, who uses a position of trust (counsellor, teacher, Boy Scout leader) to recruit children into sexual activity. Transition rings are impromptu groups set up to sell and trade photos and sex. Syndicated rings are well-structured organizations that recruit children and create extensive networks of customers who desire sexual services.[40] Sexual exploitation by these rings can devastate the child victims. Exploited children are prone to such acting-out behaviour as setting fires and becoming sexually focused in the use of language, dress, and mannerisms. In cases of extreme, prolonged victimization, children may lock onto the sex group's behaviour and become prone to further victimization or even become victimizers themselves.

In 2009, 1594 child pornography offences were reported to Canadian police, an increase of 64 percent since 1999. Though it is difficult to determine if this increase was due to a higher incidence rate, it certainly reflects changes in legislation, better police enforcement both nationally and internationally, and changes in public attitudes toward the crime.

Does Pornography Cause Violence?

An issue critical to the debate over pornography is whether viewing it produces sexual violence or assaultive behaviour. This debate was given added interest when serial killer Ted Bundy claimed his murderous rampage was fuelled by reading pornography.

Some evidence exists that viewing sexually explicit material actually has little effect on behaviour. In 1970, the National Commission on Obscenity and Pornography in the United States reviewed all available material on the effects of pornography and found no clear relationship between pornography and violence.[41] Almost 20 years later, the highly controversial U.S. Attorney General's Commission on Pornography, sponsored by the conservative Reagan administration, called for legal attacks on hard-core pornography and condemned all sexually related material—but also found little evidence that obscenity causes antisocial behaviour.[42] In Canada, University of Waterloo psychologists Marvin Brown, Donald Amoroso, and Edward Ware reported the same findings, namely that occasional exposure to pornography does not lead to changes in behaviour.[43]

The technology revolution represented by the Internet poses a major obstacle for people who want to control or limit sex-related entertainment. Should such activities be criminalized? Or are they legitimate and harmless business transactions between consenting adults?

© MARKA/Alamy

How might we account for this surprisingly insignificant association? It is possible that viewing erotic material may act as a safety valve for those whose impulses might otherwise lead them to violence.[44] Convicted rapists and sex offenders report less exposure to pornography than control groups of nonoffenders.[45]

Viewing prurient material may have the unintended side effect of satisfying erotic impulses that otherwise might result in more sexually aggressive behaviour. This issue is far from settled. A number of criminologists believe that the positive relationship between pornography consumption and sexual assault rates in various countries, including Canada and the United States, is evidence that obscenity may powerfully influence criminality.[46] Nonetheless, the weight of the evidence shows little relationship between violence and pornography per se.

Although there is little or no documentation of a correlation between pornography and violent crime, there is stronger evidence that people exposed to material that portrays violence, sadism, and women enjoying being sexually assaulted and degraded are likely to be sexually aggressive toward female victims.[47] Laboratory experiments conducted by a number of leading authorities have found that men exposed to violent pornography are more likely to act aggressively toward women.[48] The evidence suggests that violence and sexual aggression are not linked to erotic or pornographic films per se but that erotic films depicting violence, sexual assault, brutality, and aggression may evoke similar feelings in viewers. This finding is especially distressing because it is common for adult books and films to have sexually violent themes such as sexual assault, bondage, and mutilation.[49]

Pornography and the Law

Section 2(b) of the Canadian Charter of Rights and Freedoms protects free speech and prohibits police agencies from limiting the public's right of free expression. However, the Supreme Court held in *R. v. Butler* (1992)[50] that although section 2(b) protects the right to "freedom of thought, belief, opinion and expression, including freedom of the press and other media communication," such freedom is subject to interpretation under section 1 of the Charter, which states that rights and freedoms will be subject to "reasonable limits prescribed by law as can be demonstrably justified in a free and democratic society." In the *Butler* case, the Supreme Court ruled that the distribution of obscene material is sufficiently harmful to society as to restrict its freedom of expression.[51]

The Supreme Court went one step further and ruled that any media that link sex with undue exploitation, violence, or degrading or dehumanizing treatment will almost always be considered obscene and potentially harmful to society, unless, based on an argument of artistic merit, the larger benefit to the community of viewing the material outweighs the potential harm. In effect, the Court shifted the emphasis in deciding what is obscene away from simply considering what the community finds offensive to a more comprehensive consideration of "harm" to Canadian society as a whole, as in promoting antisocial behaviour:[52]

> Harm in this context means that it predisposes people to act in an antisocial manner as, for example, the physical or mental mistreatment of women by men, or possibly the reverse. Antisocial conduct for this purpose is conduct that society formally recognizes as incompatible with its proper functioning.[53]

In other words, to convict a person of obscenity, courts must now refer both to what the community has defined as intolerable, along with the potential harm of the material to Canadian society as a whole.[54]

Controlling Sex for Profit

Sex for profit predates Western civilization. Considering its longevity, there seems to be little evidence that it can be controlled or eliminated by legal means alone. Recent reports indicate that the sex business is currently booming and now amounts to more than US$10 billion worldwide per year.[55]

Although politically appealing, law enforcement crusades dedicated to controlling the sex business may not necessarily obtain the desired effect. A get-tough policy could make sex-related goods and services scarce, driving up prices and making their sale even more desirable and profitable. Going after national distributors may help decentralize the adult movie and photo business and encourage local rings to expand their activities, for example, by making and marketing videos as well as still photos or distributing them through computer networks.

An alternative approach has been to restrict the sale of pornography within acceptable boundaries. In the United States, New York City was among the first cities to enact zoning that seeks to break up the concentration of peep shows, topless bars, and X-rated businesses in several neighbourhoods, particularly in Times Square.[56] The law forbids sex-oriented businesses within 500 feet (approximately 46 metres) of residential zones, schools, churches, or daycare centres. Sex shops cannot be located within 500 feet of each other, so concentrated "red light" districts must be dispersed.

In Canada, Winnipeg and Edmonton have each implemented municipal bylaws in an attempt to regulate the prostitution trade, and many Canadian cities now license and regulate adult entertainment establishments such as sex shops, adult video stores, and "body rub" parlours.[57] In April 2010, the Fort Nelson, B.C. municipal council voted six to one in favour of licensing sex-related businesses, including an escort service, in specific, designated areas of the community.[58]

Still, rather than close their doors, sex shops often get around the law by adding products such as luggage, cameras, T-shirts, and classic films to their merchandise. Ironically, zoning statutes may not be needed as redevelopment occurs and skyrocketing downtown real estate prices make sex clubs and stores relatively unprofitable.

Technological Change

A 1993 letter to advice columnist Ann Landers gave this cry for help:[59]

> Dear Ann Landers,
>
> ... several months ago, I caught my husband making calls to a 900-sex number. After a week of denial, he admitted that for several years he had been hooked on porn magazines, porn movies, peep shows, strippers, and phone sex. This addiction can start early in life. With my husband it began at age 12 with just one simple, "harmless" magazine. By the time he was 19, it had become completely out of control. ... For years my husband hated himself, and it affected his entire life.*

A March 2005 *Dr. Phil* show provided an update to the problem, when Kiza and Chris, a young couple about to be married, discussed Chris's addiction to Internet pornography on the show. "My fiancé's addiction to porn is out of control. I don't want to marry someone who has this problem. Can you help us?" asked the young bride-to-be, Kiza. "Are you worried about marrying this guy?" Dr. Phil asked. "If he's not going to stop, yeah. Definitely," she said. "Porno is a normal guy thing," claimed Chris. "Every guy should have the right to look at porn." Chris said he'd never had any of his past girlfriends complain about it.

By the end of the discussion, Dr. Phil advised young Kiza that, "You're not ready to get married to him in a few weeks. If you do, you are asking for trouble. You will absolutely break your heart if you are married to a porn addict."

Technological change will provide the greatest challenge to those seeking to control the sex-for-profit industry. Adult movie theatres and local video stores have closed as the Internet has become the primary source for accessing and downloading pornography. Adult pay-per-view websites are now a staple of the computer industry. Internet sex services include live, interactive stripping and even interactive, on demand "cyber sex" activities.[60]

*By permission of Esther P. Lederer and Creators Syndication, Inc.

Generally speaking, Canadian courts have employed the provisions of section 163 of the Criminal Code to address the production, sale, and distribution of obscene material by any means, including the Internet.[61] However, in June 2002, Bill C-15A received Royal Assent, ushering in a series of amendments designed to address the growing problem of Internet luring and child pornography, making it illegal to communicate with a child over the Internet for the purpose of committing a sexual offence against the child, with penalties of up to five years in prison. In addition, tough new measures, accompanied by sentences of up to ten years in prison, make it illegal to "transmit, make available, export or access" child pornography in any form.[62] In 2011, Bill C-54, a bill to amend Canada's child pornography laws, passed the committee stage with the support of all parties in the House of Commons. The new bill would create mandatory minimum sentences for certain sexual crimes against children and new offences for luring children on the Internet. People convicted of such crimes would also have specific prohibitions against Internet access.[63] Despite these efforts, however, the popularity of pornography (especially on the Internet) continues to grow, overwhelming police resources available to address the problem.

LO4 Gambling

Legalized gambling is a relatively new phenomenon in Canada. A little over 100 years ago, gambling in any form was illegal everywhere in the country. However, beginning in 1892, the restrictions on gambling-type activities began to be lifted, first to allow religious organizations to operate raffles, bazaars, and bingos, and later to allow racetrack betting. (See Figure 13.1.)

Though Irish Sweepstakes tickets were a popular, though illegal, lottery operating in Canada through the 1930s and into the 1960s, it was not until 1969 that the Canadian Criminal Code was amended to allow the provinces and the federal government to operate lotteries and casinos on a charitable basis to fund "worthwhile" activities, such as the 1976 Montreal Olympics, various other recreation and sports projects, and a host of religious and charitable activities.

Today, lotteries are operated exclusively by provincial governments, in the form of "commissions" that regulate lottery activities and distribute revenues. In 1985, an amendment to the Criminal Code gave provincial governments exclusive control over gambling, including administration of computer and video-gaming devices. On the heels of the amendment, a number of provinces introduced video lottery terminals (VLTs) into bars and corner stores,

FIGURE 13.1

Net Revenue from Government-run Gambling

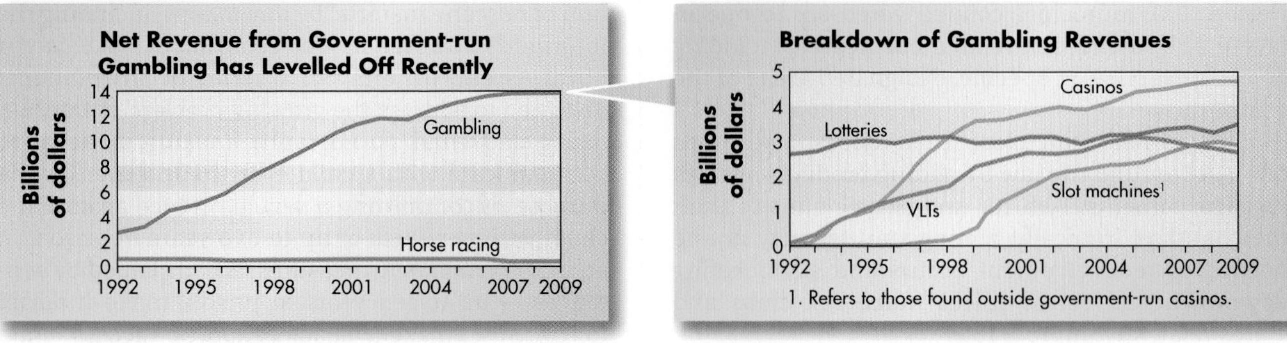

Source: Adapted from Statistics Canada publication Perspectives on Labour and Income, Catalogue 75-001-XIE2010108, vol. 11 no. 8, August 2010, page 14 (http://www.statcan.gc.ca/pub/75-001-x/2010108/pdf/11297-eng.pdf).

along with allowing racetracks to install computerized slot machines. In the late 1980s, in recognition of the sovereignty of their lands and government, First Nations people were granted the right to run permanent casinos in order to support band activities, provide funds for infrastructure development, and create employment.

According to Statistics Canada (2010), government-run lotteries, video lottery terminals, casinos, and slot machines generated $13.75 billion in net revenues in 2009. Betting on horse races generated another $355 million in revenues. In Canada, gambling is big business—in 2008, 70 percent of Canadian households engaged in at least one gambling activity in the year, spending an average of $480 over the course of the year. Gambling is now included as a component of Canadian gross domestic product, and critics claim that provincial governments, charities, sports organizations, and others have become dependent on gambling profits to make ends meet.[64]

DID YOU KNOW?

- Legalized gambling is a relatively new phenomenon in Canada.
- Provincial governments have exclusive control over gambling, generating an estimated $5.4 billion in net profits in Canada every year.
- Illegal gambling continues to be a problem. Illegal gambling offers higher potential profit margins, and is especially attractive to chronic, addicted gamblers who have been banned from legal establishments.
- An estimated 3–5 percent of the adult Canadian population has a gambling problem.
- Gambling has been linked to debt and bankruptcy, job loss, family breakdown, substance abuse, crime, and suicide.

The Law on Gambling

Section 207 of the Criminal Code gives provincial governments the exclusive right to operate or grant others the licence to operate lotteries and other games of chance, including casinos (see Figure 13.1 for revenues). Anyone else operating lotteries or games of chance without the permission of the provincial government is breaking the law. Similarly, operating a gaming or betting house (section 201); running "pools" or dice games, book-making, and taking bets on horse-racing and sports events (section 202); and placing bets for others (section 203) are illegal according to the Criminal Code, along with "cheating at play" (section 209).

Why, with so much "legal" betting and gaming going on, do individuals continue to seek out illegal forms of gambling?

Illegal gambling offers higher potential profit margins (but also higher risks); offers "games of chance" not available in licensed gambling operations; and provides an outlet for those who, because of a gambling addiction, are banned from licensed establishments.[65] Police officials and gaming regulators agree that while legal gambling formats are well regulated, illegal gambling enforcement is severely deficient. According to Statistics Canada, only 185 illegal gambling and betting-related offences were recorded by police in 2008, a 49 percent decline since 1999.[66]

The Social Costs of Gambling

In a nationwide study of gambling problems in Canada, Cox, Yu, Afifi, and Ladouceur found that the proportion of Canadians estimated to have a "moderate" or "severe" gambling problem ranged from a low of 1.5 percent of the population in New Brunswick to a high of 2.9 percent in Manitoba and Saskatchewan. The average for Canada as a whole was 2 percent.[67]

DID YOU KNOW?

- Substance abuse is an ancient practice dating back more than 4000 years.
- There is a wide variety of drugs in use today; alcohol is a major problem.
- Police report that drug offences have been on the increase since 1993.
- More than half of drug crimes are for simple cannabis possession.
- There is no single cause of substance abuse. Some people may use drugs because they are predisposed to abuse.
- There is a strong link between drug abuse and crime. People who become addicts may increase their illegal activities to support their habits. Others engage in violence as part of their drug-dealing activities.

Gambling is likely to be a problem in families that can least afford it. According to Statistics Canada, poorer Canadians spend a greater percentage of their incomes on gambling. In 2009, households earning less than $20 000 a year spent an average of about $395 on gambling, or approximately 1.9 percent of their total income. Wealthier Canadians, those earning $80 000 or more, spend about $555 each year on gambling, but only about 0.7 percent of their income.[68]

Gambling has been linked to debt and bankruptcy, job loss, family breakdown, substance abuse, and suicide. A 2010 study by Dowling and Brown of gambling and Internet usage among university students found that problem gambling was linked to psychological feelings of loneliness and anxiety as well as student stressors such as finances, friendships, and academic performance.[69] Police fear that as the problem increases, crime related to "feeding" the gambling habit will increase as well. According to a 1999 Canada West Foundation report, the types of crimes committed by problem gamblers include theft, forgery, embezzlement, fraud, credit card scams, domestic violence, break and enters, and suicide.[70]

LO5 Substance Abuse

Substance abuse is a problem found in all areas of the world. Large urban areas are beset by drug-dealing gangs, drug users who engage in crime to support their habits, and alcohol-related violence. Rural areas are important staging centres for the shipment of drugs all over the world, and are often the production sites for synthetic drugs and marijuana farming.[71] In Canada, 33 percent of young people between the ages 15 and 24 have used illegal drugs at some point in their lives.[72] In the United States, 11 percent of youth between the ages of 12 and 17 are illicit drug users.[73] In Australia, 19 percent of youths in detention centres and 40 percent of adult prisoners report having used heroin at least once; South Africa reports increased cocaine and heroin abuse; Thailand has a serious heroin and methamphetamine problem; British police have found a major increase in heroin abuse; and in Canada, cocaine and crack are considered serious urban problems.[74] Though there is little information on the prevalence of cocaine use in the general Canadian population, the 2004 Canadian Addiction Survey (CAS) revealed that almost 11 percent of Canadians aged 15 years and older had tried cocaine or crack at least once; about 2 percent reported cocaine use in the past 12 months. The prevalence of crack and cocaine use by street youth was estimated at 31 percent for both crack and cocaine in Toronto (1992); 20 percent and 33 percent, respectively, in Halifax (1993); and 85 percent for cocaine in Vancouver (1994). Of those held in Canadian federal correctional facilities, 60 percent of inmates reported using cocaine at least once during the six-month period prior to their arrest and incarceration.[75]

Another indication of the concern about drugs has been the continuing growth in the number of drug cases. Between 1999 and 2009, the number of police-reported drug crimes in Canada grew from 80 142 to 97 666, an increase of nearly 22 percent in ten years.[76] Fully 50 percent of reported drug crimes were for marijuana (cannabis) possession. Other drugs, including crystal meth, ecstasy, "date rape" drugs, LSD, barbiturates, and others are the next most popular illicit substances (8.6 percent), followed by cocaine (7.7 percent).[77] Thirty-three percent of drug charges were for trafficking, with cannabis accounting for more than half of the trafficking cases.

Despite the scope of the drug problem, some still view it as another type of victimless public order crime. There is great debate over the decriminalization or even legalization of drugs along with measures for the control of alcohol. Some consider drug use a private matter and drug control another example of government intrusion into people's private lives. Furthermore, legalization could reduce the profit of selling illegal substances and drive suppliers out of the market.[78] Others see these substances as dangerous, believing that the criminal activity of users makes the term victimless nonsensical. Still another position is that the possession of cannabis should be decriminalized; those found by police to have marijuana in their possession would be issued a ticket and fined for the offence, rather than receiving a criminal

temperance movement
The drive to prohibit the sale of alcohol in the United States and Canada, led by the Woman's Christian Temperance Union.

Prohibition
In Canada, the period from about 1915 to 1925 when the sale of alcohol was prohibited; in the United States, the prohibition period was much longer, lasting from 1919 until 1933.

conviction. Others go further to argue that the use of all drugs and alcohol should be legalized, but the sale and distribution of drugs should be heavily penalized. This would punish those profiting from drugs while enabling users to be helped without fear of criminal punishment. Alternatively, many fear the effects of legalized drugs such as marijuana. In a November 2004 article in the *National Post*, CEOs of major Canadian corporations expressed concern for what they referred to as "reefer madness" among their employees if marijuana were legalized. They felt it could lead to increases in injuries, absenteeism, and poor job performance, and could ultimately adversely affect the economy.[79]

When Did Drug Use Begin?

The use of chemical substances to change reality and provide stimulation, relief, or relaxation has gone on for thousands of years. Mesopotamian writings indicate that opium was used 4000 years ago—it was known as the "plant of joy."[80] The ancient Greeks knew and understood the problem of drug use. At the time of the Crusades, the Arabs were using marijuana. In the Western Hemisphere, natives of Mexico and South America chewed coca leaves and used "magic mushrooms" in their religious ceremonies.[81] Drug use was also accepted in Europe well into the 20th century. Recently uncovered pharmacy records circa 1900 to 1920 showed sales of cocaine and heroin solutions to members of the British royal family; records from 1912 show that Winston Churchill, then a member of Parliament, was sold a cocaine solution while staying in Scotland.[82]

In Canada, opium and its derivatives were easily obtained. Opium-based drugs were used in various patent medicine cure-alls, and recreational use of the drug was not uncommon, particularly in British Columbia, where a large population of Chinese immigrant labourers had been brought in to build the national railway. In fact, beginning in the 1820s, the British forced the Chinese government to accept opium as payment for trade goods, even going to war with China to force the issue.[83]

Alcohol and Its Prohibition

The history of alcohol and the law in Canada and the United States has also been controversial and dramatic. At the turn of the last century, a drive was mustered to prohibit the sale of alcohol. This **temperance movement** was fuelled by the belief that the purity of North American agrarian culture was being destroyed by the growth of cities. Urbanism was viewed as a threat to the lifestyle of the majority of the population, then living on farms and in villages.

The forces behind the temperance movement in Canada were lobbying groups such as the Woman's Christian Temperance Union and the Dominion Alliance for the Total Suppression of Liquor Traffic, a coalition of English Protestant groups.[84] They viewed the growing city, filled with newly arriving Irish, Italian, and Eastern European immigrants, most of them Catholics, as centres of degradation and wickedness. In 1878, the Canada Temperance Act was passed, giving local governments the right to restrict the sale of alcohol in their jurisdiction, with the result that some rural areas, towns, and cities were by law "dry," while others were "wet." During World War I, a total ban on the sale of alcohol in Canada was promoted by the Woman's Christian Temperance Union as a gesture of patriotism, and all provinces except Quebec had by 1916 imposed a ban on the retail sale of alcohol.[85] Though the province of Quebec did follow with its own ban in 1919, by the early 1920s support for **Prohibition** in Canada was on the wane, and most legislation was repealed by the end of the decade.

The situation in the United States was very different. The Eighteenth Amendment to the U.S. Constitution ushered in Prohibition in 1919. Legislation, in the form of the Volstead Act, restricted the sale of intoxicating beverages, defined as those containing one-half of 1 percent, or more, alcohol.[86] One consequence of Prohibition was the funding and growth of organized crime groups to supply illegal alcohol to a thirsty American population. Much of the alcohol was purchased from Canadian sources, which by 1925 could openly produce and sell beer, wine, and spirits.[87] Despite the exploits of Elliot Ness and his "Untouchables," American law enforcement agencies were inadequate, and officials were likely to be corrupted by wealthy bootleggers.[88] In 1933, the Twenty-First Amendment to the U.S. Constitution repealed Prohibition.

The Extent of Substance Abuse

Despite continuing efforts at control, the use of mood-altering substances persists in Canada. What is the extent of the substance abuse problem today? What should Canadians do about substance abuse?

Despite the media attention devoted to drug abuse, there is actually significant controversy over its nature and extent. Most illegal drug use by Canadians involves the possession of small amounts of marijuana. In May 2001, a federal parliamentary

Durham Regional Police announced the seizure of $40 million worth of cocaine in a joint investigation with the Canada Border Services Agency and the RCMP (December 23, 2008).

committee was struck to investigate drug use in Canada, and reported back that Canada should consider decriminalizing the "possession and cultivation of not more than thirty grams of cannabis for personal use."An April 2010 Angus Reid poll reported that 53 percent of Canadians believe that marijuana should be legalized.[89]

In 2003, Vancouver opened the first "safe injection site" for heroin and other injection drug users to combat the spread of HIV/AIDS and other bloodborne infections. In response to claims made by the federal government that the program fosters addiction and runs counter to the government's "get tough on crime" policies, the case was brought before the Supreme Court of Canada in May 2011.[90] In September of the same year, in a 9–0 decision, the court ruled in favour of the continued operation of the site, that the risk of death and disease to injection drug users outweighed any benefit that might be derived from maintaining an absolute prohibition of possession of illegal drugs at the injection site.[91]

As Figure 13.2 shows, total incidents of illegal drug use declined from a high point around 1980 until the early 1990s, when rates began to increase once again. Cannabis is overwhelmingly the drug of choice.

How can the trends in drug use be explained? The increasing trend in drug crimes is similar to a pattern previously recorded in the late 1970s and early 1980s, when the baby boomers reached the prime ages for illegal drug use; some have argued their children, the "baby boom echo," are now passing through the same phase. But why has drug use remained a major social problem? When drug use declined in the 1980s, some believed that changing perceptions about the harmfulness of drugs such as cocaine and marijuana had had an impact, reducing the likelihood that youth would try them. Others believed that widespread publicity linking drug use, needle sharing, and the AIDS virus was leading people to see drug taking as dangerous and risky. Still, statistics show that illegal drug use among Canadians is on the rise, in particular for cannabis and other drugs, including ecstasy, amphetamines, barbiturates, hallucinogens such as LSD and PCP, and anabolic steroids. For example, in December 2010, Canada Border Services Agency and the RCMP made the biggest seizure of the date rape hallucinogenic drug ketamine in Canadian history. Five men were arrested and charged with importing a controlled substance and possession for the purposes of trafficking after police discovered more than 1000 kilograms of the drug, worth more than $15 million, hidden in a shipment of coffee mugs imported into the Vancouver port from Hong Kong.[92]

It also appears that it is easier to obtain drugs, especially for younger adolescents. For example, a U.S. survey found that in 1992 about 42 percent of grade 8 students said it was easy to obtain pot; today about 47 percent say that it is easy to get that drug. In addition, parents may now be unwilling or reluctant to educate their children about the dangers of substance abuse because as baby boomers they were likely drug abusers themselves in the 1960s and 1970s.

FIGURE 13.2

Drug Offences in Canada, 1977–2007

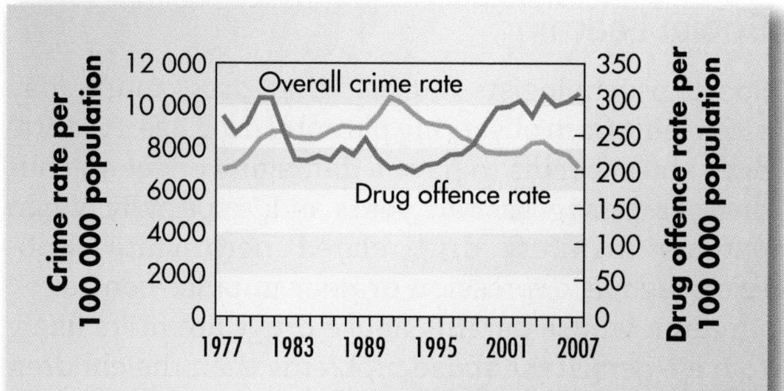

Source: Adapted from Statistics Canada Juristat - Trends in Police-reported Drug Offences in Canada, Catalogue 85-002, Vol. 29, no. 2, May 2009 (http://www.statcan.gc.ca/bsolc/olc-cel/olc-cel?catno=85-002-x&lang=eng).

The Causes of Substance Abuse

What causes people to abuse substances? Although there are many different views on the cause of drug use, most can be characterized as seeing the onset of an addictive career as either an environmental or a personal matter.

Subcultural View

Those who view drug abuse as having an environmental basis concentrate on lower-class addiction. Because a disproportionate number of drug abusers are poor, the onset of drug use can be tied to factors such as racial prejudice, devalued identities, low self-esteem, poor socioeconomic status, and the high level of mistrust, negativism, and defiance found in impoverished areas.

Residing in a deteriorated inner-city slum area is often correlated with entry into a drug subculture. Youths living in these depressed areas, where feelings of alienation and hopelessness run high, often meet established drug users, who teach them that narcotics provide an answer to their feelings of personal inadequacy and stress.[93] The youths may join peers to learn the techniques of drug use and receive social support for their habit. Research shows that peer influence is a significant predictor of drug careers that actually grows stronger as people mature.[94] Shared feelings and a sense of intimacy lead the youths to become fully enmeshed in what has been described as the "drug-use subculture."[95] Some join gangs and enter into a career of using and distributing illegal substances while also committing property and violent crimes.[96]

Psychodynamic View

Not all drug abusers reside in lower-class slum areas; the problem of middle-class substance abuse is very real. Consequently, some experts have linked substance abuse to personality disturbance and emotional problems that can strike people in any economic class. Psychodynamic explanations of substance abuse suggest that drugs help youths control or express unconscious needs and impulses. Drinking alcohol may be an indication of depression or other forms of mental illness.[97] A young teen may resort to drug abuse to reduce the emotional turmoil of adolescence, or to cope with troubling impulses.[98]

Personality testing of known users suggests that a significant percentage suffer from psychotic disorders, including various levels of schizophrenia. Surveys show that youngsters with serious behavioural problems were more than seven times more likely than those with less serious problems to report that they were dependent on alcohol or illicit drugs. Youths with serious emotional problems were nearly four times more likely to report dependence on drugs than those without such issues.[99]

These views have been substantiated by research involving a sample of 20 291 people in five large American cities. The results of this first large-scale study on the personality characteristics of abusers indicate a significant association between mental illness and drug abuse: About 53 percent of drug abusers and 37 percent of alcohol abusers have at least one serious mental illness. Conversely, 29 percent of the diagnosed mentally ill people in the survey have substance abuse problems.[100]

Genetic Factors

It is also possible that substance abuse may have a genetic basis. For example, the biological children of alcoholics reared by nonalcoholic adoptive parents develop alcohol problems more often than the biological children of the adoptive parents.[101] In a similar vein, a number of studies comparing alcoholism among identical twins and fraternal twins have found that the degree of concordance (both siblings behaving identically) is twice as high among the identical twin groups. These inferences are still inconclusive because identical twins are more likely to be treated similarly than fraternal twins and are therefore more likely to be influenced by environmental conditions. Nonetheless, most children of abusing parents do not become drug dependent themselves, suggesting that even if drug abuse is heritable, environment and socialization must play some role in the onset of abuse.[102]

In a recent study from McGill University, researchers have identified a "faulty gene" (known as CYP2A6) that may help to explain how some teenagers become more addicted to tobacco than others. The research suggests that there is no safe level and that those teens with the gene may be more susceptible to nicotine addiction even if they smoke fewer cigarettes per week.[103]

Social Learning

Social psychologists suggest that drug abuse may also result from observing parental drug use. Parental drug abuse begins to have a damaging effect on children as young as two years old, especially when parents manifest drug-related personality problems such as depression or poor impulse control.[104] Children whose parents abuse drugs are more likely to have persistent abuse problems than the children of nonabusers.[105]

People who learn that drugs provide pleasurable sensations may be the most likely to experiment with illegal substances; a habit may develop if the user experiences lower anxiety, fear, and tension levels.[106] Having a history of family drug and alcohol abuse has been found to be a characteristic of violent teenage sexual abusers.[107] Heroin abusers report an unhappy childhood that included harsh physical punishment and parental neglect and rejection.[108]

According to the social learning view, drug involvement begins with using tobacco and drinking alcohol at an early age, which progresses to experimentation with marijuana and hashish and finally to cocaine and even heroin. Although most recreational users do not progress to "hard stuff," few addicts begin their involvement with narcotics without first experimenting with recreational drugs. By implication, if teen smoking and drinking could be reduced, the gateway to hard drugs would be narrowed.

Problem Behaviour Syndrome (PBS)

For many people, substance abuse is just one of many problem behaviours. Longitudinal studies show that drug abusers are maladjusted, alienated, and emotionally distressed, and that their drug use is one among many social problems.[109] Having a deviant lifestyle begins early in life and is punctuated with criminal relationships, family history of substance abuse, educational failure, and alienation. People who abuse drugs lack commitment to religious values, disdain education, and spend most of their time in peer activities. An analysis of PBS by sociologist John Donovan found robust support for the interconnection of problem drinking and drug abuse, delinquency, precocious sexual behaviour, school failure, family conflict, and other similar social problems.[110]

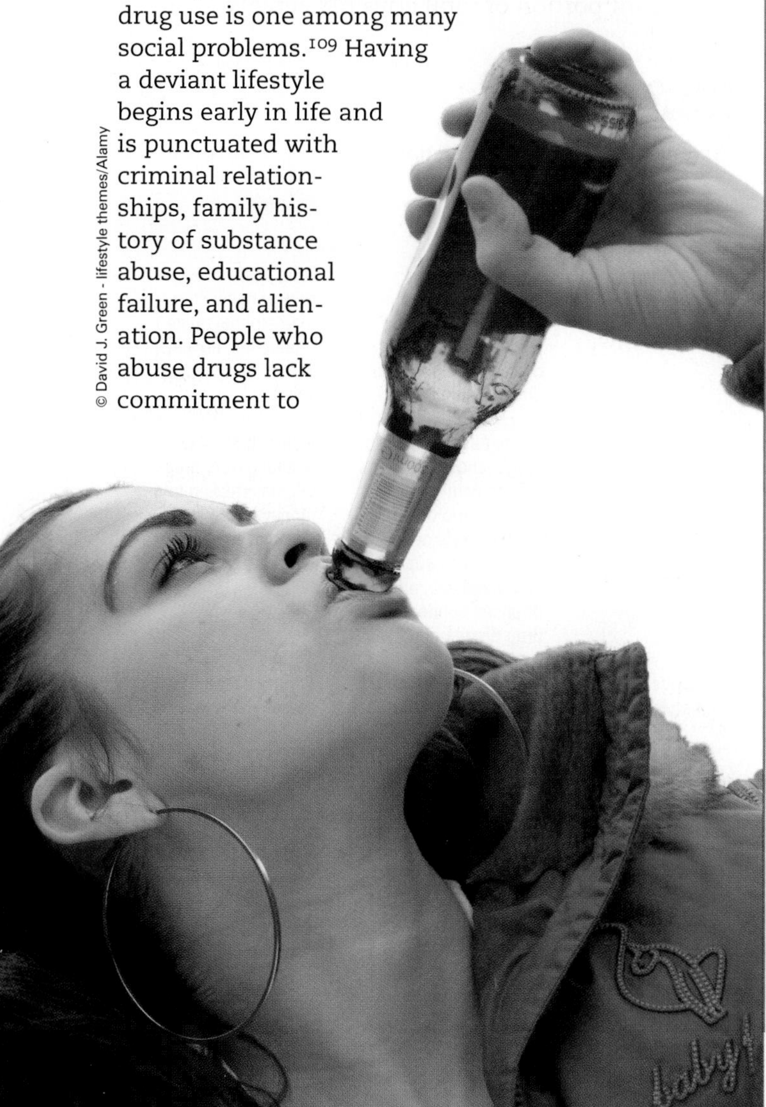

Rational Choice

Not all people who abuse drugs do so because of personal pathology. Some may use drugs and alcohol because they want to enjoy their effects: get high, relax, improve creativity, escape reality, and increase sexual responsiveness. Research indicates that adolescent alcohol abusers believe that getting high will make them powerful, increase their sexual performance, and facilitate their social behaviour; they care little about negative future consequences.[111]

Substance abuse, then, may be a function of the rational but mistaken belief that drugs can benefit the user. The decision to use drugs involves evaluations of personal consequences (such as addiction, disease, and legal punishment) and the expected benefits of drug use (such as peer approval, positive affective states, heightened awareness, and relaxation). Adolescents may begin using drugs because they believe their peers expect them to do so.[112]

Is There a Single "Cause" of Drug Abuse?

There are many different views of why people take drugs, and no one theory has proved adequate to explain all forms of substance abuse. Recent research efforts show that drug users suffer a variety of family and socialization difficulties, have addiction-prone personalities, and are generally at risk for many other social problems.[113] And although it is popular to believe that addicts progress along a continuum from using so-called gateway drugs to using ever more potent substances, that view may also be misleading. Research by Andrew Golub and Bruce Johnson shows that many hard-core drug abusers have never smoked or used alcohol. Examining a sample of more than 130 000 hard drug–using arrestees, Golub and Johnson found that the proportion who used marijuana before trying heroin and cocaine shifted significantly over time. The pathways may be different at various times and in different locales.[114]

In sum, there may be no single cause of substance abuse. People may try and continue to use illegal substances for a variety of reasons. As sociologist James Inciardi points out:

> There are as many reasons people use drugs as there are individuals who use drugs. For some, it may be a function

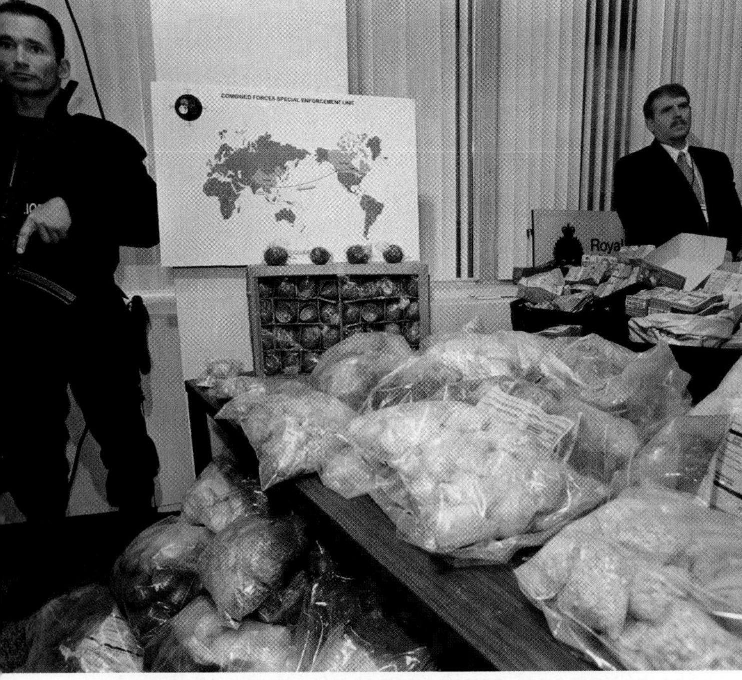

CP PHOTO/Tannis Toohey

of family disorganization, or cultural learning, or maladjusted personality, or an "addiction-prone" personality. ... For others, heroin use may be no more than a normal response to the world in which they live.[115]

Drugs and Crime

One of the main reasons for the criminalization of particular substances is the significant association believed to exist between drug abuse and crime. Research suggests that many criminal offenders have extensive experience with alcohol and drug use and that abusers commit an enormous amount of crime.[116] Statistics Canada estimates that 11 percent of homicides are related to drug trafficking,[117] and more than two-thirds of those accused of homicide had consumed drugs or alcohol at the time of the offence.[118]

Substance abuse appears to be an important precipitating factor in domestic assault. Women (and men) whose partners are "heavy drinkers" are three times more likely to be victims of spousal abuse than if their partners drank only moderately, or not at all.[119]

Although the drug–crime connection is powerful, the relationship is still uncertain because many users had a history of criminal activity before the onset of their substance abuse.[120] Nonetheless, if drug use does not turn otherwise law-abiding citizens into criminals, it certainly amplifies the extent of their criminal activities.[121] And as addiction levels increase, so do the frequency and seriousness of criminality.[122]

It is of course possible that most criminals are not actually drug users but that police are more likely to apprehend muddle-headed substance abusers than clear-thinking abstainers. A second, and probably more plausible, interpretation is that most criminals are in fact substance abusers. Drug use interferes with maturation and socialization. Drug abusers are more likely to drop out of school, be underemployed, engage in premarital sex, and become unmarried parents. These factors have been linked to a weakening of the social bond that leads to antisocial behaviours.[123] Typically, as Table 13.1 shows, the drug–crime relationship may be explained in one of three possible ways.

Despite drug seizures like the one staged in this photograph for the media, the importation and trafficking of illegal drugs remains a major source of income for organized crime.

In sum, research testing both the criminality of known narcotics users and the narcotics use of known criminals produces a very strong association between drug use and crime. Even if the crime rate of drug users were actually half that reported in the research literature, users would be responsible for a significant portion of total criminal activity.

TABLE 13.1

Summary of Drug–Crime Relationship

Drugs and Crime Relationship	Definition	Examples
Drug-defined offences	Violation of laws prohibiting or regulating the possession, use, distribution, or manufacture of illegal drugs.	Drug possession or use; cultivation, methamphetamine production; cocaine, heroin, or marijuana sales.
Drug-related offences	Offences in which a drug's pharmacologic effects contribute; offences motivated by the user's need for money to support continued use, and offences connected to drug distribution itself.	Violent behaviour resulting from drug effects, stealing to get money to buy drugs; violence against rival drug dealers.
Drug-using lifestyle	Drug use and crime are common aspects of a deviant lifestyle. The likelihood and frequency of involvement in illegal activity is increased because drug users may not participate in the legitimate economy and are exposed to situations that encourage crime.	A life orientation with an emphasis on short-term goals supported by illegal activities; opportunities to offend resulting from contacts with offenders and illegal markets; criminal skills learned from other offenders.

Source: White House Office of National Drug Control Policy, *Fact Sheet: Drug-Related Crime* (Washington, DC, 1997).

Drugs and the Law

The federal government first initiated legal action to curtail the use of some drugs in 1908, with the passage of An Act to Prohibit the Importation, Manufacture and Sale of Opium for Other than Medicinal Purposes. Criminologist Neil Boyd observes that the original impetus for the act really had very little to do with an "opium use problem." Instead, racist, anti-Chinese sentiments in the Vancouver area had blossomed into full-scale rioting over fears that Chinese labourers were taking jobs away from white workers, and action to deal with the conflict was called for. Mackenzie King, the federal minister of labour at the time, intervened and, based on complaints from citizens about opium use in the Vancouver area, resolved that some good would come from the conflict, at least in the passage of an act to restrict opium use, which King found personally distasteful.[124]

In 1911, a revised statute, the Opium and Drug Act, was introduced, which now included cocaine as a prohibited drug. In addition, the 1911 act provided for a term of imprisonment for possession of either smoking-opium or cocaine. Additional amendments in 1922 introduced the new Opium and Narcotic Drug Act, which provided for a minimum six months' term for possession, deportation of immigrants convicted of possession, and whipping of the convicted offender if so directed by the judge.[125] In 1923, marijuana was added to the act as a prohibited drug. In 1929, the penalty for possession of a prohibited drug was increased to a maximum of seven years' imprisonment.

In later years, other laws were passed to clarify existing drug statutes and revise penalties. For example, in 1961 the Narcotic Control Act was passed, which included the penalty of life imprisonment for importing or trafficking in narcotics. However, with growing drug use among the baby boomer youth population, increasing pressure was put on the federal government by parents and others to soften penalties for simple possession. Consequently, in 1969 the act was amended to provide for lesser "summary conviction" offences for possession.[126]

Throughout the 1970s, youth continued to challenge the law on drugs, and public sentiments about the use of drugs, particularly cannabis, continued to soften. Gerald Ledain, dean of the Osgoode Hall Law School, was commissioned by the federal government to review the laws on drug use, and bring forth recommendations to more effectively manage the growing problem of illegal drug use. Based on the Ledain Commission reports, in 1973 the Narcotic Control Act was amended to provide for absolute and conditional discharges as decisions of the court in drug crimes cases.[127]

The Narcotics Control Act was repealed in 1996, and replaced with the Controlled Drugs and Substances Act, which continues to govern illegal drug use in Canada today, along with the Food and Drug Act, which governs the use of legal drugs, including prescription drugs and other restricted substances.

A relatively new initiative in Canada is the emergence of drug courts. Currently there are two such courts in operation, in Toronto and Vancouver, where court-monitored treatment is emphasized over incarceration for drug-addicted offenders. The Canadian government has committed funding for at least three new drug courts with the ultimate aim of creating drug courts throughout Canada.

The federal government has also acted to control alcohol-related crimes. Spurred by groups such as Mothers Against Drunk Driving, impaired-driving laws in Canada are now among the toughest in the Western world. Under section 253 of the Criminal Code, an operator of a motor vehicle is "impaired" when the concentration of alcohol in his or her blood exceeds 80 milligrams per 100 millilitres of blood.[128] The penalties for being impaired when operating a motor vehicle range from a fine of $600 and prohibition from driving for at least one year for a first-time offence, to 90 days in jail and as much as a lifetime ban from driving for a third offence.[129]

Drug Control Strategies

Substance abuse remains a major social problem in North America. Politicians looking for a safe campaign issue can take advantage of the public's fear of drug addiction by calling for a war on drugs. These wars have been declared even when drug usage is stable or in decline.[130] Can these efforts pay off? Can illegal drug use be eliminated or controlled?

A number of different drug control strategies have been tried, with varying degrees of success. Some aim to deter drug use by stopping the flow of drugs into the country, apprehending and punishing dealers, and cracking down on street-level drug deals. Others focus on preventing drug use by educating potential users to the dangers of substance abuse (convincing them to "say no to drugs") and by organizing community groups to work with the at-risk population in their area. Still another approach is to treat known users so they can control their addictions. Some of these efforts are discussed here.

Source Control

One approach to drug control is to deter the sale and importation of drugs through the systematic apprehension of large-volume drug dealers, coupled with the enforcement of strict drug laws that carry heavy penalties. This approach is designed to capture and punish known international drug dealers and deter those who are considering entering the drug trade. A major effort has been made to cut off supplies of drugs by destroying overseas crops and arresting members of drug cartels in Central and South America, Asia, and the Middle East, where many drugs are grown and manufactured. Canadian police and other drug enforcement officials work closely with their counterparts in the United States in an attempt to stem the flow across their mutual border. Three South American nations, Peru, Bolivia, and Colombia, have agreed to coordinate control efforts. However, translating words into deeds is a formidable task. Drug lords are willing and able to fight back through intimidation, violence, and corruption when necessary. The Colombian drug cartels do not hesitate to use violence and assassination to protect their interests.

The amount of narcotics grown each year is so vast that even if three-quarters of the opium crop were destroyed, the North American market would still require only 10 percent of the remainder to sustain the drug trade.

Adding to control problems is the fact that the drug trade is an important source of foreign revenue for developing nations, and destroying the drug trade undermines their economies. More than 1 million people in Peru, Bolivia, Colombia, Thailand, Laos, and other developing nations depend on the cultivating and processing of illegal substances. The U.S. government estimates that North Americans spend more than US$40 billion annually on illegal drugs, and much of this money is funnelled overseas. Even if the government of one nation were willing to cooperate in vigorous drug suppression efforts, suppliers in other nations, eager to cash in on the seller's market, would be encouraged to turn more acreage over to coca or poppy production. For example, between 1994 and 1999, enforcement efforts in Peru and Bolivia were so successful that they altered cocaine cultivation patterns. As a consequence, Colombia became the premier coca-cultivating country because the local drug cartels encouraged local growers to cultivate coca plants. When the Colombian government mounted an effective eradication campaign in the traditional growing areas, the cartels linked up with rebel groups in remote parts of the country for their drug supply.[131] Neighbours expressed fear when, in August 2000, the United States announced US$1.3 billion in military aid to fight Columbia's rural drug dealers/rebels. Ecuador's foreign minister, Heinz Moeller, told reporters, "Our worry is that the removal of this cancerous tumor will cause it to metastasize into Ecuador."[132] With increasing pressure put on by the United States during the 1990s for countries in South America to deal with the cultivation and distribution of cocaine, by 2005 Mexico had assumed a leadership role in the cocaine distribution market. Struggles between rival drug gangs caused violence and murders in the country to spiral, with more than a dozen Canadians murdered in the country since 2000.[133]

Interdiction Strategies

Law enforcement efforts have also been directed at intercepting drug supplies as they enter the country. Border patrols and military personnel using sophisticated hardware have been involved in massive interdiction efforts; many impressive multimillion-dollar seizures have been made. Yet the American and Canadian borders are so vast and unprotected that meaningful interdiction is impossible. And even if all importation were shut down, home-grown marijuana and laboratory-made drugs such as "ice," LSD, PCP, and crystal meth could become the drugs of choice.

Law Enforcement Strategies

It has proven easier for the police to infiltrate and prosecute known traditional organized crime groups than to take on the relatively unorganized drug-dealing gangs. Police also target, intimidate, and arrest street-level dealers and users in an effort to make drug use so much of a hassle that consumption is cut back and the crime rate reduced. Approaches that have been tried include reverse stings, in which undercover agents pose as dealers to arrest users who approach them for a buy. Police have attacked fortified crack houses with heavy equipment to breach their defences. They have used racketeering laws to seize the assets of known dealers. Special police task forces have used undercover operations and drug sweeps to discourage both dealers and users.[134]

Although some street-level enforcement efforts have succeeded, others are considered failures.

Drug sweeps have clogged courts and correctional facilities with petty offenders while draining police resources. There are also suspicions that a displacement effect occurs: Stepped-up efforts to curb drug dealing in one area or city simply encourage dealers to seek out friendlier territory.[135]

Punishment Strategies

Even if law enforcement efforts cannot produce a general deterrent effect, the courts may achieve the required result by severely punishing known drug dealers and traffickers. In the United States, courts have taken a strong stand against possession and trafficking, imposing long, sometimes life sentences that have led to overflow of the prison system.[136] Many drug offenders sent to prison do not serve their entire sentences because they are released in an effort to relieve prison overcrowding.[137]

In contrast, Canada's federal Parliament introduced a bill in May 2003 to decriminalize marijuana possession, imposing instead a small fine. Significantly, drug arrests, the majority of which are for cannabis possession, dropped the same year.[138] A March 2010 EKOS poll found that 50 percent of Canadians agreed with the statement *"Possession of small amounts of marijuana for personal use should not be a crime,"* an increase of 5 percent over a June 2000 poll.[139]

Community Strategies

Another type of drug control effort relies on the involvement of local community groups to lead the fight against drugs. Representatives of various local government agencies, churches, civic organizations, and similar institutions are being brought together to create drug prevention and awareness programs.

Citizen-sponsored programs attempt to restore a sense of community in drug-infested areas, reduce fear, and promote conventional norms and values.[140] These efforts can be classified into one of four distinct categories.[141] The first involves law enforcement–type efforts, which may include block watches, cooperative police–community efforts, and citizen patrols. Some of these citizen groups are nonconfrontational: they simply observe or photograph dealers, write down their licence plate numbers, and then notify police.

A second tactic is to use the civil justice system to harass offenders. Landlords have been sued for owning properties that house drug dealers; neighbourhood groups have scrutinized drug houses for building code violations. Information acquired from these various sources is turned over to local authorities, such as police and housing agencies, for more formal action.

A third approach is through community-based treatment efforts in which citizen volunteers participate in self-help support programs, such as Narcotics Anonymous or Cocaine Anonymous. Other programs provide youths with martial arts training, dancing, and social events as alternatives to the drug life.

A fourth type of community-level drug prevention effort is designed to enhance the quality of life, improve interpersonal relationships, and upgrade the neighbourhood's physical environment. Activities might include the creation of drug-free school zones (which encourage police to keep drug dealers away from the vicinity of schools). Consciousness-raising efforts include demonstrations and marches to publicize the drug problem and build solidarity among participants.

Drug Education and Prevention Strategies

Prevention strategies are aimed at convincing youths not to get involved in drug abuse; heavy reliance is placed on educational programs that teach kids to say no to drugs. The most widely used program is Drug Abuse Resistance Education (DARE), an elementary and high school course designed to give students the skills for resisting peer pressure to experiment with tobacco, drugs, and alcohol. It is unique in that it employs uniformed police officers to carry the antidrug message to the students before they enter junior high school. The program has five major focus areas:

- Providing accurate information about tobacco, alcohol, and drugs
- Teaching students techniques to resist peer pressure
- Teaching students respect for the law and law enforcers
- Giving students ideas for alternatives to drug use
- Building the self-esteem of students

DARE is based on the concept that young students need specific analytical and social skills to resist peer pressure and refuse drugs.[142] However, evaluations show that the program does little to reduce drug use or convince abusers that drugs are harmful.[143] Although there are indications that DARE may be effective with some subsets of the population, such as children in junior grades, females, and Hispanic students, overall success appears problematic at best.[144]

Drug-Testing Programs

Some believe that drug testing of private employees, government workers, and criminal offenders helps to deter substance abuse. In the United States, employees are tested to enhance on-the-job safety and productivity. In some industries, such as mining and transportation, drug testing is considered essential because abuse can pose a threat to the public.[145]

Business leaders have been enlisted in the fight against drugs. Mandatory drug-testing programs in government and industry are common; more than 40 percent of the largest companies in the United States, including IBM and AT&T, have drug-testing programs. The American government requires employee testing in regulated industries such as nuclear energy and defence contracting.

In Canada, drug testing of employees is severely limited, and generally applies only where individuals are employed in "safety-sensitive" occupations (e.g., airline pilots) or where testing is a required condition attached to an alcohol or drug treatment program (e.g., probation or parole).[146]

Criminal defendants are now routinely tested at all stages of the justice system, from arrest to parole. The goal is to reduce criminal behaviour by detecting current users and curbing their abuse. Can such programs reduce criminal activity? At this point, the results of research evaluations of pretrial drug-testing programs are split in terms whether the programs reduce criminal behaviour.[147]

Treatment Strategies

A number of approaches are taken to treat known users, getting them clean of drugs and alcohol and thereby reducing the at-risk population. One approach rests on the assumption that users have low self-esteem and treatment efforts must focus on building a sense of self. For example, users have been placed in programs of outdoor activities and wilderness training to create self-reliance and a sense of accomplishment.[148] More intensive efforts use group therapy approaches, relying on group leaders who have been substance abusers; through such sessions, users get the skills and support to help them reject social pressure to use drugs. These programs are based on the Alcoholics Anonymous approach, which holds that users must find within themselves the strength to stay clean and that peer support from those who understand their experiences can help them achieve a drug-free life.

There are also residential programs for the more heavily involved, and a large network of drug treatment centres has been developed. Some detoxification units use medical procedures to wean patients from the more addicting drugs to others, such as methadone, that can be more easily regulated. Methadone is a drug similar to heroin, and addicts can be treated at clinics where they receive methadone under controlled conditions. However, methadone programs have been undermined because some users sell their methadone in the black market, and others supplement their dosages with illegally obtained heroin.

Other therapeutic programs attempt to deal with the psychological causes of drug use. Hypnosis, aversion therapy (getting users to associate drugs with unpleasant sensations, such as nausea), counselling, biofeedback, and other techniques are often used.

The long-term effects of treatment on drug abuse are still uncertain. Critics charge that a stay in a residential program can help stigmatize people as addicts even if they never used hard drugs; and in treatment they may be introduced to hard-core users with whom they will associate after release. Users do not often enter these programs voluntarily and have little motivation to change.[149] Supporters of treatment argue that many addicts are helped by intensive inpatient and outpatient treatment, and the cost saving is considerable.[150] Moreover, it is estimated that fewer than half of those who need drug treatment actually get it, so treatment strategies have not been given a fair trial.

Employment Programs

Research indicates that drug abusers who obtain and keep employment will end or reduce the incidence of their substance abuse.[151] Not surprisingly, then, there have been a number of efforts to provide vocational rehabilitation for drug abusers. One approach is the supported work program, which typically involves job-site training, ongoing assessment, and job-site intervention. Rather than teach work skills in a classroom, support programs rely on helping drug abusers deal with real work settings. Other programs provide training to overcome barriers to employment, including help with motivation, education, experience, the job market, job-seeking skills, and personal issues. For example, female abusers may be unaware of child-care resources that would enable them to seek employment opportunities while caring for their children. Another approach is to help addicts improve their interviewing skills so that once a job opportunity can be identified, they are equipped to convince potential employers of their commitment and reliability.

LO6 Decriminalization and Legalization

Considering these problems, some commentators have called for the legalization or decriminalization of restricted drugs. Drug enforcement costs Canadians more than $500 million each year, money that could be spent on health care or education.[152] One-half of Canadians support decriminalization of marijuana,[153] while others argue that "harm reduction" strategies, including public education and prevention, are a better means to address the drug problem than "prohibitionist" criminalizing

CP PHOTO/Kevin Frayer

Half of Canadians support decriminalizing possession of small amounts of marijuana for personal use.

approaches.[154] Certainly, the effectiveness of law enforcement to stem the flow of illegal drugs must be questioned.

Drug expert Ethan Nadelmann argues that legalization is warranted because the use of mood-altering substances is customary in almost all human societies; people have always wanted, and will find ways of obtaining, psychoactive drugs.[155] Banning drugs creates networks of manufacturers and distributors, many of whom use violence as part of their standard operating procedures. Although some believe that drug use is immoral, Nadelmann questions whether it is any worse than the unrestricted use of alcohol and cigarettes, both of which are addicting and unhealthful. Far more people die each year because they abuse these legal substances than are killed in drug wars or from abusing illegal substances.[156]

Nadelmann also states that just as Prohibition failed to stop the flow of alcohol in the United States and Canada in the 1920s while it increased the power of organized crime, the policy of prohibiting drugs is similarly doomed to failure. When drugs were legal and freely available early in the 20th century, the proportion of North Americans using drugs was not much greater than today. Most users led normal lives, most likely because of the legal status of their drug use.[157]

If drugs were legalized, the argument goes, price and distribution could be controlled by the government. This would reduce addicts' cash requirements, so crime rates would drop, because users would no longer need the same cash flow to support their habits. Drug-related deaths would decline because government control would reduce needle sharing and the spread of HIV/AIDS. Legalization would also destroy the drug-importing cartels and gangs. Because drugs would be bought and sold openly, the government would reap a tax windfall both from taxes on the sale of drugs and from income taxes paid by drug dealers on profits that have been part of the hidden economy. Of course, as with alcohol, drug distribution would be regulated, keeping drugs away from adolescents, public servants such as police and airline pilots, and known felons. Those who favour legalization point to Portugal and the Netherlands as a countries that have legalized drugs and remain relatively crime-free.[158]

This approach might have the short-term effect of reducing the association between drug use and crime, but it might also have grave social consequences. Legalization might increase the rate of drug usage, creating an even larger group of nonproductive, drug-dependent people who must be cared for by the rest of society.[159] In countries such as Iran and Thailand, where drugs are cheap and readily available, the rate of narcotics use is quite high. Historically, the availability of cheap narcotics has preceded drug-use epidemics, as was the case when British and American merchants sold opium in 19th-century China.

If juveniles, criminals, and members of other at-risk groups were forbidden to buy drugs, who would be the customers? Noncriminal, nonabusing middle-aged adults? And would not those prohibited from legally buying drugs create an underground market almost as vast as the current one? If the government tried to raise money by taxing legal drugs, as it now does with liquor and cigarettes, that might encourage drug smuggling to avoid tax payments; these "illegal" drugs might then fall into the hands of adolescents.

Full-scale legalization of controlled substances is unlikely in the near term, but further study is warranted. On the other hand, what effect would the Canadian government's policy of partial decriminalization (e.g., legalizing small amounts of marijuana) have on drug use rates? Would a get-tough policy help to "widen the net" of the justice system and actually deepen some youths' involvement in substance abuse? Can society provide alternatives to drugs that will reduce teenage drug dependency?[160] The answers to these questions have proven elusive.

Notes

Chapter 1

1. Philip Saunders, "The Missing Women of Vancouver," *CBC News Online*, 7 February 2002, www.cbc.ca/printablestory.jsp (accessed December 2011).
2. "Cost of Pickton Trial Could Rival $130-million Air India Case," *The Ottawa Citizen*, 5 December 2007 http://www.canada.com/ottawacitizen/news/story.html?id=4e9e3a1e-d690-41d1-a724-0d3416b4b65e&k=80857 (accessed 10 August 2011).
3. CBC News, "Crown Lays Out Grisly Case against Pickton, This Story Contains Disturbing Details" 23 January 2007, http://www.cbc.ca/canada/british-columbia/story/2007/01/22/pickton-trial.html#ixzz19RTpY16G (accessed 28 December 2010).
4. John Hagan and Alberto Palloni, "Sociological Criminology and the Mythology of Hispanic Immigration and Crime," *Social Problems* 46 (1999): 617–632.
5. Eugene Weber, *A Modern History of Europe* (New York: W.W. Norton, 1971), p. 398.
6. Anne Llewellyn Barstow, *Witchcraze: A New History of the European Witch Hunts* (Toronto: HarperCollins Canada, 1995).
7. Cesare Beccaria, *Essay on Crimes and Punishments,* [1764]. Translated by H. Paolucci (New York: Macmillan, 1985).
8. Described in David Lykken, "Psychopathy, Sociopathy, and Crime," *Society* 34 (1996): 29–38.
9. See Peter Scott, "Henry Maudsley" in *Pioneers in Criminology,* ed. Hermann Mannheim (Montclair, NJ: Prentice-Hall, 1991).
10. Nicole Hahn Rafter, "Criminal Anthropology in the United States," *Criminology* 30 (1992): 525–547.
11. See, generally, Robert Nisbet, *The Sociology of Emile Durkheim* (New York: Oxford University Press, 1974).
12. L. A. J. Quetelet, *A Treatise on Man and the Development of His Faculties* (Gainsville, FL: Scholars' Facsimiles and Reprints, 1969), pp. 82–96.
13. Quetelet, *A Treatise on Man,* p. 85.
14. Emile Durkheim, *The Rules of Sociological Method,* reprint ed., trans. W.D. Halls (New York: Free Press, 1982).
15. Emile Durkheim, *The Division of Labor in Society,* reprint ed. (New York: Free Press, 1997).
16. Robert Park and Ernest Burgess, *The City* (Chicago: University of Chicago Press, 1925).
17. Karl Marx and Friedrich Engels, *Capital: A Critique of Political Economy,* trans. E. Aveling (Chicago: Charles Kern, 1906); Karl Marx, *Selected Writings in Sociology and Social Philosophy,* trans. P. B. Bottomore (New York: McGraw-Hill, 1956). For a general discussion of Marxist thought, see Michael Lynch and W. Byron Groves, *A Primer in Radical Criminology* (New York: Harrow and Heston, 1986), pp. 6–26.
18. Marvin Wolfgang and Franco Ferracuti, *The Subculture of Violence* (London: Social Science Paperbacks, 1967), p. 20.
19. Thomas Gabor, "The Federal Gun Registry: An Urgent Need for Independent, Non-Partisan Research," *Canadian Journal of Criminology and Criminal Justice* 45 (2003): 489–499.
20. Wayne Kodro, "Euthanasia Case Farmer at Mercy of Canada Court," *Lancet* 357 (9253, 2001): 372; Lisa Schmidt, "60,000 Sign Petition Seeking Clemency for Jailed Latimer," *Kingston Whig-Standard,* 14 December 2001, p. 18.
21. Marvin Wolfgang, *Patterns in Criminal Homicide* (Philadelphia: University of Pennsylvania Press, 1958).
22. Hans von Hentig, *The Criminal and His Victim* (New Haven: Yale University Press, 1948); Stephen Schafer, *The Victim and His Criminal* (New York: Random House, 1968); Ezzat Fattah, *Understanding Criminal Victimization: An Introduction to Theoretical Criminology* (Scarborough, ON: Prentice-Hall, 1991).
23. Charles McCaghy, *Deviant Behavior* (New York: Macmillan, 1976), pp. 2–3.
24. John Hagan, "Crime and Deviance," in Robert Hagedorn, ed., *Sociology,* 4th ed. (Toronto: Holt, Rinehart and Winston of Canada, 1990), chap. 6.
25. Edwin Sutherland and Donald Cressey, *Criminology,* 8th ed. (Philadelphia: J. B. Lippincott, 1960), p. 8.
26. Eugene Doleschal and Nora Klapmuts, "Toward a New Criminology," *Crime and Delinquency* 5 (1973): 607.
27. Michael Lynch and W. Byron Groves, *A Primer in Radical Criminology* (Albany, NY: Harrow and Heston, 1989).
28. Howard Becker, *Outsiders: Studies in the Sociology of Deviance* (New York: Free Press, 1963), p. 9.
29. Ibid.
30. Marvin Zalman, John Strate, Denis Hunter, and James Sellars, "Michigan Assisted Suicide Three Ring Circus: The Intersection of Law and Politics," *Ohio Northern Law Review* 23 (1997): 112–138.
31. *Criminal Code* (R.S. 1985), S. 319.
32. Janice Tibbets and Leanne Dohy, "Top Court Upholds Spanking Children: Judges Set Limits on Punishment," *Calgary Herald,* 31 January 2004, p. A1.
33. Richard Barnhorst and Sherrie Barnhorst, *Criminal Law and the Canadian Criminal Code* (Toronto: McGraw-Hill Ryerson, 2004).
34. *R. v. Parks* (1992), 75 C.C.C. (3d) 287 (S.C.C).
35. *R. v. Ruzic,* http://www.lexum.umontreal.ca/csc-scc/en/pub/2001/vol1/html/2001scr1_0687.html.
36. *Criminal Code of Canada* (R.S. 1985, c. C-46) S. 83—Part II,1 Terrorism.
37. Ontario Women's Justice Network, *Arlene May—Coroner's Inquest,* http://www.owjn.org/archive/arlene.htm (accessed 20 February 2004); *Criminal Code* (R.S.C., 1985), S. 264 (1), (2), (3).
38. "Christopher's Law: A Bold Measure in Community Safety," Ontario Ministry of Community Safety and Correctional Services, http://www.mpss.jus.gov.on.ca (accessed 20 February 2004).
39. See, for example, Michael Hindelang and Travis Hirschi, "Intelligence and Delinquency: A Revisionist Review," *American Sociological Review* 42 (1977): 471–486.
40. Richard Herrnstein and Charles Murray, *The Bell Curve* (New York: Free Press, 1994).

41. Danylo Hawaleshka, "Most Aboriginal Children Are Healthy and Well-Adjusted," *Maclean's,* 4 August 2003, p. 41.
42. Anthony Petrosino, Carolyn Turpin-Petrosino, and James Finckenauer, "Well-Meaning Programs Can Have Harmful Effects! Lessons from Experiments of Programs Such as Scared Straight," *Crime and Delinquency* 46 (2000): 354–379.
43. Victor Boruch, Timothy Victor, and Joe Cecil, "Resolving Ethical and Legal Problems in Randomized Experiments," *Crime and Delinquency* 46 (2000): 330–353.

Chapter 2

1. Jim Wilkes and Nicolaas Van Rijn, "Guns Claim 4 Lives in GTA, *Toronto Star,* 3 May 2004, http://www.thestar.com; "Homicide Suspects Remain in Custody," *Vancouver Sun,* 3 May 2004, p. B3.
2. Uniform Crime Reporting Survey (Ottawa: Canadian Centre for Justice Statistics, 2004).
3. Statistics Canada, Uniform Crime Reporting Survey (UCR): Detailed Information for 2010, http://www.statcan.gc.ca/cgi-bin/imdb/p2SV.pl?Function=getSurvey&SDDS=3302&lang=en&db=imdb&adm=8&dis=2#a1
4. Shannon Brennan and Mia Dauvergne, "Police-reported Crime Statistics in Canada," 2010, *Juristat* (July 2011) Statistics Canada Cat. no. 85-002-X.
5. Samuel Perreault and Shannon Brennan, *Criminal Victimization in Canada, 2009,* Canadian Centre for Justice Statistics (Summer, 2010), vol. 30, no. 2.
6. Rémi Boivin and Gilbert Cordeau, "Measuring the Impact of Police Discretion on Official Crime Statistics: A Research Note," *Police Quarterly* (June 2011), vol. 14, iss. 2: 186–203.
7. David Seidman and Michael Couzens, "Getting the Crime Rate Down: Political Pressure and Crime Reporting," *Law and Society Review* 8 (1974): 457.
8. Jennifer L. Schulenberg, Joanna C. Jacob, and Peter J. Carrington, "Ecological Analysis of Crime Rates and Police Discretion with Young Persons: A Replication," *Canadian Journal of Criminology & Criminal Justice* (April 2007), vol. 49, iss. 2: 261–277.
9. M. Wallace, J. Turner, A. Matarazzo, and C. Babyak, *Measuring Crime in Canada: Introducing the Crime Severity Index and Improvements to the Uniform Crime Reporting Survey*, 2009, Statistics Canada website, http://www.statcan.gc.ca/pub/85-004-x/2009001/part-partie4-eng.htm (accessed 21 July 2011).
10. Ibid.
11. Statistics Canada, "General Social Survey: Victimization," *The Daily,* 28 September 2010, http:/www.statcan.gc.ca/daily-quotidien/100928/dq100928a/eng.htm (accessed 31 December 2010).
12. S. Perreault and S. Brennan, *Criminal Victimization in Canada, 2009: An Overview of Findings* (Ottawa: Statistics Canada, 2009), http://www.statcan.gc.ca/pub/85-002-x/2010002/article/11340-eng.htm#a3 (accessed 31 July 2011).
13. Rebecca Kong, "Canadian Crime Statistics," in Robert A. Silverman, James J. Teevan, and Vincent F. Sacco, eds., *Crime in Canadian Society* (Toronto: Harcourt Brace, 2000) chap. 5, pp. 63–95.
14. A pioneering effort in self-report research is A. L. Porterfield, *Youth in Trouble* (Fort Worth, TX: Leo Potishman Foundation, 1946); for a review, see Robert Hardt and George Bodine, *Development of Self-Report Instruments in Delinquency Research: A Conference Report* (Syracuse, NY: Syracuse University Youth Development Center, 1965). See also Fred Murphy, Mary Shirley, and Helen Witner, "The Incidence of Hidden Delinquency," *American Journal of Orthopsychology* 16 (1946): 686–696. For a critical perspective, see Francis T. Cullen, "Beyond Adolescence-Limited Criminology: Choosing Our Future—The American Society of Criminology 2010 Sutherland Address," *Criminology* (May 2011), vol. 49, iss. 2: 287–330.
15. Allison Ann Payne and Steven Salotti, "A Comparative Analysis of Social Learning and Social Control Theories in the Prediction of College Crime," *Deviant Behavior* (November/December 2007), vol. 28, iss. 6: 553–573.
16. John Hagan and Bill McCarthy, "Streetlife and Delinquency," *British Journal of Criminology* 43 (1992): 533–561. See also Brian P. Gendron, Kirk R. Williams, and Nancy G. Guerra, "An Analysis of Bullying Among Students Within Schools: Estimating the Effects of Individual Normative Beliefs, Self-Esteem, and School Climate," *Journal of School Violence* (April–June 2011), vol. 10, iss. 2: 150–164.
17. For example, the following studies have noted the great discrepancy between official statistics and self-report studies: Martin Gold, "Undetected Delinquent Behavior," *Journal of Research in Crime and Delinquency* 3 (1966): 27–46; James Short and F. Ivan Nye, "Extent of Undetected Delinquency: Tentative Conclusions," *Journal of Criminal Law, Criminology and Police Science* 49 (1958): 296–302; Michael Hindelang, "Causes of Delinquency: A Partial Replication and Extension," *Social Problems* 20 (1973): 471–487; Julian Roberts and William Wells, "The Validity of Criminal Justice Contacts Reported by Inmates: A Comparison of Self-Reported Data with Official Prison Records," *Journal of Criminal Justice* vol. 38, no. 5 (2010): 1031–037.
18. D. Wayne Osgood, Lloyd Johnston, Patrick O'Malley, and Jerald Bachman, "The Generality of Deviance in Late Adolescence and Early Adulthood," *American Sociological Review* 53 (1988): 81–93.
19. Jane B. Sprott, Anthony N. Doob, and Jennifer M. Jenkins, *Problem Behaviour and Delinquency in Children and Youth* (Ottawa: Statistics Canada, 2001), Cat. no. 85-002-XPE.
20. Leonore Simon, "Validity and Reliability of Violent Juveniles: A Comparison of Juvenile Self-Reports with Adult Self-Reports Incarcerated in Adult Prisons," paper presented at the annual meeting of the American Society of Criminology, Boston, November 1995, p. 26.
21. Stephen Cernkovich, Peggy Giordano, and Meredith Pugh, "Chronic Offenders: The Missing Cases in Self-Report Delinquency Research," *Journal of Criminal Law and Criminology* 76 (1985): 705–732.
22. Terence Thornberry, Beth Bjerregaard, and William Miles, "The Consequences of Respondent Attrition in Panel Studies: A Simulation Based on the Rochester Youth Development Study," *Journal of Quantitative Criminology* 9 (1993): 127–158.
23. See also Michael Hindelang, Travis Hirschi, and Joseph Weis, *Measuring Delinquency* (Beverly Hills, CA: Sage, 1981); Callie Marie Rennison and Chris Melde, "Exploring the Use of Victim Surveys to Study Gang Crime: Prospects and Possibilities," *Criminal Justice Review (*December 2009) 34 (4): 489–514.
24. Frank J. Leacy (ed.), *Historical Statistics of Canada* (Ottawa: Statistics Canada, 1983), Cat. no. 11-516-X1E.
25. Shannon Brennan and Mia Dauvergne, "Police-reported Crime Statistics in Canada," 2010, *Juristat* (July 2011) Statistics Canada Cat. no. 85-002-X.
26. Ibid.
27. Ibid.
28. Statistics Canada, "Homicide in Canada," *The Daily*, 26 October 2010.

29. Statistics Canada, "Study: Firearms and Violent Crime," *The Daily*, 20 February 2008.
30. Shannon Brennan and Mia Dauvergne, "Police-reported Crime Statistics in Canada," 2010, *Juristat* (July 2011) Statistics Canada Cat. no. 85-002-X.
31. Statistics Canada, "Criminal Victimization in Canada, 2009," *Juristat* (Summer 2010).
32. Marc Ouimet, "Crime in Canada and in the United States: A Comparison," *Canadian Review of Sociology and Anthropology*, 36 (3), 1999: 389–408.
33. Peter Carrington, "Population Aging and Crime in Canada, 2000–2041," *Canadian Journal of Criminology*, 43 (3) (2001): 331–356.
34. Susan Oh, "The Hidden Horror," *Maclean's*, 19 July 1999, p. 46; Eileen Kinsella, "Seniors, Prey of Con Artists and Brokers, Are Mad as Heck, Won't Take It Anymore," *Wall Street Journal* (Eastern Edition), 20 February 1997, p. C1.
35. Ralph Weisheit and L. Edward Wells, "The Future of Crime in Rural America," *Journal of Crime and Justice* 22 (1999): 1–22.
36. Peter Van Koppen and Robert Jansen, "The Time to Rob: Variations in Time of Number of Commercial Robberies," *Journal of Research in Crime and Delinquency* 36 (1999): 7–29.
37. Alex Sagovsky and Shane D. Johnson, "When Does Repeat Burglary Victimisation Occur?" *Australian & New Zealand Journal of Criminology* (April 2007) vol. 40, iss. 1: 1–26.
38. Ellen Cohn, "The Effect of Weather and Temporal Variations on Calls for Police Service," *American Journal of Police* 15 (1996): 23–43.
39. R. A. Baron, "Aggression as a Function of Ambient Temperature and Prior Anger Arousal," *Journal of Personality and Social Psychology* 21 (1972): 183–189.
40. Ellen Cohn, "The Prediction of Police Calls for Service: The Influence of Weather and Temporal Variables on Rape and Domestic Violence," *Journal of Environmental Psychology* 13 (1993): 71–83.
41. See, generally, Franklin Zimring and Gordon Hawkins, *Crime Is Not the Problem: Lethal Violence in America* (New York: Oxford University Press, 1997).
42. Canada Firearms Centre, *History of Gun Control in Canada*, http://www.cfc-ccaf.gc.ca.
43. Mia Dauvergne and Leonardo De Socio, "Firearms and Violent Crime," *Juristat*, 28 (February 2008): 2.
44. Michael O. Maume and Matthew R. Lee, "Social Institutions and Violence: A Sub-National Test of Institutional Anomie Theory," *Criminology* 41 (2003): 1137.
45. Victoria Brewer and M. Dwayne Smith, "Gender Inequality and Rates of Female Homicide Victimization across U.S. Cities," *Journal of Research in Crime and Delinquency* 32 (1995): 175–190.
46. Michelle Mann, "Corporate Criminals," *Canadian Business* (19 January 2004), vol. 77, iss. 2: 29; John Hagan, *Structural Criminology* (New Brunswick, NJ: Rutgers University Press, 1989); John Hagan and P. Parker, "White Collar Crime and Punishment: The Sentencing of White Collar Criminals in the Southern District of New York," *American Criminal Law Review*, 20 (1985): 259–301; C. Goff and C.E. Reasons, *Corporate Crime in Canada* (Scarborough, ON: Prentice-Hall, 1978).
47. R. Gregory Dunaway, Francis Cullen, Velmer Burton, and T. David Evans, "The Myth of Social Class and Crime Revisited: An Examination of Class and Adult Criminality," *Criminology* 38 (2000): 589–632.
48. Andrea Dottolo and Abigail Stewart, "'Don't Ever Forget Now, You're a Black Man in America': Intersections of Race, Class and Gender In Encounters with the Police," *Sex Roles* (September 2008), vol. 59, iss. 5/6: 350–364; Ivan Nye, James Short, and Virgil Olsen, "Socioeconomic Status and Delinquent Behavior," *American Journal of Sociology* 63 (1958): 381–389; Robert Dentler and Lawrence Monroe, "Social Correlates of Early Adolescent Theft," *American Sociological Review* 63 (1961): 733–743. See also Terence Thornberry and Margaret Farnworth, "Social Correlates of Criminal Involvement: Further Evidence of the Relationship Between Social Status and Criminal Behavior," *American Sociological Review* 47 (1982): 505–518.
49. Charles Tittle, Wayne Villemez, and Douglas Smith, "The Myth of Social Class and Criminality: An Empirical Assessment of the Empirical Evidence," *American Sociological Review* 43 (1978): 643–656. See also Charles Tittle and Robert Meier, "Specifying the SES/Delinquency Relationship," *Criminology* 28 (1990): 271–301.
50. Delbert Elliott and Suzanne Ageton, "Reconciling Race and Class Differences in Self-Reported and Official Estimates of Delinquency," *American Sociological Review* 45 (1980): 95–110.
51. Filomin C. Gutierrez, and Donald J. Shoemaker, "Self-Reported Delinquency of High School Students in Metro Manila: Gender and Social Class," *Youth & Society* (September 2008) vol. 40, iss. 1: 55–85. See also Delbert Elliott and David Huizinga, "Social Class and Delinquent Behavior in a National Youth Panel: 1976–1980," *Criminology* 21 (1983): 149–177. For a similar view, see John Braithwaite, "The Myth of Social Class and Criminality Reconsidered," *American Sociological Review* 46 (1981): 35–58; Hindelang, Hirschi, and Weis, *Measuring Delinquency*, p. 196.
52. Judith Blau and Peter Blau, "The Cost of Inequality: Metropolitan Structure and Violent Crime," *American Sociological Review* 147 (1982): 114–129; Richard Block, "Community Environment and Violent Crime," *Criminology* 17 (1979): 46–57; Robert Sampson, "Structural Sources of Variation in Race-Age-Specific Rates of Offending Across Major U.S. Cities," *Criminology* 23 (1985): 647–673.
53. Chin-Chi Hsieh and M. D. Pugh, "Poverty, Income Inequality, and Violent Crime: A Meta-Analysis of Recent Aggregate Data Studies," *Criminal Justice Review* 18 (1993): 182–199.
54. Robert Agnew, "A General Strain Theory of Community Differences in Crime Rates," *Journal of Research in Crime and Delinquency* 36 (1999): 123–155.
55. Wouter Steenbeek and John R. Hipp, "A Longitudinal Test of Social Disorganization Theory: Feedback Effects Among Cohesion, Social Control, and Disorder," *Criminology* (August 2011) vol. 49, iss. 3: 833–871. See also Bonita Veysey and Steven Messner, "Further Testing of Social Disorganization Theory: An Elaboration of Sampson and Groves's 'Community Structure and Crime,'" *Journal of Research in Crime and Delinquency* 36 (1999): 156–174.
56. Lance Hannon and James Defronzo, "Welfare and Property Crime," *Justice Quarterly* 15 (1998): 273–288.
57. David T. Lykken, "The Causes and Costs of Crime and a Controversial Cure," *Journal of Personality* (June 2000) vol. 68, iss. 3: 559–605; Alan Lizotte, Terence Thornberry, Marvin Krohn, Deborah Chard-Wierschem, and David McDowall, "Neighborhood Context and Delinquency: A Longitudinal Analysis," in *Cross National Longitudinal Research on Human Development and Criminal Behavior*, ed. E. M. Weitekamp and H. J. Kerner (Stavernstr, Netherlands: Kluwer, 1994), pp. 217–227.
58. Travis Hirschi and Michael Gottfredson, "Age and the Explanation of Crime,"

American Journal of Sociology 89 (1983): 552–584, at p. 581.

59. Darrell Steffensmeier and Cathy Streifel, "Age, Gender, and Crime Across Three Historical Periods: 1935, 1960 and 1985," *Social Forces* 69 (1991): 869–894.
60. Mia Dauvergne, "Motor Vehicle Theft in Canada, 2007," *Juristat* (December 2008) vol. 28, no. 10; Marnie Wallace, "Motor Vehicle Theft in Canada—2001" *Juristat* 23 (2003).
61. Shannon Brennan and Mia Dauvergne, "Police-reported Crime Statistics in Canada," 2010, *Juristat* (July 2011) Statistics Canada Cat. no. 85-002-X.
62. Gregory P. Brown and Kari Brozowski, "Golden Years? The Incarceration of the Older Offender," *Geriatrics Today* 6 (2003): 32–35.
63. Doreen Higgins and Margaret E. Severson, "Community Reentry and Older Adult Offenders: Redefining Social Work Roles," *Journal of Gerontological Social Work* (November/December 2009) vol. 52, iss. 8: 784–802. See also Julius H. E. Uzoaba, *Managing Older Offenders: Where Do We Stand?* (Ottawa: Correctional Services of Canada, 1998).
64. Margo Wilson and Martin Daly, "Life Expectancy, Economic Inequality, Homicide, and Reproductive Timing in Chicago Neighbourhoods," *British Journal of Medicine* 314 (1997): 1271–1274.
65. Ray Paternoster and Shawn Bushway, "Desistance and the "Feared Self": Toward An Identity Theory of Criminal Desistance," *Journal of Criminal Law & Criminology* (Fall 2009) vol. 99, iss. 4: 1103–1156.
66. Gordon Trasler, "Cautions for a Biological Approach to Crime," in *The Causes of Crime: New Biological Approaches,* ed. Sarnoff Mednick, Terrie Moffitt, and Susan Stack (Cambridge, UK: Cambridge University Press, 1987), pp. 7–25.
67. James Q. Wilson and Richard Herrnstein, *Crime and Human Nature* (New York: Simon and Schuster, 1985), pp. 126–147.
68. Wilson and Herrnstein, *Crime and Human Nature,* p. 219.
69. Monica Barry, "Youth Transitions: From Offending to Desistance," *Journal of Youth Studies* (February 2010) vol. 13, iss. 1: 121–136; and also Ralph C. Serin, and Caleb D. Lloyd,"Examining the Process of Offender Change: The Transition to Crime Desistance," *Psychology, Crime & Law* (May 2009) vol. 15, iss. 4: 347–364.
70. Walter Gove, "The Effect of Age and Gender on Deviant Behavior: A Biopsychosocial Perspective," in *Gender and the Life Course,* ed. A. Ross (Chicago: Aldine, 1985), p. 131.
71. Statistics Canada, "Adult Criminal Court Statistics, 2008/2009," *Juristat* (Summer 2010).
72. Cesare Lombroso, *The Female Offender* (New York: Appleton Publishers, 1920), p. 122.
73. Lombroso, *The Female Offender.*
74. Shannon Brennan and Mia Dauvergne, "Police-reported Crime Statistics in Canada," 2010, *Juristat* (July 2011) Statistics Canada Cat. no. 85-002-X.
75. Ibid.
76. Peter J. Carrington and Jennifer L. Schulenberg, "Introduction: The Youth Criminal Justice Act—A New Era in Canadian Juvenile Justice?" *Canadian Journal of Criminology & Criminal Justice* (April 2004) vol. 46, iss. 3: 219–223.
77. Elizabeth Comack and Salena Brickey, "Constituting the Violence of Criminalized Women," *Canadian Journal of Criminology & Criminal Justice* (January 2007) vol. 49, iss. 1: 1–36.
78. Lee Ellis, Shyamal Das, and Hasan Buker, "Androgen-promoted Physiological Traits and Criminality: A Test of the Evolutionary Neuroandrogenic Theory," *Personality & Individual Differences* (February 2008) vol. 44, iss. 3: 699–709; Alan Booth and D. Wayne Osgood, "The Influence of Testosterone on Deviance in Adulthood: Assessing and Explaining the Relationship," *Criminology* 31 (1993): 93–118.
79. Gisela Konopka, *The Adolescent Girl in Conflict* (Englewood Cliffs, NJ: Prentice-Hall, 1966); Clyde Vedder and Dora Somerville, *The Delinquent Girl* (Springfield, IL: Charles C. Thomas, 1970).
80. Leslie D. Leve and Patricia Chamberlain, "Female Juvenile Offenders: Defining an Early-Onset Pathway for Delinquency," *Journal of Child & Family Studies* (December 2004) vol. 13, iss. 4: 439–452; Robert Hoge, D. A. Andrews, and Alan Leschied, "Tests of Three Hypotheses Regarding the Predictors of Delinquency," *Journal of Abnormal Child Psychology* 22 (1994): 547–559.
81. Rita James Simon, *The Contemporary Woman and Crime* (Washington, DC: U.S. Government Printing Office, 1975).
82. David Rowe, Alexander Vazsonyi, and Daniel Flannery, "Sex Differences in Crime: Do Mean and Within-Sex Variation Have Similar Causes?" *Journal of Research in Crime and Delinquency* 32 (1995): 84–100; Michael Hindelang, "Age, Sex, and the Versatility of Delinquency Involvements," *Social Forces* 14 (1971): 525–534; Martin Gold, *Delinquent Behavior in an American City* (Belmont, CA: Brooks/Cole, 1970); Gary Jensen and Raymond Eve, "Sex Differences in Delinquency: An Examination of Popular Sociological Explanations," *Criminology* 13 (1976): 427–448. Jyh-Yaw Joseph Chen and David E. A. Giles, "Gender Convergence in Crime: Evidence from Canadian Adult Offence Charge Data," Econometrics Working Paper, Department of Economics, University of Victoria B.C., Canada (April 2003) http://web.uvic.ca/econ/research/papers/pdfs/ewp0303.pdf.
83. Marie Drolet, "Why Has the Gender Wage Gap Narrowed?" Statistics Canada (Spring 2011) http://www.statcan.gc.ca/pub/75-001-x/2011001/pdf/11394-eng.pdf.
84. Statistics Canada, Table 252-0029, "Youth Court Survey, Number of Cases by Sex of the Accused, Annual, 1994–2002"; Eileen Poe-Yamagata and Jeffrey A. Butts, "Female Offenders in the Juvenile Justice System, 1996," https://www.ncjrs.gov/txtfiles/femof.txt; Katherine Stevenson, Jennifer Tufts, Diane Hendrick, and Melanie Kowalski, "Youth and Crime" *Canadian Social Trends* (Summer 1999).
85. Scot Wortley, "A Northern Taboo: Research on Race, Crime, and Criminal Justice in Canada," *Canadian Journal of Criminology* 41 (1999): 261–275.
86. Ann Finn, Shelley Trevethan, Gisele Carriere, and Melanie Kowalski, "Female Inmates, Aboriginal Inmates, and Inmates Serving Life Sentences: A One Day Snapshot," *Juristat* 19 (April 1999); Statistics Canada, "Incarceration of Aboriginal People in Adult Correctional Services," *The Daily*, 21 July 2009.
87. Robert D. Crutchfield, April Fernandes, and Jorge Martinez, "Racial and Ethnic Disparity and Criminal Justice: How Much Is Too Much?" *Journal of Criminal Law & Criminology* (Summer 2010) vol. 100, iss. 3: 903–932.
88. "Singled Out: Star Analysis of Police Crime Data Shows Justice Is Different for Blacks and Whites," *Toronto Star,* 19 October 2002, p. A1.
89. Scot Wortley and Lysandra Marshall, *Race and Police Stops in Kingston, Ontario: Results of a Pilot Project* (Kingston: Kingston Police Services Board, 2005).
90. Graham C. Ousey, and Matthew R. Lee, "Racial Disparity in Formal Social Control: An Investigation of Alternative Explanations of Arrest Rate Inequality," *Journal of Research in Crime & Delinquency* (August 2008) vol. 45, iss. 3: 322–355.

91. Robert D. Crutchfield, April Fernandes, and Jorge Martinez, "Racial and Ethnic Disparity and Criminal Justice: How Much Is Too Much?" *Journal of Criminal Law & Criminology* (Summer 2010) vol. 100, iss. 3: 903–932.
92. Carol La Prairie, *Seen but Not Heard: Native People in the Inner City,* Aboriginal Justice Directorate (Ottawa: Department of Justice, 1994).
93. Ibid.
94. Ibid.
95. Gary LaFree,Eric P. Baumer, and Robert O'Brien, "Still Separate and Unequal? A City-Level Analysis of the Black-White Gap in Homicide Arrests since 1960," *American Sociological Review* (February 2010) vol. 75, iss. 1: 75–100.
96. Reynolds Farley and William Frey, "Changes in the Segregation of Whites from Blacks During the 1980s: Small Steps Toward a More Integrated Society," *American Sociological Review* 59 (1994): 23–45.
97. Marvin Wolfgang, Robert Figlio, and Thorsten Sellin, *Delinquency in a Birth Cohort* (Chicago: University of Chicago Press, 1972).
98. David P. Farrington, Maria M. Ttofi and Jeremy W. Coid, "Development of Adolescence-limited, Late-onset, and Persistent Offenders from age 8 to Age 48," *Aggressive Behavior* (March/April 2009) vol. 35, iss. 2: 150–163.

Chapter 3

1. Rosie DiManno, "The Day Tori Stafford was Murdered," *The Guelph Mercury* (10 December 2010), p. A9.
2. Criminal Victimization in Canada 2009 (Summer 2010), vol. 30, no. 2, Statistics Canada Cat. 85-002-X.
3. Department of Justice Canada, Research and Statistics Division, "Costs of Crime in Canada: An Update," http://www.justice.gc.ca/eng/pi/rs/rep-rap/jr/jr12/p7.html (accessed 28 January 2001).
4. Ibid.
5. Ibid.
6. Ibid.
7. Ross Macmillan, "Adolescent Victimization and Income Deficits in Adulthood: Rethinking the Costs of Criminal Violence from a Life-Course Perspective," *Criminology* 38 (2000): 553–588.
8. Rebecca Campbell and Sheela Raja, "Secondary Victimization of Rape Victims: Insights from Mental Health Professionals Who Treat Survivors of Violence," *Violence and Victims* 14 (1999): 261–274.
9. Peter Finn, *Victims* (Washington, DC: Bureau of Justice Statistics, 1988), p. 1.
10. Michael Wiederman, Randy Sansone, and Lori Sansone, "History of Trauma and Attempted Suicide Among Women in a Primary Care Setting," *Violence and Victims* 13 (1998): 3–11; Susan Leslie Bryant and Lillian Range, "Suicidality in College Women Who Were Sexually and Physically Abused and Physically Punished by Parents," *Violence and Victims* 10 (1995): 195–215; William Downs and Brenda Miller, "Relationships Between Experiences of Parental Violence During Childhood and Women's Self-Esteem," *Violence and Victims* 13 (1998): 63–78; Sally Davies-Netley, Michael Hurlbut, and Richard Hough, "Childhood Abuse as a Precursor to Homelessness for Homeless Women with Severe Mental Illness," *Violence and Victims* 11 (1996): 129–142.
11. Jeanne Kaufman and Cathy Spatz Widom, "Childhood Victimization, Running Away, and Delinquency," *Journal of Research in Crime and Delinquency* 36 (1999): 347–370.
12. Dina Vivian and Jean Malone, "Relationship Factors and Depressive Symptomology Associated with Mild and Severe Husband-to-Wife Physical Aggression," *Violence and Victims* 12 (1997): 19–37; Walter Gleason, "Mental Disorders in Battered Women," *Violence and Victims* 8 (1993): 53–66; Daniel Saunders, "Posttraumatic Stress Symptom Profiles of Battered Women: A Comparison of Survivors in Two Settings," *Violence and Victims* 9 (1994): 31–43.
13. K. Daniel O'Leary, "Psychological Abuse: A Variable Deserving Critical Attention in Domestic Violence," *Violence and Victims* 14 (1999): 1–21.
14. James Anderson, Terry Grandison, and Laronistine Dyson, "Victims of Random Violence and the Public Health Implication: A Health Care of Criminal Justice Issue," *Journal of Criminal Justice* 24 (1996): 379–393.
15. "Most Homicides by Rejected Men, Judge Says During Stalking Case," *Guelph Mercury,* 9 November 2004, p. A2.
16. Pamela Wilcox Rountree, "A Reexamination of the Crime–Fear Linkage," *Journal of Research in Crime and Delinquency* 35 (1998): 341–372.
17. Robert Davis, Bruce Taylor, and Arthur Lurigio, "Adjusting to Criminal Victimization: The Correlates of Postcrime Distress," *Violence and Victimization* 11 (1996): 21–34.
18. Martin Patriquin et al., "The Secret Life of Colonel Russell Williams" *Maclean's* 22 February 2010, 123 (6): 20–23; and Chris Cobb, "Ex-Colonel's Lawyers Call Lurid Courtroom Tweets 'Unnecessary'" *Calgary Herald* 24 January 2011, A2.
19. Timothy Ireland and Cathy Spatz Widom, *Childhood Victimization and Risk for Alcohol and Drug Arrests* (Washington, DC: National Institute of Justice, 1995).
20. Brigette Erwin, Elana Newman, Robert McMackin, Carlo Morrissey, and Danny Kaloupek, "PTSD, Malevolent Environment, and Criminality Among Criminally Involved Male Adolescents," *Criminal Justice and Behavior* 27 (2000): 196–215.
21. Cathy Spatz Widom, *The Cycle of Violence* (Washington, DC: National Institute of Justice, 1992), p. 1.
22. Steve Spaccarelli, J. Douglas Coatsworth, and Blake Sperry Bowden, "Exposure to Serious Family Violence Among Incarcerated Boys: Its Association with Violent Offending and Potential Mediating Variables," *Violence and Victims* 10 (1995): 163–180; Jerome Kolbo, "Risk and Resilience Among Children Exposed to Family Violence," *Violence and Victims* 11 (1996): 113–127.
23. Ibid.
24. Ibid.
25. Benjamin Bowling, *Violent Racism: Victimization, Policing and Social Context* (Oxford: Clarendon Press); James Jacobs and Kimberely Potter, *Hate Crimes: Criminal Law and Identity Politics* (New York: Oxford University Press).
26. Morton Beiser, Samuel Noh, Feng Hou, Vilet Kaspar, and Joanna Rummens, "Southeast Asian Refugees' Perceptions of Racial Discrimination in Canada," *Canadian Ethnic Studies* 33 (January 2001): 46–55.
27. Karin Wittebrood and Paul Nieuwbeerta, "Criminal Victimization During One's Life Course: The Effects of Previous Victimization and Patterns of Routine Activities," *Journal of Research in Crime and Delinquency* 37 (2000): 91–122; Janet Lauritsen and Kenna Davis Quinet, "Repeat Victimizations Among Adolescents and Young Adults," *Journal of Quantitative Criminology* 11 (1995): 143–163.
28. Denise Osborn, Dan Ellingworth, Tim Hope, and Alan Trickett, "Are Repeatedly Victimized Households Different?" *Journal of Quantitative Criminology* 12 (1996): 223–245.
29. Graham Farrell, "Predicting and Preventing Revictimization," in *Crime and Justice: An Annual Review of Research,* Michael Tonry and David Farrington, eds., vol. 20 (Chicago: University of Chicago Press, 1995): pp. 61–126.

30. Ibid., p. 61.
31. David Finkelhor and Nancy Asigian, "Risk Factors for Youth Victimization: Beyond a Lifestyles/Routine Activities Theory Approach," *Violence and Victimization* 11 (1996): 3–19.
32. Graham Farrell, Coretta Phillips, and Ken Pease, "Like Taking Candy: Why Does Repeat Victimization Occur?" *British Journal of Criminology* 35 (1995): 384–399.
33. Besserer and Trainor, "Criminal Victimization in Canada."
34. Hans Von Hentig, *The Criminal and His Victim: Studies in the Sociobiology of Crime* (New Haven, CT: Yale University Press, 1948), p. 384.
35. Marvin Wolfgang, *Patterns of Criminal Homicide* (Philadelphia: University of Pennsylvania Press, 1958).
36. Menachem Amir, *Patterns in Forcible Rape* (Chicago: University of Chicago Press, 1971).
37. Susan Estrich, *Real Rape* (Cambridge, MA: Harvard University Press, 1987).
38. Edem Avakame, "Female's Labor Force Participation and Intimate Femicide: An Empirical Assessment of the Backlash Hypothesis," *Violence and Victims* 14 (1999): 277–283.
39. Martin Daly and Margo Wilson, *Homicide* (New York: Aldine de Gruyter, 1988).
40. Rosemary Gartner and Bill McCarthy, "The Social Distribution of Femicide in Urban Canada, 1921–1988," *Law and Society Review* 25 (1991): 287–311.
41. Dan Hoyt, Kimberly Ryan, and Mari Cauce, "Personal Victimization in a High-Risk Environment: Homeless and Runaway Adolescents," *Journal of Research in Crime and Delinquency* 36 (1999): 371–392.
42. See, generally, Gary Gottfredson and Denise Gottfredson, *Victimization in Schools* (New York: Plenum Press, 1985).
43. Gary Jensen and David Brownfield, "Gender, Lifestyles, and Victimization: Beyond Routine Activity Theory," *Violence and Victims* 1 (1986): 85–99.
44. Rolf Loeber, Mary DeLamatre, George Tita, Jacqueline Cohen, Magda Stouthamer-Loeber, and David Farrington, "Gun Injury and Mortality: The Delinquent Backgrounds of Juvenile Offenders," *Violence and Victims* 14 (1999): 339–351.
45. Bonnie Fisher, John Sloan, Francis Cullen, and Chunmeng Lu, "Crime in the Ivory Tower: The Level and Sources of Student Victimization," *Criminology* 36 (1998): 671–710.
46. James Garofalo, "Reassessing the Lifestyle Model of Criminal Victimization," in *Positive Criminology,* ed. Michael Gottfredson and Travis Hirschi (Newbury Park, CA: Sage, 1987), pp. 23–42.
47. Terance Miethe and David McDowall, "Contextual Effects in Models of Criminal Victimization," *Social Forces* 71 (1993): 741–759.
48. Rodney Stark, "Deviant Places: A Theory of the Ecology of Crime," *Criminology* 25 (1987): 893–911.
49. Ibid., p. 902.
50. Pamela Wilcox Rountree, Kenneth Land, and Terance Miethe, "Macro–Micro Integration in the Study of Victimization: A Hierarchical Logistic Model Analysis Across Seattle Neighborhoods," paper presented at the annual meeting of the American Society of Criminology, Phoenix, Arizona, November 1993.
51. Lawrence Cohen and Marcus Felson, "Social Change and Crime Rate Trends: A Routine Activities Approach," *American Sociological Review* 44 (1979): 588–608.
52. For a review, see James LeBeau and Thomas Castellano, "The Routine Activities Approach: An Inventory and Critique," unpublished paper, Center for the Studies of Crime, Delinquency, and Corrections, Southern Illinois University, Carbondale, 1987.
53. Teresa LaGrange, "The Impact of Neighborhoods, Schools, and Malls on the Spatial Distribution of Property Damage," *Journal of Research in Crime and Delinquency* 36 (1999): 393–422.
54. Lawrence Cohen, Marcus Felson, and Kenneth Land, "Property Crime Rates in the United States: A Macrodynamic Analysis, 1947–1977, with Ex-ante Forecasts for the Mid-1980s," *American Journal of Sociology* 86 (1980): 90–118.
55. Terence Miethe and Robert Meier, *Crime and Its Social Context: Toward an Integrated Theory of Offenders, Victims, and Situations* (Albany: State University of New York Press, 1994).
56. Richard Felson, "Routine Activities and Involvement in Violence as Actor, Witness, or Target," *Violence and Victimization* 12 (1997): 209–223.
57. Georgina Hammock and Deborah Richardson, "Perceptions of Rape: The Influence of Closeness of Relationship, Intoxication, and Sex of Participant," *Violence and Victimization* 12 (1997): 237–247.
58. Karin Wittebrood and Paul Nieuwbeerta, "Criminal Victimization During One's Life Course," pp. 112–113.
59. Patricia Resnick, "Psychological Effects of Victimization: Implications for the Criminal Justice System," *Crime and Delinquency* 33 (1987): 468–478.
60. Dean Kilpatrick, Benjamin Saunders, Lois Veronen, Connie Best, and Judith Von, "Criminal Victimization: Lifetime Prevalence, Reporting to Police, and Psychological Impact," *Crime and Delinquency* 33 (1987): 479–489.
61. Michelle Grossman and Catherine Kane, "Victims of Crime and the Justice System," in *Criminal Justice in Canada,* ed. Julian V. Roberts and Michelle G. Grossman (Toronto: Thomson Nelson, 2004), pp. 106–119.
62. Ibid.
63. Ibid.
64. Ibid.
65. Ibid.
66. This section leans heavily on Albert Roberts, "Delivery of Services to Crime Victims: A National Survey," *American Journal of Orthopsychiatry* 6 (1991): 128–137; see also Albert Roberts, *Helping Crime Victims: Research, Policy, and Practice* (Newbury Park, CA: Sage, 1990).
67. Randall Schmidt, "Crime Victim Compensation Legislation: A Comparative Study," *Victimology* 5 (1980): 428–437.
68. Ibid.
69. Ontario Ministry of the Attorney General, "Victim/Witness Assistance Program (VWAP)," http://www.attorneygeneral.jus.gov.on.ca.
70. Pater Jaffe, Marlies Sudermann, Deborah Reitzel, and Steve Killip, "An Evaluation of a Secondary School Primary Prevention Program on Violence in Intimate Relationships," *Violence and Victims* 7 (1992): 129–145.
71. Andrew Karmen, "Victim–Offender Reconciliation Programs: Pro and Con," *Perspectives of the American Probation and Parole Association* 20 (1996): 11–14.
72. United States Department of Justice, "Growth of Victim-Offender Mediation—National Survey of Victim Offender Mediation Programs in the United States," http://www.ojp.usdoj.gov.
73. See Frank Carrington, "Victim's Rights Litigation: A Wave of the Future," in *Perspectives on Crime Victims,* ed. Burt Galaway and Joe Hudson (St. Louis: Mosby, 1981).
74. Dept. of Justice, "Victims of Crime—Table 3.2," published 22 December 2003, Dept. of Justice Canada, 2003. Reproduced with the permission of the Minister of Public Works and Government Services, 2005.
75. Sara Flaherty and Austin Flaherty, *Victims and Victims' Risk* (New York: Chelsea House, 1998).

76. Pamela Wilcox Rountree and Kenneth Land, "Burglary Victimization, Perceptions of Crime Risk, and Routine Activities: A Multilevel Analysis Across Seattle Neighborhoods and Census Tracts," *Journal of Research in Crime and Delinquency* 33 (1996): 1147–1180.
77. Leslie Kennedy, "Going It Alone: Unreported Crime and Individual Self-Help," *Journal of Criminal Justice* 16 (1988): 403–413.
78. Ronald Clarke, "Situational Crime Prevention: Its Theoretical Basis and Practical Scope," in *Annual Review of Criminal Justice Research,* ed. Michael Tonry and Norval Morris (Chicago: University of Chicago Press, 1983).
79. See, generally, Dennis P. Rosenbaum, Arthur J. Lurigio, and Robert C. Davis, *The Prevention of Crime: Social and Situational Strategies* (Belmont, CA: Wadsworth, 1998).
80. Andrew Buck, Simon Hakim, and George Rengert, "Burglar Alarms and the Choice Behavior of Burglars," *Journal of Criminal Justice* 21 (1993): 497–507; for an opposing view, see James Lynch and David Cantor, "Ecological and Behavioral Influences on Property Victimization at Home: Implications for Opportunity Theory," *Journal of Research in Crime and Delinquency* 29 (1992): 335–362.
81. James Garofalo and Maureen McLeod, *Improving the Use and Effectiveness of Neighborhood Watch Programs* (Washington, DC: National Institute of Justice, 1988).
82. Peter Finn, *Block Watches Help Crime Victims in Philadelphia* (Washington, DC: National Institute of Justice, 1986).
83. Ibid.

Chapter 4

1. Joe Fantauzzi, *ERA-Banner*, Newmarket, ON, 18 February 2011, p.1.
2. Sherri Zickefoose, "Bill Aims to Stop Metal Thefts in Alberta," *Calgary Herald*, 8 November 2010, p. B2.
3. CBC News, Wed. 14 April 2010.
4. Sherri Zickefoose, *Calgary Herald*, 8 November 2010, p. B2.
5. Julia Belluz, "The Great Copper Heist," *Maclean's*, 14 February 2011, p. 48.
6. Bob Roshier, *Controlling Crime* (Chicago: Lyceum Books, 1989), p. 10.
7. James Q. Wilson, *Thinking About Crime,* rev. ed. (New York: Vintage Books, 1983), p. 260.
8. See, generally, Derek Cornish and Ronald Clarke, eds. *The Reasoning Criminal: Rational Choice Perspectives on Offending* (New York: Springer Verlag, 1986); Philip Cook, "The Demand and Supply of Criminal Opportunities," in *Crime and Justice,* vol. 7, ed. Michael Tonry and Norval Morris (Chicago: University of Chicago Press, 1986), pp. 1–28; Ronald Clarke and Derek Cornish, "Modeling Offenders' Decisions: A Framework for Research and Policy," in *Crime and Justice,* vol. 6, ed. Michael Tonry and Norval Morris (Chicago: University of Chicago Press, 1985), pp. 147–187; Morgan Reynolds, *Crime by Choice: An Economic Analysis* (Dallas: Fisher Institute, 1985).
9. George Rengert and John Wasilchick, *Suburban Burglary: A Time and Place for Everything* (Springfield, IL: Charles Thomas, 1985).
10. John McIver, "Criminal Mobility: A Review of Empirical Studies," in *Crime Spillover,* ed. Simon Hakim and George Rengert (Beverly Hills, CA: Sage, 1981), pp. 110–121; Carol Kohfeld and John Sprague, "Demography, Police Behavior, and Deterrence," *Criminology* 28 (1990): 111–136.
11. Liliana Pezzin, "Earnings Prospects, Matching Effects, and the Decision to Terminate a Criminal Career," *Journal of Quantitative Criminology* 11 (1995):29–50.
12. Pierre Tremblay and Carlo Morselli, "Patterns in Criminal Achievement: Wilson and Abrahmse Revisited," *Criminology* 38 (2000): 633–660.
13. Ronald Akers, "Rational Choice, Deterrence and Social Learning Theory in Criminology: The Path Not Taken," *Journal of Criminal Law and Criminology* 81 (1990): 653–676.
14. Neal Shover, *Aging Criminals* (Beverly Hills, CA: Sage, 1985).
15. Robert Agnew, "Determinism, Indeterminism, and Crime: An Empirical Exploration," *Criminology* 33 (1995): 83–109.
16. Ibid., pp. 103–104.
17. Bruce Jacobs, "Crack Dealers' Apprehension Avoidance Techniques: A Case of Restrictive Deterrence," *Justice Quarterly* 13 (1996): 359–381.
18. Ibid., p. 367.
19. Ibid., p. 372.
20. Michael Rand, *Crime and the Nation's Households, 1989* (Washington, DC: Bureau of Justice Statistics, 1990), p. 4.
21. Paul Cromwell, James Olson, and D'Aunn Wester Avary, *Breaking and Entering: An Ethnographic Analysis of Burglary* (Newbury Park, CA: Sage, 1989), p. 24.
22. Ibid., pp. 30–32.
23. George Rengert and John Wasilchick, *Space, Time, and Crime: Ethnographic Insights into Residential Burglary* (Washington, DC: National Institute of Justice, 1989); see also Rengert and Wasilchick, *Suburban Burglary.*
24. Matthew Robinson, "Lifestyles, Routine Activities, and Residential Burglary Victimization," *Journal of Criminal Justice* 22 (1999): 27–52.
25. Patrick Donnelly and Charles Kimble, "Community Organizing, Environmental Change, and Neighborhood Crime," *Crime and Delinquency* 43 (1997): 493–511.
26. Ronald Clarke and Marcus Felson, "Introduction: Criminology, Routine Activity and Rational Choice," in *Routine Activity and Rational Choice* (New Brunswick, NJ: Transaction Publishers, 1993), pp. 1–14.
27. Jonathan Stempel, "Madoff Says Banks Had to Know of Ponzi Scheme—Report" *National Post,* 16 February 2011, p. A3.
28. Ronald Clarke and Patricia Harris, "Auto Theft and Its Prevention," in *Crime and Justice: An Annual Edition,* ed. Michael Tonry and Norval Morris (Chicago: University of Chicago Press, 1992), pp. 1–54, at pp. 20–21; see also Marnie Wallace, "Motor Vehicle Theft in Canada—2001," *Jursitat* 23 (January 2003) 5.
29. William Smith, Sharon Glave Frazee, and Elizabeth Davison, "Furthering the Integration of Routine Activity and Social Disorganization Theories: Small Units of Analysis and the Study of Street Robbery as a Diffusion Process," *Criminology* 38 (2000): 489–521.
30. Paul Bellair, "Informal Surveillance and Street Crime: A Complex Relationship," *Criminology* 38 (2000): 137–167.
31. John Gibbs and Peggy Shelly, "Life in the Fast Lane: A Retrospective View by Commercial Thieves," *Journal of Research in Crime and Delinquency* 19 (1982): 229–230.
32. Frederick J. Desroches, *Behind the Bars: Experiences in Crime* (Toronto: Canadian Scholars Press, 1996).
33. Ibid., p. 34.
34. Linda Deutsch, "No Plea Bargain in Jackson MD's Case," *Winnipeg Free Press*, 17 April 2010, http://www.highbeam.com/doc/1P3-2013076541.html (accessed 10 August 2011).
35. Gordon Knowles, "Deception, Detection, and Evasion: A Trade Craft Analysis of Honolulu, Hawaii's Street Crack Cocaine Traffickers," *Journal of Criminal Justice* 27 (1999): 443–455.
36. John Petraitis, Brian Flay, and Todd Miller, "Reviewing Theories of Adolescent Substance Use: Organizing Pieces in the

Puzzle," *Psychological Bulletin* 117 (1995): 67–86.
37. George Rengert, *The Geography of Illegal Drugs* (Boulder, CO: Westview Press, 1996).
38. Scott Decker, "Deviant Homicide: A New Look at the Role of Motives and Victim–Offender Relationships," *Journal of Research in Crime and Delinquency* 33 (1996): 427–449.
39. Felson and Messner, "To Kill or Not to Kill?"
40. Peter Wood, Walter Gove, James Wilson, and John Cochran, "Nonsocial Reinforcement and Habitual Criminal Conduct: An Extension of Learning," *Criminology* 35 (1997): 335–366.
41. Jeff Ferrell, "Criminological Verstehen: Inside the Immediacy of Crime," *Justice Quarterly* 14 (1997): 3–23, at p. 12.
42. Jack Katz, *Seductions of Crime* (New York: Basic Books, 1988).
43. Bill McCarthy, "Not Just 'For the Thrill of It': An Instrumentalist Elaboration of Katz's Explanation of Sneaky Thrill Property Crime," *Criminology* 33 (1995): 519–539.
44. George Rengert, "Spatial Justice and Criminal Victimization," *Justice Quarterly* 6 (1989): 543–564.
45. Ronald Clarke, *Situational Crime Prevention: Successful Case Studies* (Albany, NY: Harrow and Heston, 1992).
46. Brian Dexter, "How to Make Your Home Safe," *Toronto Star,* 19 September 2002, p. J5.
47. Barry Webb, "Steering Column Locks and Motor Vehicle Theft: Evaluations for Three Countries," in *Crime Prevention Studies,* vol. 2, ed. Ronald Clarke (Monsey, NY: Criminal Justice Press, 1994), pp. 71–89.
48. Barbara Morse and Delbert Elliott, "Effects of Ignition Interlock Devices on DUI Recidivism: Findings from a Longitudinal Study in Hamilton County, Ohio," *Crime and Delinquency* 38 (1992): 131–157.
49. Ronald Clarke, "Deterring Obscene Phone Callers: The New Jersey Experience," in *Situational Crime Prevention,* ed. Ronald Clarke (Albany, NY: Harrow and Heston, 1992), pp. 124–132.
50. Robert Barr and Ken Pease, "Crime Placement, Displacement, and Deflection," in *Crime and Justice, A Review of Research,* vol. 12, ed. Michael Tonry and Norval Morris (Chicago: University of Chicago Press, 1990): 277–319.
51. Clarke, *Situational Crime Prevention*, p. 27.
52. Ibid., p. 35.
53. Ronald Clarke and David Weisburd, "Diffusion of Crime Control Benefits: Observations of the Reverse of Displacement," in *Crime Prevention Studies,* vol. 2, ed. Ronald Clarke (New York: Criminal Justice Press, 1994).
54. David Weisburd and Lorraine Green, "Policing Drug Hot Spots: The Jersey City Drug Market Analysis Experiment," *Justice Quarterly* 12 (1995): 711–734.
55. Ian Ayres and Steven D. Levitt, "Measuring Positive Externalities from Unobservable Victim Precaution: An Empirical Analysis of Lojack," *Quarterly Journal of Economics* 113 (1998): 43–78.
56. R. Steven Daniels, Lorin Baumhover, William Formby, and Carolyn Clark-Daniels, "Police Discretion and Elder Mistreatment: A Nested Model of Observation, Reporting, and Satisfaction," *Journal of Criminal Justice* 27 (1999): 209–225.
57. R. Yeaman, *The Deterrent Effectiveness of Criminal Justice Sanction Strategies: Summary Report* (Washington, DC: U.S. Government Printing Office, 1972). See, generally, Jack Gibbs, "Crime Punishment and Deterrence," *Social Science Quarterly* 48 (1968): 515–530.
58. Robert Bursik, Harold Grasmick, and Mitchell Chamlin, "The Effect of Longitudinal Arrest Patterns on the Development of Robbery Trends at the Neighborhood Level," *Criminology* 28 (1990): 431–450; Theodore Chiricos and Gordon Waldo, "Punishment and Crime: An Examination of Some Empirical Evidence," *Social Problems* 18 (1970): 200–217.
59. Stewart D'Alessio and Lisa Stolzenberg, "Crime, Arrests, and Pretrial Jail Incarceration: An Examination of the Deterrence Thesis," paper presented at the annual meeting of the American Society of Criminology, San Diego, November 1997.
60. Jiang Wu and Allen Liska, "The Certainty of Punishment: A Reference Group Effect and Its Functional Form," *Criminology* 31 (1993): 447–464.
61. Edwin Zedlewski, "Deterrence Findings and Data Sources: A Comparison of the Uniform Crime Rates and the National Crime Surveys," *Journal of Research in Crime and Delinquency* 20 (1983): 262–276.
62. David Bayley, *Policing for the Future* (New York: Oxford, 1994).
63. For a review, see Thomas Marvell and Carlisle Moody, "Specification Problems, Police Levels, and Crime Rates," *Criminology* 34 (1996): 609–646.
64. Charles Tittle and Alan Rowe, "Certainty of Arrest and Crime Rates: A Further Test of the Deterrence Hypothesis," *Social Forces* 52 (1974): 455–462.
65. Kenneth Novak, Jennifer Hartman, Alexander Holsinger, and Michael Turner, "The Effects of Aggressive Policing of Disorder on Serious Crime," *Policing* 22 (1999): 171–190.
66. Lawrence Sherman, "Police Crackdowns," *NIJ Reports* (March/April 1990): 2–6, at p. 2.
67. Anthony Braga, David Weisburd, Elin Waring, Lorraine Green Mazerolle, William Spelman, and Francis Gajewski, "Problem-Oriented Policing in Violent Crime Places: A Randomized Controlled Experiment," *Criminology* 37 (1999): 541–580.
68. Ontario Provincial Police, *2003 Report* (Toronto: Ministry of Community Safety and Correctional Service, 2004).
69. Ed Stevens and Brian Payne, "Applying Deterrence Theory in the Context of Corporate Wrongdoing: Limitations on Punitive Damages," *Journal of Criminal Justice* 27 (1999): 195–209; Jeffrey Roth, *Firearms and Violence* (Washington, DC: National Institute of Justice, 1994); Thomas Marvell and Carlisle Moody, "The Impact of Enhanced Prison Terms for Felonies Committed with Guns," *Criminology* 33 (1995): 247–281; Gary Green, "General Deterrence and Television Cable Crime: A Field Experiment in Social Crime," *Criminology* 23 (1986): 629–645.
70. H. Laurence Ross, "Implications of Drinking-and-Driving Law Studies for Deterrence Research," in *Critique and Explanation: Essays in Honor of Gwynne Nettler,* ed. Timothy Hartnagel and Robert Silverman (New Brunswick, NJ: Transaction Books, 1986), pp. 159–171; H. Laurence Ross, Richard McCleary, and Gary LaFree, "Can Mandatory Jail Laws Deter Drunk Driving? The Arizona Case," *Journal of Criminal Law and Criminology* 81 (1990): 156–167.
71. For a review, see Jeffrey Roth, *Firearms and Violence* (Washington, DC: National Institute of Justice, 1994); and Thomas Marvell and Carlisle Moody, "The Impact of Enhanced Prison Terms for Felonies Committed with Guns," *Criminology* 33 (1995): 247–281.
72. Robert Dann, "The Deterrent Effect of Capital Punishment," *Friends Social Service Series* 29 (1935).
73. William Bowers and Glenn Pierce, "Deterrence or Brutalization: What Is the Effect of Executions?" *Crime and Delinquency* 26 (1980): 453–484.
74. John Cochran, Mitchell Chamlin, and Mark Seth, "Deterrence or Brutalization? An Impact Assessment of Oklahoma's Return to Capital Punishment," *Criminology* 32 (1994): 107–134. David Phillips, "The

Deterrent Effect of Capital Punishment," *American Journal of Sociology* 86 (1980): 139–148; Hans Zeisel, "A Comment on 'The Deterrent Effect of Capital Punishment' by Phillips," *American Journal of Sociology* 88 (1982): 167–169; see also Sam McFarland, "Is Capital Punishment a Short-Term Deterrent to Homicide? A Study of the Effects of Four Recent American Executions," *Journal of Criminal Law and Criminology* 74 (1984): 1014–1032.

75. Steven Stack, "Publicized Executions and Homicide, 1950–1980," *American Sociological Review* 52 (1987): 532–540; for a study challenging Stack's methods, see William Bailey and Ruth Peterson, "Murder and Capital Punishment: A Monthly Time-Series Analysis of Execution Publicity," *American Sociological Review* 54 (1989): 722–743.
76. Karl Schuessler, "The Deterrent Influence of the Death Penalty," *Annals of the Academy of Political and Social Sciences* 284 (1952): 54–62.
77. Thorsten Sellin, *The Death Penalty* (Philadelphia: American Law Institute, 1959); Walter Reckless, "Use of the Death Penalty," *Crime and Delinquency* 15 (1969): 43–51.
78. Ezzat Fattah, *Understanding Criminal Victimization: An Introduction to Theoretical Criminology* (Scarborough, ON: Prentice-Hall, 1991).
79. Richard Lempert, "The Effect of Executions on Homicides: A New Look in an Old Light," *Crime and Delinquency* 29 (1983): 88–115.
80. Derral Cheatwood, "Capital Punishment and the Deterrence of Violent Crime in Comparable Counties," *Criminal Justice Review* 18 (1993): 165–181.
81. Dane Archer, Rosemary Gartner, and Marc Beittel, "Homicide and the Death Penalty: A Cross-National Test of a Deterrence Hypothesis," *Journal of Criminal Law and Criminology* 74 (1983): 991–1014.
82. Isaac Ehrlich, "The Deterrent Effect of Capital Punishment: A Question of Life and Death," *American Economic Review* 65 (1975): 397–417.
83. James Fox and Michael Radelet, "Persistent Flaws in Econometric Studies of the Deterrent Effect of the Death Penalty," *Loyola of Los Angeles Law Review* 23 (1987): 29–44; William B. Bowers and Glenn Pierce, "The Illusion of Deterrence in Isaac Ehrlich's Research on Capital Punishment," *Yale Law Journal* 85 (1975): 187–208.
84. Jon Sorenson, Robert Wrinkle, Victoria Brewer, and James Marquart, "Capital Punishment and Deterrence: Examining the Effect of Executions on Murder in Texas," *Crime and Delinquency* 45 (1999): 481–493.
85. William Bailey, "Disaggregation in Deterrence and Death Penalty Research: The Case of Murder in Chicago," *Journal of Criminal Law and Criminology* 74 (1986): 827–859.
86. Steven Messner and Kenneth Tardiff, "Economic Inequality and Level of Homicide: An Analysis of Urban Neighborhoods," *Criminology* 24 (1986): 297–317.
87. Donald Green, "Past Behavior as a Measure of Actual Future Behavior: An Unresolved Issue in Perceptual Deterrence Research," *Journal of Criminal Law and Criminology* 80 (1989): 781–804.
88. Donna Bishop, "Deterrence: A Panel Analysis," *Justice Quarterly* 1 (1984): 311–328; Julie Horney and Ineke Haen Marshall, "Risk Perceptions Among Serious Offenders: The Role of Crime and Punishment," *Criminology* 30 (1992): 575–594.
89. Wanda Foglia, "Perceptual Deterrence and the Mediating Effect of Internalized Norms Among Inner-City Teenagers," *Journal of Research in Crime and Delinquency* 34 (1997): 414–442; Raymond Paternoster, "Decisions to Participate in and Desist from Four Types of Common Delinquency: Deterrence and the Rational Choice Perspective," *Law and Society Review* 23 (1989): 7–29; Raymond Paternoster, "Examining Three-Wave Deterrence Models: A Question of Temporal Order and Specification," *Journal of Criminal Law and Criminology* 79 (1988): 135–163; Raymond Paternoster, Linda Saltzman, Gordon Waldo, and Theodore Chiricos, "Estimating Perceptual Stability and Deterrent Effects: The Role of Perceived Legal Punishment in the Inhibition of Criminal Involvement," *Journal of Criminal Law and Criminology* 74 (1983): 270–297; M. William Minor and Joseph Harry, "Deterrent and Experiential Effects in Perceptual Deterrence Research: A Replication and Extension," *Journal of Research in Crime and Delinquency* 19 (1982): 190–203; Lonn Lanza-Kaduce, "Perceptual Deterrence and Drinking and Driving Among College Students," *Criminology* 26 (1988): 321–341.
90. Steven Klepper and Daniel Nagin, "The Deterrent Effect of Perceived Certainty and Severity of Punishment Revisited," *Criminology* 27 (1989): 721–746; Scott Decker, Richard Wright, and Robert Logie, "Perceptual Deterrence Among Active Residential Burglars: A Research Note," *Criminology* 31 (1993): 135–147.
91. Alex Piquero and George Rengert, "Studying Deterrence with Active Residential Burglars," *Justice Quarterly* 16 (1999): 451–462.
92. Foglia, "Perceptual Deterrence and the Mediating Effect of Internalized Norms Among Inner-City Teenagers," pp. 414–442.
93. Harold Grasmick, Robert Bursik, and Karyl Kinsey, "Shame and Embarrassment as Deterrents to Noncompliance with the Law: The Case of an Anti-Littering Campaign," paper presented at the annual meeting of the American Society of Criminology, Baltimore, November 1990, p. 3.
94. Charles Tittle, *Sanctions and Social Deviance* (New York: Praeger, 1980).
95. Green, "Past Behavior as a Measure of Actual Future Behavior," p. 803; Matthew Silberman, "Toward a Theory of Criminal Deterrence," *American Sociological Review* 41 (1976): 442–461; Linda Anderson, Theodore Chiricos, and Gordon Waldo, "Formal and Informal Sanctions: A Comparison of Deterrent Effects," *Social Problems* 25 (1977): 103–114. See also Maynard Erickson and Jack Gibbs, "Objective and Perceptual Properties of Legal Punishment and Deterrence Doctrine," *Social Problems* 25 (1978): 253–264; Daniel Nagin and Raymond Paternoster, "Enduring Individual Differences and Rational Choice Theories of Crime," *Law and Society Review* 27 (1993): 467–485.
96. Harold Grasmick and Robert Bursik, "Conscience, Significant Others, and Rational Choice: Extending the Deterrence Model," *Law and Society Review* 24 (1900): 837–861, at p. 854.
97. Grasmick, Bursik, and Kinsey, "Shame and Embarrassment as Deterrents to Noncompliance with the Law"; Harold Grasmick, Robert Bursik, and Bruce Arneklev, "Reduction in Drunk Driving as a Response to Increased Threats of Shame, Embarrassment, and Legal Sanctions," *Criminology* 31 (1993): 41–69.
98. Harold Grasmick, Brenda Sims Blackwell, and Robert Bursik, "Changes in the Sex Patterning of Perceived Threats of Sanctions," *Law and Society Review* 27 (1993): 679–699.
99. Thomas Peete, Trudie Milner, and Michael Welch, "Levels of Social Integration in Group Contexts and the Effects of Informal

Sanction Threat on Deviance," *Criminology* 32 (1994): 85–105.

100. Ernest Van Den Haag, "The Criminal Law as a Threat System," *Journal of Criminal Law and Criminology* 73 (1982): 709–785.
101. David Lykken, "Psychopathy, Sociopathy, and Crime," *Society* 34 (1996): 30–38.
102. George Lowenstein, Daniel Nagin, and Raymond Paternoster, "The Effect of Sexual Arousal on Expectations of Sexual Forcefulness," *Journal of Research in Crime and Delinquency* 34 (1997): 443–473.
103. David Klinger, "Policing Spousal Assault," *Journal of Research in Crime and Delinquency* 32 (1995): 308–324.
104. James Williams and Daniel Rodeheaver, "Processing of Criminal Homicide Cases in a Large Southern City," *Sociology and Social Research* 75 (1991): 80–88.
105. James Q. Wilson, *Thinking About Crime* (New York: Basic Books, 1975).
106. James Q. Wilson and Richard Herrnstein, *Crime and Human Nature* (New York: Simon and Schuster, 1985), p. 494.
107. Christina Dejong, "Survival Analysis and Specific Deterrence: Integrating Theoretical and Empirical Models of Recidivism," *Criminology* 35 (1997): 561–576; Paul Tracy and Kimberly Kempf-Leonard, *Continuity and Discontinuity in Criminal Careers* (New York: Plenum Press, 1996).
108. Allen Beck and Bernard Shipley, *Recidivism of Prisoners Released in 1983* (Washington, DC: Bureau of Justice Statistics, 1989).
109. Dejong, "Survival Analysis and Specific Deterrence," p. 573.
110. Paul Gendreau, Claire Goggin, Francis T. Cullen and Donald A. Andrews, "The Effects of Community Sanctions and Incarceration on Recidivism," *Forum on Corrections Research* 12 (May 2000): 10.
111. Dejong, "Survival Analysis and Specific Deterrence"; Raymond Paternoster and Alex Piquero, "Reconceptualizing Deterrence: An Empirical Test of Personal and Vicarious Experiences," *Journal of Research in Crime and Delinquency* 32 (1995): 251–258.
112. John Braithwaite, *Crime, Shame, and Reintegration* (Melbourne, Australia: Cambridge University Press, 1989).
113. Anthony Petrosino and Carolyn Petrosino, "The Public Safety Potential of Megan's Law in Massachusetts: An Assessment from a Sample of Criminal Sexual Psychopaths," *Crime and Delinquency* 45 (1999): 140–158; Owen Wood, "Sex Offender Registry," *CBC News Online,* 15 May 2003 (updated 20 June 2003), http://www.cbc.ca/news.
114. See, generally, Raymond Paternoster, "Absolute and Restrictive Deterrence in a Panel of Youth: Explaining the Onset, Persistence/Desistance, and Frequency of Delinquent Offending," *Social Problems* 36 (1989): 289–307; Raymond Paternoster, "The Deterrent Effect of Perceived Severity of Punishment: A Review of the Evidence and Issues," *Justice Quarterly* 42 (1987): 173–217.
115. Isaac Ehrlich, "Participation in Illegitimate Activities: An Economic Analysis," *Journal of Political Economy* 81 (1973): 521–567; Lee Bowker, "Crime and the Use of Prisons in the United States: A Time Series Analysis," *Crime and Delinquency* 27 (1981): 206–212.
116. Paul Gendreau, Claire Goggin, Francis T. Cullen, and Donald A. Andrews "The Effects of Community Sanctions and Incarceration on Recidivism," *Forum on Corrections Research* 12 (May 2000) 12.
117. Reuel Shinnar and Shlomo Shinnar, "The Effects of the Criminal Justice System on the Control of Crime: A Quantitative Approach," *Law and Society Review* 9 (1975): 581–611.
118. Thomas Marvell and Carlisle Moody, "The Impact of Out-of-State Prison Population on State Homicide Rates: Displacement and Free-Rider Effects," *Criminology* 36 (1998): 513–538; Thomas Marvell and Carlisle Moody, "The Impact of Prison Growth on Homicide," *Homicide Studies* 1 (1997): 205–233.
119. David Greenberg and Nancy Larkin, "The Incapacitation of Criminal Opiate Users," *Crime and Delinquency* 44 (1998): 205–228.
120. John Wallerstedt, *Returning to Prison: Bureau of Justice Statistics Special Report* (Washington, DC: U.S. Department of Justice, 1984).
121. James Marquart, Victoria Brewer, Janet Mullings, and Ben Crouch, "The Implications of Crime Control Policy on HIV/AIDS-Related Risk Among Women Prisoners," *Crime and Delinquency* 45 (1999): 82–98.
122. José Canela-Cacho, Alfred Blumstein, and Jacqueline Cohen, "Relationship Between the Offending Frequency of Imprisoned and Free Offenders," *Criminology* 35 (1997): 133–171.
123. Dennis Findlay, "Getting by with a Little Help from Their Friends," *Let's Talk* 2 (2000): 1–5; Gregory P. Brown and Kari Brozowski, "Golden Years? The Incarceration of the Older Offender," *Geriatrics Today* 6 (2003): 32–35.
124. Criminal Code, S. 753.1 (1).
125. Marc Mauer, testimony before the U.S. Congress, House Judiciary Committee, on "Three Strikes and You're Out," 1 March 1994.
126. Canela-Cacho, Blumstein, and Cohen, "Relationship Between the Offending Frequency of Imprisoned and Free Offenders."
127. Stephen Markman and Paul Cassell, "Protecting the Innocent: A Response to the Bedeau-Radelet Study," *Stanford Law Review* 41 (1988): 121–170, at p. 153.
128. James Stephan and Tracy Snell, *Capital Punishment, 1994* (Washington, DC: Bureau of Justice Statistics, 1996), p. 8.
129. Andrew Von Hirsch, *Doing Justice* (New York: Hill and Wang, 1976).
130. Ibid., pp. 15–16.

Chapter 5

1. Marie-Andrée Bertrand and Mary Jo Lakeland, "Feminists Targeted for Murder: Montreal 1989," *Feminist Issues* 11 (Fall 1991): 3–4; Marie-Andrée Bertrand and Mary Jo Lakeland, "A Criminological Analysis and Certain Interpretations of the Event," *Feminist Issues* 11 (Fall 1991): 4–10; http://massmurder.zyns.com.
2. Lee Ellis, "A Discipline in Peril: Sociology's Future Hinges on Curing Biophobia," *American Sociologist* 27 (1996): 21–41.
3. Edmund O. Wilson, *Sociobiology* (Cambridge, MA: Harvard University Press, 1975).
4. Per-Olof Wikstrom and Rolf Loeber, "Do Disadvantaged Neighborhoods Cause Well-Adjusted Children to Become Adolescent Delinquents?" *Criminology* 38 (November 2000): 1109–1142.
5. Dalton Conley and Neil Bennett, "Is Biology Destiny? Birth Weight and Life Chances," *American Sociological Review* 654 (2000): 458–467.
6. Kevin M. Beaver, Michael G. Vaughn, Matt DeLisi, and George E. Higgins, "The Biosocial Correlates of Neuropsychological Deficits: Results From the National Longitudinal Study of Adolescent Health," *International Journal of Offender Therapy and Comparative Criminology* (December 2010) 54: 878–894.
7. Anthony Walsh and Lee Ellis, "Shoring Up the Big Three: Improving Criminological Theories with Biosocial Concepts," paper presented at the annual meeting of the Society of Criminology, San Diego, November 1997, p. 16.
8. Israel Nachshon, "Neurological Bases of Crime, Psychopathy and Aggression,"

in *Crime in Biological, Social and Moral Contexts*, ed. Lee Ellis and Harry Hoffman (New York: Praeger, 1990), p. 199.
9. *Time*, 28 May 1979, p. 57.
10. Michael Krassner, "Diet and Brain Function," *Nutrition Reviews* 44 (1986): 12–15.
11. Leonard Hippchen, ed., *Ecologic-Biochemical Approaches to Treatment of Delinquents and Criminals* (New York: Van Nostrand Reinhold, 1978).
12. J. Kershner and W. Hawke, "Megavitamins and Learning Disorders: A Controlled Double-Blind Experiment," *Journal of Nutrition* 109 (1979): 819–826; Diana Fishbein and Jerzy Meduski, "Nutritional Biochemistry and Behavioral Disabilities," *Journal of Learning Disabilities* 20 (October 1987): 505–512.
13. Stephen Schoenthaler and Walter Doraz, "Types of Offenses Which Can Be Reduced in an Institutional Setting Using Nutritional Intervention," *International Journal of Biosocial Research* 4 (1983): 74–84; Stephen Schoenthaler and Walter Doraz, "Diet and Crime," *International Journal of Biosocial Research* 4 (1983): 74–84. See also A. G. Schauss, "Differential Outcomes Among Probationers Comparing Orthomolecular Approaches to Conventional Casework Counseling," paper presented at the annual meeting of the American Society of Criminology, Dallas, November 1978; A. Schauss and C. Simonsen, "A Critical Analysis of the Diets of Chronic Juvenile Offenders: Part I," *Journal of Orthomolecular Psychiatry* 8 (1979): 222–226; A. Hoffer, "Children with Learning and Behavioral Disorders," *Journal of Orthomolecular Psychiatry* 5 (1976): 229.
14. H. Bruce Ferguson, Clare Stoddart, and Jovan Simeon, "Double-Blind Challenge Studies of Behavioral and Cognitive Effects of Sucrose-Aspartame Ingestion in Normal Children," *Nutrition Reviews Supplement* 44 (1986): 144–158; Gregory Gray, "Diet, Crime and Delinquency: A Critique," *Nutrition Reviews Supplement* 44 (1986): 89–94; Diana Fishbein, "The Contribution of Refined Carbohydrate Consumption to Maladaptive Behaviors," *Journal of Orthomolecular Psychiatry* 11 (1982): pp. 17–25.
15. Mark Wolraich, Scott Lindgren, Phyllis Stumbo, Lewis Stegink, Mark Appelbaum, and Mary Kiritsy, "Effects of Diets High in Sucrose or Aspartame on the Behavior and Cognitive Performance of Children," *New England Journal of Medicine* 330 (1994): 303–306.
16. Dian Gans, "Sucrose and Unusual Childhood Behavior," *Nutrition Today* 26 (1991): 8–14.
17. James Q. Wilson, *The Moral Sense* (New York: Free Press, 1993).
18. Lee Ellis, "Evolutionary and Neurochemical Causes of Sex Differences in Victimizing Behavior: Toward a Unified Theory of Criminal Behavior and Social Stratification," *Social Science Information* 28 (1989): 605–636.
19. Lee Ellis and Phyllis Coontz, "Androgens, Brain Functioning, and Criminality: The Neurohormonal Foundations of Antisociality," in *Crime in Biological, Social and Moral Contexts*, ed. Lee Ellis and Harry Hoffman (New York: Praeger, 1990), pp. 162–193, at p. 181.
20. Alan Booth and D. Wayne Osgood, "The Influence of Testosterone on Deviance in Adulthood: Assessing and Explaining the Relationship," *Criminology* 31 (1993): 93–118.
21. Ibid.
22. Christy Miller Buchanan, Jacquelynne Eccles, and Jill Becker, "Are Adolescents the Victims of Raging Hormones? Evidence for Activational Effects of Hormones on Moods and Behavior at Adolescence," *Psychological Bulletin* 111 (1992): 62–107.
23. Booth and Osgood, "The Influence of Testosterone on Deviance in Adulthood."
24. Albert Reiss and Jeffrey Roth, eds., *Understanding and Preventing Violence* (Washington, DC: National Academy Press, 1993), p. 118.
25. Anthony Walsh, "Genetic and Cytogenetic Intersex Anomalies," *International Journal of Offender Therapy and Comparative Criminology* 39 (1995): 151–166.
26. Walter Gove, "The Effect of Age and Gender on Deviant Behavior: A Biopsychosocial Perspective," in *Gender and the Life Course*, ed. A. S. Rossi (New York: Aldine, 1985), pp. 115–144.
27. For a review of this concept, see Anne E. Figert, "The Three Faces of PMS: The Professional, Gendered, and Scientific Structuring of a Psychiatric Disorder," *Social Problems* 42 (1995): 56–72.
28. Katharina Dalton, *The Premenstrual Syndrome* (Springfield, IL: Charles C. Thomas, 1971).
29. Julie Horney, "Menstrual Cycles and Criminal Responsibility," *Law and Human Nature* 2 (1978): 25–36.
30. Diana Fishbein, "Selected Studies on the Biology of Antisocial Behavior," in *New Perspectives in Criminology*, ed. John Conklin (Needham Heights, MA: Allyn and Bacon, 1996), pp. 26–38.
31. Ibid.; Karen Paige, "Effects of Oral Contraceptives on Affective Fluctuations Associated with the Menstrual Cycle," *Psychosomatic Medicine* 33 (1971):515–537.
32. Alexander Schauss, *Diet, Crime and Delinquency* (Berkeley, CA: Parker House, 1980).
33. C. Hawley and R. E. Buckley, "Food Dyes and Hyperkinetic Children," *Academy Therapy* 10 (1974): 27–32.
34. John Ott, "The Effects of Light and Radiation on Human Health and Behavior," in *Ecologic-Biochemical Approaches to Treatment of Delinquents and Criminals*, ed. Leonard Hippchen (New York: Van Nostrand Reinhold, 1978), pp. 105–183. See also A. Kreuger and S. Sigel, "Ions in the Air," *Human Nature* (July 1978): 46–47; Harry Wohlfarth, "The Effect of Color Psychodynamic Environmental Modification on Discipline Incidents in Elementary Schools over One School Year: A Controlled Study," *International Journal of Biosocial Research* 6 (1984): 44–53.
35. Oliver David, Stanley Hoffman, Jeffrey Sverd, Julian Clark, and Kytja Voeller, "Lead and Hyperactivity, Behavior Response to Chelation: A Pilot Study," *American Journal of Psychiatry* 133 (1976): 1155–1158.
36. Deborah Denno, "Considering Lead Poisoning as a Criminal Defense," *Fordham Urban Law Journal* 20 (1993): 377–400.
37. Terrie Moffitt, "The Neuropsychology of Juvenile Delinquency: A Critical Review," in *Crime and Justice: An Annual Review*, vol. 12, ed. Norval Morris and Michael Tonry (Chicago: University of Chicago Press, 1990), pp. 99–169.
38. Terrie Moffitt, Donald Lynam, and Phil Silva, "Neuropsychological Tests Predicting Persistent Male Delinquency," *Criminology* 32 (1994): 277–300; Elizabeth Kandel and Sarnoff Mednick, "Perinatal Complications Predict Violent Offending," *Criminology* 29 (1991): 519–529; Sarnoff Mednick, Ricardo Machon, Matti Virkkunen, and Douglas Bonett, "Adult Schizophrenia Following Prenatal Exposure to an Influenza Epidemic," *Archives of General Psychiatry* 44 (1987): 35–46; C. A. Fogel, S. A. Mednick, and N. Michelson, "Hyperactive Behavior and Minor Physical Anomalies," *Acta Psychiatrica Scandinavia* 72 (1985):551–556.
39. R. Johnson, *Aggression in Man and Animals* (Philadelphia: Saunders, 1972), p. 79.
40. Jean Seguin, Robert Pihl, Philip Harden, Richard Tremblay, and Bernard Boulerice, "Cognitive and Neuropsychological Characteristics of Physically Aggressive Boys," *Journal of Abnormal Psychology*

104 (1995): 614–624; Deborah Denno, "Gender, Crime and the Criminal Law Defenses," *Journal of Criminal Law and Criminology* 85 (1994): 80–180.

41. Adrian Raine, Patricia Brennan, Brigitte Mednick, and Sarnoff Mednick, "High Rates of Violence, Crime, Academic Problems, and Behavioral Problems in Males with Both Early Neuromotor Deficits and Unstable Family Environments," *Archives of General Psychiatry* 53 (1996): 544–549; Deborah Denno, *Biology, Crime and Violence: New Evidence* (Cambridge: Cambridge University Press, 1989).
42. Diana Fishbein and Robert Thatcher, "New Diagnostic Methods in Criminology: Assessing Organic Sources of Behavioral Disorders," *Journal of Research in Crime and Delinquency* 23 (1986): 240–267.
43. Lorne Yeudall, "A Neuropsychosocial Perspective on Persistent Juvenile Delinquency and Criminal Behavior," paper presented at the New York Academy of Sciences, 26 September 1979.
44. See, generally, Jan Volavka, "Electroencephalogram Among Criminals," in *The Causes of Crime: New Biological Approaches,* ed. Sarnoff Mednick, Terrie Moffitt, and Susan Stack (Cambridge: Cambridge University Press, 1987), pp. 137–145; Z. A. Zayed, S. A. Lewis, and R. P. Britain, "An Encephalographic and Psychiatric Study of 32 Insane Murderers," *British Journal of Psychiatry* 115 (1969): 1115–1124.
45. Nathaniel Pallone and James Hennessy, "Brain Dysfunction and Criminal Violence," *Society* 35 (1998): 21–27; P. F. Goyer, P. J. Andreason, and W. E. Semple, "Positronic Emission Tomography and Personality Disorders," *Neuropsychopharmacology* 10 (1994): 21–28.
46. Diana Fishbein, "Neuropsychological Function, Drug Abuse, and Violence"; Adrian Raine, Monte Buchsbaum, and Lori LaCasse, "Brain Abnormalities in Murderers Indicated by Positron Emission Tomography," *Biological Psychiatry* 42 (1997): 495–508.
47. Pallone and Hennessy, "Brain Dysfunction and Criminal Violence," p. 25.
48. D. R. Robin, R. M. Starles, T. J. Kenney, B. J. Reynolds, and F. P. Heald, "Adolescents Who Attempt Suicide," *Journal of Pediatrics* 90 (1977): 636–638.
49. Raine, Buchsbaum, and LaCasse, "Brain Abnormalities in Murderers Indicated by Positron Emission Tomography."
50. Leonore Simon, "Does Criminal Offender Treatment Work?" *Applied and Preventive Psychology* (Summer 1998); Stephen Faraone et al., "Intellectual Performance and School Failure in Children with Attention Deficit Hyperactivity Disorder and in Their Siblings," *Journal of Abnormal Psychology* 102 (1993): 616–623.
51. Simon, "Does Criminal Offender Treatment Work?"
52. Ibid.
53. Terrie Moffitt and Phil Silva, "Self-Reported Delinquency, Neuropsychological Deficit, and History of Attention Deficit Disorder," *Journal of Abnormal Child Psychology* 16 (1988): 553–569.
54. Elizabeth Hart et al., "Developmental Change in Attention-Deficit Hyperactivity Disorder in Boys: A Four-Year Longitudinal Study," *Journal of Consulting and Clinical Psychology* 62 (1994): 472–491.
55. Eugene Maguin, Rolf Loeber, and Paul LeMahieu, "Does the Relationship Between Poor Reading and Delinquency Hold for Males of Different Ages and Ethnic Groups?" *Journal of Emotional and Behavioral Disorders* 1 (1993): 88–100.
56. Paul Verbrugge, Research and Statistics Division, Department of Justice Canada, "Fetal Alcohol Syndrome and the Youth Criminal Justice System: A Discussion Paper" 2004, 09, 10 Kenneth R. Warren and Brenda G. Hewitt (2009) "Fetal Alcohol Spectrum Disorders: When Science, Medicine, Public Policy and Laws Collide" *Developmental Disabilities* 15, 170-175.
57. J. Conry and D. K. Fast, "Fetal Alcohol Syndrome and the Criminal Justice System" (Vancouver: Fetal Alcohol Syndrome Resource Society 2000).
58. R. J. Williams, and S. P. Gloster, "Knowledge of Fetal Alcohol Syndrome (FAS) among Native in Northern Manitoba," *Journal of Studies on Alcohol,* 60 (1999), 833–836.)
59. A. P. Streissguth, F. L. Bookstein, H. M. Barr, P. D. Sampson, K. O'Malley, J. K. Young, "Risk Factors for Adverse Life Outcomes in Fetal Alcohol Syndrome and Fetal Alcohol Effects" *Journal of Developmental and Behavioral Pediatrics* 25 (4) 228–238.
60. Verbrugge, "Fetal Alcohol Syndrome and the Youth Criminal Justice System: A Discussion Paper," 2004.
61. Reiss and Roth, *Understanding and Preventing Violence*, p. 119.
62. Matti Virkkunen, David Goldman, and Markku Linnoila, "Serotonin in Alcoholic Violent Offenders," *The Ciba Foundation Symposium: Genetics of Criminal and Antisocial Behavior* (Chichester, England: Wiley, 1995).
63. Lee Ellis, "Left- and Mixed-Handedness and Criminality: Explanations for a Probable Relationship," in *Left-Handedness: Behavioral Implications and Anomalies,* ed. S. Coren (Amsterdam: Elsevier, 1990): pp. 485–507.
64. Lee Ellis, "Monoamine Oxidase and Criminality: Identifying an Apparent Biological Marker for Antisocial Behavior," *Journal of Research in Crime and Delinquency* 28 (1991): 227–251.
65. Lee Ellis, "Arousal Theory and the Religiosity–Criminality Relationship," in *Contemporary Criminological Theory,* ed. Peter Cordella and Larry Siegel (Boston, MA: Northeastern University, 1996), pp. 65–84.
66. Adrian Raine, Peter Venables, and Sarnoff Mednick, "Low Resting Heart Rate at Age 3 Years Predisposes to Aggression at Age 11 Years: Evidence from the Mauritius Child Health Project," *Journal of the American Academy of Adolescent Psychiatry* 36 (1997): 1457–1464.
67. David Rowe, "As the Twig Is Bent: The Myth of Child-Rearing Influences on Personality Development," *Journal of Counseling and Development* 68 (1990): 606–611; David Rowe, Joseph Rogers, and Sylvia Meseck-Bushey, "Sibling Delinquency and the Family Environment: Shared and Unshared Influences," *Child Development* 63 (1992): 59–67; Gregory Carey and David DiLalla, "Personality and Psychopathology: Genetic Perspectives," *Journal of Abnormal Psychology* 103 (1994): 32–43.
68. T. R. Sarbin and L. E. Miller, "Demonism Revisited: The XYY Chromosome Anomaly," *Issues in Criminology* 5 (1970): 195–207.
69. Sarnoff Mednick and Jan Volavka, "Biology and Crime," in *Crime and Justice,* ed. Norval Morris and Michael Tonry (Chicago: University of Chicago Press, 1980), pp. 85–159, at p. 93.
70. For an early review, see Barbara Wooton, *Social Science and Social Pathology* (London: Allen and Unwin, 1959); John Laub and Robert Sampson, "Unraveling Families and Delinquency: A Reanalysis of the Gluecks' Data," *Criminology* 26 (1988): 355–380.
71. D. J. West and D. P. Farrington, "Who Becomes Delinquent?" in *The Delinquent Way of Life,* ed. D. J. West and D. P. Farrington (London: Heinemann, 1977), pp. 1–28; D. J. West, *Delinquency: Its Roots, Careers, and Prospects* (Cambridge, MA: Harvard University Press, 1982).
72. West, *Delinquency,* p. 114.

73. David Farrington, "Understanding and Preventing Bullying," in *Crime and Justice,* vol. 17, ed. Michael Tonry (Chicago: University of Chicago Press, 1993): 381–457.
74. David Rowe and David Farrington, "The Familial Transmission of Criminal Convictions," *Criminology* 35 (1997): 177–201.
75. Mednick and Volavka, "Biology and Crime," p. 94.
76. Ibid., p. 95.
77. David Rowe, "Genetic and Environmental Components of Antisocial Behavior: A Study of 265 Twin Pairs," *Criminology* 24 (1986): 513–532; David Rowe and D. Wayne Osgood, "Heredity and Sociological Theories of Delinquency: A Reconsideration," *American Sociological Review* 49 (1984): 526–540.
78. Edwin J. C. G. van den Oord, Frank Verhulst, and Dorret Boomsma, "A Genetic Study of Maternal and Paternal Ratings of Problem Behaviors in 3-Year-Old Twins," *Journal of Abnormal Psychology* 105 (1996): 349–357.
79. Michael Lyons, "A Twin Study of Self-Reported Criminal Behavior," and Judy Silberg, Joanne Meyer, Andrew Pickles, Emily Simonoff, Lindon Eaves, John Hewitt, Hermine Maes, and Michael Rutter, "Heterogeneity Among Juvenile Antisocial Behaviors: Findings from the Virginia Twin Study of Adolescent Behavioral Development," in the Ciba Foundation Symposium, *Genetics of Criminal and Antisocial Behavior* (Chichester, England: Wiley, 1995).
80. Gregory Carey, "Twin Imitation for Antisocial Behavior: Implications for Genetic and Family Environment Research," *Journal of Abnormal Psychology* 101 (1992): 18–25; David Rowe and Joseph Rogers, "The Ohio Twin Project and ADSEX Studies: Behavior Genetic Approaches to Understanding Antisocial Behavior," paper presented at the annual meeting of the American Society of Criminology, Montreal, November 1987.
81. David Rowe, *The Limits of Family Influence: Genes, Experiences and Behavior* (New York: Guilford Press, 1995), p. 64.
82. R. J. Cadoret, C. Cain, and R. R. Crowe, "Evidence for a Gene–Environment Interaction in the Development of Adolescent Antisocial Behavior," *Behavior Genetics* 13 (1983): 301–310.
83. Barry Hutchings and Sarnoff A. Mednick, "Criminality in Adoptees and Their Adoptive and Biological Parents: A Pilot Study," in *Biological Bases in Criminal Behavior,* ed. S. A. Mednick and K. O. Christiansen (New York: Gardner Press, 1977).
84. For similar results, see Sarnoff Mednick, Terrie Moffitt, William Gabrielli, and Barry Hutchings, "Genetic Factors in Criminal Behavior: A Review," *Development of Antisocial and Prosocial Behavior* (New York: Academic Press, 1986), pp. 3–50; Sarnoff Mednick, William Gabrielli, and Barry Hutchings, "Genetic Influences in Criminal Behavior: Evidence from an Adoption Cohort," in *Perspective Studies of Crime and Delinquency,* ed. Katherine Teilmann Van Dusen and Sarnoff Mednick (Boston: Kluwer-Nijhoff, 1983),pp. 39–57.
85. Glenn Walters, "A Meta-Analysis of the Gene–Crime Relationship," *Criminology* 30 (1992): 595–613.
86. Lawrence Cohen and Richard Machalek, "A General Theory of Expropriative Crime: An Evolutionary Ecological Approach," *American Journal of Sociology* 94 (1988): 465–501.
87. For a general review, see Martin Daly and Margo Wilson, "Crime and Conflict: Homicide in Evolutionary Psychological Theory," in *Crime and Justice: An Annual Edition,* ed. Michael Tonry (Chicago: University of Chicago Press, 1997), pp. 51–100.
88. Lee Ellis, "The Evolution of Violent Criminal Behavior and Its Nonlegal Equivalent," in *Crime in Biological, Social and Moral Contexts,* ed. Lee Ellis and Harry Hoffman (New York: Praeger, 1990), pp. 63–65.
89. David Rowe, Alexander Vazsonyi, and Aurelio Jose Figuerdo, "Mating-Effort in Adolescence: A Conditional Alternative Strategy," *Personal Individual Differences* 23 (1997): 105–115.
90. Ibid., p. 101.
91. Margo Wilson, Holly Johnson, and Martin Daly, "Lethal and Nonlethal Violence Against Wives," *Canadian Journal of Criminology* 37 (1995): 331–361.
92. Lee Ellis and Anthony Walsh, "Gene-Based Evolutionary Theories of Criminology," *Criminology* 35 (1997): 229–276.
93. Byron Roth, "Crime and Child Rearing," *Society* 34 (1996): 39–45.
94. Deborah Denno, "Sociological and Human Developmental Explanations of Crime: Conflict or Consensus," *Criminology* 23 (1985): 711–741.
95. Glenn Walters and Thomas White, "Heredity and Crime: Bad Genes or Bad Research?" *Criminology* 27 (1989): 455–486, at p. 478.
96. Edwin Driver, "Charles Buckman Goring," in *Pioneers in Criminology,* ed. Hermann Mannheim (Montclair, NJ: Patterson Smith, 1970), p. 440.
97. Gabriel Tarde, *Penal Philosophy,* trans. R. Howell (Boston: Little, Brown, 1912).
98. See, generally, Donn Byrne and Kathryn Kelly, *An Introduction to Personality* (Englewood Cliffs, NJ: Prentice-Hall, 1981).
99. Veronique Mandal, "Schizophrenia: Widower Demands the Right to Know," *Windsor Star,* 8 October 2002.
100. David Abrahamsen, *Crime and the Human Mind* (New York: Columbia University Press, 1944), p. 137; also see, generally, Fritz Redl and Hans Toch, "The Psychoanalytic Perspective," in *Psychology of Crime and Criminal Justice,* ed. Hans Toch (New York: Holt, Rinehart and Winston, 1979), pp. 193–195.
101. August Aichorn, *Wayward Youth* (New York: Viking Press, 1935).
102. See, generally, D. A. Andrews and James Bonta, *The Psychology of Criminal Conduct* (Cincinnati: Anderson, 1994), pp. 72–75.
103. Paige Crosby Ouimette, "Psychopathology and Sexual Aggression in Nonincarcerated Men," *Violence and Victimization* 12 (1997): 389–397.
104. Robert Krueger, Avshalom Caspi, Phil Silva, and Rob McGee, "Personality Traits Are Differentially Linked to Mental Disorders: A Multitrait–Multidiagnosis Study of an Adolescent Birth Cohort," *Journal of Abnormal Psychology* 105 (1996): 299–312.
105. Seymour Halleck, *Psychiatry and the Dilemmas of Crime* (Berkeley: University of California Press, 1971).
106. Chinta Puxley, "Voice from God Told Man to Kill Passenger," *Toronto Star*, 4 March 2009, p. A15.
107. Mike McIntyre, "Family Denounces Ruling Killer Not Criminally Liable," *Winnipeg Free Press*, 3 December 2010, p.A5; CBC News, "Greyhound Bus Killer Found Not Criminally Responsible," March 5, 2009, http://www.cbc.ca/news/canada/manitoba/story/2009/03/05/mb-li-verdict.html (accessed 14 August 2011).
108. Richard Rosner, "Adolescents Accused of Murder and Manslaughter: A Five-Year Descriptive Study," *Bulletin of the American Academy of Psychiatry and the Law* 7 (1979): 342–351.
109. Richard Famularo, Robert Kinscherff, and Terence Fenton, "Psychiatric Diagnoses of Abusive Mothers: A Preliminary Report," *Journal of Nervous and Mental Disease* 180 (1992): 658–660.
110. Bruce Link, Howard Andrews, and Francis Cullen, "The Violent and Illegal Behavior of

Mental Patients Reconsidered," *American Sociological Review* 57 (1992): 275–292; Ellen Hochstedler Steury, "Criminal Defendants with Psychiatric Impairment: Prevalence, Probabilities and Rates," *Journal of Criminal Law and Criminology* 84 (1993): 354–374.

111. Marc Hillbrand, John Krystal, Kimberly Sharpe, and Hilliard Foster, "Clinical Predictors of Self-Mutilation in Hospitalized Patients," *Journal of Nervous and Mental Disease* 182 (1994): 9–13.

112. Carmen Cirincione, Henry Steadman, Pamela Clark Robbins, and John Monahan, *Mental Illness as a Factor in Criminality: A Study of Prisoners and Mental Patients* (Delmar, NY: Policy Research Associates, 1991); see also Carmen Cirincione, Henry Steadman, Pamela Clark Robbins, and John Monahan, *Schizophrenia as a Contingent Risk Factor for Criminal Violence* (Delmar, NY: Policy Research Associates, 1991).

113. J. Monahan and H. J. Steadman, "Crime and Mental Disorder: An Epidemiological Approach," in *Crime and Justice: An Annual Review of Research*, ed. N. Morris and M. Tonry (Chicago: University of Chicago Press, 1983) (pp 145–189).

114. K. S. Douglas, L. S. Guy, S. D. Hart, "Psychosis as a Risk Factor for Violence to Others: A Meta-Analysis," *Psychological Bulletin, 135* (5), 679–706.

115. Ibid.

116. S. Fazel, G. Gulati, L. Linsell, J. R. Geddes, and M. Grann, "Schizophrenia and Violence: Systematic Review and Meta-Analysis," Public Library of Science, Medicine.

117. Ibid.

118. K. S. Douglas, L. S. Guy, S. D. Hart, "Psychosis as a Risk Factor for Violence to Others: A Meta-Analysis."

119. This discussion is based on three works by Albert Bandura: *Aggression: A Social Learning Analysis* (Englewood Cliffs, NJ: Prentice-Hall, 1973); *Social Learning Theory* (Englewood Cliffs, NJ: Prentice-Hall, 1977); and "The Social Learning Perspective: Mechanisms of Aggression," in *Psychology of Crime and Criminal Justice,* ed. Hans Toch (New York: Holt, Rinehart and Winston, 1979), pp. 198–236.

120. David Phillips, "The Impact of Mass Media Violence on U.S. Homicides," *American Sociological Review* 48 (1983): 560–568.

121. UCLA Center for Communication Policy, *Television Violence Monitoring Project* (Los Angeles, 1995); Jonathan Freedman, "Television Violence and Aggression: A Rejoinder," *Psychological Bulletin* 100 (1986): 372–378; Wendy Wood, Frank Wong, and J. Gregory Chachere, "Effects of Media Violence on Viewers' Aggression in Unconstrained Social Interaction," *Psychological Bulletin* 109 (1991): 371–383.

122. K. A. Dodge, "A Social Information Processing Model of Social Competence in Children," in *Minnesota Symposium in Child Psychology,* vol. 18, ed. M. Perlmutter (Hillsdale, NJ: Erlbaum, 1986): 77–125.

123. Adrian Raine, Peter Venables, and Mark Williams, "Better Autonomic Conditioning and Faster Electrodermal Half-Recovery Time at Age 15 Years as Possible Protective Factors Against Crime at Age 29 Years," *Developmental Psychology* 32 (1996): 624–630.

124. L. Huesman and L. Eron, "Individual Differences and the Trait of Aggression," *European Journal of Personality* 3 (1989): 95–106.

125. Rolf Loeber and Dale Hay, "Key Issues in the Development of Aggression and Violence from Childhood to Early Adulthood," *Annual Review of Psychology* 48 (1997): 371–410.

126. D. Lipton, E. C. McDonel, and R. McFall, "Heterosocial Perception in Rapists," *Journal of Consulting and Clinical Psychology* 55 (1987): 17–21.

127. See, generally, Walter Mischel, *Introduction to Personality,* 4th ed. (New York: Holt, Rinehart and Winston, 1986).

128. See, generally, Hans Eysenck, *Personality and Crime* (London: Routledge and Kegan Paul, 1977).

129. Edelyn Verona and Joyce Carbonell, "Female Violence and Personality," *Criminal Justice and Behavior* 27 (2000): 176–195.

130. Hans Eysenck and M. W. Eysenck, *Personality and Individual Differences* (New York: Plenum, 1985).

131. David Farrington, "Psychobiological Factors in the Explanation and Reduction of Delinquency," *Today's Delinquent* (1988): 37–51.

132. Laurie Frost, Terrie Moffitt, and Rob McGee, "Neuropsychological Correlates of Psychopathology in an Unselected Cohort of Young Adolescents," *Journal of Abnormal Psychology* 98 (1989): 307–313.

133. David Lykken, "Psychopathy, Sociopathy, and Crime," *Society* 34 (1996): 30–38.

134. Avshalom Caspi, Terrie Moffitt, Phil Silva, Magda Stouthamer-Loeber, Robert Krueger, and Pamela Schmutte, "Are Some People Crime-Prone? Replications of the Personality–Crime Relationship Across Countries, Genders, Races and Methods," *Criminology* 32 (1994): 163–195; Heather M. Gretton, Robert D. Hare; Rosalind E. H. Catchpole, "Psychopathy and Offending from Adolescence to Adulthood: A 10-Year Follow-Up," *Journal of Consulting and Clinical Psychology* 72 (August 2004): 636–645.

135. Henry Goddard, *Efficiency and Levels of Intelligence* (Princeton, NJ: Princeton University Press, 1920); Edwin Sutherland, "Mental Deficiency and Crime," in *Social Attitudes,* ed. Kimball Young (New York: Henry Holt, 1931), chap. 15.

136. William Healy and Augusta Bronner, *Delinquency and Criminals: Their Making and Unmaking* (New York: McMillan, 1926).

137. Joseph Lee Rogers, H. Harrington Cleveland, Edwin van den Oord, and David Rowe, "Resolving the Debate Over Birth Order, Family Size and Intelligence," *American Psychologist* 55 (2000): 599–612.

138. Sutherland, "Mental Deficiency and Crime."

139. Travis Hirschi and Michael Hindelang, "Intelligence and Delinquency: A Revisionist Review," *American Sociological Review* 42 (1977): 471–586.

140. Deborah Denno, "Sociological and Human Developmental Explanations of Crime: Conflict or Consensus," *Criminology* 23 (1985): 711–741; Christine Ward and Richard McFall, "Further Validation of the Problem Inventory for Adolescent Girls: Comparing Caucasian and Black Delinquents and Nondelinquents," *Journal of Consulting and Clinical Psychology* 54 (1986): 732–733; L. Hubble and M. Groff, "Magnitude and Direction of WISC-R Verbal Performance IQ Discrepancies Among Adjudicated Male Delinquents," *Journal of Youth and Adolescence* 10 (1981): 179–183; Robert Gordon, "IQ Commensurability of Black–White Differences in Crime and Delinquency," paper presented at the annual meeting of the American Psychological Association, Washington, DC, August 1986; Robert Gordon, "Two Illustrations of the IQ-Surrogate Hypothesis: IQ Versus Parental Education and Occupational Status in the Race–IQ–Delinquency Model," paper presented at the annual meeting of the American Society of Criminology, Montreal, November 1987.

141. James Q. Wilson and Richard Herrnstein, *Crime and Human Nature* (New York: Simon and Schuster, 1985), p. 148.

142. Ibid., p. 171.

143. Richard Herrnstein and Charles Murray, *The Bell Curve: Intelligence and Class Structure in American Life* (New York: Free Press, 1994).

144. H. D. Day, J. M. Franklin, and D. D. Marshall, "Predictors of Aggression in Hospitalized Adolescents," *Journal of Psychology* 132 (1998): 427–435; Scott Menard and Barbara Morse, "A Structuralist Critique of the IQ–Delinquency Hypothesis: Theory and Evidence," *American Journal of Sociology* 89 (1984): 1347–1378; Denno, "Sociological and Human Developmental Explanations of Crime."

145. Ulric Neisser et al., "Intelligence: Knowns and Unknowns," *American Psychologist* 51 (1996): 77–101, at p. 83.

146. Susan Pease and Craig T. Love, "Optimal Methods and Issues in Nutrition Research in the Correctional Setting," *Nutrition Reviews Supplement* 44 (1986): 122–131.

147. Mark O'Callaghan and Douglas Carroll, "The Role of Psychosurgical Studies in the Control of Antisocial Behavior," in *The Causes of Crime: New Biological Approaches,* ed. Sarnoff Mednick, Terrie Moffitt, and Susan Stack (Cambridge: Cambridge University Press, 1987), pp. 312–328.

148. Reiss and Roth, *Understanding and Preventing Violence*, p. 389.

149. Kathleen Cirillo, B. E. Pruitt, Brian Colwell, Paul M. Kingery, Robert S. Hurley, and Danny Ballard, "School Violence: Prevalence and Intervention Strategies for At-Risk Adolescents," *Adolescence* 33 (1998): 319–331.

Chapter 6

1. Conway Daly, "Beating Highlights Predicament of Canada's Homeless," Canadian Press, http://www.canoe.com/CNEWSLaw0201/11_homeless-cp.html, 11 January 2002.
2. Steven Messner and Richard Rosenfeld, *Crime and the American Dream* (Belmont, CA: Wadsworth, 1994), p. 11; Patrick C. Jobes, Joseph F. Donnermeyer, and Elaine Barclay, "A Tale of Two Towns: Social Structure, Integration and Crime in Rural New South Wales," *Sociologia Ruralis*, vol. 45 iss. 3 (July 2005): 224–244.
3. Edwin Lemert, *Human Deviance, Social Problems and Social Control* (Englewood Cliffs, NJ: Prentice-Hall, 1967); and Sang-Weon Kim and William Alex Pridemore, "Poverty, Socioeconomic Change, Institutional Anomie, and Homicide," *Social Science Quarterly* (Blackwell Publishing), vol. 86 (December 2005 Supplement): 1377–1398.
4. Statistics Canada, "Cansim Table 202-0801, Low Income Cut-offs Before and After Tax by Community and Family Size, 2009 Constant Dollars, Annual (dollars) http://www5.statcan.gc.ca/cansim/pick-choisir?lang=eng&searchTypeByValue=1&id=2020801 (accessed 17 November 2011); and Armina Ligaya, CBC News Online, "The Debate over Canada's Poverty Line," (November 12, 2007), http://www.cbc.ca/news/background/economy/poverty-line.html (accessed 7 November 2011).
5. Family Service Toronto, "2009 Report Card on Child and Family Poverty in Canada: 1989–2009," http://www.campaign2000.ca/reportcards/national.
6. Myungkook Joo, "Long-term Effects of Head Start on Academic and School Outcomes of Children in Persistent Poverty: Girls vs. Boys," *Children & Youth Services Review*, vol. 32 iss. 6 (June 2010): 807–814.
7. Ibid.
8. Brooks-Gunn and Duncan, "The Effects of Poverty on Children"; Kevin K. Lee, "Urban Poverty in Canada: A Statistical Profile," *Canadian Council on Social Development* (April 2000): 2001, National Council of Welfare, *Poverty Profile 1999;* Campaign 2000, *2003 Report Card on Child Poverty in Canada*.
9. Jonathan Crane, "The Epidemic Theory of Ghettos and Neighborhood Effects on Dropping Out and Teenage Childbearing," *American Journal of Sociology* 96 (1991): 1226–1259; see also Rodrick Wallace, "Expanding Coupled Shock Fronts of Urban Decay and Criminal Behavior: How U.S. Cities Are Becoming 'Hollowed Out,'" *Journal of Quantitative Criminology* 7 (1991): 333–355.
10. Lee, "Urban Poverty in Canada: A Statistical Profile"; 2001, National Council of Welfare, *Poverty Profile 1999;* Statistics Canada, "1996 Census: Sources of Income, Earnings and Total Income and Family Income," *The Daily,* 12 May 1998.
11. Richard Sennett and Jonathan Cobb, *The Hidden Injuries of Class* (New York: Vintage Books, 1973).
12. Oscar Lewis, "The Culture of Poverty," *Scientific American* 215 (1966): 19–25.
13. Gunnar Myrdal, *The Challenge of World Poverty* (New York: Vintage Books, 1970).
14. Robin Armstrong, "Mapping the Conditions of First Nations Communities," *Canadian Social Trends* (Winter 1999): 14–18; see also British Columbia All Chiefs' Task Force Fact Sheet Aboriginal Poverty in Canada, http://www.fns.bc.ca/pdf/ACTFPovertyFactSheet_02_2010.pdf.
15. Ibid.
16. James Ainsworth-Darnell and Douglas Downey, "Assessing the Oppositional Culture Explanation for Racial/Ethnic Differences in School Performances," *American Sociological Review* 63 (1998): 536–553.
17. National Institute of Child Health and Human Development Early Child Care Research Network, "Duration and Developmental Timing of Poverty and Children's Cognitive and Social Development from Birth through Third Grade," *Child Development*, vol. 76 iss. 4 (July/August 2005): pp. 795–810.
18. William Julius Wilson, *The Truly Disadvantaged* (Chicago: University of Chicago Press, 1987).
19. Kevin K. Lee, "Urban Poverty in Canada: A Statistical Profile" (April 2000) Canadian Council on Social Development, Ottawa, Ontario; Robin Armstrong, "Mapping the Conditions of First Nations Communities," *Canadian Social Trends* (Winter, 1999).
20. See Charles Tittle and Robert Meier, "Specifying the SES/Delinquency Relationship," *Criminology* 28 (1990): 271–295, at p. 293.
21. Wouter Steenbeek and John R. Hipp, "A Longitudinal Test of Social Disorganization Theory: Feedback Effects Among Cohesion, Social Control, and Disorder," *Criminology*, vol. 49 iss. 3 (August 2011): 833–871; and Ruth Kornhauser, *Social Sources of Delinquency* (Chicago: University of Chicago Press, 1978), p. 75.
22. Clifford R. Shaw and Henry D. McKay, *Juvenile Delinquency and Urban Areas,* rev. ed. (Chicago: University of Chicago Press, 1972).
23. Ibid., p. 52.
24. Ibid., p. 171.
25. The best known of these critiques is Kornhauser, *Social Sources of Delinquency*.
26. For a general review, see James Byrne and Robert Sampson, eds., *The Social Ecology of Crime* (New York: Springer Verlag, 1985).
27. Martin A. Andresen, "A Spatial Analysis of Crime in Vancouver, British Columbia: A Synthesis of Social Disorganization and Routine Activity Theory," *Canadian Geographer*, vol. 50 iss. 4 (Winter 2006): pp. 487–502.
28. D. Wayne Osgood and Jeff Chambers, "Social Disorganization Outside the Metropolis: An Analysis of Rural Youth Violence," *Criminology* 38 (2000): 81–117.
29. William Spelman, "Abandoned Buildings: Magnets for Crime?" *Journal of Criminal Justice* 21 (1993): 481–493.

30. Keith Harries and Andrea Powell, "Juvenile Gun Crime and Social Stress: Baltimore, 1980–1990," *Urban Geography* 15 (1994): 45–63.
31. Allison T. Chappell, Elizabeth Monk-Turner, Brian K. Payne, "Broken Windows or Window Breakers: The Influence of Physical and Social Disorder on Quality of Life," *JQ: Justice Quarterly*, vol. 28 iss. 3 (June 2011): pp. 522–540.
32. Steven Messner and Kenneth Tardiff, "Economic Inequality and Levels of Homicide: An Analysis of Urban Neighborhoods," *Criminology* 24 (1986): 297–317; Charis E. Kubrin, Jerald R. Herting, "Neighborhood Correlates of Homicide Trends: An Analysis Using Growth-Curve Modeling," *Sociological Quarterly*, vol. 44 iss. 3 (Summer 2003): p. 329.
33. G. David Curry and Irving Spergel, "Gang Homicide, Delinquency, and Community," *Criminology* 26 (1988): 381–407.
34. Darrell Steffensmeier and Dana Haynie, "Gender, Structural Disadvantage, and Urban Crime: Do Macrosocial Variables Also Explain Female Offending Rates?" *Criminology* 38 (2000): 403–438.
35. Robert Bursik, "Social Disorganization and Theories of Crime and Delinquency: Problems and Prospects," *Criminology,* 26 (1988), 521–539.
36. Stephen W. Baron, "Street Youth, Unemployment, and Crime: Is It That Simple? Using General Strain Theory to Untangle the Relationship," *Canadian Journal of Criminology & Criminal Justice*, vol. 50 iss. 4 (July 2008): 399–434.
37. Scott Menard and Delbert Elliott, "Self-Reported Offending, Maturational Reform, and the Easterlin Hypothesis," *Journal of Quantitative Criminology* 6 (1990): 237–268.
38. Steven A. Kohm, "Spatial Dimensions of Fear in a High-Crime Community: Fear of Crime or Fear of Disorder?" *Canadian Journal of Criminology & Criminal Justice*, vol. 51 iss. 1 (January 2009): pp. 1–30.
39. Bilan R. Wyant, "Multilevel Impacts of Perceived Incivilities and Perceptions of Crime Risk on Fear of Crime," *Journal of Research in Crime & Delinquency*, vol. 45 iss. 1 (February 2008): pp. 39–64.
40. Wesley Skogan, "Fear of Crime and Neighborhood Change," in *Communities and Crime,* ed. Albert Reiss and Michael Tonry (Chicago: University of Chicago Press, 1986), pp. 191–232.
41. Steven A. Kohm, "Spatial Dimensions of Fear in a High-Crime Community: Fear of Crime or Fear of Disorder?"; and Stephanie Greenberg, "Fear and Its Relationship to Crime, Neighborhood Deterioration, and Informal Social Control," in *The Social Ecology of Crime,* ed. James Byrne and Robert Sampson (New York: Springer Verlag, 1985), pp. 47–62.
42. Skogan, "Fear of Crime and Neighborhood Change."
43. Ibid.
44. Finn Aage-Esbensen and David Huizinga, "Community Structure and Drug Use: From a Social Disorganization Perspective," *Justice Quarterly* 7 (1990): 691–709.
45. Allen Liska and Paul Bellair, "Violent-Crime Rates and Racial Composition: Convergence over Time," *American Journal of Sociology* 101 (1995): 578–610.
46. Wesley Skogan, *Disorder and Decline: Crime and the Spiral of Decay in American Neighborhoods* (New York: Free Press, 1990), pp. 15–35.
47. Ralph Taylor and Jeanette Covington, "Neighborhood Changes in Ecology and Violence," *Criminology* 26 (1988): 553–589.
48. Allison T. Chappell, Elizabeth Monk-Turner, Brian K. Payne, "Broken Windows or Window Breakers: The Influence of Physical and Social Disorder on Quality of Life."
49. Leo Scheurman and Solomon Kobrin, "Community Careers in Crime," in *Communities and Crime,* ed. Albert Reiss and Michael Tonry (Chicago: University of Chicago Press, 1986), pp. 67–100.
50. Wilson, *The Truly Disadvantaged*.
51. Barbara Warner and Glenn Pierce, "Reexamining Social Disorganization Theory Using Calls to the Police as a Measure of Crime," *Criminology* 31 (1993): 493–519.
52. Karen Parker and Matthew Pruitt, "Poverty, Poverty Concentration, and Homicide," *Social Science Quarterly* 81 (2000): 555–582; Scot Wortley, "Justice for All? Race and Perceptions of Bias in the Ontario Criminal Justice System—a Toronto Survey," *Canadian Journal of Criminology* 38 (October 1996): 439–468.
53. Carolyn Rebecca Block and Richard Block, *Street Gang Crime in Chicago* (Washington, DC: National Institute of Justice, 1993), p. 7.
54. Lorraine Mazerolle, Rebecca Wickes, and James McBroom, "Community Variations in Violence: The Role of Social Ties and Collective Efficacy in Comparative Context," *Journal of Research in Crime & Delinquency*, vol. 47 iss. 1 (February 2010): pp. 3–30; and Felton Earls, *Linking Community Factors and Individual Development* (Washington, DC: National Institute of Justice, 1998).
55. Donald Black, "Social Control as a Dependent Variable," in *Toward a General Theory of Social Control,* ed. D. Black (Orlando: Academic Press, 1990).
56. Robert Bursik and Harold Grasmick, "The Multiple Layers of Social Disorganization," paper presented at the annual meeting of the American Society of Criminology, New Orleans, November 1992.
57. David Klinger, "Negotiating Order in Patrol Work: An Ecological Theory of Police Response to Deviance," *Criminology* 35 (1997): 277–306.
58. Rodney Stark, "Deviant Places: A Theory of the Ecology of Crime," *Criminology* 25 (1987): 893–911.
59. Delbert Elliott, William Julius Wilson, David Huizinga, Robert Sampson, Amanda Elliott, and Bruce Rankin, "The Effects of Neighborhood Disadvantage on Adolescent Development," *Journal of Research in Crime and Delinquency* 33 (1996): 389–426.
60. Mary L. Ohmer, Barbara D. Warner, and Elizabeth Beck, "Preventing Violence in Low-Income Communities: Facilitating Residents' Ability to Intervene in Neighborhood Problems," *Journal of Sociology & Social Welfare*, vol. 37 iss. 2 (June 2010): pp. 161–181.
61. Robert Bursik and Harold Grasmick, "Economic Deprivation and Neighborhood Crime Rates, 1960–1980," *Law and Society Review* 27 (1993): 263–278.
62. Joanna C. Jacob, "Male and Female Youth Crime in Canadian Communities: Assessing the Applicability of Social Disorganization Theory," *Canadian Journal of Criminology & Criminal Justice*, vol. 48 iss. 1 (January 2006): pp. 31–60; Denise Gottfredson, Richard McNeill, and Gary Gottfredson, "Social Area Influences on Delinquency: A Multilevel Analysis," *Journal of Research in Crime and Delinquency* 28 (1991): 197–206.
63. Bronwyn Dobchuk-Land, Owen Toews, and Jim Silver, "Neighbourhood-Level Responses to Safety Concerns in Four Winnipeg Inner-City Neighbourhoods: Reflections on Collective Efficacy," *Canadian Journal of Urban Research*, vol. 19 iss. 1 (Summer 2010): 18–33.
64. Robert Merton, *Social Theory and Social Structure,* enlarged ed. (New York: Free Press, 1968).
65. Albert Cohen, "The Sociology of the Deviant Act: Anomie Theory and Beyond," *American*

Sociological Review 30 (1965): 5–14; and Eric P. Baumer and Regan Gustafson, "Social Organization and Instrumental Crime: Assessing the Empirical Validity of Classic and Contemporary Anomie Theories." *Criminology*, vol. 45 iss. 3 (August 2007): 617–663.

66. Steven Messner and Richard Rosenfeld, *Crime and the American Dream* (Belmont, CA: Wadsworth, 1994).
67. John Hagan, Gerd Hefler, Gabriele Classen, Klaus Boehnke, and Hans Merkens, "Subterranean Sources of Subcultural Delinquency Beyond the American Dream," *Criminology* 36 (1998): 309–340.
68. Robert Agnew, "Foundation for a General Strain Theory of Crime and Delinquency," *Criminology* 30 (1992): 47–87.
69. Ibid., p. 57.
70. Ibid.
71. Gregory Dunaway, "Strain, Relative Deprivation and Middle-Class Delinquency," in *Varieties of Criminology: Readings from a Dynamic Discipline,* ed. Greg Barak (Westport, CT: Praeger, 1994): 79–95; Nikos Passas, "Anomie and Relative Deprivation," in *The Future of Anomie Theory,* ed. Nikos Passass and Robert Agnew (Boston: Northeastern University Press, 1997): 62–94; and Giacinto Froggio, "Strain and Juvenile Delinquency: A Critical Review of Agnew's General Strain Theory," *Journal of Loss & Trauma*, vol. 12 iss. 4 (July–September 2007): 383–418.
72. Robert Agnew, Timothy Brezina, John Paul Wright, and Francis T. Cullen, "Strain, Personality Traits, and Delinquency: Extending General Strain Theory," *Criminology*, vol. 40 iss. 1 (February 2002): p. 43.
73. Robert Agnew and Helene Raskin White, "An Empirical Test of General Strain Theory," *Criminology* 30 (1992): 475–499.
74. Carter Hay, "Family Strain, Gender, and Delinquency," *Sociological Perspectives*, vol. 46 iss. 1 (Spring 2003): 107–135; Beverly Stiles, Xiaoru Liu, and Howard Kaplan, "Relative Deprivation and Deviant Adaptations: The Mediating Effects of Negative Self Feelings," *Journal of Research in Crime and Delinquency* 37 (2000): 64–90.
75. Robert Agnew, "Foundation for a General Strain Theory of Crime and Delinquency," *Criminology* 30 (1992): 47–87.
76. Ibid., p. 57.
77. John P. Hoffmann and Timothy O. Ireland, "Strain and Opportunity Structures," *Journal of Quantitative Criminology*, vol. 20 iss. 3 (September 2004): pp. 263–292.
78. Walter Miller, "Lower-Class Culture as a Generating Milieu of Gang Delinquency," *Journal of Social Issues* 14 (1958), 5–19.
79. Ibid., pp. 14–17.
80. Fred Markowitz and Richard Felson, "Social-Demographic Attitudes and Violence," *Criminology* 36 (1998): 117–138.
81. Jeffrey Fagan, *Adolescent Violence: A View from the Street,* NIJ Research Preview (Washington, DC: National Institute of Justice, 1998).
82. Albert Cohen, *Delinquent Boys* (New York: Free Press, 1955).
83. Ibid., p. 25.
84. Ibid., p. 28.
85. Ibid.
86. Ibid., p. 30.
87. Ibid., p. 133.
88. Richard Cloward and Lloyd Ohlin, *Delinquency and Opportunity* (New York: Free Press, 1960).
89. Ibid., p. 171.
90. Ibid., p. 73.
91. James DeFronzo, "Welfare and Burglary," *Crime and Delinquency* 42 (1996): 223–230.
92. Hamilton Police Service, C.O.P.P. 2000: Challenging Our Patrol Priorities into the Next Century (June 1999).

Chapter 7

1. Charles Tittle and Robert Meier, "Specifying the SES/Delinquency Relationship," *Criminology* 28 (1990): 271–299, p. 274; Robert Agnew, Shelley Matthews, Jacob Bucher, Adria N. Welcher, Corey Keyes, "Socioeconomic Status, Economic Problems, and Delinquency," *Youth & Society* (2008) vol. 40, no. 2: 159–181.
2. Sheldon Glueck and Eleanor Glueck, *Unraveling Juvenile Delinquency* (Cambridge, MA: Harvard University Press, 1950); Ashley Weeks, "Predicting Juvenile Delinquency," *American Sociological Review* 8 (1943): 40–46.
3. Denise Kandel, "The Parental and Peer Contexts of Adolescent Deviance: An Algebra of Interpersonal Influences," *Journal of Drug Issues* 26 (1996): 289–315; Ann Goetting, "The Parenting–Crime Connection," *Journal of Primary Prevention* 14 (1994): 167–184; John Paul Wright and Francis T. Cullen, "Parental Efficacy and Delinquent Behavior: Do Control and Support Matter? *Criminology, 39, 3* (2001): 677–705.
4. For general reviews of the relationship between families and delinquency, see Alan Jay Lincoln and Murray Straus, *Crime and the Family* (Springfield, IL: Charles C. Thomas, 1985); Rolf Loeber and Magda Stouthamer-Loeber, "Family Factors as Correlates and Predictors of Juvenile Conduct Problems and Delinquency," in *Crime and Justice: An Annual Review of Research,* vol. 7, eds. Michael Tonry and Norval Morris (Chicago: University of Chicago Press, 1986), pp. 29–151; Goetting, "The Parenting–Crime Connection"; Emma J. Palmer and Kirsty Gough, "Childhood Experiences of Parenting and Causal Attributions for Criminal Behavior Among Young Offenders and Non-Offenders," *Journal of Applied Social Psychology, 37* (4) (2007): 790–806.
5. Joseph Weis, Katherine Worsley, and Carol Zeiss, *The Family and Delinquency: Organizing the Conceptual Chaos* (Monograph, Center for Law and Justice, University of Washington, 1982).
6. Susan Stern and Carolyn Smith, "Family Processes and Delinquency in an Ecological Context," *Social Service Review* 37 (1995): 707–731.
7. Lawrence Rosen and Kathleen Neilson, "Broken Homes," in *Contemporary Criminology,* eds. Leonard Savitz and Norman Johnston (New York: Wiley, 1982), pp. 126–132.
8. James Q. Wilson and Richard Herrnstein, *Crime and Human Nature* (New York: Simon and Schuster, 1985), p. 249.
9. L. Edward Wells and Joseph Rankin, "Families and Delinquency: A Meta-Analysis of the Impact of Broken Homes," *Social Problems* 38 (1991): 71–90.
10. Nan Marie Astone and Sara McLanahan, "Family Structure, Parental Practices and High School Completion," *American Sociological Review* 56 (1991): 309–320.
11. Joseph Rankin and L. Edward Wells, "The Effect of Parental Attachments and Direct Controls on Delinquency," *Journal of Research in Crime and Delinquency* 27 (1990): 140–165.
12. Ronald Simons, Chyi-In Wu, Kuei-Hsiu Lin, Leslie Gordon, and Rand Conger, "A Cross-Cultural Examination of the Link Between Corporal Punishment and Adolescent Antisocial Behavior," *Criminology* 38 (2000): 47–79.
13. Robert Roberts and Vern Bengston, "Affective Ties to Parents in Early Adulthood and Self-Esteem Across 20 Years," *Social Psychology Quarterly* 59 (1996): 96–106.
14. Robert Johnson, S. Susan Su, Dean Gerstein, Hee-Choon Shin, and John Hoffman, "Parental Influences on Deviant Behavior in Early Adolescence: A

Logistic Response Analysis of Age- and Gender-Differentiated Effects," *Journal of Quantitative Criminology* 11 (1995): 167–192; Nancy R. VanDeMark, Lisa A. Russell, Maura Keefe, Norma Finkelstein, Chanson D. Noether, and Joanne C. Gampel, "Children of Mothers with Histories of Substance Abuse, Mental Illness, and Trauma," *Journal of Community Psychology, 33* (4) (2005): 445–459.

15. Judith Brook and Li-Jung Tseng, "Influences of Parental Drug Use, Personality, and Child Rearing on the Toddler's Anger and Negativity," *Genetic, Social and General Psychology Monographs* 122 (1996): 107–128.
16. Thomas Ashby Wills, Donato Vaccaro, Grace McNamara, and A. Elizabeth Hirky, "Escalated Substance Use: A Longitudinal Grouping Analysis from Early to Middle Adolescence," *Journal of Abnormal Psychology* 105 (1996): 166–180.
17. Carolyn Smith and Terence Thornberry, "The Relationship Between Childhood Maltreatment and Adolescent Involvement in Delinquency," *Criminology* 33 (1995): 451–479.
18. Murray A. Straus, "Spanking and the Making of a Violent Society: The Short- and Long-Term Consequences of Corporal Punishment," *Pediatrics* 98 (1996): 837–843.
19. *The Forgotten Half: Pathways to Success for America's Youth and Young Families* (Washington, DC: William T. Grant Foundation, 1988); Lee Jussim, "Teacher Expectations: Self-Fulfilling Prophecies, Perceptual Biases, and Accuracy," *Journal of Personality and Social Psychology* 57 (1989): 469–480.
20. Eugene Maguin and Rolf Loeber, "Academic Performance and Delinquency," in *Crime and Justice: A Review of Research,* vol. 20, ed. Michael Tonry (Chicago: University of Chicago Press, 1995), pp. 145–264; Richard Thompson, Jiyoung Kim Tabone, Alan J. Litrownik, Ernestine C. Briggs, Jon M. Hussey, Diana J. English, and Howard Dubowitz, "Early Adolescent Risk Behavior Outcomes of Childhood Externalizing Behavioral Trajectories," *Journal of Early Adolescence* (2) (2011): 234–257.
21. Jeannie Oakes, *Keeping Track: How Schools Structure Inequality* (New Haven, CT: Yale University Press, 1985); Marc LeBlanc, Evelyne Valliere, and Pierre McDuff, "Adolescents' School Experience and Self-Reported Offending: A Longitudinal Test of Social Control Theory," paper presented at the annual meeting of the American Society of Criminology, Baltimore, November 1990.
22. G. Roger Jarjoura, "Does Dropping Out of School Enhance Delinquent Involvement? Results from a Large-Scale National Probability Sample," *Criminology* 31 (1993): 149–172; Terence Thornberry, Melanie Moore, and R. L. Christenson, "The Effect of Dropping Out of High School on Subsequent Criminal Behavior," *Criminology* 23 (1985): 3–18.
23. Irving Janis, *Groupthink: Psychological Studies of Policy Decisions and Fiascoes* (Boston: Houghton Mifflin, 1982).
24. Delbert Elliott, David Huizinga, and Suzanne Ageton, *Explaining Delinquency and Drug Use* (Beverly Hills, CA: Sage, 1985); Helene Raskin White, Robert Padina, and Randy LaGrange, "Longitudinal Predictors of Serious Substance Use and Delinquency," *Criminology* 6 (1987): 715–740.
25. Robert Agnew and Timothy Brezina, "Relational Problems with Peers, Gender and Delinquency," *Youth and Society* 29 (1997): 84–111.
26. Scott Menard, "Demographic and Theoretical Variables in the Age-Period Cohort Analysis of Illegal Behavior," *Journal of Research in Crime and Delinquency* 29 (1992): 178–199.
27. Patrick Jackson, "Theories and Findings About Youth Gangs," *Criminal Justice Abstracts* (June 1989): 313–327.
28. Marvin Krohn and Terence Thornberry, "Network Theory: A Model for Understanding Drug Abuse Among African-American and Hispanic Youth," in *Drug Abuse Among Minority Youth: Advances in Research and Methodology,* ed. Mario De La Rosa and Juan-Luis Recio Adrados (Washington, DC: U.S. Department of Health and Human Services, 1993), pp. 29–46.
29. D. Wayne Osgood, Janet Wilson, Patrick O'Malley, Jerald Bachman, and Lloyd Johnston, "Routine Activities and Individual Deviant Behavior," *American Sociological Review* 61 (1996): 635–655.
30. Mark Warr, "Age, Peers, and Delinquency," *Criminology* 31 (1993): 17–40.
31. Sara Battin, Karl Hill, Robert Abbott, Richard Catalano, and J. David Hawkins, "The Contribution of Gang Membership to Delinquency Beyond Delinquent Friends," *Criminology* 36 (1998): 93–116.
32. Terence Thornberry, Alan Lizotte, Marvin Krohn, Margaret Farnworth, and Sung Joon Jang, "Delinquent Peers, Beliefs, and Delinquent Behavior: A Longitudinal Test of Interactional Theory," *Working Paper* no. 6, rev. (Albany, NY: Rochester Youth Development Study, Hindelang Criminal Justice Research Center, 1992), pp. 8–30.
33. Warr, "Age, Peers, and Delinquency."
34. David Fergusson, L. John Horwood, and Daniel Nagin, "Offending Trajectories in a New Zealand Birth Cohort," *Criminology* 38 (2000): 525–551.
35. Travis Hirschi and Rodney Stark, "Hellfire and Delinquency," *Social Problems* 17 (1969): 202–213.
36. T. David Evans, Francis Cullen, R. Gregory Dunaway, and Velmer Burton, Jr., "Religion and Crime Reexamined: The Impact of Religion, Secular Controls, and Social Ecology on Adult Criminality," *Criminology* 33 (1995): 195–224.
37. Lee Ellis and James Patterson, "Crime and Religion: An International Comparison Among Thirteen Industrial Nations," *Personal Individual Differences* 20 (1996): 761–768.
38. Edwin H. Sutherland, *Principles of Criminology* (Philadelphia: Lippincott, 1939).
39. See, for example, Edwin Sutherland, "White-Collar Criminality," *American Sociological Review* 5 (1940): 2–10.
40. See Edwin Sutherland and Donald Cressey, *Criminology,* 8th ed. (Philadelphia: Lippincott, 1970), pp. 77–79.
41. Sandra Brown, Vicki Creamer, and Barbara Stetson, "Adolescent Alcohol Expectancies in Relation to Personal and Parental Drinking Patterns," *Journal of Abnormal Psychology* 96 (1987): 117–121.
42. Craig Reinerman and Jeffrey Fagan, "Social Organization and Differential Association: A Research Note from a Longitudinal Study of Violent Juvenile Offenders," *Crime and Delinquency* 34 (1988): 307–327.
43. Sue Titus Reed, *Crime and Criminology,* 2nd ed. (New York: Holt, Rinehart & Winston, 1979), p. 234.
44. Gresham Sykes and David Matza, "Techniques of Neutralization: A Theory of Delinquency," *American Sociological Review* 22 (1957): 664–670; David Matza, *Delinquency and Drift* (New York: John Wiley, 1964).
45. Matza, *Delinquency and Drift*, p. 51.
46. Sykes and Matza, "Techniques of Neutralization"; see also David Matza, "Subterranean Traditions of Youths," *Annals of the American Academy of Political and Social Science* 378 (1961): 116.
47. Sykes and Matza, "Techniques of Neutralization."
48. Ian Shields and George Whitehall, "Neutralization and Delinquency Among

Teenagers," *Criminal Justice and Behavior* 21 (1994): 223–235; Robert A. Ball, "An Empirical Exploration of Neutralization Theory," *Criminologica* 4 (1966): 22–32. See also M. William Minor, "The Neutralization of Criminal Offense," *Criminology* 18 (1980): 103–120; Robert Gordon, James Short, Desmond Cartwright, and Fred Strodtbeck, "Values and Gang Delinquency: A Study of Street Corner Groups," *American Journal of Sociology* 69 (1963): 109–128.

49. Robert Agnew, "The Techniques of Neutralization and Violence," *Criminology* 32 (1994): 555–580.
50. Jeffrey Fagan, *Adolescent Violence: A View from the Street,* NIJ Research Preview (Washington, DC: National Institute of Justice, 1998).
51. Norm Desjardins and Tina Hotton, "Trends in Drug Offences and the Role of Alcohol and Drugs in Crime," *Juristat* 24 (February 2004): 1; A. Synnott, *Shadows: Issues and Social Patterns in Canada* (Scarborough, ON: Prentice-Hall, 1996).
52. Eric Wish, *Drug Use Forecasting 1990* (Washington, DC: National Institute of Justice, 1991).
53. Scott Briar and Irving Piliavin, "Delinquency: Situational Inducements and Commitment to Conformity," *Social Problems* 13 (1965–1966): 35–45.
54. Lawrence Sherman and Douglas Smith, with Janell Schmidt and Dennis Rogan, "Crime, Punishment, and Stake in Conformity: Legal and Informal Control of Domestic Violence," *American Sociological Review* 57 (1992): 680–690.
55. Albert Reiss, "Delinquency as the Failure of Personal and Social Controls," *American Sociological Review* 16 (1951): 196–207.
56. Walter Reckless, *The Crime Problem* (New York: Appleton-Century Crofts, 1967), pp. 469–483.
57. Among the many research reports by Reckless and his colleagues are Walter Reckless, Simon Dinitz, and Ellen Murray, "Self-Concept as an Insulator Against Delinquency," *American Sociological Review* 21 (1956): 744–746; Walter Reckless, Simon Dinitz, and Barbara Kay, "The Self-Component in Potential Delinquency and Potential Non-Delinquency," *American Sociological Review* 22 (1957): 566–570; Walter Reckless, Simon Dinitz, and Ellen Murray, "The Good Boy in a High Delinquency Area," *Journal of Criminal Law, Criminology, and Police Science* 48 (1957): 12–26; Frank Scarpitti, Ellen Murray, Simon Dinitz, and Walter Reckless, "The Good Boy in a High Delinquency Area: Four Years Later," *American Sociological Review* 23 (1960): 555–558; Walter Reckless and Simon Dinitz, "Pioneering with Self-Concept as a Vulnerability Factor in Delinquency," *Journal of Criminal Law, Criminology, and Police Science* 58 (1967): 515–523.
58. Travis Hirschi, *Causes of Delinquency* (Berkeley: University of California Press, 1969).
59. Ibid., p. 231.
60. Ibid., pp. 66–74.
61. Michael Wiatroski, David Griswold, and Mary K. Roberts, "Social Control Theory and Delinquency," *American Sociological Review* 46 (1981): 525–541.
62. Patricia Van Voorhis, Francis Cullen, Richard Mathers, and Connie Chenoweth Garner, "The Impact of Family Structure and Quality on Delinquency: A Comparative Assessment of Structural and Functional Factors," *Criminology* 26 (1988): 235–261.
63. Bobbi Jo Anderson, Malcolm Holmes, and Erik Ostresh, "Male and Female Delinquent's Attachments and Effects of Attachments on Severity of Self-Reported Delinquency," *Criminal Justice and Behavior* 26 (1999): 435–452.
64. Patricia Jenkins, "School Delinquency and the School Social Bond," *Journal of Research in Crime and Delinquency* 34 (1997): 337–367.
65. For a review of exciting research, see Kimberly Kempf, "The Empirical Status of Hirschi's Control Theory," in *Advances in Criminological Theory,* eds. Bill Laufer and Freda Adler (New Brunswick, NJ: Transaction Publishers, 1992), pp. 111–129.
66. Peggy Giordano, Stephen Cernkovich, and M. D. Pugh, "Friendships and Delinquency," *American Journal of Sociology* 91 (1986): 1170–1202.
67. Denise Kandel and Mark Davies, "Friendship Networks, Intimacy, and Illicit Drug Use in Young Adulthood: A Comparison of Two Competing Theories," *Criminology* 29 (1991): 441–467.
68. Stephen Cernkovich, Peggy Giordano, and Jennifer Rudolph, "Race, Crime and the American Dream," *Journal of Research in Crime and Delinquency* 37 (2000): 131–170.
69. Velmer Burton, Francis Cullen, T. David Evans, R. Gregory Dunaway, Sesha Kethineni, and Gary Payne, "The Impact of Parental Controls on Delinquency," *Journal of Criminal Justice* 23 (1995): 111–126.
70. Michael Hindelang, "Causes of Delinquency: A Partial Replication and Extension," *Social Problems* 21 (1973): 471–487.
71. Gary Jensen and David Brownfield, "Parents and Drugs," *Criminology* 21 (1983): 543–554. See also M. Wiatrowski, D. Griswold, and M. Roberts, "Social Control Theory and Delinquency," *American Sociological Review* 46 (1981): 525–541.
72. Leslie Samuelson, Timothy Hartnagel, and Harvey Krahn, "Crime and Social Control Among High School Dropouts," *Journal of Crime and Justice* 18 (1990): 129–161.
73. Alan E. Liska and M. D. Reed, "Ties to Conventional Institutions and Delinquency: Estimating Reciprocal Effects," *American Sociological Review* 50 (1985): 547–560.
74. Michael Wiatrowski, David Griswold, and Mary K. Roberts, "Social Control Theory and Delinquency," *American Sociological Review* 46 (1981): 525–541.
75. Linda Jackson, John Hunter, and Carole Hodge, "Physical Attractiveness and Intellectual Competence: A Meta-Analytic Review," *Social Psychology Quarterly* 58 (1995): 108–122.
76. President's Commission on Law Enforcement and the Administration of Youth Crime, *Task Force Report: Juvenile Delinquency and Youth* (Washington, DC: U.S. Government Printing Office, 1967), p. 43.
77. Howard Becker, *Outsiders: Studies in the Sociology of Deviance* (New York: Macmillan, 1963), p. 9.
78. Laurie Goodstein, "The Architect of the 'Gay Conversion' Campaign," *The New York Times,* 13 August 1998, p. A10.
79. Christy Visher, "Gender, Police Arrest Decision, and Notions of Chivalry," *Criminology* 21 (1983): 5–28.
80. Marjorie Zatz, "Race, Ethnicity and Determinate Sentencing," *Criminology* 22 (1984): 147–171.
81. Christina DeJong and Kenneth Jackson, "Putting Race into Context: Race, Juvenile Justice Processing, and Urbanization," *Justice Quarterly* 15 (1998): 487–504.
82. Joan Petersilia, "Racial Disparities in the Criminal Justice System: A Summary," *Crime and Delinquency* 31 (1985): 15–34.
83. Harold Garfinkle, "Conditions of Successful Degradation Ceremonies," *American Journal of Sociology* 61 (1956): 420–424.
84. Karen Heimer and Ross Matsueda, "Role-Taking, Role-Commitment and Delinquency: A Theory of Differential Social Control," *American Sociological Review* 59 (1994): 400–437.
85. Karen Heimer, "Gender, Race, and the Pathways to Delinquency: An Interactionist

Explanation," in *Crime and Inequality,* eds. John Hagan and Ruth Peterson (Stanford, CA: Stanford University Press, 1995), pp. 32–57.

86. Heimer and Matsueda, "Role-Taking, Role-Commitment and Delinquency."
87. See, for example, Howard Kaplan and Hiroshi Fukurai, "Negative Social Sanctions, Self-Rejection, and Drug Use," *Youth and Society* 23 (1992): 275–298; Howard Kaplan and Robert Johnson, "Negative Social Sanctions and Juvenile Delinquency: Effects of Labeling in a Model of Deviant Behavior," *Social Science Quarterly* 72 (1991): 98–122; Howard Kaplan, Robert Johnson, and Carol Bailey, "Deviant Peers and Deviant Behavior: Further Elaboration of a Model," *Social Psychology Quarterly* 30 (1987): 277–284.
88. John Lofland, *Deviance and Identity* (Englewood Cliffs, NJ: Prentice-Hall, 1969).
89. Frank Tannenbaum, *Crime and the Community* (New York: Columbia University Press, 1938), pp. 19–20.
90. Edwin Lemert, *Social Pathology* (New York: McGraw-Hill, 1951).
91. Ibid., p. 75.
92. Carl Pope and William Feyerherm, "Minority Status and Juvenile Justice Processing," *Criminal Justice Abstracts* 22 (1990): 327–336. See also Carl Pope, "Race and Crime Revisited," *Crime and Delinquency* 25 (1979): 347–357; National Minority Council on Criminal Justice, *The Inequality of Justice* (Washington, DC: National Minority Advisory Council on Criminal Justice, 1981), p. 200.
93. Scot Wortley, "Justice for All? Race and Perceptions of Bias in the Ontario Criminal Justice System," *Canadian Journal of Criminology* 38 (October 1996): 439–457; Scot Wortley, "Hidden Intersections: Research on Race, Crime, and Criminal Justice in Canada," *Canadian Ethnic Studies* 35 (2003): 99–117; Eric Mills, ed., *Report of the Commission on Systemic Racism in the Ontario Criminal Justice System* (Toronto: Queen's Printer for Ontario, 1995).
94. Howard Kaplan and Robert Johnson, "Negative Social Sanctions and Juvenile Delinquency: Effects of Labeling in a Model of Deviant Behavior," *Social Science Quarterly* 72 (1991): 98–122.
95. Ruth Triplett, "The Conflict Perspective, Symbolic Interactionism, and the Status Characteristics Hypothesis," *Justice Quarterly* 10 (1993): 540–558.
96. Ross Matsueda, "Reflected Appraisals: Parental Labeling, and Delinquency: Specifying a Symbolic Interactionist Theory," *American Journal of Sociology* 97 (1992): 1577–1611.
97. Suzanne Ageton and Delbert Elliott, *The Effect of Legal Processing on Self-Concept* (Boulder, CO: Institute of Behavioral Science, 1973).
98. Christine Bowditch, "Getting Rid of Troublemakers: High School Disciplinary Procedures and the Production of Dropouts," *Social Problems* 40 (1993): 493–507.
99. Melvin Ray and William Downs, "An Empirical Test of Labeling Theory Using Longitudinal Data," *Journal of Research in Crime and Delinquency* 23 (1986): 169–194.
100. Sherman and Smith, with Schmidt and Rogan, "Crime, Punishment, and Stake in Conformity."
101. Charles Tittle, "Two Empirical Regularities (Maybe) in Search of an Explanation: Commentary on the Age/Crime Debate," *Criminology* 26 (1988): 75–85.
102. Robert Sampson and John Laub, "A Life-Course Theory of Cumulative Disadvantage and the Stability of Delinquency," in *Developmental Theories of Crime and Delinquency,* ed. Terence Thornberry (New Brunswick, NJ: Transaction Press, 1997), pp. 133–161; Douglas Smith and Robert Brame, "On the Initiation and Continuation of Delinquency," *Criminology* 4 (1994): 607–630.
103. Raymond Paternoster and Leeann Iovanni, "The Labeling Perspective and Delinquency: An Elaboration of the Theory and an Assessment of the Evidence," *Justice Quarterly* 6 (1989): 358–394.

Chapter 8

1. Michael Lynch, "Rediscovering Criminology: Lessons from the Marxist Tradition," in *Marxist Sociology: Surveys of Contemporary Theory and Research*, eds. Donald McQuarie and Patrick McGuire (New York: General Hall Press, 1994).
2. Michael Lynch and W. Byron Groves, *A Primer in Radical Criminology,* 2nd ed. (Albany, NY: Harrow and Heston, 1989), pp. 32–33.
3. Ibid., p. 4.
4. James Short and F. Ivan Nye, "Extent of Undetected Delinquency: Tentative Conclusions," *Journal of Criminal Law, Criminology, and Police Science* 49 (1958): 296–302.
5. See, generally, Robert Meier, "The New Criminology: Continuity in Criminological Theory," *Journal of Criminal Law and Criminology* 67 (1977): 461–469.
6. David Greenberg, ed., *Crime and Capitalism* (Palo Alto, CA: Mayfield, 1981), p. 3.
7. "Standing Up to the FLQ Terrorists," *Maclean's,* 1 July 1999, p. 51.
8. William Chambliss and Robert Seidman, *Law, Order, and Power* (Reading, MA: Addison-Wesley, 1971), p. 503.
9. John Braithwaite, "Retributivism, Punishment, and Privilege," in *Punishment and Privilege,* eds. W. Byron Groves and Graeme Newman (Albany, NY: Harrow and Heston, 1986), pp. 55–66.
10. John Hagan and Celesta Albonetti, "Race, Class, and the Perception of Criminal Injustice in America," *American Journal of Sociology* 88 (1982): 329–355; Scot Wortley, "Justice for All? Race and Perceptions of Bias in the Ontario Criminal Justice System—A Toronto Survey," *Canadian Journal of Criminology* 38 (October 1996): 439–467.
11. Julian V. Roberts and Ronald Melchers, "The Incarceration of Aboriginal Offenders: Trends from 1978 to 2001," *Canadian Journal of Criminology* 45 (April 2003): 211–256.
12. Nicholas Kohler, Stephanie Findlay, "Life after the G20 Protests," *Maclean's*, 16 August 2010, vol. 123, iss. 31, pp. 26–27; A. Alan Borovoy, "Make Our Police More Accountable: Mass G20 Arrests Showed How Easy It Is to Abuse Power of 'Preventive Detention'" *Toronto Star*, 23 July 2010, p. A19.
13. Austin Turk, *Criminality and Legal Order* (Chicago: Rand McNally, 1969), p. 58.
14. Lynch and Groves, *A Primer in Radical Criminology*, p. 38.
15. David McDowall, "Poverty and Homicide in Detroit, 1926–1978," *Victims and Violence* 1 (1986): 23–34; David McDowall and Sandra Norris, "Poverty and Homicide in Baltimore, Cleveland, and Memphis, 1937–1980," paper presented at the annual meeting of the American Society of Criminology, Montreal, November 1987.
16. Judith Blau and Peter Blau, "The Cost of Inequality: Metropolitan Structure and Violent Crime," *American Sociological Review* 147 (1982): 114–129; Richard Block, "Community Environment and Violent Crime," *Criminology* 17 (1979): 46–57; Robert Sampson, "Structural Sources of Variation in Race-Age-Specific Rates of Offending Across Major U.S. Cities," *Criminology* 23 (1985): 647–673.
17. David Jacobs and David Britt, "Inequality and Police Use of Deadly Force: An Empirical Assessment of a Conflict Hypothesis," *Social Problems* 26 (1979): 403–412.

18. Malcolm Homes, "Minority Threat and Police Brutality: Determinants of Civil Rights Criminal Complaints in U.S. Municipalities," *Criminology* 38 (2000): 343–368.
19. Alan Lizotte, "Extra-Legal Factors in Chicago's Criminal Courts: Testing the Conflict Model of Criminal Justice," *Social Problems* 25 (1978): 564–580.
20. Terance Miethe and Charles Moore, "Racial Differences in Criminal Processing: The Consequences of Model Selection on Conclusions About Differential Treatment," *Sociological Quarterly* 27 (1987): 217–237.
21. Tracy Nobiling, Cassia Spohn, and Miriam DeLone, "A Tale of Two Counties: Unemployment and Sentence Severity," *Justice Quarterly* 15 (1998): 459–485.
22. Nancy Wonders, "Determinate Sentencing: A Feminist and Postmodern Story," *Justice Quarterly* 13 (1996): 610–648; Douglas Smith, Christy Visher, and Laura Davidson, "Equity and Discretionary Justice: The Influence of Race on Police Arrest Decisions," *Journal of Criminal Law and Criminology* 75 (1984): 234–249; Roberts and Melchers, "The Incarceration of Aboriginal Offenders: Trends from 1978 to 2001"; Alison Hatch and Karlene Faith, "The Female Offender in Canada: A Statistical Profile," *Canadian Journal of Women and the Law* 3 (1989): 432–456.
23. Thomas Arvanites, "Increasing Imprisonment: A Function of Crime or Socioeconomic Factors?" *American Journal of Criminal Justice* 17 (1992): 19–38.
24. Michael Leiber, Anne Woodrick, and E. Michele Roudebush, "Religion, Discriminatory Attitudes, and the Orientations of Juvenile Justice Personnel: A Research Note," *Criminology* 33 (1995): 431–447; Michael Leiber and Katherine Jamieson, "Race and Decision Making Within Juvenile Justice: The Importance of Context," *Journal of Quantitative Criminology* 11 (1995): 363–388.
25. Dragan Milovanovic, "Postmodern Criminology: Mapping the Terrain," *Justice Quarterly* 13 (1996): 567–610; Wortley, "Justice for All? Race and Perceptions of Bias in the Ontario Criminal Justice System—A Toronto Survey"; Commission on Systemic Racism in the Ontario Criminal Justice System, *Report of the Commission on Systemic Racism in the Ontario Criminal Justice System* (Toronto: Queen's Printer for Ontario, 1995); Zhongping Chen, "Chinese Minority and Everyday Racism in Canadian Towns and Small Cities: An Ethnic Study of the Case of Peterborough, Ontario, 1892–1951," *Canadian Ethnic Studies* (36) 1 (2004): 71–91.
26. Ian Taylor, Paul Walton, and Jock Young, *The New Criminology: For a Social Theory of Deviance* (London: Routledge and Kegan Paul, 1973).
27. See, for example, Larry Tifft and Dennis Sullivan, *The Struggle to Be Human: Crime, Criminology, and Anarchism* (Over-the-Water-Sanday, Scotland: Cienfuegos Press, 1979); Dennis Sullivan, *The Mask of Love* (Port Washington, NY: Kennikat Press, 1980).
28. Lynch and Groves, *A Primer in Radical Criminology*, p. 6.
29. This section borrows heavily from Richard Sparks, "A Critique of Marxist Criminology," in *Crime and Justice,* vol. 2, eds. Norval Morris and Michael Tonry (Chicago: University of Chicago Press, 1980), pp. 159–208.
30. Barbara Sims, "Crime, Punishment, and the American Dream: Toward a Marxist Integration," *Journal of Research in Crime and Delinquency* 34 (1997): 5–24.
31. Jeffery Reiman, *The Rich Get Richer and the Poor Get Prison* (New York: Wiley, 1984), pp. 43–44.
32. For a general review of Marxist criminology, see Lynch and Groves, *A Primer in Radical Criminology.*
33. Sims, "Crime, Punishment, and the American Dream."
34. Robert Bohm, "Radical Criminology: Back to the Basics," paper presented at the annual meeting of the American Society of Criminology, Phoenix, Arizona, November 1993, p. 2.
35. Ibid., p. 4.
36. Lynch and Groves, *A Primer in Radical Criminology*, p. 7.
37. W. Byron Groves and Robert Sampson, "Critical Theory and Criminology," *Social Problems* 33 (1986): 58–80.
38. Gregg Barak, "'Crimes of the Homeless' or the 'Crime of Homelessness': A Self-Reflexive, New-Marxist Analysis of Crime and Social Control," paper presented at the annual meeting of the American Society of Criminology, Montreal, November 1987.
39. Michael Lynch, "Assessing the State of Radical Criminology: Toward the Year 2000," paper presented at the annual meeting of the American Society of Criminology, Phoenix, Arizona, November 1993.
40. Steven Box, *Recession, Crime, and Unemployment* (London: MacMillan, 1987).
41. David Barlow, Melissa Hickman-Barlow, and W. Wesley Johnson, "The Political Economy of Criminal Justice Policy: A Time-Series Analysis of Economic Conditions, Crime, and Federal Criminal Justice Legislation, 1948–1987," *Justice Quarterly* 13 (1996): 223–241.
42. Mahesh Nalla, Michael Lynch, and Michael Leiber, "Determinants of Police Growth in Phoenix, 1950–1988," *Justice Quarterly* 14 (1997): 144–163.
43. Gresham Sykes, "The Rise of Critical Criminology," *Journal of Criminal Law and Criminology* 65 (1974): 211–229.
44. David Jacobs, "Corporate Economic Power and the State: A Longitudinal Assessment of Two Explanations," *American Journal of Sociology* 93 (1988): 852–881.
45. Harold Levy, "Professor Saw Police Beat Protester," *Toronto Star,* 23 April 2003, p. B4; Bryan Palmer, "The Riot Act: Reviving Protest in Ontario," *Canadian Dimension* 34 (September/October 2000): 29–33.
46. Richard Quinney, "Crime Control in Capitalist Society," in *Critical Criminology,* ed. Ian Taylor, Paul Walton, and Jock Young (London: Routledge and Kegan Paul, 1975), p. 199.
47. Ibid.
48. John Hagan, *Structural Criminology* (New Brunswick, NJ: Rutgers University Press, 1989), pp. 110–119.
49. Roy Bhaskar, "Empiricism," in *A Dictionary of Marxist Thought,* ed. T. Bottomore (Cambridge, MA: Harvard University Press, 1983), pp. 149–150.
50. Byron Groves, "Marxism and Positivism," *Crime and Social Justice* 23 (1985): 129–150; Michael Lynch, "Quantitative Analysis and Marxist Criminology: Some Old Answers to a Dilemma in Marxist Criminology," *Crime and Social Justice* 29 (1987): 110–117.
51. Alan Lizotte, James Mercy, and Eric Monkkonen, "Crime and Police Strength in an Urban Setting: Chicago, 1947–1970," in *Quantitative Criminology,* ed. John Hagan (Beverly Hills, CA: Sage, 1982), pp. 129–148.
52. William Chambliss, "The State, the Law, and the Definition of Behavior as Criminal or Delinquent," in *Handbook of Criminology,* ed. D. Glazer (Chicago: Rand McNally, 1974), pp. 7–44.
53. Timothy Carter and Donald Clelland, "A Neo-Marxian Critique, Formulation, and Test of Juvenile Dispositions as a Function of Social Class," *Social Problems* 27 (1979): 96–108.
54. David Greenberg, "Socio-Economic Status and Criminal Sentences: Is There an Association?" *American Sociological*

Review 42 (1977): 174–175; David Greenberg and Drew Humphries, "The Co-optation of Fixed Sentencing Reform," *Crime and Delinquency* 26 (1980): 206–225.

55. Steven Box, *Power, Crime and Mystification* (London: Tavistock, 1984); Gregg Barak, *In Defense of Whom? A Critique of Criminal Justice Reform* (Cincinnati: Anderson, 1980). For an opposing view, see Franklin Williams, "Conflict Theory and Differential Processing: An Analysis of the Research Literature," in *Radical Criminology: The Coming Crisis,* ed. J. Inciardi (Beverly Hills, CA: Sage, 1980), pp. 213–231.
56. Michael Rustigan, "A Reinterpretation of Criminal Law Reform in Nineteenth-Century England," in *Crime and Capitalism,* ed. D. Greenberg (Palo Alto, CA: Mayfield, 1981), pp. 255–278.
57. Rosalind Petchesky, "At Hard Labor: Penal Confinement and Production in Nineteenth-Century America," in *Crime and Capitalism,* ed. D. Greenberg (Palo Alto, CA: Mayfield, 1981), pp. 341–357; Paul Takagi, "The Walnut Street Jail: A Penal Reform to Centralize the Powers of the State," *Federal Probation* 49 (1975): 18–26.
58. Jack Gibbs, "An Incorrigible Positivist," *Criminologist* 12 (1987): 2–3.
59. Jackson Toby, "The New Criminology Is the Old Sentimentality," *Criminology* 16 (1979): 513–526.
60. Richard Sparks, "A Critique of Marxist Criminology," in *Crime and Justice,* vol. 2, eds. Norval Morris and Michael Tonry (Chicago: University of Chicago Press, 1980), pp. 159–208.
61. Carl Klockars, "The Contemporary Crises of Marxist Criminology," in *Radical Criminology: The Coming Crisis,* ed. J. Inciardi (Beverly Hills, CA: Sage, 1980), pp. 92–123.
62. Ibid.
63. Michael Lynch, W. Byron Groves, and Alan Lizotte, "The Rate of Surplus Value and Crime: A Theoretical and Empirical Examination of Marxian Economic Theory and Criminology," *Crime, Law, and Social Change* 18 (1994): 1–11.
64. Anthony Platt, "Criminology in the 1980s: Progressive Alternatives to 'Law and Order,'" *Crime and Social Justice* 21–22 (1985): 191–199.
65. See, generally, Roger Matthews and Jock Young, eds., *Confronting Crime* (London: Sage, 1986); for a thorough review of left realism, see Martin Schwartz and Walter DeKeseredy, "Left Realist Criminology: Strengths, Weaknesses, and the Feminist Critique," *Crime, Law, and Social Change* 15 (1991): 51–72.
66. John Lea and Jock Young, *What Is to Be Done About Law and Order?* (Harmondsworth, England: Penguin, 1984).
67. Ibid., p. 88.
68. Richard Kinsey, John Lea, and Jock Young, *Losing the Fight Against Crime* (London: Blackwell, 1986).
69. Martin Schwartz and Walter DeKeseredy, *Contemporary Criminology* (Belmont, CA: Wadsworth, 1993), p. 249.
70. Schwartz and DeKeseredy, "Left Realist Criminology."
71. For a general review of this issue, see Kathleen Daly and Meda Chesney-Lind, "Feminism and Criminology," *Justice Quarterly* 5 (1988): 497–538; Douglas Smith and Raymond Paternoster, "The Gender Gap in Theories of Deviance: Issues and Evidence," *Journal of Research in Crime and Delinquency* 24 (1987): 140–172; and Pat Carlen, "Women, Crime, Feminism, and Realism," *Social Justice* 17 (1990): 106–123.
72. Herman Schwendinger and Julia Schwendinger, *Rape and Inequality* (Newbury Park, CA: Sage, 1983).
73. Daly and Chesney-Lind, "Feminism and Criminology."
74. Janet Saltzman Chafetz, "Feminist Theory and Sociology: Underutilized Contributions for Mainstream Theory," *Annual Review of Sociology* 23 (1997): 97–121.
75. Ibid.
76. James Messerschmidt, *Capitalism, Patriarchy, and Crime* (Totowa, NJ: Rowman and Littlefield, 1986); for a critique of this work, see Herman Schwendinger and Julia Schwendinger, "The World According to James Messerschmidt," *Social Justice* 15 (1988): 123–145.
77. Kathleen Daly, "Gender and Varieties of White-Collar Crime," *Criminology* 27 (1989): 769–793.
78. Jane Roberts Chapman, "Violence Against Women as a Violation of Human Rights," *Social Justice* 17 (1990): 54–71.
79. James Messerschmidt, *Masculinities and Crime: Critique and Reconceptualization of Theory* (Lanham, MD: Rowman and Littlefield, 1993).
80. Suzie Dod Thomas and Nancy Stein, "Criminality, Imprisonment, and Women's Rights in the 1990s," *Social Justice* 17 (1990): 1–5.
81. Walter DeKeseredy and Martin Schwartz, "Male Peer Support and Woman Abuse: An Expansion of DeKeseredy's Model," *Sociological Spectrum* 13 (1993): 393–413.
82. Daly and Chesney-Lind, "Feminism and Criminology." See also Drew Humphries and Susan Caringella-MacDonald, "Murdered Mothers, Missing Wives: Reconsidering Female Victimization," *Social Justice* 17 (1990): 71–78.
83. Jane Siegel and Linda Meyer Williams, "Aggressive Behavior Among Women Sexually Abused as Children," paper presented at the annual meeting of the American Society of Criminology, Phoenix, Arizona, 1993, revised version.
84. Susan Ehrlich Martin and Nancy Jurik, *Doing Justice, Doing Gender* (Thousand Oaks, CA: Sage, 1996), p. 27.
85. Ruth Alexander, *The "Girl Problem": Female Sexual Delinquency in New York, 1900–1930* (Ithaca, NY: Cornell University Press, 1995).
86. Joan Sangster, "Girls in Conflict with the Law: Exploring the Construction of Female 'Delinquency' in Ontario, 1940–60," *Canadian Journal of Women and the Law* 12 (2000): 1–31.
87. Meda Chesney-Lind, "Judicial Enforcement of the Female Sex Role: The Family Court and the Female Delinquent," *Issues in Criminology* 8 (1973): 51–69. See also Meda Chesney-Lind, "Women and Crime: The Female Offender," *Signs: Journal of Women in Culture and Society* 12 (1986): 78–96; "Female Offenders: Paternalism Reexamined," in *Women, the Courts, and Equality,* eds. Laura L. Crites and Winifred L. Hepperle (Newbury Park, CA: Sage, 1987): 114–139; "Girls' Crime and a Woman's Place: Toward a Feminist Model of Female Delinquency," paper presented at the annual meeting of the American Society of Criminology, Montreal, 1987.
88. Hagan, *Structural Criminology*.
89. John Hagan, A. R. Gillis, and John Simpson, "The Class Structure and Delinquency: Toward a Power-Control Theory of Common Delinquent Behavior," *American Journal of Sociology* 90 (1985): 1151–1178; John Hagan, John Simpson, and A. R. Gillis, "Class in the Household: A Power-Control Theory of Gender and Delinquency," *American Journal of Sociology* 92 (1987): 788–816.
90. Brenda Sims Blackwell, "Perceived Sanction Threats, Gender, and Crime: A Test and Elaboration of Power-Control Theory," *Criminology* 38 (2000): 439–488.
91. See, generally, Lynch, "Rediscovering Criminology," pp. 27–28.
92. Lori D. Moore and Irene Padavic, "Racial and Ethnic Disparities in Girls' Sentencing in the Juvenile Justice System," *Feminist*

Criminology, vol. 5, iss. 3 (July 2010): 263–285.

93. See, generally, Stuart Henry and Dragan Milovanovic, *Constitutive Criminology: Beyond Postmodernism* (London: Sage, 1996).
94. Dragan Milovanovic, *A Primer in the Sociology of Law* (Albany, NY: Harrow and Heston, 1988), pp. 127–128.
95. See, generally, Henry and Milovanovic, *Constitutive Criminology*.
96. Bruce Arrigo and Thomas Bernard, "Postmodern Criminology in Relation to Radical and Conflict Criminology," *Critical Criminology* 8 (1997): 39–60; M. Allen, "Violence and Voice: Using a Feminist Constructivist Grounded Theory to Explore Women's Resistance to Abuse," *Qualitative Research* 11 (1) (2011): 23–45.
97. See, for example, Tifft and Sullivan, *The Struggle to Be Human*; Sullivan, *The Mask of Love*.
98. Larry Tifft, "Foreword," in Sullivan, *The Mask of Love*, p. 6.
99. Sullivan, *The Mask of Love*, p. 141.
100. Richard Quinney, "The Way of Peace: On Crime, Suffering, and Service," in *Criminology as Peacemaking*, eds. Harold Pepinsky and Richard Quinney (Bloomington: Indiana University Press, 1991), pp. 8–9.
101. Kathleen Daly and Russ Immarigeon, "The Past, Present, and Future of Restorative Justice: Some Critical Reflections," *Contemporary Justice Review* 1 (1998): 21–45.
102. Gene Stephens, "The Future of Policing: From a War Model to a Peace Model," in *The Past, Present and Future of American Criminal Justice*, eds. Brendan Maguire and Polly Radosh (Dix Hills, NY: General Hall, 1996), pp. 77–93; The Effectiveness of Restorative Justice Practices: A Meta-Analysis (2010) retrieved 27 July 2011 from http://www.justice.gc.ca/eng/pi/rs/rep-rap/2001/rp01_1-dr01_1/p5.html.
103. Daly and Immarigeon, "The Past, Present, and Future of Restorative Justice," p. 26.
104. Kay Pranis, "Peacemaking Circles: Restorative Justice in Practice Allows Victims and Offenders to Begin Repairing the Harm," *Corrections Today* 59 (1997): 74.
105. Carol LaPrairie, "The 'New' Justice: Some Implications for Aboriginal Communities," *Canadian Journal of Criminology* 40 (1998): 61–79.
106. Adapted from Kay Pranis, "Peacemaking Circles."

Chapter 9

1. Gerald Patterson and Karen Yoerger, "Developmental Models for Delinquent Behavior," in *Mental Disorder and Crime*, ed. Sheilagh Hodgins (Newbury Park, CA: Sage, 1993), pp. 150–159.
2. James Q. Wilson and Richard Herrnstein, *Crime and Human Nature* (New York: Simon and Schuster, 1985).
3. David Rowe, D. Wayne Osgood, and W. Alan Nicewander, "A Latent Trait Approach to Unifying Criminal Careers," *Criminology* 28 (1990): 237–270.
4. Lee Ellis, "Neurohormonal Bases of Varying Tendencies to Learn Delinquent and Criminal Behavior," in *Behavioral Approaches to Crime and Delinquency*, ed. E. Morris and C. Braukmann (New York: Plenum, 1988), pp. 499–518.
5. David Rowe, Alexander Vazsonyi, and Daniel Flannery, "Sex Differences in Crime: Do Means and Within-Sex Variation Have Similar Causes?" *Journal of Research in Crime and Delinquency 32* (1995): 84–100.
6. Michael Gottfredson and Travis Hirschi, *A General Theory of Crime* (Stanford, CA: Stanford University Press, 1990).
7. Ibid., p. 27.
8. Ibid., p. 90.
9. Ibid., p. 89.
10. Alex Piquero and Stephen Tibbetts, "Specifying the Direct and Indirect Effects of Low Self-Control and Situational Factors in Offenders' Decision Making: Toward a More Complete Model of Rational Offending," *Justice Quarterly* 13 (1996): 481–508.
11. David Forde and Leslie Kennedy, "Risky Lifestyles, Routine Activities, and the General Theory of Crime," *Justice Quarterly* 14 (1997): 265–294.
12. Marianne Junger and Richard Tremblay, "Self-Control, Accidents, and Crime," *Criminal Justice and Behavior* 26 (1999): 485–501.
13. Gottfredson and Hirschi, *A General Theory of Crime*, p. 112.
14. Ibid.
15. Dennis Giever, "An Empirical Assessment of the Core Elements of Gottfredson and Hirschi's General Theory of Crime," paper presented at the annual meeting of the American Society of Criminology, Boston, November 1995.
16. Robert Agnew, "The Contribution of Social-Psychological Strain Theory to the Explanation of Crime and Delinquency," *Advances in Criminological Theory* 6 (1994): 211–213.
17. David Brownfield and Ann Marie Sorenson, "Self-Control and Juvenile Delinquency: Theoretical Issues and an Empirical Assessment of Selected Elements of a General Theory of Crime," *Deviant Behavior* 14 (1993): 243–264; Harold Grasmick, Charles Tittle, Robert Bursik, and Bruce Arneklev, "Testing the Core Empirical Implications of Gottfredson and Hirschi's General Theory of Crime," *Journal of Research in Crime and Delinquency* 30 (1993): 5–29; John Cochran, Peter Wood, and Bruce Arneklev, "Is the Religiosity–Delinquency Relationship Spurious? A Test of Arousal and Social Control Theories," *Journal of Research in Crime and Delinquency* 31 (1994): 92–123; Marc LeBlanc, Marc Ouimet, and Richard Tremblay, "An Integrative Control Theory of Delinquent Behavior: A Validation 1976–1985," *Psychiatry* 51 (1988): 164–176.
18. Byongook Moon, John D. McCluskey, and Cynthia Perez McCluskey, "A General Theory of Crime and Computer Crime: An Empirical Test." *Journal of Criminal Justice*, July 2010, 38 (4) April 2010: 767–772.
19. Christian Seipel and Stefanie Eifler, "Opportunities, Rational Choice, and Self-Control: On the Interaction of Person and Situation in a General Theory of Crime," *Crime & Delinquency*, 56 (2) April 2010: 167–197.
20. Xiaogang Deng and Lening Zhang, "Correlates of Self-Control: An Empirical Test of Self-Control Theory," *Journal of Crime and Justice* 21 (1998): 89–103.
21. Alex Piquero, Raymond Paternoster, Paul Mazeroole, Robert Brame, and Charles Dean, "Onset Age and Offense Specialization," *Journal of Research in Crime and Delinquency* 36 (1999): 275–299.
22. Carl Keane, Paul Maxim, and James Teevan, "Drinking and Driving, Self-Control, and Gender: Testing a General Theory of Crime," *Journal of Research in Crime and Delinquency* 30 (1993): 30–46.
23. David Brownfield and Ann Marie Sorenson, "Self-Control and Juvenile Delinquency: Theoretical Issues and an Empirical Assessment of Selected Elements of a General Theory of Crime," *Deviant Behavior* 14 (1993): 243–264; John Cochran, Peter Wood, and Bruce Arneklev, "Is the Religiosity–Delinquency Relationship Spurious? A Test of Arousal and Social Control Theories," *Journal of Research in Crime and Delinquency* 31 (1994): 92–123.
24. Velmer Burton, T. David Evans, Francis Cullen, Kathleen Olivares, and R. Gregory

Dunaway, "Age, Self-Control, and Adults' Offending Behaviors: A Research Note Assessing a General Theory of Crime," *Journal of Criminal Justice* 27 (1999): 45–54; John Gibbs and Dennis Giever, "Self-Control and Its Manifestations Among University Students: An Empirical Test of Gottfredson and Hirschi's General Theory," *Justice Quarterly* 12 (1995): 231–255.
25. Carey Herbert, "The Implications of Self-Control Theory for Workplace Offending," paper presented at the annual meeting of the American Society of Criminology, San Diego, 1997.
26. Dennis Giever, Dana Lynskey, and Danette Monnet, "Gottfredson and Hirschi's General Theory of Crime and Youth Gangs: An Empirical Test on a Sample of Middle School Youth," paper presented at the annual meeting of the American Society of Criminology, San Diego, 1997.
27. Douglas Longshore, Susan Turner, and Judith Stein, "Self-Control in a Criminal Sample: An Examination of Construct Validity," *Criminology* 34 (1996): 209–228.
28. Deng and Zhang, "Correlates of Self-Control: An Empirical Test of Self-Control Theory."
29. Linda Pagani, Richard Tremblay, Frank Vitaro, and Sophie Parent, "Does Preschool Help Prevent Delinquency in Boys with a History of Perinatal Complications?" *Criminology* 36 (1998): 245–268.
30. Velmer Burton, Francis Cullen, T. David Evans, Leanne Fiftal Alarid, and R. Gregory Dunaway, "Gender, Self-Control, and Crime," *Journal of Research in Crime and Delinquency* 35 (1998): 123–147.
31. John Gibbs, Dennis Giever, and Jamie Martin, "Parental Management and Self-Control: An Empirical Test of Gottfredson and Hirschi's General Theory," *Journal of Research in Crime and Delinquency* 35 (1998): 40–70.
32. Vic Bumphus and James Anderson, "Family Structure and Race in a Sample of Offenders," *Journal of Criminal Justice* 27 (1999): 309–320.
33. Christopher Schreck, "Criminal Victimization and Low Self-Control: An Extension and Test of a General Theory of Crime," *Justice Quarterly* 16 (1999): 633–654.
34. Michael Benson and Elizabeth Moore, "Are White-Collar and Common Offenders the Same? An Empirical and Theoretical Critique of a Recently Proposed General Theory of Crime," *Journal of Research in Crime and Delinquency* 29 (1992): 251–272.
35. Ronald Akers, "Self-Control as a General Theory of Crime," *Journal of Quantitative Criminology* 7 (1991): 201–211.
36. Alan Feingold, "Gender Differences in Personality: A Meta Analysis," *Psychological Bulletin* 116 (1994): 429–456.
37. Gottfredson and Hirschi, *A General Theory of Crime,* p. 153.
38. Scott Menard, Delbert Elliott, and Sharon Wofford, "Social Control Theories in Developmental Perspective," *Studies on Crime and Crime Prevention* 2 (1993): 69–87.
39. Charles R. Tittle and Harold G. Grasmick, "Criminal Behavior and Age: A Test of Three Provocative Hypotheses," *Journal of Criminal Law and Criminology* 88 (1997): 309–342.
40. Douglas Longshore, "Self-Control and Criminal Opportunity: A Prospective Test of the General Theory of Crime," *Social Problems* 45 (1998): 102–114.
41. Otwin Marenin and Michael Resig, "A General Theory of Crime and Patterns of Crime in Nigeria: An Exploration of Methodological Assumptions," *Journal of Criminal Justice* 23 (1995): 501–518.
42. Bruce Arneklev, Harold Grasmick, Charles Tittle, and Robert Bursik, "Low Self-Control and Imprudent Behavior," *Journal of Quantitative Criminology* 9 (1993): 225–246.
43. Kevin Thompson, "Sexual Harassment and Low Self-Control: An Application of Gottfredson and Hirschi's General Theory of Crime," paper presented at the annual meeting of the American Society of Criminology, Phoenix, Arizona, November 1993.
44. Charles Tittle, *Control Balance: Toward a General Theory of Deviance* (Boulder, CO: Westview, 1995).
45. Marvin Krohn, Alan Lizotte, and Cynthia Perez, "The Interrelationship Between Substance Use and Precocious Transitions to Adult Sexuality," *Journal of Health and Social Behavior* 38 (1997): 87–103, at p. 88.
46. G. R. Patterson, Barbara DeBaryshe, and Elizabeth Ramsey, "A Developmental Perspective on Antisocial Behavior," *American Psychologist* 44 (1989): 329–335.
47. Joan McCord, "Family Relationships, Juvenile Delinquency, and Adult Criminality," *Criminology* 29 (1991): 397–417.
48. Paul Mazerolle, "Delinquent Definitions and Participation Age: Assessing the Invariance Hypothesis," *Studies on Crime and Crime Prevention* 6 (1997): 151–168.
49. See, generally, Sheldon Glueck and Eleanor Glueck, *500 Criminal Careers* (New York: Knopf, 1930); Sheldon Glueck and Eleanor Glueck, *One Thousand Juvenile Delinquents* (Cambridge, MA: Harvard University Press, 1934); Sheldon Glueck and Eleanor Glueck, *Predicting Delinquency and Crime* (Cambridge, MA: Harvard University Press, 1967), pp. 82–83.
50. Sheldon Glueck and Eleanor Glueck, *Unraveling Juvenile Delinquency* (Cambridge, MA: Harvard University Press, 1950).
51. Ibid., p. 48.
52. Rolf Loeber and Marc LeBlanc, "Toward a Developmental Criminology," in *Crime and Justice,* vol. 12, ed. Norval Morris and Michael Tonry (Chicago: University of Chicago Press, 1990), pp. 375–473; Rolf Loeber and Marc LeBlanc, "Developmental Criminology Updated," in *Crime and Justice,* vol. 23, ed. Michael Tonry (Chicago: University of Chicago Press, 1998), pp. 115–198.
53. G. R. Patterson, L. Crosby, and S. Vuchinich, "Predicting Risk for Early Police Arrest," *Journal of Quantitative Criminology* 8 (1992): 335–355; Rolf Loeber, Magda Stouthamer-Loeber, Welmoet Van Kammen, and David Farrington, "Initiation, Escalation, and Desistance in Juvenile Offending and Their Correlates," *Journal of Criminal Law and Criminology* 82 (1991): 36–82.
54. Raymond Paternoster, Charles Dean, Alex Piquero, Paul Mazerolle, and Robert Brame, "Generality, Continuity, and Change in Offending," *Journal of Quantitative Criminology* 13 (1997): 231–266.
55. Magda Stouthamer-Loeber and Evelyn Wei, "The Precursors of Young Fatherhood and Its Effect on Delinquency of Teenage Males," *Journal of Adolescent Health* 22 (1998): 56–65; Richard Jessor, John Donovan, and Francis Costa, *Beyond Adolescence: Problem Behavior and Young Adult Development* (New York: Cambridge University Press, 1991).
56. Marvin Krohn, Alan Lizotte, and Cynthia Perez, "The Interrelationship Between Substance Use and Precocious Transitions to Adult Sexuality," *Journal of Health and Social Behavior* 38 (1997): 87–103, at p. 88; Richard Jessor, "Risk Behavior in Adolescence: A Psychosocial Framework for Understanding and Action," in *Adolescents at Risk: Medical and Social Perspectives,* ed. D. E. Rogers and E. Ginzburg (Boulder, CO: Westview, 1992).
57. Deborah Capaldi and Gerald Patterson, "Can Violent Offenders Be Distinguished from Frequent Offenders: Prediction from Childhood to Adolescence," *Journal of*

Research in Crime and Delinquency 33 (1996): 206–231; D. Wayne Osgood, "The Covariation Among Adolescent Problem Behaviors," paper presented at the annual meeting of the American Society of Criminology, Baltimore, November 1990.

58. Terence Thornberry, Carolyn Smith, and Gregory Howard, "Risk Factors for Teenage Fatherhood," *Journal of Marriage and the Family* 59 (1997): 505–522; Todd Miller, Timothy Smith, Charles Turner, Margarita Guijarro, and Amanda Hallet, "A Meta-Analytic Review of Research on Hostility and Physical Health," *Psychological Bulletin* 119 (1996): 322–348; Marianne Junger, "Accidents and Crime," in *The Generality of Deviance,* ed. T. Hirschi and M. Gottfredson (New Brunswick, NJ: Transaction Press, 1993).
59. Robert Johnson, S. Susan Su, Dean Gerstein, Hee-Choon Shin, and John Hoffman, "Parental Influences on Deviant Behavior in Early Adolescence: A Logistic Response Analysis of Age- and Gender-Differentiated Effects," *Journal of Quantitative Criminology* 11 (1995): 167–192; Judith Brooks, Martin Whiteman, and Patricia Cohen, "Stage of Drug Use, Aggression, and Theft/Vandalism," in *Drugs, Crime and Other Deviant Adaptations: Longitudinal Studies,* ed. Howard Kaplan (New York: Plenum, 1995), pp. 83–96; Robert Hoge, D. A. Andrews, and Alan Leschied, "Tests of Three Hypotheses Regarding the Predictors of Delinquency," *Journal of Abnormal Child Psychology* 22 (1994): 547–559.
60. David Huizinga, Rolf Loeber, and Terence Thornberry, "Longitudinal Study of Delinquency, Drug Use, Sexual Activity, and Pregnancy Among Children and Youth in Three Cities," *Public Health Reports* 108 (1993): 90–96.
61. Rolf Loeber, Phen Wung, Kate Keenan, Bruce Giroux, Magda Stouthamer-Loeber, Wemoet Van Kammen, and Barbara Maughan, "Developmental Pathways in Disruptive Behavior," *Development and Psychopathology* (1993): 12–48.
62. Amy D'Unger, Kenneth Land, Patricia McCall, and Daniel Nagin, "How Many Latent Classes of Delinquent/Criminal Careers? Results from Mixed Poisson Regression Analyses," *American Journal of Sociology* 103 (1998): 1593–1630.
63. Terrie Moffitt, "Natural Histories of Delinquency," in *Cross-National Longitudinal Research on Human Development and Criminal Behavior,* ed. Elmar Weitekamp and Hans-Jurgen Kerner (Dordrecht, Netherlands: Kluwer, 1994), pp. 3–65.
64. Michael Newcomb, "Pseudomaturity Among Adolescents: Construct Validation, Sex Differences, and Associations in Adulthood," *Journal of Drug Issues* 26 (1996): 477–504.
65. Rolf Loeber and Magda Stouthamer-Loeber, "Development of Juvenile Aggression and Violence," *American Psychologist* 53 (1998): 242–259.
66. Terrie Moffitt, "Adolescence-Limited and Life-Course-Persistent Antisocial Behavior: A Developmental Taxonomy," *Psychological Review* 100 (1993): 674–701.
67. David Fergusson, L. John Horwood, and Daniel Nagin, "Offending Trajectories in a New Zealand Birth Cohort," *Criminology* 38 (2000): 525–551.
68. Ronald Simons, Chyi-In Wu, Rand Conger, and Frederick Lorenz, "Two Routes to Delinquency: Differences Between Early and Later Starters in the Impact of Parenting and Deviant Careers," *Criminology* 32 (1994): 247–275; A. K. Ward, D. M. Day, I. Bevc, Ye Sun, J. S. Rosenthal, and T. Duchesne, "Criminal Trajectories and Risk Factors in a Canadian Sample of Offenders," *Criminal Justice and Behavior* 37 (11): 1278–1300.
69. Mark Lipsey and James Derzon, "Predictors of Violent or Serious Delinquency in Adolescence and Early Adulthood: A Synthesis of Longitudinal Research," in *Serious and Violent Juvenile Offenders: Risk Factors and Successful Interventions,* ed. Rolf Loeber and David Farrington (Thousand Oaks, CA: Sage, 1998).
70. G. R. Patterson and Karen Yoerger, "Differentiating Outcomes and Histories for Early and Late Onset Arrests," paper presented at the annual meeting of the American Society of Criminology, Phoenix, Arizona, November 1993.
71. Marshall Jones and Donald Jones, "The Contagious Nature of Antisocial Behavior," *Criminology* 38 (2000): 25–46.
72. See, for example, the Rochester Youth Development Study, Hindelang Criminal Justice Research Center, 135 Western Avenue, Albany, New York 12222.
73. David Farrington, "The Development of Offending and Antisocial Behavior from Childhood to Adulthood," paper presented at the Congress on Rethinking Delinquency, University of Minho, Braga, Portugal, July 1992.
74. Joseph Weis and J. David Hawkins, *Reports of the National Juvenile Assessment Centers: Preventing Delinquency* (Washington, DC: U.S. Department of Justice, 1981); Joseph Weis and John Sederstrom, *Reports of the National Juvenile Justice Assessment Centers: The Prevention of Serious Delinquency: What to Do* (Washington, DC: U.S. Department of Justice, 1981).
75. Julie O'Donnell, J. David Hawkins, and Robert Abbott, "Predicting Serious Delinquency and Substance Use Among Aggressive Boys," *Journal of Consulting and Clinical Psychology* 63 (1995): 529–537.
76. Terence Thornberry, "Toward an Interactional Theory of Delinquency," *Criminology* 25 (1987): 863–891.
77. Ross Matsueda and Kathleen Anderson, "The Dynamics of Delinquent Peers and Delinquent Behavior," *Criminology* 36 (1998): 269–308.
78. Thornberry, "Toward an Interactional Theory of Delinquency."
79. Ibid., p. 863.
80. Terrence Thornberry, Alan Lizotte, Marvin Krohn, Margaret Farnworth, and Sung Joon Jang, *Delinquent Peers, Beliefs, and Delinquent Behavior: A Longitudinal Test of Interactional Theory,* working paper no. 6, rev, Rochester Youth Development Study (Albany, NY: Hindelang Criminal Justice Research Center, 1992), pp. 628–629.
81. Robert Sampson and John Laub, *Crime in the Making: Pathways and Turning Points Through Life* (Cambridge, MA: Harvard University Press, 1993); John Laub and Robert Sampson, "Turning Points in the Life Course: Why Change Matters to the Study of Crime," paper presented at the annual meeting of the American Society of Criminology, New Orleans, November 1992.
82. Terri Orbuch, James House, Richard Mero, and Pamela Webster, "Marital Quality Over the Life Course," *Social Psychology Quarterly* 59 (1996): 162–171; Lee Lillard and Linda Waite, "'Til Death Do Us Part: Marital Disruption and Mortality," *American Journal of Sociology* 100 (1995): 1131–1156.
83. Mark Warr, "Life-Course Transitions and Desistance from Crime," *Criminology* 36 (1998): 183–216.
84. Pamela Webster, Terri Orbuch, and James House, "Effects of Childhood Family Background on Adult Marital Quality and Perceived Stability," *American Journal of Sociology* 101 (1995): 404–432.
85. John Hagan, Ross MacMillan, and Blair Wheaton, "New Kid in Town: Social Capital and the Life Course Effects of Family Migration on Children," *American Sociological Review* 61 (1996): 368–385.

86. Sampson and Laub, *Crime in the Making,* p. 249.
87. Raymond Paternoster and Robert Brame, "Multiple Routes to Delinquency? A Test of Developmental and General Theories of Crime," *Criminology* 35 (1997): 49–84.
88. Robert Hoge, D. A. Andrews, and Alan Leschied, "An Investigation of Risk and Protective Factors in a Sample of Youthful Offenders," *Journal of Child Psychology and Psychiatry* 37 (1996): 419–424.
89. Candace Kruttschnitt, Christopher Uggen, and Kelly Shelton, "Individual Variability in Sex Offending and Its Relationship to Informal and Formal Social Controls," paper presented at the annual meeting of the American Society of Criminology, San Diego, 1997; Mark Collins and Don Weatherburn, "Unemployment and the Dynamics of Offender Populations," *Journal of Quantitative Criminology* 11 (1995): 231–245.
90. Avshalom Caspi, Terrie Moffitt, Bradley Entner Wright, and Phil Silva, "Early Failure in the Labor Market: Childhood and Adolescent Predictors of Unemployment in the Transition to Adulthood," *American Sociological Review* 63 (1998): 424–451.
91. Erich Labouvie, "Maturing Out of Substance Use: Selection and Self-Correction," *Journal of Drug Issues* 26 (1996): 457–474.
92. Mark Warr, "Life-Course Transitions and Desistance from Crime," *Criminology* 36 (1998): 502–535.
93. Robert Sampson and John Laub, "Socioeconomic Achievement in the Life Course of Disadvantaged Men: Military Service as a Turning Point, circa 1940–1965," *American Sociological Review* 61 (1996): 347–367.
94. Daniel Nagin and Raymond Paternoster, "Personal Capital and Social Control: The Deterrence Implications of a Theory of Criminal Offending," *Criminology* 32 (1994): 581–606.
95. John Laub, "Crime Over the Life Course," *Poverty Research News,* Newsletter of the Northwestern University/University of Chicago Joint Center for Poverty Research, vol. 4, no. 3 (May–June 2000).
96. Ibid.

Chapter 10

1. Gabrielle Giroday, "Homicide Unit Now Probing Brutal Beating at Pizza Shop," *Winnipeg Free Press*, 17 May 2011, p. B2.
2. David Courtwright, "Violence in America," *American Heritage* 47 (1996): 36.
3. D. M. Mares, "Civilization, Economic Change, and Trends in Interpersonal Violence in Western Societies. *Theoretical Criminology, 13* (4), 419–449.
4. Walter Gibbs and Alister Doyle, "Blast, Shootings Rock Norway; At Least 87 Dead; Arrested Man Had Right-Wing Links, Reports Say," *The Gazette* [Montreal] 23 July 2011, p. 14; Heidi Blake, "Physical Signs of Utoeya Massacre Gone, But Island's Name Stained; Public Makes First Painful Journey to Island Where 69 People Were Killed," *The Vancouver Sun* [Vancouver, B.C] 24 August 2011, p. 6.
5. CBC News, "Gunman Dead in Montreal School Rampage, 13 September 2006," http://www.cbc.ca/news/canada/story/2006/09/13/shots-dawson.html (accessed 3 August 2011).
6. Lynda Hurst, "10 Years Later, How a Massacre Changed Us All," *Toronto Star,* 27 November 1999, pp. A1 and A4.
7. Gisli Gudjonsson, Jon Fridrik Sigurdsson, Solrun Linda Skaptadottir, and Bora Helgadottir, "The Relationship of Violent Attitudes with Self-reported Offending and Antisocial Personality Traits," *Journal of Forensic Psychiatry & Psychology*, vol. 22 iss. 3 (June 2011): pp. 371–380; Richard Rogers, Randall Salekin, Kenneth Sewell, and Keith Cruise, "Prototypical Analysis of Antisocial Personality Disorder," *Criminal Justice and Behavior* 27 (2000): 234–255.
8. Dorothy Otnow Lewis, Ernest Moy, Lori Jackson, Robert Aaronson, Nicholas Restifo, Susan Serra, and Alexander Simos, "Biopsychosocial Characteristics of Children Who Later Murder," *American Journal of Psychiatry* 142 (1985): 1161–1167.
9. Dorothy Otnow Lewis, *Guilty by Reason of Insanity* (New York: Fawcett Columbine, 1998).
10. Katherine Van Wormer and Chuk Odiah, "The Psychology of Suicide-Murder and the Death Penalty," *Journal of Criminal Justice* 27 (1999): 361–370; Vivian B. Lord and Michael W. Sloop, "Suicide by Cop: Police Shooting as a Method of Self-Harming," *Journal of Criminal Justice* vol. 38 iss. 5 (September 2010), pp. 889–895.
11. Amy Murrell, Karen Christoff, and Kris Henning, "Characteristics of Domestic Violence Offenders: Associations with Childhood Exposure to Violence," *Journal of Family Violence*, vol. 22 iss. 7 (October 2007), pp. 523–532, Amy Holtzworth-Munroe and Gregory Stuart, "Typologies of Male Batterers: Three Subtypes and the Differences Among Them," *Psychological Bulletin* 116 (1994): 476–497.
12. Stephen Porter, David Fairweather, Jeff Drugge, Huues Herve, Angela Birt, and Douglas Boer, "Profiles of Psychopathy in Incarcerated Sexual Offenders," *Criminal Justice and Behavior* 27 (2000): 216–233.
13. Albert Reiss and Jeffrey Roth, *Understanding and Preventing Violence* (Washington, DC: National Academy Press, 1993), pp. 112–113; K. S. Douglas, L. S. Guy, and S. D. Hart (2009), "Psychosis as a Risk Factor for Violence to Others: A Meta-analysis," *Psychological Bulletin, 135* (5), 679–706; S. Fazel, G. Gulati, L. Linsell, J. R. Geddes, and M. Grann (2009), "Schizophrenia and Violence: Systematic Review and Meta-analysis," *PLoS Medicine,* vol. 6 iss. 8 (August 2009): pp. 1–15; P. Gendreau, T. Little, and C. Goggin (1996), "A Meta-analysis of the Predictors of Adult Offender Recidivism: What Works," *Criminology, 34,* 575–607.
14. Joan Kaufman, "Nature, Nurture, and the Development and Prevention of Antisocial Behavior Problems in Children," *Journal of the American Academy of Child & Adolescent Psychiatry* (April 2010): 300–301; Lindley Bassarath, "Conduct Disorder: A Biopsychosocial Review," *Canadian Journal of Psychiatry* 46 (September 2001): 609–616; Augustine Brannigan, William Gemmell, David J. Pevalin, and Terrance J. Wade, "Self-Control and Social Control in Childhood Misconduct and Aggression: The Role of Family Structure, Hyperactivity, and Hostile Parenting," *Canadian Journal of Criminology* 44 (April 2002): 119–142.
15. Pamela Lattimore, Christy Visher, and Richard Linster, "Predicting Rearrest for Violence Among Serious Youthful Offenders," *Journal of Research in Crime and Delinquency* 32 (1995): 54–83; Leslie Gordon Simons, Ronald L. Simons, Shannon J. Dogan, Rand D. Conger, Kim Kee Jeong and Katherine E. Masyn, "Cognitive and Parenting Pathways in the Transmission of Antisocial Behavior from Parents to Adolescents," *Child Development*, vol. 78 iss. 1 (January 2007): 335–349.
16. Robert Scudder, William Blount, Kathleen Heide, and Ira Silverman, "Important Links Between Child Abuse, Neglect, and Delinquency," *International Journal of Offender Therapy* 37 (1993): 315–323.
17. Charles Patrick Ewing, *When Children Kill* (Lexington, MA: Lexington Books, 1990), p. 22; and Ghitta Weizmann-Henelius, Matti Gronroos, Hanna Putkonen, Markku Eronen, Nina Lindberg, and Helina Hakkanen-Nyholm, "Psychopathy and Gender Differences in Childhood Psychosocial Characteristics in Homicide Offenders—A Nationwide Register-based Study," *Journal*

of Forensic Psychiatry & Psychology, vol. 21 iss. 6 (December 2010): 801–814.

18. Kathleen M. Heide, andDenise Paquette Boots, "A Comparative Analysis of Media Reports of U.S. Parricide Cases With Officially Reported National Crime Data and the Psychiatric and Psychological Literature," *International Journal of Offender Therapy & Comparative Criminology*, vol. 51 iss. 6 (December 2007): 646–675.
19. Lewis, *Guilty by Reason of Insanity*, pp. 11–35.
20. Sigmund Freud, *Beyond the Pleasure Principle* (London: Inter-Psychoanalytic Press, 1922).
21. Konrad Lorenz, *On Aggression* (New York: Harcourt Brace Jovanovich, 1966).
22. Amy Murrell, Karen Christoff, and Kris Henning, "Characteristics of Domestic Violence Offenders: Associations with Childhood Exposure to Violence," *Journal of Family Violence*, vol. 22 iss. 7 (October 2007): 523–532.
23. Michael Greene, "Chronic Exposure to Violence and Poverty: Interventions That Work for Youth," *Crime and Delinquency* 39 (1993): 106–124.
24. Marcus Felson, "Preventing Retail Theft: An Application of Environmental Criminology," *Security Journal* 7 (1996): 71–75; Marc Brandeberry, "$15 Billion Lost to Shoplifting," *Today's Coverage*, a newsletter of the Grocers Insurance Group, Portland, Oregon, 1997; C. Burrows, "Critical Decision Making by Police Firearms Officers: A review of Officer Perception, Response, and Reaction," *Policing*, 1 (3) (2007): 273–283; and John MacDonald, Geoffrey Alpert, and Abraham Tennenbaum, "Justifiable Homicide by Police and Criminal Homicide: A Research Note," *Journal of Crime and Justice* 22 (1999): 153–164.
25. Statistics Canada, "Study: A Comparison of Urban and Rural Crime Rates," 28 June 2007, http://www.statcan.gc.ca/daily-quotidien/070628/dq070628b-eng.htm.
26. Dana L. Haynie, and David P. Armstrong, "Race- and Gender-Disaggregated Homicide Offending Rates," *Homicide Studies* vol. 10 iss. 1 (February 2006): 3–32 (see three tables on p. 27); and Marvin Wolfgang and Franco Ferracuti, *The Subculture of Violence* (London: Tavistock, 1967).
27. Marvin Wolfgang and Franco Ferracuti, *The Subculture of Violence* (London: Tavistock, 1967).
28. James M. Byrne and Jacob Stowell, "Examining the Link between Institutional and Community Violence: Toward a New Cultural Paradigm," *Aggression & Violent Behavior*, vol. 12 iss. 5 (September/October 2007): 552–563.
29. Susan E. Martin, Christopher D. Maxwell, Helene R. White, and Yan Zhang, "Trends in Alcohol Use, Cocaine Use, and Crime: 1989–1998. *Journal of Drug Issues*, vol. 34 iss. 2 (Spring 2004): 333–359; and Paul Goldstein, Henry Brownstein, and Patrick Ryan, "Drug-Related Homicide in New York: 1984–1988," *Crime and Delinquency* 38 (1992): 459–476.
30. "Research Report—Substance Abuse Linked to Violent Crimes," *Alcoholism & Drug Abuse Weekly*, 7 June 2004, vol. 16 iss. 22: 7-7.
31. Ted Myers, "Alcohol and Violent Crime Re-examined: Self-Reports from Two Sub-Groups of Scottish Male Prisoners," *British Journal of Addiction*, vol. 77 iss. 4 (1982): 399–413; and James Collins and Pamela Messerschmidt, "Epidemiology of Alcohol-Related Violence," *Alcohol Health and Research World* 17 (1993): 93–100.
32. Paul E. Bellair, Thomas L. McNulty, "Gang Membership, Drug Selling, and Violence in Neighborhood Context," *Justice Quarterly*, vol. 26 iss. 4 (December 2009): 644–669.
33. D. L. James, and L. E. Glaze (2006), *Mental Health Problems of Prison and Jail Inmates,* Washington, DC: U.S. Department of Justice.
34. Mia Dauvergne, "Homicide in Canada, 2003," Statistics Canada: Cat. no. 85-002-XPE, vol. 24, no. 8 (September 2004), p. 1.
35. Dominique Eve Roe-Sepowitz, "Comparing Male and Female Juveniles Charged with Homicide: Child Maltreatment, Substance Abuse, and Crime Details," *Journal of Interpersonal Violence*, vol. 24 iss. 4 (April 2009): 601–617; "Canadian Inmates Unhealthy and High Risk," *Canadian Medical Association Journal* 171 (2004): 227.
36. *The Daily*, 26 October 2010, Homicide in Canada, Statistics Canada, http://www.statcan.gc.ca/daily-quotidien/101026/dq101026a-eng.htm (accessed 6 August 2011).
37. Martin Killias, John Van Kesteren, and Martin Rindlisbacher, "Guns, Violent Crime, and Suicide in 21 Countries, *"Canadian Journal of Criminology,* vol. 43 iss. 4 (October 2001): 429–448.
38. Mia Dauvergne and Leonardo De Socio, "Firearms and Violent Crime," Statistics Canada Cat. 85-002-X, *Juristat*, vol. 28, no. 2 (2009).
39. Ibid.
40. Mia Dauvergne, "Knives and Violent Crime in Canada," *Juristat*, vol. 30, no.1 (Spring 2010), Cat. no. 85-002-X.
41. Mia Dauvergne and Leonardo De Socio, "Firearms and Violent Crime," Statistics Canada, *Juristat*, vol. 28, no. 2 (2009), Cat. no. 85-002-X.
42. Statistics Canada, "Family Violence in Canada: A Statistical Profile" Minister of Industry, January 2011, Cat. no. 85-224-X, Table 102-0540
43. Mia Dauvergne and Leonardo De Socio, "Firearms and Violent Crime."
44. Statistics Canada, Table 102-0540, "Deaths, by Cause, Chapter XX: External Causes of Morbidity and Mortality (V01 to Y89), Age Group and Sex, Canada, Annual (Number), 2000–2007," http://www5.statcan.gc.ca/cansim/pick-choisir?lang=eng&searchTypeByValue=1&id=1020540 (accessed 11 November 2011).
45. William Green, *Rape* (Lexington, MA: Lexington Books, 1988), p. 5.
46. Susan Brownmiller, *Against Our Will: Men, Women and Rape* (New York: Simon and Schuster, 1975).
47. William Green, *Rape* (Lexington, MA: Lexington Books, 1988), p. 6.
48. Yuri Kageyama, "Court Orders Japan to Pay Sex Slaves," *Boston Globe,* 28 April 1998, p. A2.
49. Marlise Simons, "Bosnian Serb Pleads Guilty to Rape Charge Before War Crimes Tribunal," *New York Times,* 10 March 1998, p. A8.
50. Anonymous, "Congo's Rape Rate 'Astounding,'" *Winnipeg Free Press*, 12 May 2011, p. A11.
51. Canadian Centre for Justice Statistics. Sexual Assault in Canada 2004 and 2007 (Ottawa: Minister of Industry, December 2008) Cat. no. 85F0033M, no. 19.
52. Statistics Canada, "Violence Against Women: Statistical Trends," 2 October 2006 http://www.statcan.gc.ca/daily-quotidien/061002/dq061002a-eng.htm.
53. Angela Browne, "Violence Against Women: Relevance for Medical Practitioners," *Journal of the American Medical Association* 267 (1992): 3184–3189.
54. Laura Woods and Louise Porter, "Examining the Relationship between Sexual Offenders and Their Victims: Interpersonal Differences between Stranger and Non-Stranger Sexual Offences," *Journal of Sexual Aggression*, vol. 14 iss. 1 (March 2008): 61–75.
55. Sarah Hauffe and Louise Porter, "An Interpersonal Comparison of Lone and Group Rape Offences," *Psychology, Crime & Law*, vol. 15 iss. 5 (June 2009): 469–491.
56. Shannon Brennan and Andrea Taylor-Butts, *Sexual Assault in Canada 2004 and 2007,*

Canadian Centre for Justice Statistics (Ottawa: Minister of Industry, 2008) Cat. no. 85F0033M, no. 19.

57. Ibid.
58. Janet Warren, Roland Reboussin, Robert Hazlewood, Natalie Gibbs, Susan Trumbetta, and Andrea Cummings, "Crime Scene Analysis and the Escalation of Violence in Serial Rape," *Forensic Science International* 2 (1998): 56–62.
59. Pekka Santtila, Jenny Junkkila, and N. Kenneth Sandnabba, "Behavioural Linking of Stranger Rapes," *Journal of Investigative Psychology & Offender Profiling*, vol. 2 iss. 2 (June 2005): 87–103.
60. A. Nicholas Groth and Jean Birnbaum, *Men Who Rape* (New York: Plenum, 1979).
61. For other typologies, see Marita McCabe, and Michelle Wauchope, "Behavioral Characteristics of Men Accused of Rape: Evidence for Different Types of Rapists," *Archives of Sexual Behavior*, vol. 34 iss. 2 (April 2005): 241–253; and Raymond Knight, "Validation of a Typology of Rapists," in *Sex Offender Research and Treatment: State-of-the-Art in North America and Europe,* ed. W. L. Marshall and J. Frenken (Newbury Park, CA: Sage, 1997), pp. 58–75.
62. Ann Burnett, Jody L. Mattern, Liliana L. Herakova, David H. Kahl, Cloy Tobola, and Susan E. Bornsen, "Communicating/Muting Date Rape: A Co-Cultural Theoretical Analysis of Communication Factors Related to Rape Culture on a College Campus," *Journal of Applied Communication Research*, vol. 37 iss. 4 (November 2009): 465–485; see also R. Lance Shotland, "A Model of the Causes of Date Rape in Developing and Close Relationships," in *Close Relationships,* ed. C. Hendrick (Newbury Park, CA: Sage, 1989), pp. 247–270.
63. Cortney A. Franklin, "Physically Forced, Alcohol-induced, and Verbally Coerced Sexual Victimization: Assessing Risk Factors Among University Women," *Journal of Criminal Justice*, vol. 38 iss. 2 (March 2010): 149–159; and Diane Follingstad, Rebekah Bradley, James Laughlin, and Leslie Burke, "Risk Factors and Correlates of Dating Violence: The Relevance of Examining Frequency and Severity Levels in a College Sample," *Violence and Victims* 14 (1999): 365–378.
64. D. G. Kilpatrick, H. S. Resnick, K. J. Ruggierio, L. M. Conoscenti, and J. McCauley, *Drug-Facilitated, Incapacitated, and Forcible Rape: A National Study* (Charleston, SC: Medical University of South Carolina, National Crime Victims Research & Treatment Center, 2007).
65. Cortney A. Franklin, "Physically Forced, Alcohol-induced, and Verbally Coerced Sexual Victimization: Assessing Risk Factors Among University Women."
66. Crystal S. Mills and Barbara J. Granoff, "Date and Acquaintance Rape among a Sample of College Students," *Social Work*, vol. 37 iss. 6 (November 1992): 504–509.
67. Benjamin Perrin, "Hardly Draconian; A Law Professor Takes Readers through the Government's Omnibus Criminal-Justice Bill," *National Post*, 28 September 2011, p. 15.
68. Julie Allison and Lawrence Wrightsman, *Rape: The Misunderstood Crime* (Newbury Park, CA: Sage, 1993) pp. 85–87.
69. Cited in Diana Russell, "Wife Rape," in *Acquaintance Rape: The Hidden Crime,* ed. A. Parrot and L. Bechhofer (New York: Wiley, 1991), pp. 129–139, at p. 129.
70. Elaine K. Martin, Casey T. Taft, and Patricia A. Resick, "A Review of Marital Rape," *Aggression & Violent Behavior*, vol. 12 iss. 3 (May/June 2007): 329–347.
71. Jennifer A. Bennice and Patrick A. Resnick, "Marital Rape: History, Research and Practice," *Trauma, Violence, & Abuse*, vol. 4, No. 3 (July 2003): 228–246.
72. Lee Ellis and Anthony Walsh, "Gene-Based Evolutionary Theories in Criminology," *Criminology*, 35 (2) (May 1997): 229–276.
73. Ibid.
74. Laura Hensley Choate, "Sexual Assault Prevention Programs for College Men: An Exploratory Evaluation of the Men Against Violence Model," *Journal of College Counseling*, vol. 6 iss. 2 (Fall 2003): 166–176; see also Diana Russell, *The Politics of Rape* (New York: Stein and Day, 1975).
75. Kala Downs and Steven Gold, "The Role of Blame, Distress, and Anger in the Hypermasculine Man," *Violence and Victims* 12 (1997): 19–36.
76. Groth and Birnbaum, *Men Who Rape,* p. 101
77. Julie McCormack, Stephen M. Hudson, and Tony Ward, "Sexual Offenders' Perceptions of Their Early Interpersonal Relationships: An Attachment Perspective," *Journal of Sex Research*, vol. 39 iss. 2 (May 2002): 85.
78. Vanessa Vega, and Neil M. Malamuth, "Predicting Sexual Aggression: The Role of Pornography in the Context of General and Specific Risk factors," *Aggressive Behavior*, vol. 33 iss. 2 (March 2007): 104–117.
79. Richard Felson and Marvin Krohn, "Motives for Rape," *Journal of Research in Crime and Delinquency* 27 (1990): 222–242.
80. Larry Baron and Murray Straus, "Four Theories of Rape: A Macrosociological Analysis," *Social Problems* 34 (1987): 467–489.
81. Christie Blatchford, "Crying Wolf," *National Post,* 8 September 2001, pp. B1–B2.
82. Julian V. Roberts, and Renate M. Mohr, *Confronting Sexual Assault: A Decade of Legal and Social Change* (Toronto: University of Toronto Press, 1994); and Melanie Randall, "Sexual Assault Law, Credibility, and 'Ideal Victims': Consent, Resistance, and Victim Blaming," *Canadian Journal of Women & the Law*, vol. 22 iss. 2 (2010): 397–433.
83. Melanie Randall, "Sexual Assault Law, Credibility, and 'Ideal Victims': Consent, Resistance, and Victim Blaming."
84. Shannon Brennan and Andrea Taylor-Butts, *Sexual Assault in Canada 2004 and 2007*, Canadian Centre for Justice Statistics (Ottawa: Minister of Industry, 2008), Cat. no. 85F0033M, no. 19; and Lise Gotell, "Canadian Sexual Assault Law: Neoliberalism and the Erosion of Feminist-Inspired Law Reforms," http://ualberta.academia.edu/LiseGotell/Papers/279667/Canadian_Sexual_Assault_Law_Neoliberalism_and_the_Erosion_of_Feminist-Inspired_Law_Reforms.
85. Melanie Randall, "Sexual Assault Law, Credibility, and 'Ideal Victims': Consent, Resistance, and Victim Blaming," *Canadian Journal of Women and the Law* 22 (2010): 397–433.
86. Donald Lunde, *Murder and Madness* (San Francisco: San Francisco Book, 1977), p. 3.
87. S. Beattie, and A. Cotter, *Juristat: Homicide in Canada, 2009,* vol. 30, no. 3 (Fall 2010) (Ottawa: Minister of Industry) Cat. no. 85-002-X.
88. Ibid.
89. Ibid.
90. Ibid.
91. Ibid.
92. Ibid.
93. See, generally, Marc Reidel and Margaret Zahn, *The Nature and Pattern of American Homicide* (Washington, DC: U.S. Government Printing Office, 1985).
94. Rui Yang and Sigurdur Olafsson, "Classification for Predicting Offender Affiliation with Murder Victims," *Expert Systems with Applications*, vol. 38 iss. 11 (October 2011): 13518–13526.
95. Krystal Mize, Todd Shackelford, and Viviana Shackelford, "Hands-on Killing of Intimate Partners as a Function of Sex and Relationship Status/State," *Journal*

of *Family Violence*, vol. 24 iss. 7 (October 2009): 463–470; and Linda Saltzman and James Mercy, "Assaults Between Intimates: The Range of Relationships Involved," in *Homicide: The Victim/Offender Connection,* ed. Anna Victoria Wilson (Cincinnati: Anderson Publishing, 1993), pp. 65–74.

96. Angela Browne and Kirk Williams, "Exploring the Effect of Resource Availability and the Likelihood of Female-Perpetrated Homicides," *Law and Society Review* 23 (1989): 75–94.
97. Angela Browne and Kirk Williams, "Gender, Intimacy, and Lethal Violence: Trends from 1976 Through 1987," *Gender and Society* 7 (1993): 78–98.
98. Todd K. Shackelford, David M. Buss, and Viviana A. Weekes-Shackelford, "Wife Killings Committed in the Context of a Lovers Triangle," *Basic & Applied Social Psychology*, vol. 25 iss. 2 (June 2003): 137–143; and Richard Felson, "Anger, Aggression, and Violence in Love Triangles," *Violence and Victimization* 12 (1997): 345–363.
99. Alexandra Zabjek, "Albertan Guilty of Movie Script Murder," *Calgary Herald* 13 April 2011, p. 1; and Alexandra Zabjek, "Sensationalized Media Coverage Prompts Appeal," *Edmonton Journal* 11 May 2011, p. 1.
100. Sara Beattie and Adam Cotter, *Juristat: Homicide in Canada, 2009,* vol. 30, no. 3 (Ottawa: Minister of Industry, Fall 2010) Cat. no. 85-002-X.
101. Anonymous, "582 Native Women Listed Missing, Slain Report Adds 62 Names to Collection of Cases, Highlights Trauma to Aboriginal Families," *Toronto Star* 22 April 2010, p. 16.
102. Belea Keeney and Kathleen Heide, "Gender Differences in Serial Murderers: A Preliminary Analysis," *Journal of Interpersonal Violence* 9 (1994): 37–56.
103. Statistics Canada, CANSIM, Table 252-0013, "Crimes by Type of Offence," http://www5.statcan.gc.ca/cansim/pick-choisir?lang=eng&searchTypeByValue=1&id=2520013 (accessed 11 November 2011).
104. Keith Harries, "Homicide and Assault: A Comparative Analysis of Attributes in Dallas Neighborhoods, 1981–1985," *Professional Geographer* 41 (1989): 29–38.
105. Simon Doyle, "UN to Tackle Air-Rage Menace," [Final Edition] *The Vancouver Sun* 13 September 2004, p. 5.
106. Statistics Canada, CANSIM, Table 252-0013, "Crimes by Type of Offence," http://www5.statcan.gc.ca/cansim/pick-choisir?lang=eng&searchTypeByValue=1&id=2520013 (accessed 11 November 2011).
107. Jamie Komarnicki, "Police Lay Charges in Road Rage Shooting; Warning Given to Reckless Drivers," *Calgary Herald* 28 November 2008, p. 4.
108. Nico M. Trocmé, Marc Tourigny, Bruce MacLaurin, and Barbara Fallon, "Major Findings from the Canadian Incidence Study of Reported Child Abuse and Neglect," *Child Abuse & Neglect*, vol. 27 iss. 12 (December 2003): 1427–1439.
109. Harriet L. Macmillan, Ellen Jamieson, C. Nadine Wathen, Michael H. Boyle, Christine A. Walsh, John Omura, Jason M. Walker, and Gregory Lodenquai, "Development of a Policy-Relevant Child Maltreatment Research Strategy," *Milbank Quarterly*, vol. 85 iss. 2 (2007): 337–374.
110. *Family Violence in Canada: A Statistical Profile, 2011* (Ottawa: Minister of Industry, 2011) Cat. no. 85-224-X, http://www.statcan.gc.ca/pub/85-224-x/85-224-x2010000-eng.htm (accessed 6 August 2011).
111. Glenn Wolfner and Richard Gelles, "A Profile of Violence Toward Children: A National Study," *Child Abuse and Neglect* 17 (1993): 197–212.
112. Nico M. Trocmé, Marc Tourigny, Bruce MacLaurin, and Barbara Fallon, "Major Findings from the Canadian Incidence Study of Reported Child Abuse and Neglect"; and Ruth Inglis, *Sins of the Fathers: A Study of the Physical and Emotional Abuse of Children* (New York: St. Martin's Press, 1978), p. 68.
113. Martin Daly and Margo Wilson, "Violence Against Step Children," *Current Directions in Psychological Science* 5 (1996): 77–81.
114. Sandra M. Stith, Ting Liu, L. Christopher Davies, Esther L. Boykin, Meagan C. Alder, Jennifer M. Harris, Anurag Som, Mary McPherson, and J.E.M.E.G. Dees, "Risk Factors in Child Maltreatment: A Meta-analytic Review of the Literature," *Aggression and Violent Behavior* (January 2009), 14 (1): 13–29.
115. Ibid.
116. R. Emerson Dobash and Russell Dobash, *Violence Against Wives* (New York: Free Press, 1979).
117. Julia O'Faolain and Laura Martines, eds., *Not in God's Image: Women in History* (Glasgow: Fontana/Collins, 1974).
118. Dobash and Dobash, *Violence Against Wives,* p. 46.
119. Ronald Cohen, Alan Rosenbaum, Robert Kane, William Warneken, and Sheldon Benjamin, "Neuropsychological Correlates of Domestic Violence," *Violence and Victims* 15 (2000): 397–410.
120. Neil Jacobson and John Mordechai Gottman, *When Men Batter Women: New Insights into Ending Abusive Relationships* (New York: Simon and Schuster, 1998). Other research studies also report a high correlation between spousal violence and stalking (criminal harassment), including P. Tjaden and N. Thoennes, "Prevalence and Consequences of Male-to-Female and Female-to-Male Partner Violence as Measured by The National Violence Against Women Survey," *Violence Against Women* 6 (2) (2000): 142–161; J. MacFarlane, et al. "Stalking and Intimate Partner Femicide," *Homicide Studies* 3 (4) (1999) 300–316.
121. Margo Wilson and Martin Daly, "Male Sexual Proprietariness and Violence Against Wives," *Current Directions in Psychological Science* 5 (1996): 2–7.
122. Family Violence in Canada: A Statistical Profile, 2011, Minister of Industry, 2011, Cat. no. 85-224-X http://www.statcan.gc.ca/pub/85-224-x/85-224-x2010000-eng.htm.
123. Richard Rosenfeld, "Changing Relationships Between Men and Women: A Note on the Decline in Intimate Partner Homicide," *Homicide Studies* 1 (1997): 72–83.
124. Desmond Ellis and Lori Wright, "Estrangement, Interventions, and Male Violence Toward Female Partners," *Violence and Victims* 12 (1997): 51–68.
125. Federal Bureau of Investigation, *Crime in the United States, 1997* (Washington, DC: U.S. Government Printing Office, 1998), p. 28.
126. Statistics Canada, "Violent Crime in Canada," *The Canada e-Book* (11-404-XIE), based on the *2001 Canada Year Book* (11-402-XPE).
127. Maire Gannon, *Crime Comparisons between Canada and the United States,* Statistics Canada (Canadian Centre for Justice Statistics, 2001), Cat. no. 85-002-XIE, vol. 21, no. 11, pp. 5–6.
128. Caroline Wolf Harlow, *Robbery Victims* (Washington, DC: Bureau of Justice Statistics, 1989), pp. 1–5.
129. Richard Felson, Eric Baumer, and Steven Messner, "Acquaintance Robbery," *Journal of Research in Crime and Delinquency* 37 (2000): 284–305.
130. James Calder and John Bauer, "Convenience Store Robberies: Security Measures and Store Robbery Incidents," *Journal of Criminal Justice* 20 (1992): 553–566.
131. Peter Van Koppen and Robert Jansen, "The Time to Rob: Variations in Time and

Number of Commercial Robberies," *Journal of Research in Crime and Delinquency* 36 (1999): 7–29.

132. Tom Elce, *Scream 4* Review, 9 August 2011, http://www.killermovies.com/s/scream4/reviews/omm.html.
133. Section 264 (2), Criminal Code Canada.
134. Shelly Milligan, Criminal Harassment in Canada, 2009, *Juristat Bulletin,* March 3, 2011, Statistics Canada catalogue no. 85-005-X, p. 2.
135. Ibid.
136. Ibid.
137. Ibid.
138. Ibid.
139. Section 348.1, Criminal Code Canada.
140. Melanie Kowalski, "Home Invasions, Bulletin," (Canadian Centre for Justice Statistics, June 2002) Cat. no. 85F0027X1E.
141. Orest Fedorowycz, *Breaking and Entering in Canada—2002* (Canadian Centre for Justice Statistics, Statistics Canada), Cat. no. 85-002-XPE, vol. 24, no. 5.
142. "Robbery," BC Crime Trends—Police & Crime, Summary Statistics, 1989–1998, Government of British Columbia, iss. 3 (March 2000), p. 3.
143. Jack McDevitt, "The Study of the Character of Civil Rights Crimes in Massachusetts (1983–1987)," paper presented at the annual meeting of the American Society of Criminology, Reno, Nevada, November 1989.
144. Ibid., p. 8.
145. Jack Levin and Jack McDevitt, *Hate Crimes: The Rising Tide of Bigotry and Bloodshed* (New York: Plenum, 1993).
146. Statistics Canada, "Pilot Survey of Hate Crime," *The Daily,* 1 June 2004.
147. Mia Dauvergne, Katie Scrim, and Shannon Brennan, Canadian Centre for Justice Statistics Profile Series "Hate Crime in Canada 2006," Statistics Canada (June 2008), Cat. no. 85F0033M—no. 17
148. Ibid.
149. Ibid.
150. Sylvain de Léséleuc, *Criminal Victimization in the Workplace 2004* (Ottawa: Minister of Industry, February 2007) Cat. 85F0033MIE, no. 13.
151. Hubert Herring, "The Good News About 'Going Postal,'" *New York Times,* 3 September 2000, p. A3.
152. J. Barling, K. E. Dupre, and E. K. Kelloway, "Predicting Workplace Aggression and Violence," *Annual Review of Psychology*, 60 (2009): 671–692.
153. Associated Press, "Gunman Wounds 3 Doctors in L.A. Hospital," *Cleveland Plain Dealer,* 9 February 1993, p. B1.
154. James Alan Fox and Jack Levin, "Firing Back: The Growing Threat of Workplace Homicide," *Annals* 536 (1994): 16–30; and J. Barling, K. E. Dupre, and E. K. Kelloway, "Predicting Workplace Aggression and Violence," *Annual Review of Psychology*, 60 (2009): 671–692.
155. Stephen Schafer, *The Political Criminal* (New York: Free Press, 1974), p. 1.
156. Robert Friedlander, *Terrorism* (Dobbs Ferry, NY: Oceana, 1979).
157. Bruce Hoffman, *Inside Terrorism* (New York: Columbia University Press, 1998); and Walter Laquer, *The Age of Terrorism* (Boston: Little, Brown, 1987), p. 72.
158. National Advisory Commission on Criminal Justice Standards and Goals, *Report of the Task Force on Disorders and Terrorism* (Washington, DC: U.S. Government Printing Office, 1976), p. 3. and Section 83.1, Criminal Code Canada.
159. Austin T. Turk, "Sociology of Terrorism," *Annual Review of Sociology* 30 (2004): 271–86; and Paul Wilkinson, *Terrorism and the Liberal State* (New York: Wiley, 1977), p. 49.
160. Elisabeth Symeonidou-Kastanidou, "Defining Terrorism," *European Journal of Crime, Criminal Law & Criminal Justice*, vol. 12 iss. 1 (2004): 14–35; Eric Reitan, "Defining Terrorism for Public Policy Purposes: The Group-Target Definition," *Journal of Moral Philosophy*, vol. 7 iss. 2 (2010): 253–278; and Jack Gibbs, "Conceptualization of Terrorism," *American Sociological Review* 54 (1989): 329–340, at p. 330.
161. For a general view, see Jonathan White, *Terrorism* (Pacific Grove, CA: Brooks/Cole, 1991).
162. Michael Barkun, "Leaderless Resistance and Phineas Priests: Strategies of Uncoordinated Violence on the Far Right," paper presented at the annual meeting of the American Society of Criminology, San Diego, November 1997.
163. Adnan R. Khan, "Who Killed Bhutto?" *Maclean's*, vol. 21, iss. 3 (January 28, 2008): 24–29; Griff Witte, "Musharraf Denies Role in Bhutto Death; Pakistan President Insists Taliban Supporters Killed Her, Rejects Suggestion of Conspiracy," [Final Edition] *Edmonton Journal*, 4 January 2008: 4
164. Stephen Engelberg, "Terrorism's New (and Very Old) Face," *New York Times,* 12 September 1998, p. A5.
165. Bruce Hoffman, *Inside Terrorism* (New York: Columbia University Press, 1998).
166. Anonymous, "U.S. Abortionist Shot to Death at his Church; Attacked Before; Obama Health Secretary Has Ties to Slain Doctor," *National Post*, 1 June 2009, p. A2.
167. Tom Blackwell, "Sympathy for an Eco-Warrior's Fight; Wiebo Ludwig's War Story Hits the Silver Screen," *National Post* 9 May 2011, p. A3.
168. Ted Robert Gurr, "Political Terrorism in the United States: Historical Antecedents and Contemporary Trends," in *The Politics of Terrorism,* ed. Michael Stohl (New York: Dekker, 1988).
169. Amnesty International, *Annual Report,* 2011 (London, UK: May 2011).
170. This report on state action in Peru can be obtained on the Amnesty International website at http://www.amnesty.org/ailib/aipub/1996/AMR/2460396.htm.
171. Brent Smith and Gregory Orvis, "America's Response to Terrorism: An Empirical Analysis of Federal Intervention Strategies During the 1980s," *Justice Quarterly* 10 (1993): 660–681.

Chapter 11

1. Andrew McCall, *The Medieval Underworld* (London: Hamish Hamilton, 1979), p. 86.
2. Ibid., p. 104.
3. J. J. Tobias, *Crime and Police in England, 1700–1900* (London: Gill and Macmillan, 1979).
4. Ibid., p. 9.
5. Marilyn Walsh, *The Fence* (Westport, CT: Greenwood Press, 1977), pp. 18–25.
6. John Hepburn, "Occasional Criminals," in *Major Forms of Crime,* ed. Robert Meier (Beverly Hills, CA: Sage, 1984), pp. 73–94.
7. James Inciardi, "Professional Crime," in *Major Forms of Crime,* ed. Robert Meier (Beverly Hills, CA: Sage, 1984), p. 223.
8. This section depends heavily on a classic book: Wayne La Fave and Austin Scott, *Handbook on Criminal Law* (St. Paul, MN: West Publishing, 1972).
9. La Fave and Scott, *Handbook on Criminal Law,* p. 622.
10. Mia Dauvergne and John Turner, "Police Reported Crime Statistics in Canada, 2009," *Juristat* vol. 30, no. 2 (Summer, 2010), Cat. no. 85-002-X (Ottawa: Minister of Industry, 2010).
11. Margaret Loftus, "Gone: One TV," *U.S. News & World Report,* 14 July 1997, p. 61.
12. Andy Johnson, "Theft Ring up in Smoke: Cigarette Thieves Hit Here: Police," [Final Edition] *Evening Guide* [Port Hope, Ontario] 14 July 2004, p. 1.
13. Jack Harris, BDO Dunwoody LLP "Combatting Employee Theft and Fraud," *Okanagan Business Journal*, 2 May 2005.

14. Michael Lewis, "Sony Suffers Two More Hacker Attacks; Personal Information on 20 000 Customers Taken from EShop Cellphone Store's Canadian Database," *Toronto Star*, 25 May 2011, p. B2.
15. Canadian Anti-Fraud Centre: Identity Theft: Could It Happen to You? http://www.phonebusters.com/english/recognizeit_identitythe.html (accessed 17 November 2011).
16. Norman A. Wilcox Jr. and Thomas M. Regan, "Unmasking Terrorist Identity Fraud. *USA Today Magazine*, vol. 134 iss. 2724 (September 2005): 24–26.
17. Industry Canada, "STAT-USA Market Research Reports: Retail Security Overview," 29 September 2001, http://strategis.ic.gc.ca.
18. Dana Flavelle, "Stores Are Shopping for Ultimate Security; Canadian Retailers Are Losing an Estimated $8 Million a Day to Retail Theft But Many Are Starting to Fight Back in an Effort to Keep Costs under Wraps," *Toronto Star*, 29 March 2008, p. 2.
19. Mary Owen Cameron, *The Booster and the Snitch* (New York: Free Press, 1964).
20. Ibid., p. 57.
21. Lawrence Cohen and Rodney Stark, "Discriminatory Labeling and the Five-Finger Discount: An Empirical Analysis of Differential Shoplifting Dispositions," *Journal of Research on Crime and Delinquency* 11 (1974): 25–35.
22. Lloyd Klemke, "Does Apprehension for Shoplifting Amplify or Terminate Shoplifting Activity?" *Law and Society Review* 12 (1978): 390–403.
23. Erhard Blankenburg, "The Selectivity of Legal Sanctions: An Empirical Investigation of Shoplifting," *Law and Society Review* 11 (1976): 109–129.
24. Jill Jordan Siedfer, "To Catch a Thief Try This: Peddling High-Tech Solutions to Shoplifting," *U.S. News & World Report*, 23 September, 1996, p. 71.
25. "Montreal Police Bust High-tech Labs Making Fake Credit Cards," CBC News, 12 January 2007, http://www.cbc.ca/news/canada/montreal/strory/2007/01/12/mtl-fraud.htm.
26. RCMP, "Credit Card Fraud, Recognize It. What Is Credit Card Fraud?" http://www.rcmp-grc.gc.ca/scams-fraudes/cc-fraud-fraude-eng.htm (accessed 6 August 2011).
27. Royal Canadian Mounted Police, "Frauds and Scams—Counterfeiting and Credit Card Fraud," 9 July 2004, http://www.rcmp.ca/scams.
28. Mia Dauvergne and John Turner Summer, "Police Reported Crime Statistics in Canada, 2009," 2010, *Juristat*, vol. 30, no. 2 (Ottawa: Minister of Industry, 2010) Cat. no. 85-002-X.
29. Insurance Bureau of Canada. "Auto Theft" http://www.ibc.ca/en/insurance_crime/auto_theft/
30. Mia Dauvergne, Statistics Canada, "Motor Vehicle Theft in Canada" (Ottawa: Minister of Industry, 2008) Cat. 85-002-V.
31. Charles McCaghy, Peggy Giordano, and Trudy Knicely Henson, "Auto Theft" *Criminology,* 15 (1977), 367–381.
32. Kim Hazelbaker, "Insurance Industry Analyses and the Prevention of Motor Vehicle Theft," in *Business and Crime Prevention,* ed. Marcus Felson and Ronald Clarke (Monsey, NY: Criminal Justice Press, 1997), pp. 283–293.
33. Ronald Clarke and Patricia Harris, "Auto Theft and Its Prevention," in *Crime and Justice: An Annual Review,* ed. N. Morris and M. Tonry (Chicago: Chicago University Press, 1992).
34. Ian Ayres and Steven D. Levitt, "Measuring Positive Externalities from Unobservable Victim Precaution: An Empirical Analysis of Lojack," *Quarterly Journal of Economics* 113 (1998): 43–78.
35. Hazelbaker, "Insurance Industry Analyses and the Prevention of Motor Vehicle Theft," p. 289.
36. La Fave and Scott, *Handbook on Criminal Law,* p. 655.
37. Edwin Lemert, "An Isolation and Closure Theory of Naive Check Forging," *Journal of Criminal Law, Criminology and Police Science*, 44 (1953): 297-298.
38. The Canadian Anti-Fraud Call Centre, PhoneBusters, "Backgrounder: What Is Deceptive Telemarketing?" http://www.phonebusters.com/english/fraudprevention (accessed 31 October 2011).
39. The Canadian Anti-Fraud Call Centre, PhoneBusters, "Man Jailed for 8 Years in $2-M Nigerian Bank Scam," http://www.phonebusters.com/english/fraudprevention (accessed 31 October 2011).
40. Kevin Donovan, "Charity Scams Bust Public Trust," *Toronto Star*, 2 June 2007 http://www.thestar.com/News/article/220756 (accessed 6 August 2011).
41. Jerome Hall, *Theft, Law and Society* (Indianapolis: Bobbs-Merrill, 1952), p. 36.
42. La Fave and Scott, *Handbook on Criminal Law,* p. 644.
43. Ibid., p. 708.
44. E. Blackstone, *Commentaries on the Laws of England* (London: 1769), p. 224.
45. Orest Fedorowycz, "Breaking and Entering in Canada, 2002," Statistics Canada, Canadian Centre for Justice Statistics, vol. 24, no. 5 (July 2004), Cat. no. 85-002-XPE, p. 39.
46. Perreault, S. & Brennan, S., Statistics Canada, "Criminal Victimization in Canada 2009," *Juristat*, 30 (2) (Ottawa: Minister of Industry, 2010) Cat. 85-002-X.
47. Frank Hoheimer, *The Home Invaders: Confessions of a Cat Burglar* (Chicago: Chicago Review, 1975).
48. Richard Wright, Robert Logie, and Scott Decker, "Criminal Expertise and Offender Decision Making: An Experimental Study of the Target Selection Process in Residential Burglary," *Journal of Research in Crime and Delinquency* 32 (1995): 39–53.
49. Richard Wright and Scott Decker, *Burglars on the Job: Streetlife and Residential Break-ins* (Boston, MA: Northeastern University Press, 1994).
50. Simon Hakim and Yochanan Shachmurove, "Spatial and Temporal Patterns of Commercial Burglaries," *American Journal of Economics and Sociology* 55 (1996): 443–457.
51. Roger Litton, "Crime Prevention and the Insurance Industry," in *Business and Crime Prevention,* ed. Marcus Felson and Ronald Clarke (Monsey, NY: Criminal Justice Press, 1997), p. 162.
52. Graham Farrell, Coretta Phillips and Ken Pease, "Like Taking Candy: Why Does Repeat Victimization Occur?" *British Journal of Criminology*, 35 (1995), 384-399, at p. 391.
53. See, generally, Neal Shover, "Structures and Careers in Burglary," *Journal of Criminal Law, Criminology and Police Science* 63 (1972): 540–549.
54. Paul Cromwell, James Olson, and D'Aunn Wester Avary, *Breaking and Entering: An Ethnographic Analysis of Burglary* (Newbury Park, CA: Sage, 1991), pp. 48–51.
55. Statistics Canada, Cansim Table 252-0014 "Adult and Youth Charged, by Detailed Offences for Canada, Provinces and Territories, Annual, 2002," http://www5.statcan.gc.ca/cansim/pick-choisir?lang=eng&searchTypeByValue=1&id=2520014 (accessed 17 November 2011).
56. Nancy Webb, George Sakheim, Luz Towns-Miranda, and Charles Wagner, "Collaborative Treatment of Juvenile Firestarters: Assessment and Outreach," *American Journal of Orthopsychiatry* 60 (1990): 305–310.
57. Vernon Quinsey, Terry Chaplin, and Douglas Unfold, "Arsonists and Sexual Arousal to Fire Setting: Correlations Unsupported," *Journal of Behavior Therapy*

and Experimental Psychiatry 20 (1989): 203–209.

58. Leigh Edward Somers, *Economic Crimes* (New York: Clark Boardman, 1984), pp. 158–168.

Chapter 12

1. Louie Rossella, "New Trial Ordered in Massive GST Fraud Case," *Oakville Beaver*, 21 August 2008, p. 1; Allan Woods, "Masterminds of Massive GST Fraud Jailed: Bogus Car Sales: *National Post* (National Edition) 13 July 2004, p. 4; Neal Hall, "Tax Fraud Leaves $1.9 Million Tab that Will Take 163 Years to Pay," *The Vancouver Sun*, 11 April 2011, p.1, Susan Lazaruk. "Phoney GST Claims Lands Pair in Jail," *The Province*, 17 February 2011, p.15.
2. Dwight C. Smith, Jr., "White-Collar Crime, Organized Crime and the Business Establishment: Resolving a Crisis in Criminological Theory," in *White-Collar and Economic Crime: A Multidisciplinary and Crossnational Perspective,* ed. P. Wickman and T. Dailey (Lexington, MA: Lexington Books, 1982), p. 53.
3. See, generally, Dwight C. Smith, Jr., "Organized Crime and Entrepreneurship," *International Journal of Criminology and Penology* 6 (1978): 161–177; Dwight C. Smith, Jr., "Paragons, Pariahs, and Pirates: A Spectrum-Based Theory of Enterprise," *Crime and Delinquency* 26 (1980): 358–386; Dwight C. Smith, Jr., and Richard S. Alba, "Organized Crime and American Life," *Society* 16 (1979): 32–38.
4. Smith, "White-Collar Crime, Organized Crime and the Business Establishment," p. 33; Blythe Proulx, "Organized Criminal Involvement in the Illicit Antiquities Trade," *Trends in Organized Crime*, vol. 14, iss. 1 (March 2011): 1–29.
5. Mark Haller, "Illegal Enterprise: A Theoretical and Historical Interpretation," *Criminology* 28 (1990): 207–235.
6. John P. Wright, Francis T. Cullen, "The Social Construction of Corporate Violence: Media Coverage of the Imperial Food Products Fire," *Crime & Delinquency*, vol. 41, iss. 1 (January 1995): 20–36, Nancy Frank and Michael Lynch, *Corporate Crime, Corporate Violence* (Albany, NY: Harrow and Heston, 1992), p. 7.
7. Tomson H. Nguyen and Henry N. Pontell, "Mortgage Origination Fraud and the Global Economic Crisis," *Criminology & Public Policy*, vol. 9, iss. 3 (August 2010): 591–612.
8. Nikos Passas and David Nelken, "The Thin Line Between Legitimate and Criminal Enterprises: Subsidy Frauds in the European Community," *Crime, Law and Social Change* 19 (1993): 223–243.
9. For a thorough review, see David Friedrichs, *Trusted Criminals* (Belmont, CA: Wadsworth, 1996).
10. Carole Gibbs, Edmund F. McGarrell, and Mark Axelrod, "Transnational White-Collar Crime and Risk," *Criminology & Public Policy*, vol. 9, iss. 3 (August 2010): 543–560.
11. Edwin Sutherland, *White-Collar Crime: The Uncut Version* (New Haven, CT: Yale University Press, 1983), p.7.
12. Edwin Sutherland, "White-Collar Criminality," *American Sociological Review* 5 (1940): 2–10.
13. David Weisburd and Kip Schlegel, "Returning to the Mainstream," in *White-Collar Crime Reconsidered,* ed. Kip Schlegel and David Weisburd (Boston: Northeastern University Press, 1992), pp. 352–365.
14. K. Calavita, R. Tillman, and H. N. Pontell, "The Savings and Loan Debacle, Financial Crime, and the State," *Annual Review of Sociology*, vol. 23 (1997): 19–38.
15. Elizabeth Moore and Michael Mills, "The Neglected Victims and Unexamined Costs of White-Collar Crime," *Crime and Delinquency* 36 (1990): 408–418.
16. PriceWaterhouseCoopers, The Global Economic Crime Survey, Economic Crime in a Downturn, November 2009, http://www.pwc.com/en_GX/gx/economic-crime-survey/pdf/global-economic-crime-survey-2009.pdf (accessed 7 August 2011).
17. Eric Beauchesne, "Fraud Strikes Half of Firms," *Calgary Herald,* 9 July 2003, p. C1; Aaron Freeman and Craig Forcese, "Get Tough on Corporate Crime," *Toronto Star,* 17 November 1994, p. A31; Doug Fischer, "Investigator Fears Fraud Cases Ignored," *Calgary Herald,* 9 July 1994, p. A10.
18. Joe Chidley, "Camp Cupcake Has Nothing on Us," *Canadian Business*, vol. 77, iss. 20 (October 11, 2004): 4.
19. Jim Moran, "Thailand: Crime and Corruption Become Increasing Threat," *CJ International* 12 (1996): 5.
20. Sam Perry, "Economic Espionage and Corporate Responsibility," *CJ International* 11 (1995): 3–4; and Nikki Swartz, "Corporate Spying Costs $45 Billion," *Information Management Journal*, vol. 42, iss. 3 (May/June 2008): 16.
21. Marshall Clinard and Richard Quinney, *Criminal Behavior Systems: A Typology* (New York: Holt, Rinehart and Winston, 1973), p. 117.
22. Mark Moore, "Notes Toward a National Strategy to Deal with White-Collar Crime," in *A National Strategy for Containing White-Collar Crime,* ed. Herbert Edelhertz and Charles Rogovin (Lexington, MA: Lexington Books, 1980), pp. 32–44.
23. For a general review, see John Braithwaite, "White Collar Crime," *Annual Review,* 11 (1985): 1–25.
24. "Eleven Charged with Fraud and Fraudulent Manipulation of Stock Exchange Transactions,"15 February 2011, http://www.rcmp-grc.gc.ca/qc/nouv-news/com-rel/2011/02/110215-eng.htm (accessed 7 August 2011).
25. Tom Fennell, "Assumed Identities: English Police Charge a Canadian with Murder," *Maclean's,* 16 December 1996, pp. 52, 54.
26. Richard Quinney, "Occupational Structure and Criminal Behavior: Prescription Violation of Retail Pharmacists," *Social Problems* 11 (1963): 179–185; see also John Braithwaite, *Corporate Crime in the Pharmaceutical Industry* (London: Routledge and Kegan Paul, 1984).
27. "The Rise and Fall of Alan Eagleson," Canadian Broadcasting Corporation Archives, http://archives.cbc.ca.
28. James Armstrong et al., "Securities Fraud," *American Criminal Law Review* 33 (1995): 973–1016.
29. Scott McMurray, "Futures Pit Trader Goes to Trial," *Wall Street Journal,* 8 May 1990, p. C1; Scott McMurray, "Chicago Pits' Dazzling Growth Permitted a Free-for-All Mecca," *Wall Street Journal,* 3 August 1989, p. A4.
30. Douglas Goold and Andrew Willis, *The Bre-X Fraud* (Toronto: McClelland & Stewart, 1997).
31. "The Bruce Carson Affair," *National Post,* 7 April 2011, p. 5; Chantal Hebert, "Adscam and Culture of Entitlement," *Toronto Star,* 4 August 2004, p. A4; Les Whittington, "Legal Tussle Stalls Inquiry," *Toronto Star,* 10 November 2004, p. A20.
32. Rosie DiManno, "Scandal Makes Case for Civilian Oversight," *Toronto Star,* 23 January 2004, p. A20.
33. Allan Woods, "Officers Will Be Charged, Fantino Says," *National Post,* 20 April 2004, p. A12; Tracy Huffman and John Duncanson, "Case Spotlights Police Probe," *Toronto Star,* 6 November 2004, p. B1; John Duncanson and Tracy Huffman, "New Charges Laid Against Officers," *Toronto Star,* 16 October 2004, p. A17.
34. David Bruser, "Police 'Unplugged' Corruption Probe, Lawyer Says; Claims Against Drug Squad Were Ignored, Court Told, as Damage Control Bid Was Under Way on Other Unit," *Toronto Star*, 11 December 2009, p. GT1.

35. Cited in Hugh Barlow, *Introduction to Criminology,* 2nd ed. (Boston: Little, Brown, 1984).
36. Charles McCaghy, *Deviant Behavior* (New York: Macmillan, 1976), p. 178.
37. Associated Press, "Business Fraud Prevails, May Worsen, Study Says," *Wall Street Journal,* 17 August 1993, p. A4; Liane Greenberg and Julian Darling, "Employee Theft," in C.L. Cooper and D.M. Rousseau, eds. *Trends in Organizational Behavior*, vol. 3 (New York, NY: John Wiley & Sons, 1996), pp. 49–64.
38. J. Sorenson, H. Grove, and T. Sorenson, "Detecting Management Fraud: The Role of the Independent Auditor," in G. Geis and E. Stotland, ed., *White-Collar Crime: Theory and Research (*Beverly Hills, CA: Sage, 1980), pp. 221–251.
39. Jeff Bolichowski, "Physician Faces More Fraud Charges, Provincial Police Say," *The Windsor Star*, 4 December 2010, p. 3; see also Kristine DeBry, Bonny Harbinger, and Susan Rotkis, "Health Care Fraud," *American Criminal Law Review* 33 (1995): 818–838.
40. Barbara Sibbald, "MDs Get Jail Terms, Fines as New Police Squad Targets Health Fraud," *Canadian Medical Association Journal* 163 (2000): 591.
41. Marnie Ko, "A Banker with Flash," *The Report/Newsmagazine* (National Edition) (9 September 2002): 33–35, http://www.highbeam.com/doc/1G1-94199870.html (accessed 17 November 2011).
42. Tracy Huffman, "Jail Time Cut for ATM Fraud Pair," *Toronto Star,* 11 September 2003, p. A6.
43. Anonymous. "Health Centre Clerk Charged in $1M ATM Fraud," *Calgary Herald*, 12 November 2010, p. A15.
44. Michael Maltz and Stephen Pollack, "Suspected Collusion Among Bidders," in G. Geis and E. Stotland, eds., *White-Collar Crime: Theory and Research* (Beverly Hills, CA: Sage, 1980), pp. 174–98; see also the Associated Press, "British Airways and Others Settle a Suit Over Price-Fixing," *New York Times*, 8 June 2011, p. 8.
45. Tim Carrington, "Federal Probes of Contractors Rise for Year," *Wall Street Journal,* 23 February 1987, p. 50; Tony Illia, "Guilty Pleas in Midwest Concrete Cartel Probe," *Engineering News-Record*, vol. 267, iss. 7 (12 September 2011): 18.
46. A. Freeman and C. Forcese, "Get Tough on Corporate Crime," *Toronto Star,* 17 November 1994, p. A31.
47. Vincent Kiernan, "2 Incidents Put More Than 200,000 Students at Risk of Data Theft," *Chronicle of Higher Education*, vol. 52 iss. 43 (30 June 2006): A21.
48. Lorine A. Hughes and Gregory J. DeLone, "Viruses, Worms, and Trojan Horses: Serious Crimes, Nuisance, or Both?" *Social Science Computer Review*, vol. 25, iss. 1 (Spring 2007): 78–98.
49. Erik Larson, "Computers Turn Out to Be Valuable Aid in Employee Crime," *Wall Street Journal,* 14 January 1985, p. 1.
50. Clyde Wilson, "Software Piracy: Uncovering Mutiny on the Cyberseas," *Trial* 32 (1996): 24–31.
51. Susan W. Brenner, "At Light Speed": Attibution and Response to Cybercrime/Terrorism/Warfare, *Journal of Criminal Law & Criminology* (Winter 2007) vol. 97 iss. 2 (Winter 2007): 379–475.
52. Eddie Thai and Katherine Baird, "Overview of the National Agenda to Combat Organized Crime," *Public Policy Forum* (May 2007).
53. Government of Canada website, http://www.psepc-sppcc.gc.ca/policing/organized_crime/priorities/hightechcrime_e.asp (accessed 11 November 2011).
54. SeniorBusters Program, http://www. phonebusters.com/english/stopit_seniorbusters.html (accessed 11 November 2011).
55. Michael Fekete, Patricia Wilson, and Nicole Kutlesa, "Canada's Anti-Spam Law Coming into Force," Osler, Hoskin & Harcourt, 5 July 2011 http://www.osler.com/newsresources/Details.aspx?id=3614 (accessed 17 November 2011).
56. Reporting Economic Crime On-Line (RECOL), https://www.recol.ca/intro.aspx?lang=en (accessed 11 November 2011).
57. Phone Busters, the Canadian Anti-Fraud Call Centre, http://www.phonebusters.com.
58. Steven Edwards, "Madoff Gets 150 Years; Fraud Victims Cheer as Financier Sentenced in $65B Ponzi Scheme, *Star—Phoenix*, 30 June 2009, p. C5.
59. Herbert Edelhertz and Charles Rogovin, eds., *A National Strategy for Containing White-Collar Crime* (Lexington, MA: Lexington Books, 1980), Appendix A, pp. 122–123.
60. Kathleen Daly, "Gender and Varieties of White-Collar Crime," *Criminology* 27 (1989): 769–793.
61. Donald Cressey, *Other People's Money: A Study of the Social Psychology of Embezzlement* (Glencoe, IL: Free Press, 1973).
62. Ibid., p. 96.
63. Travis Hirschi and Michael Gottfredson, "Causes of White-Collar Crime," *Criminology* 25 (1987): 949–974.
64. Michael Gottfredson and Travis Hirschi, *A General Theory of Crime* (Stanford, CA: Stanford University Press, 1990), p. 191.
65. David Simon and D. Stanley Eitzen, *Elite Deviance* (Boston: Allyn and Bacon, 1982), p. 28.
66. This section relies heavily on Albert Reiss, Jr., "Selecting Strategies of Social Control over Organizational Life," in *Enforcing Regulation,* ed. Keith Hawkins and John M. Thomas (Boston: Klowver, 1984), pp. 25–37.
67. Raymond Michalowski and Ronald Kramer, "The Space Between Laws: The Problem of Corporate Crime in a Transnational Context," *Social Problems* 34 (1987): 34–53.
68. "Go Directly to Jail: White Collar Sentencing After the Sarbanes-Oxley Act," *Harvard Law Review*, vol. 122, iss. 6 (April 2009): 1728–1749; David Weisburd, Elin Waring, and Ellen Chayet, "Specific Deterrence in a Sample of Offenders Convicted of White-Collar Crimes," *Criminology*, vol. 33, iss. 4 (November 1995): 587–607; see also Steven Klepper and Daniel Nagin, "The Deterrent Effect of Perceived Certainty and Severity of Punishment Revisited," *Criminology* 27 (1989): 721–746.
69. Geis, "White-Collar and Corporate Crime," p. 154.
70. Norm Keith, *Corporate Crime and Accountability in Canada—From Prosecutions to Corporate Social Responsibility* (Markham, ON: LexisNexis Publishers, 2011).
71. Ellen Bressner and Shawn L. Graham, "Canada's First Criminal Conviction for Insider Trading," *Lexocology*, http://www.lexology.com/library/detail.aspx?g=9fea44e0-a422-42eb-9c89-5971e0f9c223, (accessed 17 November 2011).
72. Frank Pearce and Steve Tombs, "Hazards, Law and Class: Contextualizing the Regulation of Corporate Crime," *Social and Legal Studies* 6 (1997): 79–107, at p. 92.
73. See, generally, President's Commission on Organized Crime, Report to the President and the Attorney General, *The Impact: Organized Crime Today* (Washington, DC: U.S. Government Printing Office, 1986). Hereafter cited as *Organized Crime Today*; "2006 Annual Report on Organized Crime in Canada," *Trends in Organized Crime*, vol. 10, iss. 3 (September 2007): 76–88.
74. Frederick Martens and Michele Cunningham-Niederer, "Media Magic, Mafia Mania," *Federal Probation* 49 (1985): 60–68.
75. *Organized Crime Today*, pp. 7–8.
76. "Editorial: Organized Crime: Overview," *RCMP Gazette* 60 (1998): 3.

77. Criminal Intelligence Service Canada, *Annual Report,* 2009.
78. "Organized Crime Growing," *Blue Line Magazine,* February 2003, p. 16.
79. "CBC News In Depth: Biker Gangs in Canada," *CBC News,* 15 April 2009, http://www.cbc.ca/news/canada/story/2009/04/01/f-biker-gangs.html.
80. Criminal Intelligence Service Canada, *Annual Report,* 2009.
81. Donald Cressey, *Theft of the Nation* (New York: Harper and Row, 1969).
82. *Organized Crime Today*, p. 489.
83. Dwight Smith, *The Mafia Mystique* (New York: Basic Books, 1975).
84. Philip Jenkins and Gary Potter, "The Politics and Mythology of Organized Crime: A Philadelphia Case Study," *Journal of Criminal Justice* 15 (1987): 473–484.
85. Alan Block, *East Side/West Side* (New Brunswick, NJ: Transaction Books, 1983).
86. *Organized Crime Today*, p. 11.
87. Jenkins and Potter, "The Politics and Mythology of Organized Crime."
88. William Chambliss, *On the Take* (Bloomington: Indiana University Press, 1978).
89. Criminal Intelligence Service Canada, *Annual Report,* 2010.

Chapter 13

1. Sean Fine, "Porn Charges Dropped, Crown Wants Art Forfeited," *Globe and Mail,* 25 February 1994, pp. A1, A6.
2. Edwin Schur, *Crimes Without Victims* (Englewood Cliffs, NJ: Prentice-Hall, 1965).
3. Andrea Dworkin, quoted in "Where Do We Stand on Pornography?" *Ms* (January–February 1994), p. 34.
4. Jennifer E. Cobbina, and Sharon S. Oselin, "It's Not Only for the Money: An Analysis of Adolescent versus Adult Entry into Street Prostitution," *Sociological Inquiry*, vol. 81, iss. 3 (August 2011); 310–332.
5. Morris Cohen, "Moral Aspects of the Criminal Law," *Yale Law Journal* 49 (1940): 1017.
6. See Joel Feinberg, *Social Philosophy* (Englewood Cliffs, NJ: Prentice-Hall, 1973), chap. 2, 3.
7. *United States v. 12 200-ft Reels of Super 8mm Film*, 413 U.S. 123 (1973) at 137.
8. Irving Kristol, "Liberal Censorship and the Common Culture," *Society* 36 (September 1999): 5.
9. Wayne La Fave and Austin Scott, Jr., *Criminal Law* (St. Paul, MN: West, 1986), p. 12.
10. Ibid.
11. Howard Becker, *Outsiders* (New York: Macmillan, 1963), pp. 13–14.
12. See, generally, V. Bullogh, *Sexual Variance in Society and History* (Chicago: University of Chicago Press, 1958), pp. 143–144.
13. Spencer Rathus, *Human Sexuality* (New York: Holt, Rinehart and Winston, 1983), p. 463.
14. Scot Wortley, Benedikt Fischer, and Cheryl Webster, "Vice Lessons: A Survey of Prostitution Offenders Enrolled in the Toronto John School Program," *Canadian Journal of Criminology* 44 (October 2002): 369–402.
15. Monica Prasad, "The Morality of Market Exchange: Love, Money, and Contractual Justice," *Sociological Perspectives* 42 (1999): 181–187.
16. Canadian Socio-economic Information Management System, CANSIM Table 252-0051, "Incident-based Crime Statistics, by Detailed Violations, Annual (2009)" *Uniform Crime Reporting Survey*, Statistics Canada.
17. Scot Wortley, Benedikt Fischer, and Cheryl Webster, "Vice Lessons: A Survey of Prostitution Offenders Enrolled in the Toronto John School Program," *Canadian Journal of Criminology* 44 (October 2002): 369–402.
18. Federal/Provincial/Territorial Working Group on Prostitution, Report and Recommendation in Respect of Legislation, Policy and Practices Concerning Prostitution-Related Activities, Canada, December 1998.
19. Evan Wood, Jaime Schachar, Kathy Li, Jo-Anne Stoltz, Kate Shannon, Cari Miller, Elisa Lloyd-Smith, Mark W. Tyndall, and Thomas Kerr, "Sex Trade Involvement Is Associated with Elevated HIV Incidence Among Injection Drug Users in Vancouver," *Addiction Research & Theory*, vol. 15, iss. 3 (June 2007): 321–325; Kathleen N. Deering, Thomas Kerr, Mark W. Tyndall, Julio S.G. Montaner, Kate Gibson, Laurel Irons, and Kate Shannon, "A Peer-Led Mobile Outreach Program and Increased Utilization of Detoxification and Residential Drug Treatment Among Female Sex Workers Who Use Drugs in a Canadian Setting," *Drug & Alcohol Dependence*, vol. 113, iss. 1 (January 2011): 46–54.
20. Charles Winick and Paul Kinsie, *The Lively Commerce* (Chicago: Quadrangle, 1971), p. 58.
21. Linda Cusick, "Youth Prostitution: A Literature Review," *Child Abuse Review*, vol. 11, iss. 4 (July/August 2002): 230–251.
22. Linda Cusick, "Female Prostitution in Glasgow: Drug Use and Occupational Sector," *Addiction Research*, vol. 6, iss. 2 (April 1998): 115.
23. Winick and Kinsie, *The Lively Commerce,* pp. 172–173.
24. Paul Goldstein, "Occupational Mobility in the World of Prostitution: Becoming a Madam," *Deviant Behavior* 4 (1983): 267–279.
25. Mike McIntyre, "Cops Shut Wolseley Brothel," *Winnipeg Free Press*, 10 September 2009, p. A3.
26. Mireya Navarro, "Group Forced Illegal Aliens into Prostitution, U.S. Says," *New York Times,* 24 April 1998, p. A10.
27. Francine Lavoie, Caroline Thibodeau, Marie-Hélène Gagné and Martine Hébert, "Buying and Selling Sex in Québec Adolescents: A Study of Risk and Protective Factors," *Archives of Sexual Behavior*, vol. 39, iss. 5 (October 2010): 1147–1160; and Kimberly J. Mitchell, David Finkelhor and Janis Wolak, "Conceptualizing Juvenile Prostitution as Child Maltreatment: Findings from the National Juvenile Prostitution Study," *Child Maltreatment*, vol. 15, iss. 1 (February 2010): 18–36.
28. Kimberly J. Mitchell, David Finkelhor, and Janis Wolak, "Conceptualizing Juvenile Prostitution as Child Maltreatment: Findings from the National Juvenile Prostitution Study, *Child Maltreatment*, vol. 15, iss. 1 (February 2010): 18–36.
29. N. Jackman, Richard O'Toole, and Gilbert Geis, "The Self-Image of the Prostitute," in *Sexual Deviance,* ed. J. Gagnon and W. Simon (New York: Harper and Row, 1967), pp. 152–153.
30. Kimberly J. Mitchell, David Finkelhor, and Janis Wolak, "Conceptualizing Juvenile Prostitution as Child Maltreatment: Findings from the National Juvenile Prostitution Study," *Child Maltreatment*, vol. 15, iss. 1 (February 2010): 18–36.
31. Tracey Tyler, "Prostitution Laws Struck Down, *Toronto Star*, 28 September 2010, http://www.thestar.com/news/canada/article/867332--prostitution-laws-struck-down (accessed 7 August 2011).
32. Andrea Dworkin, *Pornography* (New York: Dutton, 1989).
33. Annette Jolin, "On the Backs of Working Prostitutes: Feminist Theory and Prostitution Policy," *Crime and Delinquency* 40 (1994): 60–83, at pp. 76–77.
34. Federal/Provincial/Territorial Working Group on Prostitution, Report and Recommendation in Respect of Legislation, Policy and Practices

Concerning Prostitution-Related Activities, Canada. Ottawa, Canada: Department of Justice, 1999.

35. Steven A. Kohm and John Selwood, *Sex Work and City Planning: Winnipeg's Red Light District Committee and the Regulation of Prostitution* (Winnipeg: Institute of Urban Studies, 2004). To read more about prostitution and escort services, read Matthew V. Pruitt and Amy C. Krull, "Escort Advertisements and Male Patronage of Prostitutes," *Deviant Behavior*, 32 (2011): 1, 38–63.
36. *Merriam-Webster Dictionary* (New York: Pocket Books, 1974), p. 484.
37. *Martin's Annual Criminal Code, 2012* (Aurora, ON: Canada Law Book, 2011), p. 311; Richard Barnhorst and Sherrie Barnhorst, *Criminal Law and the Canadian Criminal Code,* 4th ed. (Toronto: McGraw-Hill Ryerson, 2004).
38. Attorney General's Commission, Report on Pornography, *Final Report* (Washington, DC: U.S. Government Printing Office, 1986), pp. 837–901. Hereafter cited as Pornography Commission.
39. Stephanie Delaney, *Child Pornography and Sexual Exploitation of Children Online*, ECPAT International, September 2009, http://www.ecpat.net/ei/Publications/ICT/Child%20Friendly__Child%20Pornography_FINAL.pdf (accessed 8 November 2011).
40. Ann Wolbert Burgess (ed.) *Child Pornography and Sex Rings,* Lexington, MASS: Lexington Books, 1984.
41. *Report of the Commission on Obscenity and Pornography* (Washington, DC: U.S. Government Printing Office, 1970).
42. Pornography Commission, pp. 837–902.
43. Marvin Brown, Donald M. Amoroso, and Edward E. Ware, "Behavioral Effects of Viewing Pornography" *The Journal of Social Psychology* 98 (1976): 235–245.
44. Milton Diamond, "Pornography, Public Acceptance and Sex Related Crime: A Review," *International Journal of Law and Psychiatry*, 32 (5) (September 2009): 304–314.
45. Ron Langevin, Reuben Lang, Percy Wright, Lorraine Handy, Roy Frenzel, and Edward Black, "Pornography and Sexual Offences," *Sexual Abuse: A Journal of Research and Treatment*, 1 (3) (January 1988): 335–362.
46. Gert Martin Hald, Neil M. Malamuth, and Carlin Yuen, "Pornography and Attitudes Supporting Violence Against Women: Revisiting the Relationship in Nonexperimental Studies," *Aggressive Behavior*, vol. 36, iss. 1 (January/February 2010): 14–20; see also Drew A. Kingston, Paul Fedoroff, Philip Firestone, Susan Curry, and John M. Bradford, "Pornography use and Sexual Aggression: The Impact of Frequency and Type of Pornography Use on Recidivism Among Sexual Offenders," *Aggressive Behavior*, vol. 34, iss. 4 (July/August 2008): 341–351.
47. See Edward Donnerstein, Daniel Linz, and Steven Penrod, *The Question of Pornography* (New York: Free Press, 1987).
48. Kelly Cue Davis; Jeanette Norris, William H. George, Joel Martell, Julia R. Heiman, "Men's Likelihood of Sexual Aggression: The Influence of Alcohol, Sexual Arousal, and Violent Pornography," *Aggressive Behavior*, vol. 32, iss. 6 (November 2006): 581–589; Neil M. Malamuth, and Joseph Ceniti, "Repeated Exposure to Violent and Nonviolent Pornography: Likelihood of Raping Ratings and Laboratory Aggression Against Women," *Aggressive Behavior*, vol. 12, iss. 2 (1986): 129–137, Edward Donnerstein, "Pornography and Violence Against Women," *Annals of the New York Academy of Science* 347 (1980): 277–288
49. Gert Martin Hald, Neil M. Malamuth, and Carlin Yuen, "Pornography and Attitudes Supporting Violence against Women: Revisiting the Relationship in Nonexperimental Studies," *Aggressive Behavior*, vol. 36, iss. 1 (January/February 2010): 14–20.
50. *Martin's Annual Criminal Code, 2012* (Aurora, ON: Canada Law Book, 2011), p. 314; Barnhorst and Barnhorst, *Criminal Law and the Canadian Criminal Code*.
51. Barnhorst and Barnhorst, *Criminal Law and the Canadian Criminal Code*.
52. *Martin's Annual Criminal Code, 2012*; Barnhorst and Barnhorst, *Criminal Law and the Canadian Criminal Code*.
53. Criminal Code, Section 163 (8), *Martin's Annual Criminal Code, 2012,* p. 314.
54. Ibid.
55. Anthony Flint, "Skin Trade Spreading Across U.S.," *Boston Globe,* 1 December 1996, pp. 1, 36–37.
56. Thomas J. Lueck, "At Sex Shops, Fear That Ruling Means the End Is Near," *New York Times,* 25 February 1998, p. 1.
57. Kohm and Selwood, *Sex Work and City Planning*; J. Fraser, Report of the Special Committee on Pornography and Prostitution, vol. 2 (Ottawa: Supply and Services, 1985).
58. Sam Cooper, "Fort Nelson Licenses Escort Services Despite Opposition, *The Province*, 14 April 2010, p. A9.
59. Ann Landers, "Pornography Can Be an Addiction," *Boston Globe,* 19 July 1993, p. D36. By permission of Creators Syndicate.
60. Betsy Williams, "A Review on Cybersex Unplugged: Finding Sexual Health in the Electronic World," *Sexual Addiction & Compulsivity*, vol. 18, iss. 2 (April–June 2011): 104–106.
61. *Martin's Annual Criminal Code, 2012*, p. 332
62. Ibid.
63. Bill C-54 Protecting Children from Sexual Predators Act, An Act to amend the Criminal Code (Sexual Offences against Children), http://openparliament.ca/bills/40-3/C-54/ (accessed 1 November 2011).
64. Katherine Marshall "Gambling, 2010" (Ottawa: Statistics Canada, August 2010) Cat. no. 75-001-X, Chart A, Net Revenue from Government-run Gambling, http://www.statcan.gc.ca/pub/75-001-x/2010108/pdf/11297-eng.pdf (accessed 1 November 2011).
65. Jason J. Azmier, *Gambling in Canada: Final Report and Recommendations* (Calgary: Canada West Foundation, 2001).
66. Statistics Canada, "Uniform Crime Reporting Survey," CANSIM Table 252-0051, Incident-based Crime Statistics, by Detailed Violation 1998 to 2009 http://cansim2.statcan.gc.ca/cgi-win/cnsmcgi.exe?Lang=E&RootDir=CII/&ResultTemplate=CII/CII_pick&Array_Pick=1&ArrayId=252-0051 (accessed 1 November 2011).
67. Brian J Cox, Nancy Yu, Tracie O Afifi, and Robert Ladouceur, "A National Survey of Gambling Problems in Canada," *Canadian Journal of Psychiatry*, vol. 50 iss. 4 (March 2005): 213–217.
68. Katherine Marshall "Gambling, 2010."
69. N. A. Dowling, and M. Brown, "Commonalities in the Psychological Factors Associated with Problem Gambling and Internet Dependence," *Cyberpsychology, Behavior, And Social Networking* vol. 13, no. 4 (2010).
70. Azmier, *Gambling in Canada*.
71. Ralph Weisheit, "Studying Drugs in Rural Areas: Notes from the Field," *Journal of Research in Crime and Delinquency* 30 (1993): 213–232.
72. David Hewitt, Gary Vinje, Patricia Macneil, ed., *Horizons Three: Young Canadians' Alcohol and Other Drug Use: Increasing Our Understanding* (Ottawa: Health Canada, 1995).
73. Office of National Drug Control Policy, June 2003.
74. "British Officials Report Skyrocketing Heroin Use," *Alcoholism & Drug Abuse Weekly* 10 (17 August 1998): 7; National Institute on Drug Abuse, Community

Epidemiology Work Group, *Epidemiological Trends in Drug Abuse, Advance Report* (Washington, DC: National Institute on Drug Abuse, 1997).
75. *Canadian Addiction Survey (CAS): A National Survey of Canadians' Use of Alcohol and Other Drugs: Prevalence of Use and Related Harms: Highlights* (Ottawa, ON: Canadian Centre on Substance Abuse, 2004).
76. Statistics Canada, "Uniform Crime Reporting Survey," CANSIM Table 252-0051; and Mia Dauvergne and John Turner, *Police Reported Crime Statistics in Canada*, 2009, vol. 30, no. 2 (Summer 2010) Component of Statistics Canada Cat. no. 85-002-X.
77. Ibid.
78. Arnold Trebach, *The Heroin Solution* (New Haven, CT: Yale University Press, 1982).
79. Robert Fife, "CEOs Fear Reefer Madness," *National Post,* 22 November 2004, p. A1.
80. James Inciardi, *The War on Drugs* (Palo Alto, CA: Mayfield, 1986), p. 2.
81. See, generally, David Pittman, "Drug Addiction and Crime," in *Handbook of Criminology,* ed. D. Glazer (Chicago: Rand McNally, 1974), pp. 209–232; Board of Directors, National Council on Crime and Delinquency, "Drug Addiction: A Medical, Not a Law Enforcement, Problem," *Crime and Delinquency* 20 (1974): 4–9.
82. Associated Press, "Records Detail Royals' Turn-of-Century Drug Use," *Boston Globe,* 29 August 1993, p. 13.
83. Neil Boyd, *Canadian Law: An Introduction* (Toronto: Harcourt Brace Canada, 1998).
84. Gerald Hallowell, "Prohibition,"http://www.thecanadianencyclopedia.com, 2005.
85. Ibid.
86. McCaghy, *Deviant Behavior,* p. 280.
87. Gerald Hallowell, "Prohibition."
88. McCaghy, *Deviant Behavior*.
89. "Angus Reid Public Opinion: Majority of Canadians Would Legalize Marijuana, But Not Other Drugs," Vision Critical website http://www.visioncritical.com/category/global-opinions-and-trends (accessed 1 November 2011).
90. "Canada's High Court to Rule on Safe-Injection Site," *Canadian Press* 9 May 2011 http://www.thestar.com/news/canada/article/987998--canada-s-high-court-to-rule-on-safe-injection-site (accessed 8 August 2011).
91. "Vancouver's Injection Clinic Gets Supreme Court Blessing to Stay Open," *The Star*, 1 October, 2011, http://www.thestar.com/news/article/1062370 (accessed 1 November 2011).
92. "Date-Rape Drug Valued at $15M Seized in B.C" 26 January 2011, CBC News, http://www.cbc.ca/news/canada/british-columbia/story/2011/01/26/bc-record-ketamine-bust.html (accessed 8 August 2011).
93. Curtis, Richard, "The Improbable Transformation of Inner-City Neighborhoods: Crime, Violence, Drugs, and Youth in the 1990s," *Journal of Criminal Law & Criminology*, vol. 88, iss. 4 (Summer 1998): 1233–1276.
94. Marvin Krohn, Alan Lizotte, Terence Thornberry, Carolyn Smith, and David McDowall, "Reciprocal Causal Relationships Among Drug Use, Peers, and Beliefs: A Five-Wave Panel Model," *Journal of Drug Issues* 26 (1996): 205–228.
95. R. Cloward and L. Ohlin, *Delinquency and Opportunity: A Theory of Delinquent Gangs* (Glencoe, IL: Free Press, 1960).
96. Lening Zhang, John Welte, and William Wieczorek, "Youth Gangs, Drug Use and Delinquency," *Journal of Criminal Justice* 27 (1999): 101–109.
97. See Elsbeth Tupker, "Youth and Drugs and Mental Health: A Resource for Professionals" (Toronto: Centre for Addiction and Mental Health, 2004).
98. Sally Weinrich and Sally Hardin, "Social Support and Psychological Correlates of High School Students Who Use Illicit Drugs," *American Journal of Health Studies*, vol. 13, iss. 1 (1997): 17.
99. Substance Abuse and Mental Health Services Administration, Office of Applied Studies, "The Relationship Between Mental Health and Substance Abuse Among Adolescents," *Analytic Series: A-9*, 1999.
100. Alison Bass, "Mental Ills, Drug Abuse Linked," *Boston Globe,* 21 November 1990, p. 3.
101. D. W. Goodwin, "Alcoholism and Genetics," *Archives of General Psychiatry* 42 (1985): 171–174.
102. For a thorough review of this issue, see John Petraitis, Brian Flay, and Todd Miller, "Reviewing Theories of Adolescent Substance Use: Organizing Pieces in the Puzzle," *Psychological Bulletin* 117 (1995): 67–86.
103. Jennifer O'Loughlin, "Variant Gene Causes Students to Become Addicted to Tobacco: McGill Study," *Telegram* (St. John's, Nfld.), 24 November 2004, p. A12.
104. Judith Brooks and Li-Jung Tseng, "Influences of Parental Drug Use, Personality, and Child Rearing on the Toddler's Anger and Negativity," *Genetic, Social and General Psychology Monographs* 122 (1996): 107–128.
105. Andrew Percy, Maeve Thornton, and Patrick McCrystal, "The Extent and Nature of Family Alcohol and Drug Use: Findings from the Belfast Youth Development Study," *Child Abuse Review*, vol. 17, iss. 6 (November/December 2008): 371–386.
106. Denise Kandel and Mark Davies, "Friendship Networks, Intimacy, and Illicit Drug Use in Young Adulthood: A Comparison of Two Competing Theories," *Criminology* 29 (1991): 441–471.
107. Robert John Zagar, Kenneth G. Busch, William M. Grove, and John Russell Hughes, "Summary of Studies of Abused Infants and Children Later Homicidal, and Homicidal, Assaulting Later Homicidal, and Sexual Homicidal Youth and Adults," *Psychological Reports*, vol. 104, iss. 1 (February 2009): 17–45.
108. D. Baer and J. Corrado, "Heroin Addict Relationships with Parents During Childhood and Early Adolescent Years," *Journal of Genetic Psychology* 124 (1974): 99–103.
109. John Wallace and Jerald Bachman, "Explaining Racial/Ethnic Differences in Adolescent Drug Use: The Impact of Background and Lifestyle," *Social Problems* 38 (1991): 333–357.
110. John Donovan, "Problem-Behavior Theory and the Explanation of Adolescent Marijuana Use," *Journal of Drug Issues* 26 (1996): 379–404.
111. Jeanette Østergaard, "Learning to Become an Alcohol User: Adolescents Taking Risks and Parents Living with Uncertainty," *Addiction Research & Theory*, vol. 17, iss. 1 (February 2009): 30–53.
112. Ibid.
113. Steve Sussman, Nadra Lisha, and Mark Griffiths, "Prevalence of the Addictions: A Problem of the Majority or the Minority?" *Evaluation & the Health Professions* 34 (1) (March 2011): 3–56; and Michael Newcomb and Mitchell Earleywine, "Intrapersonal Contributors to Drug Use: The Willing Host," *American Behavioral Scientist* 39 (7) (June 1996): 823–837.
114. Andrew Golub and Bruce Johnson, "The Multiple Paths Through Alcohol, Tobacco and Marijuana to Hard Drug Use Among Arrestees," paper presented at the annual meeting of the American Society of Criminology, San Diego, November 1997.
115. Inciardi, *The War on Drugs,* p. 60.
116. Mia Dauvergne, "Trends in Police-reported Drug Offences in Canada, Statistics Canada, *Juristat*, vol. 29 no. 2 (May 2009), Cat. 85-002 _ X.

117. Josee Savoie, "Homicide in Canada, 2002," Statistics Canada, Canadian Centre for Justice Statistics, Cat. no. 85-002- XIE, vol. 23, no. 8.

118. Ibid.

119. Kathryn Graham, Sharon Bernards, Sharon Wilsnack, and Gerhard Gmel, "Alcohol May Not Cause Partner Violence But It Seems to Make It Worse: A Cross National Comparison of the Relationship Between Alcohol and Severity of Partner Violence," *Journal of Interpersonal Violence* 26 (8) (May 2011): 1503–152;3 and Besserer and Trainor, "Criminal Victimization in Canada, 1999."

120. Douglas B. Marlowe, David S. Festinger, Karen L. Dugosh, Anne Caron, Marcy R. Podkopacz, and Nicolle T. Clements, "Targeting Dispositions for Drug-Involved Offenders: A Field Trial of the Risk and Needs Triage (RANT)™," *Journal of Criminal Justice*, vol. 39, iss. 3 (May 2011): 253–260; Mark A.R. Kleiman, and Lowry Heussler, "Crime-Minimizing Drug Policy," *Journal of Criminal Justice*, vol. 39, iss. 3 (May 2011): 286–288; and Charles Faupel and Carl Klockars, "Drugs–Crime Connections: Elaborations from the Life Histories of Hard-Core Heroin Addicts," *Social Problems* 34 (1987): 54–68.

121. Carrie Oser, Carl Leukefeld, Michele Staton-Tindall, Jamieson Duvall, Thomas Garrity, William Stoops, Russel Falck, Wang Jichuan; Robert Carlson, Rocky Sexton, Patricia Wright, and Brenda Booth, "Criminality Among Rural Stimulant Users in the United States," *Crime & Delinquency*, vol. 57, iss. 4 (July 2011,): 600–621; and Michael E. Ezell, Emily E. Tanner-Smith, "Examining the Role of Lifestyle and Criminal History Variables on the Risk of Homicide Victimization," *Homicide Studies*, vol. 13, iss. 2 (May 2009): 144–173.

122. M. Douglas Anglin, Barry S. Brown, Richard Dembo, and Carl Leukefeld, "CRIMinality and Addiction: Selected Issues for Future Policies, Practice, & Research," *Journal of Drug Issues*, vol. 39, iss. 1 (Winter 2009): 89–99.

123. Paul Goldstein, "The Drugs–Violence Nexus: A Tripartite Conceptual Framework," *Journal of Drug Issues* 15 (1985): 493–506; Marvin Krohn, Alan Lizotte, and Cynthia Perez, "The Interrelationship Between Substance Use and Precocious Transitions to Adult Sexuality," *Journal of Health and Social Behavior* 38 (1997): 87–103, at p. 88; Richard Jessor, "Risk Behavior in Adolescence: A Psychosocial Framework for Understanding and Action," in *Adolescents at Risk: Medical and Social Perspectives*, ed. D. E. Rogers and E. Ginzburg (Boulder, CO: Westview, 1992).

124. Boyd, *Canadian Law: An Introduction*.

125. Ibid.

126. Ibid.

127. Ibid.

128. *Martin's Annual Criminal Code, 2012*.

129. Department of Justice Canada "Impaired Driving," http://www.justice.gc.ca/eng/pi/pcvi-cpcv/id-cafa.html (accessed 11 November 2011).

130. Andrew B. Whitford and Jeff Yates, *Presidential Rhetoric and the Public Agenda: Constructing the War on Drugs* (Baltimore, MD: Johns Hopkins University Press, 2009).

131. U.S. Department of State, 1998 International Narcotics Control Strategy Report, February 1999.

132. Clifford Krauss, "Neighbors Worry About Colombian Aid," *New York Times*, 25 August 2000, p. A3.

133. John Intini "Guns in the Sun," *Maclean's*, vol. 120 iss. 21 (4 April 2007): 23–24.

134. Jacqueline M. Drew, "Police Responses to the Methamphetamine Problem: An Analysis of the Organizational and Regulatory Context," *Police Quarterly* vol. 14, iss. 2 (June 2011): 99–123 and Government of Canada, National Anti-Drug Strategy Enforcement http://www.nationalantidrugstrategy.gc.ca/enf-app.html (accessed 11 November 2011).

135. John S. Goldkamp, E. Rely Vîlcic, "Targeted Enforcement and Adverse System Side Effects: The Generation of Fugitives in Philadelphia," *Criminology*, vol. 46, iss. 2 (May 2008): 371–409; and Mark Moore, *Drug Trafficking* (Washington, DC: National Institute of Justice, 1988).

136. Carol Kaplan, *Sentencing and Time Served* (Washington, DC: Bureau of Justice Statistics, 1987).

137. Peter Rossi, Richard Berk, and Alec Campbell, "Just Punishments: Guideline Sentences and Normative Consensus," *Journal of Quantitative Criminology* 13 (1997): 267–283.

138. Marnie Wallace, "Crime Statistics in Canada, 2003," *Juristat*, 24, 6 (Ottawa: Statistics Canada, 2001), Cat. no. 85-002-XIE.

139. CBC News, "Canadians Split on Pot, Death Penalty: Poll," http://www.cbc.ca/news/canada/story/2010/03/18/ekos-poll018.html (accessed 11 November 2011).

140. Robert Davis, Arthur Lurigio, and Dennis Rosenbaum, eds., *Drugs and the Community* (Springfield, IL: Charles Thomas, 1993), pp. xii–xv.

141. Saul Weingart, "A Typology of Community Responses to Drugs," in *Drugs and the Community*, ed. Robert Davis, Arthur Lurigio, and Dennis Rosenbaum (Springfield, IL: Charles Thomas, 1993), pp. 85–105.

142. Earl Wyson, Richard Aniskiewicz, and David Wright, "Truth and DARE: Tracking Drug Education to Graduation as Symbolic Politics," *Social Problems* 41 (1994): 448–471.

143. Ibid.

144. Dennis M. Gorman, and Charles Huber Jr., "The Social Construction of "Evidence-Based" Drug Prevention Programs: A Reanalysis of Data from the Drug Abuse Resistance Education (DARE) Program," *Evaluation Review*, vol. 33, iss. 4 (August 2009): 396–414; and Dennis Rosenbaum, Robert Flewelling, Susan Bailey, Chris Ringwalt, and Deanna Wilkinson, "Cops in the Classroom: A Longitudinal Evaluation of Drug Abuse Resistance Education (DARE)," *Journal of Research in Crime and Delinquency* 31 (1994): 3–31.

145. Mareanne Zawitz, *Drugs, Crime, and the Justice System* (Washington, DC: U.S. Government Printing Office, 1992), pp. 115–122.

146. Canadian Human Rights Commission, *Policy on Alcohol and Drug Testing* (Ottawa: Canadian Human Rights Commission, 2002).

147. Christine B. Kleinpeter, Jo Brocato, and Jeffrey J. Koob, "Does Drug Testing Deter Drug Court Participants from Using Drugs or Alcohol?" *Journal of Offender Rehabilitation*, vol. 49, iss. 6 (August/September 2010): 434–444:, Charlotte L. Powell, Deborah Bamber, and Marilyn M. Christie, "Drug Treatment in the Criminal Justice System: Lessons Learned from Offenders on DTTOs," *Drugs: Education, Prevention & Policy*, vol. 14, iss. 4 (August 2007): 333–345; and John Goldkamp and Peter Jones, "Pretrial Drug-Testing Experiments in Milwaukee and Prince George's County: The Context of Implementation," *Journal of Research in Crime and Delinquency* 29 (1992): 430–465; Chester Britt, Michael Gottfredson, and John Goldkamp, "Drug Testing and Pretrial Misconduct: An Experiment on the Specific Deterrent Effects of Drug Monitoring Defendants on Pretrial Release," *Journal of Research in Crime and Delinquency* 29 (1992): 62–78.

148. See, generally, Peter Greenwood and Franklin Zimring, *One More Chance* (Santa Monica, CA: Rand Corporation, 1985).

149. Anna Greaves, David Best, Ed Day, and Angela Foster, "Young People in Coerced Drug Treatment: Does the UK Drug Intervention Programme Provide a Useful and Effective Service to Young Offenders?" *Addiction Research & Theory*, vol. 17, iss. 1 (February 2009): 17–29.
150. Elizabeth Evans, Douglas Longshore, Michael Prendergast, and Darren Urada, "Evaluation of the Substance Abuse and Crime Prevention Act: Client Characteristics, Treatment Completion and Re-Offending Three Years After Implementation," *Journal of Psychoactive Drugs* vol. 38 (November 2006 Supplement 3): 357–367.
151. The following section is based on material found in Jerome Platt, "Vocational Rehabilitation of Drug Abusers," *Psychological Bulletin* 117 (1995): 416–433.
152. Diane Riley, *Drugs and Drug Policy in Canada: A Brief Review and Commentary* (Ottawa: Canadian Foundation for Drug Policy, 1998).
153. CBC News, "Canadians Split on Pot, Death Penalty: Poll."
154. Patricia Erickson, Diane Riley, Yuet Cheung, and Patrick O'Hare, eds., *Harm Reduction: A New Direction for Drug Policies and Programs* (Toronto: University of Toronto Press, 1997).
155. Ethan Nadelmann, "America's Drug Problem," *Bulletin of the American Academy of Arts and Sciences* 65 (1991): 24–40.
156. Ibid., p. 24.
157. Ethan Nadelmann, "Should We Legalize Drugs? History Answers Yes," *American Heritage* (February/March 1993): 41–56.
158. Caitlin Elizabeth Hughes and Alex Stevens, "What Can We Learn from the Portuguese Decriminalization of Illicit Drugs?" *British Journal of Criminology*, vol. 50, iss. 6 (November 2010): 999–1022; and Collis Parrett, "Illicit Drugs Policy: Legal and International Perspectives," *MEANJIN*, vol. 61, iss. 2 (2002): 59.
159. David Courtwright, "Should We Legalize Drugs? History Answers No," *American Heritage* (February/March 1993): 43–56.
160. C. W. J. Maris, "The Disasters of War: American Repression versus Dutch Tolerance in Drug Policy," *Journal of Drug Issues*, vol. 29, iss. 3 (Summer 1999): 493–510; and Charles B. Rangel, "Why Drug Legalization Should Be Opposed," *Criminal Justice Ethics*, vol. 17, iss. 2 (Summer/Fall 1998): 2; and Kathryn Ann Farr, "Revitalizing the Drug Decriminalization Debate," *Crime and Delinquency* 36 (1990): 223–237.

Index

Notes: Entries and page numbers in bold refer to key terms and the pages in the text on which they are defined. Page numbers followed by an *f* refer to figures; page numbers followed by a *t* refer to tables.

Q

R

Chapter in Review

To help you succeed, we have designed a review card for each chapter.

Learning Outcomes

LO1
Define criminology.

LO2
Describe the development of the discipline of criminology.

LO3
Identify the subareas that constitute the discipline of criminology.

LO4
Identify the major pers[illegible] nology and the focus [illegible]

Here, you'll find the key terms and definitions in the order they appear in the chapter.

LO5
Define common law and its relationship to the Criminal Code of Canada.

LO6
Explain the purpose of criminal law.

LO7
Define the elements of a crime.

Key Terms

absolute liability crimes 20

actus reus 18

anomie 8

biosocial theo[illegible]

capital punish[illegible]

Chicago Schoo[illegible]

classical crimi[illegible]

Code of Hamm[illegible]

common law

conflict theory

conflict view

How to use the Card:

1. Look over the card to preview the new concepts you'll be introduced to in the chapter.
2. Read your chapter to fully understand the material.
3. Go to class (and pay attention).
4. Review the card one more time to make sure you've registered the key concepts.
5. Don't forget, this card is only one of many CRIM learning tools available to help you succeed in your criminology course.

Thinking Like a Criminologist

Criminology is the scientific approach to the study of criminal behaviour and society's reaction to law violations and violators. It is [illegible] plinary field; many of its prac[illegible] trained as sociologists, anthropologists, ps[illegible] political scientists, historians, and natural scientists.

In this column, you'll find summary points supported by exhibits from the chapters.

Criminology has a rich history, with roots in the utilitarian philosophy of Beccaria, the biological positivism of Lombroso, the social theory of Durkheim, and the political philosophy of Marx.

The criminological enterprise includes subareas such as criminal statistics, the sociology of law, theory construction, criminal behaviour systems, penology, and victimology.

Criminologists believe in one of three perspectives: the consensus view, the conflict view, or the interactionist view. The consensus view holds that criminal behaviour is defined by laws that reflect the values and morals of a majority of citizens. The conflict view states that criminal behaviour is defined in such a way that economically powerful groups can retain their control over society. The interactionist view portrays criminal behaviour as a relativistic, constantly changing concept that reflects society's current moral values. According to the interactionist view, behaviour is labelled as criminal by those in power; criminals are people society chooses to label as outsiders or deviants.

The criminal law is a set of rules that specify the behaviours society has outlawed. The criminal law serves several important purposes: It represents public opinion and moral values, it enforces social controls, it deters criminal behaviour and wrongdoing, it punishes transgressors, and it banishes private retribution.

Canadian criminal law traces its origin to the English common law. In the Canadian legal system, lawmakers have codified common-law crimes into the Criminal Code. Every crime has specific elements. In most instances, these elements include both the *actus reus* (guilty act) and the *mens rea* (guilty mind)—the person's state of mind or criminal intent.

At trial, a defendant may claim to have lacked *mens rea* and, therefore, not be responsible for a criminal action. One type of defence is excuse for incapacity, such as mental disorder, automatism, or intoxication. Another type of defence is justification by reason of self-defence or entrapment.

The criminal law is undergoing constant reform. Some acts are being decriminalized—their penalties are being reduced—while penalties for others are becoming more severe.

Ethical issues arise when the questions criminologists choose to study appear biased or exclusionary. These issues may cause serious consequences because their findings can significantly impact individuals and groups.

For additional chapter links, discussions, and quizzes, see the book-specific website at http://www.icancrim2.com.

You have been experi[illegible] to identify a surefire me[illegible]

When it's time to prepare for exams, use the Card and the technique to the left to ensure successful study sessions.

CRIME AND CRIMINOLOGY

Chapter in Review

Learning Outcomes

LO1
Define criminology.

LO2
Describe the development of the discipline of criminology.

LO3
Identify the subareas that constitute the discipline of criminology.

LO4
Identify the major perspectives of criminology and the focus of each.

LO5
Define common law and its relationship to the Criminal Code of Canada.

LO6
Explain the purpose of criminal law.

LO7
Define the elements of a crime.

Key Terms

absolute liability crimes 20

actus reus 18

anomie 8

biosocial theory 7

capital punishment 13

Chicago School 8

classical criminology 5

Code of Hammurabi 16

common law 17

conflict theory 9

conflict view 15

SUMMARY

Criminology is the scientific approach to the study of criminal behaviour and society's reaction to law violations and violators. It is essentially an interdisciplinary field; many of its practitioners were originally trained as sociologists, anthropologists, psychologists, economists, political scientists, historians, and natural scientists.

Criminology has a rich history, with roots in the utilitarian philosophy of Beccaria, the biological positivism of Lombroso, the social theory of Durkheim, and the political philosophy of Marx.

The criminological enterprise includes subareas such as criminal statistics, the sociology of law, theory construction, criminal behaviour systems, penology, and victimology.

Criminologists believe in one of three perspectives: the consensus view, the conflict view, or the interactionist view. The consensus view holds that criminal behaviour is defined by laws that reflect the values and morals of a majority of citizens. The conflict view states that criminal behaviour is defined in such a way that economically powerful groups can retain their control over society. The interactionist view portrays criminal behaviour as a relativistic, constantly changing concept that reflects society's current moral values. According to the interactionist view, behaviour is labelled as criminal by those in power; criminals are people society chooses to label as outsiders or deviants.

The criminal law is a set of rules that specify the behaviours society has outlawed. The criminal law serves several important purposes: It represents public opinion and moral values, it enforces social controls, it deters criminal behaviour and wrongdoing, it punishes transgressors, and it banishes private retribution.

Canadian criminal law traces its origin to the English common law. In the Canadian legal system, lawmakers have codified common-law crimes into the Criminal Code. Every crime has specific elements. In most instances, these elements include both the *actus reus* (guilty act) and the *mens rea* (guilty mind)—the person's state of mind or criminal intent.

At trial, a defendant may claim to have lacked *mens rea* and, therefore, not be responsible for a criminal action. One type of defence is excuse for incapacity, such as mental disorder, automatism, or intoxication. Another type of defence is justification by reason of self-defence or entrapment.

The criminal law is undergoing constant reform. Some acts are being decriminalized—their penalties are being reduced—while penalties for others are becoming more severe.

Ethical issues arise when the questions criminologists choose to study appear biased or exclusionary. These issues may cause serious consequences because their findings can significantly impact individuals and groups.

For additional chapter links, discussions, and quizzes, see the book-specific website at http://www.icancrim2.com.

You have been experimenting with various techniques in order to identify a surefire method for predicting violent behaviour in consensus view 14

crime 13

criminal law 15

criminology 4

deviance 13

excuse defence 20

indictable offence 17

interactionist view 15

interdisciplinary 4

justification defence 20

mandatory sentences 13

mens rea 18

Mosaic Code 16

penology 13

positivism 6

precedent 17

rational choice theory 10

rehabilitation 13

reliable 11

social structure theory 10

socialization 9

sociological criminology 7

statutory crimes 17

summary conviction offence 17

utilitarianism 5

valid 11

victimology 13

white-collar crime 13

delinquents. Your procedure involves brain scans, DNA testing, and blood analysis. Used with samples of incarcerated adolescents, your procedure has been able to distinguish with 80 percent accuracy between youths with a history of violence and those who are exclusively property offenders. Your research indicates that if all youths were tested with your techniques, potentially violence-prone career criminals could be easily identified for special treatment. For example, children in the local school system could be tested, and those identified as violence-prone could be carefully monitored by teachers. Those at risk for future violence could be put into special programs as a precaution.

Some of your colleagues argue that this type of testing contravenes the Canadian Charter of Rights because it violates the subjects' Section 13 protection against self-incrimination. There is also the problem of error: Some children may be falsely labelled as violence-prone.

How would you answer your critics? Is it fair or ethical to label people as potentially criminal and violent even though they have not yet exhibited any antisocial behaviour? Do the risks of such a procedure outweigh its benefits?

Discussion Questions

1. What are the specific aims and purposes of the criminal law? To what extent does the criminal law control behaviour? Do you believe that the law is too restrictive? Not restrictive enough?
2. If you ran the world, which acts, now legal, would you make criminal? Which criminal acts would you legalize? What would be the likely consequences of your actions?
3. Beccaria argued that the threat of punishment controls crime. Are there other forms of social control? Aside from the threat of legal punishment, what else controls your own behaviour?
4. Would it be ethical for a criminologist to observe a teenage gang by hanging with them, drinking, and watching as they steal cars? Should the criminologist report that behaviour to the police?

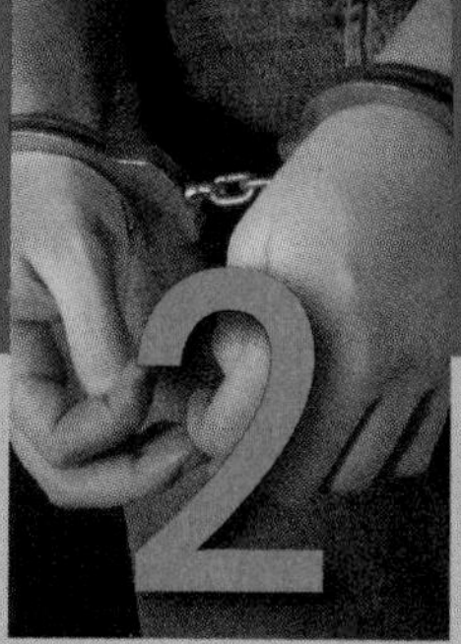

Chapter in Review

Learning Outcomes

LO1
Name three primary sources of crime statistics used in Canada.

LO2
Explain the benefits of the Crime Severity Index.

LO3
Identify the strengths and weaknesses of crime statistics.

LO4
Identify the important trends over time in the Canadian crime rate.

LO5
Identify major factors that influence the crime rate.

LO6
Define aging out or desistance.

LO7
Define racial profiling

Key Terms

aging out (desistance) 41

chronic offenders 47

Crime Severity Index 31

masculinity hypothesis 41

Personal Risk and Victimization Survey (PRVS) 32

self-report surveys 32

street crimes 38

suite crimes 39

UCR2 26

Uniform Crime Report (UCR) 26

SUMMARY

There are three primary sources of crime statistics: the Uniform Crime Reports, based on police data accumulated by the Canadian Centre for Justice Statistics; self-reports from criminal behaviour surveys; and victim surveys. The Crime Severity Index, based on the UCR data, was introduced as a new, overall measure of crime in 2009. The Crime Severity Index helps to determine the severity of police-reported crime in relation to the past and to Canada overall. The mechanics involve assigning a "seriousness" weight to each type of offence that is derived from actual sentences handed down by courts in all provinces and territories, with more serious crimes being assigned higher weight than less serious ones.

Each data source has its strengths and weaknesses. The UCR, based only on crimes reported to the police, tends to underrepresent the total amount of crime. Self-reports from criminal behaviour surveys, often conducted with young people, tend to overrepresent minor crimes such as vandalism or shoplifting, and downplay involvement in serious crimes such as sexual assault. Victim surveys may more validly represent minor types of crimes such as theft or vandalism that victims did not report to police, but more serious crimes may be underrepresented, due to victims' fear of disclosing traumatic events or fear of getting in trouble themselves.

The data sources show stable patterns in the crime rate. Ecological patterns show that crime varies by season and by urban versus rural environment. There is also evidence of gender and age gaps in the crime rate: Men commit more crime than women, and young people commit more crime than the elderly. Crime data show that people commit less crime as they age, but the significance and cause of this pattern are still not completely understood.

Similarly, racial and class patterns appear in the crime rate. However, it is still unclear whether these are true differences or a function of discriminatory law enforcement known as "racial profiling."

One of the most important findings in the crime statistics is the existence of the chronic offender, a repeat criminal responsible for a significant amount of all law violations. Chronic offenders begin their careers early in life and, rather than aging out of crime, persist into adulthood. The discovery of the chronic offender has led to the study of developmental criminology—why people persist, desist, terminate, or escalate their deviant behaviour.

For additional chapter links, discussions, and quizzes, see the book-specific website at http://www.icancrim2.com.

The provincial minister of correctional services has called a meeting to ask your advice on how to reduce the threat of repeat young offenders. Some of the more conservative members of her staff seem to believe that these young offenders need a strict dose of rough justice if they are to be turned away from a life of crime. They believe that juvenile delinquents who are punished harshly are less likely to recidivate than youths who receive lesser

Youth Criminal Justice Act (YCJA) 43

punishments, such as community corrections or probation. In addition, they believe that hard-core, violent offenders deserve to be punished; excessive concern for offenders and not their acts ignores the rights of victims and society in general.

The minister is unsure whether such an approach can reduce the threat of chronic (repeat) offending. Can tough punishment produce deviant identities that lock young offenders into a criminal way of life? She is concerned that a strategy stressing punishment will have relatively little impact on chronic offenders and, if anything, may cause escalation in serious criminal behaviours.

She has asked for your professional advice. On the one hand, the system must be sensitive to the adverse effects of stigma and labelling. On the other hand, the need for control and deterrence must not be ignored. Is it possible to reconcile these two opposing views?

Discussion Questions

1. Would you answer honestly if a national crime survey asked you about your criminal behaviour, including underage drinking and drug use? If not, why?
2. How would you explain gender differences in the crime rate? That is, why do you think males are more violent than females?
3. Assuming that males are more violent than females, does that mean that crime has a biological rather than a social basis (because males and females share a similar environment)?
4. UCR data tell us that crime rates are higher in large cities than in small villages. What does that tell us about the effect of TV, films, and music on teenage behaviour?

VICTIMS AND VICTIMIZATION

Chapter in Review

Learning Outcomes

LO1
Define victimology.

LO2
Identify major problems faced by victims of crime.

LO3
Identify major risk factors for being victimized.

LO4
Explain the victim precipitation theory, lifestyle theories, and routine activities theory.

LO5
List organizations created to assist victims of violence in Canada.

LO6
Identify victims' services programs.

LO7
Identify major legislation pertaining to victims' rights.

LO8
Describe major programs designed to prevent crime.

Key Terms

active precipitation 59

capable guardians 61

compensation 64

crisis intervention 65

cycle of violence 53

deviant place theory 61

lifestyle theories 60

motivated offenders 61

passive precipitation 59

SUMMARY

Criminologists now consider victims and victimization a major focus of study. About 7.6 million Canadians are victims of crime each year, and the social and economic costs of crime are in the billions of dollars. Like crime, victimization has stable patterns and trends. Violent crime victims tend to be young, poor, single males living in large cities, although victims come in all ages, sizes, races, and genders. Many victimizations occur in the home, and many victims are the target of relatives and loved ones.

There are a number of theories of victimization. One view, called victim precipitation, is that victims provoke criminals. More common are lifestyle theories that suggest that victims put themselves in danger by engaging in high-risk activities, such as going out late at night, living in a high-crime area, and associating with high-risk peers. Deviant place theory argues that victimization risk is related to neighbourhood crime rates. The routine activities theory maintains that a pool of motivated offenders exists and that these offenders will take advantage of unguarded, suitable targets.

Numerous programs help victims by providing court services, economic compensation, public education, and crisis intervention. The federal government and the provinces and territories have endorsed a Canadian Statement of the Basic Principles of Justice for Victims of Crime that will guide the formulation of legislations, policies, and procedures for addressing the needs of victims in the future.

For additional chapter links, discussions, and quizzes, see the book-specific website at http://www.icancrim2.com.

The assistant deputy minister of the province's Ministry of Children's Services has asked you to evaluate a self-report survey of adolescents ages 12 to 18. She has provided you with the following information on physical abuse.

Adolescents experiencing abuse or violence are at high risk of immediate and lasting negative effects on health and well-being. Of the high school students surveyed, an alarming 21 percent said they had been physically abused. Of the older students, ages 15 to 18, 29 percent said they had been physically abused. Younger students also reported significant rates of abuse: 17 percent responded "yes" when questioned whether they had been physically abused. Although girls were far less likely to report abuse than boys, 12 percent said they had been physically abused. Most abuse occurs at home; it occurs more than once; and the abuser is usually a family member. More than half of those physically abused had tried alcohol and drugs, and 60 percent admitted to a violent act. Nonabused children were significantly less likely to abuse substances, and only 30 percent indicated they had committed a violent act.

How would you interpret these data? What factors might influence their validity? What is your interpretation of the association between abuse and delinquency?

posttraumatic stress disorder 52

routine activities theory 61

suitable targets 61

target hardening 66

victim precipitation theory 59

victim–offender reconciliation programs 65

victimologists 50

victimology 50

Discussion Questions

1. Considering what you have learned in this chapter about crime victimization, what measures can you take to better protect yourself from crime?
2. Do you agree with the assessment that for young people, a school is one of the most dangerous locations in the community? Did you find your high school to be a dangerous environment?
3. Do people bear some of the responsibility for their victimization if they maintain a lifestyle that contributes to the chances of becoming a crime victim? That is, should we "blame the victim"?
4. Have you ever experienced someone "precipitating" crime? If so, did you do anything to help the situation?

CHOICE THEORY: BECAUSE THEY WANT TO

4 Chapter in Review

Learning Outcomes

LO1
State the major premises underlying choice theory.

LO2
Explain the concept of situational crime prevention.

LO3
Explain general deterrence.

LO4
Explain specific deterrence.

LO5
Explain the logic of incapacitation as a means of crime reduction.

LO6
Outline the policy implications of choice theory.

Key Terms

brutalization effect 80

choice theory 69

classical criminology 70

crackdown 79

defensible space 76

diffusion of benefits 78

discouragement 78

displacement 77

edgework 75

extinction 77

general deterrence 78

incapacitation effect 84

incarceration 83

SUMMARY

Choice theories assume that criminals carefully choose whether to commit criminal acts. People are influenced by their fear of the criminal penalties associated with being caught and convicted for law violations. The more severe, certain, and swift the punishment, the more likely it is to control crime. The choice approach is rooted in the classical criminology of Cesare Beccaria, who argued that punishment should be certain, swift, and severe enough to deter crime.

Today, choice theorists view crime as offence- and offender-specific. Research shows that offenders consider their targets carefully before deciding on a course of action. By implication, crime can be prevented or displaced by convincing potential criminals that the risks of violating the law exceed the benefits.

Deterrence theory holds that if criminals are indeed rational, an inverse relationship should exist between punishment and crime. However, a number of factors confound the relationship. For example, if people do not believe they will be caught, even harsh punishment may not deter crime. Deterrence theory has been criticized on the grounds that it wrongfully assumes that criminals make a rational choice before committing crimes, it ignores the intricacies of the criminal justice system, and it does not take into account the social and psychological factors that may influence criminality. Research designed to test the validity of the deterrence concept has not indicated that deterrent measures actually reduce the crime rate.

Specific deterrence theory holds that the crime rate can be reduced if known offenders are punished so severely that they never commit crimes again. However, there is little evidence that harsh punishment actually reduces the crime rate. Incapacitation theory maintains that if deterrence does not work, the best course of action is to incarcerate known offenders for long periods so that they lack criminal opportunity. Research efforts, however, have not proved that increasing the number of people in prison—and increasing prison sentences—will reduce crime rates.

Choice theory has been influential in shaping public policy. Criminal law is designed to deter potential criminals and fairly punish those who have been caught in illegal acts. Some courts have changed sentencing policies to adapt to classical principles, and the Canadian correctional system seems geared toward incapacitation and specific deterrence. The justice model view is that criminal sanctions should be geared precisely to the seriousness of the crime. People should be punished on the basis of whether they deserve to be punished for what they did, and not because punishment may affect or deter their future behaviour.

For additional chapter links, discussions, and quizzes, see the book-specific website at http://www.icancrim2.com.

In response to media calls for the reinstatement of capital punishment, the Attorney General of Canada has asked you, in your role as a staff criminologist, to give an expert opinion about the informal sanctions 82

just desert 86

offender-specific crime 75

probation 83

rational choice 69

recidivism 83

reintegrative shaming 84

seductions of crime 75

situational crime prevention 76

specific deterrence 83

stigmatization 84

structuring crime 71

three strikes and you're out 86

utility of capital punishment as a deterrent against murder. The last execution in Canada took place in 1962, and capital punishment was officially revoked in 1976. You make use of the Canadian statistics below to frame your opinion.

What are your conclusions, based on the available data? Did the elimination of capital punishment in Canada have an impact on the homicide rate? Why or why not? What other factors would you consider in attempting to explain increases or decreases in the homicide rate over time? Do the data indicate a need to return capital punishment?

DISCUSSION QUESTIONS

1. Are criminals rational decision makers, or are they motivated by noncontrollable psychological and emotional drives?
2. Would you want to live in a society where crime rates are quite low because they are controlled by extremely harsh punishments, such as flogging for vandalism?
3. Which would you be more afraid of if you were caught by the police while shoplifting: receiving criminal punishment or having to face your friends or relatives?
4. Is it possible to create a method of capital punishment that would actually deter murder—for example, by televising executions? What might be some of the negative consequences of such a policy?

Year	Rate*	Year	Rate*	Year	Rate*
1954	2.28	1970	2.19	1986	2.18
1955	1.50	1971	2.15	1987	2.43
1956	1.28	1972	2.34	1988	2.15
1957	1.28	1973	2.43	1989	2.41
1958	1.32	1974	2.63	1990	2.38
1959	1.16	1975	3.03	1991	2.69
1960	1.44	1976	2.85	1992	2.58
1961	1.28	1977	3.00	1993	2.18
1962	1.43	1978	2.76	1994	2.05
1963	1.32	1979	2.61	1995	2.00
1964	1.31	1980	2.41	1996	2.14
1965	1.41	1981	2.61	1997	1.95
1966	1.25	1982	2.66	1998	1.84
1967	1.66	1983	2.69	1999	1.76
1968	1.81	1984	2.60	2000	1.77
1969	1.86	1985	2.72	2001	1.78

*Homicide rate per 100 000 population.

Source: Adapted from the Statistics Canada CANSIM database, Table 253-0001 (http://cansim2.statcan.ca).

5 Chapter in Review

Learning Outcomes

LO1
Explain the basic premises of trait theory.

LO2
Explain how fetal alcohol spectrum disorder (FASD) and criminality may be linked.

LO3
Explain the relationship between genetics and criminality.

LO4
Describe the major varieties of psychological trait theories.

LO5
Describe the relationship between mental illness and criminality.

Key Terms

androgens 93

antisocial personality 108

arousal theory 98

attention deficit/hyperactivity disorder (ADHD) 96

behaviour modelling 106

behaviour theory 105

bipolar disorder 104

cheater theory 101

cognitive theory 107

disorder 103

dizygotic (DZ) twins 99

ego 102

id 102

SUMMARY

The earliest positivist criminologists were biologists. Led by Cesare Lombroso, these early researchers believed that some people manifested primitive traits that made them born criminals. Today their research is debunked because of poor methodology, testing, and logic. Biological views fell out of favour in the early 20th century. In the 1970s, spurred by the publication of Edmund O. Wilson's *Sociobiology*, several criminologists again turned to study of the biological basis of criminality. For the most part, the effort has focused on the cause of violent crime. Interest has centred on several areas: (1) biochemical factors, such as diet, allergies, hormonal imbalances, and environmental contaminants (such as lead); (2) neurophysiological factors, such as brain disorders, EEG abnormalities, tumours, and head injuries; and (3) genetic factors, such as the XYY syndrome and inherited traits. An evolutionary branch holds that changes in the human condition, which have taken millions of years to evolve, may help explain crime rate differences.

Psychological attempts to explain criminal behaviour have historical roots in the concept that all criminals are insane or mentally damaged. This position is no longer accepted. Today there are three main psychological perspectives: the psychodynamic view, the cognitive view, and the social learning perspective. The psychodynamic view, developed by Sigmund Freud, links aggressive behaviour to personality conflicts arising from childhood. According to some psychoanalysts, psychotics are aggressive, unstable people who can easily become involved in crime. Cognitive psychology is concerned with human development and how people perceive the world. Criminality is viewed as a function of improper information processing. Behavioural and social learning theorists see criminality as a learned behaviour. Children who are exposed to violence and see it rewarded may become violent as adults.

Psychological traits such as personality and intelligence have been linked to criminality. One important area of study has been the antisocial personality, a person who lacks emotion and concern for others. The controversial issue of the relationship of IQ to criminality has been resurrected once again with the publication of research studies purporting to show that criminals have lower IQs than noncriminals.

For additional chapter links, discussions, and quizzes, see the book-specific website at http://www.icancrim2.com.

According to the Canadian Criminal Code (R.S. 1985, c. C-46), a person should not be held legally responsible for a crime if the person's behaviour meets the following standard:

information-processing theory 107

latent delinquency 104

meta-analytic studies 105

minimal brain dysfunction (MBD) 95

monozygotic (MZ) twins 99

nature theory 109

neurophysiology 95

neurotic 103

neurotransmitters 97

nurture theory 109

personality 107

premenstrual syndrome (PMS) 94

primary prevention programs 110

psychodynamic (psychoanalytic) 102

psychotic 103

schizophrenia 103

secondary prevention programs 110

social learning theory 106

sociobiology 90

superego 102

testosterone 93

trait theory 90

Defence of mental disorder	16. (1) No person is criminally responsible for an act committed or an omission made while suffering from a mental disorder that rendered the person incapable of appreciating the nature and quality of the act or omission or of knowing that it was wrong.
Presumption	(2) Every person is presumed not to suffer from a mental disorder so as to be exempt from criminal responsibility by virtue of subsection (1), until the contrary is proved on the balance of probabilities.
Burden of proof	(3) The burden of proof that an accused was suffering from a mental disorder so as to be exempt from criminal responsibility is on the party that raises the issue.

"Mental disorder" is defined in the Criminal Code as a "disease of the mind"; any illness, disorder, or abnormal condition that impairs the human mind and its functioning, excluding, however, self-induced states caused by alcohol or drugs, as well as transitory mental states such as hysteria and concussion. It is a question of law for the trial judge to determine what constitutes a "disease of the mind" or a "mental disorder."

As a criminologist advising the justice minister, what modifications, if any, would you make in order to include or exclude other categories of offenders who are not excused by this definition?

Discussion Questions

1. If research could show that the tendency to commit crime is inherited, what should be done with the young children of violence-prone criminals?
2. Would you recommend that young children be forbidden to view films and video games with violent content?
3. Knowing what you do about trends and patterns in crime, how would you counteract the assertion that people who commit crime are physically or mentally abnormal?
4. Aside from becoming a criminal, what other career paths are open to psychopaths?

SOCIAL STRUCTURE THEORIES

Chapter in Review

Learning Outcomes

LO1
Explain why sociology has been the main orientation of criminologists.

LO2
Explain why social structure theory supports the idea that those living in poverty are more likely to commit crimes.

LO3
State the three branches of social structure theories.

LO4
Explain the concept of "collective efficacy."

LO5
Discuss how strain theories interpret crime.

LO6
Explain the concept of "differential opportunity."

Key Terms

"American Dream" 126

anomie 124

anomie theory 126

collective efficacy 122

concentration effect 122

cultural deviance theory 118

cultural transmission 118

culture of poverty 115

delinquent subculture 129

differential opportunity 131

focal concerns 129

general strain theory (GST) 127

SUMMARY

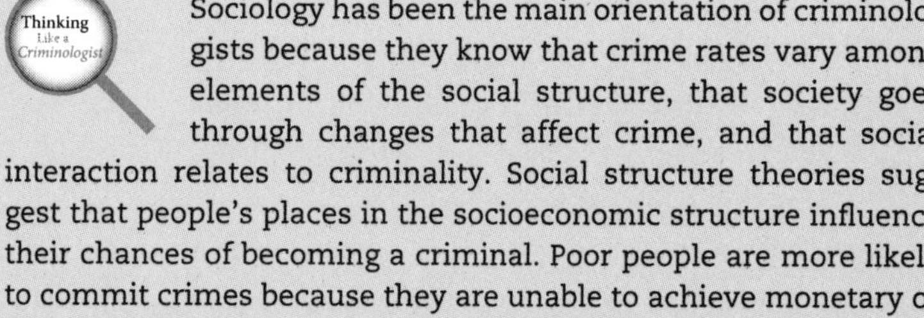

Sociology has been the main orientation of criminologists because they know that crime rates vary among elements of the social structure, that society goes through changes that affect crime, and that social interaction relates to criminality. Social structure theories suggest that people's places in the socioeconomic structure influence their chances of becoming a criminal. Poor people are more likely to commit crimes because they are unable to achieve monetary or social success in any other way. Social structure theory includes three schools of thought: social disorganization, strain, and cultural deviance theories.

Social disorganization theory suggests that slum dwellers violate the law because they live in areas in which social control has broken down. The origin of social disorganization theory can be traced to the work of Clifford R. Shaw and Henry D. McKay. Shaw and McKay concluded that disorganized areas, marked by divergent values and transitional populations, produce criminality. In response to contemporary criticisms of social disorganization theory, social ecology theory has developed. It looks at issues such as community fear, unemployment, and community deterioration.

Strain theories view crime as resulting from the anger people experience over their inability to achieve legitimate social and economic success. Strain theories hold that most people share common values and beliefs, but the ability to achieve them is differentiated by the social structure. The best-known strain theory is Robert Merton's theory of anomie, which describes what happens when people have inadequate means to satisfy their goals. Steven Messner and Richard Rosenfeld show that North American culture produces strain, and Robert Agnew suggests that strain has multiple sources.

Cultural deviance theories hold that a unique value system develops in lower-class areas. Lower-class values approve of behaviours such as being tough, never showing fear, and defying authority. People perceiving strain will bond together in their own groups or subcultures for support and recognition. Albert Cohen links the formation of subcultures to the failure of lower-class citizens to achieve recognition from middle-class decision makers, such as teachers, employers, and police officers. Richard Cloward and Lloyd Ohlin have argued that crime results from lower-class people's perception that their opportunity for success is limited. Consequently, youths in low-income areas may join criminal, conflict, or retreatist gangs.

For additional chapter links, discussions, and quizzes, see the book-specific website at http://www.icancrim2.com.

You have accepted a position in Ottawa as an executive assistant to a newly formed federal–provincial task force on urban development. The chairperson of the committee informs you that he wants to initiate a demonstration project to show that governments can have an impact on reducing poverty, crime, and drug abuse.

institutional anomie theory 126

middle-class measuring rods 130

negative affective states 127

reaction formation 131

social class 114

social disorganization theory 118

social structure theory 117

status frustration 129

strain 118

strain theory 118

stratification 114

subculture 118

transitional neighbourhood 119

underclass 115

The area he has chosen is a large inner-city neighbourhood in a Western Canadian city of more than 600 000 people. It suffers disorganized community structure, poverty, and hopelessness. There are youth gangs operating in the neighbourhood, harassing local merchants and citizens. The school system has failed to provide opportunities and educational experiences sufficient to dampen enthusiasm for gang recruitment. Stores and homes in the area are in a dilapidated condition. Commercial enterprise has fled the area. There is an uneasy truce among the varied ethnic and racial groups that populate the area. Residents feel that little can be done to bring the neighbourhood back to life. Merchants are afraid to open stores at night for fear of being robbed, and there is little hope of outside development from major retailers or manufacturers. People who want to start their own businesses find that banks will not lend them money.

One of the biggest problems has been the large low-income townhouse and apartment projects that were developed in the 1960s. These are now overcrowded and increasingly deteriorated. Even the police are reluctant to enter some of the buildings unless they arrive with backup. Drug dealing carries on openly outside some of the buildings, and residents are afraid to report dealers to the police for fear of reprisals.

You are asked to propose an urban redevelopment program to revitalize the area and eventually bring down the crime rate. You can bring any public or private element to bear on this overwhelming problem. You can also ask private industry to help in the struggle, promising them tax breaks for their participation. What programs would you recommend to break the cycle of urban poverty?

Discussion Questions

1. Is there a "transitional" area in your town or city? Does the crime rate remain constant there, regardless of who moves in or out?
2. Is it possible that a distinct lower-class culture exists? Do you know anyone who has the focal concerns Miller talks about? Were there "focal concerns" in your high school, college, or university experience?
3. Have you ever perceived anomie? What causes anomie? Is there more than one cause of strain?
4. How would Merton explain middle-class crime? How would Agnew?
5. Could "relative deprivation" produce crime among university-educated white-collar workers?

SOCIALIZATION AND CRIME

Chapter in Review

Learning Outcomes

LO1
Explain how social process theories view criminality.

LO2
Identify major family factors predictive of behaviour.

LO3
Explain how the educational process and adolescent school achievement have been linked to criminality.

LO4
Explain how peer relationships have been linked to delinquency.

LO5
Explain the difference between social learning theory and social control theory.

LO6
Explain the difference between the most prominent forms of social learning theory: differential association theory and neutralization theory.

LO7
Describe how Travis Hirschi's contemporary social control theory explains why people obey the law.

LO8
Discuss why critics have charged that labelling theory lacks credibility.

Key Terms

commitment to conformity 143

culture conflict 140

deviance amplification 150

differential association theory 139

diversion programs 154

SUMMARY

Social process theories view criminality as a function of people's interaction with various organizations, institutions, and processes in society. People in all walks of life have the potential to become criminals if they maintain destructive social relationships. Social process theory has three main branches: (1) social learning theory stresses that people learn how to commit crimes; (2) social control theory analyzes the failure of society to control criminal tendencies; and (3) labelling theory maintains that negative labels produce criminal careers.

Social learning theory suggests that people learn criminal behaviours much as they learn conventional behaviour. Differential association theory, formulated by Edwin Sutherland, holds that criminality is a result of a person's perceiving an excess of definitions in favour of crime over definitions that uphold conventional values. Sykes and Matza's theory of neutralization stresses that youths learn behaviour rationalizations that enable them to overcome societal values and norms and break the law.

Control theory maintains that all people have the potential to become criminals, but their bonds to conventional society prevent them from violating the law. This view suggests that a person's self-concept aids his or her commitment to conventional action. Travis Hirschi describes the social bond as containing elements of attachment, commitment, involvement, and belief. Weakened bonds allow youths to behave antisocially.

Social reaction or labelling theory holds that criminality is promoted by becoming negatively labelled by significant others. Labels such as "criminal," "ex-con," and "junkie" isolate people from society and lock them into lives of crime. Labels create expectations that the labelled person will act in a certain way; labelled people are always watched and suspected. Eventually these people begin to accept their labels as personal identities, locking them further into lives of crime and deviance. Edwin Lemert suggests that people who accept labels are involved in secondary deviance. Unfortunately, research on labelling has not supported its major premises. Consequently, critics have charged that it lacks credibility as a description of crime causation.

Social process theories have greatly influenced social policy. They have controlled treatment orientations as well as community action policies.

For additional chapter links, discussions, and quizzes, see the book-specific website at http://www.icancrim2.com.

Provincial politicians are debating a bill that requires the names of people convicted of certain offences, such as vandalism, soliciting a prostitute, or nonpayment of child support, to be posted in local newspapers under the heading "The Rogues Gallery." Those who favour the bill cite similar practices in the United States: in Boston, men arrested for soliciting prostitutes are forced to clean streets. In Dallas, shoplifters are made to stand outside stores with signs stating their misdeeds.

drift 141

moral entrepreneur 148

neutralization techniques 141

neutralization theory 141

primary deviance 150

reflective role taking 148

restitution 154

retrospective reading 149

secondary deviance 150

self-control 143

social bonds 143

social control theory 138

social learning theory 138

social process theory 135

social reaction theory (labelling theory) 138

socialization 135

stigmatize 146

Representatives of the Canadian Civil Liberties Association have opposed the bill, stating, "It's simply needless humiliation of the individual." They argue that public shaming is inhumane and further alienates criminals who already have little stake in society, further ostracizing them from the mainstream. According to civil liberties lawyers, shaming helps criminals acquire a damaged reputation, which further locks them into criminal behaviour patterns.

This "liberal" position is challenged by those who believe that convicted lawbreakers have no right to conceal their crimes from the public. Shaming penalties seem attractive as cost-effective alternatives to imprisonment. These critics ask what could be wrong with requiring a teenage vandal to personally apologize at the school he or she defaced and wear a shirt with a big "V" on it while cleaning up the mess. If you do something wrong, they argue, you should have to face the consequences.

You have been asked to address a provincial legislative committee on the issue of whether shaming could deter crime. What would you say?

Discussion Questions

1. If criminal behaviour is learned, who taught the first criminal? Are behaviours such as vandalism and bullying actually learned?
2. Children who do well in school are less likely to commit criminal acts than those who are school failures. Which element of Hirschi's theory is supported by the school failure–delinquency link?
3. Have you ever been given a negative label, and, if so, did it cause you social harm? How did you lose the label, or did it become a permanent marker that still troubles you today?
4. If negative labels are damaging, do positive ones help insulate children from crime-producing forces in their environment?
5. How would a social process theorist explain the fact that many children begin offending at an early age and then desist as they mature?

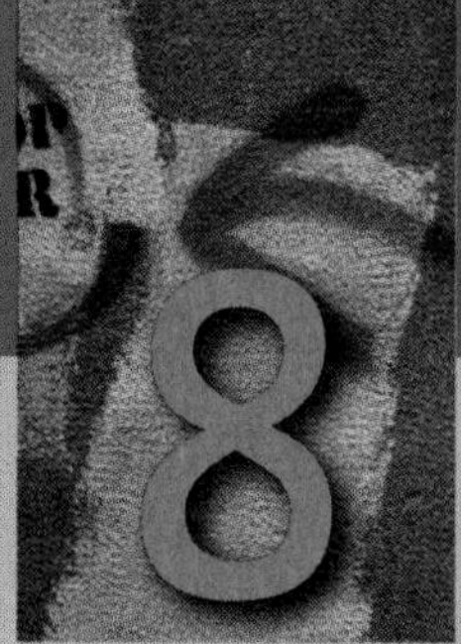

Chapter in Review

Learning Outcomes

LO1
Discuss how social conflict theorists explain the existence of crime in a society.

LO2
Explain the purpose of the legal system according to conflict theorists.

LO3
Explain why Marxist criminologists view the justice system as an army.

LO4
Describe how Marxist criminologists explain crime.

LO5
Explain how restorative justice is meant to prevent and control crime.

LO6
Explain why social conflict theorists feel the legal system is biased.

Key Terms

deconstructionist 170

demystify 165

instrumental Marxist 165

left realism 167

marginalization 164

Marxist criminology 158

Marxist feminism 168

patriarchal 168

peacemaking 171

postmodernist 170

power 160

SUMMARY

Social conflict theorists view crime as a function of the conflict that exists in society. Conflict theorists suggest that crime in any society is caused by class conflict. Laws are created by those in power to protect their rights and interests.

All criminal acts have political undertones; Richard Quinney has called this the social reality of crime. Unfortunately, research efforts to validate the conflict approach have not produced significant findings. One of conflict theory's most important premises is that the justice system is biased and designed to protect the wealthy. Research has not been unanimous in supporting this point.

Marxist criminology views the competitive nature of the capitalist system as a major cause of crime. The poor commit crimes because of their frustration, anger, and need. The wealthy engage in illegal acts because they are used to competition and because they must do so to keep their positions in society. Marxist scholars have attempted to show that the law is designed to protect the wealthy and powerful and to control the poor, have-not members of society. Branches of radical theory include instrumental Marxism and structural Marxism.

During the 1990s, new forms of conflict theory emerged. Left realism takes a centrist position on crime by showing its rational, destructive nature. Feminist writers draw attention to the influence of patriarchal society on crime. Deconstructionism looks at the symbolic meaning of law and culture. Peacemaking criminology calls for humanism in criminology.

For additional chapter links, discussions, and quizzes, see the book-specific website at http://www.icancrim2.com.

An interim evaluation of Restoration House's New Hope for Families program, a community-based residential treatment program for women with dependent children, shows that 70 percent of women who complete follow-up interviews six months after treatment have maintained abstinence or reduced their drug use. The other 30 percent, however, lapse back into their old habits.

The Restoration House program relies on restorative justice techniques in which community people meet with female drug users to discuss the harm drug use can cause and how it can damage both them and their children. The community members show their support and help the women find a niche in the community.

Women who complete the program improve their employment, reduce parenting stress, retain custody of their children, and restore their physical, mental, and emotional health. The program focuses on not only reducing drug and alcohol use but also increasing health, safety, self-sufficiency, and positive attitudes.

As a criminologist, would you consider this program a success? What questions would have to be answered before it gets your approval? How do you think the program should handle women who do not succeed in the program? Are there any other approaches you would try with these women? If so, explain.

power–control theory 170

preemptive deterrence 168

radical criminology 158

restorative justice 172

semiotics 170

sentencing circle 174

social reality of crime 160

structural Marxist 165

surplus value 164

DISCUSSION QUESTIONS

1. How would a conservative reply to a call for more restorative justice? How would a restorative justice advocate respond to a conservative call for more prisons?
2. Considering the changes that have occurred in women's role in Canadian society beginning in the 1960s, how would a power–control theorist explain recent increases in the violent crime rate among females?
3. Is conflict inevitable in all cultures? If not, what can be done to reduce the level of conflict in our own society?
4. If Marx were alive today, what would he think about the prosperity enjoyed by the working class in industrial societies? Might he alter his vision of the capitalist system?

Chapter in Review

Learning Outcomes

LO1
Describe how latent trait theorists explain criminality.

LO2
Explain what makes people commit crime according to Gottfredson and Hirschi.

LO3
Describe the two distinct elements of control according to Tittle's control balance theory and what happens when there is an imbalance.

LO4
Describe important developmental concepts of problem behaviour syndrome (PBS), pathways to crime, criminal trajectories, and continuity of crime and explain how they help us understand how criminal careers evolve.

LO5
Describe briefly how the major theories of criminal development account for the onset, continuance, and desistance of crime.

Key Terms

adolescent-limited 189

authority conflict pathway 188

control balance theory 184

covert pathway 188

developmental criminology 178

developmental theory 178

general theory of crime (GTC) 180

integrated theory 177

interactional theory 191

latent trait 179

SUMMARY

Integrated theories seek to avoid the shortcomings of single-factor theories and attempt to blend seemingly independent concepts into coherent explanations of criminality.

Latent trait theories hold that some underlying condition present at birth or soon after controls behaviour. Suspect traits include low IQ, impulsivity, and personality structure. This underlying trait explains the continuity of offending because, once present, it remains with a person throughout his or her life.

In their general theory of crime, Gottfredson and Hirschi integrate concepts from biosocial, psychological, routine activities, and rational choice theories with social control theory to come up with an overall theory of crime. According to Gottfredson and Hirschi, criminal offenders are individuals predisposed to commit crimes. The biological and psychological factors that make people impulsive and crime-prone may be inherited or may develop through incompetent or absent parenting. However, crime-prone individuals are not robots who commit crime without restraint; their days are also filled with conventional behaviours, such as going to school, parties, concerts, and religious institutions. But given the same set of criminal opportunities, such as having a lot of free time for mischief and living in a neighbourhood with unguarded homes containing valuable merchandise, crime-prone people have a much higher probability of violating the law than do noncriminals.

Developmental theories look at multiple factors derived from a number of different structural and process theories, and seek to explain how criminal careers develop and change over the life course. Examples include the social development model, interactional theory, and age-graded theory. The cause of crime constantly changes as people mature.

Early family and childhood experiences are important factors that can set the stage for later criminal behaviour. Crime can be thought of as just one among a group of antisocial behaviours that can cluster together, referred to collectively as problem behaviour syndrome (PBS).

Depending on their individual biological and psychological makeup, the environment the individual grows up in, the opportunities available to them, and the choices they make, the pathway (or trajectory) individuals will follow may be criminal or noncriminal. Different transitions and events in life can change the course of the trajectory; for example, an influential teacher, a satisfying relationship, or a good job could turn the trajectory of someone with PBS from being potentially negative and criminal to positive and law abiding. Even as the individual matures and ages, the likelihood of his or her involvement in criminal behaviour will change. Research shows that marriage and a job, and aging itself, are important reasons behind desistance, the decision to end a criminal trajectory.

For additional chapter links, discussions, and quizzes, see the book-specific website at http://www.icancrim2.com.

latent trait theory 178

life-course persister 189

life-course theory 185

overt pathway 188

problem behaviour syndrome (PBS) 187

prosocial bonds 191

pseudomaturity 189

social capital 192

social development model (SDM) 190

turning points 192

Stephen Reid grew up in a small town in Ontario, evidently a normal upbringing. In 1972 he was sent to prison after having been convicted of a string of bank robberies. Reid was a member of the notorious "Stopwatch Gang," a trio of Canadians who escaped with an estimated $15 million after staging more than 100 bank robberies across Canada and in the United States.

In 1986, while still in prison for the bank robberies, Reid published a novel, *Jackrabbit Parole*, that won him literary praise, and was responsible for his meeting and later marrying famed Canadian poet Susan Musgrave.

Upon his release from prison, Reid and Musgrave located near Victoria, British Columbia, where Reid settled into a quiet life of writing and occasional teaching and lecturing. The famous couple were frequent targets of media attention, and the subjects of at least one documentary.

In June 1999, Stephen Reid was apprehended by police and charged with attempted murder of a police officer, bank robbery, unlawful confinement, kidnapping, and various weapons charges. Disguised as a police officer, Reid had entered and robbed a Victoria bank. A wild car chase ensued as Reid attempted to flee the scene, during which he fired shots at police.

Reid was convicted and sentenced to serve another 18 years in prison. Drug use, particularly heroin and cocaine, appeared to be behind Reid's return to crime.*

Explain Reid's behaviour patterns from the general theory of crime perspective. What factors might you look for in his past to explain his return to crime?

Discussion Questions

1. Do you consider yourself the holder of "social capital"? If so, what form does it take?
2. A person maintains a 4.0 GPA throughout university. Without knowing this person, what personal, family, and social characteristics must he or she have? Another person becomes a serial killer. Without knowing this person, what personal, family, and social characteristics must he or she have? If "bad behaviour" is explained by multiple problems, is "good behaviour" explained by multiple strengths?
3. Do you believe there is a "latent trait" that makes a person crime-prone, or is crime a function of environment and socialization?
4. Do you agree with Loeber's multiple pathway model? Do you know people who have travelled down those paths?

* Jennifer Hunter, "The Jackrabbit Stumbles," *Maclean's*, June 21, 1999, p. 22.

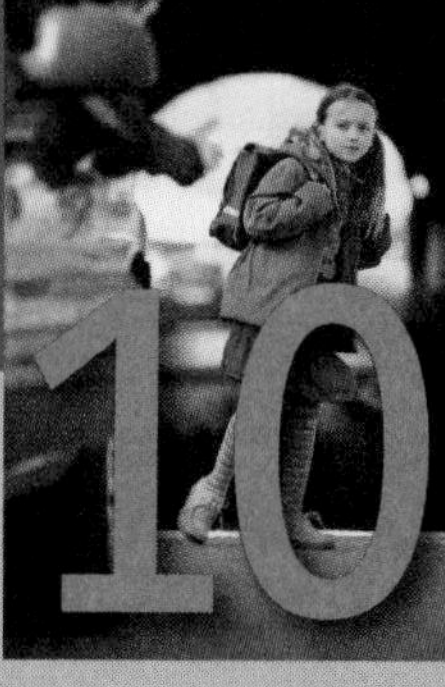

VIOLENT CRIME

Chapter in Review

Learning Outcomes

LO1
Identify the different types of interpersonal violent crime.

LO2
Name the various explanations for violent crimes.

LO3
Explain the nature of the changes in Canadian law in regard to rape.

LO4
Identify the different degrees of murder.

LO5
Explain the prevalence of assault that occurs in the family home.

LO6
Explain why robbery is considered a violent crime.

LO7
Identify emerging forms of violent crime.

LO8
Identify the forms of political violence.

Key Terms

acquaintance rape 203

assault level 1 210

assault level 2 210

assault level 3 210

child abuse 211

child neglect 211

date rape 203

disarming a peace officer 211

expressive violence 197

SUMMARY

Among the various explanations for violent crimes are the availability of firearms, human traits, a subculture of violence that stresses violent solutions to interpersonal problems, and family conflict.

There are many types of interpersonal violent crime. Rape has been known throughout history; however, the view of rape has evolved. Rape was an extremely difficult charge to prove in court; however, with the amendments to the Criminal Code in 1983, many more people have been charged and convicted. Also, victims' rights are now solidly established in Canadian law.

Murder is defined in common law as killing a human being with malice aforethought. There are different degrees of murder, and punishments vary accordingly. One important characteristic of murder is that the victim and criminal often know each other. Assault, another serious interpersonal violent crime, often occurs in the home, including child abuse and spouse abuse.

According to Statistics Canada, nearly 55 000 children and youth were the victims of a sexual offence or physical assault in 2009, 27 percent of which (14 833) were perpetrated by a family member. In six out of every ten cases in which a child or youth was victimized by a family member, the perpetrator was a parent.*

Both women and men experience spousal abuse. However, women experience more severe forms of violence, and are more than twice as likely as men to report being physically injured.**

Robbery involves theft by force, usually in a public place. Types of offenders include professional, opportunist, addict, and alcoholic robbers. Robbery is considered a violent crime because it can and often does involve violence.

Emerging forms of interpersonal violence include stalking, home invasions, hate crimes, and political violence.

Political violence is a serious problem throughout the world. Many terrorist groups exist at both the national and international levels. Hundreds of terrorist acts are reported each year in the United States alone and there is every indication that such acts will soon surface in Canada. Terrorists may be motivated by criminal gain, psychosis, grievance against the state, or ideology.

For additional chapter links, discussions, and quizzes, see the book-specific website at http://www.icancrim2.com.

The Ministry of Justice has asked you to prepare a report on sexual assault of persons under the legal age of consent because of the growing number of underage girls who have been impregnated by adult men. Studies reveal that many teenage pregnancies result

* *Family Violence in Canada: A Statistical Profile, 2011* (Ottawa: Minister of Industry, 2011) Cat. no. 85-224-X, http://www.statcan.gc.ca/pub/85-224-x/85-224-x2010000-eng.htm (accessed August 6, 2011).

** *Family Violence in Canada: A Statistical Profile, 2011* (Ottawa: Minister of Industry, 2011) Cat. no. 85-224-X, http://www.statcan.gc.ca/pub/85-224-x/85-224-x2010000-eng.htm (accessed December 6, 2011).

first-degree murder 207

gang rape 203

genocide 221

hate crime 217

homicide 207

infanticide 207

instrumental violence 197

invitation to sexual touching 204

manslaughter 207

marital exemption 204

marital rape 203

mass murderer 209

murder 207

robbery 213

second-degree murder 207

serial killer 209

sexual abuse 211

sexual assault 201

sexual exploitation 204

sexual interference 204

stalking 216

subculture of violence 199

terrorism 219

thrill killing 209

from affairs that underage girls have with older men, with age gaps ranging from seven to ten years. Some outraged parents adamantly support a law that provides additional financial grants to law enforcement agencies to help in prosecuting this form of sexual assault. These grants would allow more vigorous enforcement of the law and could result in the conviction of more than 1500 offenders annually.

However, some critics suggest that implementing these laws to punish males who have relationships with minor girls does not solve the problems of teenage pregnancies and out-of-wedlock births. Liberals dislike the idea of using criminal law to solve social problems because it does not provide for the girls and their young children and focuses only on punishing offenders. In contrast, conservatives fear that such laws give the state too much power to prosecute people for a crime that may involve a willing victim; not all cases involve much older men, and critics ask whether we should criminalize the behaviour of 17-year-old boys and their 15-year-old girlfriends. As a criminologist with expertise on sexual assault and its effects, what would you recommend regarding implementation of the law?

Discussion Questions

1. If robbers are in fact rational decision makers, what can potential victims do to reduce their chances of becoming targets?
2. What cultural values present in contemporary society promote violence? For example, is there a link between materialism and violence?
3. Are "terrorists" freedom fighters who lose?

Chapter in Review

Learning Outcomes

LO1
List the major types of theft and fraud.

LO2
Identify the role "target hardening" strategies can play in reducing the incidence of shoplifting.

LO3
Identify the difference between "false pretences" and "fraud."

LO4
Define "break and enter" and explain why victims are likely to be re-victimized.

LO5
List the motives for the crime of arson.

Key Terms

arrest by owner of property 228

arson 237

booster 227

burglary (break and enter) 234

confidence game 232

constructive possession 226

embezzlement (breach of trust) 233

false pretences 231

fence 227

fraud 231

naïve cheque forgers 232

occasional criminals 224

professional criminals 225

SUMMARY

Economic crimes are designed to financially reward the offender. Opportunistic amateurs commit the majority of economic crimes. However, economic crime has also attracted professional criminals. Professionals earn most of their income from crime, view themselves as criminals, and possess skills that aid them in their law-breaking behaviour. A good example of the professional criminal is the fence who buys and sells stolen merchandise.

Common theft-type offences include theft, fraud, and embezzlement (breach of trust). These are common-law crimes, defined by English judges, to meet social needs. Theft involves taking the legal possessions of another. The crime of false pretences is similar to theft in that it involves the theft of goods or money; it differs in that the criminal makes a false claim or statement to get victims to voluntarily give up their money or possessions. Embezzlement (breach of trust) involves people taking something that was temporarily entrusted to them, such as bank tellers taking money out of the cash drawer and keeping it for themselves. These common-law crimes have been codified into legal codes.

Shoplifting is a common form of theft involving the taking of goods from retail stores. Usually shoplifters try to snatch goods—such as jewellery, clothes, CDs, and appliances—when store personnel are otherwise occupied and hide the goods on their bodies. Retail stores are now initiating a number of strategies designed to reduce or eliminate shoplifting. Target removal strategies involve displaying dummy or disabled goods while the real merchandise is locked up. Target hardening strategies involve locking goods into place or having them monitored by electronic systems.

Break and enter, a more serious theft offence, was defined in common law as the "breaking and entering of a dwelling house of another in the nighttime with the intent to commit a felony within." This definition has also evolved over time. Today, break and enter includes theft from any structure, at any time of the day. Because break and enter involves planning and risk, it attracts professional thieves. The most competent have technical competence and personal integrity, specialize in burglary, are financially successful, and avoid prison sentences.

Arson is another serious property crime. Although many arsonists are teenage vandals, there are professional arsonists who specialize in burning commercial buildings for profit.

For additional chapter links, discussions, and quizzes, see the book-specific website at http://www.icancrim2.com.

To reduce the risk of loss during the Christmas holidays, the local Anti-Crime Unit (ACU) suggests that you do not display presents where they can be seen from a window or doorway, and put gifts in a safe place before leaving the house or taking a trip. Closing drapes or blinds during even short trips away from home is a good habit.

It is important to trick burglars into believing someone is home. If you are away, ACU suggests having lights on timers, stopping mail and newspaper delivery, and arranging to have the walkways shovelled and have a car parked in the driveway as additional security measures. Other suggestions include installing a good dead-bolt lock with at least a one-inch throat into a solid wood or steel door that fits securely into a sturdy frame, keeping doors locked, putting a chain-link fence around the yard, getting a dog, and having police inspect the house for security. Also, buy a weighted safe deposit box to secure items that cannot be replaced, and engrave your driver's licence number on your property to give police a way to contact you if your home is burglarized and the stolen items are later found.

Con artists may exploit people's generosity during the holidays by making appeals for nonexistent charities. The ACU suggests that you always ask for identification from solicitors.

As a criminologist, can you come up with any new ideas that the ACU may have failed to cover?

Discussion Questions

1. Differentiate between an occasional and professional criminal. Which one would be more likely to resort to violence?
2. What crime occurs when a person who owns an antique store sells a client an "original" Tiffany lamp that he or she knows is a fake? Would it still be a crime if the person was not aware that the lamp was a copy? Should antique dealers have a duty to determine the authenticity of the products they sell?
3. What is the difference between a booster and a snitch? If caught, should they receive different punishments? What about naïve and systematic cheque forgers?
4. What are the characteristics of the "good burglar"? Can you compare them to any other professionals?

12 Chapter in Review

Learning Outcomes

LO1
Explain how white-collar crime and organized crime are similar and how they are different.

LO2
Describe the various types of white-collar crime.

LO3
Describe some of the law enforcement strategies that government is using to combat white-collar crime.

LO4
Describe major characteristics of organized crime and the groups involved in this criminal activity.

LO5
Explain the debate about what is organized about organized crime.

Key Terms

alien conspiracy theory 258

bank fraud 249

bucketing 246

chiselling 245

churning 246

compliance strategies 255

corporate crime 243

corporate culture view 254

deterrence strategies 255

enterprise 242

front running 246

insider trading 246

SUMMARY

Thinking Like a Criminologist

White-collar and organized criminals are similar in that both use ongoing business enterprises to make personal profits.

There are various types of white-collar crime. Stings and swindles involve the use of deception to bilk people out of their money. Chiselling customers, businesses, or the government is a second common type of white-collar crime. Surprisingly, many professionals engage in chiselling offences. Other white-collar criminals use their positions in business and the marketplace to commit economic crimes. Their crimes include exploitation of position in a company or the government to secure illegal payments; influence peddling and bribery; embezzlement and employee pilferage and fraud; and client fraud. Further, corporate officers sometimes violate the law to improve the position and profitability of their businesses. Their crimes include price-fixing, false advertising, and environmental offences.

So far, little has been done to combat white-collar crime. Most offenders do not view themselves as criminals and therefore do not seem to be deterred by criminal statutes. Although thousands of white-collar criminals are prosecuted each year, their numbers are insignificant compared with the magnitude of the problem. The government has used various law enforcement strategies to combat white-collar crime. Some involve compliance strategies, which create economic incentives to obey the law. Others involve deterrence, which uses punishment to frighten potential offenders.

The demand for illegal goods and services has produced a symbiotic relationship between the public and an organized criminal network. Organized crime supplies drugs, gambling, prostitutes, and pornography to the public. It has traditionally been immune from prosecution because of public apathy and because of its own strong political connections. Organized criminals used to be white ethnics—but today Asian, Eastern European, Aboriginal, and other groups have become included in organized crime activities. The old-line "families" are now more likely to use their criminal wealth and power to buy into legitimate businesses.

There is debate over the control of organized crime. Some experts believe a national crime cartel controls all activities. Others view organized crime as a group of disorganized, competing gangs dedicated to extortion or to providing illegal goods and services. Regardless, as long as huge profits can be made, illegal enterprises will continue to flourish.

For additional chapter links, discussions, and quizzes, see the book-specific website at http://www.icancrim2.com.

People who commit computer crime are found in every segment of society. They range in age from 10 to 60, and their skill levels run from novice to professional. They are otherwise average people, not supercriminals possessing unique abilities and talents. Any person of any age with even a little skill is a potential computer criminal.

Most studies indicate that employees represent the greatest threat to computers. Almost 90 percent of computer crimes against

La Cosa Nostra 258

Mafia 258

organized crime 242

pilferage 248

price-fixing 251

restraint of trade 250

self-control view 255

virus 252

white-collar crime 242

businesses are inside jobs. Ironically, as advances continue in remote data processing, the threat from external sources will probably increase.

With the networking of systems and the adoption of more user-friendly software, the sociological profile of the computer offender may change. For example, computer criminals may soon be members of organized crime syndicates. They will use computer systems to monitor law enforcement activities. To become a "made man" in the 21st-century organized crime family, the recruit will have to develop knowledge of the equipment used for audio surveillance of law enforcement communications: computers with sound card or microphone, modems, and software programs for the remote operation of the systems.

Which theories of criminal behaviour best explain the actions of computer criminals, and which theories fail to account for computer crime?

Discussion Questions

1. How would you punish corporate executives whose product killed people, if they themselves had no knowledge that the product was potentially lethal? What if they did know?
2. Is organized crime inevitable as long as immigrant groups seek to find economic success?
3. Do the media glamorize organized crime? Do they paint an inaccurate picture of noble crime lords fighting to protect their families?

PUBLIC ORDER CRIMES

Chapter in Review

Learning Outcomes

LO1
Define a *public order crime*?

LO2
Define prostitution according to the law and think critically about whether prostitution should be legalized.

LO3
Evaluate how we decide what is pornographic and understand how the law has changed to support police in dealing with child pornography.

LO4
Know the impact, the good and the bad, of legal gambling in Canada.

LO5
Understand the role that substance abuse plays in criminal behavior.

LO6
Think critically about whether Canada should decriminalize the possession of cannabis for personal use.

Key Terms

moral entrepreneur 265

obscenity 270

pornography 270

Prohibition 276

prostitution 267

public order crime 263

temperance movement 276

victimless crime 264

SUMMARY

Public order crimes are acts considered illegal because they conflict with social policy, accepted moral rules, and public opinion. There is usually great debate over public order crimes. Some charge that they are not really crimes at all and that it is foolish to legislate morality. Others view such morally tinged acts as prostitution, gambling, and drug abuse as harmful and therefore subject to public control.

Some public order crimes are sex related, such as prostitution and pornography. In Canada, the act of prostitution itself is not illegal; instead, according to sections 210–213 of the Criminal Code, the means used to practise prostitution—"keeping a common bawdy house," "procurement," and "solicitation"—are illegal. Although prostitution has been practised for thousands of years and is legal in some areas, most countries outlaw commercial sex. There are a variety of prostitutes, including streetwalkers, B-girls, and call girls. Studies indicate that most prostitutes come from poor, troubled families and have abusive parents. However, there is little evidence that prostitutes are emotionally disturbed, addicted to drugs, or sexually abnormal. Although prostitution is illegal, some cities have set up adult entertainment areas where commercial sex is tolerated by law enforcement agents.

Pornography involves the sale of sexually explicit material intended to sexually excite paying customers. The depiction of sex and nudity is not illegal, but it does violate the law when it is judged obscene. Obscenity is a legal term that today is defined as material offensive to community standards. Thus, each local jurisdiction must decide what pornographic material is obscene. A growing problem is the exploitation of children in obscene materials (kiddie porn). There is no hard evidence that pornography is related to crime or aggression, but data suggest that sexual material with a violent theme is related to sexual violence by those who view it.

Though gambling (in the form of lotteries, VLTs, casinos, bingos, and horseracing) is legal in Canada, it is not without its problems. Gambling operations net $5.4 billion in profits every year, and it is estimated that between 3 and 5 percent of Canadians now have a gambling problem. Gambling is especially likely to be a problem in families that can least afford it, and it has been linked to debt and bankruptcy, job loss, family breakdown, substance abuse, suicide, and a host of crimes.

Substance abuse is another type of public order crime. Most countries outlaw a wide variety of drugs they consider harmful, including narcotics, amphetamines, barbiturates, cocaine, hallucinogens, and marijuana. One of the main reasons for the continued ban on drugs is their relationship to crime. Numerous studies have found that drug addicts commit enormous amounts of property crime.

Alcohol is another commonly abused substance. Although alcohol is legal to possess, it too has been linked to crime. Drunk driving and deaths caused by drunk drivers are national problems.

There are many different strategies to control substance abuse, ranging from source control to treatment. So far, no single method seems effective. Although decriminalization of the possession of marijuana for personal use has been considered, the fact that so many people already take drugs and the association of drug abuse with crime make decriminalization or legalization unlikely in the near term.

For additional chapter links, discussions, and quizzes, see the book-specific website at http://www.icancrim2.com.

According to data from two large surveys of senior elementary and high school students in Canada, there is a statistically significant correlation between illegal drug use and violence, and cannabis use was more strongly linked to violence than other drugs like alcohol or cocaine. As one would expect, males were more violent than females, and those who skipped school were also more likely to have a history of violent behaviour.

As a criminologist, what would be your interpretation of these data? What is the possible association between substance abuse and violent behaviour among youth?

Discussion Questions

1. Why do you think people take drugs? Do you know anyone with an addiction-prone personality, or do you believe that is a myth?
2. What policy might be the best strategy to reduce teenage drug use: source control? Reliance on treatment? National education efforts? Community-level enforcement?
3. Under what circumstances, if any, might the legalization or decriminalization of sexually related material be beneficial to society?
4. Do you consider alcohol a drug? Should greater control be placed on the sale of alcohol?
5. Is prostitution really a crime? Should men or women have the right to sell sexual favours if they so choose?

Synopsis OF CRIMINOLOGICAL THEORIES

Classical Theory

Origin About 1764

Founders Cesare Beccaria, Jeremy Bentham

Most Important Works Cesare Beccaria, *On Crimes and Punishments* (1764); Bentham, *Moral Calculus* (1789)

Core Ideas People choose to commit crime after weighing the benefits and costs of their actions. Crime can be deterred by certain, severe, and swift punishment.

Modern Outgrowths Rational Choice Theory, Routine Activities Theory, General Deterrence Theory, Specific Deterrence, Incapacitation

Marxist/Conflict Theory

Origin About 1848

Founders Karl Marx, Willem Bonger, Ralf Dahrendorf, George Vold

Most Important Works Marx and Friedrich Engels, *The Communist Manifesto* (1848); Bonger, *Criminality and Economic Conditions* (1916); George Rusche and Otto Kircheimer, *Punishment and Social Structure* (1939); Dahrendorf, *Class and Class Conflict in Industrial Society* (1959)

Core Ideas Crime is a function of class struggle. The capitalist system's emphasis on competition and wealth produces an economic and social environment in which crime is inevitable.

Modern Outgrowths Conflict Theory, Radical Theory, Critical Criminology, the New Criminology, Radical Feminist Theory, Left Realism, Deconstructionism, Peacemaking

Synopsis CONTINUED

Biological Positivism

Origin About 1810

Founders Franz Joseph Gall, Johann Spurzheim, J.K. Lavater, Cesare Lombroso, Enrico Ferri, Raffaele Garofalo, Earnest Hooton, Charles Goring

Most Important Works Lombroso, *Criminal Man* (1863); Ferri, *Criminal Sociology* (1884); Garofalo, *Criminology* (1885); Goring, *The English Convict* (1913); William Sheldon, *Varieties of Delinquent Youth* (1949); Eleanor Glueck and Sheldon Glueck, *Unraveling Juvenile Delinquency* (1950)

Core Ideas Some people have biological and mental traits that make them crime-prone. These traits are inherited and present at birth. Mental and physical degeneracies are the cause of crime.

Modern Outgrowths Biosocial Theory, Psychodynamic Theory, Cognitive Theory, Behavioural Theory, Evolutionary Theory

Sociological Theory

Origin 1897

Founders Emile Durkheim, Robert Ezra Park, Ernest Burgess, Clifford Shaw, Walter Reckless, Frederic Thrasher

Most Important Works Durkheim, *The Division of Labour in Society* (1893); and *Suicide: A Study in Sociology* (1897); Edwin Sutherland, *Criminology* (1924); Park, Burgess, and John McKenzie, *The City* (1925); Shaw et. al., *Delinquency Areas* (1925); Thrasher, *The Gang* (1926)

Core Ideas A person's place in the social structure determines his or her behaviour. Disorganized urban areas are the breeding ground of crime. A lack of legitimate opportunities produces criminal subcultures. Socialization within the family, school, and the peer group controls behaviour.

Modern Outgrowths Social Ecological Theory, Strain Theory, Cultural Deviance Theory, Learning Theory, Social Control Theory

Synopsis OF CRIMINOLOGICAL THEORIES

Victimization Theories (Chapter 3)		
Theory	**Major Premise**	**Strengths**
Victim precipitation	Victims trigger criminal acts by their provocative behaviour. Active precipitation involves fighting words or gestures. Passive precipitation occurs when victims unknowingly threaten their attacker.	Explains multiple victimizations. If people precipitate crime, it follows that they will become repeat victims if their behaviour persists over time.
Lifestyle	Victimization risk is increased when people have a high-risk lifestyle. Placing oneself at risk by going out to dangerous places results in increased victimization.	Explains victimization patterns in the social structure. Males, young people, and the poor have high victimization rates because they have a higher-risk lifestyle than females, the elderly, and the affluent.
Deviant places	People who live in deviant places are at high risk for crime. Victim behaviour has little influence over the criminal act.	Places the focus of crime on deviant places. Shows why people with conventional lifestyles become crime victims.
Routine activities	Crime rates can be explained by the availability of suitable targets, the absence of capable guardians, and the presence of motivated offenders.	Can explain crime rates and trends. Shows how victim behaviour can influence criminal opportunity. Suggests that victimization risk can be reduced by increasing guardianship and/or reducing target vulnerability.

Choice Theories (Chapter 4)		
Theory	**Major Premise**	**Strengths**
Rational choice	Law-violating behaviour occurs after offenders weigh information on their personal needs and the situational factors involved in the difficulty and risk of committing a crime.	Explains why high-risk youths do not constantly engage in delinquency. Relates theory to delinquency control policy. It is not limited by class or other social variables.
Routine activities	Crime and delinquency are functions of the presence of motivated offenders, the availability of suitable targets, and the absence of capable guardians.	Can explain fluctuations in crime and delinquency rates. Shows how victim behaviour influences criminal choice.
General deterrence	People will commit crime and delinquency if they perceive that the benefits outweigh the risks. Crime is a function of the severity, certainty, and speed of punishment.	Shows the relationship between crime and punishment. Suggests a real solution to crime.
Specific deterrence	If punishment is severe enough, criminals will not repeat their illegal acts.	Provides a strategy to reduce crime.
Incapacitation	Keeping known criminals out of circulation will reduce crime rates.	Recognizes the role that opportunity plays in criminal behaviour. Provides a solution to chronic offending.

Synopsis CONTINUED

Biological and Psychological Theories (Chapter 5)		
Theory	**Major Premise**	**Strengths**
Biosocial		
Biochemical	Crime, especially violence, is a function of diet, vitamin intake, hormonal imbalance, or food allergies.	Explains irrational violence. Shows how the environment interacts with personal traits to influence behaviour.
Neurological	Criminals and delinquents often suffer brain impairment, as measured by the EEG. Attention deficit/hyperactivity disorder and minimal brain dysfunction are related to antisocial behaviour.	Explains irrational violence. Shows how the environment interacts with personal traits to influence behaviour.
Genetic	Criminal traits and predispositions are inherited. The criminality of parents can predict the delinquency of children.	Explains why only a small percentage of youth in a high-crime area become chronic offenders.
Evolutionary	As the human race evolved, traits and characteristics have become ingrained. Some of these traits make people aggressive and predisposed to commit crime.	Explains high violence rates and aggregate gender differences in the crime rate.
Psychological		
Psychodynamic	The development of the unconscious personality early in childhood influences behaviour for the rest of a person's life. Criminals have weak egos and damaged personalities.	Explains the onset of crime and why crime and drug abuse cut across class lines.
Behavioural	People commit crime when they model their behaviour after others they see being rewarded for the same acts. Behaviour is reinforced by rewards and extinguished by punishment.	Explains the role of significant others in the crime process. Shows how family life and media can influence crime and violence.
Cognitive	Individual reasoning processes influence behaviour. Reasoning is influenced by the way people perceive their environment.	Shows why criminal behaviour patterns change over time as people mature and develop their reasoning powers. May explain the aging-out process.

Social Process Theories (Chapter 7)		
Theory	**Major Premise**	**Strengths**
Social Learning Theories		
Differential association theory	People learn to commit crime from exposure to antisocial definitions.	Explains onset of criminality. Explains the presence of crime in all elements of social structure. Explains why some people in high-crime areas refrain from criminality. Can apply to adults and juveniles.
Neutralization theory	Youths learn ways of neutralizing moral restraints and periodically drift in and out of criminal behaviour patterns.	Explains why many delinquents do not become adult criminals. Explains why youthful law violators can participate in conventional behaviour.
Social Control Theory		
Hirschi's control theory	A person's bond to society prevents him or her from violating social rules. If the bond weakens, the person is free to commit crime.	Explains that onset of crime can apply to both middle- and lower-class crime. Explains its theoretical constructs adequately so they can be measured. Has been empirically tested.
Social Reaction Theory		
Labelling theory	People enter into law-violating careers when they are labelled for their acts and organize their personalities around the labels.	Explains the role of society in creating deviance. Explains why some juvenile offenders do not become adult criminals. Develops concepts of criminal careers.

Synopsis OF CRIMINOLOGICAL THEORIES

Social Structure Theories (Chapter 6)		
Theory	**Major Premise**	**Strengths**
Social Disorganization Theory		
Shaw and McKay's concentric zone theory	Crime is a product of transitional neighbourhoods that manifest social disorganization and value conflict.	Identifies why crime rates are highest in slum areas. Points out the factors that produce crime. Suggests programs to help reduce crime.
Social ecology theory	The conflicts and problems of urban social life and communities, including fear, unemployment, deterioration, and siege mentality, influence crime rates.	Accounts for urban crime rates and trends.
Strain Theory		
Anomie theory	People who adopt the goals of society but lack the means to attain them seek alternatives, such as crime.	Points out how competition for success creates conflict and crime. Suggests that social conditions and not personality can account for crime. Can explain middle- and upper-class crime.
Institutional anomie theory	Material goals pervade all aspects of North American life.	Explains why crime rates are so high in North American culture.
Relative deprivation theory	Crime occurs when the wealthy and poor live close to one another.	Explains high crime rates in deteriorated inner-city areas located near more affluent neighbourhoods.
General strain theory	Strain has a variety of sources. Strain causes crime in the absence of adequate coping mechanisms.	Identifies the complexities of strain in modern society. Expands on anomie theory. Shows the influence of social events on behaviour over the life course.
Cultural Deviance Theory		
Miller's focal concern theory	Citizens who obey the street rules of lower-class life (focal concerns) find themselves in conflict with the dominant culture.	Identifies the core values of lower-class culture and shows their association to crime.
Cohen's theory of delinquent gangs	Status frustration of lower-class boys, created by their failure to achieve middle-class success, causes them to join gangs.	Shows how the conditions of lower-class life produce crime. Explains violence and destructive acts. Identifies conflict of lower class with middle class.
Cloward and Ohlin's theory of opportunity	Blockage of conventional opportunities causes lower-class youths to join criminal, conflict, or retreatist gangs.	Shows that even illegal opportunities are structured in society. Indicates why people become involved in a particular type of criminal activity. Presents a way of preventing crime.

Synopsis CONTINUED

Social Conflict Theories (Chapter 8)		
Theory	**Major Premise**	**Strengths**
Conflict theory	Crime is a function of class conflict. Law is defined by people who hold social and political power.	Accounts for class differentials in the crime rate. Shows how class conflict influences behaviour.
Marxist theory	Capitalist ownership of the means of production creates class conflict. Crime is a rebellion of the lower class. The criminal justice system is an agent of class warfare.	Accounts for the associations between economic structure and crime rates.
Instrumental Marxist theory	Criminals are revolutionaries. The real crimes are sexism, racism, and profiteering.	Broadens the definition of crime and demystifies or explains the historical development of law.
Structural Marxist theory	The law is designed to sustain the capitalist economic system.	Explains the existence of white-collar crime and business control laws.
Left realism	Crime is a function of relative deprivation; criminals prey on the poor.	Represents a compromise between conflict and traditional criminology.
Radical feminist theory	The capitalist system creates patriarchy, which oppresses women.	Explains gender bias, violence against women, and repression.
Power–control theory	Girls are controlled more closely than boys in traditional male-dominated households. There is gender equity in contemporary egalitarian homes.	Explains gender differences in the crime rate as a function of class and gender conflict.
Deconstructionism	Language controls the meaning and use of the law.	Provides a critical analysis of meaning.
Peacemaking	Peace and humanism can reduce crime; conflict resolution strategies can work.	Offers a new approach to crime control through mediation.

Integrated Theories (Chapter 9)		
Theory	**Major Premise**	**Strengths**
Latent Trait Theories		
General theory of crime	Crime and criminality are separate concepts. People choose to commit crime when they lack self-control. People lacking in self-control will seize criminal opportunities.	Integrates choice and social control concepts. Identifies the difference between crime and criminality.
Control balance	An excess or lack of control makes people crime-prone.	Shows that control is a multidimensional concept.
Developmental Theories		
Social development model (SDM)	Weak social controls produce crime. A person's place in the structure influences his or her bond to society.	Combines elements of social structural and social process theories. Accounts for variations in the crime rate.
Interactional theory	Criminals go through lifestyle changes during their offending career	Combines sociological and psychological theories.
Age-graded theory	As people mature, the factors that influence their propensity to commit crime change. In childhood, family factors are critical; in adulthood, marital and job factors are key.	Shows how crime is a developmental process that shifts in direction over the life course.